# THE SOVIETS IN WORLD AFFAIRS

LOUIS FISCHER

# *THE* SOVIETS *IN* WORLD AFFAIRS

A HISTORY
OF THE RELATIONS
BETWEEN THE
SOVIET UNION
AND THE
REST OF THE WORLD
1917-1929

ABRIDGED BY THE AUTHOR

NEW YORK VINTAGE BOOKS
A DIVISION OF RANDOM HOUSE

VINTAGE BOOKS

are published by Alfred A. Knopf, Inc. and Random House, Inc.

 Manufactured in the United States of America.

Originally published in 1930 in London by Jonathan Cape, and in 1930 by Jonathan Cape and Harrison Smith in New York. Second edition published in 1951 by Princeton University Press by arrangement with Jonathan Cape.
Reprinted by arrangement with *Princeton University Press.*

# INTRODUCTION

In 1927, when I commenced writing this book, I had established friendly relations with most of the top and middle-rank personnel of the Soviet Foreign Office. Chicherin, who succeeded Trotzky as Foreign Commissar in 1918, realized that I was compiling the story of his lifework, and gave me maximum assistance. For more than a year, I went every Sunday afternoon to his big office in the Foreign Commissariat on Kuznetsky Must and made quick longhand notes as he talked at length about Soviet negotiations and dealings with foreign countries. Throughout the working week, Chicherin of course saw an endless stream of ambassadors and aides. Yet when I entered his room each Sunday he would usually greet me with, "Last time I was saying . . ." and resumed where he had left off seven days earlier. His was an almost perfect-recall memory and he could repeat conversations that had taken place years ago.

Chicherin suffered from diabetes, bad eyesight, and muscular trouble in his right leg. He was also a hypochondriac and never wanted to be far from his physician. In 1929, he went to Berlin for a cure. I followed him; he let me come twice to his sanatorium in suburban Grunewald where, amidst insulin needles, medicine bottles, and thermometer charts, he revealed Soviet history.

In August 1929 I spent more than a week with Chicherin in Wiesbaden, Germany. My manuscript was now complete. He read it for two or three hours a day and then devoted an equal length of time to comments on what I had written. He also supplied me with supplementary data which I was able to insert.

Subsequently, in 1929 and 1930, Chicherin wrote me twenty-five handwritten letters which I have preserved. He had asked to see the proofs. In one letter he copied a page from a German book which he thought might interest me. He corrected the spelling of names and, in fine if quaint English, offered interpretations and more facts. He likewise wrote about personal matters.

"My greatest joy remains to me: playing Mozart," he

said in a letter. "He is for me the world in extract and the incarnation of the beauty of life. I am mostly in a very bad state, with some life coming back for a short time usually late in the evening."

Long before that, I had asked him to write a foreword to *The Soviets in World Affairs*. "Nobody of us can write prefaces to this book," he replied. "It is independent. And it is impossible to write a preface for a book where there is false information about the Sowjetgranaten." This was a reference to my factual account of the arms traffic from Russia to Germany in the 1920's.

I then suggested that Chicherin might use the foreword to refute my version of the Soviet grenades story. In a letter dated February 9, 1930, he again refused: "We cannot endorse in the form of a preface standpoints of yours differing from ours."

He nevertheless continued to show a touching interest in the book, reading first the proofs and then the printed volumes and expressing his views on them.

Maxim Litvinov, Chicherin's assistant until 1930 and successor from then until 1939, likewise received me in Moscow and Berlin. Most of the Moscow talks took place in his apartment in the Sugar King's Villa on the Moskva River just opposite the Czar's Palace in the Kremlin. Litvinov was a loving father, and occasionally Tania, his daughter, would sit in his lap and Misha, his boy, by his side while he told me of meetings with Briand, Lloyd George, and Sir Austen Chamberlain.

Once, when Litvinov had finished the description of the important Anglo-Soviet conference of 1924, he said, "I have told you everything I remember. The man who really knows what happened was Rakovsky."

But Rakovsky, former Soviet Ambassador to London and Paris, was in exile for Trotzkyist deviations. I had no difficulty, however, in locating Rakovsky in Saratov on the Volga.

I brought Rakovsky a letter from Litvinov. It had occurred to me that though Rakovsky knew me he might not reveal important unpublished facts about Soviet foreign policy unless he was sure that Chicherin, Litvinov, and others were doing so. I regarded Rakovsky as a loyal Bolshevik despite his official sins of opposition and I felt that he would not disclose secrets without permission. I put these doubts to Litvinov.

"What do you expect me to do?" Litvinov said. "I cannot write a letter of recommendation for you to a banished Trotzkyist."

"Then there is not much point in my going," I replied.

"Well, let me think about it," Litvinov said.

Two days later a Foreign Commissariat messenger brought me a letter. It was written and signed by Litvinov and addressed not to Rakovsky but to Theodore Rothstein, chief of the Commissariat Press Department. In it Litvinov requested Rothstein to give me every possible assistance in the preparation of a history of Soviet foreign relations. Rakovsky would know that this letter was intended for him, first, because a letter from Litvinov to Rothstein would otherwise not be in my possession, and moreover, if Litvinov had wished to give such instructions to Rothstein he would give them orally, for they met several times a day.

Rakovsky was living with his wife in a two-room suite in Saratov's best hotel. In London, Rakovsky had attended Buckingham Palace royal parties wearing silk breeches. When I knocked at his Saratov door he came out in a vest and stocking feet. He had been sleeping. I explained the purpose of my visit and presented Litvinov's letter.

"I don't need that," he said scornfully and returned it.

For eight days, for six hours each day, Rakovsky spun the exciting narrative of Soviet foreign relations. Evenings, other banished Trotzkyists called on Rakovsky in his apartment and he introduced them to me. Several times I walked with him through the streets to the public restaurant to which he was assigned; as he passed, men tipped their hats and bowed. This political "criminal" was probably the most revered person in town. In 1928, Stalinism was still relatively liberal. Oppositionists, officials, and the man in the street were not yet paralyzed by fear.

Rakovsky kept the unpublished protocols of the 1924 Anglo-Soviet conference in a huge trunk in his room. He let me make excerpts from them as well as from personal correspondence with Chicherin and prominent British and French leaders.

Rakovsky was rested, relaxed, and reflective. He shared his profound insights into world politics and showed me, as did Chicherin—but never Litvinov—how party controversies in the Soviet Union interfered with the conduct of Russia's foreign affairs.

Leo Karakhan, Assistant Foreign Commissar for the Far East, was even freer, friendlier, and more informal than Rakovsky. He had been telling me of his activities as Soviet Ambassador in China in the early 1920's. "I have something for you," he said suddenly and went back into his private office and brought out a secret file of the correspondence between him and Chicherin on the one hand and Dr. Sun Yat-sen on the other. He handed it to me.

"What can I do with these?" I asked.

"Take them home and copy them," Karakhan replied.

One letter from Karakhan to Dr. Sun Yat-sen, dated September 23, 1923, informed the Chinese leader that the Soviet government was appointing, as its representative to China, Michael M. Borodin whom the world knew as the representative of the Third International or Comintern. A *"rigidly confidential"* note, so emphasized by Dr. Sun, informed Lenin, Trotzky, and Chicherin, that he was sending Chiang Kai-shek to Moscow to obtain arms for the Chinese revolution.

Karakhan also told me, for publication, that the Soviet government financed the Whampoa Military Academy near Canton. Karakhan, a handsome, attractive Armenian, the son of a rich family and trained as a lawyer, was startlingly frank. Borodin, by contrast, was secretive and elusive. My first attempts to persuade him to talk about his part in the Chinese revolution were made in 1927. He began to confide in me in 1929, when he disclosed the detailed story which forms the basis for a long chapter in this book.

Theodore A. Rothstein, former Ambassador to Persia; Krestinsky, Soviet envoy in Berlin, and subsequently Assistant Commissar; Karl Radek, adviser to the Kremlin on foreign policy; Ambassador Gregory Sokolnikov; Adolf A. Joffe, member of the Bolshevik delegation to the Brest-Litovsk conference in 1917–1918, as well as Count Brockdorff-Rantzau, the German ambassador to Moscow—these and scores of other Russian, German, French, British, and American diplomats likewise succumbed to the normal temptation of speaking to a person who promised to record for posterity actions of which they were proud. The Sun-Karakhan-Chicherin correspondence, the Chicherin letters, and a number of statements so designated were for my guidance, and not for publication until the death of the person concerned, but in general the men and women I interviewed were generous and fearless.

The Soviet officials who gave me access to their memories and private files and to the Czarist archives had high culture and standards. They were instruments of a dictatorship, and could be tough and harsh, yet they were communicative, friendly, and responsive to friendship. The original élan and idealism of the revolution animated them. They regarded themselves as the heirs of Lenin, which probably explains why the successor of Lenin, Stalin, killed or buried alive politically those of them who failed to outwit him by dying a natural death.

*The Soviets in World Affairs* encompasses two periods:

1. Wars, insurrections, and revolutions in Russia and elsewhere, 1917 to 1921.
2. Peace and economic stabilization, 1921 to the end of 1929.

The years between 1921 and 1929, but especially between 1924 and 1929, were years of large possibilities and lost opportunities. In Europe production revived, living standards rose, hope returned; revolutionary impulses receded. But economic nationalism, and the limitations set by poverty on world markets, impeded basic economic solutions. Then, in October 1929, the Wall Street crash accelerated developments which led to the 1933–1945 era of Hitler in the old world and of Roosevelt, his Nemesis, in the new.

Even more tragic than the failure to secure the economic structure was the failure to fortify the peace. The Second World War was not inevitable; no war is. But history documents the reluctance of statesmen to bridge the gap—then undoubtedly bridgeable—between the Soviet and capitalist worlds and, too, their inability to exchange pride, vengeance, and illusory national benefits for the advantages of friendship and union among capitalist nations.

The weakness which forced the newborn Soviet republic to pay a high price for peace with the Kaiser in 1918 would have induced the Kremlin to cooperate with the victorious Allied coalition. Instead of exploring this road to reconciliation, more than a score of European, American, and Asiatic powers dispatched troops into Russia in a vain effort to crush the young republic. Subsequently, the politicians wasted years trying to collect uncollectable debts, regain nationalized property, and humble the Red revolutionaries.

While the anti-Soviet nations indulged in the follies of intervention, nonrecognition, financial boycott and commercial embargo, Moscow raised a banner on which was written the liberation of oppressed peoples, the equality of all races, and anti-imperialism. To translate program into practice, the Soviet government abolished Czarist discrimination against the more than a hundred ethnic minorities within Russia, gave independence to Finland, Poland, and the three Baltic states, surrendered the concessions and special privileges extorted by the absolute monarchy from Persia, and renounced the Czar's designs on the Turkish Straits.

When the fighting ended in 1921, the Communist regime turned inward to nurse its wounds, rebuild its ruined body, and wrestle with baffling problems of political administration.

The decade between the defeat of Soviet arms at the gates of Warsaw and 1930 was marked by revolutionary diminuendo in the world and nationalistic crescendo in Russia. The violent establishment of Communist states became impossible in Europe after 1923 and in China after 1927. Moscow accordingly concentrated on foreign propaganda whose utility was in inverse ratio to the irritation it caused abroad.

At the close of 1929, a *de facto* truce existed between the two worlds: the Communists could not destroy capitalism, and capitalism could not crush Communism. Russia had launched the first five-year plan; the West had entered on a prolonged depression. Old antagonisms persisted. But resentment against the perpetrators of foreign military intervention played no discernible part in Soviet diplomacy. Disappointment over confiscation and nonpayment of debts no longer blocked trade. The Soviet government was experimenting in peaceful symbiosis.

That is where *The Soviets in World Affairs* ends.

Ten years after 1929, Moscow signed an infamous pact with Hitler. Another decade later, Russia was an aggressive imperialist, casting a pall of fear over mankind. The contrasts between the twelve years described in this book and the present are enormous. Chapter 8, for example, opens with: "The attitude of the Bolsheviks towards the United States has always been exceptionally friendly." Other pages discuss Japan's predatory designs on China, Poland's idle hopes of expansion into the Ukraine, France's flimsy alliances in the Balkans, America's aloofness from Europe and Asia, and similar ephemeral phenomena which are as dead as they were deadly.

Yet remote as this history seems, it is the very recent prelude to the big events of today.

There is a significant and necessary interrelationship between the foreign policy carried out by Chicherin in the 1918–1929 period, by Litvinov from 1930 to 1939, and by Molotov and Vishinsky thereafter. Chicherin's antagonism to the Third International or Comintern was well known. He knew it hampered relations with bourgeois powers. Litvinov concurred in the view that Communist parties outside Russia could not make a revolution in peacetime. "The prospects of world revolution disappeared on November 11, 1918," he said to me in 1929.

But whereas Litvinov laid his sensational disarmament proposals before the League of Nations, Chicherin believed that "the whole disarmament business at Geneva is merely designed as slogans for Comintern propaganda and for internal politics. It enables us to say that we are threatened." A dictator needs foreign bogies.

Just as Chicherin made this off-the-record statement, a large dog stood up outside the window of the bar in his Wiesbaden Hotel, pawed the iron bars, and barked. "There, there," Chicherin jeered, "this is an attack on the Soviet Union. The dog provides the Comintern with a slogan."

Chicherin defended Russia's national sovereignty. "I am and always have been an absolutely undiluted, unwavering, unswerving enemy of our joining the League of Nations," he wrote me in a letter. It had apparently not occurred to him that the Soviet Union might be in a world organization yet not of it, indeed, against it.

Litvinov took the opposite position and, after he became Foreign Commissar, Russia entered the League.

Chicherin fought Moscow's adherence to the Kellogg Pact for the renunciation of war as an instrument of national policy. Litvinov advocated it, and, with Bukharin's help, won.

Chicherin recognized the importance of India and consistently cultivated the middle kingdoms of Persia and Afghanistan. He regarded a friendly Turkey as crucial to the USSR. He kept a constant watch on Outer Mongolia, which in his time became a Soviet protectorate, and supported an active Russian policy in China with a view to the expulsion of Western influences. He faced with equanimity the prospect that these Moscow attitudes might ruffle Great Britain. He foresaw an early divorce between the United Kingdom and the Dominions; the thought was fathered by the wish to see England's decline.

In Chicherin's concept, Germany was the pivot of Soviet foreign policy and Asia its special concern. He feared a nutcracker arrangement between France and Poland which would imperil Russia by reducing Germany's importance and increasing Polish aggressiveness. He was therefore anti-French and pro-Lithuanian.

In broad terms, Chicherin's policy was isolationist and anti-West, with Germany acting as a defensive bulwark for Russia while Moscow extended its influence in the Near, Middle, and Far East.

Litvinov, on the contrary, was pro-British, pro-French, pro-American, and anti-German. While still Assistant Commissar he told me he did not want big sums spent on the Red Fleet. Russian large-scale naval construction might anger Britain. "I think an agreement with England about Afghanistan and the East generally is possible," he said to me in confidence in March 1929, "but my government takes a different view."

The Soviet government was still taking the Chicherin view which reflected Russia's century-old enmity to England and her allies. But after Litvinov assumed the post of Commissar in 1930, he gradually scrapped and reversed Chicherin's diplomatic strategy. The Litvinov era was characterized by closer ties and warmer relations between the Soviet Union and the West.

Litvinov was dismissed in May 1939; ethnically, politically, and ideologically, he presented an obstacle to the conclusion of the Soviet-Nazi Pact of August 23, 1939. Stalin thereupon reverted, with amendments arising out of changed conditions, to the old-Russian-Chicherin orientation which, except for a few wartime pro-Western modifications induced by Hitler's invasion of Russia, the Kremlin has followed to this day.

There is thus a strange bond between the quiescent, defensive, anti-imperialist policy of the Chicherin period and Russia's present imperialism—a situation changed dialectically into its opposite.

At Saratov, Rakovsky revealed a clash of opinion in high Soviet circles which was resolved in 1939 in favor of imperialism. It concerned Bessarabia, a Russian province forcibly occupied by Rumania in 1918, when the Bolshevik armed forces were otherwise engaged. In 1920, just as Red troops were defeating the last counter-revolutionary armies, General Frunze, Commissar of War of the Soviet Ukraine, a Moldavian by birth, proposed the reconquest of Bessarabia. Voroshilov supported him.

Lenin consulted Rakovsky who was part Rumanian, part Bulgarian, knew the Balkans intimately, and had written a pamphlet on Bessarabia. Rakovsky opposed military action. A Russian offensive against Rumania might, he contended, precipitate a war with the Western nations. Moreover, the collapse of Rumania would involve Moscow in Balkan problems which it could not handle with its limited resources.

Although Rakovsky objected to a violent solution of the Bessarabian question, he obstructed a peaceful solution. In the summer of 1921, Trotzky urged the Politburo to recognize Bessarabia as part of Rumania and thereby heal a dangerous open wound. Litvinov sided with Trotzky; Litvinov always tried to avoid trouble. But Rakovsky demurred. By withholding a Bessarabian settlement, he argued, Rumania would be kept in a perturbed state, and Russia would win friends in Bulgaria and Yugoslavia where there was considerable hostility to Rumania.

The Trotzky-Litvinov suggestion failed of adoption. In 1924, Litvinov revived it. This, according to Rakovsky, precipitated a quarrel between him and Litvinov. That same year, Rakovsky went as Ambassador to London, and from there he continued to write memoranda to the Politburo stressing the salutary effect on Balkan politics of perpetuating Bessarabia as a "Soviet Irredenta." When Rakovsky's correspondence on this matter flagged, Chicherin chided him and begged him to continue the battle. Stalin supported the Chicherin-Rakovsky position; it finally prevailed, and on January 23, 1928, the tenth anniversary of the Rumanian seizure of Bessarabia, the Soviet press called the province "The Alsace on the Dnieper."

This seed of Soviet expansionism lay in fallow ground until 1939 when it sprouted in the warm climate of aggression which followed the Soviet-Nazi Pact.

Rakovsky told me, also in strict confidence, of inner council debates about Turkey. In 1922 Turkey, hard-pressed by the invading Greeks, knocked at the Kremlin gate. Commissar of Defense Trotzky wished to give unstinting aid. Stalin, Orjonekidze, and other Georgian and Caucasian comrades advised moderation. They recalled Turkey's occupation of the Georgian port of Batum in March 1921; they did not want a strong Turkey. Lenin backed Trotzky. Turkey received heavy Soviet supplies as well as Soviet military advisers.

Georgian nationalism colored another early episode of Soviet foreign affairs. The Soviet-Persian Treaty of Friendship of February 26, 1921, provided for the evacuation of Russian troops from the Persian province of Ghilan. Instead of withdrawing the Russian troops, Georgian Communists reinforced the Russian garrison and established a Soviet republic on Persian territory. The Teheran government complained to Soviet Ambassador Theodore A. Rothstein, who complained to Lenin. Rothstein submitted that Persia was not ripe for a proletarian revolution and that if Russia exported one to the underdeveloped country, complications would arise with England. "It seems to me you are right," Lenin replied.

Rothstein thereupon encouraged Rhiza Khan, virtual ruler and later the Shah of Persia, to overthrow the Ghilan Soviet Republic. "Among the prisoners Riza took were Russian peasants from Tula," Chicherin said to me in recounting this story. "Those," he sneered, "were the soldiers of Stalin's Ghilan Soviet Republic." (Chicherin disliked Stalin and Trotzky.)

After the Second World War, Stalin repeated the adventure, with some of the same agents, and set up a Soviet republic in Persian Azerbaijan. It, too, proved a fiasco.

Stalin's incursion into Ghilan in 1921, the 1920 Soviet military campaign to seize Poland (Stalin participated in it personally, whereas Trotzky opposed it), and perhaps the Bolshevik invasion of Menshevik Georgia in 1920, as well as Moscow's control over Outer Mongolia, may be attributable to the same tangle of nationalistic, domestic-political, personal, and ideological motivations which explain the Soviet imperialism of the post-1939 period. In the main, these early imperialistic manifestations were prolongations of defensive military actions taken during the civil war and foreign intervention. Once armies take the field, defense easily merges into offense. This induced observers to suggest that peace was desirable if only to prevent the spread of Communism. A new world war, I wrote in the conclusion to this book, "would bring revolution to Eastern Europe and as far, at least, as Vienna."

With hindsight it is therefore possible to assume that Soviet imperialism existed from the genesis of the Bolshevik regime but lay dormant from 1921 until Hitler pushed the button that started World War II.

Conquest by a foreign army, however, is not the same as a popular revolution. When the Bolshevik forces were repulsed at Warsaw in 1920, Lenin admitted that the invasion of Poland was a mistake. It was a mistake because it failed, and it failed, he said, because the Polish peasants and workers did not rise against their rulers. In the 1940's, the invasion of Poland, and of Estonia, Latvia, Lithuania, Czecho-Slovakia, Hungary, Rumania, and Bulgaria succeeded although the peasants and workers did not rise. It succeeded thanks to irresistible Soviet arms. No revolution occurred anywhere. Communism was imposed by invading hosts employing local puppets who enjoyed minority popular support. In Yugoslavia, where Tito had British weapons and an army, Russian domination was resisted and, in the end, Tito, the Yugoslav Stalin, threw off the Kremlin yoke.

Tito's defection reinforces the thesis that Soviet nationalistic imperialism and Stalinist power lust far outweigh any idealistic impulse in Moscow to better the lot of humanity through Communism.

"World Revolution" by Russian cannon and sword rather than by foreign working classes may have been implicit in Bolshevism from birth. Perhaps the chief variable between the 1917–1930 era and the present is the element of power: Russia is relatively stronger, Europe and Asia relatively weaker.

Yet today's Soviet imperialism was preceded by a metamorphosis in the character of the Soviet regime. Beginning with Lenin's death in 1924, Stalin, who is a master of dosage and patience, slowly turned the domestic-political pyramid downside up so that the powers and many of the functions of all its levels—the soviets, the trade unions, the Communist Party—flowed down into the point, the dictator, on which the structure now stands. Stalin thus achieved absolute power. And having achieved it at home, having meanwhile, moreover, substituted reactionary nationalism for progressive internationalism, he was able, when war offered an opportunity, to achieve absolute power in wide areas abroad. In Rumania, Poland, Bulgaria, and their sister colonies of the Soviet Empire, Stalin merely applied the same rules that brought him monolithic might inside Russia. Accustomed to the divorce between leadership and people in the Soviet Union, the Kremlin ignores similar circumstances in the satellites. The colonies naturally fall into the pattern of the motherland.

Ghilan was a pinpoint on the history of Soviet foreign relations. It was only twenty-five years later, when a similar pinpoint appeared in Azerbaijan, that a line could be drawn between the two points. Bessarabia was another such point. But only the post-1939 Moscovite policy in the Balkans suggests that the pinpoint was in reality a seed of the future. This is the value of history. A historian may not see, as I did not see, the full significance of the events he records; yet his work, read in the perspective of subsequent developments, can shed light on the past though he himself was not sufficiently enlightened at the time of writing.

LOUIS FISCHER

*Princeton, New Jersey*

1960

# AUTHOR'S ACKNOWLEDGMENTS

THIS BOOK traces in detail the course of Soviet foreign relations from the beginning of the Bolshevik revolution to the end of 1929. The struggle between Lenin and Trotzky and Bukharin on the signing of the Brest Litovsk treaty with Germany was studied from Bolshevik archive material. The Civil War and intervention period became clearer after a perusal of Kolchak's archives captured by the Red Army in Omsk and Irkutsk, and placed at the disposal of the writer by the Commissariat of Foreign Affairs. Litvinov showed the author his private archive of 1918. Papers and details will be found here revealing for the first time the fact and character of secret Soviet-Polish negotiations in 1919. There are also new data on Moscow's relations with Bela Kun's Communist regime in Hungary. Soviet officials and generals shared with the author their information on Enver Pasha's last mysterious adventure in Central Asia, whither he went to re-establish the empire of Tamerlane.

Chicherin, Litvinov, Rakovsky and German diplomats reconstructed the story of the Genoa Conference and the Rapallo Treaty for the author's benefit. Chicherin and Rakovsky, and lesser Soviet officials, gave him important and new material on the Lausanne Conference with Turkey in 1922–3. Soviet negotiations with England in 1924, with France in 1925, 1926, and 1927, and with Japan between 1922 and 1925 are recounted on the basis of the unpublished protocols which are quoted at length, and of conversations with the participants. The writer made a special and protracted visit to Rakovsky's place of exile, and received from him an interesting correspondence with British Labor leaders and prominent publicists, and significant side-lights on Anglo-Russian relations.

Karakhan told the author of his negotiations with China and Japan, Rothstein of his activity as Soviet minister in Persia, Aralov as Soviet ambassador in Turkey, Krestinsky in Germany, Kerzhentsev in Scandinavia, etc. Karakhan permitted the use of an unpublished correspondence with Dr. Sun Yat-sen.

A long chapter on Russia's rôle in the Chinese revolution was compiled on information from Borodin and from Chinese.

The writer discussed the subject of the book in regular meetings with Chicherin, Litvinov, Karakhan, and Rothstein. He received much assistance from German diplomats and writers, especially from Dr. Herbert von Dirksen, the German ambassador in Moscow, Ministerial Director Gaus, the legal expert of the German Foreign Office, and Herr Gustav Hilger, the economic counsellor of the German Embassy in Moscow. He talked informally on Russian questions with Mr. S. Parker Gilbert, British M.P.'s, and German, English, and American business men.

The whole manuscript or parts of it were read by Chicherin, Rothstein, Colonel John Ward, C.B., C.M.G., Borodin, Rakovsky, E. A. Adamov, keeper of archives in the Commissariat of Foreign Affairs, H. Bruce Lockhart, Dr. Von Dirksen, John C. Wiley of the United States Embassy in Berlin, Walter Duranty, Moscow correspondent of the *New York Times,* Paul Scheffer, Moscow correspondent of the *Berliner Tageblatt,* Frederick R. Kuh, Berlin correspondent of the United Press, Charlotte Kuh, Kenneth Durant, New York correspondent of *Tass,* and Sanford Griffith. All made important corrections and suggestions. To all of them, and to those many friends and colleagues and to his wife who helped him in the preparation of the volume, the author now publicly expresses a gratitude already communicated personally.

Apart from the many books, pamphlets and magazines mentioned in the notes and text, hundreds of publications were consulted. The author likewise examined the complete files of the Moscow *Izvestia* for the last twelve years, and of British, French, German and American dailies for the same period. He wishes to thank the skilled librarians in Moscow, Paris, Berlin and New York, who gave him of their advice and time.

An appendix reproduces a secret Anglo-French Convention for the division of South Russia into "zones of influence." It was supplied to the author from an official British source.

LOUIS FISCHER

1930

CONTENTS

# THE SOVIETS IN WORLD AFFAIRS

# UNION OF SOVIET SOCIALIS

AREAS ANNEXED SINCE 1939

60° N
ARCTIC CIRCLE
80° N
SPITZBERGEN (NOR.)
40° E
FRANZ JOSEF LAND
SEVER IS.
ARCTIC
BARENTS SEA
NORTH CAPE
NOVAYA ZEMALAYA
NORWAY
Murmansk
SWEDEN
KARA SEA
FINLAND
KARELO-FINNISH S.S.R.
BALTIC SEA
ESTONIAN S.S.R.
Viborg
Kara
Berlin
LATVIAN S.S.R.
Leningrad
Salekhard
Igarka
LITHUANIAN S.S.R.
DVINA R.
RUSSIAN
OB R.
POLAND
URAL MOUNTAINS
SOVIET
Warsaw
Minsk
WHITE RUSSIAN S.S.R.
Moscow
Samarovo
Kirov
Gorki
Molotov
OB R.
Kazan
Kiev
Sverdlovsk
Tobolsk
UKRAINIAN S.S.R.
RUMANIA
MOLDAVIAN S.S.R.
Kuibyshev
Toms
VOLGA R.
Odessa
Omsk
Novosibirsk
Magnitogorsk
Stalingrad
Sevastopol
Rostov
URAL R.
Istanbul
BLACK SEA
Semipalatinsk
Astrakhan
40° N
Ankara
KAZAK S.S.R.
GEORGIAN S.S.R.
Batum
LAKE BALKHASH
TURKEY
ARAL SEA
ARMENIAN S.S.R.
CASPIAN SEA
TURKESTAN
Baku
AZERBAIJAN S.S.R.
UZBEK S.S.R.
Alma Ata
Tashkent
SYRIA
TURKMEN S.S.R.
KIRGIZ S.S.R.
Ashkhabad
TADJIK S.S.R.
JORDAN
IRAQ
Teheran
IRAN
SAUDI ARABIA
AFGHANISTAN
KASHMIR
40° E

REPUBLICS
ALASKA (USA)
BERING STR.
ST. LAWRENCE I. (USA)
BERING SEA
Anadyr
80°N
60°N
NOVO SIBIRSK IS.
120°E
OCEAN
ARCTIC CIRCLE
KOLYMA R.
KOMANDORSKIE IS.
KAMCHATKA
Petropavlovsk
Verkhoyansk
Khatanga
LENA R.
Okhotsk
SEA OF OKHOTSK
KURILE ISLANDS (FROM JAPAN 1945)
Yakutsk
SOCIALIST
REPUBLIC
Nikolaevsk
SAKHALIN
KARAFUTO (FROM JAPAN 1945)
ERATED
Vitim
AMUR R.
Tygda
Biro-bijan
Khabarovsk
HOKKAIDO
Kirensk
LAKE BAIKAL
Chita
MANCHURIA
Harbin
Irkutsk
Vladivostok
TANNU TUVA 1944
JAPAN
SEA OF JAPAN
Ulan Bator
Mukden
MONGOLIAN REPUBLIC
JEHOL
KOREA
Dairen
Port Arthur
Peiping
INNER MONGOLIA
NKIANG
CHINA
Shanghai
EAST CHINA SEA
BET
1000 MILES
120°E
TRM

# 1

# THE BOLSHEVIKS MAKE PEACE

THE BOLSHEVIKS came to power in November, 1917, promising "bread to the workers, land to the peasants, and peace to all." The end of the World War, they believed, would bring all three. Therefore almost the first act of the Communist Government was to take steps towards a cessation of hostilities.

Immediate peace was demanded by the internal situation. The country was weary of fighting; the soldiers were tired of the trenches. The quick success of the Bolsheviks is explained, to a large extent, by their ability to exploit this circumstance.

> Long before the destruction of the Czarist regime (March 12, 1917), [wrote A. F. Kerensky in the *New York Times* of May 22, 1927] the army at the front had developed acute indications of disintegration. By January, 1917, more than a million deserters were roaming about in the rear of the army. In the first weeks of the March revolution the Russian army ceased to exist as a fighting force.

The Russian army, in 1917, simply commenced to demobilize itself. Not even the gilded oratory of Kerensky could stem the tide. "You, Mr. Minister," said one common muzhik-soldier to Kerensky on the Riga front, "tell us that we must fight for land and freedom. Of what good will land be to me if I am killed? All I will get will be three yards for a grave."

Kerensky did not reply to the argument. There was no reply. The peasant knew that back home his folks were expropriating the owners of large estates. That to him was more pressing business than fighting Germans, Austrians and Turks.

A Czarist general tells how he tried to persuade his peasant soldiers to remain at the front. If you open the front, he told them, the Germans will march in. "Oh," said one muzhik, "I am from the province of Pensa. They will never get as far as that." Yes, argued the general, but you will have to pay tribute. "How much?" inquired the soldiers. The general suggested an approximate figure. "That isn't much," they maintained. "We are losing much more at home now."

**THE POPULAR WILL FOR PEACE** "The army voted for peace with its legs," Lenin declared. It ran away. In November, therefore, when the Bolsheviks seized the ship of state, the Russian army was no longer an effective weapon. There could be no war because there was no army worthy of the name. "Since we could not engage in war," as Trotzky said, "we had to conclude peace. . . ."[1]

There were other factors. The Bolsheviks had opposed the World War from the very start. They considered it iniquitous and unjust. Caused by economic rivalry, aiming at ruthless aggrandizement, they believed that it would neither end wars nor destroy imperialism unless "the international war of the capitalists is transformed into a civil war against the capitalists."

Late in the evening of April 16, 1917, Lenin, Zinoviev, and thirty other revolutionary émigrés, of whom seventeen were Bolsheviks, arrived in Petrograd from Switzerland after a trip through Germany in partially sealed cars.[2] The next day Lenin addressed a meeting of Bolshevik members of the All-Russian Soviet. "It is impossible," he submitted, "to end war with a truly democratic, non-annexationist peace except through the overthrow of capitalism. . . ."

On November 8, therefore, just one day after the Bolsheviks came into power, the Government issued a decree offering peace to all the world. "The Workers' and Peasants' Government," reads the first sentence, ". . . proposes to all belligerent nations and their governments to commence immediately negotiations for an equitable and democratic peace." Definition follows. "An equitable and

[1] A. A. Joffe (ed.): *The Brest-Litovsk Peace Conference*. Complete Stenographic Record of Plenary Sessions and Session of Political Commission. Introduction by L. D. Trotzky. (Moscow, 1920), p. vi.

[2] Krupskaya, Lenin's wife, Zinoviev, and Radek, who accompanied Lenin on this trip, have written articles about it which are reprinted in *Die Reise Lenins durch Deutschland im plombierten Wagen* by Fritz Platten (Berlin, 1924).

democratic peace . . . is, according to the Government, an immediate peace without annexation (that is, without the seizure of foreign lands, without the forcible annexation of foreign nationalities) and without the payment of indemnities."

These words were penned a year and three days before that momentous November 11, 1918, on which the Armistice was signed. Yet Winston Churchill agrees that the war might have ended at this juncture. "This was undoubtedly a favorable opportunity for peace," he wrote regarding the period immediately after the Bolshevik revolution.[3] "Russia down, Italy gasping, France exhausted, the British army bled white, the U-boats not yet defeated, and the United States 3,000 miles away, constituted cumulatively a position where German statesmanhood might well have intervened decisively." He outlines the practical possibilities of such a peace; it would have been attained at the expense of Russia, the ally. And then, "Such were the elements of this great opportunity. It was the last. But Ludendorff cared for none of these things."

Strangely enough, Ludendorff talks in the same tone. In an estimate of the position of the Central Powers at the end of 1917, he says, "The Austro-Hungarian army was tired. . . . Its fighting power was small; it practically sufficed only against Italy." The political situation was serious for "only the army kept the Dual Monarchy together." Of Bulgaria the generalissimo wrote, "The nation and the army were tired of war. . . . Bulgaria would remain loyal as long as all went well with us." In Turkey conditions were no better. "She was at the end of her tether," and the strength of the whole chain suffered by reason of the extreme weakness of the weakest link. Even Germany, the strongest link, the body and trunk of the Quadruple Alliance, showed signs of extreme fatigue. "In Germany the spirit was better than in the countries of our associates, but it had obviously sunk quite appreciably, and the general atmosphere had become worse."[4]

Nevertheless, no reply was made to the Russian peace offer of November 8.

**THE ALLIES' ATTITUDE TOWARD THE SOVIET REGIME** The Allies assumed an unfriendly attitude to the new government from the very beginning. Buchanan

[3] Winston Churchill: *The World Crisis,* 1916–8, (London, 1927) II, 404.
[4] Erich Ludendorff: *Meine Kriegserinnerungen* (Berlin, 1920), p. 433.

noted in his diary for November 13 that the Bolsheviks[5] "want to stand well with the Allies" and expressed fear lest German agents "cause friction between Great Britain and Russia." Yet he would not treat with Trotzky, the Foreign Minister of an entente country. Ambassador Francis, of the United States, likewise assumed a hostile position. "The day after the fall of the Provisional Government," he tells us,[6] "I wrote in a letter to Consul-General Summers at Moscow . . . 'It is reported that the Petrograd Council of Workmen and Soldiers has named a cabinet with Lenin as Premier, Trotzky as Minister of Foreign Affairs, and Madame or Mlle. Kollontai as Minister of Education. Disgusting. . . .' " Later he wrote, "Of course, we would not, or I would not recognize any Ministry of which Lenin is Premier or Trotzky Minister of Foreign Affairs." He had not had any communication with Washington on the views of the State Department. The Bolsheviks had not as yet annulled their international debts or shown any intention of negotiating a separate peace or given any evidence of disloyalty to the Allies.

November 21, 1917, Trotzky forwarded a note to all Allied ambassadors in Petrograd (Russia was still one of the Allies), which he asked them to consider as a "formal proposal of an immediate armistice on all fronts and the immediate opening of peace negotiations." The same note was sent to all other belligerent countries.

On the previous day, a communication was sent to "Citizen Commander-in-Chief Dukhonin," generalissimo of all the Russian armies, instructing him to conclude an immediate armistice on all fronts. Dukhonin refused. In a conversation over the direct ticker-telegraph between Lenin, Stalin, Commissar of Nationalities, and Officer Krylenko in Petrograd, and General Dukhonin at Staff Headquarters in Moghilev, lasting from 2 A.M. to 4.30 A.M. November 22, Dukhonin questioned the authority of the new government to take steps leading toward peace. Thereupon, the three commissars at the other end of the wire informed him that he was discharged from his post and would soon be relieved by the new Commander-in-Chief, Krylenko. (The tape of this conversation has fortunately been preserved.)

[5] Sir George Buchanan: *My Mission to Russia and Other Diplomatic Memoirs* (London, 1923), II, 213.

[6] David R. Francis: *Russia from the American Embassy* (New York, 1921), p. 186.

November 23, a proclamation signed by Lenin and Krylenko called on all army units to enter into armistice negotiations. Simultaneously, the Bolshevik press commenced the publication of the secret diplomatic archives of the Russian Foreign Office.

That same day, Lord Robert Cecil, speaking for the British Government, declared his opposition to the Russian peace moves.

> The action taken by the extremists in Petrograd, [he said] would of course be a direct breach of the agreement of September 5, 1914, and . . . if adopted by the Russian nation would put them practically outside the pale of the ordinary council of Europe. . . . There is no intention of recognizing such a government.[7]

The Allied representatives in Petrograd took a similar position. Dukhonin had been superseded by Krylenko and the newspapers had announced the change. There was no doubt that his dismissal was final. Nevertheless, on November 23, the Allied military attachés delivered a note to Dukhonin protesting vigorously against the proposed armistice on the ground that it violated the treaty of September 5, 1914, "by which the Allies, among them Russia, agreed not to conclude a separate peace, nor to suspend hostilities one without the other. . . ." Subsequently Major Kerth, the United States Military Attaché who had not signed this note, made a similar protest "against any separate armistice that might be concluded by Russia."

A proclamation to the forces, dated "Smolni, November 24, 6 A.M." contains Trotzky's reply.

> The representatives of the Allied governments protest against a separate Russian armistice with Germany, but at the same time they do not respond to the proposal made to them by the Council of People's Commissars for an armistice on all fronts. . . .

The Russian people, Trotzky insisted, had no intention of shedding more blood in order to effect those secret, annexationist treaties which the newspapers were then publishing. They would not be bound by the dead letter of the 1914 agreement. With respect to the threat, contained in the letter of the military attachés, that the Allies

[7] Judah L. Magnes: *Russia and Germany at Brest-Litovsk. A Documentary History of the Peace Negotiations.* (New York, 1919), p. 14.

might undertake punitive measures against Russia if she concluded peace with the enemy, the workers and peasants had no fear. Their comrades in other countries, Trotzky imagined, would prevent the imperialist governments from attacking Russia simply because she "desired peace and the brotherhood of nations."

Buchanan admits that the allied military representatives told Dukhonin that Russia's defection

> might have the most serious consequences. The veiled threat contained in the last words, the envoy continues, has been interpreted to mean that we are about to call on Japan to attack Russia. It was an ill-advised step that has done us any amount of harm.

The break between the Bolsheviks and the Allies was growing wider. Not only had Lord Robert Cecil manifested his government's hostility to the Red Government, but Paris likewise, in a telegram to Berthelot, its military attaché at the Rumanian front, asked that general to inform the Russian authorities that it "would recognize no government in Russia that proved itself capable of entering into an agreement with the enemy."[8]

At home, also, political opponents of the Bolsheviks agitated against peace. The *Izvestia* of November 25 takes them to task. Addressing the "war patriots," an unsigned article says:

> You speak of a peace at the expense of Russia. But there is no peace at the expense of Russia that would be worse than a war at the expense of Russia. . . . You, sirs, are opposed to a separate peace and a separate armistice. So are we.

The same thought recurs in a note from Trotzky to the Allied military attachés,

> asserting that his government desired not a separate but a general peace, but that it was determined to have peace. It will, [the note concluded] be the fault of the Allied governments if Russia has after all to make a separate peace.[9]

**BUCHANAN FOR A SEPARATE PEACE** That a separate peace was indeed the undeniable need of the hour is conceded by Sir George Buchanan himself. On November 27 the ambassador telegraphed his Foreign Office as follows:

[8] Petrograd *Izvestia*. November 27, 1917.
[9] Buchanan, *op. cit.*

In my opinion, the only safe course left to us is to give Russia back her word and tell her people that, realizing how worn out they are by the war and the disorganization inseparable from a great revolution, we leave it to them to decide whether they will purchase peace on Germany's terms or fight on with the Allies . . .

For us to hold to our pound of flesh and to insist on Russia fulfilling her obligations, under the 1914 agreement, is to play Germany's game. Every day we keep Russia in the war against her will does but embitter her people against us.[1]

Allied policy, however, was too inflexible to permit of the move suggested by the British ambassador.[2]

**GERMANY ACCEPTS** The Central Powers did accept the Bolshevik armistice offer. On November 28 the Soviet Press announced that the Northern German command had, on instructions from the German Government, sent into the Russian lines a written acceptance of the Bolshevik invitation to negotiate an armistice. The date fixed was December 2, the interval to allow the Bolsheviks once more to "apply to our allies with the proposal to identify themselves with our peace platform and enter into common negotiations with the enemy for the conclusion of an armistice on the fronts of all belligerent nations."

Thereupon, Krylenko issued Order No. 3 ordering "Firing and fraternization to cease immediately on all fronts." Strict military discipline must be observed, and the line maintained. To be sure, "the front is starving," as the new Commander-in-Chief states in a published telegram, "the front is without clothes and boots, there is no fodder; horses are dying; there is no transport." But "peace is drawing nearer." "Yet a bit longer and we will achieve a general peace." All attention was to be concentrated on the men in the trenches. Perhaps, after all, no armistice would be signed. Russia could not remain altogether defenseless and at the mercy of the enemy.

Blindfolded Russian plenipotentiaries had entered the German trenches where the military authorities of the enemy agreed to a conference beginning December 2.

On November 30 Trotzky informed the Allied mission in Petrograd that

[1] *Ibid.*, p. 225.

[2] Colonel House relates the reaction which Buchanan's telegram created in Allied diplomatic circles. See *The Intimate Papers of Colonel House*, by Charles Seymour (London, 1928), III, 289.

military operations on the Russian front have been stopped, and asked the diplomatic representatives of the Allies in Russia to state in reply whether they desire to participate in the negotiations which will be opened on Sunday evening, December 2, at 5 o'clock.

The Allies returned no reply.

**ALLIED TACTICS IN PETROGRAD** They had decided to boycott the negotiations at Brest Litovsk. Meanwhile, however, neither the Allied nor the American Governments officially broke off relations with the Soviet authorities. The various embassies, including the British, maintained connections with the Commissariat of Foreign Affairs through so-called "unofficial" agents, and Maxim Litvinov was recognized by Downing Street as the representative of the de facto Russian Government. Trotzky himself saw Noulens, the French ambassador, and was "quite civil and correct," [3] but Buchanan wrote, "He [Trotzky] has not honoured me with a visit for fear that I should decline to receive him."

In their relations with the Allies, the Bolsheviks remained "civil and correct"—at least for a time—but when strict measures were required, Trotzky did not hesitate. Thus, for instance, he had early demanded the release of Comrades Chicherin (Ornatsky), Petrov, and others interned in Brixton Gaol, London, on the charge of pacifist propaganda, but when the request was not satisfied he issued the decree of November 30, 1917, interdicting the granting of outgoing visas to British subjects until the Chicherin episode was settled. Thereupon, the British Government assented and the prisoners left London on January 3, 1918, for Petrograd, where Chicherin immediately took up the duties of first assistant to Trotzky, and Petrov of first assistant to Chicherin.

Colonel Raymond Robins and, for a short while, General William B. Judson, served as go-betweens for the American Embassy, and in that capacity had numerous interviews with Lenin and Trotzky. Mr. Francis, the ambassador, like Buchanan and others, adopted the position of not "speaking" to the Bolsheviks while permitting responsible subordinates to engage in far-reaching negotiations. And the French refused to use the word "people's" in addressing soviet commissariats until the Bolsheviks began rejecting all correspondence that did not include it.

[3] Buchanan, *op. cit.*

This child's play, unimportant in itself, reflects the Allies' indecision vis-à-vis a situation on which another year of war depended. Generally speaking, their attitude was hostile, yet they refrained from breaking off all connections in the hope that something could still be retrieved.

**ARMISTICE NEGOTIATIONS** Parallel with this dilly-dallying in Petrograd, significant developments were taking place at Brest Litovsk. On December 2 the Bolshevik delegation, consisting of Adolf A. Joffe, chairman, Leo M. Karakhan, secretary, Leo B. Kamenev, Gregory Sokolnikov, Madame Bitzenko, Captain Mstislavsky, a working man, a sailor, a peasant, and eight military experts, arrived in the neutral zone to meet the German plenipotentiaries. (The Russians were thirty minutes late.)

The chief Russian delegates knew little if anything about military affairs. The German negotiators, on the other hand, were exclusively army men headed by Prince Leopold of Bavaria but dominated by General Max von Hoffmann. Representatives of Austro-Hungary, Turkey and Bulgaria also participated.

> Our delegates, [reads a Russian Government proclamation dated December 5, 10 A.M.] began with a declaration of peace aims with a view to which the armistice was being proposed. The enemy delegation replied that that was a matter for statesmen whereas they, as soldiers, were authorized to discuss only the military terms of the armistice and therefore could add nothing to the declarations of Czernin and von Kuehlmann [on the attitude of the German and Austrian Cabinet, respectively, to the original Russian peace proposals.—L.F.] . . . Our delegation proposed to the enemy that they ask for the necessary authority . . . (and) introduced a draft armistice agreement on all fronts . . . the chief points of which were, (1) prohibition of any transfer of troops from our front to the front of our allies, and (2) the evacuation of the Moon Sound Islands (in the Gulf of Riga) by the Germans.

The Germans replied that such terms could only be proposed to a defeated country. Germany desired an armistice only on the fronts between the Baltic and Black Seas and looked with disfavor on the interdiction of troop transfers to the Western war theatre. But the Russians insisted that "the armistice cannot serve the interests of one militarism against the other." At a second session on December 5, a truce was finally signed for the period between December 7 and December 17. Hostilities could be renewed by either party after three days' notice. Fighting was also suspended on the Moon Sound Islands, from which Petrograd could be threatened. During the ten-day truce, army units numbering a division or more could be moved only if the order therefor had been given prior to December 5.

It was agreed that armistice discussions would be resumed in Brest Litovsk on December 12. The Russians thereupon returned to their capital, leaving Karakhan behind to hold the diplomatic fort.[4]

The Bolsheviks still hoped that the Allies would join them on the reopening of the negotiations. Trotzky, as Commissar of Foreign Affairs, communicated immediately upon the conclusion of the temporary truce with the embassies of Great Britain, France, the United States, Italy, China, Japan, Rumania, Belgium, and Serbia, to the effect that

> the negotiations . . . were suspended at the initiative of our delegation for one week in order to give an opportunity during this time to inform the peoples and the Governments of the Allied countries . . .

**COMMUNIST PROPAGANDA** Meanwhile the Russians inaugurated a fiery propaganda crusade against Prussian militarism in the enemy lines and behind them. Special newspapers in the German language were printed in Petrograd and distributed in tens of thousands of copies. The Reds were trying to undermine the war patriotism and loyalty of their opponents' Western front.

Anti-militarist, anti-imperialist agitation was not, however, aimed only at the Central Powers. On December 7, the Council of People's Commissars issued a proclamation to the "Laboring Moslems of Russia and the East," signed Lenin and Djugoshvili (Stalin), Commissar of Nationalities. Apart from appeals to the faithful to rise against their "oppressors" and put an end to foreign domination of Asiatic colonies, the document contained important statements on Soviet foreign policy.

> Constantinople [it said] must remain in the hands of the Mohammedans; We announce that the agreement on the partition of Persia [August 31, 1907, between Great Britain and

[4] Karakhan has shared with the writer his reminiscences of the Brest period.

Czar's Empire] is torn up and annulled; We announce that the agreement of the partition of Turkey and the seizure of Armenia is torn up and annulled.[5]

Sir George Buchanan did not enjoy this essay of the Bolsheviks.

Mr. Lenin [he wrote] . . . incited our Indian subjects to rebellion. He placed us on a somewhat lower level than the Turks. . . . It is an unheard-of thing for a man who claims to direct Russian policy to use such language of a friendly and Allied country.

"Friendly and Allied" began to sound somewhat obsolete. The press of the Western world was fuming and foaming against the Red usurpers—and prophesying their disappearance in six weeks or six months. Why, then, recognize or treat with them?

The attitude of the Central Powers was different. Germany desired an agreement with the Russians for obvious reasons; such an agreement would weaken her enemy, strengthen her military position, and tend to fortify the spirit of the civilian population at home. She had accepted the Russian invitation to negotiations with alacrity and could not possibly, in view of public opinion, have retired from such conferences had the Allies put in an appearance. But in the absence of such a development, a separate peace with the Russians offered innumerable practical, tactical, and political advantages which Germany would be quick to exploit.

**A SEPARATE TRUCE** The separate nature of the Russian-German conversations was now no longer deniable. Trotzky blamed it on the Allies. "The responsibility for the separate character of the armistice," he declared, "rests entirely on those governments which have hitherto refused to announce their armistice and peace terms."

On December 13 armistice conversations commenced in Brest Litovsk, and centered around three questions, (1) the transfer of troops, (2) naval matters, (3) fraternization between opposing forces.

The Russians were uncompromising on the first point, and the Germans soon agreed not to move any troops

[5] Kluchnikov and Sabanin (eds.): *International Politics in Modern Times. Treaties. Notes, and Declarations.* Publication of the Commissariat of Foreign Affairs (Moscow, 1926), II, 94.

from the Eastern front to the Western front for a whole month until January 14. The Central Powers likewise made considerable concessions with respect to fleet operations, and, finally, "organized" fraternizing was officially countenanced by the representatives of German militarism to whom the very idea was revolting. "The exchange of views and newspapers is to be permitted." To be sure, "there must not be present at any one time more than twenty-five unarmed persons from each side," but twenty-five was enough for the Russians' anti-war propaganda purposes.

Furthermore, Turkish and Russian troops were to be withdrawn from Persia; immediate exchange of civil and military prisoners was provided for; both parties pledged to open peace negotiations without delay. . . . The armistice would remain in force at least until January 14, but continued operative unless seven days' notice was given by either contracting party.

Fighting had commenced in the South between Red forces and Dutov, Kaledin, Kornilov and other insurgent generals. Relations between Petrograd and the Ukrainian, bourgeois Rada government were highly strained. Anti-Bolshevik parties were lifting their heads and sabotaging Bolshevik efforts to establish order. On December 19, Petrograd was declared in a state of siege so as to permit the police to cope with rowdies who sacked wine, whisky and vodka stores, and drank their contents as a preliminary to riotous conduct throughout the town. In the provinces, the extension of Communist authority met with resistance from the bourgeoisie, the Social revolutionaries, etc. The internal situation made peace imperative.

The armistice was a fact. Russia was on the eve of the peace conference. The Bolsheviks wished it to be a general meeting for the re-establishment of peace throughout Europe; some Germano-Austrian diplomats inclined favorably towards the same eventuality. Throughout 1917 Austria had engaged in secret peace negotiations with France and England.[6] In Germany the desire for victory was still strong, but the confidence in success had slightly waned, and reserve strength was diminishing. Before de-

[6] Prince Sixte du Bourbon: *L'Offre de Paix Separee de l'Autriche (Decembre 5, 1916–Octobre 12, 1917) avec deux lettres autographes de l'Empereur Charles et une note autographe du Comte Czernin.* (Paris, 1920). Also, August Demblin: *Czernin und die Sixtus Affaire* (Munich, 1920).

parting for Brest, both Kuehlmann and Czernin made statements which reflected a desire for universal peace. It soon became clear, however, that the peace with Russia would be a separate peace. The Allies would be absent.

The refusal of the Allies to attend made it incumbent on the Germans to conduct the conference with an eye to Germany's future military tasks and thus confirmed the control over German foreign policy exercised by the Ludendorff-Hindenburg organization. The civilians had enjoyed a short period of ascendancy that reflected war-weariness and wavering. Even the militarists, for that brief moment, might have rejoiced in the prospect of dropping their heavy burdens. But now they proposed to use Russia's collapse as a lever to break through in France and Flanders.

**PEACE NEGOTIATIONS** The Bolsheviks went to the Brest Litovsk peace conference in a revolutionary mood. Trotzky gave the delegates a "send-off" in his famous "Appeal to the Workers, and the Oppressed and Bled Peoples of Europe." Soviet Russia's dominant motives in Brest, he advertised, would be first, "the quickest possible cessation of the shameless and criminal war which was murdering Europe," and, secondly, "to give every possible aid to the working class of all countries to destroy the rule of capitalism and to seize the government with a view to a democratic peace and the socialist remolding of Europe and all humanity."

Almost in the very hour of the opening of the Brest Litovsk peace conference—December 22, 1917—Trotsky announced in Petrograd that "yesterday a freight car full of propaganda for peace and socialism was dispatched to Germany." "Although we are negotiating peace with Germany," declared the Foreign Commissar, "we continue to speak our usual revolutionary tongue." The next day, he announced, a new Hungarian Communist daily would commence to appear.

These were the activities of the so-called "German agents." Sir George Buchanan gave Trotzky a bill of relative health when he said "even if he does take money from the Germans for his own purposes he is not their agent." The unproved accusation that Lenin, Trotzky, and the Bolsheviks generally were paid or unpaid accomplices of the Germans played its important role during the war, but it need scarcely occupy us at this late day. . . . Certainly the stenographic record of the Brest Litovsk peace conference contains no proof of Bolshevik sympathy for Germany or Austro-Hungary.

**STRANGE CONTRASTS AT BREST** Two worlds met in the citadel town. The most perfect representatives of law and *Ordnung* sat across the green table, and occasionally the dinner-table, from men who only a few months previously had stolen through Germany on false passports. Groomed diplomats to whom a prison sentence was the blackest badge of degradation negotiated with Bolsheviks with long records in Russian jails as well as German, and some of whom (Kamenev and Radek) were fated, a few months later, to suffer foreign incarceration again. The spokesman of the most disciplined and apparently most permanent government on earth broke lances here with the leaders of a child republic whose lease of life was uncertain.

Militant Communism faced organized militarism; the tempest of revolt encountered the rock of conservatism; the rough spirit of the lowest masses came into contact with the arrogance of the highest classes. It promised to be a battle.

The Russian delegation consisted of Joffe, Kamenev, Madame Bitzenko, Professor Pokrovsky, the "court" historian of the Bolsheviks, Karakhan, M. P. Veltman-Pavlovich, and four military specialists, as well as a worker, a sailor, a soldier, and a peasant who were there as useless exhibits of the new Russian democracy. The visitors were housed in barracks within the Brest fortress and ate with the Germans in the officers' mess.

I shall never forget the first dinner with the Russians, [writes General Hoffmann][7] I sat between Joffe and Sokolnikov, the present Commissar of Finance. Opposite me sat the worker who was obviously embarrassed by the large quantity of silver-ware. He tried to catch this and that with the various utensils, but he used the fork exclusively for the purpose of cleaning his teeth. Diagonally opposite, next to Prince Hohenlohe sat Madame Bitzenko, and next to her the peasant, a thoroughly Russian phenomenon with long grey locks and a tremendous, primeval-forest beard. On one occasion, the orderly could not refrain

[7] Max von Hoffmann: *Der Krieg der versaeumten Gelegenheiten* (Munich, 1924).

from a smile when, asked whether he wanted red wine or white, he inquired which was stronger, for it was the stronger brand that he would want.

> Joffe, Kamenev, Sokolnikov, above all the first, [writes Hoffmann] made an exceptionally intelligent impression. They spoke with enthusiasm of their task of leading the Russian proletariat to the peak of happiness and prosperity.

The Bolsheviks, according to the general, even confided to him their plans for world revolution.

The leading German delegates were State-Secretary of Foreign Affairs von Kuehlmann and Major-General Hoffmann; the chief of the Austro-Hungarian representatives was Foreign Minister Count Czernin; the Grand Vizier, Talaat Pasha, had come from Constantinople with his Foreign Minister Achmed Nessim Bey; last, the Bulgarians with Minister of Justice Popov and two ambassadors.

**THE DISCUSSIONS** The peace conference opened at 4.24 P.M., December 22. The first word from a Russian was the demand for public sessions. Trotzky had promised that "they would meet in conference under a bell-glass." A little opposition was beaten down and Russia won the first skirmish.

At the initial plenary session lasting only forty-nine minutes the Russians read a declaration of principles on which a general world peace was to be based. On Christmas Day, von Kuehlmann for the Quadruple Alliance, identified himself with the Russian program. Before the thirty-three minutes' sitting was closed, Joffe deftly criticized the limitations which the German statement sought to put on the Russian principles, agreed however that a basis for further negotiations was already available, and proposed a ten-day recess in order to give Russia's Allies an opportunity to join the conference. On the 28th, after a half-hour session, the conference adjourned for a week.

The interval between this initial exchange of views and the body of the conference is of outstanding interest. Bolshevism had its ears to the ground listening for the sounds of a popular will to peace. In a speech in Petrograd, Trotzky had stated that there could be no real peace without the help of the workers of the Central Powers. They were negotiating with the Kaiser as with a foe; he was a "tyrant" towards whom they "preserved their irreconcilable enmity." Unless the masses forced the German militarists to concessions, perhaps they would have to fight. Could Russia fight? "I think we could," replied the commissar, and the audience applauded wildly.

The *Izvestia,* on the other hand, turned its attention to the peoples of the Allied countries. The Bolsheviks doubted the sincerity of the Central Powers' acceptance of the Russian peace principles. Therefore, "the refusal of our Allies to participate in the peace talks ties the Russian revolution hand and foot in its struggle for a general, democratic peace."[8]

Obviously, the Russians were afraid of the terms the Germans would force on them if they returned to Brest Litovsk alone. There is a tremor of uncertainty in the voices of Petrograd and a fear that their hope in the Allies would not be fulfilled. For on December 28, M. Pichon, the new French Foreign Minister, in addressing the Chamber, gave expression to sentiments of which the Bolsheviks had not been in complete ignorance. He said:

> Germany is trying to involve us in her Maximalist (Bolshevik) negotiations. After suffering as we have, we cannot accept peace based on the status quo. . . . Russia may treat for a separate peace or not. In either case the war will continue for us.

**GERMANS SUSPECTED OF DUPLICITY** The spirit in Petrograd reflected the first encounter at Brest. In the Christmas session, the Germans had agreed to the Bolshevik principle of self-determination with certain reservations; they maintained that in Poland, Lithuania, Courland and Livonia—then under German military occupation—the will of the people had already been expressed. The Russians, however, called such expression a travesty of the principle, for there could be no free self-determination under the shadow of the rifles and machine guns of a foreign army. Pokrovsky had said at Brest Litovsk that there was no use the Central Powers talking about non-annexation when they were in control of eighteen Russian provinces where they tried to "persuade" the populace that it desired Kaiser rule.[9] Self-determination?—Yes, said General Hoffmann. But when one of the Russian military

[8] *Izvestia,* December 27, 1917.
[9] Hoffmann, *op. cit.*

attachés asked him at dinner just what territory the Germans would evacuate, Hoffmann replied, "Not one millimeter."[1] That was December 28. Germans consider it a black-letter day.

> On December 28, 1917, [writes Prince Max von Baden] we committed an irreparable mistake; we aroused in the whole world and in the German masses the impression that, in contradistinction to the Russian attitude, our agreement to the principle of the self-determination of nations was insincere and a mere shield for annexationist designs. We refused the Russian demand for free, unconstrained plebiscites in the occupied territories on the ground that Courland, Lithuania, and Poland had already voted. Never should we have spoken of the arbitrarily created or arbitrarily enlarged national councils as organs of popular representation.[2]

The *Izvestia,* discussing the same problem, speaks of the Germans, as "wolves in sheeps' clothing," and the atmosphere becomes more and more electric. Trotzky makes a last appeal to the Allies to enter the conference, even promising that pre-war annexations—Ireland, India, Egypt, Indo-China—would not be subjected to revision.

**COLONEL ROBINS** Colonel Raymond Robins of the American Red Cross Mission in Russia believed that the distrust towards Germany which prevailed in Petrograd could be exploited by the Allies for their own ends. He was in contact with the leaders of the Red regime together with his secretary, Alexander Gumberg, who was well recommended. During December he had

> been working under the verbal instructions of the ambassador of the United States in conference with Lenin and Trotzky and other officers of the Soviet Government seeking to prevent the signing of a German peace at Brest Litovsk.[3]

Robins' fundamental idea was expressed in a suggested communication to the Commissar of Foreign Affairs, dated January 2, 1918.

> At the hour, [it reads] the Russian people shall require assist-

[1] M. H. Pokrovsky: *Russian Foreign Policy in the Twentieth Century,* (Moscow, 1926), p. 74.

[2] Prince Max von Baden, *Erinnerungen und Dokumente* (Berlin, 1927), p. 191. Karl Helfferich, Vice-Chancellor of Germany during the war, likewise testifies to the insincerity of Germany's "Self-determination" policy in his *Der Weltkrieg.* Vol. 3 (Berlin, 1919).

[3] *Bolshevik Propaganda.* Hearings before a Sub-committee of the Committee of the Judiciary. United States Senate, February 11, 1919, to March 10, 1919. (Washington, 1919), p. 1009.

ance from the United States to repel the actions of Germany and her allies, you may be assured that I will recommend to the American Government that it render them all aid and assistance within its power. If upon the termination of the present armistice Russia fails to conclude a democratic peace through the fault of the Central Powers and is compelled to continue the war I shall urge upon my government the fullest assistance to Russia possible. . . . I may add, however, that if Russian armies now under command of the people's commissaires commence and seriously conduct hostilities against Germany and her allies, I will recommend to my government the formal recognition of the de facto government of the people's commissaires.

This document was drafted by Robins and approved and initialled by Ambassador Francis, but never sent. Another paper, likewise approved by the envoy, was to inform Washington of the break in the negotiations at Brest—if and when such break occurred—and suggest immediate aid. That, too, was never sent.

Meanwhile, a split seemed imminent in the ranks of the Central Powers. Czernin was under orders from the Emperor Karl to bring home a peace under any circumstances, for only peace could save the Dual Monarchy. The Russians' stern opposition to the Kuehlmann-Hoffmann attitude on Poland, Lithuania, etc., endangered the future of the conference, and, to impress his Berlin colleagues with the seriousness of the situation, Czernin threatened to conclude a separate peace with the Bolsheviks. Hoffmann's nervous system was stronger and he laughed, but the matter was most important and the Germans felt obliged to define their stand—first of all, among themselves. Accordingly, the delegates repaired from Brest to Berlin and took counsel with their chiefs.

On January 2, a Crown Privy Council discussed the Brest Litovsk conference. Von Kuehlmann reported; then the Kaiser talked on Poland and echoed Hoffmann, the last man who had spoken to him on the matter. He objected to the General Headquarters' plan for pure undisguised annexation. "General Ludendorff contradicted these objections in a somewhat vehement manner." Ludendorff completely lost control and yelled at the Kaiser. In the face of this attack, Wilhelm acted like a schoolboy in the presence of a bully. He grew white. He grew quiet. He would wait for the Staff's report. Later "the Chief War Lord" suggested meekly that Ludendorff himself might go to Brest for a while. But the general was no "babbler."

He rudely rejected the idea. (Hindenburg supported Ludendorff, though a bit more politely.)

At this meeting, Hindenburg and Ludendorff advised more rapid and energetic conduct of the negotiations at Brest so that the fate of the Border states already in the possession of Germany would be settled by their being definitely separated from Russia and awarded to the Central Powers."[4]

The next day, the Kaiser, under threats of resignation from Hindenburg and Ludendorff, approved their policy. Kuehlmann, however, was cynically instructed to effect the ends desired by the militarists "by the more amicable way of the Right of the Self-Determination of the Peoples."[5]

**THE FOURTEEN POINTS** While the Russian delegation was returning to Brest after the recess, President Wilson made his famous speech to the United States Congress in which he enunciated the Fourteen Points. During the summer of 1917 and immediately after the Bolshevik revolution Colonel House had attempted without success to persuade the Allies to make a statement of their war aims that would placate Russian public opinion and perhaps win the sympathy of German Liberals. From these efforts probably sprang the President's wish to formulate a liberal statement of World War aims. But it is not generally known that Wilson's address on the Fourteen Points was provoked by the proceedings at Brest Litovsk and, indeed, inspired from Petrograd. Colonel Robins, we recall, was "working" against the separate Russo-German peace. He had practically convinced Mr. Francis. He also talked to Edgar G. Sisson, later the sponsor of the notorious "Sisson documents." Sisson was the Petrograd representative of George Creel's Committee on Public Information, the official American propaganda bureau. On January 3, Sisson, probably acting on the suggestion of Robins (who subsequently disavowed him as a distributor of forged papers) wired to Creel urging that Woodrow Wilson "restate anti-imperialistic war aims and democratic peace requisites of America . . ." in brief, "placard" paragraphs. These he would "get fed into Germany." "Need is for internal evidence that the President is thinking of the

[4] Hoffmann, *op. cit.*
[5] *Ibid.*

Russian and German common folk . . . and that he is talking to them. Can handle German translating and printing here" through the Bolshevik agencies which were distributing revolutionary propaganda in Germany and the German army.[6]

Wilson complied on January 8.

Once more, as repeatedly before, the spokesmen of the Central Powers have indicated their desire to discuss the objects of the war and the possible bases of a general peace. Parleys have been in progress at Brest Litovsk between Russian representatives and the Central Powers to which the attention of all the belligerents has been invited for the purpose of ascertaining whether it may be possible to extend these parleys into a general conference with regard to terms of peace and settlement.

After declaring that "the Russian representatives were sincere and in earnest," the President expounded the view that while the earlier statements of Central Power principles has been made by liberal diplomats, the German side at Brest now expressed the spirit and intentions of those who "insist upon conquest and subjugation."

Then, answering the challenge to define Allied war aims, President Wilson gave the world his celebrated Fourteen Points. Points VI and XIII referred directly to the subjects under discussion at Brest Litovsk:

VI. The evacuation of all Russian territory and such a settlement of all questions affecting Russia as will secure the best and freest co-operation of the other nations of the world in obtaining the unhampered and unembarrassed opportunity for the independent determination of her own political development and national policy and assure her of a sincere welcome into the society of free nations under institutions of her own choosing; and, more than a welcome, assistance also of every kind that she may need and may herself desire. The treatment accorded Russia by her sister nations in the months to come will be the acid test of their good will, of their comprehension of her needs as distinguished from their own interests, and of their intelligent and unselfish sympathy.[7]

XIII. An independent Polish state should be erected which shall include the territories inhabited by indisputably Polish populations.[8]

[6] *Russian-American Relations (R.A.R.). March 1917–March 1920. Documents and Papers.* Compiled and edited by C. K. Cumming and W. W. Pettit (New York, 1920).

[7] How Russia's sister nations passed this test is related in the following chapters dealing with foreign intervention on Soviet territory.

[8] H. W. V. Temperley: *A History of the Peace Conference of Paris,* (London, 1920), I, 433.

The President's speech was placarded on the walls of Petrograd. It was printed on a hundred thousand Russian posters and three hundred thousand Russian handbills. The American Y.M.C.A. availing itself of Bolshevik aid, distributed one million copies throughout the Russian lines and another million, in German, within the German trenches on the Eastern front. All the papers published the statement in full. Its contents were wired to Trotzky at Brest who radioed them to "ALL, ALL, ALL."

The Bolsheviks, to be sure, distrusted Wilson's "empty phrases." They suspected in fact, and the official *Izvestia* aired these suspicions, that the Allies were prepared to let Germany satisfy her appetite in the East and consume Poland, Lithuania, etc., in order to make the peace in the West easier. Nevertheless, Wilson's message was good propaganda and the Russians exploited it.

There is no proof that the Fourteen Points address ever had the remotest effect on Allied policy towards Russia. There is no indication that the Fourteen Points played any role at Brest Litovsk. It was a voice of peace crying in a wilderness of shot, shell and blood, and slogans of "no peace without victory." It was words unaccompanied by acts. Ludendorff and Hindenburg loomed like large black shadows over the discussions in the citadel town; the spirit of Wilson was vague and unavailing.

**THE BATTLE OF WORDS** This was the stage setting for the resumption of negotiations. Nothing since the first act of the Brest drama had improved the Russians' position. The Allies had not changed their views, and no revolution had developed in the Central countries. The Bolsheviks were discouraged. If they went to the conference in December hoping vaguely that home pressure would force the Germans to grant them an honorable peace, the enemy delegations' cynical hypocrisy had disillusioned them. Von Kuehlmann's friendly phrases were neither as decisive nor important as Hoffmann's interpretation of non-annexation and self-determination. This was the prospect that faced the Communists on their return to Brest. What, then, was the sense of bargaining or negotiating? The Germans would not surrender their spoils. This had been made clear by the first session of the conference. Now only one trump remained in the hands of the Russians—propaganda.

As the train bearing the men from Petrograd drew into Brest Litovsk, Karl Radek commenced throwing pamphlets in German to the German soldiers who lined the tracks. This action was a sort of adventurous announcement of the intentions of the Bolsheviks.

Now commenced the famous and historic battle of words. Brest was a podium. From it the Bolsheviks issued their multitudinous, fiery appeals to "ALL." If they talked little to the frock-coated diplomats or be-medalled generals who sat opposite them at the green table, they talked much to the workers, soldiers and peasants of the entire world. Hoffmann stormed against attacks on German militarism, the Kaiser, etc., in the Russian Press and at Russian demonstrations. Trotzky told him, in effect, to mind his own business. Politeness was gone. Friendly relations were gone. Trotzky, who now headed the Russians, gave instructions for the Bolshevik delegation to take its meals separately from the enemy representatives. There were no more little discussions à trois or à quatre as there had been in December to thrash out knotty problems in personal, unrecorded conversations. Von Kuehlmann suggested ironically that Trotzky would soon put the Russian delegation in a monastery.

Sentences exchanged at public sessions were frequently curt and sharp. Talks were proceeding, on one occasion, about the evacuation of neutral Persia by Turkey, Germany's ally. Von Kuehlmann suggested that Russia might urge similar action on her "friend" England. Whereupon Trotzky flashed back: What about Belgium, whose neutrality had been violated? . . . The Germans drafted a preamble for the German-Russian peace treaty. It contained the usual formula "In order to establish peace and friendship." Trotzky objected to the second word. They were not in Brest to establish "friendship" but only to make peace. . . .

Hoffmann was insisting that the question of Poland, Lithuania, and Courland had already been settled. The Kaiser's army was in control and would not get out. Von Kuehlmann tried to justify this violence by reference to "the more amicable way of the right of self-determination." Are there, then, two German governments, Trotzky inquired, one in Berlin represented by Kuehlmann and the other at General Army Headquarters represented by Hoffmann which really determines the policy of the country?

Everybody knew this was so: Ludendorff could not only defy Chancellor Hertling, he could overawe and shout down the Kaiser himself. If that were the case, Trotzky proposed, why not call a spade a spade? "We are revolutionists," he said, "but we are also realists. We prefer to speak of annexations rather than use a pseudonym for the real thing."

The issue was Poland, Lithuania, Courland, Estonia, and other parts of the former Russian empire under German occupation. The Bolsheviks laid no claim to these districts. They could become independent. But the resolutions of hand-picked Landtags meeting under the muzzles of German rifles was not to be internationally recognized. The Russians proposed evacuation, the construction of a national government by the co-operation of all political parties, finally a plebiscite.

Hoffmann felt outraged. With a studied effort to offend, he said, "I must, first of all, protest against the tone of these remarks. The Russian delegation talks as if it represents the victor who has occupied our country. I want to point out that the facts are just reversed."

In the oratorical and dialectical contest which raged for weeks, the Germans and Austro-Hungarians were no match for the soap-box Russians whose chief business in life had been polemics. Count Czernin ailed too much to cut a great figure. Von Kuehlmann handled a difficult job well. Yet Trotzky towered far above him. Even Hoffmann, all his hate notwithstanding, must certify to Trotzky's versatility, culture, energy, industry, eloquence, and determination. The Germans did not like him; he was dictatorial and irritating. "His (Trotzky's) tone became more and more provoking although no real power stood behind him. He always appeared in the role of the one who demands," wrote Ludendorff. "I sat in Kreuznach as if on coals,"[9] the Quartermaster-General adds, for he wished to settle the situation in the East, and commence active preparations for the great March offensive in Flanders. Yet neither Hoffmann's gruffness nor Kuehlmann's suavity could force Trotzky to accelerate the tempo at which he wished the conference to move forward.

Kuehlmann,[1] born at Constantinople into a prominent family, was a brilliant statesman with a fine mastery of

[9] Erich Ludendorff; *op. cit.*, p. 443.
[1] Thomas Rodes: *The Real von Kuehlmann* (London, 1925).

social theory, law, and history. He was readily drawn by Trotzky into long, abstract discussions which led to no practical results and thus played into the hands of the Communists, who were trying to prolong the conference in the hope that revolutionary developments in Germany and Austro-Hungary might improve their position.

While they negotiated with the Central Powers, therefore, the Bolsheviks openly strained every nerve to provoke uprisings on the territories of those Powers. Three and a half years of suffering had fertilized the soil and prepared it for the propaganda of the Russians. It was the Central Governments' realization of the dangers of their internal situation, as well as their fear of the most unfavorable effect a breakdown of the conference would have on world opinion and, more particularly, on their military position, that forced them to tolerate Trotzky's oratory and Bolshevik procrastination. The failure of the peace negotiations would have had a bad press at home and was sure to cause popular disfavor. The state of affairs was volcanic. Even passively this circumstance reacted to the advantage of the Russians at Brest and gave their time-killing strategy a longer lease of life.

Soon enough the seeds scattered from the wireless towers at Brest and Petrograd began to sprout on the friendly soil of peoples dragged down by years of hopeless contest. On January 16, Czernin noted "desperate cries for food from Vienna." The next day's entry in his diary reads, "Bad news from Vienna and vicinity. Big strike movement . . . reduced flour ration." [2]

Large and important political strikes broke out in Berlin on January 28, and about the same time in Hamburg, Kiel, Dortmund, Mannheim, and Munich. These took place "against the wishes of the majority of the German Labor leaders and seemed to presage important results for the Bolsheviks at Brest and elsewhere." [3] A general strike movement likewise started in Austria, while the food situation in Hungary began to grow serious. Austro-Hungary's heart was not in the war, and when its stomach became empty trouble loomed. Frantic telegrams were exchanged between Vienna and Brest. Without peace, the

[2] Count Czernin: *Im Weltkriege* (Berlin, 1919), p. 323.

[3] H. W. V. Temperley (ed.): *History of the Peace Conference of Paris.* Vol. I. Published under the auspices of the Institute of International Affairs, in six volumes (London, 1920).

Dual Monarchy was doomed. The Germans, too, were not altogether certain that the strikes would not develop into rebellion.

**THE UKRAINIAN ISSUE** Austria needed bread. "In order to prevent a state of famine," writes General Hoffmann, "Berlin had to be asked for aid. Notwithstanding its own want, Berlin assisted, but in consequence Count Czernin naturally was deprived of the possibility of threatening to conclude a separate peace with Trotzky, or even try to do so. On the other hand, the separate peace with the Ukraine which I had looked upon as a measure that might force Trotzky to sign a peace, now became, as a means of obtaining bread, a vital necessity for Count Czernin."

Hungry Austro-Hungary thus sold its independence at Brest for the flour Berlin could spare. But in the final analysis, famine could be staved off only with the help of shipments from the Ukraine, the "granary of Europe." The Ukraine now became the chief issue of the conference.

The Ukraine had been proclaimed an autonomous, separate republic in accordance with the Bolshevik declaration that any part of the former Russian empire could exercise the right of independence even to the extent of secession. A "Rada" government was thereupon established at Kiev in which the outstanding figures were Vinnichenko and Simon Petlura. It was from the first anti-Bolshevik, received aid from France, and aroused the ire of Petrograd by giving succor to Kaledin's counter-revolutionary forces in the Don while obstructing the progress of Red forces sent against him. Nevertheless, when a delegation from the Rada appeared in Brest Litovsk on January 9 in reply to the Bolshevik appeal to all belligerent nations to join in the conference, Trotzky recognized that delegation's authority to speak in the name of an independent Ukraine.

The Ukrainians messed with the Germans, and maintained friendly relations with the Central Powers' representatives whose greatness awed them. They were unskilled in the dangerous diplomatic game. Besides, the tenure of their government was insecure, and they wished to conclude a hasty peace and thus gain German support for the crumbling Cabinet at Kiev.

Kuehlmann and Hoffmann would have been happy to meet the desires of the Rada. They wanted a peace with the Ukraine as a threat over Petrograd's head. But Austro-Hungary objected. A separate treaty with the Ukraine would involve the Dual Empire in territorial difficulties with a new national unit which, as neighbor, was sure to be a source of incessant irritation. Then the bottom fell out of Austro-Hungary's bread-basket. Vienna was ready even for a peace with the Ukraine.

Czernin authorized Hoffmann to negotiate with the Ukrainians, for he could not bring himself to do it. At this juncture, Trotzky and Kamenev left for Petrograd. The Third Congress of Soviets was meeting in the capital and the commissars would be asked to report not only on the proceedings at Brest but as well on the revolutionary situation in enemy lands. Moreover, the Communist Party had to take its definite stand on future policy at the conference.

A document from the archives of the Central Committee presents details of a session on January 22 which discussed the problems of Brest Litovsk. Lenin said:

> At a former meeting (on January 21) three points of view were advanced: (1) sign a separate, annexationist peace, (2) wage a revolutionary war, (3) declare the war ended, demobilize the army, but do not sign the peace. . . . The first (Lenin's) proposal was supported by 15 votes, the second by 32, the third (Trotzky's) by 16.

Lenin was in favor of signing a German peace.

> The position of the Germans on the islands of the Baltic is such that in an offensive they could capture Reval and Petrograd with naked hands. By continuing the war under such circumstances we strengthen German imperialism. We will have to conclude peace in any case, but the terms will be worse if they will not be signed by us.

Lenin was out-voted.

Lenin saw matters clearly. He called Trotzky's formula "No war but no peace," an "international political demonstration" which they could not afford. "If the Germans begin to advance," he argued, "we will be forced to sign any peace presented." Nor could they put their trust in the German proletariat. "Germany, you see," was his plea, "is only pregnant with revolution, but here in Russia a perfectly healthy child—the socialist republic—has already been born, and we may kill it if we start a war."

The ballot taken at this meeting of the Central Committee produced the following results: For a revolutionary war 2, against 11, not voting 1. For dragging out the negotiations 12, against 1. For Trotzky's formula 9, against 9.

The instructions Trotzky was to take back to the Brest conference accordingly amounted to this: there was to be no war, and the talks were to be prolonged as much as possible. No other definite instructions for future tactics were given. Under the circumstances, Trotzky was free to put his own policy into effect if and when the occasion arose. Lenin did not favor that policy, but did not energetically oppose it. He was ready to give it a trial.

**A SECRET ANGLO-GERMAN AGREEMENT AT RUSSIA'S EXPENSE?** The three alternatives which presented themselves to the minds of the Bolsheviks: an annexationist peace, a revolutionary war, and "no war, no peace," indicate that as early as January 1, when Trotzky quitted Brest for Petrograd, the Russian Government considered the conference situation critical. The Germans were appearing as frank annexationists and militarists. They had agreed to the principle of non-annexation and then insisted on the indefinite occupation of the Russian Border states. They had accepted self-determination and then submitted that self-determination had already taken place, though the expression of "popular" will was in reality the voice of Baltic-German land barons and of German agents. They had consented to the formula of no indemnities, but at Brest they were preparing to present a bill to the Russians which, as Trotzky estimated in his address to the Third Soviet Congress, would amount to between four and eight billion rubles. It was a "Shylock" account, Trotzky complained, and he believed, and with him most of the Communists, that it, as well as the other hard terms were "tacitly approved in London." This idea of the Bolsheviks that the British and Germans had an agreement whereby the latter would be permitted conquests in the East in order to make them "more conciliatory in the negotiations with their British and American fellow-capitalists" had gained much ground in Petrograd.

There is no proof that an "agreement" had taken place between the two mighty opponents on a peace at the expense of the revolution. But that the idea was entertained in London and perhaps elsewhere can no longer be doubted. We have the testimony of Churchill, British Secretary of State for War, and of Sir Henry Wilson, Chief of the British General Staff. Churchill is discussing the conditions which made peace with Germany possible toward the end of 1917.

> The immense conquests,[4] [he writes] which Germany had made in Russia, and the hatred and scorn with which the Bolsheviks were regarded by the Allies, might well have made it possible for Germany to make important territorial concessions to France, and to offer Britain the complete restoration of Belgium. The desertion by Russia of the Allied cause, and the consequent elimination of all Russian claims created a similar easement in negotiations with both Austria and Turkey.

Early in 1918, Sir Henry Wilson was in England engaged in important conversations with the diplomats.

> Wilson afterwards saw Bonar Law, [writes his biographer, basing himself on copious diaries][5] who was thinking about peace terms and believed that Germany might be disposed to restore Alsace-Lorraine to France and to make other concessions if given a free hand on the Russian side. . . .

H. Wickham Steed refers to the same subject in his *Through Thirty Years*.[6]

The Russians were convinced that a "deal" at their cost had actually been reached. This certainly did not contribute towards a feeling of confidence.

**A SEPARATE GERMAN PEACE—WITH THE UKRAINE** Trotzky was returning late on the night of January 26 to rejoin his colleagues at Brest, and resume the sittings of the German-Austrian-Russian Political Commission which had been adjourned on his departure on January 18. Some circumstances, he thought, had improved their position. The Bolsheviks had won victories in the struggle with Kaledin and other Russian counterrevolutionaries. In the Ukraine, the bourgeois Rada had been overthrown, Kiev entered by Bolshevik troops and an Ukrainian Soviet set up. Moreover, there were labor troubles and food riots in Austria, Hungary, and Germany. Nevertheless, he could make no fiery promises. The dele-

[4] Winston Churchill: *The World Crisis,* 1916–8 (London, 1927).
[5] Major General Sir C. E. Callwell: *Field-Marshal Sir Henry Wilson: His Life and Diaries* (London, 1927), p. 49.
[6] H. Wickham Steed: *Through Thirty Years, 1892–1922,* Vol. 2 (London, 1924).

gation would work for an honest peace; the government would continue to demobilize the army and form a Red Guard. Germany could not undertake an offensive against them, because her soldiers would disobey. If that proved not to be the case, however, they would call to the World Proletariat. "Do you hear?" the Communist would shout, and the answer would come, "I hear." (It proved to be a sorry illusion, this faith in the solidarity of the non-Russian workers.)

Parallel with the discussions and deliberations in Petrograd, discussions and deliberations took place in Berlin and Vienna. Czernin went to see his Kaiser and talk to the Austro-Hungarian Parliament. Speaking on January 24, he said, "I demand not a square metre or a penny from Russia." Poor man, he may have been telling the truth. He did not want territory or tribute, but his German ally did, and he was too weak to resist. The condition of his country was such that he could no longer oppose the separate peace with the Ukraine urged by General Hoffmann. Though somewhat disturbed by telegraphic messages from Brest to the effect that most of the Ukraine had been captured by Soviet Ukrainian troops and a new Red Government established in Kharkov which disputed the right of the Ukrainian delegation then at Brest to negotiate in the name of the Ukrainian Government, Czernin now enthusiastically advocated a "wheat peace" with the Kiev Rada. Flour was the prime requisite.

In Berlin the next day, Kuehlmann addressed the Reichstag. His statement was preceded by a long address of Hertling, who replied point by point to Wilson's Fourteen Points. With respect to No. 6, which called for the "evacuation of all Russian territory," the Premier declared that, in view of the Allies' refusal to participate in the peace negotiations, they had no right to intervene. He indicated that Russian territory would not be evacuated. Hertling's speech as well as the debate that followed showed clearly that the militarist clique was firmly in the saddle. Among other orators, Gustav Stresemann, later Minister of Foreign Affairs, supported the tactics of General Hoffmann and defended the fictitious self-determination of Lithuania on the ground that "70 to 80 per cent of her inhabitants were illiterate."

On the 30th of January the sessions at Brest were resumed. Trotzky had brought with him, as he announced the moment the conference reopened, Medvediev and Shakhrai, representatives of the new Soviet Government of the Ukraine. Two Ukraines now met at Brest, a bourgeois Ukraine and a Bolshevik Ukraine. The former was fast losing territory and power. The rooms they occupied in Brest, Trotzky declared, were the only space over which the plenipotentiaries of the Kiev Rada had any right to dispose—and those rooms they were assigned by the German commandant. "Judging by the reports from the Ukraine that I had before me," writes General Hoffmann, "Trotzky's words seemed unfortunately not to be without foundation." For the Rada Government had lost Kiev and fled, and it no longer possessed even a shadow of authority. Nevertheless, the Germans considered these "difficulties" as merely temporary and transitory, since "we," according to Hoffmann, "could support it with arms and establish it again." This is indeed what happened. On February 9, the Central Powers signed a separate treaty with the delegates of the defunct Rada. Without delay, the Rada Cabinet, which had escaped to the town of Zhitomir, "invited" the Germans to its rescue, and the German army complied with this expression of "popular will" by setting up an anti-Soviet Government.

February 9 saw a crucial historical session. The Russians, of course, knew of the negotiations with the Rada. They told the enemy delegates that there was no sense in signing a treaty with a non-existent government. To which both Kuehlmann and Czernin replied that their information from the Ukraine did not conform with Petrograd's. We know now, from General Hoffmann's memoirs ("the Rada Government . . . no longer possessed even a shadow of authority") that it did. The statesmen were lying. Moreover, Czernin has to his credit this remarkable syllogism: "We have recognized the government of the Ukrainian Rada. For us, therefore, it exists."

The Germans were now ready to press Russia for a decision on the peace treaty. On January 18, the Central Powers had presented a map showing their proposed new Russian boundary in the West. They likewise declared that they could not evacuate the occupied territories (Poland, Lithuania, Courland, and parts of Livonia and Estonia) immediately or at the end of the hostilities between the Quadruple Alliance and the Western Entente.

When these demands were announced, in rather ultimative form, Trotzky had left for Petrograd. The impression in the capital, it will be recalled, was a painful one, and the Communists, though divided on a definite program, instructed their delegation at Brest to "kill" time but prevent war. From January 30, when he returned to the conference, till February 9, Trotzky killed time beautifully but not without help from the Germans. They were anxious first to come to terms with the Ukraine and to suppress revolutionary outbreaks at home. So the conversations dragged on with interest yet without result; Trotzky even introduced the philosophy of Hegel into the debate.

On February 9, it was no longer possible to postpone detailed deliberation of the boundary proposed by Germany. A Territorial Commission was thereupon appointed. The yellow line on an official German military map made it clear that the Central Powers were insisting on the renunciation by Russia of all the Baltic States, Poland, and of the Moon, Dago and Oesel Islands in the Baltic Sea from which Petrograd could easily be attacked. Admiral Altvater, the Russian expert, protested that such a frontier could be desired by Germany and Austro-Hungary only for purposes of military offense against Russia. (This General Hoffmann denied. He required hundreds of miles from the pre-war German boundary for defensive purposes, he said.)

The German militarists wished to dictate the conditions of surrender, but, since that was impossible, they did not want peace. The proof is Ludendorff's. "At our meeting on the 4th and 5th of February (in Berlin)," he writes,[7] I got State Secretary von Kuehlmann to promise that he would break with Trotzky twenty-four hours after the signing of the peace treaty with the Ukraine." Now the peace with the deposed Rada Government had been signed. Ludendorff accordingly telephoned to Brest asking Kuehlmann to keep his promise. Kuehlmann, however, refused.

That very day, Kuehlmann received a telegram from the Kaiser. It had come to the attention of the General Headquarters—which informed the "Chief War Lord"—that a radiogram from Petrograd to the German army called upon the soldiers to disobey their officers, according to Ludendorff, and to murder their officers, according to

[7] Erich Ludendorff, *op. cit.,* (Berlin, 1920). Page 445.

Hoffmann. Enraged, the Kaiser demanded that Kuehlmann present an ultimatum to the Russians insisting on a settlement within the next twenty-four hours. Kuehlmann again refused.

Kuehlmann hoped that under the impression of the Ukrainian treaty and with the aid, perhaps, of one or two minor territorial concessions, he could persuade the Russians to sign a treaty in the near future which would satisfy German expansionist designs as well as Germany's World War requirements. He therefore urged Wilhelm to desist, but if the Emperor would not change his mind, he, Kuehlmann, would resign. If no reply were forthcoming until 4.30 that afternoon, the State Secretary, as he wired Berlin, would keep the Kaiser's ultimatum in his pocket. Kuehlmann waited till 4.30. There was no reply. There was no ultimatum.

On the next day, the 10th of February, however, Trotzky brought the historic Brest Litovsk Conference to a close.

Immediately on the opening of the session of the Political Commission, consisting of representatives of Russia, Germany, and Austro-Hungary, von Kuehlmann referred to the alleged summons to insubordination sent out by the Russian High Command. Trotzky said he knew nothing about such an order; he did know that Germany was distributing Russian newspapers among Russian soldiers which agitated the Soviet Government. The meeting then passed to the business of the day: the report of the Boundary Committee. But there was no report because the Committee had not agreed.

**NO WAR AND NO PEACE** Obviously, the Germans would insist, sooner or later, on Russian acceptance of their territorial demands. In view of the Ukrainian treaty and of the ruthless suppression of the German labor strikes, such insistence was likely to come soon. Trotzky wished to anticipate it. Before taking the decisive step, however, the Soviet delegation consulted Petrograd. On the morning of that day Karakhan went to the telegraphic apparatus and called the capital. Stalin answered the summons. He was told of the impending move and gave his approval.

Trotzky therefore arose and said:

"The hour of decision has arrived. The peoples wait

impatiently for the result of the peace negotiations at Brest Litovsk. . . . If the war was ever waged for self-defense, it has long ago ceased to be that for both sides. When Great Britan conquers African colonies, Bagdad and Jerusalem, it cannot be a war of defense; when Germany occupies Servia, Belgium, Poland, Lithuania, Rumania, and the Moon Islands it cannot be a war of defense. This is a war for the division of the world."

"We," he continued, "no longer wish to participate in this purely imperialistic war where the designs of the propertied classes are being effected with human blood. Our relation to the imperialism of both camps is equally irreconcilable. . . ."

Further, "In expectation of the hour, which we hope is near, when the oppressed working classes of all countries will seize power as has the proletariat of Russia, we are taking our army and our people out of the war. . . . At the same time, we declare that the terms offered us by the Government of Germany and Austro-Hungary are in fundamental contradiction to the interest of all nations. . . . The peoples of Poland, Ukraine, Lithuania, Courland and Estonia regard these conditions as a violation of their will for Russia; these terms mean a permanent menace. . . . We refuse to sanction the conditions which the imperialism of Germany and Austro-Hungary is writing with the sword on the bodies of live nations. We cannot place the signature of the Russian revolution under terms which carry with them oppression, sorrow, and misery for millions of human lives."

"We are out of the war but we refuse to sign the peace treaty," said Trotzky.

This was the end. The Brest Litovsk peace conference between Russia and the Central Powers had failed to produce a peace treaty. The delegations packed their bags.

**THE OFFENSIVE** Ludendorff and Hindenburg were now bent on subjugating Russia. Without waiting, therefore, the expiry of the agreed seven-day notice period, the German armies on the Eastern Front commenced to advance into Russia.

The decision to do so was arrived at in a special conference held on February 13 at Homburg, the country home of the Kaiser. Dramatis personæ: Wilhelm, the

Chancellor, the Vice-Chancellor, von Kuehlmann, Hindenburg, Ludendorff, the Chief of Staff of the Imperial Navy. The military wanted "clarity" in the East. "No war but no peace" was too vague a situation to satisfy them. Besides, they wished to prevent any renewal of warfare by Russia with the help of her Allies. Ludendorff preferred a "swift, powerful blow" which might yield them large supplies of captured war materials.

The blow had to be swift in order to prevent Russian recovery, no matter how slight. From the strategic point of view, the military clique was undoubtedly right in arguing at Homburg that though all forces were needed in the Western theater, uncertainty in Russia would require them to maintain a sizeable army to watch events there, whereas a quick move to paralyze the Bolsheviks militarily and compel them to sign a peace treaty might be expensive for a while but highly profitable before long.

German divisions immediately began occupying more Russian territory. As the Germans came on, the Russian troops turned and fled. Two hours after the beginning of the advance, the Germans had crossed the strategic Dvina and proceeded in the general direction of Petrograd. Soon large sectors of Livonia and Estonia were occupied. Simultaneously an Austrian army penetrated into the Ukraine.

**LENIN'S POLICY** It was time for Petrograd to act. On February 17, when the capital had already been informed that German airplanes had flown over Dvinsk and German divisions received marching orders, the Central Committee of the Communist Party was summoned to the Smolni Institute. When it convened on the 18th, information was at hand of the general German advance. This was no time for talk. Even the Russians realized that. Each fraction was limited to two speakers and each speaker to five minutes. The question was: "Shall we wire the Germans and sue for peace?" Zinoviev and Lenin spoke for the affirmative; Trotzky and Bukharin for the negative. After twenty minutes, the vote was taken, and Lenin's motion to dispatch an immediate telegram to Germany was defeated by six ballots against seven. Trotzky and Bukharin had won.

The Central Committee re-convened that same evening. Trotzky reported the capture of Dvinsk and further incursions into the Ukraine, and proposed an inquiry to the Central Powers on their demands. A debate followed. First Lenin spoke. They could wait no longer. They were losing equipment and territory. You cannot jest with war. The revolution was not coming yet in Germany, and the Germans would not stop. If the Germans were insisting on the overthrow of the Bolshevik regime, resistance would be the only alternative. But that was not the case, and so to wait meant the surrender of the revolution, for the enemy would not halt before it had taken the capital and points inland.

Lenin was followed by Uritzky, Trotzky, Stalin, and Bukharin. The leader then undertook the rebuttal. He criticized Bukharin first. Bukharin who had originally favored the Trotzky "no war, no peace" program, now stood for a revolutionary war. Lenin ridiculed the notion. They were not ready for it. A "permanent peasant war" against Germany was a "Utopia." That was possible in civil warfare but not in a struggle with a mighty foreign power. "If we give up Finland, Livonia, and Estonia, the revolution is still not yet lost."

After Lomov had spoken in support of the revolutionary war, a vote was again taken on the Lenin motion of an immediate offer of peace to Germany. Ballots cast *for* were those of Lenin, Trotzky, Smilga, Stalin, Sverdlov, Sokolnikov, and Zinoviev; *against:* Bukharin, Dzerzhinsky, Joffe, Lomov, Uritzky, and Krestinsky. Seven to six. Lenin had won the day by the passing of Trotzky to his side.

Early the next morning, a radio was broadcast from Petrograd to Berlin. It protested against the offensive and against the unannounced suspension of the armistice; and finally declared Bolshevik readiness, under constraint, to sign a dictated peace.

This message was received at the German wireless station of Koenigs Wusterhausen at 9.12 A.M. that very day and immediately acknowledged by General Hoffmann. Nevertheless, the German army continued to advance. On February 21 detachments had pushed forward to within 70 miles of Riga; German cavalry was approaching Mohilev, the former Russian General Headquarters, and a Turkish army was driving into the Caucasus.

The Bolsheviks were convinced that the Germans and

Austrians would not stop till they had taken Petrograd and Kiev and overthrown the revolutionary government. Accordingly, the orders were issued for the waging of a holy revolutionary war "for the defense of the republic against the bourgeoisie and imperalists of Germany." On February 22 the Central Committee met again for a sitting of extraordinary interest. Were they to permit the Germans to take the capital and ride rough-shod over the workers' soviets? What alternative presented itself to the Bolsheviks?

**TROTZKY'S SOLUTION** Trotzky offered a solution. He proposed that the Bolsheviks ask the Allies for aid against the Germans. The Bolsheviks wished to retain complete freedom of foreign policy but would otherwise accept Allied conditions. At the same time, Trotzky tendered his resignation as Commissar of Foreign Affairs. Bukharin opposed the acceptance of Allied terms. Lenin could not attend the session but sent a rough slip of paper on which he had scribbled in ink: "Please add my vote *in favor of* the receipt of support and arms from the Anglo-French imperialist brigands. Lenin." Trotzky's recommendation was approved by 6 votes against 5.

Trotzky had been conferring with Captain Sadoul of the French Military Mission, with Colonel Robins of the American Red Cross, and with R. H. Lockhart, the British High Commissioner. He wished them to help organize a Red Army and to assist in building up a new front against the Germans. In fact, conversations with this in view had been proceeding for several weeks, ever since it had become clear that the Central Powers would agree to none but an annexationist peace.

Chicherin told the writer that Sadoul and Ruggles of the French and American armies came to him at the height of the German offensive. Chicherin went with them to Lenin, where it was agreed that if the Germans advanced beyond Pskov, Allied military units would blow up the bridges and destroy all war materials along the line of the enemy's march. Subsequently the Bolsheviks suggested the transfer into the interior of larger stores of steel and other metals in Petrograd and Petrozavodsk in Karelia. This second arrangement, however, was frustrated by the vacillating and many-sided policies of the Western Powers.

Above all, the Bolsheviks wished to keep alive the revolution. If a special train from Ludendorff or financial aid and advice from the Allies serve this end, the Communists felt justified in accepting them. The Bolsheviks were not certain of their tenure in office. Lenin experienced the joy of a child when the Soviet Government broke the record of the Paris Commune in 1871 by living through its seventy-first day. Help from the outside would strengthen the regime. Support could come only from the Allies. In return for such support, the Bolsheviks would under no condition have re-entered the war. But had the Germans threatened the very existence of the Red state by invading its heart and center, and had the Allies come to the rescue, the Western Entente would have been aided immeasurably, for such a development, even without active Russian participation in the war, would have forced the Germans to maintain heavy forces on the Eastern front. Merely by taking something from the Allies, the Bolsheviks would have been giving much more to the Allies. Sadoul, Lockhart and Robins grasped this point and worked incessantly towards co-operation between their countries and Petrograd.

The French Military Mission in the Russian capital, with the exception of Sadoul, had always been objectionable to the Bolsheviks. General Niessel was publicly accused of participating in anti-Soviet conspiracies and, on one occasion during a very stormy interview, Trotzky simply put him out of his office. After the January 30 break at Brest, however, this relationship changed. The French were persuaded that there was no pact between the Communists and the Hohenzollerns. Conversations proceeded between the French and Trotzky as well as between Lockhart and Robins and Trotzky. Robins had gained the support of Sisson, and of Major T. D. Thacher and Major Allen D. Wardwell of the Red Cross Mission who joined him in urging "prompt recognition of Bolshevik authority and immediate establishment of a modus vivendi making possible generous and sympathetic co-operation."

All these efforts came to naught. Perhaps, had time permitted, even Allied officials at home might have been persuaded of the wisdom of a friendly course, but on February 23 the Germans finally reacted to the Bolsheviks' urgent plea for peace.

On the morning of the 23rd, the German terms, sent from Berlin on the 21st, arrived in Petrograd by courier. They stipulated the acceptance of the German territorial settlement proposed at Brest, plus modifications at the expense of Courland; the complete demobilization of the Russian army and of the newly-formed Red Guard; the retirement of the Russian fleet to Russian harbors, the renewal of the Russian-German commercial agreement, and the free export, without tariff, of ores, the interdiction of all propaganda against the Central Powers, recognition of the German treaty of peace with the Ukraine, the withdrawal of Russian troops from the Ukraine and Finland, "assistance" to Turkey to re-establish her Anatolian frontiers, indemnities that would amount to several billions, and the support by Russia of German commissions for war prisoners and war refugees.

These conditions, the message concluded, must be accepted within forty-eight hours. Russians plenipotentiaries were to start for Brest without delay and there, after three days, sign a peace which must be ratified within two weeks.

The demands precipitated a bitter fight in the Communist Party and in the Central Executive Committee of the Soviet Government, for opposition to the signing of the peace persisted, despite Lenin's formal victory. The discussions that shook the party are not only of historic importance; they throw light on the psychology of the Communists.

The Central Committee of the Communist Party met that day. Lenin arose first. He demanded the acceptance of the terms. He demanded that the "policy of revolutionary phrases" and of revolutionary war be dropped. Otherwise he would resign from the Government and from the Central Committee. This was his ultimatum. He would not withdraw it.

Trotzky followed Lenin and argued that a revolutionary war was inconceivable in the absence of unity within the party. Bukharin insisted on such a war. Lenin flayed the Bukharinites, though he conceded the necessity of preparing for a revolutionary war. He, of course, wanted a Red Army and would defend the regime whenever the need arose, but at that moment the best defense was capitulation.

It was a lengthy discussion. Finally Lenin presented three questions:

| The votes were cast as follows: | (1) Shall we immediately accept the German Terms? | (2) Shall we prepare for a Revolutionary War? | (3) Shall we consult the voters of Petrograd and Moscow? |
|---|---|---|---|
| Lenin | Yes | | |
| Stasova | Yes | | |
| Zinoviev | Yes | | |
| Sverdlov | Yes | | |
| Stalin | Yes | | |
| Sokolnikov | Yes | | |
| Smilga | Yes | Yes | Yes 11 |
| Bubnov | No | Unanimously | No 0 |
| Uritzky | No | | Not Voting 4 |
| Bukharin | No | | |
| Lomov | No | | |
| Trotzky | Not Voting | | |
| Dzerzhinsky | Not Voting | | |
| Joffe | Not Voting | | |
| Krestinsky | Not Voting | | |

By a plurality, accordingly, the Bolsheviks had decided to bow to the will of the Germans. Thereupon Bukharin, Lomov, Bubnov, V. Jakovlev, Piatakov and V. M. Smirnov resigned from the Central Committee and from their government offices and issued a statement "reserving for themselves the freedom of agitation (against the peace) within the party as well as outside its ranks." Efforts by Lenin, Trotzky, and others to dissuade them were of no avail. A split in the Communist party seriously threatened, but Lenin was convinced of the wisdom of his course and followed it unflinchingly. He sent plenipotentiaries to meet the Germans.

En route to Brest, the Russian delegation, on February 25–6, passed through Pskov, 257 versts from Petrograd, and found it in the occupation of German troops. The German offensive had not even been stopped by the Bolshevik acceptance of Berlin's ultimative peace demands.

**PEACE AT THE TIP OF A SWORD** On February 28 the Soviet delegation arrived in Brest. Its personnel, however, was changed. Trotzky had refused to attend. Joffe, who opposed the Lenin policy, declined to accept any political responsibility for the delegation's acts, and went only as an adviser. The members were Sokolnikov, G. I. Petrovsky (later President of the Ukraine), George Chicherin, and Karakhan as secretary. The Germans sent von Rosenberg, and the Austro-Hungarians Dr. Gratz, both officials of second rank. The discussions did not promise to be of any great interest.

They opened on March 1. Von Rosenberg warned that they had only three days and would have to work "intensively." Sokolnikov replied that he was ready to dispense with all commissions and technicalities and to accept the terms which Germany, arms in hand, was dictating to the Russian Government.

Most of the talking was now done by the Germano-Austrians. Sokolnikov contented himself with two or three remarks lasting no more than one or two minutes, and with two formal declarations. The Russians painfully sought to avoid every impression that the treaty was the result of an agreement, of a give and take, of discussion. It was a peace handed them on the point of a sword, they said. Sokolnikov therefore tried to have the session over as quickly as possible. The Germano-Austrians, in addition to the terms contained in the ultimatum delivered in Petrograd on the 23rd, now added the demand that Russia renounce Batum, Kars, and Ardagan and prepare the way for their absorption by Turkey. There was no use objecting. The Germans were still advancing into Russia and the Ukraine. The Russian army was being demobilized. Allied spokesmen were talking about aid but not giving it.

On March 3 the peace treaty was signed by the plenipotentiaries of Russia and her four enemies. The German representative thereupon announced that the offensive would be immediately discontinued. It was—but only in Russia. German and Austrian armies proceeded on their march into Soviet Ukraine.

Kaiser Wilhelm said, in a congratulatory telegram to Chancellor von Hertling: "The German sword wielded by great army leaders has brought peace with Russia." Then Wilhelm II expressed his "deep gratitude to God, Who has been with us." The sword and God.

How serious the German threat to Petrograd had been may be judged from the fact that on February 23 the Government offices began preparing for evacuation. On February 26 the United States Embassy moved inland to Vologda, where it was soon joined by most of the Allied Missions. A few day later, March 5, the Bolsheviks decided to transfer their capital to Moscow, and on March 11 the chief organs of the Soviet Government established themselves in the ancient Kremlin.

**ALLIED EFFORTS TO FRUSTRATE THE BREST TREATY** The Allies did not wish to see the treaty ratified. And they tried to prevent it, albeit very half-heartedly. The Allies had made several efforts to win the Bolsheviks for the war. On one occasion the Americans offered Commander-in-Chief Krylenko 100 rubles for every Russian soldier he would place at the front against the Germans. Krylenko rejected this deal in cannon fodder. Subsequent endeavors are on the records of Robins, Sadoul, and Lockhart. But the most determined Allied effort came immediately after the signature of the Brest Litovsk peace treaty.

On March 5, two days after the signing, Robins saw Trotzky at Smolni. A conversation ensued in which the Russian inquired about the attitude of the American Government. He encouraged Robins to believe that if the Bolsheviks could receive economic and military aid from the Allies they would not ratify the peace. Robins wanted a statement in writing. He got it at four o'clock that afternoon.[8] In case, it said, the Soviets refuse to ratify the peace, or if the Germans advance despite the peace, or if the Soviets renounce the treaty before or after its ratification, "it is very important for the military and political plans of the Soviet power for replies to be given to the following questions:

" 'Can the Soviet Government rely on the support of the United States of North America, Great Britain and France in the struggle against Germany?' What would be the nature of this assistance; what, in particular, would America do 'should Japan—in consequence of an open or tacit understanding with Germany or without such an understanding'—occupy Siberia? Would England send aid to Murmansk and Archangel? The only condition named by Trotzky was complete independence in foreign and internal affairs to be directed in 'accord with the principles of international socialism.' "

Robins took this paper and, together with his secretary

[8] Reproduced in the U.S. Congressional Record for January 29, 1919.

Gumberg, went to Lenin's office, where he was "assured of the genuineness of the position" as outlined in the Trotzky document. Thereupon he went to see Bruce Lockhart, the British High Commissioner. Lockhart, too, had interviewed Trotzky that morning. Later that day he sent a secret and confidential telegram to the Foreign Office in London. He proposed aid to Russia from the Allies and warned that if "the Allies are to allow Japan to enter Siberia, the whole proposition is hopeless . . . this action (Japanese occupation) is quite unnecessary at the present moment as far as safeguarding supplies from Siberia is concerned." Furthermore,

> If ever the Allies have had a chance in Russia since the revolution, the Germans have given it to them by the exorbitant peace terms they have imposed on them. And now when Germany's aims have been unmasked to the whole world, the Allies are to nullify the benefits of this by allowing the Japanese to enter Siberia. If His Majesty's Government does not wish to see Germany paramount in Russia, then I would most earnestly implore you not to neglect this opportunity. . . . Please show this telegram to the Prime Minister [Lloyd George] and Lord Milner.[1]

The Trotzky statement to Robins was submitted by wire to the State Department in Washington, and later, on March 9, Ambassador Francis sent two telegrams to the Secretary of State of the United States drawing attention to the serious consequences that would result from a Japanese invasion of Asiatic Russia. "The Soviet Government," he added, "is the only power which is able to offer resistance to the German advance. . . ."

Was Trotzky consciously misleading the Allied and American representatives into believing that the Bolsheviks would fight if assisted? The commissar wished to gain time. He wished to gain good will in quarters which would determine how soon Allied intervention in Russia would commence. He wished, perhaps, to exploit the Allies' desire to prevent the ratification of the peace in order to win their disapproval of the impending Japanese adventure in the East. Moreover, the party congress was then in session. It might reject the German terms. That would have meant war, and Trotzky wanted to assure himself of foreign aid. But beyond all those considerations, it must have been uppermost in his mind that the Ger-

[1] *R.A.R.*, page 82.

mans could not be trusted to keep hands off Bolshevik Russia. It was conceivable that they would attack whether or not the Soviet ratified the peace. And indeed there is reason to believe that if the mammoth German offensive on the West front had not been initiated just at this juncture, the Russian revolution would have been doomed without outside assistance. Trotzky was not misleading Robins, Lockhart, and Sadoul. He did not promise them that Russia would join the ranks against the Central Powers. He merely wished to know what might be expected from the Allies if the Bolsheviks were forced to go to war in order to save the revolution.

**THE BOLSHEVIKS QUARREL** That such a revolutionary war was possible is clear from the unanimous vote of the Central Committee on February 23 in favor of preparing for it. Lenin would have been reconciled to it as a necessity. Bukharin made a virtue of it. He and his followers saw no other alternative. They had left the Central Committee and organized their own paper, *The Communist*,[2] which daily printed violent attacks on Lenin's policy. At the party congress, March 6–8, the battle was long and bitter. Trotzky played a relatively minor role. The real struggle was between Lenin and Bukharin who led the "young," Left, Communists. Trotzky spoke for ratification.

The "Left" faction was vociferous. Outside the congress its views and acts were seconded by the Left Social Revolutionaries, who were even registering men for the revolutionary front. At the sessions the storm raged. Obolensky-Ossinsky argued that if they ever let the Germans get on Russias' back they would ride her not for a breathing-space but for years. Lenin's promises to the contrary were "empty phrases." Madame Kollontai believed that both the Germans as well as the Bolsheviks would regard even the ratified treaty as a scrap of paper. Therefore "Long Live the Revolutionary War." (Applause)[3].

Bukharin made his final speech under a continuous heckling fire from Lenin. Bukharin argued that there

[2] *The Communist* appeared daily in Petrograd between the 5th and 19th of March under the editorship of Bukharin, Radek and Uritzky; and in Moscow from April to June, as a weekly, under the editorship of Bukharin, Ossinsky, Radek, and V. M. Smirnov.

[3] *Stenographic Record of the Proceedings of the Seventh Communist Party Congress*. March 6–8, 1918. (Moscow, 1928).

were two possibilities: to organize completely and then fight, or to organize while fighting. His program excluded the first and called for the second. Lenin wished both. Events were on the side of Lenin. The army had almost disappeared. The Germans were upon them. Transport, food supply, and finances were disorganized. The Communist Party was divided. The international proletariat failed to revolt. The Russian bourgeoisie lay in wait for an opportunity to spring at the Red regime and bear it to the ground. These were the leader's arguments. They were unanswerable except with wild appeals to revolutionary enthusiasm which, Lenin said, was out of place in judging a hard, practical situation.

Accordingly, when the vote was taken, 28 votes were cast for the Lenin resolution demanding immediate ratification; 9 votes of the Bukharinites were entered against the resolution; and one delegate refrained from voting. Lenin was the victor by a big majority. This decision was followed by the election of a new Central Committee. Bukharin was chosen a member and Uritzky and Lomov candidates (substitute members). These three adherents of the "Left," revolutionary war wing, however, immediately announced their refusal to accept the offices. Pleas by Lenin and Zinoviev to remain did not move them.

The battles for ratification were now almost won, but there was still the Congress of Soviets. This body, the highest government authority in Soviet Russia, met from March 14 to 16 in Moscow. Its word was final. Here the Left Communist opposition to Lenin was reinforced by the Left social revolutionaries and other anti-Bolshevik parties.

While the congress was in session, it received a message from Woodrow Wilson dated Washington, March 11. Sverdlov, first President of the Soviet Republic, read the document to the delegates.

> May I not take advantage, [was the characteristic beginning] of the meeting of the Congress of the Soviets to express the sincere sympathy which the people of the United States feel for the Russian people at this moment when the German power has been thrust in to interrupt and turn back the whole struggle for freedom and substitute the wishes of Germany for the purposes of the people of Russia? Although the Government of the United States is unhappily not in a position to render the direct and effective aid it would wish to render, I beg to assure the

people of Russia through the Congress that it will avail itself of every opportunity to secure for Russia once more complete sovereignty and independence in her own affairs and full restoration to her great rôle in the life of Europe and the modern world. The whole heart of the people of the United States is with the people of Russia in its attempt to free themselves for ever from autocratic government and become masters of their own life.[4]

On the evening of the second day of the Congress, Robins was sitting on a step leading to the platform. He looked around and Lenin motioned to him. "What have you heard from your Government" (in reply to the Trotzky questions)? inquired the Russian. "Nothing." "What has Lockhart heard?" "Nothing." Lenin wished to know what the Allies would do, not say, to help the Bolsheviks. But he realized that there was no sense in expecting help from that quarter. "Neither the American Government nor any of the Allied Governments will cooperate, even against the Germans, with the workmen's and peasants' revolutionary government of Russia." So he said to Robins, and so saying he rose to the rostrum to make his final speech on ratification. The Congress was with him. Mensheviks, social revolutionaries, and the "Left" Communists opposed the peace. Nevertheless, the Lenin resolution was adopted by 784 votes to 261. A national congress had approved the leader's strategy in signing the treaty of March 3 at Brest.

**A "TILSIT PEACE"** Napoleon, in 1807, humiliated Alexander I, Czar of Russia, and Friedrich Wilhelm, King of Prussia, by forcing upon them shameful, self-destructive terms of peace. The treaty was signed in Tilsit. A few years later the Russians and Prussians annulled the agreement and avenged themselves against the great conqueror. In all his speeches, Lenin referred to the Brest Litovsk Treaty as a "Tilsit Peace." It would not last long, he predicted.

It did not. On November 9, 1918, less than nine months after the ratification of the Brest Peace, the Kaiser was overthrown and a Social Democratic Government established in Berlin. By Point XV of the Armistice which ended the World War, the Germans were forced to renounce the Brest Litovsk Treaty and all its benefits. The

[4] *Current History*. New York. Vol. VIII, Part 1, 49.

Bolsheviks annulled the treaty two days later, on November 13. The Versailles Peace confirmed the cancellation.

**THE KAISER AND THE BOLSHEVIKS** Under the Brest Treaty, normal diplomatic relations were established between the signatory countries. Count Mirbach was appointed German ambassador to Moscow, and Adolf A. Joffe Russian ambassador to Berlin. But Joffe was a revolutionist. He wanted to precipitate an insurrection against the government to which he was accredited. Acting in perfect bad faith—he admitted it in January, 1919—he worked assiduously against the Imperial Government. More than ten Left Social Democratic newspapers were directed and supported by the Soviet Embassy in the German capital. The embassy bought information from officials in various German ministries and passed it on to radical leaders for use in Reichstag speeches, in workers' meetings and in the Press. Anti-war and anti-government literature was sent to all parts of the country and to the front. Tons of literature were printed and clandestinely distributed by Joffe's office. "It is necessary to emphasize most categorically," Joffe wrote in an almost unknown memorandum,[5] "that in the preparation of the German revolution, the Russian Embassy worked all the time in close contact with the German Socialists." Leaders of the German Independents discussed most matters of revolutionary tactics with Joffe, who was an experienced conspirator. In a radio message, dated December 15, 1918, broadcast by Joffe to the revolutionary soviets of Germany, he admitted having paid 100,000 marks for the purchase of arms for the revolutionists and announced that he had established in Germany a 10,000,000 ruble fund for the support of the revolution, which was entrusted to Oskar Kohn, a Socialist deputy.[6]

But Bolshevism harmed the Kaiser's cause in more ways than this. Churchill testifies that "the German prisoners liberated from Russia by the Treaty of Brest Litovsk returned home infected by the Lenin virus. In large numbers they refused to go again to the front.[7]

Joffe's activities brought down upon him the wrath

[5] *Vestnik Zhizni*, No. 5. (Moscow, 1919).

[6] A general confirmation of Soviet Russia's role in the German revolution will be found in Trotzky's *Terrorismus und Kommunismus. Anti-Kautsky* (Hamburg, 1920), p. 104.

[7] *The World Crisis*, 1916–8. II. 491.

of the German Government. Prince Max of Baden avers that Berlin wished to strengthen the majority Social Democrats led by Ebert, Scheidemann, and Noske, against the more radical Independent Socialists. Ebert had a secret pact with the prince about future policy. The Social Democrats even contemplated the preservation of the monarchy. But the defeated army was turning red. The sailors at Kiel had hoistered the crimson flag. The Independent Socialists would become serious rivals of the Ebert-Scheidemann party if quick action were not taken. These considerations, however, could not be employed to bring about Joffe's ejection. Nor did the German Government base that action on the Soviet envoy's anti-Kaiser efforts. Scheidemann suggested instead that a box in Joffe's diplomatic post from Moscow be caused to burst in Berlin. Revolutionary circulars were discovered in it. But these circulars, the Austrian Social Democratic *Klassenkampf* revealed on December 1, 1927, "were neither written, nor printed, nor packed, nor dispatched from Russia. They were, in fact, inserted into the diplomatic box by the Imperial (German) police; they were written in Germany by Comrade Levi." Many other statements tend to confirm the suspicion that although Joffe was heavily laden with revolutionary guilt these particular circulars in his diplomatic mail originated with the Prussian Police. On November 5, accordingly, Joffe and his staff received orders to evacuate the Berlin Embassy and return to Russia. . . . The Socialists who succeeded the Kaiser continued his policy, and German relations with Moscow were only resumed in 1922.

Here ends the story of the Brest Litovsk peace.

The Brest Litovsk Conference was an attempt to arrive openly at an open covenant. There was no such meeting before it nor since. It is unique in world history.

# 2

# ALLY AND ENEMY

"My Government still considers America an ally of the Russian people," said Ambassador Francis after the Brest Peace had been signed.[1] And although Wilson's cordial message to the Soviet Congress was said to be a maneuver to strengthen the opponents of Lenin and of the treaty, the President's words nevertheless put the United States on record as entering the friendliest intentions towards the new workers' and peasants' government. Also Mr. Balfour, British Secretary of State for Foreign Affairs, in a speech to the House of Commons on March 14, referred to England, France, etc., as "Russia's Allies." This fiction persisted during years of foreign military intervention.

**THE RAPE OF BESSARABIA** The foreign interventionists in Russia were the Germans and the anti-Germans. But as a prelude to the chief events of the period, a little side-show was ènacted far to the south-east. When the Bolshevik revolution broke out, Bessarabia, a border province fated to play an important role in subsequent Soviet foreign affairs, boiled with partisan fighting. Petrograd's arm was too short and its voice too weak to command attention. Jassy, the temporary Rumanian capital, was near. Its statesmen had signed a peace with Germany which relieved them of the war burden. Soon after the New Year of 1918, accordingly, Rumanian troops began occupying Bessarabia. Moldavian patriots offered

[1] Interview published March 22, 1918, in the American bulletins issued by the Committee on Public Information of the United States in Moscow. Reproduced by *Russian-American Relations* (*R.A.R.*). *March,* 1917–*March,* 1920. *Documents and Papers* (New York, 1920), p. 95.

resistance, but on January 26 the seizure of all Bessarabia by Rumania was an accomplished fact.

This action produced a Soviet "Irredenta," an "Alsace on the Dnieper" as the official Moscow press wrote on January 26, 1928, a decade after the event.

**GERMAN OCCUPATION** The seizure of Bessarabia created a thorny international problem. In 1918, however, its significance paled beside the advance of the Germans into Russia. The giant military machine rolled over thousands of square miles of territory, and nobody, not even the usually self-assured Bolsheviks, were certain that it would stop before it got to the Urals. And while Lenin and his followers waited anxiously for Germany's reply to their acceptance of her terms, while, later, the empty formalities of the treaty of peace signature were being enacted at Brest Litovsk, the great monster moved forward ominously. Already, in the north, Reval and Pskov had been taken; further south, in White Russia, the cities of Minsk and Orsha.

General Hoffmann admits in his memoirs that he, at that time (spring, 1918), advocated the capture of Moscow and the overthrow of Bolshevism by German arms. But troops were needed in Flanders for the famous March, 1918, drive which crumpled the Allied line, and Ludendorff vetoed his subordinate's plan. The offensive into Russia, accordingly, ceased when the Petrograd plenipotentiaries attached their names to the "Peace of Violence" on March 3.

In the Ukraine, on the other hand, the agreement with the Rada offered a cynical legal basis for further penetration. "If the Central Powers, who had made peace with the Ukraine for the sake of bread wanted to get bread, they had to go and fetch it," said Hoffmann.

In the middle of March, Kiev fell; and early in April, Kharkov. Soon all the Ukraine and the Crimea were prostrate, and the German-Austrian power even extended as far east as Taganrog and Rostov-on-the-Don, where they established friendly contact with the White Guard General, Krasnov.

Even the compliant Rada now seemed too independent to the military representatives of Berlin and Vienna. Accordingly they shelved it and raised up Hetman Skoropadski, a figure head with monarchist sympathies, as ruler of the country.

Before long, however, it developed that bayonets might occupy a country but could scarcely collect wheat, butter and eggs. Whole provinces seethed with militant discontent, and the Germans experienced difficulties in obtaining bread.

Was the muzhik anti-German or pro-Bolshevik? He may have been both or neither, but he was not prepared to feed an invading army variously estimated at between 300,000 and 600,000 men, and, in addition, to sell for export at prices dictated by the foreign buyer.

Moreover, the German military in the Ukraine returned confiscated land to former owners and favored the rich peasants above the poor. Nothing irritated the rural masses more. Bands of Bolsheviks and Left Social Revolutionaries, operating underground, nourished these feelings and fanned the fire of muzhik resentment. Insurrections broke out in many localities. Passive resistance was the least of the forces with which the Central armies had to cope. In Odessa an airplane factory was set on fire. Numerous munition dumps were exploded and trains wrecked. Partisans combed the country for isolated units of enemy soldiers and even attacked railway stations. Disaffection was wholesale. Strikes multiplied.

The Germano-Austrians met the situation with a terror which made people more sullen but no less determined.

As a bread-collecting venture, consequently, the Central Powers' occupation of the Ukraine was more or less disappointing. Count Czernin wrote[2], that in nine months this "granary of Europe" yielded them only 113,421 tons of flour, of which 57,392 tons were shipped to Austro-Hungary. In addition, the invaders obtained 172,349,556 kilograms of other articles such as butter, fats, cheese, fish, eggs, horses, sugar, etc. All in all, 24,000 freight cars filled with goods were dispatched to Central Power territories, and it is estimated that half as much more was smuggled across the frontier. These quantities were not without significance. They staved off the actual starvation of thousands of citizens in the Dual Monarchy but did not prevent its collapse or rescue the situation for its associates. They enabled the Germans to eat more meat in 1918 and supplied the army with 140,000 badly needed horses, but could not so strengthen the Central Powers as to prevent the disaffection of the civil population nor the collapse of the front.

[2] Czernin: *op. cit.*, p. 345.

**THE GERMANS SEEK OIL** While the Germans and Austrians occupied the Ukraine, German and Turkish troops were making themselves at home in the rich and strategic Caucasus. This region had attracted the attention of Constantinople long before Brest Litovsk. As a matter of fact, the Turkish campaigns against the armies of Grand Duke Nicholas in the territory between the Black and Caspian Seas cost the Porte more lives than any other Ottoman activity during the war. But when Russian resistance was broken and the Brest Peace signed, the armed forces of the Sultan were free to wander where they pleased in the much-coveted Caucasus. Early in April Kars was occupied; and on April 15, Batum, the gateway of the Caucasus, fell into Turkish hands.

Turkey was Germany's ally, but not always a reliable one. Moreover, the Caucasus was too valuable economically to surrender even to a faithful associate. From a purely military point of view, no German reinforcements were required in this theater. The Turks were pouring whole divisions into an area where a few regiments could have maintained control, and yet the Germans felt constrained to put in a personal appearance because, as Ludendorff explains,

> this was demanded by our supply of raw material. The behavior of the Turks in Batum had again proved that we could not depend on them in this matter. They had taken all available stores for themselves. We could therefore expect oil from Baku only if we fetched it ourselves.

The streets of German cities, Ludendorff wrote, were dark; the activities of German military airplanes circumscribed for want of petroleum. And submarine warfare depended on oil. To cover Germany's petrol deficits, it was accordingly decided that "the Batum-Tiflis-Baku railway be put in operation by Colonel von Kress with the consent of the Turks. Naturally the decisive question was how we could get to Baku."[3]

Baku may have presented some difficulty to Ludendorff's mind, but the entrance into Georgia was facilitated by the Menshevik Party. Soon after the opening of the Turkish offensive, the nations of the Caucasus seceded from Russia, declared themselves autonomous, and set up a "Trans-Caucasian Federation" consisting of Georgia, Armenia, and Azerbaijan.

[3] Ludendorff, *op. cit.*

The Mensheviks of Georgia were the spiritual fathers of this new state. The Mensheviks called themselves Georgian Nationalists. Nevertheless, they had demanded Georgia's secession from the Czar's empire. Menshevik leaders such as Tscheidze and Tseretelli played important roles in the Kerensky Government. They never raised their voices in favor of the separation of Georgia and the Caucasus from the body of Russia. But when the Bosheviks seized the government the Menshevik leaders proclaimed the independence of Georgia and her neighbors.

However, before the Georgian Republic was much more than a month old, its authorities had invited the Germans to give them the comfort of their presence. On May 25, accordingly, three thousand German troops under von Kress, now General, landed in the Georgian port of Poti and on the very same day the Trans-Caucasian Federation was officially declared non-existent, and Noi Jordania, the Menshevik leader, read the Declaration of Independence of the Georgian Republic.[4] Three days later, Chenkeli, its representative, gave form to this "independence" by signing an agreement with the Germans by the terms of which the railways and naval equipment of the country were surrendered to the Germans for the duration of the World War. Subsequently, a pact was signed between Turkey and Georgia giving the former the right to carry petroleum free of charge over the Batum-Baku pipeline. Thereafter, until the Germans left, Georgia was a willing tool in the hands of the invaders.

Germans and Turks now established themselves for a prolonged stay. Supplementary units came from Germany and additional Turkish troops were brought in from other fronts. "The Turks are sacrificing all Arabia, Palestine, and Syria to these boundless undertakings of theirs in the Caucasus," Limon von Sanders, the Commander-in-Chief of the Turkish armies in Syria, complained to Count von Bernstoff, German ambassador in Constantinople. Turkey planned to annex the Caucasus, and the Sultan's Government, completely under the domination of Enver

[4] The intrigues which accompanied this episode are described by Joseph Pomiankowski, Austro-Hungarian Field-Marshal in Turkey during the World War, in his *Der Zusammenbruch des Ottomanischen Reiches*. (Vienna, 1928), pp. 361–2.

Pasha, sent Pan-Turanian propagandists deep into Dagestan and even into the Crimea.

**BAGDAD TO BAKU** Meanwhile, a great Turkish force concentrated on Baku. A German detachment advanced into Northern Persia to occupy Tabriz, and a Turkish army made its first steps into Azerbaijan. Local Bolsheviks had set up a government in Baku soon after the November, 1917, coup. But the regime was opposed by the moderate Tartar Nationalists or Mussafatists who had actually dispatched a delegate to Major-General Dunsterville in Enzeli, Persia, to pray for his assistance.

Dunsterville had started out from Bagdad in February of that year with a company of British officers. Russia had not yet signed the Brest Litovsk Peace. Her position as an ally still carried some weight in London. There could be no announcement, therefore, of any intention to invade her territory. It was merely given out that the "Dunsterforce"[5] would prevent a "German march on India." Later, however, Sir Percy Sykes, Inspector-General in Persia, aired the correct version.[6] He explained that no large force could be moved 800 miles across desert from Bagdad to Baku. "The authorities therefore decided to dispatch a military mission to reorganize the sound elements of the country into a force that would prevent the Turks and their German masters from reaching Baku . . ."

This was an unusual move, bold in conception and difficult of execution but much to the taste of the adventurous Dunsterville.

Before the middle of the summer, the Dunsterforce had traversed the desert in forty motor-cars and pitched its tents in Enzeli, where it waited an opportunity for a leap across the Caspian. This came in August. On the 13th of the month, the Bolsheviks, faced by a united bourgeois and Menshevik opposition, left the Government, and three days later, Dunsterville, with about a thousand men and much artillery, appeared on the scene as the guest of the Mussafatists.

Several weeks later, however, great masses of Turkish

[5] Major-General Dunsterville: *The Adventures of the Dunsterforce,* 1920. London, 1921.

[6] Sir Percy Sykes: "Persia," *Encyclopedia Britannica,* 1922. Vol. 32.

infantry closed in on the city and a bombardment commenced. Thereupon Dunsterville took to his ships and returned to Persia without firing a shot. (September 13, 1918.) The Turks immediately occupied Baku, and immediately denationalized the oilfields which a Communist decree of May had declared State property.

**A BRITISH SALT LAKE** The Caspian Sea, nevertheless, remained under British control, thanks to General Denikin, an officer of the Czar's General Staff who had served Kerensky but fled south to the Kuban on the advent of the Bolsheviks. There, in December 1917, with headquarters at Jekatrinodar (now Krasnodar), he organized a Cossack army and later pushed down as far as Derbent on the Caspian. The Caspian fleet thus fell into his hands. He placed it at Britain's disposal. "Commodore Norris had taken charge of the Imperial Caspian Navy and on behalf of General Denikin's anti-Bolshevik government held command of the Caspian Sea.[7]

The Caspian was practically a British lake. The Bolsheviks, to be sure, were in Astrakhan, at the mouth of the Volga, and occasionally sallied forth with their inferior flotilla to challenge the British seamen, but the British ruled supreme along the Persian coast of the Caspian and in Transcaspia.

A small Anglo-Indian force under General Malleson had advanced into Transcaspia from Meshed in Persia, and set up a Menshevik-Social Revolutionary Government at Askhabad, hard on the Persian frontier, with whose sanction they fought Bolshevism in Turkestan and tried to occupy Tashkent. They took Merv and its famous oasis and even looked into the waters of the historic Oxus, but never became masters of Bokhara or Khiva.

When Dunsterville evacuated Baku and returned in Commodore Norris's ships to Enzeli, some of his men were carried straight across the Caspian to Krasnovodsk to join General Malleson's force.[8] The stay of the Turks in Baku and the Caucasus was too short-lived to permit them to threaten this British army. On the other hand,

[7] W. E. R. Dickson: *East Persia, A Backwater of the Great War.* (London, 1924), p. 62.

[8] General Malleson is notorious in the Soviet mind for the summary execution of twenty-six Baku commissars delivered to him at Krasnovodsk by his comrade-in-arms Dunsterville during the latter's brief sojourn in the oil city.

the British in Transcaspia were too weak to dispute Turkish domination of Baku or Turkish-German rule in the Caucasus.

All the time the Turks concentrated on Baku, Adolf Joffe protested to Talaat Pasha, who was then in Berlin, against such violation of the Brest agreement. The Moscow Government likewise sent Leonid Krassin to the German Staff Headquarters to remonstrate with Ludendorff.[9] The Grand Vizier and the Generalissimo, however, gave Soviet diplomats no satisfaction, and, on September 20, soon after the capture of the oil city, Moscow announced that it ceased to be bound by the Brest Litovsk Treaty as far as Turkey was concerned. None the less, the Sultan's troops continued the conquest of Azerbaijan, thus adding to the Russian territory held by the Central Powers.

**GERMANY'S CONQUESTS IN RUSSIA** The Quadruple Alliance was now master of an enormous fraction of the former Russian Empire. Apart from the territories handed over to Germany by the Brest Treaty (Poland, Lithuania, Courland, Livonia, and Estonia) and to Turkey (Kars, Batum, Ardagan), armies of the Central Powers had occupied all of the Ukraine, including the Don Basin, rich in iron and coal, and all of the Caucasus with its petroleum resources. A continuous belt of country, from the Gulf of Finland and the Baltic to the Black, Azov and Caspian Seas, comprising approximately 400,000 square miles and inhabited by about 60,000,000 people, had fallen into foreign hands. It had accounted for much of Russia's export grain, most of her oil, and at least 80 per cent of her coal and iron, as well as most of her sugar and tobacco. Moreover, it contained large centers of steel, chemical and textile manufacture. These conquests left Bolshevik Russia with only one port, except those on the distant Arctic, but even that port, Petrograd, was not free from the menace of German occupation. Danger threatened from the direction of Finland.

**RED AND WHITE IN FINLAND** On December 4 the Helsingfors Senate declared Finland an independent republic and applied to Russia for recognition. Swinhuvud, the head of the new government, went personally to see

[9] G. Sokolnikov: *The Brest Peace.* (Moscow, 1928), p. 11.

Lenin in Petrograd. He laid his case before the leader and, on the same day—December 31—the Council of People's Commissars approved. January 4, Finnish recognition by the Soviet Republic was officially proclaimed. Germany, Sweden, and France soon followed suit.

This bourgeois Finnish government was pro-German. In October and November, 1917, a German cruiser and a U-boat landed munitions in Finland, and no sooner had the Swinhuvud Cabinet been formed than negotiations commenced for undisguised German intervention. At the same time, Helsingfors demanded the recall of the Russian troops still quartered in Finland.

Events moved quickly. A workers' general strike was called throughout the country, and on January 27 the White Cabinet fell. A Red Government succeeded it. The anti-proletarian elements concentrated in the north where, under Mannerheim, a general in the Czar's army, they gathered a considerable fighting force. The proletarian government had at least 60,000 guards of its own, but it could also lean for support on the Russian troops. With these on the scene the Whites' cause remained hopeless.

At Brest Litovsk, von Kuehlmann and von Hoffmann tried to persuade the Bolsheviks to withdraw their army. But the Bolsheviks were anxious to bolster the Soviet regime in Finland, which in the absence of a strong Communist Party, required the extra prop. Then came the German offensive and the German ultimatum demanding the immediate evacuation of the Russian army.

On March 3, the very day when the Bolsheviks agreed to retire their armed units from the Aaland Islands and Finland and their fleet from Finnish waters (as soon as the ice permitted), the Germans landed on the islands and, a month later, "at the request of the Finnish (White) Government," according to General Mannerheim, "units of the powerful and victorious German army disembarked on Finnish soil to expel the Bolshevik monsters."

The Reds struggled stubbornly but unsuccessfully against the combined strength of the Germans and White Finns, and on April 29, after three days of sanguinary street fighting, Helsingfors succumbed. On May 12, after more killing, Viborg, to which the Soviet Government had fled, was captured and partially gutted. Viborg is but a short ride from Petrograd.

Thus ended the Soviet regime in Finland.[1] What followed reflected little credit upon German rule. The country began to starve. Russia had been its source of bread. In the second place, a White Terror was inaugurated which holds its place among the bloodiest in post-war Europe. General von der Goltz, who commanded the German occupational forces, made no attempt to curb Mannerheim. To be sure, he was a guest and could not interfere in internal Finnish affairs. Yet he was able to "persuade" the freedom-loving Finns that they wished to establish a monarchy and that they wished to offer the crown of that monarchy to none other than a German prince, Friedrich Karl of Hesse. Finland thus became a vassal state.

The presence of several divisions of German soldiers in Finland constituted a perpetual threat to Petrograd. But Petrograd was a hungry city which foreign conquerors would be required to feed. In a general German offensive for the capture of Moscow and Central Russia, nothing could be simpler than to march across the narrow strip of territory from Viborg to Petrograd. In the absence of such a drive, a constant Damoclean sword over the city was more effective than actual possession. The Germano-Finn combination accordingly turned its attention farther north and deployed in the direction of Kem and Murmansk on the Arctic Ocean.

**GERMANY'S INTERVENTIONIST POLICY** The Central Powers wanted bread and raw materials from the Ukraine and the Caucasus.

The Quadruple Alliance, furthermore, wished to prevent the formation of an Eastern front. A million or more German troops had been transferred to France and Flanders before the Brest armistice. They had made possible the great offensive of March 17, 1918, which nearly brought the Kaiser's armies within reach of the Channel ports. A counter-move by the Allies was inevitable. No forces could be diverted from the West; it would be a decisive summer.

[1] The Soviet Government of Finland left behind it a document unique in the annals of international diplomacy; an agreement between two unfederated socialist republics. On March 1, the Red Governments of Helsingfors and Moscow signed a treaty of mutual friendship. It provided that disputes arising between the contracting parties be settled by an arbitration court whose chairman would be appointed by the Central Committee of the Swedish Left Social Democratic Party.

Accordingly, Russia must be maintained in a state of military paralysis.

German policy shifted with movements of armies and changed in a day or a week. At this juncture (April–May, 1918) it appeared as if the Germans were intent on occupying Moscow and overthrowing the Bolsheviks.

Moscow in German hands might have meant one of two things: the absolute precluding of an Eastern front and the economic enslavement of the country, or a second Ukrainian situation. As a matter of fact, the Left Social Revolutionaries never ceased advocating the annulment of the Brest Litovsk Treaty as a means of provoking a German occupation of Moscow. They then proposed to raise the standard of revolt against the foreigners, precipitate insurrections as in the Ukraine, sabotage, harass the invader, and by all these means not only strengthen the revolutionary spirit in Russia but even hasten the revolution in Germany. Whether this calculation was correct or not is of no moment; that civil, partisan war, however, would have followed German seizure of Moscow was undoubted. Faced with this prospect, the Germans proceeded warily.

In April, units commenced creeping slowly northward from the Ukraine in the direction of Moscow. Orel, Kursk, Voronezh, and near-by districts were entered. When Moscow protested in Berlin, Wilhelmstrasse replied that it knew nothing of such movements. Perhaps it did not. The military were acting on their own, and using irregular German bands instead of ordinary army regiments. Nevertheless, Moscow's heightened diplomatic resistance rather sobered Ludendorff, who, above all else, wished to avoid active Bolshevik opposition.

The German authorities in the Ukraine had obstructed the conclusion of an armistice between Soviet Russia and Skoropadski Ukraine. They had preferred to leave the situation in flux so that a slight push might any day deliver Moscow into their hands. But Berlin now realized that the consequent state of uncertainty magnified Germany's difficulties with the peasantry. Moreover, the Americans were arriving in France and the Allies were preparing a grand attack. Germany could no longer waste attention or energy in Russia and the Ukraine. She needed certainty and clarity. On June 12, accordingly, the Ukraine and Soviet Russia signed an armistice which inaugurated a period of greater moderation in Germany's dealings with the Bolsheviks.

**ALLIED INTERVENTION** If the chief desire of the Germans was to prevent the creation of an Eastern front, the chief desire of the Allies was to create one. In a Note on the war addressed to the Imperial War Cabinet, Churchill outlined his plans for the further prosecution of the World struggle. "There are two perfectly simple things to do. . . . (1) Above all things reconstitute the fighting front in the East; (2) make a plan for an offensive battle in France in 1919." The Secretary of State for War apparently attached as much importance to the former as to the latter proposal, for "If we cannot reconstitute the fighting front against Germany in the East, no end can be discerned of the war. Vain will be all the sacrifices of the peoples and the armies. . . ."[2]

How did Churchill propose to re-establish the anti-German line in the former Czarist Empire? Obviously, he and his friends could avail themselves either of Allied forces or of anti-Bolshevik forces within Russia. But a combination of the two was the wiser course. The country would be invaded and the invaders would rouse elements opposed to Bolshevik policy.

Furthermore, there were the Czecho-Slovak prisoners in Russia proper. They had served, unwillingly, in the Austro-Hungarian army which fought against General Brusilov and been taken captives. In addition, counter-revolutionary generals like Denikin could be mobilized for the attempt to renew fighting in Russia.

This was the interventionists' plan. But the plan involved the destruction of the Soviet regime.

**AN ALTERNATIVE POLICY** An alternative suggested itself to some Allied representatives. Perhaps it would be more advisable to gain the favor of the Bolsheviks. Perhaps, if the Allies supported the Russians in the organization of their army and economy, the resistance of Moscow to the Germans would be stiffened, and in a crisis the Soviets might conceivably resist a German armed force. But even if this did not occur, Allied assistance to Soviet Russia would make her a source of danger to Germany and compel Germany to maintain larger forces in the east

[2] Winston Churchill: *The World Crisis,* 1916–18. (London, 1927).

as a guarantee against unwelcome developments. These Allied representatives (Lockhart, Robins, etc.) believed that their side would gain more by keeping Russia a friend than by making her an enemy. It was a policy based on the assumption that the Red State was stable and that the Bolsheviks were honest men even if deluded extremists.

Colonel Robins, testifying before the United States Senate Committee on his activities in Russia subsequent to the November revolution: "We went to the representatives of the Allied military missions and urged that we enter into negotiations at that time with Trotzky . . ." with a view to preventing unguarded military supplies from falling into German hands. But the

> gentlemen of the allied missions threw up their hands and said, "What! Work with this German agent, thief and murderer Government? Nothing doing! And, anyhow, Robins, we might think of it if they had any real power, but they have not. They will not last but three months longer." [3]

Robins received aid and moral support from General William B. Judson, the chief of the United States Military Mission, "and because he went to see Trotzky," Robins testifies, "in order to arrange to prevent raw materials from going into the Central Empires, he was summarily recalled. . . ." The Soviets also wished the Allies to take hold of their transportation system. There was an American railway mission in the Far East: Trotzky said to Robins, "You send in your mission. We will give you control of the Trans-Siberian at all points. We will make any man you designate assistant commissioner of ways and communication. . . ." It was a simple proposition. "The American ambassador thought well of it"; he (Francis) wired the State Department on March 9, that

> Trotzky asserted that neither his Government nor the Russian people would object to the supervision by America of all shipments from Vladivostok into Russia and a virtual control of the operations of the Siberian railway.

Lenin sent Colonel Robins a long memorandum on May 14 adumbrating a "Plan for Russian-American Commercial Relations" which suggested United States co-operation in the construction of electric power stations at Volkhov

[3] *Bolshevik Propaganda.* Hearings before a sub-committee of the Committee of the Judiciary. United States Senate, February 11, 1919–March 10, 1919. (Washington, 1919), p. 787.

and Skvir, the digging of the Volga-Don Canal, the exploitation of coal-mines, and in the development of seal hunting, of lumbering, of Siberian railways, etc., etc. In the same document Lenin "guarantees that the military stores which are on hand in Russia will not be sold to Germany.[4]

Bolshevik policy was based on the wish to attract foreign financial assistance for the difficult task of rehabilitating and developing the country. But of greater importance was the political motive; the more support the Soviets received from the Allies the better they could resist German demands. Also, the Communists may have imagined that they could gain by arraying one or more of the Allied powers against the others.

**ALLIED POLICIES** The outstanding war aim of the Allies in Russia was the formation of an eastern front to prevent German concentration in the west. But agreement was lacking on whether this could best be achieved by co-operating with the Bolsheviks or by antagonizing them. Generally speaking, the representatives of the Allies in Moscow were at least realistic; the statesmen at home, already under the influence of counter-revolutionary emigres, and affected by the "Bolsheviks are German agents" propaganda which they themselves had inspired, had a distorted view of the Russian scene. In Vologda and Moscow as well as in the Allied and associated capitals sharp differences of opinion prevailed. The Japanese Embassy had already left Russia, and thus proclaimed its impending active hostility to the Soviet regime. The other nations vacillated. In the case of the United States, Colonel Robins, acting for Mr. Francis in Moscow, was friendly; Mr. Francis in Vologda was less friendly, Secretary Lansing in Washington was cold. He approved very few of Robins's or Francis's co-operation suggestions. Or, in the case of France, Captain Sadoul and the other military attachés were helpful, M. Noulens, sitting in Vologda, nursed a rising bitterness toward Bolshevism, and Clemenceau was frankly hostile. He refused to allow Kamenev entrance into France as Soviet envoy despite the fact that Noulens, the French ambassador in Russia, had visa-ed his passport. Yet at the same time Litvinov was in London as recognized plenipotentiary of the Soviet Government

[4] *R.A.R.* p. 211.

and the recipient of verbal notes from the Foreign Office and letters from Austen Chamberlain and other state officials.[5]

Nor was England's policy free of internal contradictions. Bruce Lockhart had committed himself to co-operation. He trusted the sincerity of the Communist leaders and in an official letter to Colonel Robins dated Moscow, May 5, 1918,[6] he enumerated the important instances in which Trotzky, acting for the Government, "has shown his willingness to work with the Allies." Lockhart, however, could not convince London to adopt his course or accept his advice. Or, to put it more correctly, he could not convince everyone in London. While Churchill, for instance, was arranging Allied intervention in Russia, Lloyd George sent Sir William Clark to discuss trade problems with Chicherin. These were two varying methods of coping with "German domination of Russia." Sir William, in fact, was engaged in conversations with the commissar when British troops landed on Soviet territory. Then, of course, he hastily returned home, disavowed by events. But there is a more astounding circumstance on record: Allied military attachés actually helped to organize the Red Army which later shot down Allied troops.

**ALLIES HELP THE RED ARMY** Even prior to the German offensive in March, the Bolsheviks had realized the need of a dependable army. The Czarist army represented too rotten a foundation, yet some of its healthy elements could be saved. Moreover, workers' guards had been formed; revolutionary units had sprung up spontaneously throughout the country to defend the Red regime. There were also wild Cossack regiments that volunteered to serve under the Soviet banner, and Communist Letts, and the sailors who had turned the fleet over to the Bolsheviks. These were the nuclei.

In January, 1918, the Council of People's Commissars decreed the formation of a workers' and peasants' army; in February, officers' training corps were established and the real work commenced of welding all the scattered forces into a centralized fighting apparatus; in March, on the 16th of the month, Leon Trotzky, who had left the Foreign Office, was appointed People's Commissar of War.

[5] The writer was privileged to examine Mr. Litvinov's private archive of this period.
[6] *R.A.R.*, p. 203.

Lenin had always been favorable to the "receipt of support and arms from the Anglo-French imperialist brigands." The Central Committee of the Communist Party concurred. Trotzky conducted the negotiations. They were twofold: economic and military. The Bolsheviks needed an army. Plenty of men volunteered, and former Czarist officers too (some because they wanted jobs, others because they were sympathetic—but all were carefully watched by trustworthy Communist "Political Commissars"). Expert advice, however, was lacking as well as technical knowledge and, above all, supplies. Accordingly, contact was established with the Allied military attachés. During March, April, and May, 1918, most interesting conversations proceeded. As early as March 11 Colonel James A. Ruggles, Chief of the American Military Mission, had a "satisfactory interview with Trotzky," as Francis reported, "but no definite program (was) adopted." Within ten days Captain Riggs, Moscow representative of Ruggles who had proceeded to Vologda, wired his superior officer: "Sadoul and I had interview Trotzky to-day and yester-day. Soviet Government asks French Military Mission for inspector instructors for new army." The next day, Robins informed Francis that the "French mission here has accepted Trotzky offer and is making assignment of officers for inspection work for Soviet army." Forty-eight hours later, not only French, but "American, French, English and Italian officers . . . are now co-operating with Trotzky."[7] This was not the sort of neutrality the Central Powers expected after the ratification of the Brest Litovsk Treaty, but Russia was looking after her selfish interests.

The military attachés, very naturally, did not act without the knowledge and approval of their Governments. Ambassador Francis, for instance, "authorized Ruggles to instruct Riggs to render active assistance in organizing Soviet army."[8] Lockhart likewise wrote approvingly of the Soviets' invitation "to us to send a commission of British naval officers to save the Black Sea Fleet" and "to co-operate in the reorganization of the new army."[9] Sadoul also acted on instructions from higher authorities and his Italian colleague did too, no doubt.

The Allies entertained no love for Bolsheviks and had

[7] *R.A.R.* pp. 97, 107, 108, 110.
[8] *R.A.R.* p. 117. [9] *R.A.R.* p. 203.

no special desire to further the revolution. They believed the Red Army would help fight Germany. This explains their support.

The Allies did not persuade themselves, however, that the Red Army could do the job unaided. London, Paris, Rome and Washington were contemplating intervention in Soviet Russia with their own armies. At first, they thought they could obtain the Kremlin's approval. With this in view, the British War Cabinet, meeting on April 22 under Lloyd George's chairmanship, "decided that Smuts should go to Kola [Murmansk—L.F.] to see Trotzky."[1] Smuts, for some unrecorded reason, did not undertake this strange mission, but on May 2 Ambassador Francis, while encouraging friendly relations with his left hand, "recommended the intervention in a cable" to the State Department with his right,[2] and on the next day asked Colonel Robins, "Do you think the Soviet Government would oppose Allied intervention if they knew it was inevitable?"[3] Francis inquired. But Lockhart was sure. He was convinced that "a policy of Allied intervention, with the co-operation and consent of the Bolshevik Government, is feasible and possible."[4] Lockhart may not have been very far from the mark—at the moment. A small British landing had been made at Murmansk in March to cope with the northern advance of the Germano-Finns. Moscow, it was clear, would resist intervention aimed at the revolution or undertaken with a view to the permanent occupation of Soviet territory. But if the Allies limited their military efforts on Russian soil to fighting against a real German offensive, the Communists were prepared to sit by passively until their own interests came under fire.[5]

For a moment, therefore, the British War Cabinet, Mr. Francis and Mr. Lockhart toyed with the idea of obtaining Russian acquiescence to their interventionist designs. Acquiescence would have simplified matters. Obviously, however, such a notion could be entertained only so long as the purpose of intervention was anti-German. Nobody expected the Bolsheviks to agree to intervention against the Bolsheviks.

The Allies had already recommended, encouraged and

[1] Callwell: *Field-Marshal Sir Henry Wilson: His Life and Diaries,* (London, 1927), p. 93.
[2] Francis, *Russia from the American Embassy,* p. 266.
[3] *R.A.R.,* p. 162 [4] *R.A.R.,* p. 203.
[5] See Chicherin's statement to the writer on p. 85.

aided the Japanese invasion of Asiatic Russia in April without asking Bolshevik acquiescence. May and June, nevertheless, constituted the critical period in which the "Little Interventionists" who envisaged intervention in Russia as a strictly anti-German move, and the "Big Interventionists" to whom an invasion would serve the purpose of destroying Bolshevism and Russia and the Germans as well, fought for control. Towards the end of June 1918, the latter had won and the problem of Bolshevik consent to intervention disappeared. This decision, indeed, had been foreshadowed by the Japanese-British landing in the Russian Far East.

**JAPANESE INTERVENTION** Japan's invasions of Soviet Russia in April and subsequently were frankly annexationist. Almost immediately after the original peace summons of the Bolsheviks, and before even a truce with Germany had been negotiated, the Allied military attachés warned that Japan might undertake punitive measures against Russia. Brest Litovsk was a respite; the Allies refrained from overt hostile acts while it continued. Yet all the time Tokyo intrigued.

As an ally of Great Britain, Japan automatically adhered to the Western Entente. But Japan was pro-Japan, and neither pro-Entente nor anti-German. The moment Russia collapsed, Japan girded her loins for new acquisitions in the Czar's Asiatic domains. The Island Empire had ambitions in Siberia. England wished to weaken Russia by reducing her size and driving her away from the seas. Japan and Britain, therefore, were well met in the Anglo-Japanese Alliance of 1911. And when the revolution broke out, the two countries immediately commenced to plan the seizure of Russian land on the Pacific. France concurred. Foch, in an interview with Mr. Grasty[6] urged Japan and the United States to meet Germany in Siberia.

America barred the way. It was part of America's foreign policy to weaken Japan's position on the mainland. Japanese intervention in Siberia would, therefore, offend the United States, and the United States could not be offended for she was just then beginning to ship large quantities of supplies and men to the European battlefields. Accordingly, a campaign to win Woodrow Wilson was inaugurated.

[6] *New York Times,* February 26, 1918.

The matter was not simple. The President's single-track mind saw only the French front. Even if there was no fundamental consideration of policy against Japan's control of Siberian territory, he could not grow enthusiastic about a "side show" far from the field of war. His propaganda speeches and his army were calculated to defeat Germany. And he was being assured that intervention in Asiatic Russia would only strengthen Germany. "Japanese invasion would . . . eventually make Russia a German province," Francis wired Washington on March 9. The Bolsheviks preferred Germany to Japan. Trotzky said, "I, of course, object to both armies, but if there is not other alternative, I say, better the German army than the Japanese. . . . If Japan sends an army force she will not withdraw it. . . ."[7] The President decided against Japanese intervention.

> One of the last acts of the Supreme War Council on March 17 had been to send a cable to President Wilson, urging him to agree to Japan undertaking operations in Siberia, a matter to which both the British War Cabinet and the British military authorities attached very great importance.[8]

Why? Because the Germans might occupy Siberia.

Does this bear examination? Not in its extreme form, but few presented the extreme form. Few people asserted that a German army would march straight across Russia, traverse the Urals and invest Siberia from there to Vladivostok. It is an eleven-day trip, in normal times by express train, from Moscow to the Pacific. The armed forces of the Central Powers were in Reval, Pskov, and Vilna at the time. Ludendorff was more interested in Channel ports than in Pacific ports. Every sensible statesman knew that the German General Staff would not waste its divisions in the Farthest East.

**GERMAN PRISONERS IN SIBERIA** Accordingly, the press of Allied countries began to teem with tales of armed German prisoners in Siberia. Not a regular German army, but the tens of thousands of Germans captured by Russia in the war and transferred to Siberia for safe keeping—these would seize Siberia and hold it for the

[7] Leon Trotzky. *Collected Works*. Vol. XVII, Part I, 'The Soviet Republic and the Capitalist World.' (Moscow, 1926).
[8] Callwell, *op. cit.*, p. 71.

Kaiser. Against these Japan asked permission to advance.

When such stories commenced circulating, Ambassador Francis and Mr. Lockhart, both of whom opposed Japanese intervention, were taken by a natural desire to investigate the rumors. They accordingly sent Captain W. L. Hicks of the British Mission in Moscow, and Captain William B. Webster, military attaché to the American Red Cross Mission in Russia, to Siberia. The two officers left Moscow on March 19, remained away more than a month, and on April 26 submitted a "Report of English and American officers in regard to arming of Prisoners of War in Siberia."[9] They said:

> We used every means possible in making investigations. We consulted with various Allied consuls, with the Swedish and Danish Red Cross representatives, with the Russian Secret Service, with the Y.M.C.A. men working in the prison camps, with the Soviets in charge of prisoners, and, finally, with prisoners of war, both civil and military, many of whom were personally known to Captain Webster in his work as American Embassy Delegate in Central Siberia during 1916–7.
>
> Our investigations carried us to Irkutsk, Chita, Dauria, Krasnoyarsk, and Omsk. . . .
>
> We did not deem it necessary to go further east then Chita on the Amur line, inasmuch as Major Walter Drysdale, the American Military Attaché in Peking, whom we met in Irkutsk had just made this trip, stopping at all places where prisoners of war were interned, and reported that none of them had been armed and that they were all well guarded. . . .
>
> We found at Omsk that three sets of prisoners consisting of Hungarians, Czechs and Slavs had been incorporated into the Revolutionary Red Army. . . . The first party, consisting of 434 men, was sent to the Manchurian Front and here we were able to see and talk with them. A second unit, consisting of about 300 men, was later sent to this same front, and while we were in Omsk we interviewed the third set, consisting of 197 men. This made a total of 931 prisoners who have been officially armed for military purposes. In no other part of Siberia was this being done . . .

Moreover,

> The Central All-Siberian Soviet, at Irkutsk, stated that naturally such a number was limited and that they would guarantee that not more than fifteen hundred prisoners of war would be armed in all Siberia. . . . They submitted this guarantee in writing. . . . The Omsk Soviet confirmed this guarantee. . . .

[9] *R.A.R.*, pp. 177 *et seq.*

We can but add that after seeing the armed prisoners and the type of men they are, that we feel there is no danger to the Allied cause through them.[1]

Nine hundred and thirty-one prisoners had been armed in Siberia several thousand miles from Japan and as many miles from Moscow. Tokyo, therefore, deemed it necessary to send a whole army.

On April 4, Francis wired to Robins as follows:

After two sessions of two hours each with military attachés and Garstin (a British captain), the Allied ambassadors agreed to cable their respective governments, advising against Japanese intervention or interference for present. I had done so a day or two before.

Yet on the very next day, Japanese and British troops landed in Vladivostok. George Chicherin, Soviet Commissar for Foreign Affairs, tells what followed.

"April 16 a so-called Far Eastern Government was formed in Peking with Horvath[2] as Prime Minister and Admiral Kolchak[3] as Minister of War. On the next day, Japanese spies were arrested in Irkutsk and it was discovered that the Japanese consul was implicated in the espionage. On the following day a counter-revolutionary plot was unearthed in Vladivostok and documents were found throwing light on the role of the Entente in the formation of the counter-revolutionary Siberian Government. April 25 the Soviet Government demanded that England, France, and the United States recall their consuls from Vladivostok and investigate their activities and explain the relation of those Powers to the counter-revolutionary moves of their agents in Russia."[4]

**CONTRADICTIONS** The trend of Allied diplomacy now began to emerge. Washington opposed, London and

[1] In a memorandum which Dr. Masaryk, later President of the Republic of Czecho-Slovakia, placed before Mr. Roland S. Morris, United States Ambassador in Tokyo, after a trip across Siberia, he wrote (on April 10, 1918), "Nowhere in Siberia, between March 15 and April 2, did I see armed German and Austrian prisoners. The anarchy in Siberia is no greater than in Russia." See T. G. Masaryk, *Die Welt Revolution. Erinnerungen und Betrachtungen.* 1914–18 (Berlin, 1925), p. 214.

[2] Director of the Chinese Eastern Railway.

[3] Admiral Kolchak had served with the Black Sea Fleet under the Czar. On trial before the Cheka in January, 1920, he testified that he was sent to England by Kerensky, in August, 1917. There he met Jellicoe. From London he proceeded by British cruiser to Ottawa and thence in a special car

Paris openly supported, Japanese intervention. At the same time, Allied officers drilled the Red Army which would soon be shooting down Japanese and other Allied soldiers.

Francis, Noulens, and the other Allied envoys in Vologda cabled on April 4 against intervention. Yet the Governments of Noulens and Lockhart were for intervention. Then the diplomats in Russia experienced a sudden change of heart. Noulens advocated intervention on April 22, Francis on May 2. However, having committed themselves and having been committed by their Governments to a policy of intervention without consulting the Bolsheviks, they proceeded to consult the Bolsheviks, though they knew that their countries would intervene whether the Bolsheviks agreed or not, and in the case of England, that the Government had already intervened.

The Japanese tried to exploit anti-German hysteria to obtain United States sanction of their aggression. When this failed they justified themselves by citing the mysterious murder of a Nipponese businessman in Vladivostok.

Balfour assured the world that Japanese intervention was in Russia's interests. . . . His assurances were doubted.

"If Japan should decide to take Vladivostok, Harbin, and Russia's territory in the Extreme East," wrote the *Manchester Guardian* on February 28, "it will not be to please the French or to help the Allies. It will be because Japan has long desired to possess these places and thinks Russia's plight is her opportunity."

Japan harbored designs on all Siberia and not only on one port. But the killing of a single citizen in Vladivostok did not warrant penetration a thousand miles inland. For that a better justification was required. Presently it appeared in the form of the Czecho-Slovaks. These would now offer the excuse for large-scale Allied intervention in Siberia.

---

to New York and Washington. "I was guest of the nation," he declared. In the capital, he interviewed the President and naval officers. His mission was to persuade the chiefs of the United States to attack the Dardanelles and enter the Black Sea. From America he returned to Japan, where he received an invitation from the British to join their army on the Mesopotamian front. The admiral accepted but *en route* a telegram intercepted him at Singapore "ordering" him to retrace his steps and come to Peking. There he was told by the British that he would serve better by putting himself at the disposal of the anti-Bolshevik leaders in the Chinese Capital. This he did.

[4] George Chicherin: *Two Years of Soviet Foreign Affairs*. Small pamphlet published in Moscow, 1920, p. 11.

**THE CZECHO-SLOVAKS** The Czecho-Slovak revolt was one of the strangest episodes in the history of the Russian revolution. It supplies a most important clue to the policy of the foreign Powers towards Bolshevism. . . . From the very beginning of the World War, the Czechs and Slovaks, who fought against Russia in the Austro-Hungarian armies, deserted en masse to the enemy. They had a strongly developed national feeling; they hated the Dual Monarchy and hoped the war would end with its destruction and their constitution as an independent State; moreover, as Slavs they felt a kinship to the Russians.[5]

These Czech and Slovak prisoners were pro-Ally. They and their cousins who had lived in Russia as civilians accordingly proposed to form a corps and fight side by side with the forces of the Czar. Delegations approached the "Little Father," who spoke pleasant words in reply but took no action—the Czecho-Slovaks were republican and Roman Catholic. Moreover, as Chicherin once suggested to the writer, Petrograd did not wish to close the door to a separate peace with Austro-Hungary by supporting one of the Dual Monarchy's disaffected minorities.

Finally Czarist autocracy was overthrown and succeeded by the Provisional Government. The Czecho-Slovak politicians in Petrograd and with them the French Military Mission, particularly General Janin, now increased their pressure on the Russians to permit the formation of the proposed force, and on April 22, Dukhonin ordered the mustering of the Czecho-Slovak prisoners.[6]

Dr. Masaryk, later President of the Czecho-Slovak republic, who was then in Russia, desired to have an independent army, and he desired it to fight in France. "Accordingly I came to an agreement with the French Military Mission," writes Masaryk—it was in May, 1918, "to send 30,000 prisoners to France. . . . We were promised . . . that the transports would be sent via Archangel as soon as possible." French discipline was introduced, and French liaison officers were attached to the entire corps.

A significant detail: When Masaryk visited General

[5] The Serbs in the Austro-Hungarian Army acted in much the same manner and the Russian Government soon allowed the organization of a Serbian Legion on Russian soil.

[6] Masaryk, *op. cit.*, p. 427. My account of the early history of the Czecho-Slovak army follows Dr. Masaryk's. Close reference was also made to Edward Beneš, *Der Aufstand der Nationen*. (Berlin, 1928). Beneš was a trusted co-worker of Masaryk during the World War.

Headquarters on October 9, it was "explicitly agreed with Dukhonin that our army would be used only against the *foreign enemy*."[7] (Italics mine.—L.F.). This was Masaryk's "chief principle of non-intervention" in Russian internal affairs. He intended the Czecho-Slovak army only for the struggle with the Central Powers.

As soon as it became clear that Russia was intent on making peace with the Central Powers and that the Czecho-Slovaks could no longer fight Germany and Austria on Russian territory, Masaryk and his supporters decided to move out of the Ukraine, where the army was concentrated, into Russia. The idea was to proceed "from Kiev to France by way of Siberia—a fantastic plan," Dr. Masaryk asserts. And, now that the Czecho-Slovaks were no longer a part of the Russian army and no longer received rubles from Petrograd, Masaryk went to Moscow to see to it that his 50,000 men were absorbed into the French army. "The point was," he adds, "to secure our army financially." The Czecho-Slovaks, who had no funds of their own, now went on the payroll of Paris. "We were financially dependent on France and the Allies," writes Masaryk.[8]

> I had thought of the war against the Bolsheviks and against Russia. I would have attached myself and our corps to an army which would have been strong enough for a struggle against the Bolsheviks and the Germans, and which would have defended democracy.

Almost immediately after the Bolshevik revolution, Masaryk intimates, pressure was put on the Czecho-Slovaks to place themselves at the disposal of the Allies in *Russia*. "England would have preferred to see us in Russia or, actually, in Siberia."

Now comes a sensational revelation.


> I had thought of the war against the Bolsheviks and against Russia. I would have attached myself and our corps to an army which would have been strong enough for a struggle against the Bolsheviks and the Germans, and which would have defended democracy.


"There was only one possibility for the fight against the Bolsheviks—the mobilization of the Japanese." It follows plainly that the leader of the Czecho-Slovaks was ready to take up arms against the Bolsheviks if the Japanese did so.

[7] Masaryk, *op. cit.* [8] *Ibid,* p. 198.

Toward the end of April, when the Germano-Austrian occupation made it impossible for them to remain in the Ukraine, the Czecho-Slovaks began their famous "Anabasis" to Vladivostok. On the eve of this movement, their leaders received 80,000 pounds sterling from the British (Masaryk admits this), and 11,000,000 rubles from the French consul in Moscow,[9] thus completing their dependence on the Allies.

No sooner had the Czecho-Slovaks entered upon their adventure than the Bolsheviks commenced disarming them. This was done in accordance with a previous agreement, and when Masaryk heard in Tokyo that the Russians had relieved his corps of its arms, he wrote in a secret memorandum to Roland S. Morris, American envoy in Tokyo, "This report is very favorable: the army is *en route* to France and needs no weapons because it will be re-equipped there."[1] Nevertheless, the Czecho-Slovaks refused to give up all their weapons. Their opposition was a violation of an agreement between their own leaders and the Soviets.

The agreement was concluded on March 26 and provided, according to Edward Beneš, for the departure of the Czecho-Slovaks to France "as a group of free citizens who, for protection against counter-revolutionary attacks, were to take a limited number of arms with them." In his book Beneš further reports that the Soviets showed their good-will by allowing the ex-prisoners to obtain military supplies from the stores at Archangel when they reached that port on their way to France. "Lavergne won Trotzky's approval through the aid of Sadoul," writes Beneš. That was on May 7. Yet three weeks previous, on April 13, 1918, "at the military conference, the view of a part of the commanders of the first [Czech] division was adopted against surrendering the arms at the next station to the Bolsheviks—in accordance with the agreement with the Soviets." Benes then relates how the troops hid their weapons. "The branch of the [Czecho-Slovak] National Council knew of this," he says accusingly, "but tolerated it in silence." Later, Dr. Maxa and Chermak, Czech representatives in Moscow, wired to the corps to fulfil the terms of the treaty which they had signed with the Commissariat of War. But no heed was paid to their remonstrances.

[9] M. P. Price, *My Reminiscences of the Russian Revolution,* (London, 1921), p. 292.
[1] Masaryk, *op. cit.,* p. 216.

Frequently, attempts are made to explain the hostility between the Czecho-Slovaks and the Bolsheviks by the incident at Cheliabinsk when a Hungarian prisoner, who apparently provoked the Czechs, was murdered by them on the railway track. But that occurred on May 14, while the decision to resist Bolshevik efforts to disarm them "in accordance with the agreement" had been adopted on April 13. Beneš does not deny that Russian White officers had found pivotal positions in the corps from which they could influence the mood of their Slav brethren. Allied attachés likewise had a hand in the matter. But according to Masaryk and Beneš, the Bolsheviks were not at fault.

Frequently, misinformed persons suppose that the Bolsheviks disarmed the Czechs in reply to German pressure. There certainly is no documentary proof, and the Bolsheviks deny it. Even Paposhek, Beneš' secretary, admits that the first known German representations to Moscow were made on May 28—whereas the disarmament agreement between the Communists and the Czecho-Slovaks dates back to March 26, when the Germans, according to Paposhek,[2] had forgotten about the existence of the ex-prisoners' corps.

The fact is that the Czecho-Slovaks who were themselves not reactionary had put their lot in the hands of reactionaries and served reactionary purposes. Many of the Czecho-Slovak leaders expressed extreme displeasure with subsequent developments. Masaryk himself disapproved of the alliance between his army and the monarchist Kolchak. But such disapproval nowise changed the circumstances.

In the end, the Czecho-Slovaks never reached France. After various experiences, which will be referred to below, the Czecho-Slovaks occupied Vladivostok on June 28. They had fought their way across Siberia and seized the railway in doing so. Why did they not ship to France? The road was clear; the port was theirs. Their goal was France. Why did they turn back to join Kolchak? Why did they begin to move eastward? The answer is, assuming that the ex-prisoners themselves were innocent and sincere, that their masters, the Entente, did not intend to allow their departure for France. The Czecho-Slovaks were too valuable an asset in the anti-Bolshevik struggle to be transported to the Western front.

Of necessity, the Czecho-Slovak battalions were stretched

[2] "The Causes of the Czecho-Slovak Offensive in 1918." Published in the Prague Monthly, *Volia Rossii,* VIII–IX, 1928.

out along a far-flung line, so that, when the trouble started, they were in a position to occupy in quick succession Novo-Nikolaevsk, Omsk and Cheliabinsk in Siberia on May 25, Pensa in European Russia on May 30 and Samara on the Volga on June 8.

> The events taking place on the Volga and along the Siberian Railway [M. Philips Price, Moscow correspondent of the *Manchester Guardian,* wired his paper on June 11] are a clear proof that the Czecho-Slovak forces are not engaged in innocent self-protection from Bolshevik terrorism. It is significant that in every town to which they come in East Russia and Siberia they arrest the local soviets and set up an authority, relying upon the Cadets, Right Social Revolutionaries and Cossack officers.

This interference in internal Russian affairs seems to have met with the hearty approval of Ambassador Francis, who wrote from Vologda to his son Tom on June 4, saying:

> I am now planning to prevent if possible the disarming of 40,000 or more Czecho-Slovak soldiers, whom the Soviet Government has ordered to give up their arms under penalty of death. . . . I have no instructions or authority from Washington to encourage these men to disobey the orders of the Soviet Government. . . . I have taken chances before, however.[3]

Thus encouraged, the Czecho-Slovaks became an undisguised counter-revolutionary force.

In a lecture delivered in Moscow on June 16, Trotzky, Soviet Commissar of War, explained that since the Czecho-Slovaks were commanded by counter-revolutionary officers and since they possessed Russian weapons, "I made the condition that all arms be returned to the Soviets. I decided to permit each echelon to keep a few rifles for the maintenance of order; they agreed. . . . Later we learned that this condition was not fulfilled," and that non-fulfilment caused most of the friction between the soldier-prisoners and the local Soviet authorities.

Then the Japanese, in April, took temporary charge of Vladivostok. The Bolsheviks feared co-operation between the Japanese and Czecho-Slovaks with a view to the conquest of Siberia. Accordingly, Trotzky continued:

[3] *Russia from the American Embassy,* by David R. Francis. New York, 1921, p. 303.

I informed their representatives and the representatives of the French Mission that we could not send them to Vladivostok but were prepared to carry them to Archangel and Murmansk. We demanded that France and England tell us how many ships they could make available at Archangel. . . . I waited for a reply but received none and thereupon declared that France and England bear nine-tenths of the responsibility for what is now happening. I got no reply to my direct question to the chief of the French Mission as to whether the French would remove the Czecho-Slovaks. In answer to my inquiry whether England agreed to transport the Czecho-Slovaks on her vessels, I was told, "The situation is difficult. We have no free ships." . . . I waited and the Czecho-Slovaks waited many weeks for the reply of the French Government. . . . The bourgeois press maintains silence about these facts.

Radek discussed the same subject with Philips Price on June 6.

The Soviet Government, he said, is also ready to consult the Allies on the question of the future of the Czecho-Slovaks. One thing, however, we will not endure, and that is that Soviet Russia should become a prey to any military adventurer who gets enough foreign money and machine-guns. Precisely because we know that Allied Military Missions have been trying to use the Czecho-Slovaks for subversive purposes, we have decided to insist on disarming them. If the Allies are really so anxious to get the Czecho-Slovaks out of Russia, why do they hold up transport in Vladivostok and refuse to allow some 10,000 Czecho-Slovaks, who have already arrived there, to depart for the West?[4]

The only reply to the question posed by Radek was: "The Allies did not want the Czechs to leave Russia."

Data adduced by Dr. Beneš, in his *Der Aufstand der Nationen,* makes the whole matter 100 per cent clear. It had been understood that the Czecho-Slovak corps was to fight in France. But as early as April 1, 1918, the British Ministry of War forwarded a memorandum to Beneš in which doubt was expressed whether "these troops . . . could come as far as Europe. They should therefore be employed in Russia or Siberia." Beneš did not like the idea. France too opposed: Paris was perturbed about the Western front and wanted reinforcements; England, however, thought of weakening Russia.

On May 10 Beneš saw Arthur J. Balfour in London. The British Secretary of State for Foreign Affairs intimated that the Czecho-Slovaks in Siberia might remain there.

[4] Price, *op. cit.*, p. 296.

Five days later Lord Robert Cecil expressed the same wish.

London, meanwhile, brought pressure on Clemenceau to accept its plan of using the Czecho-Slovaks as the basis of an interventionary force against the Bolsheviks. The activities of the French Military Mission in Russia tended in the same direction. During the first week in June, writes Beneš, "the French military representatives, Vergé and Guinet,[5] who had received urgent telegrams from Paris, refused to guarantee the transport of the troops to France." Definite instructions were sent to General Lavergne from Paris on June 20 to keep the Czechs in Russia, and a week later he was ordered to mobilize around the Czecho-Slovak nucleus all counter-revolutionary elements, to seize the Trans-Siberian Railway and to prepare for Allied intervention—which eventuated in July and August. This complete identification of the French policy with the British found expression in a note from Clemenceau to Pichon on July 12.[6] This decision of June 20, moreover, marks the complete victory of the "Big Interventionists."

On June 28, the Czecho-Slovaks, "Without warning or provocation of any kind, seized the city [Vladivostok], disarmed the Red Guard and drove out the Soviet Government."[7] And on July 12 the Czecho-Slovaks commenced moving westward, that is, back into Siberia. "The real motives for this change of front on the part of Czechs have been the subject of some debate," writes Norton.[8] "The stated reason was hardly sufficient to cover all the circumstances. It did not explain the capture of Yakutsk, far from the line of the railroad, where there were, and had been, no Czechs. It did not explain the advance of the Czechs against the Russian forces in the Ussuri Valley, with whom they had been on the best of terms, immediately after the seizure of Vladivostok. It did not explain the attacks along the Amur railway from the West. It did not explain the determination to hold the Volga line, and even to advance into Russia itself. . . .

[5] Guinet was chief of the French Mission attached to the Czechs. His role and that of the French generally in the Czecho-Slovak affair is discussed in *Notes sur la Revolution Bolchevique. Quarante Lettres de Jacques Sadoul.* (Paris, 1922), pp. 94 *et seq.*

[6] Beneš, *op. cit.*, p. 514.

[7] Henry Kitredge Norton, *The Far Eastern Republic of Siberia,* London, 1923, p. 67.

[8] *Ibid.*

"The efforts of the Bolsheviks to detain them [that is, to prevent them from joining the Japanese at Vladivostok. —L.F.] were hardly sufficient to warrant the change of front, for those efforts had been wholly futile. . . .

"The other explanation offered, and this is universally believed by the Siberians, is that the Czechs were prevailed upon by the Allies and under the urgence of France, to attack the Russians from the rear in return for recognition and assistance. This hypothesis covers all the circumstances already mentioned, and receives additional support from the later action of the Allies. France recognized the Czecho-Slovak Republic on June 30. Great Britain followed on August 13. The United States granted recognition on September 2, and Japan on September 9."

The Czecho-Slovak armed battalions had "renounced their ambition to fight the Germans in France" for the task of fighting the Russians in Russia. Coming up from the south, one branch of the line moved into Siberia while another penetrated deep into Russia. During July they captured Ufa, Verkhni-Uralsk, Simbirsk, Yekatrinburg, and, early in August, Kazan. Having taken Samara on June 8, a strong Czecho-Slovak force entrenched itself in the Volga district and slowly crept up the great river in the direction of Moscow.

**THE PLAN TO OVERTHROW BOLSHEVISM** Lenin had said, during the Brest Litovsk debate, that if they lost Petrograd they could retreat to Moscow, if they lost Moscow they could retreat to the Urals, and if they lost the Urals they could retreat to Vladivostok. But only two or three months later, the Czecho-Slovaks held Vladivostok and the Urals, Krasnov was trying to capture the lower reaches of the Volga, the Germans were in the Caucasus, the Crimea, the Ukraine and Finland, Denikin was in the Kuban, Dutov was on the march. This period was the Bolshevik zero hour in the Civil War. They controlled less territory than ever before or ever after. Moscow was surrounded by a small blotch of red. The rest of the country was white, black, black-white-red, etc.

History was in a feverish haste. Events followed one another kaleidoscopically. The plan to forge an iron ring around the red capital quickly matured. There were battles, insurrections, assassinations, invasions—two most exciting months.

A map and the chronology of events reveal the outline:

July 1. British-French landing in Murmansk.
July 6. Assassination of Count Mirbach, German ambassador in Moscow.
July 6. Left Social Revolutionist insurrection in Moscow.
July 6. Anti-Bolshevik uprising in Jaroslav.
July 9. Anti-Bolshevik risings in Murom, Ribinsk and Arzamas.
July 25. Allied diplomats leave Vologda for Archangel.
July 29. Assassination of Eichhorn, Commander-in-Chief of German forces in Ukraine.
August 1. Allied landing in Archangel.
August 6. Czecho-Slovaks take Kazan.
August 24. White plot against Soviets revealed in Moscow.
August 30. Uritzky, prominent Bolshevik, assassinated in Petrograd.
August 30. Attempt on life of Lenin in Moscow.

It is almost a straight north-south line from Archangel to Moscow. The only important towns on the route are Vologda and Jaroslav. Ribinsk is near Jaroslav. It is almost a straight east-west line from Kazan to Moscow. The only important towns on the route are Arzamas and Murom. If all these points fell into the hands of the Allies or their Russian supporters, Moscow and with it the Bolshevik regime were doomed.

The preparatory work was to be carried out by the Right Social Revolutionaries and Savinkov.

But circumstances intervened which upset all calculations. The Archangel landing came too late, and the Jaroslav rising failed; so did the Ribinsk mutiny. And the Czechs were delayed en route to Kazan.

Jaroslav was the key to the situation. The ancient city lies on the Archangel-Moscow route and also on the Volga. Savinkov led the attack personally. It commenced at 2 A.M. on the morning of July 6. Tanks, heavy artillery, and airplanes were employed in a struggle which lasted twelve days and resulted in the well-nigh complete gutting of the town. Finally, the Social Revolutionaries surrendered. Many, including Savinkov, had previously fled, but Jaroslav was Savinkov's greatest fiasco. With the walls of its historic buildings crumbled the high hopes of the Allies to destroy Bolshevism before it had become sufficiently entrenched. Now there was nothing left for the Entente diplomats to do in Vologda or anywhere on

Soviet territory. They accordingly proceeded to Archangel despite insistent urgings by Chicherin to come to Moscow, urgings reinforced by a personal visit to the ambassadors of Karl Radek and Arthur Ransome, then correspondent of the London *Daily News*.[1]

It was Trotzky who objected to the presence of Allied diplomats at Vologda, and Chicherin accordingly warned the ambassadors that Vologda might at any time be subjected to White bombardment.

**THE ASSASSINATION OF MIRBACH** The opening of the sanguine Jaroslav revolt synchronized with an event of great moment—the assassination of Count Wilhelm Mirbach, the German ambassador in Moscow.

On the afternoon of July 6, Mirbach sat in his office on the ground floor of the embassy when two Russians asked to see him. They came from the Cheka, the Extraordinary Commission for the Struggle with Counter-Revolution, and urged pressing business. On being ushered into the presence of the Count, Blumkin and Andreiev produced their documents, signed by Dzerzhinsky, the Chief of the Cheka, and counter-signed by an assistant. Before these could be examined, however, Blumkin drew a revolver and shot at Mirbach and his two attachés. The ambassador immediately rushed to an adjoining room, but was overtaken by a bullet which struck him in the back of the head. To make matters certain, Blumkin then hurled a hand-grenade at the diplomat and, without stopping to retrieve caps or portfolios, both assassins jumped through the window—Blumkin broke a leg in the fall—and escaped in a waiting auto to the headquarters of the Left Social Revolutionary Party.

Immediately the news of the count's death reached Dzerzhinsky, he and Karakhan proceeded to the embassy. It was clear that his signature had been forged by Blumkin who, though he indeed worked in the Cheka, was known as a Left Social Revolutionary. Accordingly, Dzerzhinsky dashed across town to the brigade headquarters of the Social Revolutionary Popoff where he and Latziz, his assistant, demanded the surrender of the assassins. The Bolsheviks personally searched the house and smashed some doors in the process, but when the assassins were

[1] *Correspondance diplomatique. Se rapportant aux Relations entre la République Russe et les Puissances de l'Entente.* 1918 (Moscow, 1919).

not found Dzerzhinsky threatened to arrest the Social Revolutionaries present unless they delivered Blumkin and Andreiev. In lieu of a reply the Social Revolutionaries disarmed the commissar and his companions and "temporarily detained" them in the cellar of the building.

> I organized the Mirbach affair from the beginning to the end, [Marie Spiridonova, Social Revolutionary leader, boasted in her cross-examination by the Cheka on the 10th] We, [she explained, referring to the Central Committee of her party] adopted a resolution on the necessity of assassinating Count Mirbach as part of a plan we had accepted of annulling the Brest Treaty of peace.[2]

Another part of the plan was an insurrection on the following day. The Left Social Revolutionaries, operating from their staff headquarters in the Morosov Palace on Triekhsviatitelsky Street, seized the central post office, patrolled the streets of a section of the city, and arrested all Bolsheviks they could lay hands on. They proposed to take Lenin and Trotzky prisoners and then seize the government. The revolt, however, was poorly organized and indifferently directed. On the night of the 7th, a battalion of faithful Letts, commanded by Peterson, captured the Social Revolutionary headquarters, arresting most of the heads of the party.

In their proclamation which accompanied this episode, in their statement to the Cheka and at the Soviet Congress which opened just two days prior to the assassination, the Left Social Revolutionaries admitted that their purpose was to provoke war against Germany. There is no doubt that they intended the murder of Mirbach (which Blumkin subsequently confessed having executed on orders from the Left Social Revolutionary Central Committee) as a provocation to the Central Powers. It was hoped that the Germans would retaliate by occupying Moscow, and this step, in turn, would justify an Allied attack on the capital.

Some Bolsheviks believe that the Left Social Revolutionaries acted under Allied instructions. But the Left Social Revolutionaries were as resolutely opposed to Entente imperialism as they were to German. They thought that the Brest Peace doomed the revolution to destruction. To

[2] *Red Book.* Published by the Cheka in Moscow in 1919, but immediately withdrawn from circulation. P. 200.

save it, they proposed precipitating a partisan war in Russia much like that which worried the Germans in the Ukraine. Mirbach would be shot. Prestige would demand revenge. The Germans would march into Moscow; the Allies would march too; both imperialisms would lose and the European revolution would be hastened. It was a puerile, impossible, unpolitical plan, but it was not an Allied plan. The most one can concede is that the ambassadors in Vologda may have been aware of the Left Social Revolutionaries' intentions (spies were ubiquitous), and timed the revolts in Jaroslav, etc., and the landings in Murmansk and Archangel to synchronize with the Mirbach affair. This was Savinkov's hypothesis too.

During the same period, according to Cheka charges levelled early in September, Bruce Lockhart, the British High Commissioner, was engaged in planning the assassinations of Lenin, Trotzky, and other Communist leaders, and in an effort to bribe the Lettish Guards to strike a blow against the revolution. Lockhart was arrested, despite the protest of Chicherin, and expelled from the country.

That Lockhart had previously been strongly opposed to Allied intervention in Russia is proved by documentary evidence. But intervention with Bolshevik sanction appealed to him as feasible, and when this sanction was not forthcoming, his Government nevertheless proceeded with plans calculated to destroy the Communist leaders, capture Moscow, and overthrow the Soviet regime. But in conversation with the writer, Lockhart categorically denied that he had plotted the assassination of Lenin and other Russian leaders, or in any way furthered, or given encouragement to, such plans.

**INTERVENTION IN NORTH RUSSIA** The Allied scheme for the capture of Moscow failed not only because the Jaroslav revolt was suppressed but also because the Anglo-French-American landing in Archangel came too late. Foreign troops commenced disembarking in Murmansk during the latter half of June, and on the 1st of July the occupation was complete. Had events proceeded according to program, Archangel would have fallen into Allied hands no more than ten days later. Instead, a whole month elapsed.

> There was a danger, [said Churchill in the House of Commons on July 29, 1918] of Archangel becoming a submarine base for

the Germans, and the danger of the loss of all that great mountain of stores we had accumulated there in order to keep that means of contact with Russia, and for all these reasons, combined with the fact that it was hoped the Czechs would make their way out by that route, the Allies in 1918, as an essential military operation and as part of the war, decided to occupy Archangel and Murmansk and put an inter-Allied force on shore there.

German U-boats were, it is true, operating in north Russian waters. So were Allied men-of-war. But the submarines had never attempted to establish a permanent base. A U-boat can sink ships and shell a town intermittently but it cannot deposit enough soldiers on shore to capture that town. Moreover, why in order to prevent the establishment of a German base, did the Allies require 12,000 armed individuals? Why did they need to penetrate a few hundred miles inland and occupy all intervening territory?

The second "reason" is equally lame. There were, it is true, some stores at Murmansk and "great mountains of stores" at Archangel. Far back in February the Bolsheviks had suggested to Robins that they be removed inland, and when no agreement was reached on the matter, they undertook the task themselves. The Russians were as anxious as the Allies to prevent the supplies from becoming a German prize. Yet when the Soviets commenced transporting these military goods to safer centers, the Allies protested. On March 4, 1918, Douglas Young, British consul in Archangel, wrote:

> The British Government regards all the stores on hand in Archangel as the exclusive property of the Allies and not of Russia. . . . The stores cannot become the property of the Russian Government even in part.[3]

In much the same tone, Ambassador Francis telephoned to Colonel Robins on March 30 saying:

> Authoritatively informed that large shipments being made to interior from Archangel where immense accumulations of munitions and other supplies furnished by Allies on credits repre-

[3] Translated from the original Russian translation which I saw in the possession of M. Kedrov, the Soviet commissar in charge of the removal of the stores.

sented loans since repudiated, but Russian Government claims ownership nevertheless. Such position untenable. . . .[4]

Ambassador Francis testified before the U. S. Senate Overman Committee on March 8, 1919, that "the Bolsheviks were shipping a hundred cars a day out of Archangel and sent them to Kotlas, sent them down to Vologda, and to Petrograd and Moscow. . . ."[5] This activity was prosecuted with vigor in the spring of 1918 under the eyes of Allied consuls, who must have known that the material remaining at Archangel or Murmansk in July–August was too small in quantity to justify the landing of an army.

The Bolsheviks, harried as they were, could scarcely prevent an Entente landing in the North. Chicherin therefore made it clear to the ambassadors that while the Bolsheviks objected to intervention, they would resist foreign landings only in case they were directed against the Communist Government. In June—it was before the Mirbach assassination—Chicherin tells the writer, he sent one of his subordinates, a Left Social Revolutionary named Vosnisensky, to Vologda to interview the Allied missions there. Vosnisensky saw Noulens, who spoke frankly of his proposed "Little" intervention for anti-German purposes and of "Big" intervention for anti-Bolshevik purposes. He likewise saw Sir F. O. Lindley, the British envoy. He informed both Noulens and Lindley, under instructions from Moscow, that the Soviets would not resist landings of foreign troops on the Arctic provided they moved inland in the direction of Finland against the German forces there. But if they proceeded towards Petrograd or Moscow, the Bolsheviks would be forced to fight.

Chicherin sent numerous notes to London and Washington on the subject of the Murmansk and Archangel occupations. Between the lines, the same policy can be read. The Communists, because they had no other choice, were prepared to countenance Allied descents not aimed directly against them.

In view of these facts, neither the thesis that intervention was a World War measure aimed at the Germans, nor Churchill's U-boat excuse, nor his stores story, will bear examination. To the confirmed interventionist for

[4] *R.A.R.*, p. 122.
[5] *Bolshevik Propaganda.* Hearings . . . p. 976.

intervention's sake, the anti-German motive had become subordinate to the anti-Bolshevik.

The Germans' war power was beginning to decline rapidly. Bulgaria was crumbling; Allenby rained heavy blows at the Turks; the Allies had stayed Hindenburg's offensive in the West, and Foch even directed one or two successful counter-offensives. On June 24, von Kuehlmann declared in the Reichstag that the war could not be ended by military means, and though the statement cost him his position it attested to Berlin's waning self-assurance. This lack of confidence was mirrored in the reaction to the Mirbach incident. The Bolsheviks expected severe reprisals; even the taking of Moscow. The Wilhelmstrasse, as a matter of fact, demanded Bolshevik permission to dispatch a battalion to guard Dienezhni Pereulok 5 where Mirbach had been killed, and in high Bolshevik quarters this was interpreted as the introduction to more sinister measures. The Kremlin, nevertheless, protested violently against the German demand and Germany, whose hands were full elsewhere, everywhere, retreated. An exchange of notes took place in the second fortnight of July, and finally both parties agreed on the increase of the embassy's personnel to 300. The added staff was to arrive in groups of thirty without arms or uniforms.

This was a diplomatic victory for Chicherin. It pointed to Germany's weakness. Indeed, Karl Helfferich, who quietly appeared in Moscow on the 28th of July as Mirbach's successor, had strict instructions to follow a conciliatory policy of economic rapprochement. Helfferich's own attitude was extremely aggressive. No sooner had he arrived in Moscow than he established contacts with White elements and decided that Germany would act most wisely if she pooled her strength with the counter-revolutionaries in order to give the Bolsheviks that "light blow" which, in his opinion, would have sufficed to overthrow them early in August. He would not have signed the supplementary agreements envisaged by the Brest Treaty and he would have catered to the "undivided Russia" sentiments of the Whites by returning the Baltic provinces. His plan of an anti-Communist putsch engineered by German brains and gold also included military operations by Czarist generals in South Russia and the bribing of the Lettish regiments in the capital. To all this the ambassador confesses in his three-volume opus on the "Weltkrieg."

**A BOLSHEVIK OFFER TO GERMANY** Early in August, Chicherin, on behalf of the Soviet Government, made a most significant proposition to Helfferich. The commissar suggested that the Germans march an army into Russia. The Bolsheviks, according to this plan, would open a corridor for the Germans, who could enter the country from Finland and, while avoiding such cities as Petrograd and Petrozavodsk, advance to stem Allied penetration southward from Murmansk and Archangel. At the same time, German forces from the Ukraine were to resist General Alexeev's efforts to extend his influence north of the Don.[6]

General Alexeev, Chicherin explained to the writer on one occasion, received comfort from the German forces in the Ukraine despite the fact that he was pro-Entente. The Bolsheviks wished to destroy this united front of the Powers against the revolution. Moreover, the Brest Litovsk Supplementary treaties, then in preparation, envisaged the return to the Soviets of the railways leading to Rostov-on-Don. These, highly important to the Russians as a link with the Caucasus, were, however, in the hands of General Alexeev, and the Germans were thus offering Moscow something they did not have. But the supplementary agreements represented a quid pro quo, and since the Bolsheviks gave real values they asked in return more than empty promises. They wanted the Germans to take the railways from Alexeev, the White counter-revolutionary. This was one of the salient features of Chicherin's proposal to Helfferich.

This strange offer would never have been made had Moscow known, as it might have known, how quickly Imperial Germany was nearing her doom.

The reason for the Bolsheviks' proposal is clear; they were attacked on all sides; the Allies had definitely determined on intervention and might again repeat the Jaroslav-Vologda-Archangel and Kazan-Murom-Armazas scheme for the capture of Moscow. The Communists wished to win foreign support and only Germany could give it.

Helfferich, however, in his extreme Moscowphobia, never even submitted Chicherin's offer to his Government. Soviet diplomats subsequently discovered that the Berlin

[6] These facts, told me by Chicherin, are referred to casually by Helfferich in his *Weltkrieg*.

Foreign Office was completely ignorant of the suggestion.

The German Government, however, would never have entered upon such an adventure. It was negotiating in friendly manner with Joffe. It disapproved of Helfferich's machinations with the Russian Whites, and the ambassador was, in fact, recalled to Berlin during the first week of August. The German General Staff as well as the civilian authorities had no desire to complicate the eastern situation by destroying the Soviet regime and establishing a pro-German monarchist substitute which would inevitably be subjected to Allied attack. At a meeting with the Kaiser in Spa on July 2, 1918, Ludendorff stated definitely that they "must make no attempt to overthrow the Bolsheviks at the present moment," and the Chancellor agreed.[7] In like manner, Germany could not have wished to intercede on behalf of the Bolsheviks and thus provoke a bitter struggle with the Allies in Russia when she needed every soldier to prevent defeat in France.

Meanwhile, the fear struck into the Germans' hearts by the murder of Mirbach had not disappeared. Convinced that the Allies would succeed in occupying Moscow, some members of the German embassy's staff evacuated their families to the home country. Helfferich left Moscow on the 6th of August. The next day a number of the embassy's departments moved to Petrograd, where they were closer to the border. A week later they went still farther and took up their abode on territory occupied by the Germano-Finns, leaving a few representatives in Moscow. These movements were scarcely proofs of strength or indications of offensive intentions. Moreover, Germany's position in the Ukraine, especially after the assassination of General Eichhorn and as a result of the subversive activities of Piatakov's underground Bolshevik agents, grew increasingly alarming.

This decline of the Reich's strength was reflected in three supplementary agreements which Berlin and Moscow signed on August 27 in accordance with the stipulations of the original Brest Treaty.[8]

[7] Secret protocol of the meeting published in the Berlin *Rote Fahne*, November 6, 1928.

[8] From the official German and Russian texts deposited in the Commissariat of Foreign Affairs.

In these

| *Germany promised to* | *Soviet Russia promised to* |
|---|---|
| | Pay six billion marks in goods, bonds, and gold.[9] |
| Evacuate White Russia. | |
| Occupy no more Russian territory. | |
| Evacuate Rostov and part of the Don. | Renounce sovereignty over Estonia and Latvia. |
| Give Russia access to the sea via Reval, Riga and Windau, and | |
| Surrender Baku to the Russians. | Sell Germany 25 per cent of Baku's oil yield, and |
| | Take cognizance of Germany's recognition of an independent Georgia. |

This was much better than Brest. Yet the rapid sinking of the Central Powers warranted a bigger victory for Moscow. Co-operation between the Entente and the Russians at this juncture would have permitted the Kremlin to defy Berlin at every point; it would have weakened Germany and given the advantage to the Western Powers. The Allies, however, had made war on the Soviet State, and the attacks of the Czecho-Slovaks, the landings in Murmansk, Archangel, and Vladivostok undermined Bolshevism's diplomatic defenses against the Germans.

Despite Soviet warnings that foreign invasion would be met with armed resistance, troops continued to land and by July 1, 4,000 British, French, American, and Serb soldiers had invested Murmansk. Within a fortnight the entire district had been occupied, including Kandalaksha, about 150 miles south of Murmansk, and Kem, near by Kandalaksha. On August 2 a landing was made at Archangel, where, on the same day, and under the protection of Allied cruisers and Allied soldiers, the Soviet was overthrown and a coalition government set up under the presidency of N. V. Chaikovsky.

[9] The Soviet Government actually paid 120,000,000 rubles gold to Germany in two shipments during August and September. Viewed retrospectively, this was the height of folly. Germany was on her last legs and could never have forced Russia to pay. But Joffe misinformed Moscow on the strength of the Central Powers. He did not expect that their collapse was so imminent.

This was the first case of large-scale intervention in Soviet Russia by oversea armed forces of the Allied Powers. At Vladivostok a few hundred Japanese and fifty British came on shore, but did not overthrow the Bolshevik Government nor attempt to penetrate inland. Here, however, there were more than 10,000 men (further reinforcements came later), and their activity consisted in the establishment of authorities opposed to the Bolsheviks as well as the conquest of territories far from the coast.

It is no surprise to find Englishmen, Frenchmen, Serbs and Italians among these forces. But Americans? Had not President Wilson strenuously opposed Japanese intervention in Siberia? Had he not expressed sympathy and friendship for the Soviet Government?

American diplomacy was transparent:

May 2. Mr. Francis advocated intervention in a secret cable.
May 31. Mr. Francis made a public statement to the effect that "The policy of my Government is not to intervene in the internal affairs of Russia."
May 31. Mr. Lansing cabled Mr. Francis: "The friendly intentions of the United States towards Russia . . . will not be changed under the influence of accusations. . . nor through any denials of diplomatic privileges . . ."
June. American troops landed in Murmansk.

**WOODROW WILSON AND INTERVENTION** Wilson had opposed Japanese intervention in the Far East because of America's traditional Far Eastern policy. The President's position was not determined by any interest in the revolution or the Moscow regime. If it had been, he could not have allowed intervention in the North. Having approved of intervention in Murmansk, it would have been inconsistent to disapprove of it in Siberia. Yet Wilson did continue to object to Japanese occupation in Siberia. Clearly, his motives were anti-Japanese rather than pro-Bolshevik.

Strong British pressure was being brought on Wilson to join the contemplated Siberian adventure. At a War Cabinet meeting in London on June 19, Sir Henry Wilson, Chief of the Imperial General Staff, "again said that I would have to ask for the withdrawal of Poole [the British general in charge of the Arctic expedition.—L.F.] and of all his command if the Japanese did not come in, as we shall lose all our men at Pechenga, Murmansk, and Archangel."[1] This statement is noteworthy because it draws attention to the connection in the minds of the military between these two very distant fronts and because mention is made on June 19 of men at Archangel when they actually disembarked in that city only on August 2. (This delay contributed materially to the failure of the Allies to capture Moscow in July.) Yet, despite the Commander-in-Chief's arguments for assistance to the Japanese, Lloyd George "hangs back for some unaccountable reason."[2] The unaccountable reason was the President of the United States. The Cabinet, accordingly, decided to cable to Woodrow Wilson, "urging upon (him) the need of Japanese intervention in Siberia."[3]

But the President remained firm. A month later, on July 16, the same British War Cabinet deliberated upon the same question.

> . . . A. J. B. [Arthur J. Balfour], Sir Henry Wilson notes in his diary, "brought up [Lord] Reading's objection to Knox[4] going to Siberia, saying President Wilson was opposed to it. I was very angry, and Lloyd George and Bob Cecil backed me; so Knox goes to-night by New York and Vancouver.

Lloyd George and Cecil backed Sir Henry because they knew Wilson was weakening. The next day, in fact, the United States State Department sent notes to the Powers in which it expressed preliminary agreement with intervention.[5]

Paris, London and Tokyo had forced Wilson's hand. The Allies, tired of Woodrow Wilson's obstructions, had determined to defy him. They decided to march into Asiatic Russia over Washington's veto. And rather than lose all control of and touch with the Siberian situation, the President agreed to participate. As a characteristic compensation, however, the official announcement of August 3 said that the "Government of the United States has, therefore, proposed to the Government of Japan that each of the

[1] Callwell, *op. cit.*, 109.
[2] *Ibid.*
[3] Callwell, *op. cit.*
[4] General Knox, then already designated to command the British forces about to be landed in Siberia.
[5] F. L. Schuman: *American Policy toward Russia Since 1917*, (New York, 1928), p. 103.

two governments send a force of a few thousand men to Vladivostok." On the same day, the Japanese Government accepted the "proposal"; on the same day a detachment of British landed in Vladivostok; a week later came four French companies. On the 12th of August, the Japanese arrived, and on the 15th the Americans.

Strangely enough, the official United States statement of August 3 opened with anti-interventionist arguments.

> In the judgment of the Government of the United States, [it began]—a judgment arrived at after repeated and very searching consideration of the whole situation—military intervention in Russia would be more likely to add to the present sad confusion than cure it, and would injure Russia, rather than help her out of her distress.

Then why intervene?

> Such military intervention as has been most frequently proposed, [it continues] even supposing it to be efficacious in its immediate object of delivering an attack upon Germany from the east, would . . . be more likely to turn out to be a method of making use of Russia than to be a method of serving her. Her people, if they profited by it all, could not profit in time to deliver them from their present difficulties. . . . We are bending all our energies now to the purpose. . . . of winning on the Western front and it would . . . be most unwise to divide or dissipate our forces.

These are unanswerable contentions against intervention. But since the Japanese and British were not to be arrested, the American Government joined. It imagined that it could keep Tokyo in check and therefore proposed that the number of men be limited to a "few thousand." By some mistake, however, the United States broke the agreement and sent in 8,500 troops instead of 7,000.[6] Thereupon, on the ground that they were no longer bound, the Nippon militarists increased their forces in Siberia to 73,400. Subsequent protests by Secretary of State Colby were of no avail.

**AMERICAN-JAPANESE FRICTION** Sharp conflicts soon developed between the American and Japanese chiefs in Siberia. The United States may have joined the forces of reaction in Russia, but its purpose in intervening was certainly not territorial aggrandizement. Japan, on the

[6] E. A. Ross: *The Russian Soviet Republic,* (New York, 1923), p. 154.

other hand, was plainly laying the groundwork for future annexations to round out her war-time gains in China. Accordingly, the more aggressive Japan's moves became, the more cautious grew the attention of the American authorities in Siberia. This was also due, in part, to the statesmanlike conduct of Major-General William B. Graves, head of the American Expeditionary forces.

The intentions of the Japanese were clear. By the end of August they had, in addition to the men landed at Vladivostok, 30,000 soldiers in North Manchuria and 6,000 at Manchuli, on the Manchurian-Siberian frontier. Early in September they had proceeded as far west as Irkutsk. The whole Baikal region lay at their feet.

More and more Japanese troops kept coming into the country. But it was impossible to check their numbers. For if the American or British or French Government placed a captain in charge of its men at a certain point, Japan was certain to send a colonel. If the others sent a colonel, Tokyo never failed to dispatch a general. The Commander-in-Chief of all the Allied forces in Siberia was, accordingly, General Otami, a member of the Supreme Military Council of Japan. All troop movements were reported to him, but the Allies were unable to obtain information with regard to movements of Japanese troops. Allied military operations required the approval of the Commander-in-Chief. Japanese operations were not even brought to the attention of the Allies.

Within a few months Japan held the railway line from Vladivostok to Chita and her faithful ally, Ataman Semenov, had gained control of the district between Manchuli and Chita. At the same time, the Czecho-Slovaks were in command of the country west of Chita as far as the Urals, and beyond too.

Under these circumstances anti-Bolshevik groups could work with facility. A number of governments were set up at various places but only one pretended to national significance. That was the "Provisional All-Russian Government" appointed at Ufa on September 22, 1918, by the so-called "State Assembly," and consisting of Astrov, N. D. Avksentiev, Boldirev, Vologodski and N. V. Chaikovsky, the chief of the Archangel Cabinet who, it is important to note, was included in the Ufa list because of the kinship between the two districts under Allied control and of the intention ultimately to unite both regions and all Russia in one counter-revolutionary state. The "directors," as they were called, now moved to Omsk and began to organize their administration. Vladivostok recognized its authority as did Irkutsk, and most of that part of Siberia which the Czecho-Slovaks had occupied. Semenov, the Japanese puppet, however, remained hostile, while General Horvath, who supervised the Chinese Eastern Railway by the grace of the Japanese, offered only paper allegiance. Omsk, nevertheless, became a power to reckon with.

**ADMIRAL KOLCHAK** Admiral Kolchak had arrived in Omsk in September and was appointed Minister of War of the Omsk Government. Nevertheless, he caused the directors of that government to be arrested on the night of November 18 and declared himself "Supreme Ruler of Russia." A group of officers had engineered the coup.

Kolchak now commenced to mobilize an army to overthrow the Bolsheviks in Russia. Speaking of Kolchak's forces, Mr. Churchill said in the House of Commons, on May 29, 1919, "In the main these armies are equipped by British munitions and British rifles, and a certain portion of the troops are actually wearing British uniforms."

With the rise of Kolchak, the pretense of democratic opposition to the Bolsheviks disappeared. All the generals in the Ukraine, the Don, the Kuban and the Caucasus, whether pro-German or pro-Entente, were frankly reactionary and autocratic, and, for the most part, enthusiastically monarchist. Krasnov, Alexeev, Dutov, Denikin, Kornilov, Kaledin and the others never even claimed to have popular support.

**WHY INTERVENTION?** There were three categories of interventionists:

1. The Churchill, "Big Intervention" brand who saw Bolshevism as a menace and wished to overthrow it. The desire to create an Eastern front against the Germans was a sincere motive in their case, but behind it was their hatred of the Bolsheviks.

2. The Japanese, who were not interested in the overthrow of Bolshevism but rather wished to see a state of

Russian disorder and weakness from which they could extract advantages.

3. The doubters who favored only the "Little Intervention," that is, intervention against the Germans.

Intervention on a large scale became possible when the "Big Interventionists" won the approval of the "Little Interventionists." and in June–July came the intervention which the Lloyd Georges thought "Little" but which the Churchills knew would be "Big." For in June and July the Germans were withdrawing many thousands of troops from the Eastern front to the Western. The Entente no longer feared the "Germanization" of Russia. But the menace of Bolshevism remained.

Intervention found the Soviets standing alone on a small piece of territory faced by a combination of Russia's bourgeoisie and a group of foreign countries. They had little money, an imperfect organization, a weak army, limited experience, and insufficient military equipment. The enemy disposed of huge financial resources, expert military leadership, boundless supplies of arms, munitions and stores, great stretches of territory (Siberia, the Ukraine, the Caucasus, the North, etc.), and the richest agricultural, raw-material producing and industrial sections of the country.

Yet in the end, victory came to the Soviets. Singlehandedly they fought England, America, Japan, Serbia, Italy, Czecho-Slovakia, the Baltic States, Kolchak, Denikin, Petlura, the Mensheviks, Yudenich, Wrangel, Semenov, Kalmikov, and a host of lesser forces, and won.

To understand how they did it is to understand the secret of Soviet Russia's persistence to the present day.

# 3

# "BIG" ALLIED INTERVENTION

NOVEMBER, 1918, marks a milestone in the history of the Soviet Civil War. The rise of Kolchak, the fall of the Kaiser, and the close of the World War represent the dawn of a new phase.

The Kolchak coup introduced clarity into the internal Russian conflict. It became a struggle between the establishment of the new and the restoration of the old. In like manner, the Armistice revealed the true character of foreign intervention. After the defeat of the Central Powers, the "German menace" could no longer be offered as an excuse for Allied interference. If Allied troops had entered Russia to reconstruct th Eastern front or to prevent military supplies from falling into German hands or to defeat the sinister designs of armed enemy prisoners, then the Armistice should have signalled the beginning of evacuation. Instead, Allied support to counter-revolutionaries increased considerably after the Armistice.

By this time, the White Russian emigrés had consolidated their influence in foreign political circles. Not unlike their prototypes in the French revolution, these counter-revolutionary nobles, landlords, industrialists, and bankers fled abroad immediately after the Bolshevik upheaval and created, in London, Paris, Washington, etc., salons and unofficial centers of anti-Soviet activity. With their wealth and social position, they quickly won the ear of important personalities in government positions, and became the accepted sources of information on Russian questions. The emigrés affected the course of Soviet international relations from the very beginning. Even during Brest Litovsk their influence was not negligible. And as the Powers slowly moved towards a more and more anti-Bolshevik stand, the Whites' status gained force. They were consulted. They lobbied. They volunteered advice. And "they" included the whole gamut from the Grand Dukes Nicholas and Cyril to Miliukov and Kerensky.

Everywhere, except in Germany, governments continued to deal with and regard as representative the diplomatic envoys of the Czarist and Provisional Governments. Official exchequers advanced money to ambassadors and financial agents of pre-1917 regimes in Russia who spoke in the name of non-existent governments.

White emigrés became the advisers of foreign offices and Cabinet Ministers. The counter-revolutionaries had one aim: to unseat the Bolsheviks. When this aim was adopted by the Western Powers towards the end of the World War, a perfect entente arose in which the role of the Russians must not be underestimated.

It was natural that the Allies should concentrate more attention on Russia when they had finished with Germany. The Great Powers felt that Moscow represented an idea the spread of which constituted a danger to their hegemony. During the War their energies were divided. Now fleets, armies, munition factories, war offices, newspapers, and Cabinets could be more readily mobilized for the battle against Bolshevism.

This motive was frankly admitted in a British General Staff memorandum dated February 4, 1919, which declared that Bolshevik success in the Archangel campaign "would give the Bolsheviks' cause an impetus which would be felt not only in Siberia and South Russia but throughout the civilized world."[1]

**THIN ICE** Sir Henry Wilson, writing officially to Winston Churchill, said:

> Having been initiated as an anti-German measure, the signature of the German Armistice robbed the campaign of its original purpose. It may then be asked why did we not immediately withdraw our troops from North Russia in November, 1918. There were two main obstables in the way of doing this. In the first place, owing to climatic conditions, we could not be sure

[1] British Blue Book. Cmd. 818. *Army, The Evacuation of North Russia.* (London, 1919) p. 23.

of being able to remove the whole force from Archangel before the port was closed by ice.[2]

But Murmansk, where part of the Allied forces was stationed, is open all the year round. The Gulf Stream keeps it free of ice. Why were not the soldiers sent home through Murmansk? Or, why were not the soldiers at Murmansk sent home? The Murmansk units gave the Archangel detachment no protection or cover. Besides, why did not evacuation take place in the spring season when ships could enter and leave? Why was the British occupational army retained in North Russia until October, 1919, and then removed not because the military wished but because pressure at home and in the exiled battalions compelled evacuation?

Sir Henry proceeds with his second reason.

> In the second place,[3] [writes the Field-Marshal] the prosecution of our anti-German policy had involved us in obligations to those loyal Russians who had remained true to the Allied cause and had thereby compromised themselves with the Soviet Government.

This holds as little water as the ice argument. The only persons who "remained true to the Allied cause" were so few in number that they could have been carried off on troop ships, as in fact they finally were. That the "loyal Russians" constituting the Northern Government lacked all mass support is testified by Ambassador Francis himself, who on one occasion "had to tell the President [Chaikovsky] . . . that if the Allied forces were withdrawn from Archangel, the officials of the new government would be driven into the Arctic Ocean."

**THE BOLSHEVIKS' FIRST VICTORY** Bolshevik prospects did not seem bright. The bullets that temporarily felled Lenin struck horror into the hearts of the Kremlin leaders. For a moment it appeared as if the end had come. But they girded their loins for a great effort. On September 2 the Central Executive Committee of the Soviet Government placed the entire country under martial law, and three days later the Council of People's Commissars announced the initiation of the Red Terror as a weapon against the Savinkov organization and other

[2] British Blue Book. Cmd. 818. *Army, The Evacuation of North Russia.* (London, 1919).
[3] *Ibid.*

opponents of the revolution. "Death to all traitors," "Merciless war on the foreign invaders" were the new slogans. The Bolsheviks fought with all the fierceness of a beast at bay.

While the Cheka mowed down conspiring Whites operating on Bolshevik territory, the Red Army and Navy moved against the Czecho-Slovaks. Petrograd workers and units of the Baltic fleet were brought from the Neva River, through the intricate canal system which makes it possible to go by water from Petrograd to Persia, and concentrated on the Volga near Kazan. At the same time, land forces led personally and inspired by the fiery eloquence of Trotzky, bore down on the same Tartar city. On the 10th of September the town fell.

The Commissar of War now ordered Tukhachevsky to take Simbirsk by September 12. On that date, a telegram to Trotzky read: "Command executed. Simbirsk captured. Tukhachevsky." By October the entire Volga district had been cleared, and the Czecho-Slovaks were in retreat towards the Urals.

Three weeks remained before the Volga would be closed by ice. Fuel was needed from the south to give light and heat to Central Russia. Grain was needed to keep it from starvation. "Mother Volga" would bring life to the revolution. The flotilla from Petrograd worked feverishly, loading, unloading, transshipping. Contagious enthusiasm reigned. Victory had encouraged them to unusual efforts.

That autumn saved the Bolsheviks from becoming a mere episode. But this was, as yet, no time to take stock, for the enemy had massed troops on several fronts, and triumphs on one did not guarantee safety.

Drilling became ubiquitous and Red armies multiplied. One pursued the Czecho-Slovaks, another dealt with Krasnov, another kept watch in the Ukraine, still a fourth struggled with the Allied forces at Murmansk and Archangel. Simultaneously, Red bands and peasant partisans harrassed Semenov and Kalmikov in Eastern Siberia. They had no contact with Moscow, but were not less opposed to the counter-revolution. Bolshevik defense began to present an obstacle to the foreign interventionists and their Russian allies. The balance remained decidedly in the Communists' disfavor. Nevertheless, their slow uphill climb had commenced.

All the time, without relaxing its vigilance on internal

affairs, the Kremlin kept a sharp look-out for signs of international revolution. In this respect, nothing had changed since Brest Litovsk, for all Bolsheviks from Lenin down continued to believe that the new regime in Russia could only be saved by similar upheavals abroad. The collapse of the Central Powers therefore brought encouragement to Moscow.

**MOSCOW AND THE KAISER** Late in September the Bulgarian front was smashed by Allied attacks. The Germans in France and Flanders were retreating in the face of Foch's hammering blows.

> This news,[4] [writes M. P. Price, an eye-witness] evoked wildest excitement in Soviet Russia. The *Izvestia* came out with great spreadlines announcing the "Collapse of World Imperialism" and the coming of the social revolution. At a special meeting of the Moscow Trade Union Council on the following day I heard Lenin make a long speech on the international situation. He offered the support of a million Red soldiers and all the material resources of the Soviet republic . . . to the German workers if they should overthrow the Kaiser's Government and get into difficulties with the Entente.

When Prince Max von Baden became German Chancellor and accepted Wilson's Fourteen Points, the Bolsheviks cried, "He will not stay long. Liebknecht will see to that." The eyes of Red Russia were fixed on Karl Liebknecht, on Rosa Luxemburg and on other Communist leaders abroad. But the Bolsheviks were convinced that once the revolution was loosed, it would not remain within the confines of the Central Powers. They consequently spared the Allies in their propaganda no more than they did the German Imperialists. Woodrow Wilson was the hero of the hour. He spoke words that thrilled whole nations. The Bolsheviks remained skeptical. They suspected that he was a man of words—and words only. A note accordingly was dispatched to Washington which sought to dispel the "Wilson illusion" which might, the Communists thought, check that spirit from which revolutions spring.

**LENIN v. WOODROW WILSON** The document is

[4] M. P. Price: *My Reminiscences of the Russian Revolution,* (London, 1921), p. 343.

altogether unique in diplomatic correspondence.[5] It reviewed the Fourteen Points and Wilson's several statements of sympathy for the Soviet republic. The President's words had been high-minded protestations of friendship. Yet the United States Government, it said, assisted the Czecho-Slovak adventure. The result was famine in Central Russia.

This was the first thing that the working men and peasants of Russia experienced in practice from your Government and that of your allies after the promises made by you in the beginning of the year. And after that they experienced another thing–the invasion of the North of Russia by the troops of your Allies in which American troops participated, the occupation of Russian territory without any cause and without any declaration of war . . .

You have promised, Mr. President, [the communication continued] to help Russia secure full and unhindered opportunity for the adoption of her independent decision with regard to her own political development and her national policy. But in reality this assistance expressed itself in the fact that the Czecho-Slovak troops and soon afterwards your own troops and those of your Allies attempted at Archangel, at Murmansk, in the Far East, to force upon the Russian people the government of the oppressors . . .

The acid test of the relations between the United States and Russia has not given exactly the kind of results that one would have expected after your message to Congress, Mr. President. [Nevertheless] Our experience has helped us create a firmly-welded, disciplined Red Army which is growing every day in strength and is learning to defend the revolution.

Mr. Wilson, at the time this note was sent, had made the armistice with Germany conditional on her withdrawal from occupied territories.

We are ready, Mr. President, [wrote Radek] to conclude an armistice on these conditions, and we request you to inform us as to the time when you, Mr. President, and your Allies intend to remove your troops from Murmansk, from Archangel and from Siberia.

[5] When the Political Bureau decided on the note, Lenin instructed Radek to draft it and outlined its contents. Then Radek's effort was submitted to Chicherin who introduced the lofty sarcasm which distinguishes it. Thereupon, it was re-submitted to Radek, who added polish and finishing touches. The note was forwarded to Wilson through the Norwegian Embassy. Printed in *R.A.R.*, pp. 258 ff., and in *Bolshevik Propaganda*. Hearings before a Subcommittee of the Committee of the Judiciary, United States Senate. February 11, 1919, to March 10, 1919 (Washington, 1919).

The note then passed to a most arrogant disquisition on wider, international problems.

> You demand the independence of Poland, Serbia, Belgium, and freedom for the people of Austro-Hungary. . . . But strangely we do not notice in your demands any mention of freedom for Ireland, Egypt, India, or even the Philippine Islands.

The League of Nations had been heralded by Wilson; it would end all wars. But, argued this Communist manifesto, wars were made by capitalists seeking profits, markets, dividends. Why not establish a real League by first overthrowing capitalism?

> Thus, Mr. President, though we know from experience what your promises mean, [the note read] still we have placed ourselves upon the ground of your proposition with regard to international peace and the League of Nations, only we have endeavored to deepen your propositions that they could not bring results contradictory to your promises, as has happened with your promise of help for Russia. We have tried to formulate your proposition for the League of Nations so specifically as to prevent the League of Nations from turning out to be a league of capitalists against the nations. . . .

Then the note undertakes a frontal attack.

> We have had to do [it says] with the President of the assault upon Archangel and of the invasion of Siberia. We have also had to do with the President of the Peace Programme of the League of Nations. Is not the first of the two the real President who actually directs the policy of the American capitalist Government?

Turning now to less academic matters, the Soviet message puts some questions and demands "exact and entirely business-like answers."

> Do the Governments of America, Great Britain, and France intend to cease calling for the blood of Russian people and the lives of Russian citizens, if the Russian people will agree to pay them for it and to buy themselves off by ransom. . . . And if so what kind of tribute from the Russian people is it that the Governments of America, Great Britain, and France demand?

There follow important hints on the debt question.

> We would especially like to learn what are the demands of your French Allies with regard to those milliards of rubles which the Paris bankers advanced as loans . . . to the criminal Government of the Czar. . . . The Russian people, who are exhausted

by war and who have not yet had time to enjoy the benefits of the popular Soviet Government and to improve their economic affairs, will not be able to pay in full to the bankers of France the tribute for the milliards spent by the Czar's Government against the interests of the people. . . .

Do your French Allies present the demand for the payment to them of a part of this tribute in installments, and if so what part? . . .

But if . . . you should give us no answer to our fully definite and specific questions, we will draw from it the entirely undeniable conclusion that . . . your Government and those of your Allies intend to get out of the Russian people tribute both in cash and in the natural wealth of Russia and in territorial aggrandizement.

This unusual note was a combination of pure revolutionary propaganda and shrewd diplomacy. The Bolsheviks hoped that their offer to pay old debts would pave the way to negotiations and to a cessation of armed foreign intervention. Neither the Allies nor Wilson, however, vouchsafed a reply.

Meanwhile, high hopes dashed by the sudden realization of defeat created an explosive atmosphere in Central Europe. Insurrections began to multiply. On November 2 a revolution broke out in Hungary. On the 8th the sailors of the German fleet at Kiel mutinied and on the 9th the German revolution was a fact. Two days later the Armistice ended the bloodiest war in world history.

The Armistice brought increased concern to the Bolshevik leaders. Lenin said to Chicherin, "Now *das Weltkapital* will start an offensive against us."[6]

The Armistice required the Germans to evacuate territories occupied by virtue of the Brest Treaty and in subsequent conquests. When partial German evacuation commenced in December, 1918, Skoropadsky, the German puppet in Kiev, was overthrown by Petlura, the Minister of War of the Central Rada, who had been imprisoned by Skoropadsky but released a few weeks before the Armistice. The gradual withdrawal of the Germans now increased the area over which the Reds and the Petlurists fought for the domination of the Ukraine. Meanwhile, the French arrived on the scene.

Obviously, intervention could no longer be explained on anti-German grounds. Premier Clemenceau, moreover,

[6] Related to the writer by Chicherin. Lenin used the German word. He said, "Na nas idyot das Weltkapital."

did not usually mince words. Addressing himself to General Franchet D'Esperey, Clemenceau wrote: "I hereby enclose a letter which presents a general plan for the economic isolation of Bolshevism in Russia with a view to provoking its fall." Subsequently, on December 13, M. Clemenceau said in a telegram:

"The inter-Allied plan of action is not of an offensive character, but it simply interdicts to the Bolsheviks access to the Ukraine regions, the Caucasus, and Western Siberia, which are economically necessary to them for their endurance, and where elements of Russian order are being organized."

And again, on December 21, he wired:

"The plan of action of the Allies is to realize simultaneously the economic encirclement of the Bolsheviks and the organization of order by the Russian elements."[7]

Clemenceau proceeded to instruct his general to draw up a program of attack in consultation with General Berthelot, formerly chief of the Allies' armies in Rumania, Transylvania, and South Russia. Clemenceau's message to Franchet D'Esperey was dated October 27, 1918,[8] when he felt thoroughly confident of the "imminent capitulation" of Germany. The Allies, plainly, intended losing no time in dealing with the Bolshevik problem.

The plan was elaborated in October; activities commenced in November. The foreign Powers took the initiative. They had their designs and issued their orders independently of Russian advisers or Russian Whites. Yet to ignore native anti-Bolshevik forces would have been folly, and the Allies accordingly hastily summoned the representatives of all counter-revolutionary elements for a special conference in Jassy, Rumania. The invitations, which came from the French, reached several score of Cadets, Monarchists, Social Revolutionists, etc., in Kiev and Odessa, whither they had fled from Bolshevik rule, and urged them to attend the meeting to discuss the question of "aid for Russia in the struggle with Bolshevism."[9]

[7] Read by M. Pichon, French Minister of Foreign Affairs, in the Chamber of Deputies, December 29, 1918.

[8] Published in the Paris *Matin* for June 17, 1919.

[9] The details of this meeting are taken from a description of the Jassy Conference by M. S. Margulies, one of its participants, printed in his book *A Year of Intervention,* Berlin, 1923. They conform with the facts from other sources.

**THE JASSY CONFERENCE** The conference in Jassy, the temporary Rumanian capital, lasted seven days and ended on November 24. It decided to request the Entente Powers to dispatch an expeditionary force of 150,000 men into Russia for the overthrow of the Soviets. The assembled Whites, moreover, agreed on the necessity of a personal dictatorship in Russia. Sharp differences of opinion arose on the choice of the dictator, the alternatives being ex-Grand Duke Nicholas and Denikin. After prolonged discussion, the mantle of authority was placed on the shoulders of the latter.

Denikin had been waiting impatiently for Allied assistance. He was poorly armed and exposed to Bolshevik attacks which gave him no rest. His goal was the rich Ukraine and then the heart of Russia, Moscow. But without munitions and money such moves would be irresponsible adventures. Finally, on November 22, he received information by radio that an Allied squadron had entered the Black Sea; the next day it anchored at Novorossisk; three days later, French and British agents presented themselves to Denikin. At the official reception, the representative of Paris announced Denikin's appointment as head of the armed Russian forces in South Russia and promised all possible aid to "the fraternal and allied Volunteer Army."

Soon afterwards, Denikin received from General Scherbachev a report, dated November 16, of the latter's conference with General Berthelot in Bucharest at which the French commander promised to land twelve French and Greek divisions in Odessa within a few days. This Allied force would quickly occupy Kiev, Kharkov, the Donetz Basin, Krivoi Rog, and the Kuban in order to give the Volunteer and Don armies "the possibility of organizing themselves more firmly and of being free for wider active operations." The tempo of Allied troop shipments, however, left Denikin ill at ease, and on December 7 he urged Franchet D'Esperey to rush at least two divisions to the regions of Kharkov and Yekaterinoslav. A week later, the promised French and Greek divisions had not yet landed and Denikin therefore requested the Allies to prevent the Germans from evacuating Kharkov for the time being. He feared the capture of that city by the Bolsheviks or the Petlurists.

Finally, on December 17, the first French landing took

place in Odessa. Gradually the entire Ukrainian coast of the Black Sea and a belt of territory reaching back about 100 miles from it were occupied by some 12,000 troops including Algerians, Senegalians, Poles, and Greeks. The force was well equipped with tanks, airplanes and artillery, and could rely for support on an Anglo-French fleet consisting of three dreadnoughts, eight cruisers, twelve torpedo-boats and a number of transports. In the Crimea, in addition, some French soldiers, a battalion of Greeks and several thousand colored troops had taken command of the situation.

**BRITISH AND FRENCH ZONES IN RUSSIA** French influence was confined to the Ukraine and the Crimea in accordance with a Franco-British agreement entered into on December 23, 1917, by the terms of which North Russia, the Baltic States, the Caucasus, the Kuban, and the eastern part of the Don region fell to the lot of England.[1]

On November 16, accordingly, the British who had been driven out of Baku in September by the oncoming Turks, returned from Persia in the vessels of the Denikin fleet. The flagship flew the national banners of Great Britain, the United States, France—and of the long-deceased Czarist Empire. A week later, a British division landed at Batum on the opposite side of the Caucasian isthmus.

Baku now replaced Meshed as the base for the British expeditionary forces under General Malleson in the Transcaspia, and more troops were transported across the sea to that far-off Central Asiatic province. At the same time, and in view of the policy confirmed in the agreement of December 23, 1917, the British stretched out a finger to the Baltic. An English squadron sailed up the Baltic, touched at Libau and Riga, and, on December 12, anchored at Reval, where it unloaded thousands of rifles and a quantity of cannon for the Estonian army. Thus supported, the bourgeois Government of Estonia felt secure. In Finland, too, a reactionary Cabinet resisted the Bolsheviks and even contemplated an advance on Petrograd.

Remained Latvia and Lithuania. Here local Communist factions endeavored to set up a Soviet regime and

[1] For text see *Appendix*.

hoped that the Russian Red Army would march to their assistance. Bolshevik troops entered both these little States in January, 1919. France and England, fearing the westward flow of Communism, immediately pressed the late enemy into service, and ordered Germany to keep her tired forces in Latvia and West Lithuania.

**THE BOLSHEVIKS SURROUNDED** With the exception of Latvia and Lithuania, where, however, the Germans under von der Goltz soon ejected the Russians, the encirclement of Soviet Russia which Clemenceau had planned was now complete. On the west, Russia was cut off from the outside world by the Baltic buffers, the Germans, the British fleet and by Poland; on the north, by British, French, American, Italian and Serbian troops; on the south, by the French in the Ukraine, Denikin in the Kuban, and the British in Caucasia and Transcaspia; on the east, finally, by the Japanese and their faithful atamans in Eastern Siberia, and by the Czechs and Kolchak in Western Siberia.

The Bolsheviks, of course, felt that sooner or later revolutions in other countries would reinforce their position. Yet the example of the German revolution had proved that a so-called "revolutionary" regime could be as anti-Communist as Wilhelm II. For the moment, therefore, they were thrown back on their own strength.

# 4

# THE PARIS PEACE CONFERENCE

"The effect of the Russian problem on the Paris [Peace] Conference . . . was profound: Paris cannot be understood without Moscow. Without ever being represented at Paris at all, the Bolsheviki and Bolshevism were powerful elements at every turn. Russia played a more vital part at Paris than Prussia." —*Woodrow Wilson and World Settlement: Written from his Unpublished and Personal Material,* by Ray Stannard Baker. London, 1923. II, p. 64.

THE EYES of the world were now fixed on Paris where the mapmakers and nation-carvers would endeavor to create a new Europe and new empires. Woodrow Wilson, breaking the presidential precedent of remaining in the country whose chief executive he was, had decided to attend in person. He and his staffs sailed on the *George Washington* from New York and arrived in Paris on December 13. During the latter part of the same month, London enjoyed the privilege of fêting him.

Two days after Christmas, the King tendered a banquet to the President in Buckingham Palace. It so happened that David R. Francis, who had quit Archangel, likewise received an invitation. And in one of the happiest moments of his life he brushed sleeves with George V. "Mr. Ambassador," said the monarch politely, "what do you think we ought to do about Russia?" Francis replied that the Allies must overthrow the Bolshevik Government. "The King rejoined by telling me he thought so too, but President Wilson differed from us."

Wilson kept Francis at arm's length and refused to

grant him an audience. As an advocate of the "little intervention," he saw no reason for the presence of Allied troops in Russia after the Armistice. The President was thinking of negotiations with the Bolsheviks. As a preliminary step, he sent W. H. Buckler, attaché to the United States Embassy in London, to speak with Litvinov in Stockholm.

The commissar outlined to Buckler a number of definite proposals which he wired to the President. The result came with almost lightning speed for, though Wilson's emissary left London as late as January 1, or thereabouts, action with a view to invite the Russians to Paris was taken on January 5.

On that day the British Embassy in Paris sent an identical memorandum to the French, Italian, Japanese, and American Foreign Offices which suggested that a message be forwarded to the Bolsheviks in Moscow, and to all other governments in Russia requesting them to call a truce for the duration of the Paris Peace Conference and to delegate representatives to the Conference.

Immediately S. Pichon, French Foreign Minister, rejected the suggestion. "It fails," he said, "to take into account the principles which have not failed to dominate its [the French Republic's] policy and that of the Powers in Russia." The regime of the Bolsheviks was "criminal," and it did not "represent in any degree that of a democratic government." Furthermore, Moscow could not claim to be recognized as a regular government when it had negated "all the principles of public and private right."

**RUSSIA AT VERSAILLES** Russia occupied the Paris Peace Conference the very day it convened. On January 12 the peacemakers assembled. Among them were Foch, General Weygand, Field-Marshal Sir Henry Wilson, and General Bliss for America. Foch immediately urged a quick peace with Germany in order to free the Allies' hands for an anti-Bolshevik crusade. He wished to crush Bolshevism by force. He would send a large American Army commanded by an American into Poland; he would use the Russian prisoners in Germany.

Woodrow Wilson objected. Communism was indeed "a social and political danger," but "there was great doubt in his mind whether Bolshevism could be checked by arms."[2] He proposed to negotiate with the Muscovites.

No one wanted Russia represented at the Peace Conference. Lloyd George simply desired to summon the Russians to Paris "somewhat in the way that the Roman Empire summoned chiefs of outlying tributary States to render an account of their actions."[3] The Entente would listen to testimony and pleas and claims, then send the Russians home, and adopt its decisions.

The French Government opposed the presence of Bolsheviks in Paris. "They would convert France and England to Bolshevism,"[4] said Mr. Lloyd George in re-stating the French objection. The Welshman laughed, but Clemenceau and Pichon insisted, and the statesman being the guests of France, could not be rude.

However, Mr. Sazonov, the Czar's Foreign Minister, had the ear of some delegates. He was Kolchak's Foreign Minister. Savinkov had also appeared on the scene with credentials from Kolchak. Besides, there were Prince Lvov of the provisional government in Petrograd; Maklakov, the Czar's ambassador; Chaikovsky, who had fled from a too trying post in Archangel, and a host of other prominent Russians of various shades from monarchist white and Cadet grey to Kerensky pale pink. Red remained anathema.

The French refused to negotiate with the Bolsheviks. This grew out of their attitude on intervention. They were unalterably committed to the collapse of the Communist regime. The British camp, however, was not united. Lloyd George, representing the civilians or "Frocks" as Sir Henry Wilson sneeringly styled them, feared the consequences of a war against Russia on the heels of the exhausting conflict with Germany.

The Prime Minister of England is speaking. Woodrow Wilson, Baron Sonnino of Italy, Mr. Balfour, M. Clemenceau and M. Pichon are gathered in the latter's office around the large flat desk near the fireplace (January 16). They debate the British proposal for a discussion with the several Russian factions. He does not wish to recognize the Bolsheviks, says Lloyd George. Nor does he wish

[2] Ray Stannard Baker, *Woodrow Wilson and World Settlement: Written from his Unpublished and Personal Material,* London, 1923. I, 166.

[3] *Ibid.*

[4] Minute of the Conversation in Pichon's office in the Quai d'Orsay on January 16, 1919, reproduced in the Hearings before the Committee on Foreign Relations in the U.S. Senate, Senate Document 106, p. 1235.

them to attend the conference of the Powers. He wants information which Sazonov cannot supply. All the Russians in Paris are anti-Bolshevik partisans. He would like to hear the other side too; hence his suggestion.

All this involved the problem of intervention. Why was the British Premier opposed to it? "There is one report that the Bolsheviks are stronger than ever, that their internal position is strong and their hold on the people stronger. . . . It is also reported that the peasants are becoming Bolsheviki. It is hardly the business of the Great Powers to intervene either in lending financial support to one side or the other, or in sending munitions to either side." Moreover, "the hope that the Bolshevik Government would collapse had not been realized."

Lloyd George believed that "the Bolsheviki movement is as dangerous to civilization as German militarism." His opponents both at home and in the French Government immediately inquired, "And did we not destroy German militarism? Surely Lenin is not stronger than Wilhelm. If we could smash Germany we can unquestionably overthrow the handful of men who reign from the Kremlin."

If they proposed to kill Bolshevism by the sword, answered Lloyd George, "the armies would mutiny. . . . The mere idea of crushing Bolshevism by a military force is pure madness. Even admitting that it is done, who is to occupy Russia?"

"Kolchak and Denikin," was the ready reply of his opponents. Churchill, Noulens, Foch, and the French and British military, still put their trust in the anti-Bolshevik elements of Russia. But Lloyd George, with an instinct that explains much of his political success, already sensed the inferior quality of the Russian White leaders.

"Mr. Lloyd George asked who was there to overthrow the Bolsheviki?" says the official summary of the meeting in Pichon's office.[5] "He had been told that there were three men, Denikin, Kolchak, and Knox. In considering the chances of these people to overthrow the Bolsheviki, he pointed out that he had received information that the Czecho-Slovaks now refused to fight; that the Russian army

[5] Minute of the Conversation in Pichon's office in the Quai d'Orsay on January 16, 1919, reproduced in the Hearings before the Committee on Foreign Relations in the U.S. Senate, Senate Document 106, p. 1235.

was not to be trusted. . . . If the Allies counted on any of these men, he believed they were building on quicksand. He had heard a lot of talk about Denikin, but when he looked on the map he found that Denikin was occupying a little backyard near the Black Sea. Then he had been told that Denikin had recognized Kolchak, but when he looked on the map, there was a great solid block of territory between Denikin and Kolchak. Moreover, from information received it would appear that Kolchak had been collecting members of the old regime around him, and would seem to be at heart a monarchist."

Intervention, therefore, was no solution. And "it would be manifestly absurd," said Lloyd George frankly, "to come to any agreement and leave Paris when one-half of Europe and one-half of Asia is still in flames. Those present must settle this question or make fools of themselves."

**DISAFFECTION IN THE ALLIED ARMIES** The Premier's wisdom was dictated by fear. "If a military enterprise were started against the Bolsheviki," he declared, "that would make England Bolshevist, and there would be a Soviet in London." At the same meeting:

> President Wilson stated that he would not be surprised to find that the reason why British and United States troops would not be ready to enter Russia to fight the Bolsheviki was explained by the fact that the troops were not at all sure that if they put down Bolshevism they would not bring about a re-establishment of the ancient order.
>
> We are sitting on the top of a mine which may go up at any minute, wrote Sir Henry Wilson in his diary for January 17. Ireland to-night has telegraphed for some more tanks and machine guns and is evidently anxious about the state of the country.

On the 22nd, noting proceedings at a London Cabinet Meeting, he said:

> I emphasized the urgency of the situation, pointing out that unless we carried out our proposals we should lose not only our army of the Rhine, but our garrisons at home, in Ireland, Gibralter, Malta, India, etc., and that even now we dare not give an unpopular order to the troops, and discipline was a thing of the past. Douglas Haig said that by February 15 we would have no army in France.

Leaders commenced to waver. Sir Henry Wilson spoke with Lloyd George in Paris on the 1st of February and then made this entry: "Prime Minister wants to clear out of Constantinople, Batum, Baku, Transcaspia, and out of Syria." No mention of Siberia and Archangel. On the same day, the Field-Marshal wrote, "Had a long talk with A. J. B. [Balfour]. I find him in favor of clearing out of the Caucasus and of Constantinople and of Syria, but not of Mosul."

The next day news came to Paris of riots in Glasgow and strikes in London and Liverpool. French labor too was restive. In January, the General Federation of Labor as well as the permanent administrative committee of the French Socialist Party adopted resolutions which indicated their opposition to Russian intervention. Moreover, the poilus had had enough of the trenches. On February 3 Foch admitted to Sir Henry Wilson that "his men won't stand it much longer, and will demobilize themselves as the Belgians are doing."

These developments introduced a new note into the conversations of the statesmen at Paris. They had come to that city on the heels of triumph and expected nothing more than the simple job of nation-slicing and map-carving. Instead, disillusioned and suddenly awakened nations stirred with an unprecedented spirit of revolt and protest.

"The Bolshevist danger was very great at the present moment," said Clemenceau, according to the official summary of the Council of Ten's deliberations at Paris on January 21, 1919.

> Bolshevism was spreading. It had invaded the Baltic Provinces and Poland, and that very morning they received very bad news regarding its spread to Budapest and Vienna. Italy, also, was in danger. The danger was probably greater there than in France. If Bolshevism, after spreading in Germany, were to traverse Austria and Hungary and so reach Italy, Europe would be faced with a great danger. Therefore, something must be done against Bolshevism.

Clemenceau saw that as a representative of one system of society he must advocate war upon a rival system with militant intentions against his own. President Wilson, too, was of this point of view and at the same meeting he said, "As Baron Sonnino has implied, they were all repelled by Bolshevism and for that reason they had placed armed men in opposition to them,"[6] thus giving the lie to the anti-German excuse.

The Allies had just waged a successful war against a great and strong enemy. A puny group of extremist-propagandists was defying them in Moscow. How simple it would be to crush them. There were thousands of airplanes, tanks, cannon. Millions of soldiers in arms. The sea was open and transport unlimited. A force of 150,000, it was estimated, could put a White Government in power in Russia and thus ensure the domination of capitalism.

But armies refused to fight.

> The Canadian soldiers, Lloyd George declared at the Conference on January 21, would not agree to stay and fight against the Russians. Similar trouble had also occurred among the other Allied troops. And he felt certain that, if the British tried to send any more troops, there would be mutiny.

Then the British Premier, turning to Woodrow Wilson and Clemenceau, asked what contributions America and France would make towards the raising of a volunteer army of 150,000 to combat Bolshevism. "President Wilson and M. Clemenceau each said none." Lloyd George now put the same question to M. Orlando, and "M. Orlando agreed that Italy could make no further contributions."

These were unanswerable arguments against intervention. Telegrams from home kept worrying the nervous diplomats in Paris with labor unrest and army disaffection. The trouble was, as Clemenceau said, that "the Allies were in need of a speedy solution . . . their populations could stand no more."

**THE PRINKIPO PLAN** Accordingly, the meeting of January 21 instructed Woodrow Wilson to draft a plan for a conference of all Russians parties somewhere in Salonika or the Island of Lemnos. The condition of attendance would be a cessation of hostilities on all internal Russian fronts.

Deep in their hearts, many of the participants in the Paris Peace parley hoped that these Russian talks would never eventuate. M. Pichon and the French Foreign Office

[6] Printed in full as it was read to the U.S. Senate Foreign Relations Committee in *The Bullitt Mission to Russia,* by Wm. C. Bullitt. (New York, 1919), p. 24.

were particularly antagonistic. Clemenceau would have favored the immediate formation of the cordon sanitaire by supplying money and munitions to Poland, the Baltics, Rumania and Czecho-Slovakia. But the Quai d'Orsay, as well as the French militarists, pressed for intervention. Balfour too looked upon the Salonika or Lemnos idea as a maneuver. He thought the Bolsheviks would refuse, "and by their refusal they would put themselves in a very bad position." Sonnino, on the contrary, thought the Bolsheviks would be first to come. Therefore, perhaps, he fought the proposal. President Wilson believed that Allied liberalism in deigning to speak with Bolsheviks would "bring about a marked reaction against Bolshevism." Clemenceau thought the reverse might be the case.

On the 22nd, Wilson submitted the plan for a conference of all Russian factions on Prinkipo or Prince's Island, near Constantinople. The opening was set for February 15.

The British agreed to send Sir Robert Borden to Prinkipo. Wilson decided to delegate William Allen White, and Italy, M. Teretti. But the British General Staff opposed the measure, and the French Foreign Office hastily began to sabotage the meeting. Sir Henry Wilson and M. Pichon were as certain as Lloyd George that the mobilization of a large Allied army for war in Russia was impossible. But they had faith in Kolchak and Denikin and they thought that funds and munitions plus military advice would help the White defeat the Reds.

It had been decided to invite the Bolsheviks to Prinkipo. There is a suggestion that the first piece of sabotage by the enemies of this move was the failure to transmit the invitation. Moscow was never summoned to the conference. But on the 23rd of January, the powerful radio station in the Soviet capital picked up an unaddressed news item announcing the decision of the Peace Conference to convene a Russian truce parley. Five days later, Chicherin broadcast a message to Wilson complaining that his Government had not been invited. No reply was received and the Bolsheviks thereupon, on February 4, acting on the assumption that they were invited, wired their acceptance.[7]

[7] Printed in the full original Russian text in Vol. II of *International Politics,* by J. V. Kluchnikov and Andrei Sabanin, an official collection of documents published by the Commissariat of Foreign Affairs. (Moscow, 1926), pp. 221–3.

**BOLSHEVIK COMPROMISES** This radiogram contains important statements.

*With respect to foreign loans:* "The Soviet Government first of all declares its readiness to make concessions in this matter to the demands of the Entente Powers. It does not refuse to recognize its financial obligations to its creditors in Entente countries. . . ."

*With respect to interest:* "In view of the difficulties of the Russian Soviet Republic's financial position and its insufficient foreign credits, the Russian Soviet Republic proposes to guarantee the payment of interest on its loans with a definite quantity of raw materials. . . ."

*With respect to concessions:* "The Soviet Government is prepared to grant citizens of Entente countries mining, lumbering and other concessions. . . ."

*With respect to territorial settlement:* "The Russian Soviet Government does not, under any conditions, intend excluding from these discussions the examination of the question of annexations by the Entente Powers of Russian territory."

*With respect to propaganda:* "The Russian Soviet Government . . . declares its readiness, if necessary, to include in the general agreement with the Entente Powers a pledge of non-interference in their internal affairs."

The policy which allowed of these compromises represented a repetition of Lenin's tactics during the Brest Litovsk period. Russia needed peace and the Bolsheviks had decided to buy it at a great price in the confidence that the sacrifice was temporary.

The Bolsheviks miscalculated. The saving revolution in Europe did not materialize. Had the Allies, therefore, accepted the Moscow offer contained in the February 4 radio, much of Russian and world history might have been totally different. Certainly the Moscow reply to the Prinkipo proposition offered advantages to the capitalist world which exceed by far anything that has been wrenched from the Bolsheviks from that day to this.

"The Bolsheviks," the President thought, "had accepted, but had accepted in a way that was studiously insulting." He read into the Moscow rejoinder this Bolshevik view: "We are dealing with perjured governments whose only interest is in striking a bargain, and if that is the price of European recognition and co-operation, we are ready to pay it."

What about Lloyd George?

I never saw a man more angered than Mr. Lloyd George, who said, 'We cannot let that insult go by. We are not after their money or their concessions or their territory. That is not the point. We are their friends who want to help them and must tell them so.' We did not tell them so, continues Wilson, because to some of the people we had to deal with the payment of foreign debts was a more interesting and more important matter. . . .[8]

Though allegedly insulted and infuriated, both Mr. Wilson and Mr. Lloyd George liked the Soviet reply so much that they went on supporting the Prinkipo project, and when it failed, the idea of Bolshevik payments and concessions continued to have such an appeal that they supported the Prinkipo plan in modified form, not once but twice.

Pichon and the French Foreign Office, however, were bent on sabotaging the Prinkipo meeting. Mr. William C. Bullitt, attached to the American Commission to Negotiate Peace, who was in daily touch with Secretary of State Lansing, Colonel House, and other prominent United States diplomats in Paris, testified before the Committee on Foreign Relations of the United States Senate that

The French—and particularly the French Foreign Office, even more than M. Clemenceau . . . were opposed to the idea [of Prinkipo—L.F.], and we found that the French Foreign Office had communicated to the Ukrainian Government and various other anti-Soviet Governments that if they were to refuse the proposal, they would support them and continue to support them, and not allow the Allies, if they could prevent it, or the Allied Governments, to make peace with the Russian Soviet Government.

The anti-Bolshevik Government rejected the Prinkipo suggestion, or failed to accept it by February 15, thus automatically cancelling the invitation.[9]

[8] President Wilson made these statements to a private meeting of the Democratic National Committee held in the White House on February 28, 1919, during his short visit to the United States. They were first published years later by Joseph P. Tumulty, the President's private secretary in his *Woodrow Wilson As I Know Him*. (London, 1922), p. 374. The President's address, in the course of which he said, incidentally, that the Bolsheviks were "the most consummate sneaks in the world," was an appeal to the committeemen to support the League of Nations as a counterpoise against Communism.

[9] The Governments of Latvia, Lithuania and Estonia accepted. So did the Soviet Government of the Ukraine. Georgia refused to attend, as did Kolchak, Denikin, and Archangel. The last three sent a joint reply on February 19, 1919.

During February the interventionists continued to work with zeal. Early in the month, Wilson discovered from a memorandum which "he had from unimpeachable sources" that the French Government press was instructed "to emphasize chaotic conditions in Russia."[1] But the real opportunity came to the enemies of Bolshevism when Wilson sailed for America on February 15 and Lloyd George proceeded to London shortly afterwards to deal with serious labor difficulties. Colonel House substituted for the President, and Winston Spencer Churchill sat in the seat of the mighty Premier.

"The first thing that Winston Churchill did [on February 18] was to demand instant action against Russia, and he practically supported Foch's Napoleonic scheme, which was now resurrected with new determination, for applying military force against Soviet Russia."[2]

Churchill wired Lloyd George for support of his proposal. Instead he received a reprimand. For Lloyd George and the Americans had not yet admitted defeat and planned to resurrect the Prinkipo suggestion for a Russian conference. In fact, it had occurred to Wilson in the days when he saw the Prinkipo idea dying to send a representative to Lenin. The choice fell on William C. Bullitt.

**MR. BULLITT'S SECRET MISSION** The Bullitt Mission was secret. Only the British knew of it in advance. Before proceeding to Russia on official instructions from Lansing and House, Bullitt consulted these gentlemen as well as English diplomats regarding the terms that appeared acceptable to the Allies. The representatives of both Powers agreed on several fundamental principles: cessation of hostilities, economic relations with Russia, feeding Russia, withdrawal of Allied armies, debt settlement.

Bullitt left Paris on February 22, accompanied by Captain Walter Pettit, of the American Military Intelligence Service, and Lincoln Steffens, an eminent American journalist. He arrived in Russia on March 8, spent a week in the country, and held several conference with Lenin, Chicherin, Litvinov, and with Menshevik and Social Revolutionary leaders who told him they were opposed to intervention.

[1] Baker, *op. cit.*, 297.
[2] *Ibid.*

The Bolsheviks took Bullitt's mission extremely seriously. On March 13, 1919, for instance, Chicherin wrote to Rakovsky, who was then in the Ukraine: "The decision is very important. If we do not reach an understanding, the policy of blockade will be pressed with vigor. They [the Allies.—L.F.] will send tanks, etc., to Denikin, Kolchak, Petlura, Paderevski, etc." Four days later Chicherin wrote again to Rakovsky: "He [Bullitt] doesn't believe big concessions can be put over in Paris."[3]

Bullitt brought back an impression of a regime which was rapidly consolidating itself around Lenin and the Communist Party. He also brought back the Soviet Government's peace proposals drafted by Litvinov, approved by Lenin, and handed to Bullitt by the latter on March 14. The Bolsheviks suggested a conference and an armistice pending its convocation. All de facto governments in Russia would remain in control of the territory they now held until and if the inhabitants voted a change; the economic blockade was to be lifted; the Soviet and other Russian Governments would "recognize their responsibility for the financial obligations of the former Russian Empire." It is an interesting index to Russian distrust of the French that Chicherin told Bullitt that "The Soviet Government is most anxious to have a semi-official guarantee from the American and British Governments that they will do their utmost to see to it that France lives up to the conditions of the armistice." Bullitt refused to accept this special request.

Before Bullitt left, it occurred to Litvinov to make an interesting suggestion about debts. Litvinov, who always had placed considerable hope in the possibility of cordial American-Russian relations, proposed that the United States take over all Russia's obligations to the European Powers and cancel a corresponding volume of the Allied debts to the United States. Such a procedure, Litvinov reasoned, would simplify Russia's relations with the Allies and give the Bolsheviks only one creditor from whom they might expect to receive better terms of payment. With Lenin's consent, this proposition was made orally to Bullitt as a possible alternative to individual settlements with the several countries.[4]

Mr. Bullitt wired detailed reports of his mission as soon as he reached Helsingfors. They were examined

[3] These letters are from Rakovsky's private files.
[4] Related to the writer by Litvinov.

by Secretary Lansing and Colonel House. Lloyd George and Balfour saw copies. On his return to Paris, late in March, he submitted a written report at the request of the President.

Bullitt believed that the Bolshevik proposal presented "an opportunity to make peace with the revolution on a just and reasonable basis—perhaps a unique opportunity." He recommended immediate action.

According to Bullitt's testimony before the Senate Committee, House, Lansing, General Bliss and Henry White of the American Peace Delegation all thought it highly desirable to attempt to bring about peace on the basis of the Moscow proposition. They told him so after a long discussion on the day following his return to Paris. The next morning he breakfasted with Lloyd George, General Smuts, and Sir Maurice Hankey, the Secretary of the Council of Ten. The Premier thought the matter of extreme importance but "did not know what he could do with British public opinion." The interventionists were busy in the House of Commons. Thinking aloud at the breakfast-table, he suggested that he would send Lord Lansdowne to Moscow, who might bring home tidings that would impress the electorate and thus enable Lloyd George to adopt some definite policy. Then he thought Robert Cecil might go; before the next course had been served he thought of Smuts, then again of the Marquis of Salisbury as special ambassador to the Bolsheviks.

Subsequently, Bullitt learned that Balfour favored his plan. Colonel House told him that Orlando had been won for it. But the French still knew nothing—not officially. Thus the Peace Conference worked. Nobody dared to accept a definite programme and push it through. Statesmen avoided responsibility and killed time.

Bullitt never spoke to President Wilson about the Bolshevik plan. The night after his return to the French capital, House telephoned to Wilson suggesting that he receive his own envoy. The President promised to do so the next evening. The next evening Wilson "had a headache." A day later Colonel House explained that Wilson had a one-track mind and was too occupied with Germany at present to be able to discuss Russia. So he left the whole matter to Colonel House.

Wilson was not inclined to take a committing step. Lloyd George stood in terror of his voters. On the one hand, Labor opposed intervention. On the other hand, the bourgeois parties opposed a pact with the Communists.

**WOODROW WILSON SUGGESTS FEEDING COMMUNISTS** The British Premier felt called upon, in the circumstances, to adopt the tactics of indecision. The Americans, however, resolved to make one more attempt; they would feed the Bolsheviks.

Much of Wilson's peace program at Paris may have been conceived as a check to Bolshevism. He revealed his purposes on the *George Washington*'s first trip to France. In an ornate cabin on the top deck and in the presence of his co-workers, the President frequently spoke from the depths of his mind. "The poison of Bolshevism," he said on one such occasion, "was accepted because it is a protest against the way in which the world has worked. It was to be our business at the Peace Conference to fight for a new order . . ." "What did he mean by a new order?" asks Ray Stannard Baker, Wilson's keeper of documents. "There were two great central ideas in his programme . . . (1) the right of self-determination of peoples . . . (2) . . . a league of nations." As Herbert Hoover wrote in a letter to Oswald G. Villard, editor of the New York *Nation,* on August 17, 1921, "the whole of American policies during the liquidation of the armistice was to contribute everything it could to prevent Europe from going Bolshevik or being overrun by their armies."

Wilson's liberalism was the Allies' sharpest weapon against Communism. They wielded it poorly and blunted its edge. But the Prinkipo scheme and the Bullitt Mission were consistent moves of the President to weaken Bolshevism by fair treatment. This same motive inspired the sponsors of the plan to feed Russia.

**HOOVER AND THE BOLSHEVIKS** Professor Fridtjof Nansen, the well-known Norwegian Arctic explorer and statesman, was in Paris mobilizing support for famine relief in Russia. His greatest recruit was Herbert Hoover, head of the American Relief Association then operating in Belgium. On March 28, 1919, Hoover sent a long memorandum to Wilson outlining his views on the Bolshevik menace and urging that some "neutral of international reputation for probity and ability" (Nansen) be allowed to "create a second Belgian Relief Commission for Russia" on condition that the Bolsheviks cease their military operations. This proposal would be made only to the Communists. That it was conceived as an anti-Bolshevik measure appears from Hoover's own words:

> If such an arrangement can be accomplished it might at least give a period of rest among the frontiers of Europe and would give some hope of stabilization. Time can thus be taken to determine whether or not this whole system [Bolshevism.—L.F.] is a world danger, and whether the Russian people will not themselves swing back to moderation and themselves bankrupt these ideas.[5]

Feeding would afford an opportunity of discovering the facts, and full stomachs might destroy the Reds.

A few days later Hoover and Nansen drew up a letter to Woodrow Wilson asking for a definition of the political terms on which the Peace Conference would approve relief measures. On April 9, Orlando, Lloyd George, Wilson, and Clemenceau (the "Big Four") addressed a reply to Professor Nansen stating that their only condition was the cessation of hostilities and the complete suspension of the transfer of troops and military supplies. (Clemenceau signed "with some reluctance.")

Immediately the news became public, a storm of opposition arose. The "Russian Political Conference," a White organization, entered a protest to the Council of Four signed Prince Lvov, Sazonov, Maklakov, and N. Chaikovsky. "The proposition to feed our enemies," they complained, "comes when the moment of victory is near for us." The reactionary press of the world likewise protested. So did the French Foreign Office, Clemenceau's formal signature notwithstanding. The result of this relief enterprise, Pichon submitted on April 16, "would be a moral and material reinforcement of the iniquitous Bolshevik Government." He therefore insisted that only the non-Soviet sections of Russia be fed. Hoover rushed into the controversy with an appeal to the counter-revolutionaries to remember that "the newly born democracies [*sic*] of

[5] H. H. Fisher, *The Famine in Soviet Russia, 1919–23,* New York, 1927. Page 14. This is the official story of the A.R.A. in Russia.

Siberia, Finland, Estonia, Lettland, Livonia, Poland, Ruthenia, Rumania, Armenia, Serbia, Bulgaria, and Austria, and other nationalities which surround Bolshevik Russia must have a breathing spell to build up some stability." Food and necessities and the relief-armistice would relieve them of "the constant threat of Bolshevist invasion" and give them time to set up "orderly governments." But Hoover's voice was not heard.

Meanwhile, Nansen sent a wireless to Lenin in which he quoted the "Big Four's" reply. This was not a simple matter. The Allied radio stations, according to Nansen,[6] refused to transmit the message. He appealed to the Norwegian Government but its radio was not yet communicating with Russia. Then he decided to go himself to Moscow. En route, the authorities in Berlin consented to send the communication, and when he reached Norway Chicherin's reply awaited him. It was dated May 7. It accepted the proffered aid, offered to pay for it, and expressed thanks to Nansen, but suspecting "foul play," suggested the convocation of a conference to discuss all political and military problems involved. Nansen considered the Bolshevik reply a basis for negotiations and wired Chicherin to that effect. William Allen White likewise considered the Bolshevik demand for a conference a just one, and wrote, "so when the proposition came to the Bolsheviki to stop where they were winning and keep on losing where they were losing, they refused. The food did not go in."[7] "In my opinion," writes Nansen in *Russia and Peace,* "this was regrettable. . . . I am convinced that if these negotiations had attained their object the state of affairs in Europe would have been entirely different from what we see to-day." But the Allied statesmen did not look far into the future. At that moment Kolchak was moving on Moscow, according to the newspapers, and negotiations with the Bolsheviks were therefore considered unnecessary.

The purposes of the Bullitt Mission and of Nansen's feeding plan—both variations of the Prinkipo proposal—were defeated by Kolchak's successes. These victories of the Admiral enabled the Entente, for the first time since the end of the World War, to adopt a definable position towards the Russian question.

The new policy—which was maintained from April,

[6] Dr. Fridtjof Nansen: *Russia and Peace,* (New York, 1924).
[7] *Syracuse Herald,* June 15, 1919.

1919, to the end of the Russian Civil War—was twofold: few foreign troops, but much foreign money, ammunition, and advice.

**EUROPE ON THE VERGE OF REVOLT** February and March of 1919 were the most ominous period in Europe's troubled post-war existence. The whole continent seemed on the brink of a social upheaval that threatened to sweep all governments into the ashbin of history. The nations were hungry and disillusioned; the armies were tired and unwilling to drill or fight or do guard duty; the statesmen were confused.

This state of affairs permitted of no concentration of forces against Russia. "The war to end wars" had barely closed, yet in the spring of 1919 the world was torn by more than a dozen armed conflicts. The late enemy required feeding, and in March the Allies assembled at Paris decided to send bread into Germany. For Bolshevism marched over the land and if Germany succumbed, capitalism in Europe would lose one of its firmest supports. On March 21, a Hungarian Proletarian Government was proclaimed in Budapest under the leadership of Bela Kun. Bavaria, which boiled all through February and March, established a Soviet Government on April 5. And the Third or Communist International (Comintern) first met in Moscow in the first week of March, 1919, to encourage the Red tide.

These developments, more particularly the Hungarian Communist revolution, gave the interventionists an excuse for a new campaign against Bolshevism. Foch presented a plan for the military encirclement of the Hungarians with the aid of Rumania and Czecho-Slovakia, and French generals in Constantinople established an effective food blockade of the revolutionary country. The British and French interventionists in Paris renewed their pressure on the assembled diplomats for a crusade against Russia and pointed to the outbreaks in Central Europe as indications that the menace could only be crushed by force—otherwise it would be upon them in very few months.

The anti-interventionists did not, however, regard armies as an effective weapon against the spread of the new order. The Peace Conference in early April had not yet settled the critical Fiume question with the Italians nor the equally troublesome Shantung question with the

Japanese. The German treaty was not ready; the French were violently anti-Wilson; Lloyd George vacillated; there was no unity. At this time the subject of a renewal of the World War caused the "Big Four" serious worry. "Would the Germans sign?" was the problem of the hour. Clemenceau favored maximum pressure upon Germany. Lloyd George and Wilson felt that such tactics would drive Germany into the arms of Russia. A Russian-German-Japanese Entente was frequently rumored.

A secret memorandum circulated by Lloyd George on March 25 for the "Considerations of the Peace Conference" stressed the danger of a bloc between Moscow and Berlin and although, as Clemenceau showed in an immediate secret reply, this was but a plea for the placation of Germany at the expense of France instead of at the expense of Britain, the Georgian memorandum served as an answer to the interventionists; Europe was too unsettled to permit of an armed expedition against Bolshevism.

Conscious of the sacrifices its citizens had made during the War, the French Government early disapproved of sending its nationals to fight in Russia. Its policy was to let others do and die; Paris would pay—and supply the powder. This was the cordon sanitaire idea.

The British interventionists, both of the anti-Bolshevik, class-conscious school of Churchill, as well as of the anti-Russian, Indian Office school of Lord Curzon and Milner, originally planned to destroy the Soviet Government by directing a British army against it. But the disturbing events which followed the Armistice, the opposition of Labor and the obstruction of Lloyd George deterred them. They too, thereupon, decided to have recourse to only financial and material assistance; men would not go except in most urgent cases.

As early as January 26, Sir Henry Wilson, Chief of the Imperial General Staff, wrote to Lloyd George that he

> was in favor of clearing out of Omsk now, if France would agree, and getting ready to clear out of Murmansk and Archangel next summer, but on the other hand I would want to strengthen our position on the line Batum-Baku-Krasnovodsk-Merv.

On February 12, the British War Cabinet discussed the Russian question and showed "no disposition to approve of warlike operations being undertaken against the Bolsheviks."[8] Later in the same month Sir Henry Wilson presented a memorandum to the British Government advising "evacuation of Archangel, instructional staffs only with Denikin and Kolchak, and handing over Transcaucasia to Italy." A few days later, Sir Henry was back in Paris and had a ninety-minute interview with Foch. The Frenchmen, who a month previous had entertained "Napoleonic" schemes for the conquest of Russia, now agreed with Wilson on evacuation. Moreover, "he has no belief in either Denikin or Kolchak—and I am afraid I agree," Sir Henry noted.

At this time, the British force in North Russia boiled with discontent. Russian conscripts had turned on their British officers and shot them. British soldiers disobeyed orders and declined to fight. Americans demanded ships for home. Meanwhile, the Red Army crept slowly forward, reducing the distance between the Allied armies and the sea. Labor M.P.'s in London called loudly for evacuation.

**THE FRENCH IN SOUTH RUSSIA** In the French garrison in the Ukraine the situation was equally disquieting. The French military had probably conceived of the occupation of the Ukraine as a mere process of relieving the Germans at a quiet guard-post. But Germany's task had never been so simple. Moreover, the Austro-Germans had commenced to evacuate before the French arrived, and when they finally did come on the scene, they found the Bolsheviks and Petlurists poised to give them battle. This precipitated trouble. The French were not prepared to shed their blood.

During March, 1919, the Red Army advanced on Kherson. In the struggle which ensued the French lost 400 men and 14 officers. The result was the hasty evacuation of Kherson and Nikolaiev and the concentration of the entire French force in Odessa.

The French had occupied the hinterland of Odessa as far as Kherson in order to ensure their food supply. With Kherson and Nikolaiev in enemy hands, the situation in the great seaport became precarious, the more so

[8] Callwell: *Field-Marshal Sir Henry Wilson. His Life and Diaries*, (London, 1927), II, 169.

as the Communists in Odessa were planning an insurrection in conjunction with radical elements in the Tricolor fleet.

Red troops were closing in on Odessa. General d'Anselme, commander of the French troops, wired Paris about the "excellent condition" of the enemy forces and of the critical food situation in the city. A starving civil population and casualties in fighting back the Bolsheviks stared Pichon and Clemenceau in the face. The parliamentary opposition was demanding evacuation. Accordingly, on the 2nd of April, d'Anselme received instructions to leave South Russia within forty-eight hours. The next morning a panicky evacuation commenced. April 6 a Soviet Government had already been established while the French occupational army was steaming in the direction of Constantinople. Later in April, the foreigners likewise departed from the Crimean Peninsula.

The disaffection in the French fleet and garrison offer only partial explanation for this sudden evacuation. Marty, the French Communist, has exaggerated the importance of the mutiny in the French Black Sea fleet as well as his own role in the incident. Neither was the military situation very critical. Only one division was located at Odessa. One or two additional divisions covered by the guns of the navy would have made Odessa impregnable. But the French were disillusioned with both Denikin and Petlura. They were disagreeably surprised by the knowledge that the situation required fighting. Above all, however, evacuation was the result of pressure at home and the realization that the French army would not spill its blood on foreign soil for a cause which had not won its heart. Subversive Bolshevik propaganda sowed disaffection among the French troops on land.

The first week of April, 1919, therefore, marked the end of grandiose French plans for intervention in Soviet Russia. Similarly, British plans for the evacuation of South Russia and the Caucasus began to mature. The evacuation of the French, and the British preparations for evacuation as well as the decision of both these great Powers to restrict their future activities in Russia, should in the ordinary course of events have given support to the faction at the Paris Peace Conference which favored negotiations with the Bolsheviks.

**KOLCHAK ADVANCES** This would indeed have been the effect but for important Kolchak victories. On March 6 the army of Kolchak, anticipating offensive intentions on the part of the Red Army, attacked in full force from the Ufa-Perm line against a weak Bolshevik center and broke through the enemy defenses. Kolchak had 112,000 men massed on his Ural front; the Soviets faced him with 96,000 soldiers. The Fifth Army of the Bolsheviks soon commenced to retreat towards the Volga, and Kolchak's forces rushed headlong after it.

These Kolchak advances were widely heralded and exaggerated by the friendly press of Europe and America. Newspapers and experts counted the days that separated Kolchak from Moscow.[9] As a matter of fact, Moscow was never threatened. The Bolshevik setback, to be sure, was serious. Several large units were crippled; about 14,000 men were lost. Further Kolchak advances might have produced a critical situation. But in the third week of April, the "Supreme Ruler's" forward movement had been checked, and early in May, Red forces were registering small successful counter-offensives. A reorganized Red Army, hastily reinforced with Communists, now held the line and allowed no further progress into Central Russia.

The changed situation, however, found no echo in the Western Press, and throughout April and May—indeed even on through the summer—Europe slept securely in the confidence that it would awake some day to read the announcement of Kolchak's capture of Moscow and the overthrow of Bolshevism.

On April 16, when his troops were still moving towards the Volga, Lloyd George defended himself against verbal attacks in the House of Commons. He was still opposed to intervention. Of course, they could conquer Russia if they wished. But the expense would be excessive. "I would rather see Russia Bolshevik until she sees her way out," declared the Premier, "than see Britain bankrupt. And that is the surest way to Bolshevism in Britain."

"To attempt military intervention in Russia," he reiterated, "would be the greatest act of stupidity that any Government could possibly commit. But then I am asked

[9] For an account of the misstatements regarding White army victories see the special supplement of the *New Republic* (New York), entitled "A Test of the News," by Walter Lippmann and Charles Merz. August 4, 1920.

why do you support Kolchak, Denikin, and Kharkov?" (Lloyd George mistook the capital of the Ukraine for a counter-revolutionary leader. Later in the same speech he referred to "General Kharkov.") His answer was that these people had opposed Germany.

At the Peace Conference on January 16, Lloyd George had spoken his distrust of the Russian "White" hopes. Kolchak was a monarchist, he had argued; besides, he had no contact with Denikin. The British statesman asked consideration for these facts in a speech advocating the Prinkipo plan. Subsequently, for similar reasons, he had given unofficial approval to the Bullitt Mission. But in March, news of Kolchak's victories was broadcast through Europe. Lloyd George cooled towards Bullitt. So did President Wilson. And in April, the Welshman rudely disavowed Bullitt. Kolchak was approaching Moscow, the papers screamed. Accordingly, Lloyd George backed the winning horse. On January 16 he could not see why anyone should support Kolchak. On April 16 he was trying to convince Parliament that Kolchak, Denikin and "Kharkov" ought to be supported.

The military, naturally, were quick to take advantage of the civilian change of heart, and on the very day Lloyd George addressed the House of Commons we find Sir Henry Wilson writing to Churchill, Secretary of State for War, advising recognition of Kolchak.[1]

The movement to recognize Kolchak now gathered momentum and the Peace Conference yielded to the pressure. The statesmen had completed the German peace and handed a neatly bound copy to Count Brockdorff-Rantzau on May 7 in the Versailles Hall of Mirrors. Much to the relief of all Allied leaders, the Germans had not rejected the terms. Hearts and minds, accordingly, were now freer for the Russian problem, and on May 26 the Supreme Council, consisting of Clemenceau, Lloyd George, Orlando, Woodrow Wilson, and Saionji, addressed a joint note to Admiral Kolchak[2] laying down the law to the "Supreme Ruler of All the Russias." They opened with several statements hardly worthy of great men. "It has always been the cardinal axiom of the Allied and Associated Powers," they said, "to avoid interference in the

[1] British Blue Book Cmd. 818. *Army. The Evacuation of North Russia,* (London, 1919), p. 31.

[2] *Ibid.*

internal affairs of Russia." Then, in immediate contradiction, they refer to intervention during the War, they admit maintaining forces in Russia since the Armistice and announce that "they are prepared . . . to continue their assistance."

This flouting of the truth is only equalled by the distortion of fact that follows. The note speaks of the Peace Conference's effort to establish peace "by inviting representatives of all the warring governments within Russia" to a conference. The reference, of course, is to Prinkipo. Wilson knew that the Bolsheviks had accepted this proposal. Kolchak had flatly rejected it. Yet in the communication to Kolchak, Woodrow Wilson and the other statesmen of Versailles stated that "this proposal . . . broke down through the refusal of the Soviet Government."

The note then outlined the conditions under which the Allies were prepared to help and recognize Kolchak. Will Kolchak and his friends call the Constituent Assembly "as soon as they reach Moscow," institute free elections, guarantee that the Czarist regime will not be re-established, recognize the independence of Finland and Poland, Estonia, Latvia, Lithuania, and Caspian and Caucasian Republics, agree to permit the Peace Conference to settle the Bessarabian question, join the League of Nations, and finally, abide by his declaration of November 27, 1918, to pay Russia's foreign obligations?

Kolchak made reply on June 4. He accepted the conditions. But Kolchak, being a sincere partisan of an "undivided Russia" could scarcely reconcile himself to the thought of losing all the Baltic and Caucasian provinces and perhaps Bessarabia to boot. He therefore resorted to a clever ruse. Was he not a staunch democrat? Was he not affirming in this reply that the Constituent Assembly would be the highest sovereign institution of the land? How then could he himself determine questions of international relations, boundaries, autonomy, etc.? That must be left to the Assembly. He thus avoided a rejection of the Allied terms and evaded a definite enunciation of policy. Kolchak's only concession was the recognition of Polish independence. He condescended to this concession at the urgent request of Colonel John Ward, the British Army representative at Omsk. Colonel Ward tells the writer that in framing the reply to the Big Four, Kolchak faced the united opposition of his uncompromising royalist supporters, who, but for Colonel Ward's aid in drafting the document, would have made it an unequivocal reflection of their reactionary views.

But by the time Kolchak's answer reached Paris, the Red Army had thrown him back towards the Urals. His chances of reaching Moscow were nil. The thought of recognition was therefore dropped, and on June 12 the Supreme Council sent him a bored letter acknowledging his rejoinder and promising support.

The Allies' definite alignment with Kolchak and their pledge of aid precluded further conversations with the Bolsheviks and should have closed the period of direct intervention. But the militarists objected to such logic and tried to discover excuses for the continued stay of foreign troops in Russia. Thus, on May 4, General Ironside, commander of the British forces at Archangel, received orders from London, sent with Lloyd George's approval, to effect a junction with the Czech General Gaida who presumably, in connection with Kolchak's short-lived success, planned to push up from the Perm region to Kotlas.

President Wilson, too, rushed to support the presence of American forces in Siberia. They were needed there to protect the railway mission of John F. Stevens, which railway mission kept the lines running that brought Kolchak munitions and food.[3]

Thus, the end of the Peace Conference saw America and the Allies committed to a definite anti-Bolshevik policy. It saw them committed to Kolchak. They had, it is true, decided not to intervene with their own troops. But in no case did the Great Powers withdraw all their forces from Russia immediately after the adoption of a non-intervention policy. England, in fact, sent reinforcements.

For practical purposes, the British had now accepted the French cordon sanitaire idea. This indeed became the policy of the entire Western world: help the Russian border states and help the Russian Whites fight their battles without foreign troops.

[3] Reply of Wilson to Senate Resolution concerning American troops in Siberia, June 26, 1919. *R.A.R.*, p. 343.

# 5

# THE ALLIES AND THE WHITES

EVERY ONE of the counter-revolutionary governments in Russia received assistance from an Allied Power or a group of Powers. The Bolsheviks fought unaided. The reliance of the Whites on outside help testifies to that intrinsic weakness which ultimately spelled their defeat and disappearance.

**WHITE DIFFICULTIES** The anti-Soviet regimes were destroyed by the Red Army. But in the final analysis, they came to grief by reason of their own shortcomings.

Kolchak's reign was ended by village uprisings in his rear. Denikin perhaps would have reached Moscow but for obstructions by the Ukrainian peasantry. Kolchak promised that the land problem would be solved in the future by the Constituent Assembly. The Siberian peasants refused to wait for the fulfilment of this vague prophecy. Denikin even commenced the restitution of confiscated land to former owners. General Lukomsky, Denikin's closest co-worker, refers in his memoirs[1] to the robberies perpetrated by Denikin's forces in the villages, and to "the irresistible awakened appetites of the landowners approved by the local authorities" which played into the hands of Bolshevik agents who organized successful revolts against Denikin at the most critical period of his advance on Moscow.

The Whites realized the importance of Russia's hundred

[1] A. S. Lukomsky: *Memoirs,* (Berlin, 1932), II.

million peasants. But they were bound by bonds of past experience, sympathies, and ideology to the richer classes. They could not satisfy the economic demands of the muzhiks.

Another problem which the White Governments failed to solve was of nationalities. Practically all the armed attempts to overthrow Bolshevism originated on the periphery of Russia where large numbers of the population were not Great Russian. Yet the leaders of these armed attempts were almost invariably Great Russian and wrote "Great Undivided Russia" on their banners. The national minorities protested.

In the Ukraine, the autonomy movement was strongest. Petlura posed as its standard-bearer. But when Denikin moved into the Ukraine in 1919, Petlura left off fighting the Bolsheviks and, for a while, concentrated all his hostility on the Great Russian restoration.

**RED DIFFICULTIES** Though aided by such objective conditions, the task facing the Soviets was difficult. The country they controlled was completely blockaded. Transport was seriously crippled. Epidemics raged. Cut off from Western Europe and from domestic sources of oil, coal, iron, bread and other necessities, Central Russia's industries suffered woefully. Famine threatened.

The Bolsheviks fought on a front which completely encircled them. The Red Army had first claim on all supplies. In 1920, according to official figures, the armed forces consumed 25 per cent of the flour, 60 per cent of the fish, 60 per cent of the meat, 40 per cent of the fats, 100 per cent of the tobacco, 90 per cent of the men's shoes, and 40 per cent of the cotton goods of the entire country. The strength of the army increased from 435,000 in December, 1917, to 1,500,000 in the middle of 1919, to 5,300,000 in 1920.

The exigencies of civil war necessitated the rationing of the civil population. This system plus the concentrating of attention on the requirements of the army characterize the economic arrangement known as the Military Communism. "Militant" Communism as applied to this period is a misnomer. The Russian term is "voyenni" or "relating to war" and cannot possibly be translated "militant." Nor was the system militant in conception or intention.

The unity of the Communist Party culminating in the

unquestioned leadership of Lenin permitted the singleness of purpose that paved the way to Bolshevik victory in the Civil War. Moscow had one policy and it was always strictly adhered to. The Whites were divided among themselves.

**"WEDGING IN"** The second phase of the Civil War began late in 1918 with the end of the World War, the rise of Kolchak, the retirement from Russia of the armies of the Central Powers, and the opening of the Dardanelles and the Baltic to Allied vessels. It changed the face of the war against Moscow.

The northern Archangel front had, by this time, sunk to secondary importance as a result of climatic conditions and because Moscow was impregnable. And in view of the expansion opportunities offered in the West and South, the Bolsheviks neglected Kolchak for the Baltic and Ukraine-Don fronts.

**WAR IN THE BALTICS** The situation in the Baltics became fluid immediately after the Armistice. It will be recalled that von Kuehlmann had insisted at Brest Litovsk that Estonia, Latvia, Lithuania, and Poland were already "self-determined." The Bolsheviks, however, declined to accept "self-determination" that had found its highest expression in an application, on April 12, 1918, for incorporation into the German Reich. Two days later the Kaiser granted their "request" and accepted them into the "Imperial family." And when the representatives of the new little vassals approached Joffe in Berlin during May, for recognition of their "independence," he, naturally, denied both the fact and the petition.

These Baltic governments remained in power as long as German troops continued in occupation. But the moment the regular divisions began to withdraw, Soviet forces followed in their footsteps. At the same time, the civil population organized for self-government.

On December 23, 1918, the Soviet Government at Moscow recognized the Lithuanian, Latvian, and Estonian Soviet Republics and offered them "all necessary aid and support." Except in Latvia, however, soviets did not yet exist in these provinces.

Latvia did have her own revolutionary army. Vatzetis, the Commander-in-Chief of the Red Army, a Lett not untainted with Latvian nationalism, had, early in 1918, withdrawn Lettish Communists from the Ukrainian, Don, and Ural fronts to organize them into Latvian Rifles who now became a Latvian Red Army. On January 5, 1919, the workers of Riga, Latvia's capital, seized the city and proclaimed a soviet state. The new Latvian Red unit rushed to its support. Other Red forces advanced into Estonia, Lithuania, and White Russia.

In Estonia, White forces stemmed the tide, drove out the Bolsheviks, and created a convenient spring-board for General Yudenich's attempt to take Petrograd later in the year. In White Russia the Red Army met resistance from the Poles; in Latvia and Lithuania, from the Germans.

**"HUNS" "HELP" ALLIES** The Armistice had permitted the Germans to maintain their forces in the Baltic provinces. The Treaty of Versailles confirmed this arrangement. That document, in Article 433, abrogated the Brest Litovsk "Peace of Violence" and ordered the withdrawal of German troops "as soon as the governments of the principal allied and associated Powers shall think suitable, having regard to the internal situation of those territories." The Allies, who did not wish or were not able to employ their own soldiers in the Russian border states, had decided on making use of the Germans to prevent the spread of Bolshevism westward. There was the danger that Soviet influence in Lithuania might reach contiguous Prussia and from there join hands with Spartacism in other sections of Germany. The Ebert Cabinet in Berlin gladly served the Allies in this matter and, though it withdrew part of the tired regular forces, it financed the irregular, volunteer battalions of von der Goltz.

During the month of March, 1919, the Germans and Latvian Whites registered several important successes against the Bolshevik forces and thereupon commenced an encircling movement in the direction of Riga. An Allied note dated April 23 demanded that these German activities cease. But the warning was not heeded. On May 4, accordingly, the Allies insisted with Berlin that von der Goltz be recalled. Instead, the General captured Riga eighteen days later.

Foch, in a communication dispatched June 18, ultimately ordered the Germans to stop their advance into Estonia and to evacuate the Latvian ports of Libau and Windau, and all Russian territory. But von der Goltz was sure of his ground. He knew he could not easily be suppressed by Allied arms. Perhaps he even thought that Paris and London would not sincerely intercede on behalf of the Bolsheviks by forcing his withdrawal. The fact is that the German forces remained near Riga and as late as September 27 the Supreme Council threatened to exert economic pressure on all of Germany unless she compelled von der Goltz to retire. He finally did so in December.

Finland, at this juncture, possessed a bourgeois government which had won Allied recognition. In Estonia, a bourgeois government held its own with the help of a British squadron and of White Russian troops. The Latvian soviet republic was destroyed through the instrumentality of von der Goltz's cohorts, while in Lithuania, the Germans and the Poles prevented the establishment of a Red regime.

The Bolshevik effort to thrust westward thus ended in complete failure. Thereafter, few developments of moment took place on the Baltic front until Yudenich's advance in the summer of 1919 and the Polish offensive in 1920.

**WHITE v. RED IN THE UKRAINE** Events in the South assumed infinitely greater importance and magnitude. Here too the strategy of the Bolsheviks consisted of "wedging in" between the departing Germans and the oncoming Entente forces. The Allies, on the other hand, wished to avoid a vacuum into which the Bolsheviks might rush, and attempted to delay German evacuation.

But the Germans failed to stay on—thanks to the mutinous attitude of their soldiers, and Allied aid materialized slowly and insufficiently. General Franchet d'Esperey had promised twelve divisions, but only one arrived in Odessa, for a limited stay. The Bolsheviks therefore had only Petlura to reckon with. But Petlura was responsible for the German occupation from which the peasants had suffered. Moreover, the Ukrainian proletariat supported Bolshevism, and the muzhik, until grain requisition commenced, sided with the Soviets. The Bolsheviks, accordingly, experienced comparatively little difficulty in establishing their power throughout the greater part of the Ukraine during the winter and spring of 1919. January 3, Kharkov was taken; January 12, Chernigov; February 5,

Kiev; in March, the French lost Nikolaiev and Kherson; and on April 5, a soviet was set up in Odessa after its evacuation by the French and capture by Ataman Gregoriev, a rough peasant partisan whose alignment with Bolshevism reflected the friendship of the peasant masses for the Bolsheviks.

*Soviet Russia Wishes to aid Soviet Hungary* The Red Army now made ready to enter the Crimea and, in April, successfully pursued the remnants of Petlura's force to the East Galician frontier, capturing Zhitomir, Kamenetz-Podolsk, and Tiraspol. From a military point of view, the Bolsheviks were now in a position to do one of two things:

(1) March an army into Rumania and recapture Bessarabia, or

(2) March to the assistance of Soviet Hungary.

These possibilities tempted Moscow greatly. In fact, on March 26, Vatzetis, the Soviet Commander-in-Chief, wired Antonov-Avseenka, in charge of the Kiev operations, to limit his activities on the Rumanian front, to destroy Petlura, and move towards East Galicia and Bukovina in order to establish "direct, intimate contact with the Soviet armies of Hungary."[2]

Revolutions had broken out in Hungary and Bavaria. Checked on the Baltic front, the Bolsheviks, it appears, were bent on penetrating into the Balkans and so come to the aid of Hungary. For, on Allied inspiration, Rumania was making war on Bela Kun's soviet state. This war threatened the life of Bolshevism in Hungary. The Russians, moreover, realized that Communism in Budapest and in all of South-Eastern and Central Europe would be tremendously stimulated if they gave direct military assistance to Bela Kun or distracted the Rumanians with an offensive into Bessarabia. The Bolsheviks planned both moves. Red Budapest was in constant radio communication with Moscow, using Kharkov as a relaying center. Airplanes flew regularly from Hungary to the Ukraine, bringing leaders or reports and taking back suggestions, Soviet legal codes as models, and mail. A Bolshevik offensive would establish direct geographical contact with Bela Kun, bring Bessarabia back to Russia, perhaps inspire a revolution in Rumania and affect the affairs of the entire Balkan peninsula at least.

[2] Quoted from the archives of the Soviet War Commissariat.

Europe's post-war history might have been totally different had these projects been effected or even initiated. However, a number of circumstances intervened to prevent the fruition of these plans to carry the red banner through Europe.

Early in March Kolchak broke through the Ural front and commenced advancing into the Volga region. During April, the Admiral's progress grew menacing, and the Bolsheviks were compelled to reinforce their eastern front with troops from the south. This weakened their ability to extend into Hungary—an undertaking which would probably have involved them in wars with East Galicia and perhaps with Czecho-Slovakia.

Furthermore, just when he had been ordered to march towards Bessarabia, Ataman Gregoriev suddenly deserted the Bolsheviks, and set out on his short-lived career as an independent partisan marauder and perpetrator of anti-Jewish pogroms which ended with his murder by Makhno.

Finally, the Red Army's winter and spring campaigns of 1919 against Krasnov and Denikin in the Don-Kuban district had not been decisively successful, and in April and May there were indications that these forces intended ambitious offensives eastward and northward. Under the circumstances, the thought of a major offensive towards Soviet Hungary was abandoned. By May, to be sure, Kolchak had been checked, but before Moscow could recover from the extra efforts required for this task, it was called upon to cope with Denikin. In May, too, Yudenich commenced moving from his line near the Estonian-Russian border, and crept forward towards Gatchina and so close to Petrograd, the hearth of the revolution, that he actually printed currency for distribution upon its capture.[3]

May, 1919, was the critical month in the history of the Soviet civil war. Kolchak regarded his reverses as temporary and expected to push ahead and join forces with General Miller, who, after Chaikovsky's retirement in favor of the more congenial pursuit of playing diplomat in Paris, had become head of the Archangel Government. Denikin was driving up in the direction of Kharkov and Moscow, while Yudenich menaced Petrograd.

**FOREIGN AID FOR KOLCHAK** Yudenich, Denikin,

[3] A fresh unused 1,000-ruble note of this currency is in the possession of the writer.

Kolchak, and all the more important White leaders owed whatever successes they achieved to Allied help. To try to prove this is, as the Russian saying goes, like trying to break through an open door. No effort was made to conceal it. No effort could have been made to conceal the fact, for instance, that foreign troops were stationed in Siberia. Of the non-Russians 5,600 were British, 7,500 American (official figure), 760 French (official figure), 2,000 Italian, 4,000 Serb, 55,000 Czecho-Slovak, 10,000 Polish, 4,000 Rumanian, and 28,000 Japanese. The commander-in-chief of all the interventionists' strength with Kolchak was at one time the British General Knox and later the French General Janin. Sir Henry Wilson noted in his diary for April 29, 1919, that he had spent time in the morning "considering a message I am sending to Kolchak advising him as to the strategy of his summer campaign."

America, though she lagged behind England, France and Japan, likewise lent a helping hand. On April 26, 1919, Serge Ughet, financial agent of the former Russian Government in Washington, wired to Omsk suggesting that the "Supreme Ruler" make a declaration of liberal policies in order to win United States public opinion.[4] On July 24 of the same year, Ughet informed his superiors in Siberia that while the U.S. Secretary of War was not anxious to sell uniforms and other war materials, he would give him quantities of rifles at cost price and on twelve months' credit. Mr. Ughet admitted to the writer that a hundred locomotives paid for by the United States Treasury were shipped by him to Vladivostok and Novorossisk.[5]

In July, 1919, when the Paris Peace Conference had under consideration the question of Kolchak recognition, President Wilson ordered Roland S. Morris, the American ambassador in Tokyo, to proceed to Siberia and report on conditions there. The envoy arrived in Omsk on July 21, remained in the country three weeks (on July 31 he interviewed the authorities of the University of Perm, who

[4] These telegrams are from the secret archives of Kolchak's Ministry of Foreign Affairs, which were seized by the Red Army when it captured Omsk and Irkutsk. The writer has been able to avail himself fully of all the documents contained therein by courtesy of the Soviet Commissariat for Foreign Affairs where the Kolchak documents are now deposited.

[5] See article entitled "Kerensky," New York *Nation* of April 27, 1927.

told him that Kolchak's was an undemocratic, military regime), and advocated recognition. The *Springfield Republican* of August 24 supplied further details. Morris's statement on Kolchak's government, it said, was rather pessimistic, nevertheless he favored recognition if the admiral could hold out another month. "By the time this report could be acted upon, however, Kolchak had met with serious reverses in Western Siberia. Morris cabled urging haste to save the situation . . ."[6]—but it was too late, and Wilson waited watchfully.

*Britain and Denikin* The United States gave little assistance to Denikin, although Admiral McCully represented Washington at Yekatrinodar. Great Britain, on the other hand, was generous to the leader of the Volunteer Army. Since the soldiers' frame of mind did not encourage the dispatch of masses of rank and file to Russia, Churchill, as Secretary of State for War, reconciled himself to military missions. One such body, consisting of 2,000 commissioned and non-commissioned officers, functioned with Denikin. Its duties, Churchill explained in the House of Commons, "are confined to advice and supervision in the distribution and use of British materials." The next day, December 17, 1919, Churchill added: "Every effort has been made by the Mission to re-organize the railways, and with the same object technical materials to the value of 500,000 pounds sterling and commodities and clothing to a similar value are being sent out by the War Office."

Though support of this nature was important, British aid assumed far greater proportions. ". . . very valuable assistance is being given by the Allies to General Denikin's army in South Russia," says the *Manchester Guardian* of May 21, 1919, quoting Reuter. "Great Britain is supplying complete equipment with arms and guns for 250,000 men." King George pinned the Order of the Bath on Denikin through his chief officer at Yekatrinodar, General H. C. Holman.

*Foreign Aid to Yudenich* There is equally strong evidence of foreign help to Yudenich. Wiring from Riga, Walter Duranty, *New York Times* correspondent, stated that "Yudenich's advance was made possible by four British tanks and British crews."[7]

[6] H. K. Norton, *The Far Eastern Republic of Siberia,* (London, 1923), p. 88.

[7] Quoted by *Soviet Russia,* a New York weekly, on December 13, 1919.

On August 26, 1919, Nabokov, Kolchak minister in London, wired Omsk that "the army of Yudenich received from England complete war equipment for one division." September 16, Sablin, a well-known monarchist, informed Kolchak that "a ship has arrived in Reval with clothing and full equipment for 30,000" (men).[8] This was the time of Yudenich's hottest preparations for his second drive on Petrograd. A telegram in the archives of the Omsk Foreign Office from its London agent reports his audience with Churchill who, in the Russian's presence, ordered sent to Yudenich "arms, clothes, shoes and medical supplies" for 20,000 soldiers in addition to materials already forwarded. Also, 10 light and 16 heavy cannons, and 15 airplanes. (October 18.)

**THE HIGH COST OF INTERVENTION** A British White Paper gives England's total outlays for naval and military purposes in Russia from the Armistice to October 3, 1919, as amounting to no less than 94,830,000 pounds sterling. Baron Consuke Hayashi, Japanese Ambassador to Great Britain, told a Labor delegation on June 15, 1921, that Japanese intervention in Siberia, which he styled "an unfortunate movement," had cost his government 70,000,000 or 80,000,000 pounds sterling during the last three years.[9] What shares the United States and France contributed to the billion and more dollars spent on foreign interference in Russian affairs is not known, but French assistance was probably not even second to that of the British, for while Paris sent few missions and fewer poilus to the Whites within Russia, she spent fortunes in preparing Poland, Rumania, and Czecho-Slovakia for anti-Bolshevik adventures.

The Allies likewise interceded diplomatically. Thus Churchill, according to a telegram from Nabokov to Kolchak, dated June 13, 1919, undertook to persuade Finland to join Yudenich's offensive.[1] Similarly, Maklakov telegraphed from Paris on April 1, 1919, concerning French negotiations with Estonia with a view to a joint Yudenich-Estonian drive on Petrograd.[2] And, September 18, 1919, Sablin informed Omsk that "British Government

[8] From the secret archives of the Ministry of Foreign Affairs in Omsk.

[9] "Attacks on Russia during 1921." Pamphlet published by the British 'Hands off Russia' Committee (London, 1921).

[1] From Kolchak's Secret Archives.

[2] *Ibid.*

(had) instructed its agent in Reval to seriously warn Estonian Government against concluding peace with (the) Bolsheviks."[3] Professor Dennis, among others, confirms the fact that the Western Powers tried to induce Finland to join Yudenich in attacking Petrograd,[4] and the Council of Five of the Paris Peace Conference is on record as having put pressure on the same country to the same end.

**THE CO-ORDINATION OF THE FOUR WHITE FRONTS** Too often the activities of the numerous counter-revolutionary groups in the Russian Civil War are regarded as disjointed, independent affairs. The truth is that common plans frequently existed and that at least the major anti-Bolsheviks had constituted themselves into a closely knit union recognizing one leader and one general purpose. That leader was Admiral Kolchak, and the general purpose was the re-establishment of a "great undivided Russia" presumably with a constitutional monarchy as the form of government.

Denikin announced his allegiance to Omsk just as foreign help began making itself felt in his camp. His Army Order #45 issued May 30, 1919, said: "I subordinate myself to Admiral Kolchak as Supreme Ruler of the Russian State and as Supreme Commander of the Russian armies." This statement which, in view of imperfect telegraphic connections, could not be transmitted directly from Yekatrinodar, was relayed through Constantinople on June 15 and stamped "Received" in Omsk on June 20.[5] Exactly a week later, the "Supreme Ruler" wired his thanks to Denikin in unusually lyric language.[6]

The critical month of May, 1919, marked by increased and more or less successful military activity against the Bolsheviks, likewise seems to have been devoted to the consolidation of the White political situation and the raising of Kolchak's prestige. All the threads meet in Sazonov's hand. Sazonov had been the Czar's foreign minister. He was also Kolchak's Foreign Minister. But he spent all his time abroad—most of it in Paris. During May he paid a ten-day visit to London. The Peace Con-

[3] *Ibid.*
[4] Alfred L. P. Dennis: *The Foreign Policies of Soviet Russia* (New York, 1924).
[5] From Kolchak's Secret Archives.
[6] *Ibid.*

ference was still sitting. The Big Four deliberated the question of Kolchak recognition, and Sazonov wished to strengthen his British ties. Apparently the sojourn pleased him greatly and he so informed his master in a telegram dated June 1 and decoded and typewritten on Omsk Ministry of Foreign Affairs stationery on June 5. He had seen the King in private audience, he had twice held conferences with M.P.'s "of various parties." The British Government, he said, was ready to help, but Labor must not be antagonized by reactionary moves in Siberia. The same message[7] shows Sazonov's concern not only for the Siberian situation but also for the Archangel and Yudenich fronts.

These diplomatic victories, however, were not matched by similar triumphs on the field of battle. Kolchak, it will be remembered, lost heavily in May after initial gains in March and April. By the end of July, the Supreme Ruler's prospects seemed so dark that he wished to resign, and at a conference in Omsk asked the Allied representatives to transfer his authority, title and responsibilities to Denikin. Only after earnest pleas from the foreigners and their promises to grant more aid did he consent to remain.

Unaware of the sad turn of events in Siberia, Denikin struggled with the problem of reconciling his allegiance to Kolchak and an "undivided Russia" with his own desire for power and with the Cossacks' yearning for autonomy. Soon after he had officially recognized Omsk, therefore, he consulted the admiral telegraphically. Neratov, Denikin's Foreign Secretary, wired to Kolchak's envoy in Athens, who in turn transmitted the message to Siberia. Under date of July 6, we read:

> Neratov wires #870: The Commander-in-Chief [Denikin.—L.F.] requests you forward to Admiral Kolchak: 'In view of my subordination to you as Supreme Ruler and Supreme Commander it is now necessary, until the fronts will actually be united to decide the following questions: (1) the limits of my authority in civil and military administration, in legislation, and in judicial affairs; (2) the organization and activity of departments in the field of foreign relations . . .'

In view of the difficulty of communicating with Omsk, a delegation was being sent to Paris under General Drago-

[7] From Kolchak's Secret Archives.

mirov to describe conditions in South Russia to Kolchak over a direct wire and obtain his instructions.

Dragomirov supplied Sazonov with all the information available on the separationist tendencies of the populations in Denikin's territory and on the concessions that were required by his Commander-in-Chief's amour propre. A lengthy correspondence ensued and there was no final decision until December, 1919, when Kolchak, expelled from Omsk and about to be deserted by his followers and executed, wired from Irkutsk to Sazonov a hasty "In reply to yours of November 8 I agree to conditions." But Kolchak's agreement was of no importance. For in December, 1919, Denikin, as well as he, were about to fade into the historical past.

One thing the Dragomirov mission did accomplish. It won a rise in salary for Denikin. On August 22, a telegram from Sazonov to Kolchak pointed out that Denikin was receiving only 2,250 rubles a month and wanted more. Across the document on to which this message is decoded, the "Supreme Ruler" wrote in green ink his resolution in favor of giving Denikin as much as the assistant Commander-in-Chief in Omsk received, and signed "Admiral Kolchak, August 26, 1919."[8] Such subordination by Denikin, amounting almost to humiliation, could scarcely have been voluntary. It apparently reflected Allied insistence on interdependence and co-ordination.

How closely Kolchak identified himself with Denikin may be seen from a proclamation he made during the latter's successes. "We," he announced, "have taken Kiev, Odessa, Tambov, Kolzov, Yeletz, and will take Chernigov and Kursk. . . ."

*Archangel and Kolchak* The relation between the Northern Archangel Government of Chaikovsky-Miller and the Omsk "Supreme Ruler" was likewise close, thanks to the wish of the British that it be so, and "General Miller . . . drafted at the end of March, 1919, a letter which recognized Admiral Kolchak as dictator."[9]

On account of the small number of foreign troops, of the unreliability of the Russian troops, of the hostility of the local population and of unfriendly climatic and terrain conditions, the northern front, throughout 1919, played only a secondary role—as a sort of arm or branch of

[8] From Kolchak's Secret Archives.
[9] James Mavor: *The Russian Revolution* (London, 1928).

the Kolchak Eastern front. Therefore, and as a result of Labor opposition, the British decided in March, 1919, to liquidate it.[1] But this was displeasing to the military, who sought to postpone evacuation. The difficulty of withdrawal served as the excuse. The generals explained that in order to bring away the troops already there, you had to have more troops. So, where the British had a rifle strength of 3,905 in North Russia and a ration strength of 6,832 on January 2, 1919,[2] the force numbered 18,400 in the autumn when evacuation finally took place. Thus reinforced in order ostensibly to end the expedition, the commanders proceeded not to evacuate but to carry out the expedition's "original intention of joining hands with the Czechs on the Perm-Vologda railway."[3] In June General Ironside therefore opened an offensive in the direction of Kotlas in order to establish contact with Kolchak. This occurred months after the decision to withdraw.

The British military justified the offensive as a protection for their contemplated evacuation. They feared a Red Army attack that would hinder it. But the Bolsheviks had repeatedly offered to sign an armistice in order to facilitate evacuation. Moreover, the guns of the British cruisers lying in the White Sea could easily have afforded sufficient cover for the embarkation of several thousand soldiers and of several thousand Russian civilians.

**YUDENICH AND KOLCHAK** Yudenich too recognized the "Supreme Ruler" and was subject to instructions from Omsk. It was announced in Reval on August 19, that "the new Government of Yudenich recognizes its temporary and district character and declares its agreement with Admiral Kolchak and with the program adopted by him and by General Denikin."

**YUDENICH AND DENIKIN** To complete the united front of the four big White leaders there is the link between Yudenich and Denikin to which Lloyd George alluded in the House of Commons on December 18, 1919, when he said "General Yudenich, who is acting more or less in concert with General Denikin . . ."

[1] British Blue Book. Cmd. 818. *Army. The Evacuation of North Russia.* (London, 1919).
[2] *Ibid.*
[3] *Ibid.*

There was, then, a tie between Kolchak and the three other fronts, between Archangel and Yudenich and Kolchak, between Yudenich and Archangel and Denikin, and between Denikin and Yudenich and Kolchak.

The interdependence of the counter-revolutionary groups, product of a common political ideology and aim, in turn resulted in a co-ordination of military activities which, in view of poor communications and the distances between fronts, could only have been planned for in some foreign capital after consultation with Kolchak's agents. The first attempt at such military co-ordination was made in the spring of 1919 when Allied assistance began to assume great importance, and its first-fruits were the notable successes gained during the critical May month of 1919 around Petrograd and in the Ukraine.

**YUDENICH AT PETROGRAD'S GATES** Yudenich commenced his offensive at daybreak on May 13, found the Soviet forces unprepared, and registered appreciable forward pushes. On the 25th, Bulak-Balakhovich, later of pogrom fame in White Russia, took Pskov with the aid of Estonians. The White army was supported by a well-planned conspiracy hatched in Petrograd by two reactionary organizations called the "National Center" and the "Resurrection Union." Thanks to their efforts, one regiment in the Red Army mutinied, the fort of Red Gorka raised the flag of revolt and fired on Kronstadt and on the Soviet fleet. Grey Horse Fort followed suit. In Petrograd a railway strike was contemplated. The counter-revolutionaries even placed agents in Red Army staff headquarters.

This plot was discovered by the Cheka in June and wholesale arrests followed. The revelations produced a deep effect on the Petrograd proletariat and thousands offered their services against Yudenich. These enthusiastic recruits soon checked Yudenich's advance. By June and the early part of July the White offensive, so auspiciously begun, had been halted—both favorable and unfavorable developments on this front were rapid because the distances were small.

A Soviet counter-offensive which commenced in August met with almost instantaneous success owing to the retirement of the Estonians—not for military but for political reasons. They simply turned about and left the front open for the Bolsheviks to march ahead. The result was the complete paralysis of Yudenich's forces.

**"THERE IS NO ESTONIA"** N. N. Ivanov, a member of Yudenich's Cabinet, has preserved a most interesting conversation on this question between himself and his chief which took place early in 1919. The discussion turned to relations with Estonia. "There is no Estonia," Yudenich explained. "It is a piece of Russian soil—a Russian province. The Estonian Government is a gang of criminals who have seized power, and I will enter into no conversations with it."[4] Such an attitude arose naturally from his Great Russian belief in an "undivided" Russia. Estonia was of course aware of Kolchak's and Yudenich's hostility towards the national aspirations of the border states of the former Czarist Empire. The Estonians realized that the victory of Bolshevism would not threaten their independence while the victory of the Whites would.

**CABINET FORMATION IN FORTY MINUTES** The defection of the Estonians and the support of Petrograd factory hands had defeated Yudenich's first effort, yet neither he nor the Allies despaired of final victory. The condition of achievement, however, was reorganization, and with this in view General March, of the British Army, arrived dramatically in Reval on August 10. The same evening he invited eleven leading White Russians to his apartment. Then, in the presence of the American and French military attachés, he ordered the assembled leaders to form a new Government in forty minutes. He drew his watch. It was 6.20 P.M. as he spoke: the cabinet must be ready at 7. Moreover, this new Government would be required to sign an agreement with Estonia immediately and on the spot.

Faced with such an ultimatum, the Yudenich group meekly complied. The British saw plainly that the General would never take Petrograd until some settlement was patched up between him and Estonia. But the incident provoked Kolchak's jealousy. Forthwith, Sazonov protested against Yudenich's independence in foreign affairs,

[4] N. N. Ivanov: *Events outside Petrograd in 1919,* Archives of the Civil War (Berlin, 1921).

and against an agreement with Estonia which was more than military in character.

If Yudenich's situation was difficult, England's was complicated and anomalous. On the one hand she supported Kolchak and Yudenich, to whom independent border nations were anathema; on the other hand, she supported those border nations out of her desire to weaken her age-long enemy, Russia, and drive the Muscovite Power away from the seas. Yet military expediency required that the two elements, the restorationists and the natural enemies of the restorationists—the Estonians—be made amicable bed-fellows. It was impossible.

**DENIKIN'S DISTANT OFFENSIVE** Fortune smiled on Denikin more warmly than on his friend in Reval. In May, he moved forward rather rapidly in three directions: towards Tsaritsin to unite with Kolchak on the Volga, towards Voronezh and Kharkov to take Moscow, and towards Odessa and Crimea to occupy the Ukraine.

Denikin was favored by mutinies in the Red Army. Ataman Gregoriev's revolt exposed the southern Ukraine to anti-Bolshevik attack. In the same month of May, Makhno, who commanded a corps in the army, started an insurrection against Bolshevism and attacked the very units to which he had formerly adhered, thus opening a breech for Denikin's advance on Kharkov. Such disaffection in the Red Army's ranks was not accidental; it reflected opposition to Moscow's peasant policy on the part of the richer muzhiks of the Ukraine who were displeased when the Bolsheviks requisitioned grain for the fighting forces.

Denikin enjoyed another advantage—he had cavalry, whose moves were quick and deadly. The Bolsheviks possessed little until later in the campaign. During September Trotzky gave out his famous summons, "Proletarians, to horse," and Budenny's mounted Cossacks began to play a decisive role in Soviet strategy. Until then the dashing divisions of Mamontov's and Shkuro's cavalry sowed devastation throughout Soviet Ukrainian territory.

The Bolsheviks were faced not only by 150,000 fairly well organized troops of Denikin but also by the Poles and by Petlura. Moreover, the Red Army was forced to spend considerable energy in battling with Makhno and numerous bandit, pogromist chiefs.

Denikin made swift progress. The campaign was long and bitterly fought with many trying contests and advances and retreats on both sides, but until October success remained with the Volunteer Army. From May till October he moved forward in the direction of Moscow and the Bolsheviks could not stop him. On September 20 he captured Kursk (330 miles from Moscow), October 5 Chernigov, and October 14 Orel (245 miles from Moscow).

Moscow was alarmed.

**DENIKIN'S END** Denikin had lengthened his line and proceeded far from his base. To refresh his spent army, he was forced to conscript among the local population which was neither loyal nor ready to fight. He even pressed Red Army prisoners into the ranks. Moreover, the peasants began to understand his pro-landlord policy and harassed his rear. The Bolsheviks, on the contrary, now threw enthusiastic workers into the front line and brought up reserves from other theaters. Finally Denikin's greatest political difficulty, apart from village uprisings, was the disaffection of the inhabitants of Terek, Dagestan and Kuban, who resented his policy towards national minorities.

A further blow to Denikin's cause was the deflection of Allied ammunition from him to D'Annunzio. Entente arms were frequently shipped to Russia in Italian vessels, the seamen on which had organized in trade unions led by a certain Jiulietti. During the Genoa Conference in 1922, Chicherin met Jiulietti together with D'Annunzio. In 1919 D'Annunzio had founded a republic at Fiume on near-Soviet lines. He thought of making Italy the leader of national revolutionary movements; he planned an alliance between Italy, Germany and Soviet Russia. At the time, and even later, he maintained contacts with Italian Communists, notably Bombacci. Jiulietti, who knew D'Annunzio and Bombacci well, persuaded his Italian sailors to divert shiploads of war materials from Denikin's Black Sea ports to the pink free state of Fiume.

Apart from these difficulties, a split had developed in Denikin's own camp. Two factions struggled for control—

the pro-Entente Cadets, and the Russian monarchists whose sympathies went out to the Hohenzollern dynasty.

Thus weakened, Denikin began to decline. In November a general retreat developed. Soon the Volunteer Army was fighting for its existence—not in the Ukraine but in the Don region. The Red Army swept ahead irresistibly in all directions; Budenny's cavalry advanced rapidly, and by March, 1920, Denikin was back in the Northern Caucasus, where his adventure saw its inception in 1918.

This was the end of Denikin. A remnant of his army under General Baron Wrangel saved itself by rushing into the Crimean bottle and inserting the cork at Perekop. Thousands of stragglers trekked across the Caucasian Mountains into Georgia—but the Volunteer Army as such had passed into history. In May, 1920, Denikin himself appeared in London and began to write his valuable many-volumed memoirs.

**KOLCHAK'S END** While these kaleidoscopic events were unfolding on the Southern front, another Red force pounded at Kolchak. The "Supreme Ruler" had become a sorry spectacle; even the Allies despaired of his success and informed him that they would henceforth concentrate their support on Denikin. The Siberian peasants refused to enter his ranks. Partisan bands operated everywhere to the detriment of the White divisions.

Under the circumstances, the Red Army's advance was determined by its own rapidity of movement. It quickly traversed the Ural plateau during the early autumn, and by October had conquered much of Western Siberia. Omsk fell without a struggle. The admiral himself fled with his gold and some archives in the direction of Irkutsk to the Baikal region.[5] His followers deserted, and no less than 100,000 prisoners were counted by the Bolshevik forces in these operations.

The "Supreme Ruler," his dreams of supremacy and ruling miserably dashed, surrendered himself to General Janin, the French officer in charge of the Allied forces in Siberia. Janin, in turn, handed him over to the Bolsheviks because they threatened to annihilate his corps if he did

[5] Part of the archives of the Kolchak Ministry of Foreign Affairs was abandoned in Omsk and seized by the Bolsheviks. The remainder travelled to Irkutsk and became Soviet property upon the capture of that city. These documents are now in the vaults of the Commissariat of Foreign Affairs in Moscow.

not.[6] The Bolsheviks thereupon tried him before a Revolutionary Tribunal, found him guilty, and shot him at five in the morning of February 7, 1920.

Western Siberia had gone "Red." The Japanese held the Maritime Provinces and Vladivostok. Between the two a sort of buffer state was establishd on April 6, 1920, with a capital at Chita. Alexander Krasnoschekov, recently arrived from Chicago, was chosen president of this "Far Eastern Republic."

During the Red Army's operations against Kolchak in the Ural region, one of its sections bent sharply to the south, and, instead of pursuing the Admiral's main force, undertook a bold move in the direction of Turkestan. Within three months, these troops had penetrated into the distant Trans-Caspian region, captured Krasnovodsk on the Caspian (February 6, 1920), and paved the way for the immediate setting up of a Soviet Government. Thus, another tremendous slice of Russian territory was relieved of White influence and of foreign intervention.

**YUDENICH TRIES AGAIN** The Bolsheviks were making a determined stand against Denikin around Orel. They were busy liquidating Kolchak's army. Moscow seemed threatened. At this juncture, Yudenich began to menace Petrograd which, for the revolution, was almost as vital as Moscow. By October 16, his soldiers had taken Gatchina and approached the suburbs of Peter's "Paris of the North."

Almost panicky, the Bolsheviks rushed young cadets and the most reliable Communist units to Petrograd. Trotzky himself appeared on the scene and faced the possibility of stubborn street fighting within the limits of the town. Every house would become a fortress, he proclaimed.

Factories organized for defense; barricades were thrown up in the southern suburbs. The fleet hurried into the Neva—into the heart of Petrograd. At the same time, the front, not far from the limits of the town, received reinforcements.

The Whites used tanks which the Red Russians had never seen. But progress became impossible in the face of the Bolsheviks' will to win, and Yudenich soon yielded.

[6] H. K. Norton: *The Far Eastern Republic of Siberia,* (London, 1923), p. 93.

The first fortnight in November saw the crisis: first standstill, then retreat, then retirement to Estonia and to inactivity. The bitter winter had arrived now and resumption of operations was inconceivable. . . . A heavy burden fell from Moscow's shoulders. Kolchak, Denikin, and Yudenich were no more.

**OIL** There remained at this juncture—early in 1920—the Poles on the Russo-Polish frontier, Baron Wrangel in the Crimea, and the British in Georgia.

Georgia is one of the most illuminating phases of the Russian civil war; it involves British policy in the Near East, oil, empire, and Menshevism.

With the World War Armistice, the Turks and the Germans evacuated the Caucasus. By the secret Anglo-French agreement of December 23, this region acquired the status of a special British zone of influence, and the British therefore made haste to occupy it.

Why did they go in?

> After the Armistice, [writes Arthur Moore, a well-known British authority on Asiatic problems, in the London *Times* of July 10, 1922] we poured troops into the Caucasus which is largely Musulman. Far across the Caspian we had troops even in the famous Merv. At first these had a stabilizing influence, and we announced that we had come to keep the Bolshevists away. But as soon as the Bolshevist menace began to materialize, it was we who faded away. Why, then, did we go there at all? Islam knows the answer. We went to try to get hold of the Baku oil-fields, but we were not prepared to fight for them.

**THE ITALIANS AND THE CAUCASUS** London decided to resign in favor of the Italians. "Lloyd George still wants the Italians to go to the Caucasus," wrote Sir Henry Wilson on May 5, 1919, "although he told [President] Wilson their presence there would create 'hell'—which pained my cousin." And at a meeting of the Peace Conference on May 5th, Sir Henry Wilson declared that "the Italian military and naval mission must now be at Constantinople on its way to Batum-Baku to make arrangements for taking over."[7]

But a bit later in the month the Italians entertained

[7] Callwell: *op. cit.*, II, 188.

some doubts about the wisdom of accepting this "theater of disturbance," as Sir Henry, who was making the gift, called the Caucasus. Opposition to the Caucasian adventure, indeed, may have been one of the causes of the fall of the Orlando Cabinet and the rise of Nitti.

> When I assumed the direction of the Government in June, 1919, [writes Nitti] an Italian military expedition was under orders for Georgia. The English troops, who were in small number, were withdrawing. Italy had, with the consent of the Allies, and partly by her own desire, prepared a big military expedition. . . . Georgia is a country of extraordinary natural resources, and it was thought that she would be able to furnish Italy with a great number of raw materials which she lacked. What surprised me was that not only men of the Government, but intelligent financiers and men of very advanced ideas [the reference is to Socialists.–L. F.] were convinced supporters of this expedition.[8]

Nitti fought the project. He regarded Georgia a natural part of Russia. "Georgia before the war formed part of the Russian Empire," he says, "and no country of the Entente had considered that unjust."[1] Why, therefore, this sudden interest in the independence of Georgia?

The whole story of Italy's role or contemplated role in the Caucasus is veiled in mystery. The plan must have been the result of a quid pro quo, the details of which are not available. Nor do we know the real reasons why Nitti stood out against it. Apparently, however, his obstructions succeeded and autumn saw the British still in the Caucasus. The question of withdrawal, nevertheless, remained pressing, and on September 2, the Cabinet discussed it. "Curzon favored our leaving a brigade there. So did Milner; but Bonar Law, Montagu, Austen, and I opposed this."[2]

**THE BRITISH AND THE CAUCASUS** So the matter remained suspended for several months. The British Government was divided and did nothing. The smashing of

[8] Francesco S. Nitti, *Peaceless Europe,* London, 1922. Page 147. Nitti is mistaken about the riches of Georgia. It is a rough, mountainous province whose only raw materials of importance to foreign countries is manganese. But Georgia controls Europe's access to Baku, the great oil field. Nitti was probably under the impression that Baku belonged to Georgia.

[1] *Ibid.*

[2] Callwell: *op. cit.,* II, 219.

Denikin, however, made some action imperative and the problem now commenced to cause "sharp disagreement in Cabinet circles."[3]

Curzon had gone to Paris with Lloyd George. Under Curzon's pressure, the Allies, on January 11, recognized the de facto government of Georgia and Azerbaijan. This was their answer to the Denikin debacle. In December, at a session of the League of Nations, England had refused to take such a step. Recognition of these separationist states would have riled Denikin, the patriot of an "undivided Russia." When he had fallen, recognition offered the possibility of continued resistance to Bolshevism. And this is indeed what Curzon wished. "Curzon now wants to hold Batum-Baku, and Montagu backs him."[4] Curzon had won Montagu to his point of view; the ex-Viceroy of India was working hand in hand with the Secretary of State for India. To them, obviously, Georgia and Azerbaijan were important not so much for their significance in the petroleum struggle as out of imperial considerations. With the Caucasus and the Trans-Caspia in England's grip, Afghanistan could not be defiant. India would be safe.

Having recognized Georgia and Azerbaijan, the Supreme Council called in their representatives who "told the Frocks the same ridiculous cock-and-bull stories they had told me and Beatty, and for Lloyd George's benefit and Winston's anger, they added that they feared and hated Denikin, who was a Czarist." On the basis of these "cock-and-bull stories," nevertheless, the meeting "decided to arm, equip, and feed the Georgians, Azerbaijanese and Armenians."[5]

The idea of intervention was not yet dead at this late day. Again it is Sir Henry Wilson who, and with winning military frankness, makes this cynical statement:

> It is amazing to see the Frock mind. In St. James's Palace is sitting the League of Nations, their principal business being the limitation of armaments. In Downing Street is sitting the Allied Conference of Lloyd George, Millerand, Nitti, and a Japanese, who are feverishly arming Finland, Baltic States, Poland, Rumania, Georgia, Azerbaijan, Armenia, Persia, etc.

[3] *Ibid.*
[4] Callwell: *op. cit.*, II, 223.
[5] *Ibid.*

The British force in the Caucasus gradually dwindled—the Generals withdrew detachments quietly as the need arose. Nevertheless, Curzon persisted. He coaxed one postponement after the other from the Cabinet, hoping, probably, that some accident would retrieve his position. Finally, it was no longer tenable and Curzon applied to Paris and Rome for support. These agreed to dispatch tiny units, whereupon all but two British battalions were removed from the Caucasus. They held Batum. A month later, April, 1920, the Red Army took Baku, and Azerbaijan became an autonomous soviet republic.

In April the historic San Remo Conference convened. According to Nitti, "the possibility was discussed of an expedition by Great Britain, France, and Italy to defend at least the oil production" of the Caucasus. But the verdict was "No." In fact, despite opposition from Curzon and Berthelot of the Quai d'Orsay, the meeting decided on April 23, 1920, to evacuate Batum.

Undaunted, Curzon, when he got back to London, continued his stubborn battle for the maintenance of even the two battalions at Batum. And it was not a foolish point of view. For in British circles, the idea gained ground that if they left Batum, Persia would be next. Lloyd George actually favored the evacuation of both. Others proposed concentration in Iraq, which seemed about to blow up. Curzon stubbornly stood by his guns and at a cabinet meeting as late as June 18 showed inclinations to resign, together with Milner, in case Persia should be surrendered.

Curzon and his friend were finally overruled; the English garrison left Batum on July 7, 1920, after the city had been transferred to the sovereignty of the Georgian Menshevik Republic.

Menshevik Georgia became Soviet Georgia in February, 1921.

**GREAT BRITAIN** In Georgia and the Caucasus generally, British policy aimed at acquiring invaluable petroleum deposits and at enlarging the size and rounding out the periphery of the empire. Baku, as Chicherin put it, is "a finger pointing to Asia." (His eye was on the physical shape of the Aspheron Peninsula.) Baku was also the world's largest oilfield.

Russia and Britain were ancient rivals. The "bear that

walks like a man" never loved the lion, nor did the lion wish to lie down with the bear. The hate was written in history; it took its origin deep in the center of Asia where the two empires met.

But there is nothing static or unchangeable in world politics, and on August 31, 1907, when Russia was exhausted from the 1905 revolution and the war with Japan, and England looked about for allies against the looming menace of Germany, the confirmed enemies called a truce and signed a treaty (delivering Afghanistan to the "protection" of England, declaring Tibet forbidden ground for both Powers, and outlining British and Russian "zones of influence" in Persia) which paved the way to the British-Russian alliance that found its highest expression in World War co-operation.

The Bolshevik revolution broke the truce. The old rivalry reappeared. The old hatred was enhanced. New hates appeared. For to the British, Soviet Russia seemed to combine the former menace of Russia with the novel threat of Communism. British statesmen may have been aiming at the old antagonist, the bear, when they seemed to be pointing a shot at the red revolutionist.

Arch-interventionists like Churchill repeatedly urged the League of Nations to undertake an anti-Russian crusade.[6] In such cases, he obviously would paint Russia not as a rival of Britain in Central Asia but as a menace to civilization and a power for evil in Europe.

Long after it had become manifestly clear that Bolshevism would persist in at least a part of Russia, London statesmen continued the struggle for the separation from Russia of her Asiatic provinces. In this phase, the imperial, anti-Russian motive was unquestionably predominant.

Speaking at the Guildhall on November 10, 1919, Lloyd George referred to Bolshevik victories against the Whites and said: "You must not imagine that I am reading from the present situation any sort of prediction that the Bolshevists are going to conquer the whole of Russia. I do not believe it. (Cheers.) The free peasantry of the South have in their hearts a detestation of Bolshevism, and I do not believe that the Bolshevists will conquer that aversion."

Even Lloyd George, who was an interventionist of mod-

[6] See, for instance, his speech before the British Russian Club quoted in the London *Times* of July 19, 1919.

erate enthusiasm compared with Churchill or Milner or Curzon, wished to see Russia divided irrespective of whether or not Britain would later rule the parts.

**JAPAN** Japan aimed to undermine Russia's strength. Nippon statesmen occasionally did refer to Bolshevism and the "danger to civilization," but more often they were agreeably silent or cynically indifferent to the world's opinion of their ventures in Siberia.

Japan did not want Russian unity. The four great Far Eastern Powers are Britain, America, Japan and Russia. Geographically, the position of the last is the strongest, for she sits firmly on the Asiatic mainland and is contiguous with the problem country of Asia, China. A Russia restored to pre-War dimensions could check Japan's annexationist plans in China, in Manchuria and Mongolia, in much the same manner as she might cause embarrassment to the British Empire in Central Asia.

During 1918, especially, but in 1919 as well, Japan dreamt Pan-Asiatic dreams. Chicherin tells the writer that the Bolsheviks found Japanese agents as far west as Uzbekstan and Bokhara, and he considers Baron Ungern-Sternberg, who fought the Bolsheviks first in Siberia and then in Mongolia, an ideologist and supporter of this Pan-Asiatic movement. Even partial success, however, was inconceivable if Russia got back on her feet. Hence Tokyo's efforts to hinder Russian unification.

But Japan's political considerations were heavily loaded with economic ballast. Japan required new fields for economic conquest. In Japan's career as an interventionist in Russia, the economic factor was more potent than in the case of any other Power. Her motives too were less disguised. She was the first to begin. She was the last to retire.

**THE UNITED STATES** The United States was the least aggressive of the Powers in the Russian Civil War. She coveted no Russian territory. Her business and financial stakes in Russia were comparatively insignificant.

The United States opposed, in principle at least, all measures that might prejudice the integrity of Russia. She long refused to recognize the Baltic republics. She failed to recognize the Caucasian republics. She obstructed Japanese intervention in Siberia. A strong Russia could check an aggressive Japan. Therefore America preferred a strong Russia to a dismembered Russia.

Despite President Wilson's friendly messages to and concerning the Bolsheviks, American troops began to land in North Russia in June, 1918. Yet Wilson continued to bar the way to the invasion of Siberia. His policy then was not anti-interventionist, but anti-Japanese, and the anti-Japanese motive tended to restrain any existent American tendencies towards militant anti-Bolshevism.

The history of American intervention in Siberia is replete with conflicts with the Japanese. The immediate stimulus may have been trivial or important. Fundamentally, the trouble lay deep in the antagonism between the two countries in Manchuria and Asia generally.

The struggle for domination in Manchuria is a story of railroads. This was the "most serious bone of contention" between Japan and America. These are the facts:

When the Czar fell, the Kerensky Government asked Washington to operate the Chinese Eastern Railway for it. The United States gladly sent over a commission headed by Colonel John F. Stevens to undertake the task. After the advent of the Bolsheviks, the Allies considered themselves the ad hoc heirs of the line, took it over, and asked America to run it for the time being.

Japan refused to consent. And Semenov, the Japanese puppet who held Chita and the surrounding territory, immediately began to plunder the property and obstruct traffic. The ataman was a specialist in such activities and did his duty well. Negotiations opened. There were protests, notes, diplomatic demarches. Finally, on February 10, 1919, Frank L. Polk, acting Secretary of State, informed Ishii, the Mikado's envoy in Washington, that America accepted the terms of the Japanese memorandum of January 9th.[7] By these terms, Colonel Stevens remained president of the technical management of both the Chinese Eastern and the Trans-Siberian railways, as far as the latter was not in Bolshevik hands, while an inter-allied force would guard them. It was further agreed that American soldiers would guard the eastern spur of the Trans-Siberian and Japanese soldiers the Chinese Eastern. The Japanese command, however, failed to co-operate with

[7] *R.A.R.*, pp. 276 ff.

Stevens and endless friction ensued from which business and American-Japanese relations suffered grievously.

The Japanese resented the presence of an American expeditionary force in Siberia which interfered with their aggressive intentions. On one occasion, for instance, a considerable number of Kalmikov's Cossacks mutinied against the Japanese puppet and surrendered to the Americans. The Japanese objected to such protection. General Graves turned a deaf ear. On another occasion, Semenov kidnapped Boris Skvirsky, who later directed the Soviet Information Bureau in Washington, and began rushing him towards the Chinese border. Graves sent an armored auto in pursuit and rescued the Russian.

Like the Japanese, Kolchak too disliked the conduct of the Americans. He frequently complained against their "radicalism." One such protest was made in February, 1919. Another, dated December 12, 1919, is a report to Kolchak from an agent in Vladivostok who explains (1) that the United States soldiers are infected with Bolshevism, (2) that most of them are Jews from the East Side of New York City who constantly agitate for mutinies, (3) that it is not inconceivable that the Bolsheviks may receive support from the American Army, and (4) that the propaganda of the Y.M.C.A. is a preparation for Bolshevism.

The United States expeditionary force, and the American railway experts were finally withdrawn in accordance with a State Department declaration dated January 17, 1920.

American intervention in Siberia was a fruitless, dismal tragedy-comedy. Similarly in North Russia.

**FRANCE** French interventionist policy in Russia has been subjected to considerable misinterpretation by the Bolsheviks.

France was not a very active participant in the civil war.

France was not interested only or primarily in debt payment.

France was not interested in the maintenance of a united Russia.

Generally, French policy is summarized thus: France had lent great sums of money to Czarist Russia. Only a strong Russia could settle these debts. Therefore she played a prominent role in the struggle within Russia, but not, as in the case of England and Japan, with a view to the dismemberment of the country. . . . All this is incorrect.

France had 750 officers and men in Siberia, about 2,300 soldiers in Archangel, and, for three months, some 12,000 in the Ukraine, of whom 4,000 were Poles, 1,500 Russians, and 2,000 Greeks. But the majority of the remaining 4,500 "Frenchmen" hailed from the African and Asiatic colonies of the Third Republic.[8] This was the entire extent of French intervention.

The big White chiefs, Kolchak, Denikin, and Yudenich, were protégés of England. Churchill gave them almost everything they ever possessed. Wrangel is the exception. He was a French tool.

The leadership of the Czech army also lay in French hands. Its advisers were French. Masaryk admits its financial dependence on French francs. This, however, represents an early commitment of Clemenceau's before the World War had been won and when the army was truly destined for the French front. Noulens had other intentions, and when the Cezcho-Slovaks remained to fight against the Bolsheviks in Russia, France could not possibly have dropped the burden. (The bills, nevertheless, became a nuisance.) Most of what may appear on the books as French subsidies to Kolchak was actually paid for the maintenance of the Czechs.

France's outstanding part in the civil war was her expedition to Odessa in the early part of 1919. With a Franco-Hellenic-Polish-Rumanian force, France made ready to occupy her zone in Russia. The Ukraine and the Crimea constituted the French zone by the terms of "L'accord Franco-Anglais du 23 décembre 1917, définissant les zones d'action française et anglaise."

This document is frequently referred to by Denikin in his memoirs, by General Lukomsky in his memoirs, by numerous White authors as well as by Soviet writers. Its terms were actually put into practice.[9] It is significant first for its date. December 23, 1917. Less than two months after the Bolshevik revolution, eleven months before the

[8] A month before evacuation, the force was increased to a rifle strength of approximately 35,000.

[9] See Appendix for text.

end of the World War, Great Britain and France met to dismember Russia. Allied representatives still sat in Petrograd urging resistance to German demands at Brest Litovsk, offering assistance to the Red Army, and speaking of Russia as an ally. At the same time, allied representatives sat in Paris dividing the carcass of the bear.

The Caucasus, part of the Don, the North Russian timber belt, and the Baltics fell to England's lot; Poland, the Ukraine and the Crimea were the share of France. Alone the fact that Paris signed such a treaty proves that the policy of an undivided Russia was no longer hers.

Republican France and Czarist Russia were close friends. France needed a strong Russia as a balance against Germany. But a strong Bolshevist Russia could of course not be trusted to serve French purposes. Had there not been suggestions of a Russian-German military alliance? Paris, therefore, sponsored Poland. A well-financed, well-advised Poland would be more tractable than any kind of Russia and would herself be interested in serving French anti-German purposes.

Poland had a sad history and therefore unlimited ambitions. She dreamt of the frontiers of 1772. Pilsudski, her national hero, visualized a country stretching from the Baltic to the Black Sea, and including Lithuania and the Ukraine.

By sponsoring Poland, France ipso facto identified herself with Polish plans. This consideration induced Paris, in 1919, to send an expedition to the Ukraine and Crimea rather than to some other parts of Russia. Even during the life of the Franco-Russian alliance, Chicherin tells the writer, Paris encouraged Ukrainian separatists. The commissar declares that France availed herself of the services of the Freemasons and, with the help of a certain Markotun, organized lodges in the Ukraine which soon extended their influence to the Don region.

France had tremendous financial stakes in the Ukraine and the Don. Before the war, 32.6 per cent of all foreign capital invested in Russia was French. Professor Ohl of the Soviet Commissariat of Finance, who examined the records of the Czarist Exchequer and takes his figures from that official source,[1] places the total French investment in antebellum Russia at 731,746,600 rubles, of which

[1] P. V. Ohl: *Foreign Capital in Russia,* (Petrograd, 1922), p. 10.

43.3 per cent fell to the mining and 21.6 per cent to the metallurgical industry.

These industries are concentrated in the Ukraine and the neighboring Don region, part of which likewise entered into the French zone; and as a matter of fact, 80.4 per cent of French capital in metallurgy was invested in South Russia, and 79.5 per cent of French capital in mining was invested in the Donetz Basin.[2] French interventionists aimed to safeguard these interests and secure them for their French owners.

One reason for France's uncompromising policy towards the Bolsheviks was her fear of Bolshevism. It might seize Poland as it had Hungary. From Hungary it could conceivably spread to the little allies that Paris had mobilized in the Balkans.

France never developed any enthusiasm for intervention in Russia, because her statesmen, especially Clemenceau, preferred the policy of the cordon sanitaire. Let Poland do the job, and Rumania, and Czecho-Slovakia, the "Tiger" argued. France did not put her heart into the expedition to Odessa.

Yet certain phenomena accompanying this expedition are extremely helpful in interpreting French policy. The Ukraine was the bridge over which Denikin had to pass in order to reach Moscow. Denikin stood for an undivided Russia. England showed him every kindness. Nevertheless, (or shall we say—therefore) the French were rather unkind to the general.

There was continual friction between the French command in Odessa and Denikin's Volunteer Army. When the French arrived in the city, they drove out the Petlurists who held the town in slipshod fashion and set up their own civil government despite protests. "We simply had the usual occupation," Lukomsky of Denikin's staff complains.[3]

The French checked Denikin's every step. In January, 1919, for instance, he wished to move his headquarters from Yekatrinodar to Sevastopol in order to prepare for the Ukrainian offensive. But Franchet d'Esperey (whom the Russians soon christened "Franchet Désespéré") wired: "I find that General Denikin should be with the Volunteer Army and not in Sevastopol where French

[2] *Ibid.*
[3] General Lukomsky, *Memoirs,* (Berlin, 1922). Vol. II.

troops are stationed which are not under his command."[4]

The French also offended Denikin by entering into negotiations with Petlura. Denikin's relationship to Petlura is characterized by a September 5, 1919, telegram from his foreign expert Neratov to Kolchak, in which he writes that he had informed the local representatives of the Allied missions that the Petlurists were a dangerous movement. "To recognize Petlura," the wire said, "and work together with him would be to recognize the dismemberment of Russia."[5]

The Denikinites never made any secret of this attitude. It was a corollary of their restorationist philosophy. Nevertheless, the French entered into relations with Petlura, the enemy of Russian unity, and as time went on, the relations between the French and Denikin became worse while relations with Petlura grew better.

Subsequently, when Poland was fighting as an ally and under the dictation of France against Soviet Russia and trying to wrest the Ukraine from Bolshevik rule, Petlura co-operated with the Poles. Petlura had previously been an enemy of the Poles. His change of heart may have had its inception during the months of contact with the French in Odessa.

France, to be sure, may not have been so deeply interested in dismemberment as England and Japan. She herself had no such territorial ambitions in Russia. Yet she was the sponsor of Poland which had.

A revision of the common conception of France's attitude towards a strong Russia, requires a change in our emphasis on the importance of debt payment. If Pilsudski had succeeded, with French aid, in annexing the Ukraine, Lithuania and White Russia from Soviet Russia, Soviet Russia would not have been in a position to repay if she wished. The Ukraine is Russia's source of bread, iron, coal and steel. A Ukraine-less Russia is a Russia seriously handicapped economically. This France knew—yet was not deterred. Debts were not uppermost in her mind.

**SOVIET RUSSIA'S POLICY IN THE CIVIL WAR** It is one of the most interesting phases of the revolution that a nation which had left the trenches and deserted from the World War because it was war-weary, rebounded

[4] *Ibid.*
[5] From Kolchak's Secret Archives.

lightly into the battle only a few months later. The "Peace" slogan on which the Communists rode into power in November, 1917, made way for enlistment and mobilization agitation in January and February, 1918. How did it happen that civil war, intervention, blockade, epidemics, and famine did not bring Lenin to his fall? In August, 1918, Bolshevism tottered. Communists sitting in the Kremlin could imagine the knife at their throats. Moscow was surrounded by an ever-narrowing iron ring formed by Allied, Czecho-Slovak and counter-revolutionary troops, while within the walls of the capital, assassins, plotters, and international adventurers sought to undermine the foundations of the new republic. How did the Bolsheviks annihilate this powerful enemy?

During the Brest Litovsk Conference, the Soviet leaders saw the Civil War coming. And it was one of the great strokes of Lenin's genius that he insisted on a "breathing-space," no matter how brief. He wanted the peasants to go to their fields, the workers to their tools. If it was only for a month, or two or three, they would discover in the interval who was their enemy and who their friend. The "breathing-space" would show them the gains and losses from the revolution. Life moved quickly in those days. Men saw clearly in a week what might otherwise require years of study and debate. Soldiers returned from the World War trenches realized that the revolution had been made by people of their own kind, and for their kind. The "boss," the exploiter, the landlord—all of them, rightly or wrongly, the personification of what the Russian under-dog detested—had been swept away. The romance of the revolution captured simple souls. In its first period its newly-found power and freedom intoxicated all who drank at its spring. And from this "inebriated" state they were called upon to fight the Whites and foreigners who, it was said, came to relegate the workers and peasants to their former status of ruled instead of ruling.

To the great mass, Bolshevism was part promise and part fulfilment. From the revolution had come peace, land, and a new form of ownership. But it also painted a glorious future which attracted and provoked. The enemies of Communism had nothing thrilling or inspiring to offer. Lenin operated on credit. His capital was a promissory note on coming years. The Whites on the other hand could appeal only to the record of that past which they wished to enthrone again. Psychologically, the position of the Bolsheviks was stronger.

The Soviets enjoyed the advantage of a united command. The Communist Party was supreme. The leadership of Lenin and Trotzky was unquestioned. Differences of opinion existed. When they arose they were frankly thrashed out and removed. But the camp of the Whites showed a diametrically opposed picture.

The difficulty of co-ordinating the efforts of Estonia and Yudenich, of Petlura and Denikin, and, in general, of reconciling the important White leaders with the restive ethnic groups which sought autonomy, must be regarded as one of the chief contributing causes of the counter-revolution's failure.

Geography further handicapped the counter-revolutionaries. Despite attempts at co-ordination which had more political significance than tactical advantage, not one of the four White fronts—Kolchak, Denikin, Yudenich, Archangel—ever established contact with any other. The Bolsheviks, however, fought from a compact center well supplied with transportation facilities and possessing the best railway junction in the country—Moscow. Shifting of troops from a quiet front to a troubled sector was comparatively simple. For the Whites, it was practically impossible.

All these circumstances enabled the Red Army to defeat the Whites despite its inferior equipment and less-experienced officers.

Notwithstanding their weakness, the Russian Whites might still have won the battle against Bolshevism had the foreign Powers been in a position to give them unlimited support. A force of 100,000 British or French or American volunteers could undoubtedly have overthrown the Communist regime early in the Civil War—though it could not have guaranteed against a resurgence of the Soviets or against its own inoculation with the "Lenin virus." Yet when England did intervene, her armed units were small and, later, unreliable. The French expedition to Odessa consisted of more Algerians, Rumanians, Poles and Greeks than real natives of the republic, who, like the Americans in Archangel and Siberia, murmured loudly against their forced exile. Only Japan gave of her strength without reserve or fear.

# 6

# WHITE POLAND v. RED RUSSIA

POLAND let slip a unique opportunity in 1919. Throughout the autumn of that year, the 12th Russian Army faced a hostile Polish army in the neighborhood of Minsk and Bobruisk. When Denikin came within a dangerous proximity of Moscow, the Bolshevik High Command drew heavily on this unit for reserves, and thus seriously weakened its potential resistance. The Poles took no advantage of this development. "A slight effort in the fall of 1919," writes General Kakurin,[1] would have enabled Poland to regain her 1772 frontiers in the Ukraine. But Pilsudski did not make the slight effort.

This strange conduct Kakurin explained to me as follows: A Polish attack at the time of Denikin's greatest success might have given him Moscow. But the re-establishment of a reactionary Russia constituted a danger to Poland. For even if Denikin had submitted to the will of the Allies to maintain a separate Poland, he would never have parted with the Ukraine, or Lithuania, or White Russia—on all of which Pilsudski had designs.

Count Alexander Skrzynski, Polish Foreign Minister in 1922–3 and from 1924 to 1926, confirms the Kakurin hypothesis.

> Undoubtedly, [he writes] [2] Denikin would have received with great gratitude the help of the Poles, but only on the understanding, scarcely concealed, that such help was forthcoming from the Poles as faithful subjects of Russia.

[1] N. Kakurin: *How the Revolution Fought,* (Moscow, 1926), II, 321.
[2] Count Alexander Skrzynski: *Poland and Peace,* (London, 1923), p. 39.

Denikin reasoning in this way, the Poles could have no interest in giving him help. That is why his episode was played out independently of the evolution of Polish Eastern Policy.

Nothing could be plainer: two anti-Bolshevik interests hated one another so cordially that they refused to co-operate against the common enemy.

The idea of a possible Russo-Polish agreement was first suggested to Chicherin by Wieckovski, who came to Moscow early in 1919. Wieckovski talked of a united front between Russia and Poland against the outside world. He stated definitely that Poland, at any rate, would not support Denikin.

**A SECRET POLISH–RUSSIAN ARMISTICE** Julian Markhlevsky was a prominent Polish Communist. The end of 1918 found him in Germany. But Noske, the Social Democratic Minister, issued a death warrant for him; and Markhlevsky, rejecting the alternative of an airplane escape to Holland, fled in the disguise of an agricultural worker to his native country.

In Warsaw, Markhlevsky met an old acquaintance, Josef Bek, assistant Minister of Interior and member of the innermost political circle in Poland. Bek had access to the all-powerful Pilsudski. Markhlevsky pressed home the danger to Poland which a White Russia would constitute. He inspired articles to that effect in the Polish Press, notably an editorial in the Warsaw *Rabotnik* of June 11, 1919, entitled "Kolchak." The Admiral, the counter-revolutionary generals and the Czarists generally, would never countenance an independent Poland. Pilsudski saw the logic of this argument and permitted Markhlevsky to continue his work. After a while, the Polish authorities even delegated an officer to accompany Markhlevsky to the Russian border on his way to consult with Lenin.

The Bolsheviks fully approved of the activity which Markhlevsky had commenced on his own initiative. Before long, he was ordered to return to Poland. On July 5, 1919, the radio operator at Detskoe- (formerly Tsarskoe-) Selo sent a slip of paper to Chicherin in which he announced that he had repeated a message to the Ministry of Foreign Affairs in Warsaw and received a receipt[3]; the message

[3] This document was in the possession of Mrs. Markhlevsky, who kindly permitted the writer to copy it and other material left by her deceased husband.

stated that a certain Kujavsky would soon cross the Polish-Russian frontier. Kujavsky was Markhlevsky.

Kujavsky-Markhlevsky went to a forest near Bialovesh. There he met Count Kosakovsky. Everything was kept in deep secret. This happened in July.

Subsequently, in October, 1919, a Polish and Soviet delegation met at Mikashevitch near Lutsk. Officially they were Red Cross missions occupied with the knotty problem of the exchange of prisoners. But Markhlevsky had a credential signed Chicherin and dated October 4, 1919, which authorized him to "conduct negotiations with the representatives of the Polish Government on all questions that have arisen or may arise" between the two States, and especially to ascertain "the basis of an agreement which would guarantee peaceful relations between the Polish Republic and the Russian Socialist Federated Soviet Republic.[4]

Markhlevsky and his assistants remained at Mikashevitch from October 9 to December 22. They lived in a train and held their sessions with the Poles on the sidings of the tiny railway station. And while Markhlevsky talked prisoners with the official Polish representatives, he now and then—four times during the period—received visits from a mysterious gentleman named Colonel Berner. The Colonel was a confidant of Pilsudski and spoke in the name of the statesman-general. They discussed the old question: would Poland refrain from attacking Soviet Russia while the Bolsheviks were engaged by Kolchak, Denikin, Yudenich and other Whites? The advantages were as clear to the Russians as to the Poles. Markhlevsky and Berner likewise exchanged views on a future Polish-Russian frontier. Indeed, so much progress was registered that the situation seemed to require a personal meeting between Pilsudski and Markhlevsky. This was actually agreed upon.

Both Pilsudski and Markhlevsky were passionate hunters. According to the scheme, they would meet "by accident" while engaged in a chase in the thick woods of Eastern Poland.

Much of this mystery, secrecy and make-believe is explained by Pilsudski's position with respect to the Allies, more particularly France. Poland had her own federationist

[4] Photographic copy obtained from the Lenin Institute in Moscow.

plans, but their success was predicated on the defeat of the Russian Whites. France, however, egged Warsaw on. The policy of cordon sanitaire required another attack on Soviet Russia; required it before the Bolsheviks could recuperate from the White attacks.

Accordingly, Pilsudski, in order to keep the goodwill and financial backing of Paris, saw himself forced to create the impression of warlike intentions against the Bolsheviks, even when for a moment he preferred a peaceful course. The Poles therefore moved their troops about, and, during the whole period in which Markhlevsky negotiated with Colonel Berner, sought to act as if they were preparing for battle with the Russians.

The purpose of the Markhlevsky discussions was a Polish-Russian armistice lasting at least till Denikin collapsed. This conformed with Poland's best interests. Yet France, in her desire to overthrow the Soviet regime, and with no understanding for the welfare of Poland, wished to precipitate the struggle without delay. And therefore Pilsudski was compelled to deceive Paris while his agent parleyed with Markhlevsky.

The meeting between Markhlevsky and Pilsudski never took place. Pilsudski's internal enemies opposed it, and he feared the effect abroad. Yet Markhlevsky's mission did postpone the opening of the war, and, according to Chicherin, kept the Polish army on the Polish side of a line demarcated by Markhlevsky and Berner.

The Poles bided their time until Moscow had annihilated most of its enemies. During the whole of 1919 they pushed forward into Soviet territory. On April 19, 1919, Polish troops occupied Vilna, the capital of Soviet Lithuania, and on August 8 they entered Minsk, the center of Soviet White Russia, deep in the heart of Russia. The Russian-Polish line now ran along the Berezin River, touching Bobruisk and Mozir. Here it remained from August to December while the Bolsheviks dispatched Denikin and while Markhlevsky negotiated with Pilsudski's lieutenants. The Poles loyally fulfilled their pact with Moscow.

**SOVIET PEACE OFFERS** But by the beginning of 1920 the anti-Bolshevik military movement in Russia was in its death struggles. Poland now proposed to act.

These intentions did not remain secret, and the Conmissariat of Foreign Affairs in Moscow consequently commenced to pour out peace notes, settlement proposals, armistice suggestions, etc., etc.

In December, 1919, it became clear that the Poles had no intention of renewing the Markhlevsky talks, then about to adjourn for the Christmas holiday. An important peace offer was accordingly sent to Warsaw by Chicherin on December 22, 1919, in which he declared the "firm wish of the Soviet Government to end all its conflicts with Poland." Immediate negotiations were proposed. "Peace between Poland and Russia is a life necessity for both countries," the note appeals. The "Soviet Government is convinced that all differences between them can be removed by a friendly agreement."[5]

This note was never answered.

Lenin, Chicherin and Trotzky, in the name of the Council of People's Commissars, issued a declaration to the Polish Government and the Polish nation on January 28, 1920, which warned that the Allies were driving Poland into "an unwarranted, senseless and criminal war with Soviet Russia." To avoid all possible misinterpretation, the Moscow Government reaffirmed: that it "unconditionally recognizes the independence and sovereignty of the Polish Republic"; that it entertained no aggressive intentions; that the Red Army would not advance beyond the then existing line; and that the Soviet State had not concluded agreements with Germany or any other Power aimed directly or obliquely against Poland.[6]

This almost humiliating declaration brought no results. Patek, the Minister of Foreign Affairs, merely acknowledged it on February 4 and promised a reply.

On February 2 the Central Executive Committee of the Soviet Republic again appealed to the Polish people. "The Russian nation," it said, "thirsts for peaceful construction, thirsts for a system of peace under which there will be no place for war between countries." Once more peace negotiations were urged.

Chicherin radioed a further peace offer to Patek on March 6.

Finally on March 27 Patek informed Chicherin that

[5] *Red Book*. Collection of Documents on Russian-Polish Relations from 1918 to 1920. Published by the Commissariat of Foreign Affairs (Moscow, 1920), p. 82.

[6] *Ibid*.

the Polish Republic was ready to enter into negotiations with Russian plenipotentiaries, and named the date and place: April 10—Borisov. To let the Russian delegates pass through the firing zone, the Poles would interrupt hostilities in the Borisov sector for twenty-four hours.[7]

Moscow replied on the very day Patek's message arrived, and expressed pleasure at Poland's acquiescence. But why a truce for only twenty-four hours and only in one small segment of the front? "We, for our part," wrote Chicherin, "see no reason that would justify new human sacrifices and the continuation of bloodshed. . . ." What kind of a peace conference could take place amid the roar of cannon and the screams of the wounded?

**POLAND'S POLICY** Were the Poles sincere? Count Skrzynski, Polish ex-Foreign Minister, says No.

> The [Soviet] proposals for peace, [he declares] were not given any serious consideration. . . . When, however, parliamentary and democratic policy did not permit them to be left without an answer, the question of the place where the negotiations might be held was raised in such an offensive spirit that the whole question stopped at that point.[8]

Almost the identical words are employed by H. H. Fisher, a neutral commentator and the official historian of the American Relief Association.

> The Poles, [he affirms] did not give them [the Soviet peace proposals] serious consideration, and the reply which the Government ultimately and reluctantly made was so offensive in spirit and so extravagant in its demands that peace on the basis of the Soviet's terms, which were by no means unreasonable, was obviously not desired.[9]

Patek knew the Borisov suggestion was unacceptable. Therefore he made it. After he became Polish Minister to Moscow, Patek told the writer that at the time the Borisov proposal was made the Poles held a highly favorable military position—presumably for the coming offensive. A truce for a longer period than twenty-four hours and at a different place would have permitted the Bolsheviks to strengthen their defense.

[7] *Red Book.*

[8] Skrzynski: *Poland and Peace,* p. 40.

[9] H. H. Fisher: *The Famine in Soviet Russia, 1919–23,* (New York, 1927), p. 32.

In a desperate attempt to save the situation, Chicherin thereupon proposed that the discussions take place in Warsaw or Moscow or Petrograd or an Estonian town. Patek, however, remained adamant.

The Poland which rejected peace because it prepared for war needed peace no less than Soviet Russia. The inclusion of many millions of non-Poles within her territories made the political situation chaotic. The economic position might have given every reason for pause. Hoover's A.R.A., at the instigation of the Paris Peace Conference, distributed over $50,000,000 worth of food in Poland during February–August, 1919. It continued its relief measures in 1920 while Poland continued her war preparations. In June of that year, the A.R.A. was feeding 1,315,000 children.[1] At that time, Pilsudski's army had penetrated deep into the Ukraine. Foreign relief committees were giving clothing and shoes to hundreds of thousands. Poland, the chief sector of the cordon sanitaire, counted no less than 34,000 cases of typhus in January, 1920—a catastrophe with which the Polish Government was powerless to cope. Yet the Warsaw authorities dreamt of foreign conquests. And the Paris diplomats who had refused to feed Soviet Russia unless she pledged to cease fighting back her enemies, vigorously pushed their relief program in Poland without attempting to check the aggressive plans of her statesmen.

Mr. Herbert Asquith put the matter succinctly in the House of Commons on August 10, 1920. "There she was six months ago," he said of Poland, "a population stricken with disease and famine, and it is no exaggeration to say, on the verge of national bankruptcy, and it was under these circumstances that she started this campaign." "Her avowed object," he continued, "was to get rid of the comparatively limited frontier, not an ungenerous frontier . . . and to go beyond it to the ancient boundaries of the Poland of 1772. . . . As I say, it was a purely aggressive adventure. . . . It was a wanton enterprise."

Poland's plans were crystallized into one word—"Federalism."

Federalism (its most eminent exponent was Pilsudski) was an audacious, romantic scheme for the solution of the eastern border-lands question by the creation, at the expense of Russia, of

[1] H. H. Fisher: *America and the New Poland,* (New York, 1928).

a series of independent States–Lithuania, White Russia, Ukraine —federated with and under the hegemony of Poland.[2]

The question of Poland's frontiers had not been settled. Neither the Foch line demarcating the boundary between Poland and Lithuania (July 27, 1919) nor the Curzon line secretly drawn by the Supreme Council on December 8, 1919, was accepted as final by Polish leaders. Poland had successfully defied the Peace Conference in the matter of Eastern Galicia, and her politicians did not intend to accept from the world's diplomats less than they thought obtainable by force of arms.

"Polish opinion by this time," says Professor Fisher, "was intoxicated with the doctrine of 'federalism' which could not be realized except by war."[3]

Ostensibly, the Poles were interested in liberating their eastern neighbors from the "yoke of Bolshevism," but Professor Fisher, among others, affirms that "this grandiose scheme unfortunately ignored the fact . . . that such neighbors as the Ukrainians and the Lithuanians would welcome almost any fate in preference to Polish rule, however disguised."[4]

No less a Polish patriot than Count Skrzynski exposes the hypocrisy of the federationist idea.

> The nations [he writes] which according to this theory Poland wanted to liberate from Russian servitude did not have any definite wishes about the matter, and even if they did not particularly care for Russia, they had less affection for Poland.

**PETLURA, THE POLES, AND THE POPE** So, while Moscow rained negotiations proposals, Warsaw searched the map for allies. Petlura was an easy conquest. In 1919 the Bolsheviks had pushed him out of the Ukraine into East Galicia. Haller's Polish legions pushed him back again into the Ukraine. Even before the Soviets had finally destroyed Denikin, they easily found the little energy necessary to strip Petlura of any vestige of power, following, and authority. In December, 1919, therefore, the "Hetman" appeared in Warsaw. The Poles welcomed him, fêted him, and came to an understanding with him that later assumed definite form in the treaty of April 23, 1920, in which Petlura renounced all claims to East Galicia

[2] *Ibid.*
[3] *Ibid.*
[4] Fisher: *The Famine in Soviet Russia,* p. 33.

and accepted, in return for Polish aid, the doubtful gift of leadership in a future non-Soviet Ukraine. Many of Petlura's faithful supporters considered his surrender of East Galicia treason to the Ukrainian nationalist cause, and M. Levitzky, for instance, the Hetman's minister in Copenhagen, resigned his post to take up cudgels against his former chief.[5]

**ENGLAND'S CHANGED ATTITUDE** Petlura's alignment with Poland afforded Pilsudski little encouragement for his Napoleonic adventure. He required more potent allies. Accordingly, in January, 1920, we find Patek, the Polish Minister of Foreign Affairs, lobbying for help in the British capital. His reception was cold.

The victories of the Bolsheviks over Denikin, Kolchak and Yudenich in the last quarter of 1919, coupled with the rising tide of labor unrest and imperial disaffection, affected London deeply. Churchill, who had never enjoyed the full support of Lloyd George nor the complete backing of the Curzon school, was now branded an expensive failure. Lloyd George decided to try another tack. He would withdraw the blockade around Soviet Russia.

The blockade had become completely effective in January, 1919, when the Scandinavian countries, yielding to Allied pressure, withdrew their diplomatic missions from Moscow and expelled Litvinov and Vorovsky. Thereafter, for almost a year, Russia could neither buy nor sell abroad. She needed food, clothing, anaesthetics and medicines to cope with typhus and other epidemics; she was ready to pay for them with gold and goods, but the Allies insisted on the blockade. As late as October, 1919, the Paris Peace Conference requested the German Government to join the blockade and at the same time addressed notes to twelve neutral countries reminding them of their responsibility to maintain Russia's isolation with undiminished vigilance. Only three months later, on January 16, 1920, the Peace Conference, then nearing its natural death, lifted the blockade, and announced that it would grant facilities to the Russian co-operatives to import goods in exchange for grain and other commodities.

[5] Levitzky, later the leader of the Ukrainian Movement in Poland, gave the writer an explanation of his position in an interview which took place in Lemberg in November, 1926. This important subject will be dealt with in a subsequent chapter.

This significant development in the history of Soviet Russia followed upon an important exchange of view between the French and British Governments which, in turn, led to conversations and negotiations between English and Soviet statesmen on the subject of a trade agreement.

The trade discussions between Russia and England dovetail closely with the military movements in the Polish War. London's mood changed with the fortunes of the Red Army, for England sat on two stools. Lloyd George said "Thumbs down" one moment and "Thumbs up" the next.

At the Versailles Peace Conference the Premier advocated peace negotiations with Moscow. Then Kolchak began winning, and Lloyd George bet on the Admiral. But before long it became obvious that the "White hopes" were a hopeless lot and could never drive the Communists from their capital. At best, they would hold some salients of the Russian periphery.

Convinced of the permanence of the Soviet regime, Lloyd George's mind now turned to business. Britain's strength was her world trade. Russia represented a market. Manufacturers, merchants and workers clamored against the Government's impracticable policy towards Moscow. Lloyd George accordingly commenced to toy with the idea of a commercial understanding. This did not move him to discard the interventionist strategy of the Government whose chief he was. He continued to support it—or at least not to oppose it. But, while permitting it to run its expensive course, he prepared an alternative policy.

**THE FRENCH POLICY OF "PARALLEL LINES"**

The beginnings were small, yet it is interesting that they occurred as far back as September, 1919. The Peace Conference still sat. Anglo-French antagonism had not yet grown to full stature. The British Government consequently went through the gestures of consulting France on her attitude towards this important problem.

In notes dated September 25 and October 23, 1919, Downing Street inquired "what measures the French Government intended to take to establish its demands against Russia and to protect the rights and claims of its nationals." The Quai d'Orsay made reply November 3, and emphasized the expediency of co-operation on the part of the two governments with a view to establishing on parallel lines, and by similar methods of tabulation, a common statement based on corresponding principles of right which the two countries are justified in asserting against Russia.[6]

Great Britain, however, sought trade, and though for a time she made concessions to the French point of view, there was no intention in London to hang too tightly to Millerand's apron strings. Lloyd George had decided to bridge the gap between his Government and Lenin's. The appointment of Maxim Litvinov was opportune.

**LITVINOV'S ACTIVITIES ABROAD** On November 14, 1919, Litvinov received from Lenin credentials to negotiate peace with the succession States of the former Russian Empire and with the other countries. On the same day he was authorized to negotiate with the Powers for the exchange of prisoners. The next morning, Loenid Krassin, Commissar of Trade and Industry, appointed Litvinov his plenipotentiary in the Scandinavian countries. Thus equipped as a diplomat, humanitarian, and State merchant, Litvinov prepared for the West in an effort to establish a modus vivendi between the Communist and Capitalist worlds. Lenin felt that Russia's military victories against the Whites might have persuaded the Allies to enter into contact with Moscow.

Arrived in Copenhagen, Litvinov sent peace proposals to the Allied legations and endeavored to establish touch with the foreign diplomats in the Danish capital. Soon Litvinov was busily engaged conducting negotiations with a host of Powers.

As an opening wedge to a more ambitious program, the exchange of civil and military prisoners first occupied attention. Lloyd George had delegated O'Grady, a Labor M.P., to negotiate with Litvinov. Elaborate discussions completed, the two representatives signed an agreement on February 12, whereby England agreed to supply ships not only for her own prisoners in Russia but for those of all the Allies and neutrals as well. During the same period, Litvinov arranged the exchange of prisoners with

[6] *Correspondence between His Majesty's Government and the French Government respecting the Anglo-Russian Trade Agreement.* British White Paper. Russia No. 2 (1921). Cmd. 1456. (London, 1921).

the Scandinavian States, Austria, Hungary, Switzerland, Holland, Belgium, Italy, and France.

Simultaneously, Litvinov devoted considerable attention to the resumption of trade relations. On one occasion, he handed O'Grady a series of definite proposals. The M.P. returned the envelope unopened. Officially, his functions were limited to facilitating the exchange of prisoners. The unofficial O'Grady-Litvinov discussions, however, played an important role as ice-breaker for the subsequent Anglo-Russian trade agreement conferences and for the Supreme Council's decision of January 16, 1920, to lift the blockade.

This fiat sanctioned commercial transactions only with the Russian Co-operatives in order, apparently, to avoid contamination through direct dealings with the Bolsheviks. For Moscow, this was one of the best jokes in ages, and years later Chicherin could not refrain from a chuckle as he talked with me about it. The Soviets had taken over all the co-operatives and state-ified them. When the Peace Conference placed its stamp of approval on the co-operatives, therefore, the Bolsheviks, smiling at the folly of this self-delusion, appointed some of their best diplomats, Krassin, Litvinov, Nogin and Rozovsky, to negotiate with the Allies on behalf of the Centrosoyus, the central co-operative organization. They were to proceed to London. But London refused to receive Litvinov.

At the beginning of their diplomatic relations with the Western Powers the Bolsheviks resented personal discrimination against one of their plenipotentiaries. It was often assumed that Litvinov had been arrested and expelled from England for conducting propaganda. But he actually went to Brixton Jail in August, 1918, as a hostage for Lockhart who had been imprisoned in Moscow. On the door of Litvinov's cell hung a sign which read "Military Guest of His Majesty." Litvinov remained in confinement some eight or ten days. During that time and subsequently until he voluntarily departed for Bergen, Norway, Litvinov was never molested or deprived of the special diplomatic privileges he enjoyed in common with foreign envoys. Accordingly, the *Daily Mail's* agitation against Litvinov as an "agent" seemed little ground to Moscow for barring him from England in 1920, and instructions were given for the entire delegation to proceed to Copenhagen. If the Allies wished to negotiate with the Russian Co-operatives, that is, with the Soviet Government, they could send representatives to the Danish capital.

This was in April. In the same month a significant little conference took place at Geneva. At the suggestion of France, the neutrals met there to adopt a common policy towards commercial relations with Russia and to enter the united front contemplated by Paris. French diplomacy was eminently successful, and a resolution adopted on April 17, 1920, announced that the delegations of Denmark, Holland, Norway, Sweden and Switzerland were "convinced that it is of the greatest importance that the countries above mentioned should address their claims to Russia in the same style and showing a complete unity of opinion."[7] A larger and more important meeting was convoked at Paris on June 10, 1920. Ten countries, including England, were represented. This conference, too, agreed on the advisability of common action with respect to Russia and even outlined the constitution of an "International Office" which would undertake the task of settling debts and repairing damages.

Such being the dominant atmosphere, the Allies sent a mixed commission to Copenhagen in April, 1920, to deliberate with the Russians. But the varied wishes, policies, and designs of the several States, and the fact that France was too absorbed in the Polish offensive to be interested in Russian trade, made practical achievements unlikely. Mr. E. F. Wise, the chairman of the Allied commission, accordingly hinted that Lloyd George would welcome a personal chat with Krassin.

**CURZON PLEADS FOR WRANGEL** Here one glimpses an interesting interplay of forces in British domestic politics. It was April, 1920. The Bolsheviks had destroyed Denikin. A Soviet republic had been set up at Baku. Lord Curzon trembled lest the Russians step over into Persia or attack his garrison in Batum. He would not have been averse to the undermining of Russian strength by means of a joint attack by Poland and by

[7] *Correspondence between His Majesty's Government and the French Government respecting the Anglo-Russian Trade Agreement.* British White Paper. Russia No. 2 (1921). Cmd. 1456. (London, 1921).

Wrangel who had bottled himself up in the Crimea with the desperate remnants of Denikin's volunteer army. Perhaps, also, Curzon's mind harked back to the Palmerstonian days when Britain's avowed aim was the wresting of the Crimean Peninsula from the rule of the Czar.[8] At any rate, he intervened on behalf of Wrangel at a time when Lloyd George opposed such intervention and stood on the threshold of tête-à-tête negotiations with Soviet spokesmen.

On April 11 Curzon radioed Moscow urging the cessation of operations against Wrangel. The Bolsheviks made quick to welcome this message as the beginning of diplomatic relations (theretofore, at best, only trade and prisoners' negotiations had taken place), and suggested that Litvinov be invited to London for a discussion of the entire complex of outstanding problems between the two countries. Chicherin added another bit of characteristic Bolshevik "humor"; Curzon had requested an amnesty for Wrangel's forces. The Russians asked the release of the Hungarian Communists arrested when the Bela Kun regime fell on August 2, 1919.

In lieu of a reply, the British fleet began shelling Soviet Black Sea towns. Moscow protested and recalled England's declared intention of refraining from granting aid to Wrangel. There was an exchange of notes, but nothing definite developed. By this time Krassin was en route to London on Lloyd George's invitation.

All the while Poland hunted for allies. The possibility of finding them was narrowed by the Peace Conference's decision to lift the blockade, by a corresponding United States decision on March 7, 1920, and by Lloyd George's tactics.

Developments in the Baltics further prejudiced Poland's chances of success in this search. On February 2, 1920, the Soviet Government signed a treaty of peace with Estonia.

**SOVIET RUSSIA'S FIRST PEACE TREATY** It was Moscow's first peace agreement (Brest Litovsk was not an agreement). More than that—"our treaty with Estonia," as Chicherin put it in a report delivered at the February,

[8] Philip Guedalla: *Palmerston,* (London, 1926), p. 360.

1920, session of the Russian Central Executive Committee (VTZIK), "developed into a dress rehearsal, so to speak, for an understanding with the Entente, into the first attempt to break through the blockade, and into the first experiment in peaceful co-existence with bourgeois States." The peace with Estonia thus represents a milestone in the history of Soviet foreign affairs. Estonia became Russia's window opening toward Europe. Through it, for four whole months, went all of Bolshevik trade with the West.

The Bolshevik-Estonian pact strengthened the moderates in Britain who urged a more friendly strategy towards Russia. The Soviet negotiators proceeded on the assumption that the words spoken at Dorpat (Juriev), the conference town, were heard on the banks of the Thames and therefore not only paid Estonia 15,000,000 rubles in gold as indemnity but offered the little republic valuable concessions. The Communists wished to impress the world, more particularly England, with their conciliatory purposes.

At first they found this somewhat difficult, for the Estonians presented exorbitant demands. But the moment the Supreme Economic Council in Paris sanctioned trade with Russian Co-operatives, Estonia quickly deflated her claims and agreement became possible.

Estonia broke the ice. And since the succession countries sometimes had a tendency to hang together, the example of Estonia was soon followed by all the rest.

**LITHUANIA AND LATVIA FALL IN LINE** Lithuania needed no coaxing. The rumbling of Polish war drums terrified the tiny country which long ago suspected Poland of the desire to gobble her up and the Allies of favoring this. Foreign Minister Voldemaras accordingly suggested negotiations to Moscow on March 31 on condition of Soviet recognition of Lithuanian sovereignty over Vilna, Kovno, and Grodno. Peace conferences began in the Bolshevik capital on May 7; a treaty was signed on July 12. The Russians acceded to most of Kovno's territorial demands, above all, to the adhesion of Vilna, and agreed to pay Lithuania 3,000,000 gold rubles in consideration of her share in the State funds of the Czarist Government.

Latvia next fell in line. At the conference which opened in Moscow on April 16, both parties found themselves armed with the same scholarly volume by Pastor Billenstein on ethnographic distribution in the border regions. Disputes were therefore few. Moscow consented to grant Riga 4,000,000 gold rubles and a 100,000 desyatin lumber concession in settlement of all outstanding accounts. The treaty was signed on August 11 and led to the immediate establishment of normal diplomatic relationships.

**FINLAND SIGNS** Finland offered the greatest difficulties. She had territorial ambitions. In 1918, her delegates met Joffe in Berlin and asked him not only for the entire Murmansk Peninsula but for Petrograd and Petrozavodsk in Karelia as well. And Finland claimed Pechenga on the ground of a promise given by Alexander II to Finnish courtiers back in 1864, and, in particular, on the ground that Moscow had granted Pechenga to Soviet Finland in 1918.

Russia and Finland had been at war and hostilities continued as late as 1920. This too complicated negotiations, but after numerous preliminaries the final conference opened in Juriev on June 12—in the midst of the Polish War.

The Finns insisted on Pechenga. The Bolsheviks finally acquiesced; the Finns, in return, reconciled themselves to the loss of Eastern Karelia which had organized as a "Labor Commune" under the paternal attention of Lenin. These territorial adjustments paved the way to the general treaty of October 14, 1920.

Huge breaches had now been introduced into anti-Soviet ranks by the deflection of England, half-hearted though it remained, by the deflection of Estonia, and—in the spring of 1920—by the inclination of practically every one of the Baltic States, Poland's best prospects, to open negotiations with Moscow.

Warsaw, nevertheless, was sanguine. It had not shot its bolt against the new Russian republic. Poland could depend on some assistance; she could trust Petlura but knew his limited power. She was given to understand that Wrangel would seek to divert Bolshevik strength by activities in the Crimea and the Ukraine. The Georgian Mensheviks too had representatives in Warsaw; they were party friends of Pilsudski. Italy, according to Chicherin, sent airplanes and uniforms. But Poland's best bet, obviously, was France.[9]

On December 24, 1919, Clemenceau was thus quoted by the *New York Times:* "Not only will we not make peace, but we will not compromise with the Government of the Soviets." And on February 5, 1920, the *New York Times* said:

> France cannot get away from the theory, of which Marshal Foch is the advocate, that the Allies ought to send a Polish army to Moscow. She wants Rumania and Poland to stage a war against Lenin and Trotzky, not for the primary purpose of protecting Poland, but for the primary purpose of crushing the Soviets.

**RUMANIA FAILS POLAND** France attempted to mobilize Rumania. But Rumania felt too uneasy about her hold on Bessarabia and too anxious about the enmity of Hungary. Rumania, in fact, listened with one ear to Muscovite peace bids.

The French proposed to kill three birds with one stone: to settle Rumanian-Hungarian differences; to sign a profitable pact with Hungary; and to win Hungary for the anti-Soviet war of the Poles. The conversations with these ends in view were of course secret, but one able journalist, Robert Dell, suspected some such deal at the time it was being planned.

> The Quai d'Orsay [he wrote] is making desperate efforts to prevent Rumania from entering that alliance [Yugoslavia's defensive alliance against Hungary] and to reconcile her with Hungary. But the Rumanian Government has discovered that France has secretly promised to Hungary that part of Banat transferred to Rumania by the Treaty of Trianon.[1]

In consideration of such kindly treatment at the hand of Millerand, Hungary would, Mr. Dell wrote, place herself at the disposal of France and at the side of Poland against Soviet Russia.

What constituted a suspicion years ago is now an established fact. In 1927, Lord Rothermere, the British

[9] The nature and quantity of French aid to Poland in 1920 is discussed in detail in *Pologne, Pologne . . .* , by Olivier d'Etchegoyen, Paris, 1925, p. 300. M. d'Etchegoyen was attached to the French Military Mission in Poland.

[1] London *Nation,* September 11, 1920.

newspaper king, engaged in a campaign for the modification of the Treaty of Trianon to the advantage of Hungary. That could only be done at the expense of the members of the Little Entente, the special protégés of France. French journals therefore raised a cry of protest. To France the whole chain of Versailles treaties, of which Trianon forms a link, was inviolable. Whereupon, September 28, 1927, *Magyarsag,* a Budapest daily, published the contents of a memorandum dated April 15, 1920, and signed by Maurice Paleologue, General Secretary of the French Foreign Office, as well as by Sir Francis Barker for England, in which the essence of conversations was recorded that had proceeded between the French and Hungarian Governments on this complex of questions: Hungary would march an army of 100,000 men into Poland through Karpatho-Rus. France would equip and lead the force. Hungary would receive twelve important cities seized from her by Rumania. Nevertheless, Paris undertook to effect a peaceful settlement between Budapest and Bucharest. Incidentally, the French were to obtain a lease of Hungary's railroads. *Magyarsag* wished to show that France had not always regarded as sacred the boundaries fixed in the Treaty of Trianon.

Events now took an interesting turn. Diamandi, the Rumanian Minister in Paris, inquired of Paleologue whether the **Magyarsag's** revelations were true. Paleologue replied in the negative. This Budapest could not tolerate, and accordingly caused to be published a theretofore secret document dated June 24, 1920, in which Fouchet, the French envoy in Budapest, outlined to the Hungarian Foreign Minister, Count Teleki, the territorial changes proposed by France and England at the expense of Rumania.

Further doubts were impossible. France definitely did try to align Hungary with Poland against Russia in 1920, and planned to pay for the service with arbitrarily transferred towns and populations. She hoped Rumania could be rewarded in some other quarter.

Rumania suspected and held aloof. Hungary hesitated till it became too late. Mutual hostility paralyzed the potential power of both against the great Red enemy. Czecho-Slovakia, moreover, protested against the deal because it threatened to strengthen her enemy, Hungary, and involved the transportation of Hungarian troops through her territory.

**THE WAR COMMENCES** Though Rumania and Hungary failed her, Poland, counting on Petlura, on Wrangel and most on Millerand, opened the attack. Nobody declared war. But on April 26, 1920, Pilsudski issued a proclamation which began: "At my orders, the army of the Polish Republic has moved forward and penetrated deep into the Ukraine." The offensive thus heralded was quickly successful.

Kiev, the ancient Ukranian capital, fell into Polish hands on May 8. The capture of a city so far in the interior of the country so soon after the opening of the campaign meant that Pilsudski had met no resistance. The Bolsheviks were caught unprepared. They were still engaged by the remnants of Denikin's forces.

**BRUSILOV, BUDENNY, TUKHACHEVSKY** The Red Army, however, soon struck back.

A defensive war with Poland was a popular cause among almost all classes of the population, and even avowed anti-Bolsheviks enlisted in Soviet regiments. General Brusilov, of World-War fame, himself accepted an appointment in the Russian Staff and issued an appeal to White officers to volunteer their services. The Bolsheviks harnessed national sentiments to their own chariot.

The Red Army's blows were quick and sure. On June 13, the Pilsudski legions abandoned Kiev and turned their faces westward. Budenny's cavalry now threatened to cut the Polish lines at Zhitomir. His lancers sowed dismay within the enemy ranks and havoc throughout all Poland. Pilsudski himself declares that Budenny created the impression of some "legendary and invincible power."

At the same time, General Tukhachevsky, aged 27, commanding the main Soviet army of 150,000 men on the fields of Smolensk where Napoleon once destroyed the Czar's last bulwark on the road to Moscow, took the offensive. Success was immediate. The Polish Field Headquarters evacuated Minsk on July 11, and the important railway center of Vilna fell after stubborn fighting on July 14. The Polish retreat in the direction of Warsaw continued with undiminished haste, and the Red

Army, its right flank covered by friendly Lithuania, advanced an average of twenty kilometers a day between July 4 and July 20.

On July 4, too, the Polish southern army, which had taken Kiev and invested the Ukraine, rushed back to the Bug at a daily speed of some ten kilometers.

These rapid developments completely demoralized the Poles. "The Government trembled," says Pilsudski.[2] Tukhachevsky's march, the Marshal writes, represented "a terrible kaleidoscope." Even before it commenced, Budenny's slashing attacks had driven despair into the highest Polish army quarters, and Pilsudski relates how at a conference in Belvedere Palace during the last week of June, General Sheptitzki, his Chief-of-Staff, declared that the war had been lost and advised an immediate peace at any price.[3] Despair grew to hopeless panic when the youthful Tukhachevsky's Red flood began to move menacingly towards Warsaw.

At this juncture, Premier Grabski and Foreign Minister Patek rushed to Western Europe to beg on the doorstep of the Allies. The prospective philanthropists were England and France. But England was in the midst of serious conversations with Moscow representatives.

**KRASSIN'S "DECLARATION OF WAR"** E. F. Wise had asked Krassin to come to London. Krassin came in May, and first saw Lloyd George on the last of the month. It had been announced that these talks would be limited strictly to questions of trade. But the two statesmen went straight to the heart of the problem—to politics.

Krassin outlined business possibilities but suggested that Soviet Russia could scarcely concentrate on commercial operations while engaged in a war with Poland. Would not England, therefore, refrain from assisting Pilsudski? (The Poles were then in Kiev.)

Lloyd George thereupon enunciated a detailed political program. The Bolsheviks must not send agents into Asia Minor, Persia, Afghanistan, and India. They must not harm the British garrison in Batum or the Menshevik Government of Georgia. They must not fight against

[2] Joseph Pilsudski: *1920* (Moscow, 1926). The account in this chapter of the military events of the period follows Pilsudski's own description.
[3] *Ibid.*

Wrangel in the Crimea or against the Balkan States. They must not help Kemal Pasha. (The British Premier was preparing Greece for a war against Turkey.) In return for these "must nots" Lloyd George offered the Russians the privilege of buying and selling in England.

On June 9, Krassin met Lloyd George again, and read him a sternly-worded note which contained Moscow's reply to British demands. Krassin affirmed that the Bolsheviks were prepared to discuss Russia's foreign obligations. But there was also Allied indebtedness to be considered. Had not the Powers helped Kolchak, Denikin, etc.? The interests of the widowed and orphaned victims of that intervention seemed more pressing than the claims of the rich European investors in Russian enterprises. Allied operations had undermined Russia's economic strength. This circumstance must be thrown into the balance. At all events, there must first be a peace conference to regulate all political difficulties, a conference at which the Soviet Republic would enjoy equal rights.

Lloyd George interrupted the reading of Krassin's statement with the cry, "This is a declaration of war." Nevertheless, the talks continued.

It was now time for Downing Street to type a paper. This it did on July 1, and the memorandum, Lloyd George stated, required an answer before the Allied representatives met at Spa on July 7. The memorandum proposed four things:

(1) Mutual renunciation of hostile acts and hostile propaganda;

(2) Mutual repatriation of prisoners;

(3) Soviet recognition of Russia's indebtedness; and

(4) Exchange of trade delegations. The British Government would agree to anybody except Maxim Litvinov.

The Russians accepted these proposals in a brief note dated July 7, and for further negotiations delegated Leonid Krassin, Leo Kamenev, Vladimir Miliutin, and Theodore Rothstein. But the Moscow reply intimated that it preferred separate discussions with England because the inclusion of French problems would complicate the settlement with Britain.[4]

## LLOYD GEORGE DISCIPLINES A PRIME MINISTER

Lloyd George took Krassin's note with him to Spa.

[4] The foregoing account of the Lloyd George-Krassin talks is from official Soviet sources.

Here Allied and German statesmen were gathered to discuss current problems. Hither, therefore, repaired Grabski and Patek. The British Premier met the Polish Prime Minister alone on July 10. "Your army is at present on territory which does not appear to be Polish," the Welshman barked as he opened the conversation. Grabski could do nothing but affirm. At that time the Pilsudski legions still stood approximately 125 miles to the east of their own frontier.

Throughout the conversation, Lloyd George made

> all his observations in curt, peremptory tones. He dwelt with great emphasis on the fact that Poland was surrounded by enemies, Russian, German, and Czech. . . . He recalled to Mr. Grabski that Poland was still dependent on the Allied good will for a favorable settlement of the Upper Silesian, Eastern Galician, and Danzig questions. He effectively cowed the Polish Premier, who returned from the interview crestfallen and nervous.[5]

Grabski, however, could explain to the British statesman that his country's army was beginning a hasty retreat in thorough demoralization; that his "Government trembled"; that the Reds would soon be on Polish soil unless stopped by the Allies. This was a cogent argument. For however much Lloyd George may have desired trade, and however much he may have hated to help Poland while she acted under French dictation, he could not permit the Bolsheviks to overthrow the Polish Republic and thus establish contact with Germany.

The upshot of the confrontation of the two Premiers amounted to a promise that Britain would help if Poland's independence and integrity were threatened.

France was more friendly. "French policy, unlike ours [England's] was consistently and unambiguously pro-Polish," writes Mr. Kennedy. "France had, unlike Britain, encouraged Poland's original offensive in May."

Lloyd George could not remain unaffected by the warmth of French affections for Poland. Nor did Grabski's warning of a Bolshevik invasion leave him indifferent. Accordingly, the British commenced diplomatic intervention, and on July 11, the day after the Grabski-George tête-à-tête, Moscow was informed by radio that England would act if Poland were threatened, and suggesting that

[5] These impressions were given to Mr. A. L. Kennedy by Prince Sapieha, Polish Foreign Minister, five days after the interview and are published in his *Old Diplomacy for New,* p. 322.

the Bolsheviks send representatives to London to negotiate peace.

In the House of Commons, sarcastic comments were heard of the eternal readiness of the Allies to support invasions of Russian territory and, in contrast, their sudden pacifism when the Red Army gained a victory. The Kremlin, however, agreed to discuss peace terms with Poland direct, seeing no reason why the talks must take place under Anglo-French supervision. Nor did Moscow agree that the Baltic States, with all of which it was engaged in peace negotiations, be invited to a Polish-Russian conference. Finally, the proposal, contained in the radio, that Wrangel be given an armistice and that his troops be permitted to remain in the Crimea while he came to London to outline his terms, was summarily rejected.

These points of view were elaborated in Chicherin's reply of July 18. "Impertinent," said the French Premier on reading it. "Impudent," wrote Sir Henry Wilson.

Their wrath notwithstanding, Paris and London advised Poland to enter into direct negotiations—which she did on July 22. Representatives of the two belligerents met at Baranovitchi on the 1st of August to discuss an armistice and on the same day the Soviet delegation arrived in London. Lloyd George received Krassin and Kamenev on the 4th. While the three were thus closeted, Churchill came to the Premier's door. Lloyd George did not admit him (it would have been a strange confrontation), but sent out a note in which he wrote, "I have told them that if they don't stop their advance in Poland I shall order the British fleet into the Baltic at once."[6] The next day Winston Churchill told Sir Henry Wilson that Lloyd George was considering the question of giving military aid to Baron Wrangel.

**THE CRISIS** The situation became serious. If Poland crashed, anything might happen. The French were ready to act. The British threatened to act. London had not even waited for the Bolsheviks to sin. Before the Red Army violated Polish territory, a special official British mission, headed by Lord d'Abernon, ambassador in Berlin, and including Sir Maurice Hankey, Secretary of the Cabinet, and General Sir Percy Radcliffe, of the Imperial Staff,

[6] Callwell: *op. cit.*, p. 255.

arrived in Warsaw. On the same day, July 25, came a French committee led by M. Jusserand and counting as its most important member General Weygand, Chief of Foch's Staff. The French continued to send munitions, as did the British.

Meanwhile the Red forces pressed forward irresistibly. A second Curzon note of July 20 had warned the Bolsheviks not to advance beyond the so-called Curzon Line drawn by the Supreme Council on December 8, 1919. The frontier thus demarcated passed from Grodno to Bialostok, to Brest Litovsk, then south along the Bug River. The Russian Army approached this line on July 24, and crossed it on July 27. Brest Litovsk fell into its hands on August 1.

**FOREIGN LABOR HELPS** Everywhere in Europe the proletariat was aroused. Campaigns to prevent the forwarding of war materials to Poland developed in all transit countries. Working men in Czecho-Slovakia stopped and searched trains moving in the direction of the Polish frontier and refused to pass them when munitions were discovered. Danzig, the most important port for Polish traffic, witnessed stirring scenes. Longshoremen and sailors went on strike. Ships stood in the harbor for days upon days waiting for dockhands who sometimes did not come; and British troops had to be employed in the unloading of supplies. (Bonar Law admitted the fact in the House of Commons.)

During the latter half of July, Lloyd George inclined many degrees towards the French thesis of active hostility towards Bolshevism, and he even contemplated military assistance for Pilsudski and Wrangel. The British trade unions objected strenuously to such measures. They wanted no war on the Soviet Republic. Not only did they obstruct the shipment of munitions to Poland: they organized a serious movement to paralyze any effort the Government might undertake on behalf of the Warsaw regime.

**PEACE IS UNPOPULAR** The Poles did nothing to help Lloyd George. The meeting in Baranovitchi came to naught because the Warsaw representatives claimed they were unauthorized to discuss important questions. French advice was against peace. After the Baranovitchi failure, both sides agreed to meet in Minsk. The Poles, however, were not inclined to keep the appointment for August 10, and "only persistent pressure by the Allies' representatives in Warsaw kept them at their decision to proceed." Lord d'Abernon exerted most of the pressure, according to A. L. Kennedy.

Meanwhile, Lloyd George tried to persuade the French to agree to an armistice between Poland and Russia. But France still thought she could beat Bolshevism. Millerand, Foch, and Berthelot met Lloyd George at Lympne, England, to discuss the matter (August 8). The British Premier read the draft terms of a truce, but "Millerand," writes Sir Henry Wilson, who attended, "followed with a clear statement that he would not deal with the Bolsheviks, that their word and signature were worth nothing, and that they had neither honor nor laws."

The French succeeded in impressing the impressionable mind of Lloyd George. Negotiations were scheduled to begin at Minsk on August 10 or 11. Suppose these conversations failed through no reason of the Poles, but because the Russians submitted terms that prejudiced the independence of Poland. Then, Lloyd George finally agreed, he would help Warsaw with ammunition and advice, he would support Wrangel, and he would break off the trade discussions with Krassin and Kamenev.

On the 10th of August, an exciting day, the British Prime Minister was back in London. In the morning a Labor delegation waited on him. Bevin, of the Transport Workers' Union, spoke. "They had no hesitation in laying their cards on the table, and if war were carried on directly in support of Poland or indirectly . . . there would be a match set to explosive material, the result of which none of them could foresee."

All day the House of Commons talked Russia and Poland. At 5 P.M. Lloyd George appeared to make his statement on the results of the Lympne Conference in the mansion of Sir Philip Sassoon.

Mr. Asquith immediately took him to task. Suppose the negotiations at Minsk broke down as a result of Bolshevik harshness? But on such a matter there would always be two opinions. One party would blame the Russians for the failure; the other the Poles. For the rest, the ex-Premier launched into a bitter attack on Poland's aggressiveness and declared that he could well understand the Bolsheviks for wishing to guarantee their country against another attack by the Poles. Lord Robert Cecil, too, criticized the Poles as well as the British Government, which threatened to punish the Russians for invading Poland, but had not tried to stop Poland from invading Russia.

For hours the M.P.s continued the debate on the Russian-Polish War. While this battle of words continued, a document came into the Prime Minister's hand signed by Kamenev which contained a summary of the peace terms to be offered to the Poles by the Bolsheviks at Minsk. They appeared moderate. Lloyd George summoned the Cabinet from Parliament and took counsel with them. At 10 P.M. he and his ministers returned to the front bench where he read the Kamenev paper. The Polish Army was to be reduced to 60,000 plus a civilian militia. Arms not required by these units were to be surrendered to Russia. War industries were to be demobilized. War victims or their families in Poland would receive free farms. For its part, the Soviet Government agreed, as it had agreed in its note of July 18, to give Poland more land than foreseen by the Curzon Line decision.

These terms, according to Lloyd George, changed the situation, and he wired Poland to accept. But Kamenev had wilfully omitted from the document a most important item of the Bolshevik demands: that the civilian militia, numbering perhaps 200,000, would consist only of working men. This was revolutionary propaganda and not a peace term, for Moscow obviously knew that no bourgeois government would accept such a condition. The Russians, plainly, did not want peace on August 10. They were on the crest of a wave of victory, and of revolutionary enthusiasm. Throughout Soviet Russia resounded the cry, "*Dayosh Varshavu,*" "Warsaw must be taken." The Bolsheviks saw visions of a Soviet Poland. Kamenev wished to prevent British interference. He felt that Russia's relations with the British Government and even with the British proletariat were too weak to stand the announcement of the workers' militia demand.

Lloyd George's advice to the Poles to consent to Moscow's terms naturally angered the French. They reacted by recognizing Wrangel on August 11 as the Government of South Russia.

The terms which the Muscovites proposed to present for Polish signature at Minsk were intended not as a road to peace but as a stepping-stone to revolution. Yet, though the Poles knew nothing of these conditions, their delegates never appeared at Minsk on the 10th or 11th or thereafter. The fault for the non-occurrence of the Minsk armistice conference was therefore mutual. Neither Warsaw nor Moscow was interested in peace conferences. The one felt that dismal defeat could be stayed; and the other that glorious revolution waited in the offing.

The issue, accordingly, would be decided on the field of battle. Tukhachevsky's army continued its unopposed march on Warsaw while, to its rear, attempts were being made to lay the foundations of a Soviet regime in Poland.

### THE FAILURE TO MAKE WHITE POLAND RED

These attempts were directed by a "Polish Provisional Revolutionary Government" consisting of Felix Dzerzhinsky, the head of the Soviet Cheka, Julian Markhlevsky, Felix Kon, and Unschlicht, Assistant Commissar of War, who, however, did not participate because of an accident which detained him in hospital. The writer was able to discuss the activities of this "Provisional Government" of Poland with Kon, its only surviving member.

Dzerzhinsky, Markhlevsky, and Kon moved forward with the Red Army, organizing Soviets as they went. Their greatest success was at Bialostok, a large industrial center. Here the workers were with them; a government authority was organized, a daily newspaper published, innumerable proclamations issued,[7] and plans made for further expansion. But between Bialostok and Warsaw no big proletarian city lay across the Army's path. Poland's industry is concentrated in the capital, in Lodz, Lemberg, Cracow, but not in the district traversed by Tukhachevsky's forces. Thus Kon explained the failure of the Polish working class to seize the opportunity offered it by the presence of the Red Army. On the other hand, the confiscation of grain by the Bolshevik divisions who had been separated from their base in the rapid advance, antagonized the peasant population. The Bolsheviks lost the support of the village without gaining the support of the towns.

To be sure, one reason for the Red invasion, recognized

[7] These proclamations and other interesting material on the work of the "Revolutionary Government" are contained in a pamphlet written by the late editor of the Moscow *Izvestia,* I. Stepanov-Skvorzov, who was then a war correspondent, entitled *With the Red Army in Bourgeois Poland.* (Moscow, 1920).

in the House of Commons and elsewhere, was Russia's desire to destroy the Pilsudski's legions and prevent a resumption of aggressive activities. "Woods incompletely cut down quickly rise again," wrote General Serge Kamenev, Commander-in-Chief of the Red Army—the more so since French and British fertilizers were being supplied. The revolutionary motive, however, predominated. Moscow believed that the Polish masses would rise and overthrow their Government.

An invincible Red Army marching to the heart of Poland. Russia united behind it, with even the petty bourgeoisie supporting the Soviets. The German proletariat still tingling from its victory over the reactionary Kapp-Ludendorff putschists by means of a lightning general strike. The British trade unions threatening to call a general strike; staid English Labor leaders using revolutionary phrases. Europe not stabilized. Its World War wounds were open, and balm more distant than ever after the failure of the Peace Conference to establish real peace.

Under the circumstances, Bolsheviks would not be Bolsheviks if they did not wish and try to exploit the situation for revolutionary expansion.

**POLAND GIRDS HER LOINS** The Red Army's threat to Warsaw united the Polish bourgeoisie. Whole parties had been opposed to Pilsudski's invasion of the Ukraine. If the Russian forces had stopped at the Polish frontier, these internal difficulties, aggravated by a defeated, demoralized army and a discredited leadership, could conceivably have brought the regime to ruin. But the moment national territory felt the tramp of foreign troops, parties buried their swords, petty differences were forgotten, and a strong government emerged. On July 24, Grabski fell. V. Witos, a popular peasant leader, took his place.

Similarly, thousands rushed to the defense of Warsaw, especially the Polish student youth. If, from a narrow military view-point, these raw recruits constituted very inferior reinforcements, their spirit strengthened the morale of the Polish army.

These factors, taken cumulatively, determined the issue of the struggle between the two contending armies. No military move by Pilsudski and no assistance from French Staff generals can account for the precipitate retreat of the Red forces from the immediate vicinity of Warsaw. Pilsudski himself, who is not inclined to minimize his contribution, devotes many pages of *1920* to the details of his counter-maneuver in the latter fortnight of August, mentioning Weygand only very incidentally, but fails to create the impression that his activities alone forced the Russians to retire. The Red Army's advance towards Warsaw proved a military debacle because it was a political mistake.[8]

**LENIN ADMITS HIS ERROR** Lenin admitted the error in a conversation, during the winter of 1920, with Clara Zetkin, the German Communist leader, who noted his words faithfully.[9] Lenin said:

> Yes, what happened in Poland had to happen . . . our unbelievably brave, victorious advanced guard could receive no reinforcements from the infantry, could receive no munitions, not even stale bread and other prime necessities from the Polish peasantry and petty bourgeoisie. These . . . saw in the Red Army soldiers not brother-liberators but foes. . . . The Polish revolution on which we reckoned failed. The peasants and workers, stultified by the partisans of Pilsudski and Dashinsky, defended their class enemies, permitted our brave Red Army soldiers to die of starvation, and ambushed and killed them.
>
> . . . all the talents of Budenny and of other revolutionary army leaders could not counterbalance our military and technical shortcomings and, even less, our false political reckoning: our hope in the Polish revolution.
>
> Incidentally, [Lenin went on] Radek foretold how everything would happen. He warned us. I was terribly angry with him, and called him a defeatist—but in the main he has proved to be right. He knows the situation in the West better than we do and he is talented. He is very helpful to us. . . .
>
> Do you know that the conclusion of peace with Poland in the beginning met with serious opposition in much the same way as the conclusion of the Brest Litovsk Peace? I had to fight a hard battle because I favored the adoption of peace terms which

[8] Not a few Bolshevik military experts favored at least a temporary halt of the Red Army at Poland's ethnographic frontier which was reached about the end of July. Vladimir Melikov, of the Soviet War Academy presents the arguments of these experts in a forceful volume entitled *Marne, Vistula, Smyrna* (Moscow, 1928), in which, comparing the battle near Warsaw with the battle of the Marne in 1914, he claims that both von Kluck outside the French capital and Tukhachevsky outside the Polish capital should have stopped betimes to straighten their lines and reorganize their rears.

[9] Clara Zetkin: *Lenin* (Moscow, 1925).

were undoubtedly favorable to Poland and very difficult for us.

I myself think [Lenin continued] that our situation made it by no means necessary to conclude peace at any price. We could have carried on through the winter. But I believed that from a political point of view it was wiser to make concessions to the enemy. The temporary sacrifices of a bad peace seemed to me cheaper than the prolongation of war. In the end, our relations with Poland only gained from this. To be sure, pacifist slogans are only empty excuses. Nothing more than excuses. We are using the peace with Poland in order to descend upon Wrangel with all our strength and give him such a crashing blow that he leaves us alone for ever.

**"THE MIRACLE OF WARSAW"** Without the political miscalculations of the Bolshevik leaders, "The Miracle of Warsaw" would never have been possible. For the situation in the capital was so threatening that the foreigners decided to find a safer home, and on August 13, the d'Abernon Mission, the Jusserand Mission, and the entire diplomatic corps, with the exception of the Papal Nuncio Ratti who later became Pope Pius XI, left for Posen. In Warsaw all was chaos.

The main Soviet army, far from its base and fatigued by forced marching, stood north of Warsaw. But instead of converging on the capital, Tukhachevsky moved in the direction of Thorn and Danzig in order to cut off the Polish munition supplies. On the 15th the Red Army operated in the vicinity of Plotzk, Novo-Georgievsk, and Vlotslavsk, only about 50 miles from the edge of Warsaw.

Tukhachevsky, following the strategy of General Paskevitch-Irivansky who took Warsaw for the Czar in 1831, had made the Polish Corridor his main objective and there concentrated his maximum strength. Simultaneously, the Soviet encircling movement against Warsaw continued to develop. The Vistula was reached on August 16. The program, at this point, called for an uprising of the Warsaw proletariat. Dzerzhinsky, Markhlevsky, and Kon were at Vischkova, quartered in the house of a priest from which they could see the roofs of the capital. In an hour this Provisional Revolutionary Cabinet might have entered the Belvedere Palace in Warsaw and set up a Soviet regime.

As if political failure were not enough, the Bolshevik command was guilty of serious military blunders. In the first place, Tukhachevsky had directed his main force into a vacuum. He marched into an area where the enemy's troops were not. Pilsudski thus won relief from attack and obtained the possibility of freely maneuvering.

Budenny committed an equally disastrous mistake. Warsaw constituted the chief goal. With it Poland would have fallen into Bolshevik hands. The cavalry general, however, had permitted himself to be side-tracked in order to seize Lemberg, the center of East Galicia. Then on the 12th of August, he received orders to move on Warsaw. He was unable to obey the order.[1] And he had with him half of the Red Army in Poland. If he had proceeded to Warsaw, Pilsudski's counter-attack would have been impossible. But when the Poles actually commenced operations, they found neither Tukhachevsky nor Budenny. Pilsudski rushed around in an auto all day trying vainly to discover the enemy. He accordingly moved northward, and, advancing from the Ivangorod-Lublin line, took Sedletz on the 17th and Lomzha on the 22nd, thereby outflanking the Soviet Army.

Part of the Red force now stood in danger of capture, and accepted the only other alternative: internment in German East Prussia. Many units, however, fought their way through the Polish lines, suffering heavy losses of men and material in the process.

**THE WAR ENDS** Armistice negotiations now assumed a different hue. The Soviet Government abandoned the demands of Minsk, and took up a more conciliatory attitude. Peace talks opened in Riga on September 21. The Bolsheviks were anxious for a quick settlement. They wished to free their forces for the struggle with Wrangel. To gain an immediate peace, therefore, the Communist spokesmen at Riga offered Poland a better frontier than the Curzon Line—provided the proposal was accepted within ten days. The Russians even agreed to make a serious and perhaps over-hasty sacrifice of far-reaching international importance: they permitted the Poles to run a corridor between the Soviet republic and Lithuania.

These concessions formed the basis of a preliminary understanding on October 5 which was embodied seven days later in a preliminary treaty. During this intervening

[1] Stalin's role in this matter is described in RUSSIA REVISITED, by Louis Fischer. (New York, 1957).

week, the Poles, in defiance of the League of Nations, seized the city of Vilna from the Lithuanians—a move which the defeat of the Bolsheviks facilitated.

On March 18, 1921, the final Treaty of Riga was signed by Dombski for Poland and Joffe for Soviet Russia. It confirmed the territorial settlement of the previous October whereby the Poles obtained a frontier hundreds of miles to the east of the Curzon Line with approximately 3,600,000 inhabitants in the intervening area of whom no more than a million were Poles. (This frontier was more religious than ethnographic and coincides, roughly, with the division of the population into Roman Catholics and Greek Catholics.) It pledged mutual absention from aggression and intervention; it mutually guaranteed cultural and religious rights to national minorities; Moscow promised to return art and cultural treasures stolen from Poland by the Czar at the time of the division of 1772; Poland received 30,000,000 rubles as her share in the Romanov's gold reserve, and locomotives, etc., to the value of 29,-000,000 rubles as her share in the railway wealth of the monarchy. But though Moscow thus gave to Poland, as it had to the Baltic states, of the assets of the Empire, it agreed at Riga, as it had in the negotiations with the other secession countries, to liberate Poland from any responsibility for Russia's liabilities and foreign debts. . . . The treaty was ratified at Minsk on April 20.

**THE BARON IN THE BOTTLE** Baron General Peter von Wrangel was the last of the White Mohicans. The Bolsheviks entertained a special dislike for him because of the harm he had wrought by diverting their attention during the Polish War. When the Poles had agreed to peace, therefore, the Russians threw themselves upon the Baron with all their might and bitterness.

The British Government testified to its interest for Wrangel in Curzon's request for an amnesty and armistice for the General's forces. British ships carried Denikin officers from Georgian to Crimean ports. A British military mission under General Percy attended on Wrangel. On August 19, 1920, Wrangel, and his Chief of Staff, according to information presented to the House of Commons by Lieutenant-Commander Kenworthy,[2] were "offi-

[2] *Parliamentary Debates,* 1920, Vol. 133. August 9–October 29.

cially received and entertained at dinner on board His Majesty's ship *Ramillies*." . .

The following letter outlines England's Wrangel policy of neutrality in offense and aid in defense:

*June* 5, 1920.

YOUR EXCELLENCY,

I beg to inform you that I have received a message from my Commander-in-Chief, Admiral de Robeck, in which he directs that His Majesty's ships are not to take part in any offensive operations which you may commence against the Red forces, but that they may assist your forces in the event of a Red attack on the Crimea. I have the honour to remain, Sir,

Your Excellency's Obedient Servant,
(Signed) G. HOPE,
Rear-Admiral.

To His Excellency General Baron Wrangel,
Commander-in-Chief of the Armed Forces of South Russia.

French support assumed a more intense, less interrupted, and more enthusiastic character. France finally had found a White who, unlike Denikin, Kolchak, Chaikovsky, Miller, and Yudenich, was not a British puppet. She therefore took him to her bosom and nursed his "On to Moscow" dreams. But more direct motives played the decisive role. Wrangel's task consisted in diverting Bolshevik attention from the Poles. Their attacks would synchronize.

Moreover, since nobody in Western Europe at that time foresaw the possibility of a united Russia under Soviet rule, France planned her little independent-coal-and-iron state in the Ukraine. This constituted Wrangel's immediate goal.

When the remnant of Denikin's army sought refuge in the Crimea under Wrangel it was a poorly equipped body of stragglers. A few months later, it had been supplied with the wherewithal for a year's struggle against the Bolsheviks. The supplies came from England and France—much of the equipment later fell into the hands of the Red Army with the mark of the manufacturer easily discernible.

Wrangel commenced serious military operations in May, 1920, when the Bolsheviks were occupied with the invasion of the Poles. The Baron commanded thousands of experienced Kuban and Don horsemen. In fact, his army consisted almost entirely of highly trained and hardened Denikin officers for whom the Crimea was the last desperate stand. They were at bay with their backs to the deep sea.

The Soviets considered the Crimean southern front of secondary importance as compared to Poland. Wrangel, accordingly, was able to come out of the bottle and advance into the Ukraine in the direction of the Don coal region. He also attempted landings in the Kuban.

By August, the Muscovites began to take him seriously. That month a new cavalry division consisting largely of Communists was organized, and many troops were moved from the Polish theater. Airplanes played their role as well as armored trains—all of them of Entente manufacture and captured in the Denikin or Kolchak debacle.

During August and September, Wrangel continued to attack, but owing to dissensions in his own ranks and disaffection in his rear, success did not crown these efforts. Wrangel had an army 75,000 strong. Its equipment was excellent. He was able to demand the attention of no less than 150,000 Red soldiers, many of whom had to be transferred from the Polish front at the height of the campaign against Pilsudski. This was his outstanding service to the anti-Bolshevik cause.

The preliminary peace with the Poles in October permitted Red concentration against the White Crimean forces and on October 15 the Reds took the offensive. The Bolsheviks planned by a daring coup to capture the neck of the bottle and block Wrangel's retreat into the Crimea. A bloody, seven-day battle ensued in which the Baron lost 20,000 prisoners and much cannon. But Wrangel's strategy was superior to the Bolsheviks' and in the end he maintained his line of communication and withdrew into the flask with the Bolsheviks following hot on his heels.

One of the most sensational struggles of the Civil War now developed for the command of the neck of the bottle. Both sides fought heroically. Trench warfare was resorted to, and years later the writer could see the dug-outs and the heavy cannon on the surrounding fields. By the 10th of November, the entire Crimean peninsula had fallen into Soviet hands, and Wrangel hastily took to his ships, Russian and Allied ships, which carried his homeless, defeated warriors to Constantinople and various centers of the Balkans where for years they continued to exist as loose units ready to serve counter-revolutionary interests in any part of the world, be it Morocco, China, or the Soviet Union.

**THE END OF THE CIVIL WAR** The end of 1920 marked the end of the Russian internecine war. On February 7, 1920, Kolchak was executed in Irkutsk. His army thereupon ceased to play any important role. In March, 1920, the remnants of the Chaikovsky-Miller regime at Murmansk and Archangel liquidated or evacuated to England. During the same month, Denikin's army definitely suffered annihilation in the Caucasus, and on April 27 the Bolsheviks took the oil city of Baku.

Then started the war with Poland which closed with the Treaty of Riga in October, 1920. Almost immediately, Wrangel disappeared from the map of Soviet Russia. And then Makhno. By the beginning of 1921, therefore, only the Japanese remained in the Far East. But these in no way even remotely threatened the existence of the Soviet regime.

An era of peace now dawned for the Bolsheviks.

# 7

# THE ARMISTICE BETWEEN TWO WORLDS

THE VICTORIES and defeats of the Red Army governed the progress of trade negotiations in London for many months. At the moment of Bolshevik success, in July, 1920, Lloyd George and Kamenev stood nearest agreement. When Tukhachevsky threatened Warsaw, and London saw the possible necessity of more energetic intervention on behalf of the Poles, negotiations ceased. When the Russians retreated hastily to their own frontier or crossed the Prussian frontier, the British expelled Leo Kamenev on the ground of propaganda. This was on September 10.

But it was characteristic of Lloyd George that after making this concession to the Right, he proceeded to inject strong political flavor into the economic discussions with Krassin.

British public opinion, in October, 1920, urged the resumption of the Anglo-Russian conferences. Some people opposed. In Parliament it was submitted that British war prisoners in the Soviet Republic had not yet been repatriated. The charge of Bolshevik propaganda in the East was heard. But on October 26 Bonar Law announced for the Cabinet that "Trade relations have been renewed by other Governments, and this Government must do its best to get its share of the trade."

"Other countries are pinching all the trade," exclaimed Mr. W. Thorne from his seat in the Commons when he heard Bonar Law's statement. Nevertheless, the Government continued to refuse export licenses to British merchants and manufacturers. Though officially removed, the blockade remained in force.

The gold blockade was an even more disturbing fact.

Famine had spread over Russia. She had no grain to export. Her industries, exhausted by war requirements and other circumstances, produced practically nothing for foreign consumption. The Bolsheviks could therefore pay only with gold for their purchases abroad.

**BOLSHEVIK GOLD** The Czar's yellow metal reserve amounted to almost a billion dollars. Half of this huge treasure melted away during the World War and the Kerensky regime; about $500,000,000 remained when the Bolsheviks assumed power. In February, 1918, when the Germans, following on the temporary failure of the Brest Litovsk Conference, opened an offensive into Russia, the Bolsheviks hastily removed approximately 50 per cent of their gold reserve to Kazan. There it was captured by the Czecho-Slovaks, who subsequently transferred it to Kolchak.

The remaining $200,000,000 in bullion and coin lay safely within the vaults of the State Bank in Moscow and Petrograd. Sixty million dollars were foolishly paid to Germany in accordance with the Brest Litovsk supplementary treaties. On the other hand, $230,000,000 of the gold fund seized by the Czechs in Kazan fell into the Bolsheviks' hands when they overthrew Kolchak. Production added tiny quantities as did the confiscation of church ornaments for the relief of famine sufferers. So that, when the outside world began to think of business relations with Soviet Russia in 1920 and 1921, the State held in its possession roughly $500,000,000 of the precious metal.

Europe suffered from lack of gold. The Bolsheviks thought, accordingly, that the countries of Europe would raise a cry of joy the moment Moscow announced its readiness to ship gold. But a gold blockade began instead —largely on the initiative of France.

France, England, and the United States refused to accept Soviet gold, and the tactics of the powerful banks of these countries were adopted by the financial institutions of smaller nations. France threatened to seize Russian bullion on the high seas.

The Bolsheviks had to deal with petty merchants in Reval who naturally underpaid. Finally, on May 15, 1920, Krassin signed an agreement with the Swedish Nydqvist and Holm Trust according to which, on deposit of 25,-000,000 gold kronen, the Soviet Government would buy 100,000,000 kronen worth of locomotives and machines. This broke the blockade but by no means ended it, for the Powers, and especially France, continued to exert pressure against the shipping of Russian gold to Western countries.

Soviet orders now commenced to find ready bidders in Scandinavia, Germany, etc. Other countries were "pinching" the trade England might have obtained. Lloyd George felt the desire of British manufacturers to compete for the Russian market. But he first sounded the authorities in Paris. Paris, however, proposed common action, a united front, parallel lines, corresponding principles, and co-operation between Britain and France in dealing with Russia.

**A "DAWES PLAN" FOR RUSSIA** France, moreover, had a scheme whose general philosophy, outline, and even terminology, resemble, strangely enough, those of the Dawes Plan of later years. It was elaborated in a note from A. Briand dated November 25, 1920.[1]

The French Government stated that it "has no objection to the resumption of commercial relations between individuals." But since individuals in Soviet Russia were prevented by the state monopoly of foreign trade from engaging in business with foreign countries, the French Government was actually saying that it did have objection to commercial relations with the Russian republic.

Besides, Paris would make the resumption of commercial relations conditional upon the settlements of debts. There could be no dealings with a country which had repudiated its obligations. France seemed concerned less with the funding of Moscow's indebtedness than with the control of the economic fate of the country; hence her "Dawes Plan." Paris wanted "international supervision over or intervention in the affairs of Russia"—"a delicate problem."

Knowing that the Soviet Government was agreeable to a debt settlement, the French submitted that "without

[1] *Correspondence between His Majesty's Government and the French Government respecting the Anglo-Russian Trade Agreement.* British White Paper. Russia, No. 2 (1921). Cmd. 1456. (London, 1921).

effective guarantees, without a special organization charged to direct the execution of the engagements incurred, all assurances might remain a dead letter."

The special international organization would:

"Centralize the operations of conversion and transfer."

"Organize and employ, on the widest possible scale, payment by means of compensation in kind."

"Whenever it would be practicable," continued the French note, "reparation would be carried out by the restoration and restitution in their entirety of the impaired property, rights and interests, in their original shape."

But if properties could not be restored, or if the actual owner refused such restoration, indemnification would be effected by "the assignment of unworked assets or of concessions" or by "the surrender of securities" equal in value to the sum lost by the foreign capitalist through expropriation.

France did not want money. "Indemnification must therefore be sought particularly by methods which foster the exploitation of the resources of the country." The French Government aimed at the peaceful conquest of Russia's resources. The psychology which lay beneath this plan never forsook the French. In modified and unmodified form, it reappeared at the Genoa Conference and at subsequent direct discussions between Moscow and Paris.

The British, however, paid no attention to what seemed to them a fantastic scheme. They did not even answer this note until June 24, 1921, three months after the conclusion of the Anglo-Russian Trade Agreement, when Hardinge of Penshurst speaking for Curzon of Kedleston stated that "His Majesty's Government are unable to agree . . . that the resumption of trade with Russia and the recognition of Russian debts should not be dealt with independently." As to the "Dawes Plan," the note declared that "these principles are so general in nature that . . . considerable discussion will be required as to the details of the procedure whereby they may be given practical effect."

Meanwhile the statesmen in London proceeded with their negotiations with Krassin. The chief incentive was the desire to prevent other countries from "pinching" all the trade; the chief obstacle was fear lest the Bolsheviks conduct propaganda along the outposts of the British Empire in Central Asia.

**THE BOLSHEVIKS SUMMON ISLAM TO A HOLY WAR** Bolshevik propaganda in the East took concrete form in a unique assembly convened in Baku during September, 1920. Zinoviev and Radek, President and Secretary of the Comintern, and Bela Kun came from Moscow to inspire this "Congress of the Peoples of the East." It was an odd gathering, a museum of Oriental costumes, a Babel of tongues, a confusion of ideas and aims.[2]

Lenin once upon a time took pencil in hand and figured out that the United States, Britain, France, and Japan with a population of about one-quarter billion were ruling countries and colonies with a population of two and a half billion. This is the lesson Lenin's disciples brought to the Baku congress.

Soviet supporters pointed to the freedom and cultural autonomy granted to the Tartars, the Bashkirs, the Kirghizi and all other nationalities in Russia. Other peoples, they urged, must strive towards a similar goal.

The Comintern's policy had been outlined by Zinoviev on the evening of September 1. It was past midnight when his address drew to a dramatic close. "The Communist International," he announced, "turns to-day to the peoples of the East and says to them: 'Brothers, we summon you to a Holy War first of all against British Imperialism.' " "Jehad, Jehad," the delegates thundered. Every man in the hall jumped to his feet. Studded daggers were drawn, Damascan swords unsheathed, revolvers brought out of their holsters and lifted on high while their owners yelled "We swear," "We swear."

Despite this oath of arms, the Holy War was conceived as a non-military offensive directed by the Council of Propaganda and Action created by the Congress to match the Council of Action of the British trade unions. "The infantry of the East would reinforce the cavalry of the West."

The eastern nations which concerned the Congress above all were Turkey, Persia, Afghanistan, and India. In these, England's role was most important. Therefore Brit-

[2] *Stenographic Record of the Congress at Baku of the Peoples of the East.* (Moscow, 1920).

ish imperialism stood in the foreground of the assembly's attention, while France received only secondary consideration.

This meeting went down into history as the "First Congress of the Peoples of the East." It established a permanent organization on the assumption that annual or periodical gatherings would follow. But the first congress remained the only congress. The establishment of normal diplomatic relations between the Governments of Eastern countries and the Government of Russia began to take precedence over the relations between the revolutionary movements in Eastern countries and the revolutionary movement of Russia. Comintern psychology receded though it fought for its place in the sun, and, more and more, revolutionary possibilities were sacrificed to the Soviets' desire for treaty contacts with non-revolutionary states.

**AFGHANISTAN** A Young Afghan movement had developed during the World War which was anti-British and progressive, and which had won the support of the Emir's third son Amanullah. Some of the Young Afghans showed sympathies for a German military mission which came to Kabul in 1916, and Emir Habibullah accordingly sentenced Amanullah to death. The prince evaded the executioner. In February, 1919, the Emir was killed by an unknown hand, although rumor implicated Nadir Khan, Amanullah's uncle. After the murder, Amanullah reappeared on the political scene, and his mother persuaded the troops to pronounce him king.

Amanullah had Pan-Islamist sympathies. But above all his inspiration came from the Indian revolutionary movement. He was a modernist. He wished to make his country sovereign in foreign affairs, and to introduce content into the nominal independence of his Government in internal affairs. Under the circumstances, Amanullah turned to Moscow. This he did in a flowery letter of greeting addressed to "His High-Born Mr. President of the Great Russian Republic" on April 21, 1919. Lenin replied from Moscow on May 27, 1919, congratulating the "independent Afghan people heroically defending itself against foreign oppressors," and suggesting the exchange of diplomatic officers as opening "wide possibilities for mutual aid against any attack by foreign bandits on the freedom of others."

The Bolsheviks were too occupied with their own Civil War to grant assistance of a practical military nature. Moreover, no geographic contact then existed between Afghanistan and Soviet Russia. When the Third Afghan War commenced in May, 1919, therefore, Amanullah faced the foe alone. Nevertheless, the Afghans won, though the month's struggle ended with British troops on Afghan soil. England required every soldier and every ounce of energy to cope with her difficulties in Ireland, Egypt, Iraq, and India. The war with Afghanistan, in which Amanullah received encouragement from Hindu nationalists, created much ferment in India. The army, too, had become restive. London consequently withdrew from the conflict and agreed, in the preliminary peace treaty of August 8, 1919, to return Afghanistan her complete independence and her freedom of action in foreign as well as in domestic affairs.

Conversations with a view to the establishment of diplomatic relations commenced immediately in Kabul and Moscow. Russia's attitude was elaborated in a letter of November 27, 1919, from Lenin to "His Majesty the Emir of Afghanistan.[3] Lenin wished to encourage the Pan-Islamic tendencies of Amanullah Khan.

At present, [he wrote] flourishing Afghanistan is the only independent Moslem state in the world, and fate sends the Afghan people the great historic task of uniting about itself all enslaved Mohammedan peoples and leading them on the road to freedom and independence.

Then as to Great Britain:

"The Workers' and Peasants' Government of Russia instructs its embassy in Afghanistan," said the Bolshevik Premier, "to engage in discussions with the Government of the Afghan people with a view to the conclusion of trade and other friendly agreements the purpose of which is not only the buttressing of good neighborly relations in the best interests of both nations, but together with Afghanistan the joint struggle against the most rapacious imperialistic government on earth—Great Britain, the in-

[3] Copies of this and the Lenin letter cited above were obtained by the writer from the Soviet State Archives. Neither has ever before been published in any language.

trigues of which, as you correctly point out in you letter,[4] have hitherto disturbed the peaceful and unhindered development of the Afghan people and separated it from its closest neighbors.

"In a conference with your extraordinary ambassador, the worthy Mohammed Wali Khan," Lenin continued, "I learned that you are prepared to enter into negotiations in Kabul on the question of a treaty of friendship and also that the Afghan people wishes to receive military aid against England from the Russian people. The Workers' and Peasants' Government is inclined to grant such assistance on the widest scale to the Afghan nation, and, what is more, to repair the injustice done by the former Government of the Russian Czars . . . by adjusting the Soviet-Afghan frontier so as to add to the territory of Afghanistan at the expense of Russia."

Quiet negotiations continued, and on February 28, 1921, the Soviet-Afghan Treaty was signed in Moscow.

**PERSIA** At Brest Litovsk the Russians promised to evacuate the forces that had been stationed in Persia by the Czarist Government. On January 14, 1918, Trotzky, as Commissar for Foreign Affairs, informed Teheran that the Bolsheviks no longer considered the one-sided treaty of 1907 binding and were prepared to annul all special privileges granted previous Russian Governments by Persia.

These measures encouraged Persian statesmen to ask similar concessions from Great Britain. The Shah's ministers accordingly dispatched a note to London in February, 1919, demanding the nullification of the 1907 agreement, a revision of the customs settlement of 1903, and Persian participation in the Versailles Peace Conference. This move was resented in London, and instead of surrendering her "sphere of influence" in South Persia, Great Britain proceeded to occupy the former Russian "sphere of influence" in North Persia, and the Dunsterforce established itself in Enzeli. Persian Cabinets now began to come and go with sensational rapidity. The whole country was held under control by British rifles—"a Persia picketed on all sides with British forces," says Lord Curzon's authorized

[4] This Lenin communication, the draft of which was prepared by Karakhan, is a reply to a message from Amanullah brought to Moscow by Mohammed Wali Khan.

biographer[5]—military, political and financial control by Great Britain. In accordance with the terms of the Anglo-Persian agreement of August, 1919, a British military mission arrived in the country in December, 1919, and three months later the financial mission of Armitage Smith and Balfour appeared on the scene to take charge of Persian fiscal affairs.

Beginning with the spring of 1919, England used Persia as a spring-board for attacks on Russia. Persia was the base for the British and Indian troops which operated against the Bolsheviks in Turkestan and Baku. Moreover, British control in Persia enabled the Denikin flotilla to operate freely in the Caspian under the supreme command of Admiral Norris.

The Red Army entered Baku on April 27, 1920, whereupon the Denikin squadron fled to the Persian port of Enzeli with the Red Fleet, commanded by F. Raskolnikov, hot on its heels. Raskolnikov was a fiery spirit who, after his capture in a Baltic naval battle, had been complimented by England's insistence on exchanging him for no less than eighteen officers.

Raskalnikov arrived outside Enzeli, warned the Persian authorities that he was about to shell the town, and then proceeded to bombard Denikin's vessels and the British military positions on land. Having thus crowned his pursuit with victory, Raskolnikov entrenched himself in the Persian province of Ghilan in order to prevent the return of the British from Kasvin. The Shah felt a new man when he heard the firing in Ghilan, he told Theordore A. Rothstein, the Soviet ambassador in Teheran, on May 26, 1921, and the Medjelis, he added, was encouraged to refuse the ratification of the Anglo-Persian Treaty.[6]

But instead of evacuating after a normal period of occupation, Communists rushed across the sea from Baku, and before long a so-called Soviet Republic of Ghilan was established with headquarters in Enzeli and Resht. The Persian Government in Teheran naturally protested against such infringement of its territorial integrity, and in reply Chicherin tried to explain that this was merely a local incident. The fact of the matter is that the Caucasian

[5] The Earl of Ronaldshay: *The Life of Lord Curzon.* (London, 1928). III, 212.

[6] Mr. Rothstein read to the writer from this chapter in his diary.

comrades had got out of hand; Moscow ordered them to withdraw from Persia, but they remained. Indeed, the "Soviet Republic of Ghilan" continued to exist until October, 1921. In June of that year it even commenced, in concert with prominent Communists in Georgia, to march on Teheran, and both Moscow and Theodore A. Rothstein had to exert unusual pressure to force them to desist from their plan.[7]

This adventure disturbed Soviet-Persian relations but could not destroy the cordial atmosphere established by Moscow's policy toward Teheran.

Soviet Russia's policy toward Persia was clearly outlined on June 26, 1919, in a note from Karakhan to the Persian Government which was delivered to the Shah's minister by Kolomietzev, Soviet representative in Persia before official recognition had taken place. This document[8] is significant because it defined in 1919 the principles and concessions accepted in the treaty of 1921. The Soviet Government, said the note, wished to make good the damage done by the former Czarist State, and hoped that Teheran would find means of collecting compensation for corresponding damage by the "imperialist Government of England."

Concretely Moscow announced that, (1) all Persian debts to the Czarist Government were annulled, (2) Russian interference in Persia's income from customs, post and telegraph was at an end, (3) all Russian official and private concessions in Persia were void, (4) the Russian Bank in Persia with all its inventory, branches, land, etc., was declared the property of the Persian people, (5) all the roads, electric stations, port equipment, railway lines, etc., built and owned by Russia were transferred to the Persian nation, and (6) capitulations ceased to exist.

Persia, however, was in no position to reply to this gesture. For in June, 1919, the country had been completely occupied by Britain, a Czarist consul still lived in the Russian Legation, and Kolomietzev barely escaped from Teheran with his life. (He was later killed by Whites on an island in the Caspian.) The Shah's Government was tied hand and foot. It exercised no freedom of action in

[7] Further details on this episode will be found in *Men and Politics. An Autobiography*. by Louis Fischer. (New York, 1941).

[8] A copy of the note was supplied to the writer from the archives of the Soviet Commissariat of Foreign Affairs.

foreign affairs, and a resumption of relations with Russia was unthinkable.

Only when the Caucasus was cleared of the British, when Raskolnikov drove the English forces out of North Persia, and when, for this reason as well as out of a variety of larger imperial considerations, the British military decided to retire to Kasvin—at about the time of the evacuation of Batum—only then, in July, 1920, did a new Cabinet come to power in Teheran which could dare enter into negotiations with Soviet Russia. A Persian envoy appeared in Moscow on October 25, 1920.

The negotiations proceeded so smoothly and quickly that on November 28 the Soviet Government appointed Theodore A. Rothstein its plenipotentiary representative in Teheran.

England's prestige rapidly waned with the withdrawal of British troops. The situation thus created encouraged nationalist forces in Persia, and on February 21, Riza Khan, then War Minister, but later self-appointed Shah, engineered a coup d'état and set up a government. This Cabinet immediately announced the abrogation of the one-sided Anglo-Persian "Agreement" of August, 1919, and twenty-four hours later (February 26, 1921) its representative in Moscow signed the Soviet-Persian Treaty.

The treaty[9] opened with a fiery declaration in which Moscow condemned and rejected the aggressive policy of the Czarist regime, and promised to refrain from any interference with the internal affairs of Persia. Nevertheless, it was agreed that if any third Power (read Great Britain) were to violate Persian territory with a view to using it as a base for an attack upon Soviet Russia, Russian troops might temporarily assume positions on Persian soil.

**PROPAGANDA** These negotiations between Soviet Russia on the one hand and Persia and Afghanistan on the other were conducted simultaneously with the London conversations between the British and Krassin, which, for the most part, partook of a commercial character. But the moment a political issue arose, Lloyd George lifted the situation out of the hands of Sir Robert Horne and himself wrestled with the bear.

[9] Official Russian text, see *International Politics,* Part III. A collection of treaties, notes and declarations by Kluchnikov and Sabanin. (Moscow, 1928).

The whole complex of political questions was condensed into one word: "Propaganda." . . . In the autumn of 1920, a group of Whites active in London, conceived the idea of printing imitation copies of the Moscow Bolshevik daily *Pravda* and shipping them into Soviet Russia for anti-Communist agitational purposes. British Government institutions lent their aid to this project, and in the course of events the matter came up for discussion in the House of Commons. Replying to a question directed to the Home Secretary, Mr. Shortt admitted on March 3, 1921, that the Director of Intelligence "assisted them [the Whites—L.F.] to the extent of arranging for the removal of the English printer's name from the news-sheets and for their being forwarded to an address in one of the countries bordering on Russia." To match this aid on the part of England to the enemies of the Soviet State, there stands the charge that Kamenev brought diamonds into the United Kingdom which he passed on to the London Labor newspaper, *The Daily Herald*. The propaganda shoe, in other words, fitted the other foot as well.

**THE LAST PHASE** While pro-Soviet Members of Parliament and newspapers stressed the importance of Russian trade as a partial cure for British unemployment, opponents submitted that Russia had no money, that her economy was destroyed, and that trade would not develop rapidly enough to solve Britain's domestic problems. Moreover, the question of "stolen oil" then arose for the first time. "Will it be competent for Soviet Russia," asked Major Barnett on November 22, 1920,[1] "to barter in exchange for British manufactured goods petroleum stolen from British oil companies at Baku?"

Exaggerated claims were made. Sir Donald Maclean stated in the House of Commons[2] that "it is much more beneficial to us to trade with Russia than with the United States." Several authorities were disturbed by reports of a tremendous lumber and mining concession granted by Moscow to the American, Washington Vanderlip, in North-Eastern Siberia and Kamchatka. Rumor had it that the Bolsheviks offered contracts for the exploitation of the oilfields of Grosni and Baku.

All these factors tipped the balance in favor of the

[1] *Parliamentary Debates,* 1920, Vol. 135.
[2] *Ibid.,* 1921, Vol. 138.

conclusion of the agreement. England was in the throes of an economic depression. When Krassin, accordingly, placed orders for textiles in Manchester, or arranged with the Armstrong Company for the complete overhauling of 1,500 locomotives in a period of five years, he was making propaganda for a quick settlement between Moscow and London. Krassin himself believed that the circumstance which probably ended all the delays was the contract given German factories in March, 1921, for the delivery to Russia of 600 locomotives. "Quite likely this very circumstance—the fear of losing big orders, impelled the British Government to instruct Sir Robert Horne to sign the Russian-English Treaty of March 16, 1921."[3]

**THE ANGLO-RUSSIAN TRADE AGREEMENT** The preamble of the Anglo-Russian Commercial Treaty[4] made it plain that the two signatory Powers considered it a "preliminary agreement. . . ." But even the preliminary treaty was subject to the mutual renunciation of hostile action and official propaganda. More particularly, the Russian Soviet Government promised to refrain "from any attempt by military or diplomatic or any other form of action or propaganda to encourage any of the peoples of Asia in any form of hostile action against British interests or the British Empire, especially in India and in the Independent State of Afghanistan." The British Government gave a similar undertaking "in respect of the countries which formed part of the former Russian Empire and which have now become independent. . . ."

Then followed a mutual renunciation, for all practical purposes a British renunciation, of the policy of blockade or of otherwise obstructing the resumption of trade.

The treaty provided for the exchange of semi-diplomatic and commercial representatives, and in Article IX—the most important in the agreement—created the basis of British-Russian trade by pledging the British Government "not to initiate any steps with a view to attach or to take possession of any gold, funds, securities or commodities not being articles identifiable as the property of the British Government which may be exported from Russia. . . ." Further, the Lloyd George Cabinet promised not to discriminate in any way against the importation, transforma-

[3] L. B. Krassin: *Questions of Foreign Trade,* Moscow, 1928.
[4] Kluchnikov and Sabanin, *op. cit.,* Pt. III.

tion or disposal of precious metals (gold or silver) brought into the United Kingdom from Soviet Russia.

The agreement between Communist Russia and Capitalist England brought about a radical change in Moscow's relations to other countries.

> The British trade treaty [wrote Krassin] was a signal to the majority of European states, and towards the end of 1921 Soviet Russia had negotiated commercial agreements and treaties with Sweden, England, Germany, Finland, Estonia, Latvia, Lithuania, Poland, Norway, Czecho-Slovakia, Austria, and Italy. Commercial representations in Constantinople, Angora, Teheran, and China opened the possibility of establishing some trade connections with the East.

The blockade had been broken. Soviet Russia began to make her first feeble steps in the direction of a normal economic life.

**A MILESTONE IN SOVIET HISTORY** The signing of the Anglo-Russian Trade Agreement divides the Bolshevik revolution, as far as foreign affairs are concerned, into two periods. It was a truce between two worlds. It said (in effect): "We are natural enemies. We hate one another. But, though we tried, we failed to destroy one another. The struggle cannot continue. Let us call a halt."

Such an armistice demanded a mutual grounding of arms. Therefore, the bourgeois state indicated its willingness to refrain from armed attacks on the Soviet Republic and expected in return that the Bolsheviks would stop their propaganda attacks on the British Empire.

For years Britain had been engaged in the serious business of overthrowing the Soviet Government by means of armies, guns, navies, etc. Now she guaranteed herself against attempts by Communists to overthrow the British Government with leaflets, soapbox orators, newspapers, etc.

Here was the old Lion *v.* Bear competition, with the lion a bit more worried because the bear had a new weapon. Governments can send armies to cope with armies. But they cannot so easily cancel unequal treaties or surrender capitulation privileges.

The most successful chapter of Bolshevik propaganda in Persia was the Soviet Government's cancellation of Russia's special interests in Persia, the return of Russian concessions, and the negotiation of a fair treaty. The worst bit of Bolshevik propaganda in Afghanistan was Moscow's early recognition of Afghan independence.

Such propaganda, of course, nobody could prohibit to the Soviet State. Yet it was easy and very effective.

**THE COMMUNIST INTERNATIONAL AND THE SOVIET GOVERNMENT** The question whether the Soviet Government is organizationally connected with the Communist International is of little practical importance until and unless the Soviet Republic admits the fact. The admission is, however, not likely to be forthcoming.

Of tremendous historic significance, on the other hand, is the influence of Comintern psychology on the Soviet Government. In 1917, at the time of the establishment of the Bolshevik regime and even before the Comintern had been founded, the Soviet Government never conceived of the possibility of insular existence in a capitalist sea. The Russian Revolution would be the beginning of the world revolution. Bolsheviks were then ready to sacrifice the best interests of the Red regime in Russia for the sake of the creation of Red regimes elsewhere. This was the essence of Soviet policy at Brest Litovsk. Only the realization, thanks to the hammering logic of Lenin, that the situation abroad did not warrant sanguine revolutionary hopes, impelled the Communist Party to accept a peace that would safeguard the national revolution in Russia instead of furthering an upheaval throughout Europe.

This appreciation of the importance of the Russian Revolution rose with the increasing stability of the Bolsheviks' regime and the reduction of revolutionary possibilities outside. Some leading Communists, especially among those directly responsible for the execution of foreign policy, despaired of world revolution the moment the World War Armistice was signed. But 1919 brought renewed hope. The disturbed state of Europe, the setting up of Soviet authority in Bavaria and Hungary, and the difficulties facing the diplomats at Paris, seemed to improve the prospects of a mass uprising. And the Bolsheviks, who now saw themselves surrounded by White and Allied armies and who knew the awful economic condition of their country, felt that revolution in the West was the only salvation of the revolution in Russia. Therefore the special concern for the Baltic States and the desire to establish military contact with Bela Kun in Budapest. Yet already at that time another tendency existed at Moscow which, inspired with greater confidence in the regime, insisted that the interests of the Russian Revolution were paramount. When the Soviets in Russia could be successfully defended against attack by a concentration of energy, the weakening of that defense for the sake of carrying the revolution to other lands was considered a luxury.

Then came the Polish War. Originally, for the Bolsheviks, it was a war of defense. But it developed, when the Red Army entered Polish territory, into an attempt to carry revolution to Poland and perhaps Germany. The Bolsheviks could not resist the temptation of planting the Red Flag in Warsaw which the advance of their army offered them.

The Soviet-Polish War was a setback for the world-revolutionary tendency in Soviet politics. The year 1920 marks the beginning of World Revolutionary diminuendo and of National Revolutionary crescendo. The first did not disappear altogether nor did the second capture control. But a dynamic situation developed in which the one gave way while the other gained ground. This is a generalization. Sometimes, Comintern psychology became uppermost. Yet the larger tendency was in the other direction.

**THE "ARMISTICE"** The Western world's condescension to peaceful symbiosis with the Soviet regime arose (1) from that world's failure to destroy the Soviet regime by force, and (2) from the economic necessity of exploiting business opportunities latent in Russia.

The Soviet regime's condescension to peaceful co-existence with the Western world arose (1) from the failure of the international revolution to eventuate, and (2) from the miserable economic situation in Soviet Russia.

From 1918 to the spring of 1921 Russia had suffered under Military Communism. Its drastic measures had enabled the Bolsheviks to carry the war against the Whites and the Poles to a successful close. Yet these very measures impoverished the country, and introduced economic chaos and political disaffection.

**NEP** Accordingly, when the hostilities against Poland and Wrangel ceased, Lenin began to plan the elimination of Military Communism. Discussion within Communist Party ranks on this question had proceeded for several months when matters came to a head as a result of an insurrection of the peasant-sailors in the fortress of Kronstadt which commands the sea entrance to Petrograd, and by revolts in Tambov and other provinces. Clearly, Bolshevik relations with the village needed quick doctoring, and Lenin decided to administer a radical cure. The medicine was called NEP.

The New Economic Policy, or NEP, announced in March, 1921, represented a sharp departure from previous methods. Its basic innovation was the legalization of domestic trading by individuals. The peasants won the right to sell their grain and to buy manufactured goods with the proceeds.

The Leninist strategy proposed to lead industry over the NEP bridge of State capitalism towards real Communism, and, while easing the peasant situation through the re-introduction of private trade, to move the village slowly forward in the direction of socialization by means of co-operatives and the mechanization of agriculture. At the same time, Lenin's policy of concessions to foreign capitalists, adumbrated as early as 1919, now received more serious attention in Moscow.

Just as the recession of Comintern psychology signified a political retirement after the successful but costly Civil War, so the NEP represented a shifting of the economic front. Both these changes date approximately from the spring of 1921, and, when coupled with the Anglo-Russian Trade Agreement and Soviet treaties with Afghanistan and Persia of February–March, 1921, constitute an important turning-point in the history of Soviet internal conditions and of Bolshevik foreign affairs.

All these reforms and events seemed to Western Europe to indicate that the Communists were either ready to capitulate and come to terms with foreign capital, or that a bit of pressure, some kindness, and some promises could bring them to such a state of mind. Hence the Genoa Conference of April, 1922.

# 8

# AMERICA, JAPAN, AND SOVIET RUSSIA

FROM THE beginning, Moscow believed that America's anti-Soviet sentiments were less deep-seated than those of the other Powers, and that the Far Eastern situation might induce a more cordial relationship in Washington toward the Government of Russia.

Special treatment was therefore accorded American business interests. The properties of the International Harvester Company, the Westinghouse Brake Company, and the Singer Sewing Machine Company, were not confiscated in 1918 and 1919 when all other foreign firms suffered nationalization by Communist fiat.

The attitude of Woodrow Wilson for a time encouraged the Bolsheviks in their misconceptions. In June, 1918, Litvinov's observations in London had convinced him that the Soviets could expect only hostile intervention from Britain and France. He therefore requested Lenin to empower him to go to the United States. Such authorization was duly sent, but, on application, Litvinov was refused a visa.

When Washington B. Vanderlip came to Moscow in 1920 he was looked upon by the Russians as the forerunner of a host of billionaire Americans who would apply their capital and capitalist experience to building up a Communist State. Vanderlip bargained for oil, coal, fishing, and forest concessions of an estimated value of $3,-000,000,000 in Kamchatka and Eastern Siberia. The location of the proposed concession areas was significant;

the Russian leaders spoke with Vanderlip of their relations towards Japan and China, and intimated to him that Russia supported the Open Door policy in all parts of China—presumably against Japan.

America's objection to Japanese expansion no doubt accounts, in part, for Washington's insistence on Russian territorial integrity. The State Department consistently refused to follow the lead of Great Britain in recognizing the Baltic and Caucasian republics. More especially, however, United States diplomacy rejected the idea of Japanese aggrandizement in the Russian Far East.

The Bolsheviks disliked the protracted presence of Japanese troops on Russian soil. Their forces, however, were spent after the trying Civil War, and when Tokyo intimated in talks with Krasnochekov, the chief of the pro-Soviet factions in Eastern Siberia, that Japan would be ready to evacuate the Trans-Baikal region on condition that no Communist Government were established there, Moscow gladly and cynically instructed its supporters in Siberia to set up a "democratic" republic. This organization, which subsequently became the Far Eastern Republic with capital at Chita, thus constituted a buffer between Russia and Japan.

Japan remained in Vladivostok, the Maritime Provinces, and in the northern half of the island of Sakhalin.

"On the 28th of July, 1920, the Japanese Government received a note from the United States, indicating that the American Government approved the Japanese decision to evacuate Trans-Baikalia and reserved its opinion regarding Vladivostok because of lack of information concerning the situation there, but failed completely to understand the occupation of northern Sakhalin."[1]

This démarche by the Democratic Secretary of State Colby was met by an assurance from Ambassador Shidehara that the occupation would be temporary. Yet it was not lifted for many months, and on May 31, 1921, the Republican Secretary of State Hughes again protested,[2] and was again assured of the eventual Japanese withdrawal. Washington's motives were anti-Japanese. In any event, the Soviets rejoiced, and were confirmed in their

[1] F. L. Schuman: *American Policy Toward Russia since 1917,* (New York, 1928), p. 209.
[2] *Ibid.*

optimism on the future of American-Soviet relations.

**HARRY F. SINCLAIR** These considerations probably played a decisive role in the Sinclair oil concession. The preliminary concession, granted by the Far Eastern (Chita) Republic on May 14, 1921, and ratified on January 7, 1922, gave the Sinclair Exploration Company the right to exploit the petroleum resources of the northern, (Russian) half of Sakhalin and to construct two ports on its eastern coast.

Here was Russia telling a big American concern with considerable political influence to go in and get the island's oil. Here were the Bolsheviks offering an American company the possibility of building two harbors right under the nose of Japan—harbors where, if the necessity arose, ships flying the "Stars and Stripes" might coal and "oil." Obviously Chita, which of course acted in concert with Moscow, meant this as a bid for an understanding with Washington.

President Harding then sat in the White House. Fall, Denby, and Daugherty were in the President's Cabinet. Harry F. Sinclair knew them intimately. He promised the Bolsheviks United States recognition—whether by previous agreement with his high-placed friends no one can say. But the fact is that the Bolsheviks made the permanence of the Sakhalin concession, as of the Vanderlip concession, conditional upon the establishment of normal diplomatic relations between themselves and Mr. Sinclair's government.

Moscow expected Washington to understand. Moscow supposed Washington would be glad to align Russia on its side in the Far Eastern struggle for a balance of power.

**THE WASHINGTON ARMS CONFERENCE** America's protests against Japanese occupation may have encouraged the Soviets in their belief that a rapprochement was in the making. But the Washington Conference on the Limitation of Armaments (November 12, 1921–February 6, 1922), which was largely a conference on Far-Eastern problems, brought cruel disillusionment. The Soviet Republic received no invitation. Moscow protested its right to participate—but without avail.

A "trade" delegation from the Far Eastern (Chita) Republic, however, received admission to Washington if not to the conference. The Japanese-controlled Merkulov Government in Vladivostok, Russian monarchist groups, and Miliukov Cadets likewise sent representatives.

When, in connection with the Siberian question, the matter of Japanese occupation arose for consideration, Secretary of State Hughes told the conference that the United States Government saw no necessity for continued occupation. Baron Shidehara reacted to United States pressure by affirming that "it is the fixed and settled policy of Japan to respect the territorial integrity of Russia and to observe the principle of non-intervention in the internal affairs of that country. . . ."[3] Also, the military occupation of the Russian Province of Sakhalin is only a temporary measure and will naturally come to an end as soon as a satisfactory settlement of the question shall have been arranged with an orderly Russian Government."

**CHARLES E. HUGHES FIGHTS FOR RUSSIA** Mr. Hughes was not pleased. Japan had promised during more than a year that the occupation was only "temporary." The formula of a settlement with "an orderly Russian Government," moreover, permitted of wide interpretation. The Secretary of State submitted that the

> public assurances given by the two Governments at the inception of the joint expedition [to Siberia] nevertheless required the complete withdrawal of Japanese troops from Russian territory—if not immediately after the departure of the Czecho-Slovak troops, then within reasonable time . . .

Mr Hughes added the wish that "the divergence of views between the two Governments might be removed with the least possible delay," and expressed "the hope that Japan will find it possible to carry out within the near future her expressed intention of terminating finally the Siberian expedition and of restoring Sakhalin to the Russian people."

The net result however, amounted to zero. The Japanese pocketed Mr. Hughes's insinuations but showed no intention of leaving Eastern Siberia or Northern Sakhalin.

**THE OTHER SIDE OF THE MEDAL** Early in 1920, the United States Government sent food and war supplies

[3] *Conference on the Limitation of Armaments.* Official Protocol of the Sessions. (Washington, 1921), pp. 340–54.

to the Poles. "General Tasker H. Bliss and Secretary of War Baker insisted that such aid was essential to check the spread of Bolshevism and save civilization."[4] But the Soviet-Polish war had not commenced, and Poland was yet to reject all Bolshevik peace overtures.

While the Polish offensive into the Ukraine was still in progress,

> Hugh Gibson, first American Minister to Poland, then in the United States, sought to refute the charge of imperialism and emphasized the warm friendship of the United States for the Poles. . . . A Polish loan of $50,000,000 was soon floated successfully with the approval of the State Department.[5]

The American Government gave moral comfort to the Poles in addition to financial and material succor. This took the form of a much-quoted note from Secretary of State Bainbridge Colby to Baron Cammillo Romano Avezzeno, Italian Ambassador in Washington, on August 10, 1920, which outlined American policy towards Russia for several years to come.

**THE STATE DEPARTMENT ENUNCIATES ITS RUSSIAN POLICY** Colby averred in his note that he "recoils" from the "recognition of the Bolshevik regime," and the "dismemberment of Russia." The Secretary then urged that all decisions of vital importance to Russia, especially "those concerning its sovereignty over the territory of the former Russian Empire, be held in abeyance," until Russia is no longer "helpless in the grip of a non-representative Government, whose only sanction is brute force."

Colby followed with a warning to Russia not to take herself wholly out of the pale of the friendly interests of other nations by the pillage and oppression of the Poles." Then a slashing attack:

Mr. Colby ascribed to the Bolsheviks declarations to the effect that "they have not the slightest intention of observing such undertakings [with foreign Powers.—L.F.] or of carrying out such agreements." Without citing his authority for this assertion, the Secretary proceeds to affirm that "they have not only avowed this as a doctrine, but have exemplified it in practice."

[4] Schuman, *op. cit.*, p. 176.
[5] *Ibid.*, p. 178.

On August 10, 1920, the date of the Colby note, the Soviet republic stood in treaty relationship with only two countries: Estonia—agreement concluded on February 2, 1920—and with Lithuania—agreement concluded on July 12, 1920. The record showed no violation of the two treaties.

> Moreover [wrote Mr. Colby] . . . the Bolshevik Government is itself subject to the control of a political faction with extensive international ramifications through the Third International, and this body, which is heavily subsidized by the Bolshevik Government from the public revenues of Russia, has for its openly avowed aim the promotion of Bolshevist revolutions throughout the world. The leaders of the Bolsheviki have boasted that their promises of non-interference with other nations would in no way bind the agents of this body.

Colby then proceeded to summarize his own note and to define "territorial integrity" as referring to the area of the former Russian Empire with the exception of Finland, Poland, and Armenia. He omitted Estonia, Latvia, and, most particularly, Lithuania. The Poles, who had designs on Lithuania, were deeply pleased.

The French Government, which backed Poland, thanked Mr. Colby for his note. So also the Polish Government for his "valuable moral support." Whereupon it was announced that the American State Department approved the aims of Baron Wrangel, the Czarist General and rejoiced in the "common objective of the French and American Governments."[6]

**THE BOLSHEVIK REPLY** Bolsheviks loved an argument too much to have permitted a note like Colby's to go unanswered. Chicherin as well as Ludwig K. Martens, Soviet diplomatic agent in New York, issued replies.

Martens's statement first drew attention to the circumstance that the policy enunciated by the United States differed from that of a number of European Governments which, "yielding to the demands of the workers," had shown a tendency to "revise their previous misjudgments of Russia, and to adopt a policy of adjustment." The attitude of America, Martens affirmed, was conducive to perpetuating in Europe a state of poverty and war. Were it to prevail with the Allies "there would be no hope of peace in Europe." "Fortunately, however . . . the

[6] Schuman: *op. cit.*, p. 182.

European masses will make peace, in spite of insatiable imperialistic ambitions of their own rulers, and in spite of any interference from the American Government."

Nor could the Colby declaration change Russia's internal policy. "The naïve hope," wrote Martens, "expressed in some quarters, that this note may affect the purposes and actions of the Russian people, can only arise from ignorance of the facts, and is too ridiculous for serious consideration."

Then Martens dealt with American recognition of Russia. International law and international practice do not make recognition synonymous with approval. During Woodrow Wilson's administration, however, America's desires to affect the destinies of Central and South American republics grew apace, and recognition was granted or withdrawn as reward or punishment for conformance or non-conformance with Washington's wishes. President Wilson applied this measure to Soviet Russia as well, and the result, obviously, had to be the refusal to recognize. But "no Government has ever based its foreign relations upon this principle," Martens charged, "and if the American Government now assumed to do so, we repeat that this is a principle which the Soviet Government emphatically repudiates."

Moscow was establishing relations with capitalist countries, "but we do not ask them to approve our institutions nor can they expect us to approve theirs." Had the American Government approved of the Czar's tyrannical regime, Martens asked, or of the Mikado's?

Nor could Mr. Martens accept as sincere America's protested concern for Russia's territorial integrity. Such a policy was scarcely in accord with the self-determination of Latvia, Estonia, and Lithuania.

Chicherin's cabled reply, submitted by Martens, likewise made much of this point. Why, Chicherin wondered, had Colby been prepared to offer independence to Poland, Finland, and Armenia, but not to Latvia, Estonia, and Lithuania? He could only think that it was "probably due to lack of information concerning national conditions in Eastern Europe." As for the Soviet Government, it "unwaveringly upholds the right of national self-determination of the working class of every nationality, including the right of secession and of forming separate states."

Satisfied that the outside world was still poorly acquainted with the system of government in his country, Chicherin exploited the Colby challenge to explain the democratic nature of the Soviet regime as opposed to "the absolute domination of strongly organized political parties which are completely subservient to the leading financial groups" in capitalist countries. He denied that freedom of the Press or assemblage could exist under bourgeois conditions. He asserted that it was the capitalist State that rested "on brutal force." Moreover, he rejected the innuendo that the Soviet ruled "against the will of the masses." That, he said, is "sheer absurdity." For how, but for the solid support of the population, he asked, could the Bolsheviks have persisted through a long Civil War in which the united forces of a hostile world were pitted against them?

Then the Commissar for Foreign Affairs turned to the subject of diplomatic privileges. To Mr. Colby's charge of their abuse, Chicherin said, "Not a single fact can be quoted in support of this calumny."

Finally, in a peroration, Chicherin expressed the hope that the Colby policy would be superseded.

**A RED DIPLOMAT IN NEW YORK** The psychology and idealogy reflected in the Colby note explain America's treatment of the Martens Mission.

Ludwig C. A. K. Martens, born of German and Russian parents, had engaged in engineering activities in Germany before the War, but was also known in Bolshevik circles; 1916 found him in the United States.

Moscow came upon the idea of availing itself of Martens's services, and sent him the necessary credentials dated January 2, 1919. These, together with a long memorandum on the origin, character and pacific intentions of the Soviet Government, he forwarded to the State Department on March 19, 1919. The State Department ignored them.

The State Department still recognized and dealt with Boris Bakhmetiev, Kerensky's envoy, as the rightful plenipotentiary of the Russian State despite the fact that the Government which had appointed Bakhmetiev had been dead for sixteen months and that its members had dispersed to the four corners of the earth. Bakhmetiev and Serge Ughet, his Financial Agent, were frankly White.

Mr. Ughet admitted in conversation with the writer that he sent locomotives to Vladivostok for Kolchak and to Novorossisk for Denikin. Locomotives and munitions—all paid for by the United States Treasury from credits placed at the disposal of the Kerensky regime.

Since Martens was accorded no diplomatic status, he attempted to perform the second half of his task: the establishment of contacts with American business firms. Offices were opened in New York City, but the State Department hastened to announce that "the Government of the United States had never recognized the Bolshevik regime at Moscow," and that "it is deemed proper to warn American business men that any concessions from the Bolshevist authorities probably could not be recognized as binding on future Russian Governments." Here the speculation on the probable fall of the Soviet Government is patent.

Mr. Martens's sojourn in the United States coincided with what Louis F. Post, Assistant Secretary of Labor, characterized as "the deportations delirium of 1920" during which thousands of foreigners were exiled, and thousands more, suspected of Radicalism, Anarchism, Bolshevism, etc.—among them Sacco and Vanzetti—thrown into prison on insufficiently substaniated charges. Martens's offices were raided, he was arrested, his files searched, his employees examined, and his alleged activities subjected to sensational press attacks.

These activities on the part of the Department of Justice, the New York State "Lusk Committee," and private detective agencies severely handicapped the Bolshevik "ambassador's" endeavors to do business, and, though he succeeded in aligning a number of Senators and intellectual leaders, the inevitable end came on January 22, 1921. On that day Martens and his staff sailed from New York on the *Stockholm*. He left on his own volition and at his own expense, and was not served a warrant of deportation.

**HARDING SUCCEEDS WILSON** The election of Warren G. Harding as President and his appointment of Charles Evans Hughes as his Secretary of State introduced into the Russo-American situation little welcome change for the Bolsheviks. But Moscow thought it would. Moscow failed to realize the comparative continuity of

American foreign policy. On March 31, 1921, accordingly, exactly seventeen days after the inauguration, Litvinov forwarded to Washington a Soviet plea for the establishment of normal political and business relations between the two countries.

Mr. Hughes soon replied:

> It is manifest to this Government [he wrote] that in existing circumstances there is no assurance for the development of trade. It is only in the productivity of Russia that there is any hope for the Russian people and it is idle to expect resumption of trade until the economic bases of production are securely established. Production is conditioned upon the safety of life, the recognition of firm guarantees of private property, the sanctity of contracts and the rights of free labor.
>
> If fundamental changes are contemplated, involving due regard for the protection of persons and property and the establishment of conditions essential to the maintenance of commerce, this Government will be glad to have convincing evidence of the consummation of such changes, and until this evidence is supplied this Government in unable to perceive that there is any proper basis for considering trade relations.

**HERBERT HOOVER ON RUSSIA** The new Secretary of State denied the possibility of an exchange of goods between a capitalist and a non-capitalist nation. This was a novel note, unheard of during the Wilson administration and little heeded in Europe. Hughes sent his answer to Litvinov on March 25. Nine days previously the British Government had signed a commercial treaty with Moscow which facilitated the exchange of goods, including gold, and which provided for a final political settlement. Apparently, therefore, the Old World entertained quite different ideas.

The principle enunciated by Hughes may have been Herbert Hoover's. For the newly appointed Secretary of Commerce had declared on March 21, 1921, that

> The question of trade with Russia is far more a political question than an economic one so long as Russia is under the control of the Bolsheviki. Under their economic system, no matter how much they moderate it in name, there can be no real return to production in Russia, and therefore Russia will have no considerable commodities to export and, consequently, no great ability to obtain imports. . . . That requires the abandonment of their present economic system.

Thus, in almost identical phraseology, Hughes and

Hoover sought to establish the principle that since a Bolshevik regime was incapable of producing goods there could be no sense in making provision with it for the exchange of goods.

**HOOVER FAMINE RELIEF** Though Herbert Hoover had an oft-expressed aversion for the political and economic forms of Bolshevism, he nevertheless answered immediately to the heartrending cry from Russia for food.

By the summer of 1921 no less than 25,000,000 people suffered hunger in the Volga River region. On July 13, Maxim Gorki, the well-known author, appealed to "All Honest People" for prompt aid to the Russian nation. "Give bread and medicine," he urged.

A conference of European Government representatives, after meeting in Paris and Brussels, declared that it would weigh the question of relief for the starving if the Soviets first acknowledged their debts.[7] The United States made no such condition. Instead Herbert Hoover announced that the American Relief Administration would render assistance forthwith.

Hoover's American Relief Administration (A.R.A.) spent upward of $60,000,000 for the aid of the sufferers from September, 1921, when actual operations commenced, to July, 1923, when they ceased. Of this sum, $11,357,000 was supplied in gold by the Soviets. There can be no doubt that millions of men, women, and children, would have died but for the quick, efficiently-organized service rendered by the Hoover organization.

The Bolsheviks suspected Hoover. They knew his anti-Bolshevik bias because he had made no secret of it. They knew also that Captain Gregory of the A.R.A. had been instrumental in overthrowing the Soviet regime in Hungary. Gregory boasted of the achievement.[8] They said Congress appropriated $20,000,000 for Russian relief which was really farmer relief. (Middle West corn was being stuffed into fires in lieu of kindling wood.) Most of the A.R.A. food-stuffs came from America despite the fact, the Communists argued, that European prices and transportation costs were cheaper.

[7] H. W. V. Temperley, ed., *A History of the Peace Conference of Paris,* Vol. VI. Published under the Auspices of the British Institute for International Affairs. (London, 1924), p. 326.

[8] *World's Work,* New York, June, 1921. "Stemming the Red Tide," by T. T. C. Gregory.

These and other complaints made the rounds. Difference of temperament and language, and the complete failure of the Americans to grasp Bolshevik psychology probably accounted for some of the misunderstanding. On many occasions, the relief workers were not treated with the consideration and cordiality their services entitled them to expect. Yet on the whole, the amount of friction and the number of disputes was very small, and mutual distrust notwithstanding, no serious incidents marred the work.

When the A.R.A. finally departed, the Government tendered its leaders a banquet at which Dzerzhinsky and other prominent Bolsheviks drank the health of the Americans.

# 9

# THE GENOA CONFERENCE

LLOYD GEORGE is usually regarded as the father and sponser of the Genoa Conference. He no doubt envisaged it as the crowning glory of his political career, and as the best weapon with which to win Liberal and Labor support for the impending General Election. But Briand may have been equally anxious to issue the invitation.

The policy of consortiums for Russia belonged primarily to Paris. Lloyd George always preferred direct negotiations by individual countries. Downing Street and British business interests had registered some progress in their discussions with the Bolsheviks and scarcely required French assistance at that stage. General discussions, in fact, might interfere with success.

Moreover, Briand wished to arrive at a working agreement which would enable Germany to pay reparations without stops, starts, moratoria, and ultimata. Liberal treatment of Germany, however, would, in his opinion, increase the risk of German recovery and therefore of revenge.

**BRIAND'S FALL** Briand, accordingly, made his goal a British guarantee to France against German attack. At Versailles, both Great Britain and President Wilson had expressed a readiness to share such a guarantee. But the rejection, by the United States Senate, of the Paris Peace Treaty ended that possibility, and at Cannes, when the proposition was renewed, England stood alone.[1]

[1] Short studies of the Cannes Conference will be found in *The Rise of the German Republic,* by H. G. Daniels (London, 1927); in *Through Thirty Years, 1892–1922,* Vol. II, by H. Wickham Steed (London, 1924); and in *Von Versailles zur Freiheit,* by Freiherr von Rheinbaben (Berlin, 1927).

Many of the preliminaries of this security pact were discussed between drives on the Cannes golf-course and remain secret. But it is known that while France demanded a many-sided alliance, including provisions regarding Russian-Polish and Russian-German relations, Lloyd George would go only to the length of a guarantee against unprovoked attack.[2] This was far less then Poincaré and his friends desired. Poincaré even contemplated "a constant entente . . . between the respective General Staffs."[3] The anti-Briand opposition in Paris, moreover, and the French Nationalists and industrialists, had for some time weighed the advisability of occupying the rich Ruhr region in Germany. That would be better security, they felt, than any signature of Lloyd George; it would likewise facilitate reparations collections.

Poincaré worked feverishly in Paris, and before long, circumstances warranted a hasty summons to Briand to return from Cannes to Paris. In the capital, the cards were so stacked against him that resignation remained the only choice. With him fell the British guarantee, and as a result reparations disappeared from the Genoa agenda. At a subsequent tête-à-tête with Lloyd George in Boulogne in February, Poincaré made doubly sure that reparations would be reserved for his own solution—Ruhr occupation.

**GENOA RESERVED FOR RUSSIA** The proposed Genoa Conference thus became a purely Russian matter. On the second day of the Cannes meeting, the assembled diplomats decided to convene a European Economic Conference at Genoa and to invite the Soviet Republic. Thereupon, on January 7, 1922, the Italian Government forwarded to Moscow a note which especially urged the "personal participation" of Lenin.[4] Russia quickly accepted the invitation "with pleasure" and assured the Powers that even if the necessity of coping with the famine prevented the attendance of "Citizen Lenin," the Bolshevik plenipotentiaries would be armed with sufficient authority to facilitate the work of the conference. Lenin was actually named chief of the delegation to satisfy Lloyd George's wish that "big men meet big men," but he never proposed to attend. His health had suffered. The Bolsheviks,

[2] British Blue Book. *Papers respecting Negotiations for an Anglo-French Pact*. Cmd. 2169. (London, 1924).

[3] *Ibid.*, p. 131.

[4] *Genoa Conference. Stenographic Account, Materials and Documents.* Publication of the Commissariat of Foreign Affairs. (Moscow, 1922).

furthermore, feared attempts on his life by the Whites in Europe.

The initiators of the Genoa Conference, notably Lloyd George and, originally, the French, entertained plans for a far-reaching settlement with the Bolsheviks. The economic and political reforms introduced in Russia in 1921 encouraged the belief that the Soviets were ready to come to terms, perhaps to capitulate completely and beg for foreign support. The great famine strengthened that conviction.

Besides, the Allies believed that the revision of the Bolsheviks' attitude towards domestic capitalism as evidenced in the New Economic Policy (NEP) entailed a reconsideration of their position towards foreign capitalism. Herein lay the clue to the Genoa Conference.

**TOP-HATS AND SILK GLOVES** The Bolsheviks were ready to make compromises. Weary from three and a half years of world war, two and a half years of civil war and foreign intervention, and two years of a hermetic blockade, Russia staggered under the blow delivered by the widespread famine. Severe trials faced the Communists; they therefore sought aid beyond their borders.

Moscow's behavior fed the high hopes which the Western nations set on Genoa. For when the Communist delegates appeared in Berlin and later in the Italian seaport wearing top-hats and cut-aways, the bourgeois world said, "These outward forms have a deep and symbolic meaning. They herald a change in conviction."

**THE TRUCE BETWEEN TWO WORLDS ON PAPER**
A Cannes resolution declared that

> nations can claim no right to dictate to each other the principles on which they are to regulate their systems of ownership, internal economy, and government. It is for every nation to choose for itself the system which it prefers in this respect.[5]

During the years of intervention, such tolerance was of course inconceivable. But in 1922 a resolution admitting the possibility of the co-existence of two diametrically opposed systems of economy and government spelled progress. It indicated that the Allies meant peace and

[5] *Resolutions Adopted by the Supreme Council at Cannes, January, 1922, as the Basis of the Genoa Conference.* British White Paper. Cmd. 1621. (London, 1922).

business. It reflected the conviction, in some quarters at least, that a Red Russia would be less dangerous than a great, "united" White Russia. This applied especially to England and Poland, and, to the extent that Poland's interests were dear to France, it applied to France. Japan would naturally have said "Amen." Only the United States disagreed. To America, a weakened Bolshevik Republic was less desirable than a strong, bourgeois Russia that could resist Japan. The United States refused to attend the Genoa Conference.

**FRENCH v. BRITISH POLICY** It did not require excessive prevision to see that Genoa would be still another battlefield for French and British divergent policies. The whole history of the post-war period had been a series of disputes between the erstwhile allies. Indeed, Anglo-French antagonism began with the Versailles Peace Conference where the two chief victors wrangled over the spoils of war. Subsequently, controversies developed over Russia and over Lloyd George's trade agreement with the Bolsheviks. Mosul was another irritant. The fact that France gave arms to Kemal Pasha while England urged Athens to make war on him drove the two countries further apart than ever. Finally, France and Britain clashed on the most vital of Western European problems: Germany and reparations.

Anglo-French friction had become a chronic feature of European politics by the beginning of 1922.

**RUSSO-GERMAN "ALLIANCE"** On March 25, 1919, Lloyd George had secretly circulated a memorandum among a few members of the Paris Peace Conference. The text remained unknown, except to a very limited circle. In it, the British Prime Minister said:

> The greatest danger that I see in the present situation is that Germany may throw in her lot with Bolshevism and place her resources, her brains, her vast organizing power at the disposal of the revolutionary fanatics whose dream it is to conquer the world for Bolshevism by force of arms. This danger is no mere chimera.

When this secret document came to the desk of Clemenceau in 1919, he declared that it was intended as a means of extracting concessions for Germany from France instead of from England Lloyd George wished to convince the French that a too stern peace treaty would drive Germany into the arms of Russia. Why, then, did Lloyd George give this document to the British Press on March 25, 1922, on the eve of the Genoa Conference? Presumably for the same reason. But also to warn Poincaré that stern treatment of Russia would drive her into the arms of Germany.

Lloyd George realized that Poincaré's policy towards Russia would, if it prevailed at Genoa, make agreement with Chicherin impossible. His preliminary maneuvering therefore aimed to induce a more conciliatory attitude towards Moscow in the Quai d'Orsay. Moreover, Lloyd George believed that Russia's internal difficulties presented the finest opportunity for economic penetration by Great Britain herself.

**THE URQUHART CONCESSION** Krassin's entrance into London in 1920 had been the signal for a large number of concession applications, the most significant of which originated with Leslie Urquhart, the chairman of the Russo-Asiatic Corporation, and from Deterding, the president of the Royal Dutch-Shell Petroleum Company. These received encouragement from the Bolshevik emissary.

In 1921, Mr. Urquhart undertook a trip to Moscow to discuss his concession with the Soviet chiefs. Before the revolution, his firm had controlled what was probably the richest mining area in rich Siberia. It covered 4,000 square versts in the Ural and Altai regions and yielded gold, silver, copper, lead, and zinc. It boasted extensive forests and fisheries, coal deposits, and industrial plants. The Bolsheviks had confiscated it. Urquhart wanted it back.

The British Government looked with favor upon Urquhart's negotiations with Krassin, and Mr. Urquhart was attached to the English delegation to the Genoa Conference.[6]

**THE ROYAL DUTCH CONCESSION** Deterding's Royal Dutch-Shell likewise held properties in Czarist Russia. He was one of several huge investors who had

[6] The writer discussed this matter with Mr. Urquhart in 1926 in London.

been attracted by the country's unfathomable oil wealth.

The Bolsheviks had nationalized the fields and thus dispossessed Deterding and all foreign and Russian owners. Yet the Anglo-Russian Trade Agreement of March, 1921, and the NEP of March, 1921, inspired the hope in British business leaders that this action was not irrevocable, or, at least, that some method could be devised whereby they could save their properties and the Bolsheviks their faces; by concessions, perhaps, which, it was thought, would be a veiled form of restitution.

The Royal Dutch, accordingly, established contact with Krassin. But the Royal Dutch knew that Downing Street's assistance would be not without value. Lord Curzon, British Secretary of State for Foreign Affairs, was found ready to help, and he caused his Under-Secretary Ovey, later envoy to Moscow, to write this letter:[7]

FOREIGN OFFICE.
19*th October,* 1921.

Monsieur Krassin,
SIR,

The Marquis Curzon of Kedleston is informed by Colonel J. W. Boyle that the Royal Dutch-Shell group are anxious to obtain a concession from the Soviet Government for the production of oil from their properties in South Russia and the Caucasus.

I am directed to inform you that it is with the full approval and support of His Majesty's Government that Colonel Boyle has addressed himself to you on this subject. His Majesty's Government trust that these negotiations may result in an early and satisfactory settlement.

I am,
Sir,
Your most obedient servant,
(Signed) ESMOND OVEY.

Such intercession did not leave the Bolsheviks unimpressed. Soon Colonel Boyle, who had served as an intermediary between Rakovsky and the Rumanians in 1918, made a trip to Baku, and before long the conversations with Krassin had apparently reached a point where the Royal Dutch even submitted a draft contract.

The Genoa Conference cannot be understood without full appreciation of the import of the Shell concession. The difficulties it encountered were not only typical of

[7] Copied by the writer from the original in the archives of the Soviet Embassy in London.

relations between Russia and the outside world: they actually were the difficulties of the conference itself and affected the outcome of the meeting as much as any single factor. A settlement with the former owners of Russian oil properties, however—either through compensation or concessions or through outright restitution—involved the whole principle upon which the larger question of Russian foreign obligations would be solved. This principle had not yet been defined. There were, in fact, several principles proposed by several Powers. The Allies disagreed among themselves. Under the circumstances a concession to the Royal Dutch would have prejudiced the final settlement in a manner inevitably favorable to the British principle. The French, moreover, insisted that Russia's creditors must act in concert and seek a solution along "parallel lines" rather than square their accounts with the Russians individually as Deterding wished to do.

There was, in addition, very direct opposition to the concession itself on the part of petroleum associations. The Standard Oil Company of New Jersey as well as French and Belgium oil men objected to a Deterding concession because it would have weakened their own claims on the Soviet Government. And since the oil firms of America, France and Belgium enjoyed the goodwill of their Foreign Offices. it first became embarrassing and then impossible for the Royal Dutch-Shell or Lloyd George to press the business of the Deterding trust before at least the outline of a general economic settlement with Russia had been fixed by all the conference members.

Finally, Sir Henri Deterding's plan for obtaining monopoly rights to the liquid wealth of the Caucasus was temporarily forced into the background by a larger scheme for exploiting all the resources of Russia and satisfying all the claims of all former Russian investors. Enter the "Europa Consortium."

## A EUROPEAN CONSORTIUM FOR THE SOVIETS

This "International Corporation" actually formed the basis of official, inter-government negotiations. At Cannes, in fact, the Supreme Council declared that it "approves of the establishment of an International Corporation . . . for the purpose of the economic reconstruction of Europe" and the Governments represented agreed to contribute

10,000 pounds sterling each towards financing the work of the organizing committee.[8]

At the January 12 session of the Cannes Conference, Walther Rathenau, the German delegate, urged his nation's right to join.

> Germany [he submitted] was the more fitted to contribute towards the reconstruction since she was acquainted with the technical and economic conditions and with the customs of the East. . . . The path entered upon seems to me the right one [he added]. An international syndicate, indeed a private syndicate. [The beginnings should be made with transport; then the sources of production, raw materials.][9]

This was the scheme in outline. Late in December, 1921, on the eve of the Cannes assembly, important industrialists and bankers from England, France, Italy, Belgium, and Japan met in Paris under the chairmanship of the French Minister Loucheur to discuss it. An investment of twenty million pounds sterling was foreseen. Germany would be invited—to help her pay reparations. American participation was also sought.

Such a far-reaching venture required legal guarantees from the Soviets as well as a modification of the system of justice in Russia. An international body of experts, representing the several Allied Governments, accordingly met in London in March to deal with this problem. The result of their labor was the "London Memorandum" intended as the ground-work on which the structure of Genoa would be erected.[1]

In a note dated February 15, 1922, the French Government urged the introduction of "an actual system of capitulations" for Russia. This suggestion was consonant with the French "Dawes Plan" for Russia and the solicitude of France not so much for the settlements of her debt with Russia as for the economic exploitation of the country by foreign capital.

"Capitulations," accordingly, became the cue for the authors of the London Memorandum. For no matter who

[8] *Resolutions Adopted by the Supreme Council at Cannes, January, 1922, as the Basis of the Genoa Conference.* British White Paper. Cmd. 1621. (London, 1922).

[9] Walther Rathenau: *Cannes und Genua,* (Berlin, 1922).

[1] For complete text see *Papers Relating to the International Economic Conference. Genoa, April–May, 1922.* British Blue Book, Cmd. 1667. (London, 1922).

summoned these experts, or who advocated the "International Corporation," any attempt to deal collectively with the Russian problem would obviously proceed under the sign of the French principle of joint action along parallel lines.

The London Memorandum accordingly prescribed the following for Russian acceptance: (1) A foreigner could be arrested only in the presence or with the consent of his consul; (2) no searches could be undertaken in the homes or plants of foreigners; (3) sentences passed upon foreigners by Russian courts could be executed only with the approval of their consuls; (4) Soviet labor laws would not maintain in plants owned or managed by foreigners, but wages might be fixed by joint employer and employee commissions "if necessary"; (5) foreigners could, when signing a contract, name the country under whose legal code disputes arising under the contract were to be adjudicated; in such instances the Russian court was bound to be guided by that code.[2] The experts, furthermore, envisaged the creation of free zones in a number of ports or of free "treaty" ports as in China.

The ground having thus been prepared, Russia having agreed, further, to recognize and pay her debts, to restitute confiscated foreign properties, to grant concessions, to submit her currency to foreign control and, probably, to permit the establishment of a powerful foreign bank in Moscow, the "International Consortium" could begin its work.

The "Europa Consortium," as it came to be styled after America refused to adhere, would grant credits for the stabilization of the ruble, finance concession undertakings, and itself participate in railway operation and construction as well as in the production of raw materials for manufacture in Western European countries.

The Allies had thus sketched their ideal solution of the Bolshevik problem.

On January 27, 1922, Chicherin told the Central Executive Committee in Moscow that the Bolsheviks would not accept co-operation with bourgeois States which "took

[2] Reference to these questions is made in a *Telegram from M. Chicherin, Moscow, to the Governments of Great Britain, France and Italy respecting the Genoa Conference.* British White Paper. Cmd. 1637. (London, 1922).

the form of economic domination over Russia."[3] The consortium, he said, represented a danger to the Soviet Republic.

This expression of Bolshevik policy, however, remained unheeded in the West. Far more serious was American rejection of the idea of the corporation. And before even the Genoa Conference convened, the Germans, who soon began to be accepted as a most important pillar of the consortium, quarrelled among themselves. Hugo Stinnes, who was regarded as an industrial "wizard" and who regarded himself as a great statesman (who, therefore, obtained diplomatic assignments from the German Government), had originally favored the plan of the "International Consortium." His participation figured in the preliminary discussions. But as Genoa drew nearer his attitude changed together with that of such gigantic industrial concerns as Krupps, Otto Wolff, etc. The German banks, on the other hand, as well as the light industries, and particularly the electric companies with whose workings and requirements Rathenau, the Foreign Minister, was intimately acquainted, continued in their support of the international project.

This division in the German business world no doubt colored the deliberations of the German Parliament. We find, for instance, that Gustav Stresemann, then leader of the Volkspartei, the party of the heavy industrialists, and later Minister of Foreign Affairs, took issue with Rathenau in a Reichstag debate on March 29, 1922.[4] Stresemann favored direct negotiations with the Bolsheviks. Rathenau, however, still clung to the proposed "Europa Consortium" though his advocacy of it as a monopoly concern for Russian business had weakened considerably.

Even the Allies were divided; when Germany wavered, hope of agreement vanished. At Genoa the "International Corsortium" still lingered in the minds of some diplomats, experts, and commission members. It may have been em-

[3] *Genoa Conference. Stenographic Account, Materials, and Documents.* Publication of the Commissariat of Foreign Affairs. Moscow, 1922, p. 17. Chicherin tells the writer that Felix Deutsch, the prominent German industrialist, had sketched the general idea of an international consortium to Krassin long before the Cannes Conference. The Bolsheviks then objected and the Germans never mentioned it again.

[4] Official Reichstag stenographic report.

ployed as an argument. But as an active political factor and as a big, unprecedented economic possibility it was dead.

## BOLSHEVIK NEGOTIATIONS WITH GERMANY

Many ties bound the Russians and Germans in this period. The Bolsheviks branded the Versailles Peace Treaty as unjust, vindictive, imperialistic; neither their Marxist principles nor their interpretation of the secret treaties they had published in 1917 enabled them to accept the Allied verdict written into Versailles of Germany's sole war guilt; they had rejoiced when Woodrow Wilson accepted their "no annexations, no indemnities" formula, and rejected a peace which meant to Germany loss of territory and colonies and the payment of reparations. Such a stand was the greatest possible comfort to Germany. It was identical with her own stand though she realized that the Russians started from a premise diametrically opposed to her own.

The Bolsheviks' opposition to Versailles established not merely this sentimental link, but also an economic and political bond between Russia and Germany.

It is almost a formula which holds for all time that when Germany's Western horizon is dark she turns to the East for light. With Bismarck and with other German statesmen, the Eastern orientation was a matter of policy rather than of necessity. Before the War, there were years when the Wilhelmstrasse would deliberately have turned its back on the western half of Europe to court Czarism. Always, after the First World War, the attitude of the Western Powers towards Germany determined her policy towards Soviet Russia.

In 1921, therefore, when, the Germans believed, France sought their economic and political ruin, the German Government decided to undertake measures which would lead to cordial relations with the Bolsheviks.

The Bolsheviks saw the possibilities which Germany's state of mind and condition offered them. To win her from the "capitalist united front" against the Soviet Republic, they stressed the plethora of economic opportunities which awaited the country that came to Russia with intentions of a purely business nature.

Such co-ordination of effort might extend to military industries as well. The Russians were especially interested in the development of an air fleet, and negotiations initiated during this period ultimately resulted in the establishment near Moscow, very quietly, of an airplane factory by Professor Junkers, the director of the famous Junkers plant in Dessau, Germany. This arrangement functioned for a number of years—until the Russians felt industrially more independent.

The Bolsheviks had no objection if the Germans reaped benefit from the Junkers contract or from similar agreements. They looked upon Germany as a weakened object of Entente Imperialism, and to strengthen Germany meant not merely the stiffening of resistance against that powerful combination but the buttressing of a force which might act as a check against Poland were Pilsudski to undertake another offensive into the Ukraine—an eventuality that obsessed the Bolshevik brain.

The conversations which ultimately led to the Rapallo Treaty commenced in a Berlin prison cell occupied by Karl Radek in 1920. There he was visited by important German personalities, among them Rathenau and Felix Deutsch. Begun on his own initiative in such surroundings, they were continued by Radek during several visits from Moscow to Berlin after his liberation. The Germans originally proposed to grant credits to Russia in exchange for Russia's renunciation of her claims on Germany under the Treaty of Versailles. Moscow objected to this formula on the ground that it could meet the German demand only in consideration of the cancellation of German State and private loans to the Czarist Empire. Germany's relations to the Allies strengthened the Russian position. The reparations problem was an open wound. Ultimata abounded. At the very time the Soviet delegation arrived in Berlin en route to Genoa (March, 1922), German public opinion was incensed by the policy of the Allied Military Control Commission which consisted in swamping German ministries with hundreds of notes on every alleged or actual incident in the zone of occupation. The advent of Chicherin, Litvinov, Krassin, Radek, Joffe and Rakovsky, therefore, caused a flutter in the German capital. They were ready to speak with Germany on terms of equality. They offered quid pro quos.

The wheels thus oiled, negotiations proceeded quickly and soon German and Russian legal experts were busy drafting a treaty. The fundamental lines of the document which later became known as the Rapallo Treaty were agreed upon then and there—in Berlin during March. Complete accord on the question of the socialization of German properties in Russia (Article 2) and especially on most-favored-nation treatment (Article 4) had not yet been reached, but these serious differences of opinion might have been ironed out had the Germans been prepared to sign in Berlin.[5]

Baron von Maltzan, chief of the Eastern Section of the Foreign Office, energetically pressed for the immediate conclusion of the treaty. He found support in numerous influential quarters. But Rathenau hesitated. He still hoped that Genoa would yield some results in the field of reparations. He feared the effect on England. Nor had he lost all faith in the consortium. With his financial mind, his concentration upon the most immediate problem of war tribute, and with his very Western temperament which could never quite harmonize with Russian manners, Rathenau advocated postponement.

The Russians, for their part, wished to sign the treaty in Berlin. They realized, of course, that such a Soviet-German agreement would have confronted the Allies, on the eve of Genoa, with an unwelcome fait accompli. But the Bolsheviks, Chicherin tells me, put very little faith in the outcome of the conference. They felt that it rested on a misunderstanding, on the supposition, in foreign quarters, that the NEP represented the Thermidore of the Communist Revolution. They believed, moreover, that the French would sabotage the assembly and that Lloyd George's chief interest in the meeting was that of saving his Coalition Cabinet, "the donkey with two heads,"[6] although it is difficult to understand how with his knowledge of Poincaré's attitude, Lloyd George could have expected the conference to succeed. Even before it opened,

[5] The writer's information regarding the negotiations leading to the Rapallo Treaty is derived from lengthy conversations with Chicherin, Litvinov, and with Herr Gaus, a high official of the German Foreign Office, who wrote the final text of the treaty, as well as from Count Harry Kessler's account in his book, *Rathenau, Sein Leben und Sein Werk,* which, I am authoritatively assured, is based on Baron von Maltzan's notes and on interviews with the leading German negotiators. I was also able to discuss the subject with Mr. E. F. Wise, Lloyd George's secretary at Genoa, and Paul Scheffer, the *Berliner Tageblatt's* correspondent in Moscow.

[6] The British Prime Minister's role at Genoa is dealt with, "much too generously," as he himself says, in *The Genoa Conference,* by J. Saxon Mills. London.

the Russians despaired of reaching an understanding with the Allies at Genoa. They attended in order to assert Russia's natural position on the international stage, and, perhaps, to establish normal relations with individual countries. Little could be lost by participating in the conference. Yet the possible gain, according to Bolshevik conception, was far less than a treaty with the Germans offered. Since it takes two to make a bargain, however, the Moscow-Berlin compact had to wait.

**THE GENOA CONFERENCE OPENS** On April 10 the world listened for Chicherin's speech. Chicherin began by saying that the Soviet delegation had come to Italy in the interests of peace and of European economic reconstruction.[7] He spoke a perfect French, and then translated his statement into English. He looked the part more of the retiring scholar than of a savage propagandist, and seemed to have unimpeachable manners. What he said irritated Barthou, the chief French delegate.

Chicherin emphasized the tremendous and unexploited natural wealth of Russia. The Soviet Government was prepared to "open its frontiers . . . for the creation of international traffic routes," and to grant "concessions of all kinds throughout the territory of the Federated Socialist Soviet Republic of Russia (R.S.F.S.R.)," and particularly in Siberia. Moscow, he announced, had, in conformance with the recently adopted New Economic Policy (NEP), already undertaken measures in the "domain of international legislation," which offered "the legal guarantees necessary for economic collaboration between Soviet Russia and States based on private property."

But economic reconstruction would be handicapped "by the menace of new wars," the commissar feared. Therefore the Soviet delegation "intend to propose, in the course of the conference, the general limitation of armaments" and the outlawry of the "most barbarous forms" of fighting "such as asphyxiating gas and aerial warfare, as well as the use of means of terrorizing peaceful populations."

This was the passage that infuriated Barthou. He felt

[7] Complete text in *International Economic Conference of Genoa. Provisional Verbatim Record. First Plenary Session.* (Official conference document in Italian, French, and English.) (Genoa, 1922).

obliged to "make a short but very definite statement," which he hoped, however, would not "give rise to an incident."

What Chicherin suggested, Barthou declared, was not on the agenda. If therefore "the Russian delegation propose to discuss this question [of disarmament], they will find themselves faced not only with a reservation and protest, but with an absolute denial, definite, categorical, final, and decisive on the part of the French delegation."

Chicherin sprang to his feet. At the Washington Disarmament meeting, he stated, Briand had said "that the reason why France opposed disarmament was the state of armament in Russia. We were therefore led to suppose that if Russia did consent to disarm, the reason cited by M. Briand would ipso facto disappear."

For a few moments it looked as if the Genoa Conference would die on the day of its birth. Indeed, but for a dramatic effort by Lloyd George, which required all his great diplomatic and forensic talent, the Chicherin-Barthou incident may have adjourned the meeting sine die. The British Prime Minister, however, skillfully poured oil on the very troubled waters, and then provoked a few laughs which restored outward peace.

**IN THE VILLA D'ALBERTIS** The Russian question soon dominated the conference completely. Three days after the opening incident, Wickham Steed, editor of the London *Times,* wired his paper that "Genoa has become a stage for the Bolshevists," and on the 16th he registered his distress over the circumstances that the Russians "are the arbiter of the conference."

The important discussions, however, took place not in plenary session or in the many political and technical commissions that were organized, but privately and secretly in Lloyd George's villa.

"The negotiations in the Villa d'Albertis," Chicherin said to me, "are the only thing that happened at Genoa" —as far as Allied-Russian relations are concerned. Then the Commissar for Foreign Affairs gave the writer the following summary of the meetings in the British Prime Minister's home:

Lloyd George participated on behalf of England, Barthou for France, Jaspar for Belgium, Schanzer for Italy, and Chicherin, Litvinov, and Krassin for Russia. The Allied representatives began by placing their views before the Bolsheviks. Then what Lloyd George called the "Little Soviet" was created—that is, Litvinov and Sir Sidney Chapman went down into the garden to discuss rival claims. They tried to find a formula for the negotiations, but, as Litvinov subsequently admitted to the writer, they failed. The Russian discussed debt payments at the end of a rather lengthy moratorium, and concessions and credits. Sir Sidney, however, had not been prepared to listen to stern Bolshevik demands and sine qua nons.

Litvinov, furthermore, explained that Russia would recognize her foreign obligations provided her counter-demands of 50 billion francs for damages done by Allied intervention during the Civil War be placed in the scales.[8]

"If you came to Genoa with that, you need not have come at all," Lloyd George said to Chicherin when this declaration was brought to his attention. Nevertheless, the talks continued. The Russians submitted that the Allies were responsible for destruction wrought by Allied armies in Russia especially since officially no state of war had existed, and that these Bolshevik claims must be set up against Russia's debt to foreign countries.

The Allied statesmen finally agreed that in view of her services to the Allied cause during the World War and taking into consideration her economic situation, Russia's war debts would be wiped from the slate if Moscow waived her counter-claims.

When this was put in writing, however, the war debts were not completely but only partially erased.

Another cause of discord was Russia's pre-war obligations. These the Bolsheviks consented to pay—assuming considerable reduction—but only on condition that the Allies grant credits. In the sunny halls of the Villa d'Albertis, the Soviet Republic announced the principle that has guided it in debt negotiations from that day to this: We pay if you give.

The Bolsheviks argued that it would be idle for them to accept the burden of foreign debt payments when they were unable to make such payments. But credits from abroad would yield a profit when invested by the Rus-

[8] See *Les Réclamations de la Russie aux Etats responsables de l'Intervention et du Blocus*. Official Soviet Publication. (Genoa, 1922).

sians in the reconstruction of their country, and out of that profit regular transfers could be made on account of debt settlement.

The "Big Soviet" in Lloyd George's villa discussed this question of credits, but the written Allied proposals submitted to the Communist plenipotentiaries contained no mention of them.

The knottiest problem the statesmen were called upon to solve was that of the nationalization of private property in Soviet Russia. Here no formula or principle could be found to bridge the gap between the French and British points of view and between these and the Russian position. The Bolsheviks refused compensation, and of course restitution.

In the end, therefore, the secret conclave in the Villa d'Albertis ended without a definite agreement but with the understanding, to which the Russians attached great importance, that in a final settlement the Bolshevik counter-claims would be juxtaposed to Russia's war debts and used to cancel them in part if not in their entirety.

**THE GERMANS FEAR A CONSPIRACY** Throughout the conversations in the Villa d'Albertis the German delegation was in a state of extreme nervousness—it suspected that Russia would assert her rights under Article 116 of the Versailles Treaty and demand reparations of Germany together with the Allied Powers. "The Allied and Associated Powers," reads the pertinent paragraph of Article 116, "formally reserve the rights of Russia to obtain from Germany restitution and reparation based on the principles of the Present Treaty." Insistence by Russia on this right would have meant not only a heavy increase in Germany's international financial burdens, but, what was almost as important, the political isolation of Germany.

Chicherin and Litvinov assure me that the question of reparations was never even broached in Lloyd George's villa, and prominent Germans with whom I have discussed the matter admit that the suspicion rested on a fundamental misconception of Bolshevik psychology.

At a Press conference in Genoa after the Rapallo Treaty was signed, one journalist asked Rakovsky, the Soviet spokesman, whether the new treaty did not conflict with the Treaty of Versailles. "Treaty of Versailles?" said Rakovsky as if trying to recapture a vague memory, "Treaty of Versailles? I know nothing about it." The Bolsheviks had no official knowledge of the Paris Peace, they did not recognize Versailles, they rejected the principles on which it was based, and abhorred its spirit. Under the circumstances, they could not conceivably have attempted to draw advantages from it or from Germany's defeat in the World War.

The Germans, however, suffered under an unenviable psychological pressure during these days; nobody wished to see them or talk with them. A funereal atmosphere filled the Hotel Eden where the German delegation was quartered. From the very beginning of the Genoa Conference the Germans had felt very much alone and as the days of the Villa d'Albertis conversations followed one another, Rathenau and Wirth were so despondent that they even weighed the advisability of requesting Berlin for orders to return home.

On April 13, the first day of the secret conclave in Lloyd George's villa, Rathenau made three requests for an interview with the British Prime Minister; two were in writing, one by telephone. All were refused. Then Chancellor Wirth tried—but in vain.

That same day, Baron von Maltzan of the German Foreign Office and Dufour of the German Embassy in London discussed the matter with E. F. Wise, one of Lloyd George's secretaries. The Germans informed Wise of the Berlin draft of the proposed Russo-German treaty (later the Rapallo Treaty). They likewise told him that Lord D'Abernon, the British envoy in Berlin, had been apprised of the progress of these Berlin negotiations and of the fact that the Germans regarded them as a defense against the possible operation of that terrible Article 116. This was a frank hint for transmission to Lloyd George that the Germans would feel compelled to sign a separate treaty with the Bolsheviks if the meetings in the Villa d'Albertis essayed to give content to Article 116. Yet the Germans were not at all certain that the Russians would now be willing to enter into an agreement with them.

The next day, April 14, the conference in the Lloyd George villa continued, and the Germans continued distraught. Meanwhile Chicherin and Litvinov saw Wirth frequently and gave him an impression of pleasure with the way in which the talks in the Villa d'Albertis were proceeding.

The situation had now become quite unbearable for the Germans. Again the leaders of the German delegation tried to establish contact with Lloyd George, and again they failed. German isolation was complete. Something had to be done.

**RATHENAU AND MALTZAN** The German delegation was divided. At one pole stood Walther Rathenau, Minister of Foreign Affairs; at the other von Maltzan, chief of the Russian division of the Wilhelmstrasse. He found support in Wirth. Maltzan was Rathenau's subordinate, but he made up in energy and will-power what he lacked in rank. Maltzan was a strong, dominating, forward individual with no wish to understand details, legal formulæ or bureaucratic red tape. He accepted responsibility with alacrity; Rathenau with great caution. Rathenau was analytic and meticulous; a student, thinker, orator, and writer.

Rathenau still hoped that some modus vivendi on reparations would be found with the Entente. Carl Bergmann, the German expert, was busy discussing the subject in a Genoa hotel with Seydoux, the French delegate.[9] All realized that a compact with the Bolsheviks would torpedo these efforts.

But Maltzan dismissed these, to him minor, considerations. He wished to avoid an agreement between Russia and the Western world. He wanted Russia on the side of Germany and felt that objective conditions favored such an alignment. He wanted friendship for Russia without sacrificing good relations with England, and saw in this double orientation Germany's only escape from foreign control.

It is not impossible that Maltzan never believed that the Bolsheviks were discussing reparations in the Villa d'Albertis. He may never have thought that Article 116 of Versailles would be applied to the detriment of Germany. Yet he used the argument for its effect on Rathenau, who was most susceptible to anything concerning reparations.

The Germans, in any event, realized that an agreement

[9] Carl Bergmann: *The History of Reparations,* (London, 1927).

between Russia and the Entente would be disastrous even if Article 116 did not become operative. For it would have created for Germany a state of permanent isolation which would be far more intolerable than the isolation they were experiencing during these very unpleasant days in Genoa.

Rathenau, being an extremely sensitive man, felt the offense of that isolation more keenly perhaps than other German plenipotentiaries. Maltzan played on that feeling. The results seemed to justify further talks with the Russians.

**THE RAPALLO TREATY** On the third day of the Villa d'Albertis conversations, Maltzan made an appointment to meet Rakovsky and Joffe at 10 A.M. in a Genoese café. The Germans skilfully sounded the Muscovites on the resumption of their Berlin treaty negotiations. Obviously, he said, there could be no question of German industrial assistance to Russia in case of an understanding with the Allies. Maltzan likewise pressed the point of certain political advantages. Rakovsky and Joffe replied that they attached great importance to co-operation with Germany, and that Russia was not at all averse to signing a treaty with Berlin. (The Germans immediately reported this possibility to members of the British delegation.)

Saturday evening the atmosphere in the Hotel Eden was blacker than ever. For rumor had it that the negotiations in the Villa d'Albertis stood on the verge of successful conclusion. In sour spirit, the German delegation went early to bed.

At one in the morning—it was Easter Sunday—a telephone call from Joffe awakened Maltzan. Would not the Germans come to Hotel St. Margherite, the Russian headquarters in Rapallo, at 11 the next morning, Joffe asked, to resume the Berlin conversations? "And what about the Villa d'Albertis negotiations?" Maltzan inquired. Those, came the reply across the wire, were proceeding satisfactorily, though no agreement had yet been reached. A recess had been declared over Easter Sunday and Monday.

Maltzan now aroused the entire German delegation and the famous "pajama party" took place which preceded the Rapallo Treaty. They conferred from one until three in the morning. Rathenau still opposed a separate pact with the Russians, though his opposition had weakened. Maltzan enthusiastically favored it. Wirth sided with him. One consideration was, "What will Berlin say?" for they knew in Genoa that President Ebert and the Social Democrats were convinced Westerners and would object to a treaty with the Bolsheviks. (Ebert's objections were ironed out in long telephone conversations later in the day.)

Finally the German delegation decided to motor to Rapallo, and at 7 A.M. they phoned the decision to Chicherin. At 7.30, with characteristic caution, the Germans tried to pass on this information to the British. But Mr. Wise could not be reached.

At noon on Easter Sunday, an automobile bearing Rathenau, Maltzan, and State Secretary von Simson drew up in front of the Hotel St. Margherite. Later Wirth came, and Gaus and others. A conference between Chicherin and Rathenau first dealt with general principles, and then Litvinov retired into a quiet chamber with Maltzan and Gaus to formulate the exact text.

Despite a protracted intermission for lunch and several little recesses to permit the two delegations to determine their own policies on disputed subjects, the treaty was ready for signing at 5 P.M., and at 6.30 P.M. Chicherin and Rathenau affixed their signatures to the historic document.

By the terms of the Rapallo Treaty, "Germany and the R.S.F.S.R. mutually renounce compensation for their war damages" and "for civil damages . . . caused by the forcible measures of the State authorities of the other party." Germany thus recognized the Bolshevik act of nationalization and forfeited all claims to compensation for damages resulting from that act.

Article 2 practically repeats the same German renunciation of claims upon the R.S.F.S.R. and the same recognition of Bolshevik expropriatory measures, but adds the highly important condition "that the Government of the R.S.F.S.R. does not satisfy similar claims of other States." As long as Russia paid no debts or reparations to other Powers, Germany would present no claims. But the moment Moscow essayed to satisfy the claims of England or France or the United States or even Luxemburg, Germany would be entitled, by this provision, to similar treatment.

Article 3 provided for the resumption of diplomatic and consular relations. No mention is made of *de jure* recognition because that had already been granted at Brest Litovsk.

The most-favored-nation principle found mutual approval in the next article, while in Article 5 the German Government promised to assist private German firms—with State-guaranteed credits?—in the extension of their contracts with the Soviets.

Subsequently, the Soviet Republic of Ukraine signed a similar treaty with Berlin in which it renounced its special claims on account of damages caused by the German occupation in 1918.

**THE SIGNIFICANCE OF THE RAPALLO TREATY**

Both delegations were extremely pleased with their achievement. The treaty was significant, first, as an unspoken protest of the anti-Versailles Powers against the Versailles Powers—and herein lies one explanation of the storm which the treaty loosed against Germany. But in the agreement there was likewise implicit close co-operation between Russia and Germany. This constituted the real object of French, Belgian, and other protests.

The treaty robbed the Entente of one of its most effective weapons against Moscow and Berlin: pressure by isolation. Germany, for once since the war, had discarded her role of passive object and taken the initiative in foreign policy. That move interfered with the Allies' plans with respect to Russia; a Russia befriended by Germany, the statesmen argued in their disappointment, could offer greater resistance to Western schemes for economic penetration by means of consortia, concessions, debt collections, "Dawes" schemes, etc.

The negotiations in the Villa d'Albertis had gone awry. Debts, credits, and property formed the obstacles to an agreement. The Bolsheviks had contrived to create a contrary impression on the Germans who were embittered and suspicious by reason of their mistreatment at Genoa.

The Germans might have waited until the complete failure of the Russians in Lloyd George's villa was common property. The British and the French might have informed the Germans of the failure. As it happened, the Bolsheviks adroitly utilized the short moment between the interruption of their discussions with the Allies and the inevitable resumption of the Allies' contact with the Germans to lead the Germans to the ink-well and quill.

The Germans probably lost little thereby. Germany's independence in concluding the treaty won her respect and consideration from the Versailles nations. As a result of the Genoa Conference, says Count Harry Kessler, Germany once more joined the ranks of the Great Powers. This German authority even maintains that Germany was the only country that benefited from the conference. Russia was prevented from joining a concert of Western Powers; England drew closer to Germany and further away from France; new confidence inspired German foreign policy. But the chief gain was the bond forged between Moscow and Berlin.

**THE NEW SITUATION** The Rapallo Treaty created a new and more difficult situation for the Allies. They had come to Genoa for the sole purpose of reaching a working agreement with Soviet Russia. They had presented certain demands in the Villa d'Albertis; Russia had rejected them. But the British, French, Italians and Belgians felt that Chicherin could not, in view of economic conditions at home, return to Moscow without some pledge of foreign assistance. Now, suddenly, he had received it from the Germans. That made pressure on Russia less effective and a one-sided agreement with Russia more distant. Allied assurance that the Communists could be compelled to accept outside help on the outsiders' terms and that the Red Republic would be opened to European exploitation began to wane.

The new situation widened the breach among the Allies. New alignments developed and new strategies were brought into play. After the Rapallo Treaty, negotiations continued between the Allies and Russia on the questions of debts and private property. Another talk over the teacups even took place in the park of the Villa d'Albertis where Lloyd George, Worthington-Evans, and Lord Birkenhead discussed the old problems with Chicherin and Litvinov. But the agreement with the Germans constituted an obstacle to an agreement with the other Powers. In Article 2 of the Rapallo document, Germany recognized the Bolsheviks' nationalization law, and renounced all private and governmental claims arising from it "provided the Government of the Russian Soviet Federative Socialist Republic does not satisfy similar claims of other States." Any understanding with the Allies on debts would therefore, ipso facto, cancel this, perhaps the most important stipulation of the Russo-German compact, and, furthermore, constitute a voluntary assumption by Russia of financial obligations vis-à-vis Germany which, for all practical purposes, were annulled by the letter of the Rapallo Treaty.

**THE ALLIED MEMORANDUM OF MAY 2** Early in the Genoa Conference, a serious difference of opinion appeared between the British and the Franco-Belgians. It is succinctly put by Wickham Steed in his wire from Genoa on April 28.

> The British view [he says] seems to be that the Allies can accept the Bolshevist principle of nationalization provided that private properties which have been seized be returned to their owners on a ninety-nine years' lease. The Belgian view is, on the contrary, that the maintenance of the freehold principle is essential. . . .

Belgium and France demanded full restitution of private property; the British would have contented themselves with a century concession.

The memorandum of May 2 said: "France, by reason of the effort which she is obliged to make in order to restore her own devastated areas, cannot at this moment afford direct financial assistance for the reconstruction of Russia." Here, above the signatures of the Great Powers, is one explanation of French tactics—France had too little money to invest in a grandiose scheme like a "Dawes" Plan or "Europa Consortium" or any other form of large-scale economic domination in Russia. She could therefore wait, and in the meantime insist on her maximum demands, safe in the assurance that the Bolsheviks would not accept them. The position, and policy, of Belgium were not dissimilar.

In the Bolshevik reply to the memorandum of May 2, the Russian delegation could not

> refrain from expressing its surprise that Powers like France, in which are found the majority of the small holders of Russian bonds, should have insisted most upon the restitution of property, thus subordinating the interests of the small holders of Russian bonds to those of certain groups who demand the restitution of property.

This, Chicherin observed, indicated that the Paris Government was prepared to sacrifice a large number of petty capitalists for the sake of a small number of big capitalists. The Bolsheviks emphasized, in their memorandum of May

11,[1] that "the Russian Government is determined to respect the interests of the small bondholders"; but Poincaré and Barthou were not impressed.

The Quai d'Orsay's position, however, did not lack rhyme and reason. Huge French—and Belgian—investments had been made in the Don and Ukrainian coal and metallurgical industries—the same investments which played their role in the geography of French interventionist and *cordon sanitaire* efforts. There was another factor. It was oil.

**PETROLEUM POLITICS** When the talks in the Villa d'Albertis failed, there followed the memorandum of May 2 which Belgium did not sign and which France did not approve—which, in effect, was accordingly a British product. Article VII of the memorandum presented the British proposals for meeting the problem of Soviet nationalization of foreign property. This article, more than any other, frustrated all efforts toward agreement.

By its terms, the Soviet Government was required to restore confiscated properties, and, where that was impossible, to pay compensation. "In cases in which the Russian Soviet Government cannot give back the property it shall not be entitled to hand it over hereafter to other parties." Each plot must be returned to its proprietor, or, where that is impossible, it must lie unused. Since such a scheme might prove unworkable, however, the very next paragraph of the article annuls it. "If the exploitation of the property," it reads, "can only be ensured by its merger in a larger group, the preceding provision shall not apply." Now the road was open to merger-concessions of the type which the Royal Dutch proposed to obtain in the Caucasus.

Obviously, Deterding could not adopt the Bolshevik method of dispossessing fellow-capitalists. He, accordingly, planned to absorb them into his concession and permit them to help finance the undertaking. But this arrangement would have obliged him to accept the partnership of the Standard Oil, since it too claimed a portion of Baku. To block such preferential treatment of the Shell's chief rival in the world oil industry, the British injected yet a third paragraph into the mooted article which defined a "pre-

[1] Full text in British Blue Book, Cmd. 1667. 1922.

vious owner" as a company controlled by foreign nationals "at the date of nationalization." The date of nationalization was 1917. The Standard Oil had bought its claim in 1920. The claim of the Standard Oil thus suffered cancellation under Article VII, and the American trust was effectively barred from participation in the merger-concession contemplated by the Royal Dutch. French interests consisting of papers purchased on the Paris Bourse subsequent to 1918 were similarly excluded.

**DETERDING'S CONCESSION** Article VII, in effect, paved the way to a Soviet concession to the Royal Dutch-Shell in which some small companies might participate but not Deterding's chief rival, the Standard Oil.

Henri Rollin, special Genoa correspondent of the Paris *Temps,* now wired his newspaper a long and sensational story in which he definitely affirmed that the Shell concession had already been signed. Excitement knew no bounds. Denials, affirmations, and declarations filled the air.

"The Press is full of oil to-day," telegraphed the Paris correspondent of the London *Times* on May 7. "Movements of oil magnates and alleged draft agreements to sign which the Bolsheviks are only awaiting the end of the conference." The Quai d'Orsay was aroused.

> . . . the French have at last awakened to the desirability of being specially represented at Genoa in the matter of oil, [continued the correspondent] and M. Laurent-Eynac, Under-Secretary of State for Aeronautics [and in 1920 Chief Commissar for Petroleum Affairs.—L.F.] has gone there to keep an eye on the proceedings of foreign oil negotiations.

With him went General Gassouin, president of the Standard Franco-Americaine, the Standard Oil subsidiary in France, and M. Pineau, head of the oil section of the French Ministry of Commerce.

But the French, prior to the Bolshevik revolution, had invested very little in the Russian oil industry. The official Czarist figure is 51,115,000 rubles. Belgian participation amounted to 6,812,500 rubles.[2] No large French or Belgian companies operated in the Caucasus before the War.

[2] Professor P. V. Ohl: *Foreign Capital in Russia,* (Petrograd, 1922). p. 105. The compilation is based on the records of Czarist ministries.

French petroleum efforts at Genoa therefore aroused the suspicion that France acted as the "Prætorian guard"[3] for the Standard Oil trust.

This now became the central idea of a hypothesis on which a number of observers essayed to fathom the secret of the Genoa Conference.

The London *News of the World,* owned by Lord Riddell, a personal friend of Lloyd George who himself attended the Genoa Conference and in all probability received his inspiration, if not his information, from the chief of the British delegation, wrote on May 6:

"The Standard Oil Company, one of the greatest secret forces of the world, is now fighting to prevent a Russian settlement on lines which they believe would give British oil interests virtual control of the great Russian oil industry."

> It is believed [the paper explains] that before the publication of the story [of the Shell concession.—L.F.] American oil interests had been active in Belgium and Paris, warning the Governments concerned against so-called British greed. Belgium's demand for the return of private property without leaving Russia the option of compensation, and the French amendment to the Russian memorandum may both have been thus influenced. It is also known that American oil interests brought pressure to bear at Washington to obtain a declaration from the American Government in favor of an open-door policy in Russia.

Mr. Bedford, of the Standard Oil Company, had declared himself in favor of the open door in Russia. "A fair and equal economic opportunity" was his formula. Mr. Bedford interviewed Mr. Hughes in the Washington State Department at this juncture. A few days later, on May 11, R. W. Child, United States ambassador in Italy, issued a statement in Genoa in which, after referring to the petroleum issue and to America's policy of protecting "in Europe and elsewhere American citizens who have properties and rights that require protection," he announced that "the United States will never consent that any scheme whatsoever, national or international, shall be applied unless it takes account of the principle of the open door for all and recognized equal rights for all."

The reference is obviously to the rumored Deterding concession, "Any scheme whatsoever, national or inter-

[3] Berlin *Lokal Anzeiger,* May 11, 1922.

national," is quite clear in its connotation. The open door meant, in this instance, equal rights in the Caucasus for Mr. Bedford's Standard Oil.

The intimate relationship between the open-door principle, the Standard Oil, the Deterding concession in Russia, the State Department and Mr. Child on the one hand, and the French and Belgian attitude towards nationalized private property on the other, naturally did not escape Wickham Steed, the editor of the London *Times*.

"As regards the Standard Oil," he telegraphed on May 9, "which wields great influence in the United States, it must be remembered that its acquisition of the oil rights of the Nobel Brothers in South Russia some time ago gives it a distinct status in Russian oil negotiations.

"This status," he continued, "clearly lends point to the support given by the United States to the French and Belgian attitude in regard to private property in Russia, as also to the polite invitation which the leading delegations here have received from the American ambassador" concerning the open door.

Great Britain knew, from a regretted experience, that the United States must not be defied when it championed the principle of the open door. Downing Street had been taught that lesson in the eighteen months' controversy over the Mesopotamian and Palestinian oilfields, a controversy which ended with victory for the State Department and Standard Oil.[4] America's political and economic influence had become too powerful since the War, and European States were too dependent on financial arrangements with Wall Street and Washington to permit of effective resistance against the serious wishes of the United States Government and United States business interests.

Mr. Child's activity on behalf of the open door was, accordingly, the finita la commedia of Genoa. The United States would not tolerate a concession to a British company that barred the Standard; therefore Deterding could accept none. Under the circumstances, a solution of the problem of private property, the most difficult obstacle to relations between Russia and the Western Powers, was impossible. The conversations in the Villa d'Albertis had

[4] *Correspondence between His Majesty's Government and the United States Ambassador respecting Economic Rights in Mandated Territories.* British White Paper. Cmd. 1226 (London, 1921).

proven that no modus vivendi on debts or credits could be found. The conference was a failure.

The two worlds, to be sure, now had a better understanding of one another. They had worked, dined, and laughed together. Practically, the conference established several principles: that Moscow would recognize and pay pre-war debts; that the Bolsheviks would grant concessions to former owners but would refuse to compensate them directly or restitute their property outright; that the Soviets would withdraw their counter-claims if they received credits; that Great Britain would not demand the restitution of nationalized property; and that the Powers would cancel or reduce Russia's World War obligations in consideration of her counter-claims. This represented an advance. But nothing was definitely settled. Genoa brought no concessions, no credits, no debt agreements, and no *de jure* recognition of the Soviet Government.

# 10

# IN THE ROYAL DUTCH CAPITAL

FOLLOWING a Bolshevik suggestion, which Lloyd George seized with avidity in an attempt to avoid the political consequences of defeat, the Genoa Conference decided to resurrect itself at The Hague in June.

The United States refused to attend. Germany was not invited. The British Government's attitude on private property remained the same as in Genoa. The French Government's attitude remained unchanged.

Obviously, therefore, the second act of Genoa could achieve success only if the Bolsheviks radically modified their previous position. The Western Powers trusted in the Russian economic crisis to make the Communists more conciliatory. Yet no prominent statesmen ventured the risk of failure by attending the Hague Conference in person.

The pomp and publicity of Genoa would not be The Hague's. Unlike Genoa, it would not be honored with the blessing of the Pope or the presence of Prime Ministers, Foreign Ministers and Archbishops. Nor would the world look to it so eagerly for the inauguration of a new era of European economic reconstruction.

**BOLSHEVIK POLICY** The Bolsheviks were pessimistic. "We expected little from The Hague," wrote Radek.[1] From the beginning we doubted the success of the conference, said Sokolnikov, a member of the Soviet delegation.[2]

[1] Moscow *Pravda* editorial, July 18, 1922.
[2] *Izvestia,* July 25, 1922.

Nevertheless, and in view of their desire to reach an agreement with the Western Powers, Litvinov, the chief of the Soviet representatives to The Hague, took with him to the conference proposals which, the Bolsheviks thought, might pave the way to a settlement.

The Bolsheviks considered their position more moderate than that of the Soviet delegation at Genoa. At Genoa the Bolsheviks demanded Government loans or Government credits. In The Hague "we changed our demands to such an extent," said Litvinov at the July 14 session of the Sub-Commission on Credits, "that we now agree to ask credits only from the industrialists. These, however, must have a Government guarantee."[3]

During the Genoa Conference, moreover, "we categorically refused to return that [private] property. We even refused to discuss the question of compensation."[4] In The Hague, Litvinov accepted the principle of compensation for the former owners of nationalized property.

The non-Russian and Russian sections of the Hague Conference approached the problem from diametrically opposed extremes. Litvinov promised favorable consideration for the interests of former owners if Moscow first obtained credits. Sir Philip Lloyd Greame (later Sir Philip Cunliffe-Lister), chief of the British experts and chairman of the Sub-Commission on Private Property, regarded the satisfaction of the former owners a necessary preliminary to the granting of credits.

**THE BOLSHEVIK ARGUMENT** The Soviet Government would not hear of unconditional, permanent restitution of private property. "The question of the restitution of private property . . . is utopian," said Krassin.[5]

The non-Russians therefore inquired what form of compensation the Bolsheviks contemplated.

Moscow proposed to grant concessions and to make compensation. It consented to grant concessions not because it accepted the principle that the properties belonged to their former owners, but in order to hasten the economic rehabilitation of Russia. The Bolsheviks, however,

[3] *Hague Conference: June–July, 1922. Complete Stenographic Report.* Published by the Commissariat for Foreign Affairs. Moscow, 1922. p. 165.
[4] *Ibid.*, p. 164.
[5] *Ibid.*, p. 48.

would under no condition return to each foreign company the plant it had previously held. They would merely open bids for concessions to certain mines, oilfields, fisheries, forestries, factories, etc. Former owners could apply; so could people who had never done any business in Russia. The Soviet delegates at The Hague promised, however, that the former owners would receive favored treatment in view of their valuable experience. This was no small advantage, Litvinov repeatedly stated at the sessions, and it was obvious from the attitude of the Bolsheviks that many of the properties that would revert to foreign management would be transferred, in the form of concessions, to their former owners. A *Pravda* editorial of June 17 made the same point and explained that once Russia was interested in attracting foreign capital she could have no desire to boycott the former owners.

The Russian delegation at The Hague submitted to the Sub-Commission on Private Property a long list of the plants and natural resources the Soviet Government intended to open to foreign exploitation.[6] It began with oilfields, and listed mines, chemical, electrical, and match industries, and farms. It included property formerly operated by foreigners but also properties formerly owned by the Russian state. It did not include all properties formerly operated by foreigners. The Bolsheviks argued that some nationalized plants had been completely destroyed in the intervention period, while some were of such special importance that the Soviet Government wished to retain them.

The Bolshevik delegation likewise examined into the question of compensating former owners with money or bonds.[7] And it wished, even before the Hague Conference closed, to arrive at a concrete debt settlement which would stipulate the total liability and the conditions of payment.

But no concessions would be granted, no compensation paid, and no debts refunded unless the Soviet Government obtained credits.

The Russians, first, justified their claims to credits on moral grounds. Intervention, they argued, did more harm to Russia than the revolution to foreigners. But

[6] *Ibid.*, pp. 218 ff.
[7] *Ibid.*, p. 46.

while revolution resembled a phenomenon of nature governed by its own laws of uncontrollable operation, intervention was a deliberate, voluntary act. Those responsible for it therefore bore an obligation to contribute towards the removal of the debris.

The damage caused by intervention Litvinov estimated at 39 to 50 billion gold rubles. "The war of 1914–17," he said, "and the interventionist wars of 1918–20, swalled five-twelfths of the national wealth of Russia."[8] The first stage of reconstruction which the Bolsheviks now contemplated required, according to Communist experts, a foreign credit of 3,224,000,000 gold rubles.[9]

"How can I answer any question regarding the compensation of foreign owners," Litvinov asked at the conference, "without knowing what will be the financial position of the Soviet Government three or five years from today?"[1] "If I told you," he added, "that we would pay compensation within a year or two, nobody would believe me. But given some knowledge of the probable measure of foreign aid, the Bolsheviks would undertake a detailed consideration of payments to former owners of nationalized properties and to the holders of Russian bonds."

**THE POSITION OF THE NON-RUSSIANS** The non-Russians at the Hague Conference replied that by acceding to the demands of the foreigners the Bolsheviks would re-establish confidence in their good faith and stability and thereby receive something of far greater value than Government-guaranteed loans or credits. The world must know, Sir Philip Lloyd Greame declared, that industry in Russia was being conducted efficiently and profitably; then it would give financial assistance.

> The entire problem of attracting foreign capital for the restoration of a given branch of industry [he said] will depend on two conditions: on the employment of good managers for the exploitation of the plants, and on a guarantee of the viability of these enterprises.[2]

In a word, "it was absolutely clear to him," to Sir Philip, "that it would be impossible to find either Government or private credits as long as private property owners were not granted satisfactory terms."[3]

[8] *Hague Conference. June–July, 1922. Complete Stenographic Report.* Published by the Commissariat for Foreign Affairs. Moscow, 1922, p. 134.
[9] *Ibid.*, p. 133.
[1] *Ibid.*, p. 69.
[2] *Ibid.*, p. 36.
[3] *Ibid.*, p. 44.

The essence of the non-Russians' program was: Dispel the uncertainty and distrust with which the outside world looks at Soviet Russia. Private investment would follow naturally.

During the greater part of the Hague Conference, the relationship of the British and the Italians to the Bolsheviks was more cordial than that of the French and the Belgians. This difference arose from a divergence of opinion on the most important subject which engaged the conference: the question of private property. At Genoa, Lloyd George had accepted the lease or concession principle. The French had insisted on unconditional restitution.

The problem of "Restitution or Concession" had torpedoed the Genoa Conference. Rather than yield one inch of the British position, Lloyd George had permitted the conference which was to have been the crowning glory of his political career to end in failure. The British Prime Minister had endangered the Entente and incurred the enmity of France by his insistence. His antagonism to the Franco-Belgian thesis of restitution continued after Genoa. It had undergone no change as late as June 10.

Yet on July 12, during the course of a session of the Sub-Commission on Private Property at The Hague, the British Government executed a sudden volte face and adopted the Paris-Brussels viewpoint. Sir Philip Lloyd Greame said:

> It has been perfectly plain to everybody that the only effective form of compensation for seized property within the power of the Russian Government to make at the present moment is the restitution of the property concerned wherever possible. . . . We came here to learn what could be restored.

Cattier, the Belgian expert, agreed. "The Russian Government," he declared, "must restore the property or give real compensation. There is no other alternative."

As long as the possibility existed that the British advocacy of concessions might prevail, the negotiations at The Hague enjoyed some prospect of success. But when the intransigent Franco-Belgian policy of restitution was adopted by the British, the situation became hopeless. Immediately, the impasse in the Sub-Commission on Private Property communicated itself to the Sub-Commissions on Debts and Credits, and on the 14th of July all three had discontinued their activities.

**A NEW BOLSHEVIK PROPOSAL** Although the Russians at The Hague had offered terms far more moderate than those of Genoa, Litvinov would not allow the delegates to disperse without making one more attempt to reach a settlement. He therefore insisted that a plenary session of the conference be convened to listen to a new Bolshevik proposal.

When his request was granted, Litvinov informed the conference that he proposed, if the experts agreed, to request his Government for new instructions—to inquire of Moscow "whether the Russian Government consents to recognize the obligations of the former Russian Government to foreign citizens even if credits . . . would not be available at the present time?" Credits had been the Bolshevik *sine qua non.* Now the head of the Soviet delegation at least admitted the possibility of the withdrawal of this condition. He would likewise inquire whether Moscow would, in the absence of credits, grant compensation, in the form of concessions or of equally concrete values, to former owners of sequestrated property.

Litvinov first aired this suggestion at a private dinner at which he, Leslie Urquhart, Sir Sidney Chapman and Krassin were present. In the session, Sir Philip Lloyd Greame attached "extra-ordinary importance" to Litvinov's plan and felt that it "represented a new epoch in their negotiations." But Cattier, who expressed the Franco-Belgian view, gave the Litvinov declaration a different and less favorable interpretation. At this juncture, the chairman, however, interrupted the discussion and asked the Russians when the reply from Moscow might be expected. Within four days to a week, Litvinov answered. Herewith, the first and only plenary session of the Hague Conference adjourned.

The non-Russian representatives had not tried to dissuade Litvinov from consulting his Government. They had, in some instances, declared their interest in his proposal. They knew that not even a telegraphic reply could be placed before them before four days. Yet on July 20, twenty-four hours after Litvinov had appeared before the plenary session, the non-Russians met and declared the Hague Conference closed. At the same time they adopted a resolution recommending that all Governments refrain from assisting their nationals in acquiring properties in

Russia which had not belonged to those nationals prior to the Bolshevik act of expropriation. Mr. Cattier, who moved this resolution, stated that the United States Government approved of its contents and had authorized him to make a public announcement to that effect.

**THE UNITED STATES AND THE HAGUE** Why should the American Government have been so eager to make known its agreement with the resolution? What was the exact meaning and significance of the resolution? Why did the conference adjourn immediately after receiving an "epoch-making" proposal from the Russians which may have provided a more promising basis for further negotiations? Why did the British, after persistently defending the concessions policy, unexpectedly accept the restitution principle?—All these puzzles suggest that even more happened at the Hague Conference than is revealed by its stenographic record. . . .

France had loaned most money to pre-war Russia. Yet France was most opposed to the repayment of Russia's pre-war loans as proposed by Chicherin in Genoa and by Litvinov in The Hague. Even to France, whose financial stake in Russian debts was far greater than in Russian private property, the chief issue remained private property.

The United States, on the contrary, lent very little to the Czar's Government. Nor did Americans invest heavily in Russian industry. Moreover, such property as United States nationals had held—the Luberetzky factory of the International Harvester Company and the Petrograd plant of Westinghouse Brake—had never undergone nationalization. The only large American interest involved in the Soviet treatment of private property was the claim to Baku which the Standard Oil purchased from Nobel, a Russian citizen, in 1920. Even those authorities who dispute the right of a State to alienate the wealth of foreigners, concede that law and precedent are on the side of a Government which confiscates the property of its own citizens. And the Russians would add that in buying a claim to oilfields subsequent to the decree of nationalization from a seller who was no longer the owner, the Standard Oil speculated on the fall of the Soviet Government or the cancellation of the Nationalization Act.

The Standard Oil claim was the only American interest

involved in M. Cattier's motion of July 20 which the United States State Department had, by procedure uncommon in diplomacy, seen fit to endorse.

**BEHIND THE SCENES** On June 15, 1922, the very day the Hague Conference assembled, the Franco-Belgian Petrol Syndicate organized in Paris. The foundation of this syndicate had been laid at Genoa by M. Laurent-Eynac, an official representative of the French Government.[4] The chairman of the syndicate's first meeting was M. Pineau, director of the Essences and Pétroles Service of the French Ministry of Commerce. He had accompanied Laurent-Eynac to Genoa.

The new syndicate immediately sent "delegates" to The Hague who "put themselves at the disposal of the French and Belgian experts."[5] Mr. H. G. Trew of the British Spies Petroleum Company, Ltd., and Richard R. Tweed of the Baku Consolidated Oilfields, Ltd., likewise proceeded to The Hague, "and behind the official doors conversations followed with Sir Henri Deterding and other representatives [Mr. Samuel and Colonel Boyle.—L.F.] of the Royal Dutch-Shell combination. One fancies that this was the Hague Conference which really mattered."[6] It was convened, according to the Paris *Temps,* by Sir Henri Deterding "through the President of the Hague Conference [the official one.—L.F.] and the various delegations."

This petrol council held parallel meetings with the Hague Conference, and observers hinted that its deliberations were not without their effect on the official sessions.

The Bolshevik concession proposal at the Hague Conference satisfied none of the oil interests. It certainly did not please Deterding, who, in Genoa, had envisaged the possibility of Shell control over all of Baku and Grozni whereas the Russian offer in The Hague limited him to the lands his company had previously worked. Litvinov, moreover, made no definite pledge that all the expropriated owners would obtain leases to their former properties, nor did he outline concession terms that were concrete and acceptable. The petrol council, conferring behind the scenes in the Royal Dutch capital, accordingly closed its ranks and

[4] Paris *Journée Industrielle,* May 20, 1922, and *Matin,* May 19, 1922.
[5] *Le Courrier des Pétroles.* Paris, July 22, 1922.
[6] Davenport and Cooke: *The Oil Trusts and Anglo-American Relations,* London, 1923.

presented a united front of opposition towards Moscow's concessions policy.

The unanimity in "the Hague Conference which really mattered" corresponded with the unexpected agreement between the Anglo-Italian and Franco-Belgian sections of the official conference: the Royal Dutch rejected the Bolshevik ideas on concessions, and Sir Philip Lloyd Greame accepted the Paris-Brussels thesis of restitution.

Faced by a new alignment of harmonious forces, the Russians resurrected their Genoa formula of a merger-monopoly concession.

> The Bolshevik spokesman [reads a Hague telegram to the London *Daily Telegraph* of July 18] today made an important admission that Russia, instead of returning the various oil properties to their original owners, intended to form one general company to carry on all operations. The oil company which gets the contract to operate all the oil fields will be asked to satisfy the other claimants.

This announcement had all the earmarks of Soviet concessions policy. In 1925, the Soviet Government gave such a blanket lease to W. A. Harriman, of New York, for the Chiaturi manganese deposits, leaving Harriman to reach his own settlement with the previous foreign exploiters.

When the Soviet renewal of the merger-monopoly concession offer became known in The Hague, Sir Henri Deterding immediately attempted to win the Franco-Belgian Syndicate and the lesser British companies for the merger. He would readily have amalgamated with these in order to exclude his chief world rival, the Standard Oil.

The Belgians, it was said,[7] received Sir Henri's advances coldly, but the French reacted more favorably. The Royal Dutch-Shell controlled a large fraction of the French internal oil market and could, moreover, influence Parisian political and journalistic circles. France may also have responded to the possibility of debt payments which Litvinov's declaration to the plenary session of the Hague Conference opened for her.

But it was only for a moment. On the 20th, M. Cattier, the Belgian delegate, presented his motion. The State Department proclaimed America's agreement, and France and Britain followed. After the events of Cannes and

[7] *Courrier des Pétroles*. Paris, July 22, 1922.

Genoa, and in view of the Franco-British friction which characterized that period of post-war European politics, a common policy with America conformed more with Poincaré's taste—and offered him greater advantages—than joint action with England.

Throughout the Hague Conference, the question of private property dominated the proceedings. Debts, which involved far greater sums, were subordinated to it. And of the properties concerned, oilfields played the most conspicuous role.

**SOVIET INTERPRETATION OF HAGUE CONFERENCE'S FAILURE** Returning from The Hague, Litvinov told the foreign journalists in Berlin that the reply of the Soviet Government to his intended telegraphic inquiry from The Hague would have satisfied England and a number of other countries. For this very reason, he said, the non-Russians dispersed before Moscow's answer could have been received. They did not wish to demonstrate their lack of unity.[8]

Lloyd George was, at this period, involved in the Greco-Turkish war situation where France had it within her power seriously to undermine British prestige and perhaps even cause England territorial losses. Lord Curzon, the British Foreign Minister, vehemently opposed his Prime Minister's tactics and sought, with some success, to strengthen the Anglo-French entente.[9] Curzon's policy, therefore, did not tolerate friction with Poincaré on the Russian question. The Anglo-Russian Trade Agreement of March 16, 1921, Curzon's biographer tells us, "had always been looked on by Lord Curzon with feelings of cold disfavor."[1] The former Viceroy of India never trusted the Bolsheviks to refrain from propaganda in Asia. India was always uppermost in his mind, and the interests of India demanded a settlement with Turkey which Poincaré would not prevent. Co-operation with Paris therefore became a cardinal element in Curzon's foreign outlook. And especially since he attached little value to better relations with Soviet Russia, the failure of the Hague Conference through British agreement with France had no terrors for Curzon;

[8] *Izvestia.* Moscow, July 27, 1922.

[9] The Earl of Ronaldshay: *The Life of Lord Curzon,* Vol. III, Chap. XVII. (London, 1928).

[1] *Ibid.,* p. 354.

on the contrary, he saw the advantage of such a development.

Lloyd George had lost much influence since Genoa. In October, 1922, the Conservatives, under the leadership of Bonar Law, Curzon, and Austen Chamberlain, would force his resignation. In July, therefore, he was unable to insist on his Russian policy. Even at Genoa, at the height of his power, he failed to overcome Franco-Belgian-American resistance. Now the prospect was nil. Therefore the Hague Conference failed, said the Russians.

The chief economic explanation of the failure at The Hague, the Russians declared, was European bankruptcy. The Governments of the West gave Moscow no credits because they had none to give, ran the Bolshevik refrain. "The collapse of the conference," said Sokolnikov, "can be attributed mainly to the utter financial impotence of the reactionary French Government."[2]

Chicherin and Krassin conferred with American diplomats in Europe during this period, and Krassin gathered the impression that the United States would use every means at its command to prevent Britain from exploiting the economic possibilities of Russia.[3] This, he believed, offered another explanation of their inability to reach a settlement at The Hague.

According to Krassin, German inflation and the fall of the mark likewise affected the situation. A financial catastrophe in Germany, he said, would constitute a menace to all the Powers, but especially to England on account of her maritime trade. London therefore wished to check any aggressive French measures against Germany and could do so best by maintaining the entente with France. To England and to Europe generally, Russia consequently became a problem of only secondary importance.[4]

It is not impossible, however, that Poincaré fought a settlement with Russia partly out of fear that it would stabilize European politics and prevent French occupation of the Ruhr.

**BOLSHEVIK ESTIMATES OF THE FUTURE** The Bolsheviks felt that they were thrown back on their own resources. The task was now greater than they had at first

[2] *Izvestia*, July 25, 1922.
[3] *Ibid.*, August 8, 1922.
[4] *Ibid.*

fancied. They had planned to place a fraction of the responsibility of reconstruction upon foreign industrialists, and to finance at least a part of their own lion's share of the undertaking by the attraction of foreign capital. They had miscalculated. They would have to shoulder the entire burden themselves.

Russia in 1921 was a ruin. The World War, the Civil War, the Polish-Russian War, intervention, the blockade, and the famine which was a result of all these and of an unprecedented drought, had undermined industry, trade, and agriculture. The writer first saw Russia in the autumn of 1922. The gradual uphill climb had commenced. But the wounds of the recent past were ubiquitous. Trains moved slowly and irregularly. Railway rolling stock was badly in need of repair and replacement, and the station "hospitals" were overfilled with "sick" locomotives that had been crippled serving the fronts. The streets of Moscow required paving, and houses wanted plastering and general renovation. People looked haggard and poorly dressed. The outskirts of Petrograd represented a forest of dead smoke-stacks. Hundreds of factories throughout the country were idle and thousands were therefore unemployed. Hordes of homeless waifs, whose life-history rang like a monotone: "Father killed in battle, mother died in the famine," combed the cities and the country-side.

Food, however, was plentiful, and each day as one wandered through the streets gathering impressions in the new, strange surroundings, one noted more stores that had shed the boards from their plate glass and commenced to fill their show windows with eagerly sought goods. Most of these shops had been closed since 1918. Every day, too, the newspapers announced the re-opening of more and more mines and plants.

Upbuilding now became Moscow's primary concern. The Bolsheviks riveted their attention on the domestic scene and felt that Allied policy had isolated them.

Nevertheless, the Soviet Government did not despair of an agreement with Great Britain, Italy, and other countries whose attitude at The Hague had impressed the Russian delegation as relatively cordial. As long as France pursued her anti-Soviet strategy, and as long as she found encouragement in Brussels and Washington, joint conferences with a view to collective settlements could achieve no practical results. Acting on this assumption, the Bolsheviks adopted the slogans of separate agreements with governments and separate contracts with private capitalists.

The Bolsheviks were particularly hopeful about England. But they reckoned without Lord Curzon. They expected that the Royal Dutch, twice thwarted at Genoa and The Hague, would knock at their door again. Instead Sir Henri Deterding joined in a world boycott of Caucasian petroleum.[5] They intended to give Leslie Urquhart a concession to his previous vast holdings in Siberia and believed such action would affect the British Government's policy. But the Turkish situation interfered.

Despite a very expressed Bolshevik desire to agree with the Powers, objective conditions or the policies of those Powers frequently prevented agreement. Moscow hoped, but was not very sanguine. The Soviet Government, as Trotzky said, now intended "to work and to wait."

[5] Discussed in detail in Chap. IV of *Oil Imperialism,* by Louis Fischer. New York, 1926.

# 11

# DISARMAMENT AND BOLSHEVISM

THROUGHOUT the greater part of 1922 Lenin was confined in bed by the mysterious workings of a combination of complicated maladies which were destined to demand his life. But in October a marked improvement occurred, and on November 1 he appeared unexpectedly in the throne room of the Czar's palace in the Kremlin where the Central Executive Committee was in session. He entered unobtrusively and, in order not to interrupt Krylenko's report on legal matters, slipped quietly into a chair near the door. Then the delegates discovered him and an ovation followed. With a walk that resembled a run he moved to the platform where, holding a little watch in the hollow of his hand—for his physicians had limited him to an hour's speech—he began his address. "We greet the Red Army," were his first words. The Bolsheviks had the day previous taken Vladivostok on the far-off Pacific. "The last forces of the White Guards," Lenin announced, "have been thrown into the sea."

Long negotiations in Dairen and Chang Chun between Russia and Japan had preceded the occupation of the Siberian Maritime Provinces by Red troops. There was no raison d'être now for the Far Eastern (Chita) Republic, and on November 14, 1922, this artificial buffer adhered to the Russian Socialist Federated Soviet Republic (R.S.F.S.R.). Moscow ruled from the White Sea to the Black, from the Baltic to the Pacific, over a territory that comprises one-sixth of the earth's dry surface. Foreign forces were left only in Northern Sakhalin. And, except for skirmishes in Turkestan with Enver Pasha, the Civil War had drawn to a close.

The gradual diminution of internecine fighting in Russia had warranted a corresponding weakening of the Red Army, and in August, 1922, Leon Trotzky, the Commissar of War, was able to announce that the strength of the Soviets' armed forces had fallen from 5,300,000 to 800,000. "Further reduction," however, "required serious changes in the international situation." It required a general reduction of armaments.

After Chicherin's failure to precipitate a disarmament debate at Genoa, Moscow despaired of drawing the big Powers into a discussion of the question, but hoped, nevertheless, to achieve practical results by convening a meeting of Russia's immediate neighbors. With this end in view, Litvinov addressed invitations on June 12, 1922, to Poland, Estonia, Latvia, and Finland to examine with Russia "the proportionate reduction of respective armaments." Time and place were left open.

While accepting in principle, these states urged postponement in deference to the League of Nations which intended to deal with the subject of disarmament at a forthcoming session. The Bolshevik reply doubted whether "the so-called League of Nations" was anxious or able to effect a limitation of armaments; yet Litvinov consented to delay the opening until November 30—in Moscow.

Litvinov invited Rumania while at The Hague, but Bucharest demanded Russian recognition of its suzerainty in Bessarabia as a condition of attendance. The Bolsheviks refused: the Moscow Disarmament Conference would not concern itself with political or territorial problems; it must remain unfettered by previous conditions; Bessarabia, moreover, had been seized illegally. Rumania therefore absented herself, agreeing only that Poland make declarations on her behalf at the sessions. The non-attendance of Rumania, according to the Bolshevik view, should have made disarmament more acceptable to Poland, for it meant that while the Polish army would be reduced, the army of Rumania, Poland's ally, would remain intact.

## THE BOLSHEVIK APPROACH TO DISARMAMENT

In 1922 the process of Soviet economic reconstruction had commenced, and the Communists wished to devote to it all their energy. They were too weak and poor to fight. The disarmament of Russia's neighbors would not make peace absolutely certain, but it would prejudice the situation in favor of peace. The Red Press, moreover, intimated that Soviet counsels hoped the effect of the Moscow Conference would spread and perhaps lead to general disarmament.

A French blow at Germany—which the Bolsheviks considered not unlikely—might, in their opinion, involve the rest of Europe. A peace move, especially if it were participated in by Poland, a neighbor of Germany and an ally of France, would conceivably exert a formidable influence on the trend of political events on the Continent.

The counter-revolutionary movement within Russia was, for combatant purposes, definitely moribund. But the idea of the *cordon sanitaire* was not dead, and Poland represented a longest and strongest segment of the barrier. Poland had incurred the undying enmity of the Lithuanians by seizing Vilna, which they regarded as their capital and as one of their chief cultural centers. The question of Polish disarmament therefore involved Lithuanian disarmament, and any question that concerned Poland and Lithuania was a life interest to the remaining Baltic States.

It made little practical differences to Russia whether Latvia had an army of 20,000 or 30,000 men or whether there were 15,000 or 25,000 Estonians under arms. But without at least the partial demilitarization of all the States just outside the Soviet periphery, no one State would consent to disarm.

Immediately the conference opened on December 2, Litvinov therefore proposed that all the participants reduce their land forces 75 per cent within the next eighteen to twenty-four months, disband all irregular military formations, and limit armament expenditures.[1]

## THE OPPOSITION OF THE SECESSION STATES

The invited countries had previously met to determine their policy at the conference. Poland naturally dominated such meetings and her influence sufficed to exclude Lithuania. First Finland, Estonia, and Latvia gathered in Reval, in August, to decide on a common strategy towards Poland and towards Russia. The next month, representatives

[1] *Conférence de Moscou pour Limitation des Armaments.* Edition du Commissariat du Peuple aux Affaires Etrangères. (Moscow, 1923) p. 47.

of these three nations and Rumania discussed the Moscow disarmament problem with Polish statesmen in Warsaw. In October a similar preliminary conference took place in Reval—without Rumania. It resembled a dress rehearsal for the Moscow deliberations.

"The Polish delegation," President Norutovitch of Poland told newspaper correspondents, "will be guided in Moscow by the line of conduct worked out at the Reval Conference of the border States."[2] This was a bad beginning, the Russians commented, and when Prince Janus Radziwill, the Polish plenipotentiary, referred to "the rich experience of the League of Nations in disarmament projects,"[3] they feared that the outlook had been darkened. What, they asked, had the "so-called League of Nations" ever done to further disarmament? The prince with the Lithuanian surname and the Roman Christian name added the pessimistic prediction that "our work will not be easy," but it could be "useful."

Moscow believed that an agreement with the Baltic States on disarmament was a relatively simple matter. But "they lack the courage to break with Poland and march their own way. . . . If the Moscow Conference fails, the entire responsibility will fall on Poland's shoulders."[4]

Throughout the conference, Poland defended what has since become known as the French thesis of "Security First." An atmosphere of mutual confidence must be established. Then treaties of non-aggression may be concluded, and arbitration agreements signed. These would, in turn, usher in an era of moral disarmament in which, and only in which, material disarmament would be feasible. All the invited States supported this principle, and Lithuania even argued that since League membership had not prevented her from being invaded nor Poland from invading her, she could trust solely in the strength of her army.

The Baltic countries and Poland consistently refused to discuss land disarmament until all outstanding political issues were solved by negotiation. But they wished to add the question of naval disarmament to the agenda of the conference.

[2] *Izvestia,* November 28, 1922.
[3] *Ibid.,* December 3, 1922.
[4] *Pravda,* December 12, 1922.

Russia had limited the scope of the conference to armies, just as the United States had limited the Washington Disarmament Conference to fleets. Naval disarmament was not a question the Bolsheviks could discuss with their neighbors only. The Soviet Navy, weak, outmoded, and ill-equipped though it was, could probably have resisted an assault by any of the little Powers on the Baltic or even by a combination of all those Powers. But Russia's coastline is 39,000 kilometers long. On her sea-coast, for every practical purpose, she is the neighbor of Great Britain, France, Germany, Japan, and even the United States, as well as of Sweden, Norway, Denmark, Turkey, and Rumania. Yet now the Poles and Balts alone demanded the inclusion of naval disarmament into the program of the Moscow conference.

**MOSCOW COMPROMISES** Faced with a united front of the invited Powers, Moscow yielded not merely on this point which involved no question of principle, but agreed, after some wrangling, to the priority of political discussions. The Bolsheviks would, in the circumstances, sign new treaties, accept new arbitration regulations, and go through all the motions of moral disarmament whose efficacy they doubted, if, at the same conference, definite steps were taken in the direction of material disarmament which the Russians viewed as "the first condition of moral disarmament." Russia, Litvinov repeatedly averred, does not wish the conference to end only with additional affirmations, and another sealed document. She "does not wish to attach her signature to phrases which hide the absence of real achievement."

Assuming a subsequent agreement on disarmament that would be included in it, the Soviet delegation and the delegations of Poland, Latvia, Finland, and Estonia now adopted a convention providing for mutual abstention from armed aggression, neutrality in case any country not a party to the convention would commit an act of aggression against one of the signatory Powers, and the peaceful arbitration of all conflicts. This was the first and only time in its history that the Soviet Government accepted the principle of international arbitration in political matters. The articles of ratification, it was agreed, would be deposited in Christiania (Oslo) because the Communists objected to Berne.

The conference thereupon settled down to deliberate

upon the subject for which it had been convened—land disarmament.

**RUSSIAN DISARMAMENT PROPOSAL** Litvinov, and Victor Kopp, the second Soviet representative, stated that Moscow desired to refrain from radical changes and 75 per cent reductions which might meet the disapproval of other States, and therefore proposed, as an initial move, to reduce her army in 1923 from 800,000 to 600,000 if the invited countries made proportional reductions. Military budgets, moreover, would be limited to a sum equal to the number of individuals in the force multiplied by 400 rubles. Such limitation, the Bolsheviks submitted, would prevent the expenditure of huge funds on technical equipment in order to cancel the effect of decreased man-power.

In accordance with the Soviet plan, Poland thereupon declared its intention of cutting her army to a strength of 280,000, Finland to 28,000, Latvia to 19,000 and Estonia to 16,000, while Lithuania, which originally rejected the scheme on the ground of her dispute with Poland, later accepted without presenting detailed data.

The Moscow Disarmament Conference was now ready for its bomb-shell sensation. When the delegates had all gathered in the conference hall of the Commissariat of Foreign Affairs, Victor Kopp arose, and, reading from a paper, declared that Poland had, in reply to a League of Nations questionnaire, informed Geneva on June 22, 1922, that the number of effectives in her army was 275,367 men and 18,377 officers, making a total of 293,744. If she now proposed to reduce her army to 280,000 effectives, the reduction would amount to only 13,000 or 4.5 per cent instead of the prescribed 25 per cent. Poland, Kopp charged, had put her army strength at 370,000 in order to nullify the effect of the reduction proposed by the conference.

Prince Janus Radziwill protested. "The Polish delegation," he said, "did not object to the figure given by the Russian delegation for the reduction of the Russian Army." A discussion of the Polish figures will bring no results. "The Polish delegation refuses to answer questions concerning Poland's budget for the present year." No explanation was offered for the discrepancy between Warsaw's data to Geneva and to Moscow.

Information at the disposal of the Soviet Government,

moreover, was to the effect that Latvia's army at the time of the conference consisted of 19,500 and Estonia's of 14,000 men, so that when the former proposed to cut its armed force to 19,000, the reduction equalled only 2½ per cent; while Estonia, according to Russian data, would actually obtain international sanction for an army increase of 14 per cent.[5]

On these rocks the Moscow Disarmament Conference foundered. Since it was impossible to find the mathematical basis for reduction of armaments, there could be no reduction, and since Litvinov had emphasized times without number that the non-aggression and neutrality convention had been accepted by the Soviets conditionally and only in order to win the invited nations for the cause of disarmament, the convention, now that disarmament had failed, remained unsigned.

Thus ended the conference. It produced a better feeling between Russia and Lithuania, and more understanding between Russia and Latvia, Estonia, and Finland. Moscow's relations with Poland suffered.

[5] *Official Report of the Commissariat of Foreign Affairs for the Year 1922.* (Moscow, 1923).

# 12

# REVOLUTIONARY RUSSIA AND REVOLUTIONARY TURKEY

RUSSIA is both Oriental and Occidental. The World War deprived Russia of her most developed Western provinces —Poland, and the Baltic States. The revolution, under compulsion, moved the nation's capital from Petrograd, "the Paris of the North," to Moscow, the Byzantine city. The armed hostility of the West towards the Soviet regime caused the Communists to look eastward for relief—especially since the repercussion of Bolshevism in Asia found expression in a nationalist protest against Russia's imperialist foes.

Simultaneously, however, the Bolsheviks trusted in the European proletariat to rise and overwhelm the interventionist Governments. Moscow's highest hopes were reposed in the "cavalry of the West." The "infantry of the East," the tens of millions of Moslems, Mongols, and Hindus, would constitute only the rearguard. But the direction of the frontal attack was westward.

The overthrow of Czarism, the disappearance of the nobility, and the discarding of the Oriental pomp and regalia connected with these institutions, as well as the weakening of the Greek Catholic Church, in origin and character Eastern, served as influences towards Westernization. Further factors operating in the same direction were the introduction of the Latin alphabet and script in Transcaspia and the Caucasus, the fight against the veil in Turkestan, increased literacy, and, above all, the growing industrialization and modernization of the city, and, partly, of the village.

In foreign affairs, Russia's orientation can never be wholly Eastern or wholly Western. It must be both. Yet differences of emphasis are inevitable and result from changing circumstances. The Polish War, the Anglo-Russian Trade Agreement, the prospect of commerce with Europe which opened the inauguration of the NEP, and the expectations inspired by the Genoa Conference undoubtedly drew Russia's attention to the West, and away from the Middle East, and away from her special interest in developments that could antagonize possible sources of credits, loans, and business. Comintern psychology and Eastern political orientation were in *diminuendo*. But the failure of the Genoa and Hague meetings, the failure even of the Moscow Disarmament Conference, and the distressing difficulty of establishing any sort of normal, regular relations with European states, provoked a reversal of feeling in Moscow. This, together with the remarkable recrudescence of the Turkish nationalist movement under Kemal Pasha at a time when Russian economic rehabilitation had not yet progressed sufficiently to demand the indispensable co-operation with Europe of a later day, produced a definite change of political emphasis. The East was again trump—the inevitable corollary was the renewal of the struggle with England which the attitude of Lord Curzon seemed to encourage.

The Soviet rejection of the Urquhart concession on the ground that Great Britain was pursuing an anti-Turkish policy, throws a bright light on the mentality of this period.

**THE STORY OF ENVER PASHA** The Bolsheviks had, from the very beginning, adopted an extremely cordial and helpful attitude towards Kemal Pasha. And Kemal Pasha displayed an active sympathy for the Soviet Government.

Enver and Kemal nursed an old hatred for one another.

During the World War, in fact, Enver was the actual ruler of the country, and with Talaat Pasha and Djemal Pasha constituted a dictatorial triumvirate. His name was a power to conjure with from Berlin to Bagdad, and his reputation as a vigorous, imaginative leader of men had spread even to the borders of India. Kaiser Wilhelm knew his influence. The Sultan-Caliph did his bidding.

In this period, Mustapha Kemal was merely an army commander. But he was a stormy petrel. He had quarrelled with Enver Pasha during the War of Tripoli and again during the Balkan Wars. In the course of the World War, after Kemal had repulsed the British on the bloodiest sector of the Gallipoli front, a sharp disagreement arose between him and Enver on the subject of army organization, and Kemal, whose military genius could not be spared, was sent to the Mesopotamian-Palestinian front "in disgrace." There he came into conflict with the German General von Falkenhayn and, much to Enver's chagrin, resigned from the army. But Liman von Sanders, Falkenhayn's successor, persuaded Mustapha Kemal to return. And when the Sultan's forces were crushed by General Allenby, Kemal received a commission from von Sanders to hold Adana and re-organize the Turkish Army. Here he made the first steps towards his future position as Turkey's national hero.

A week before the armistice between Turkey and the Western Entente, Kemal appeared in Constantinople and soon received the important appointment of Inspector-General of Anatolia.

While Kemal was rising to power, Enver was falling into disgrace. His armies had met miserable defeat in the Caucasus; his policies, it was claimed, had caused the collapse of his country. In 1919, he was condemned to death.

He escaped and tried to reach Odessa. But a storm arose on the Black Sea, broke the mast of his little sailing vessel and obliged him to return to Turkey. Bent on reaching Russia, however, he made his way to Germany, where he secretly boarded his own airplane in an effort to fly to Moscow. The machine crashed. He spent some time in a prison in Kovno, and a few weeks in another in Riga.[1] Finally, in 1920, he reached Moscow.

Enver had been preceded to the Soviet capital by Djemal Pasha, his colleague in the famous triumvirate, by Halil Pasha and by Semi Bey. What were these prominent Turks seeking in Russia? At the Baku Congress of Eastern Peoples a declaration was read from Enver Pasha in which he protested that he "hated and cursed German imperialism and the German imperialists as much as he

[1] *Stenographic Record of the First Congress of Eastern Peoples.* (Petrograd, 1920), p. 110.

did British imperialism and the British imperialists." He was a friend of the Soviet Republic and of the Soviet idea, he said; he favored the revolution and would fight in the interests of oppressed peoples.

But the Congress did not believe Enver, nor did the Bolsheviks. Djemal had been easier to handle. Djemal entertained no immediate anti-Kemalist ambitions. The British were fighting the Communists. A state of active hostility existed between Russia and England. Afghanistan at the time was engaged in a struggle for independence with England. Moscow, accordingly, directed Djemal Pasha's attention towards Kabul.

At Kabul, Djemal immediately won high regard and exercised considerable influence over Amanullah Khan. The constitution of Afghanistan was largely his work. He likewise assisted in the organization of the Afghan army.

Enver had wilder flights of fancy than Djemal. His imagination swept all of Asia. His ambitions were boundless. . . . In Moscow he always wore an unusually high black tarboosh to detract attention from his low stature.

The Bolsheviks knew Enver's talents as a military and political leader. They knew also that he was an adventurer. But Enver was violently anti-British. England had destroyed the Turkish Empire and annexed part of Turkey's Arabian domains. England was largely responsible for the defeat of Turkish arms in the World War. England, moreover, wished to drive "the Unspeakable Turk" out of Europe.

The Bolsheviks first attempted to reconcile Enver and Kemal. The attempt failed. Then they thought they could use Enver as they had used Djemal. Enver, speculating on the old Russian hatred for Great Britain and on the possibilities of the new hostility between Red Moscow and Imperial London, came to the Soviet capital in the expectation of receiving sympathy and support. An excellent partnership might have sprung up if Enver's dreams had fitted into Bolshevik plans. But the only field for Enver's activities was Afghanistan—far too narrow for a man of his nature.

Enver's mind's-eye swept empires. He dreamt of reestablishing the kingdom of Tamerlane. He saw himself the ruler of a realm embracing Chinese Turkestan, Russian Turkestan, Kazakstan, and Afghanistan. Then, like

Alexander the Great, he would march through the Khyber Pass into India and strike a mortal blow at the British Empire. He would be the Napoleon of Asia.

He hid these ambitions. For while they were anti-British they also involved Soviet territory. Enver felt, furthermore, that the success of his Pan-Turanian Empire depended on his conquest, first, of the center of the Turanian world—Turkey. He must overthrow Kemal Pasha.

But while Enver chafed under months of idleness in Moscow, the Russians were cementing their relations with Kemal. In the beginning, Enver Pasha tried to act as an intermediary in the Russo-Turkish negotiations and to put himself in the position of the real representative of Turkey. "Mustapha Kemal," he would say, "is weak. He is known neither at home nor abroad. I, on the other hand, have a reputation throughout Turkey and Europe. Every child in the Moslem world knows the name of Enver Pasha."

The Bolsheviks did not listen to him, probably because they did not trust him completely. They were thorough Kemalists. Moscow and Ankara grew closer and closer together, and when the Soviet-Anatolian Treaty of March 16, 1921, was signed, Enver felt that his chances of supplanting Kemal with Bolshevik assistance were gone.

Early in the summer of 1921, he announced, therefore, that he wished to go to the Caucasus. Enver lived in Russia as the guest of the Soviet Government; it could not deny him freedom of movement. He was accordingly given a saloon car in which to travel south. Before he went, however, he gave Chicherin a personal undertaking that he would not get into touch with his friends in Turkey, or work against Kemal.

Enver's supporters had come across the Turkish border to meet him in Batum. He was still influential in the Turkish Army, in church quarters—for Kemal was an avowed opponent of Pan-Islamism and of the Sultan-Caliph—and with the upper classes. A full-fledged Enverist congress now took place in Batum which, the Russians learned, planned a coup d'état against the Kemal regime. Kemal protested to the Bolsheviks, and when, shortly after the meeting, Enver tried to make his way into Turkey, the Soviet authorities detained him by force.

Enver was violently angry and swore revenge, but maintained outwardly friendly relations with the Russians. He said, however, that he would not return immediately to Moscow but go instead to Transcaspia to meet Djemal Pasha who was on his way back from Kabul. He also wanted to hunt in Bokhara—for what he did not say. In the city of Bokhara he still appeared officially to Soviet representatives, and then suddenly he vanished.

Before long, he assumed the leadership of the Basmachi who were in revolt against Bolshevik rule in Bokhara. A Young Bokhara Party, very much akin to the Young Turks and the Young Afghans, had sprung up before the World War. In 1910, and again in 1913, Young Bokharan insurrections took place against the local Emir, who was the Czar's representative in Central Asia. Considerable anti-Russian sentiment actuated the Young Bokharans. When the World War broke out, for instance, they burned a big bull in the streets of Samarkand as a symbol of what they hoped would happen to Czarism in consequence of the conflict, and when Kerensky assumed power, a delegation of rich Bokharan merchants petitioned him to abolish the emirate. Miliukov objected to such a move. The result was a growth of sympathy for the Bolsheviks among the Young Bokharans.

Throughout the early phase of the Communist revolution, Moscow had no contact with Bokhara. But the expulsion of British interventionist troops and the defeat of the Whites in Siberia and Turkestan encouraged the Young Bokharans to continue their struggle against the unpopular emir, and in September, 1920, a three-day revolution flared up which forced him and his female and boy harems to flee to Afghanistan.

This upheaval left the feudal khans and the pro-emir party dissatisfied. They could prey on many of the peasants who had suffered economic distress throughout the Civil War from lack of contact with Russia on which Bokhara depends for bread and to which it sells its cotton. The peasants likewise resented the anti-religious ardor of the Bolsheviks.

Enver Pasha now put himself at the head of these insurgents or Basmachi and opened his war against the Bolsheviks. He tried to infect the Basmachi with his Pan-Turanian ideology, and sent emissaries to Kabul where his cause won the sympathy of those court circles which would not have been averse to the annexation of Bokhara by Afghanistan. Enver mobilized an army and concentrated his great talents on the fulfilment of a life's ambition. He spent almost a year in Bokhara. His movement, however, gathered little momentum. The re-establishment of geographical connections with Central Russia promised to remove the chief grievances of the Basmachi, and Pan-Turanianism struck no root.

Enver was a general of the German school and a master of modern military tactics. But in the mountains of East Bokhara his strategy almost invariably improved the position of the Red forces sent to destroy him.

On the night of June 14, 1922, he attacked in the region of Derbent, where Alexander and the Romans had marched centuries before. General Kakurin, who commanded the Bolshevik force, estimates that Enver had no more than 3,000 men and little cannon, whereas the Soviet division was 8,000 strong and enjoyed the advantages of superior artillery and trained cavalry. Enver suffered defeat.

Kakurin now pressed Enver's shattered band deep into the mountains, and before long the Turkish leader had turned south towards the Afghan border. Here the Red Army operated in small patrols which combed the intricate defiles for rebellious Basmachi.

One such patrol of approximately 100 horsemen entered a narrow pass on August 4, 1922, and saw in front of it a large group of Bokharans seated on the ground in a circle. When the Bokharans spied the Red unit they immediately gave battle and repulsed the assailants. But one gunner, assisted by two comrades, carried a single piece of light field artillery to the top of a low hill where he was able to hold the Basmachi at bay. Meanwhile, another Red Army patrol, attracted by the booming mountain echoes of the firing, galloped to the scene, and a struggle ensued which resembled the combats of King Richard the Lion-Hearted and his medieval knights. The warriors hacked one another to pieces with scimitar and saber, and wrestled for their lives on the rocky ground. Finally, the remnant of the Basmachi retreated, leaving their dead on the field of battle.

When the Red soldiers examined the corpses, they found that all the Basmachi khans were dressed in long richly colored Bokharan robes and typical Central Asiatic headgear. But one had worn high military boots, breeches, and a tightly-buttoned blue jacket. On his finger was a valuable signet ring. They examined his papers. There were three letters from Berlin written in a woman's hand, a notebook, and scraps of paper on which orders had been scribbled in Turkish. The dead man was Enver Pasha.

His possessions were taken to Tashkent, photographed, and deposited in the military museum. The body found burial in the distant mountain pass in a grave that is unmarked and now unknown.[2]

According to information subsequently obtained, the conference in the defile which the Soviet patrol had discovered was a meeting of the most important Basmachi khans and sheiks. Enver had decided to give up the struggle and retire to Afghanistan—but not for ever. It was his farewell discussion with the fighting chiefs to whom he proposed to transfer the command; it took place near Baldjhan—only 80 kilometres from the Afghan frontier.[3]

The relations between Moscow and Ankara had always been cordial. But Mustapha Kemal urged nothing less than a treaty of military and political alliance. Such was the purport of a letter he addressed to Moscow on April 26, 1920, in which he declared his readiness to "participate in the struggle against foreign imperialism which threatens both countries."[4]

The Bolsheviks felt that permanent alliances with non-Communist states were a dangerous liability. They could, conceivably, put the Bolsheviks in a position of supporting a State that was persecuting Communists and trade unionists, or adopting other tactics offensive to Soviet citizens.

In the case of Turkey in 1920, an alliance would have required the Red Army to march against the Greeks in Asia Minor. But Russia was tired, and still had its own battles to fight against Poland, Wrangel, and the Mensheviks in Georgia.

Moscow therefore rejected Kemal's offer of an alliance.

[2] The writer's information regarding Enver's stay in Russia and his last adventure was obtained from General Kakurin, Chicherin, Karakhan, Zuckerman, the Chief of the Middle East section, and Pastukhov, the Chief of the Near East section of the Commissariat of Foreign Affairs.

[3] Djemal Pasha, who had made peace with Kemal, left Moscow for Ankara on July 5, 1922. On the 22nd he was killed by Armenians in Tiflis. He was buried, with honors, in Turkey. Talaat Pasha, the third member of the famous triumvirate, met death in Berlin at the hands of Armenians on March 15, 1921.

[4] Kluchnikov and Sabanin: *International Politics of Modern Times: Treaties, Notes and Declarations,* (Moscow, 1928). Vol. III, Part I, p. 26.

Chicherin suggested instead, in a note of June 2, 1920, the establishment of regular diplomatic relations.[5]

But Turkey needed more than political collaboration and moral support. Bekir Semi, the Turkish Foreign Minister, himself traveled to Moscow, and there, on November 16, 1920, appealed for material aid.

The Turks were hard pressed. In May, 1919, the Greeks had landed in Smyrna and occupied the city and the vicinity. The invasion of Anatolia, however, inspired a Turkish nationalist protest which the Sultan's Government in Constantinople was powerless to check. Kemalist congresses organized throughout the country, and on April 23, 1920, the Nationalist Assembly, which adopted the famous Nationalist Pact, met in Ankara.

Turkey now had two parallel governments. While the Constantinople Cabinet existed feebly under Allied guns, and signed the Peace Treaty of Sèvres at Allied dictation (August 10, 1920), the Anatolian regime improved its relations with France and stiffened its resistance to the Greek invasion. By the beginning of 1921, Kemal had organized a regular army.

In these activities, Kemal enjoyed the valuable assistance of the Bolsheviks. "It need no longer be a secret," Karakhan said to the writer, "that we helped Kemal with much cannon, money, arms, and military advice." Thus reinforced, the Kemal Government succeeded in complicating Greek forward movements, and the result was an Allied summons to both Turkey and Greece to engage in armistice negotiations. But the conference which opened in Paris on February 21 closed, without achievement, in London on March 23, and the next day the Greek army in Asia Minor resumed its advance.

Despite Bolshevik military co-operation with Kemal, however, the Moscow negotiations for a Russo-Turkish treaty did not proceed with the expected ease. Batum barred a settlement.

Batum had been a part of Turkey until the war of 1877–8, when it was ceded to the Czar. Kemal now claimed the city. The Menshevik authorities of Georgia had previously offered him Batum as the price of an alliance with them against the Bolsheviks. Mustapha Kemal saw the obvious disadvantage of such a bargain, yet when the negotiations commenced in Moscow he insistently de-

[5] *Ibid.*

manded the surrender of Batum to Turkey. On one occasion, a three-weeks' rupture of the negotiations occurred on this account, and though the negotiations were resumed, the problem remained unsolved.

While the fate of the treaty thus hung in the balance, Turkish troops under Karabekir took advantage of the disorder following the fall of the Menshevik Government of Georgia and entered Batum on March 11, 1921.

Batum is the natural port of export for Baku petroleum and is the terminus of the Baku-Batum pipe-line. Batum, too, is the Western World's door to the Caucasus. The Bolsheviks, fresh from their experiences with Allied intervention, feared the renewal of foreign attack and felt that so strategic a city as Batum could not be ceded even to a friendly power.

For a moment, the issue threatened to provoke armed hostilities between two countries which, in other fields, stood in a relationship of temporary military allies. Red troops closed in on the city, and their commander. Kjubisheff, parleyed politely but firmly over cups of black coffee with the Turkish general. Finally, the counsel of peace prevailed, and five days after Karabekir marched into Batum, the Russian-Turkish Treaty was signed in Moscow which provided for his evacuation. Batum went to the Russians and, in exchange, Kars and Ardagan were ceded to Turkey. The treaty likewise took cognizance of "the solidarity between them in the struggle with imperialism," regulated the Caucasian frontier between Turkey and Russia, mentioned Constantinople as a part of Turkey, stipulated the convocation of a conference on the fate of the Straits, and declared the mutuality of interests between "the nationalist liberating movement of the peoples of the East and the struggle of the workers of Russia for a new social system."[6] It was at this time that Kemal actually organized his own Communist Party in Turkey and commenced to harass the Communists who adhered to the Comintern.

From March to September, 1921, the Greek Army pushed forward into Anatolia, and in July the Kemal Government was forced to desert its own capital. In August the Greeks had entrenched themselves along the entire line of the Sakaria River. Here Kemal resolved

[6] Kluchnikov and Sabanin: *International Politics of Modern Times: Treaties, Notes and Declarations,* (Moscow, 1928). II, 94–5.

to make his stand, and in September he succeeded in throwing the enemy back from the river. Chicherin immediately wired congratulations.

Kemal had fought the Greeks to a standstill, but victory required the recapture of almost the entire country from the Sakaria to the sea. Again he appealed for Bolshevik aid.

On December 13, 1921, Michael Frunze, then Commander-in-Chief of the Soviet forces in the Ukraine and later Trotzky's successor as Commissar of War, arrived in Ankara, where he was received with extraordinarily warm protestations of friendship. He came, it was announced, to negotiate an agreement between the Soviet Republic of Ukraine—then "autonomous" in foreign affairs, and Turkey. But his short visit, of twenty-three days, was used to arrange for heavy shipments of Russian munitions and for the mapping out of a detailed plan of campaign against the Greeks in which, if need be, Red officers would participate.

Shortly after Frunze's departure, Aralov, the new Soviet envoy, came to Turkey. From the day he first set foot on Turkish soil, he later told the writer, till his arrival in the capital, he was welcomed by the population with every mark of affection, and Aralov felt as much at home as if he had never left his own country. Subsequently, he visited the front with Kemal Pasha, took the salute at parades, addressed the soldiers, urged the officers to added efforts, and distributed thousands of comfort bags to the army. Part of the Allied military equipment captured by the Bolsheviks from Yudenich, Denikin, Miller, Kolchak, and other White leaders was now in use in the Turkish forces. Kemal sent greetings to the Red Army and Aralov praised Kemal's Army.

Turkey likewise received French military aid. Franklin-Bouillon's mission, in fact, had established intimate relations with Ankara which the Turks even tried to use as a means of bridging the gulf between France and Russia.

Aided by the Russians and the French and strengthened by the rise of national feeling in Anatolia, Kemal began to advance rapidly during the summer of 1922. As each victory became known, Moscow sent a congratulatory telegram.

In September, the Turkish Army recaptured Smyrna

after a precipitous Greek retreat, and threw the enemy into the sea. Simultaneously, Kemal reached out in the direction of Stambul, and refused to recognize the neutral zone which the British had declared at Chanak.

These military events cost two monarchs their thrones. On September 27, a revolution broke out in Greece which forced King Constantine to flee. On November 1, the National Assembly at Ankara declared that the Sultan-Caliph had "passed into history."

The Greco-Turkish War came to a close by the armistice signed at Mudania on October 11. It was clear to the Allies that a victorious Turkey would reject the Treaty of Sèvres which had merely been presented to Constantinople for signature. Now a treaty would have to be negotiated.

Accordingly, Great Britain, France, Italy, Japan, Yugoslavia, Rumania, Bulgaria, Soviet Russia, Soviet Ukraine, Soviet Georgia, and Turkey agreed to meet for a conference to open in Lausanne, in December, 1922. The Soviet republics were invited only after Moscow's sharp protests against their exclusion from deliberations on a subject of vital interest to them, and even then their participation was limited to discussions affecting the future of the Straits and of Constantinople.

**RUSSIA AND CONSTANTINOPLE** Before the Bolshevik revolution, the relations between Russia and Turkey represented an almost unbroken tradition of enmity, due, in great measure, to the Czar's and Miliukov's designs on Constantinople (now Istanbul).

The Romanoffs, protectors of the Greek Catholic Church, were bent on liberating Constantinople, the ancient center of their religion from the hands of the Turks and from the domination of the infidels. But more important was the political and economic factor. Russia wanted Constantinople to prevent hostile navies from entering the Black Sea and attacking the Crimea or the Caucasus. Constantinople would bring Russia a long step nearer the warm waters and warm countries of the Mediterranean.

The Russians believed, moreover, that they needed the Straits for their export trade. For approximately five months of the year, the port of Leningrad (Petrograd) is closed by ice. Murmansk, although an open port, had no railway connection with the south before 1916, while Riga and Libau were far from Russia's grain belt. It thus lay within the power of the British Navy or of Turkey to prevent Russian exports from reaching the outside world by blocking the Straits during the extended period when Petrograd is closed by ice. Such was the case once during the Turko-Italian War, when Russia lost hundreds of millions of rubles by being unable to ship her surplus grain.

Political and economic motives were frequently hidden under the cover of Pan-Slavic idealism. The Czar strove to reach Constantinople and the Straits by sea, but also to win the friendship of Bulgaria and Serbia in order to approach Turkey by the land route. The protagonists of Pan-Slavism were advocates of the Eastern expansion of Russia; they were generally anti-Westerners and therefore opponents of industrialization.

Before the War, Great Britain fought Russia's southward and eastward tendencies in Afghanistan, Persia, China, Tibet, and the Straits. Turkey resisted them on her own territory, and Austro-Hungary in the Balkans, but the most serious obstruction was England.

**UNIVERSAL PRINCIPLES** A summary of the pre-war history of the Straits demonstrates (1) that Great Britain generally preferred closed Straits which prevented Russia from coming out into the Mediterranean, and trusted that in time of necessity her navy could sweep away any legal or military obstructions to passage, (2) that Russia desired closed Straits when she was weak and at such periods sought the support of Turkey, but set her heart on open Straits for herself and did not hesitate to antagonize Turkey when she felt more conscious of her power, and (3) that Russia and England are the two countries most interested in the status of the Straits.

The World War radically changed the situation for Russia. France and England depended on Russian military efforts while Sazonov felt that Turkeys' position as an ally of the Central Powers gave him the moral right to demand the cession of Constantinople and the Straits to the Russian Empire.[7]

[7] E. A. Adamov: *Constantinople and the Straits,* I, 16. Moscow, 1925. This book of two volumes, published by Professor Adamov, the Keeper of the Archives of the Commissariat of Foreign Affairs in Moscow,

On November 13, 1914, the day after Turkey entered the World War, Count Benckendorff, Russia's ambassador to the Court of St. James, broached the matter in an audience with George V. "Constantinople must be yours," King George agreed.

Several months later, Czar Nicholas drew aside M. Paleologue, the French ambassador, at a royal reception, and said to him:

I feel that I have not the right to impose the terrible sacrifices of war on my people without granting them, in recompense, the realization of their age-long dream. Therefore, Monsieur Ambassador, I have made my decision. I will effect a radical solution of the problem of Constantinople and the Straits. The solution which I indicated to you in November is the only possible and practical one. The city of Constantinople and Southern Thrace must be incorporated into my Empire. . . . You know [Nicholas continued], that England has already informed me of her agreement. King George has said to my ambassador: "Constantinople must be yours."[8]

King George's acquiescence notwithstanding, Great Britain proposed to bargain and delay. Powerful influences in England objected strenuously to the emergence of Russia into the Ægean and Mediterranean.

Impatient to witness the "realization of age-long dreams," Sazonov reduced Russia's demands to paper, on March 4, 1915, and in a memorandum to Paleologue and to Sir George Buchanan, the British ambassador in Petrograd, declared that every solution of the Straits problem would be

insufficient and temporary if the city of Constantinople, the western coasts of the Bosphorus, the Sea of Marmora and the Dardanelles, as well as Southern Thrace to the line of Enos-Midia, will not be included into the Russian Empire.

Sazonov likewise asked, "in view of strategic requirements," for

---

contains hundreds of hitherto unpublished documents taken from the files of the Czarist Ministry of Foreign Affairs which throw precious light on the diplomatic history of the period from 1908 to 1917. Although these volumes, and the companion volume, *The Partition of Asiatic Turkey*, by E. A. Adamov (Moscow, 1924), are known to a few scholars on World War origins, they are, unfortunately, not available in translation to Western countries.

[8] Maurice Paleologue: *La Russie des Tsars pendant la Grande Guerre* (Paris, 1921) I, 314.

a part of the Asiatic shore limited by the Bosphorus, the Sakaria River and a point on the coast of Ismid Bay yet to be determined, as well as the islands in the Sea of Marmora and the islands of Imbros and Tenedos . . .[9]

These Russian claims marked the beginning of Allied partition of the Ottoman Empire. France replied on March 8 to Sazonov's memorandum promising that the "Imperial Government could fully depend on the friendly attitude of the Government of the Republic in the solution of the problem of Constantinople and the Straits in accordance with the wishes of Russia." But on the 14th of March, Paleologue informed Sazonov that France wished, in exchange for this kindness, "to annex Syria, including the district of the Gulf of Alexandretta and Cilicia as far as the Taurus Mountains." The French ambassador, who went to see the Czar at General Headquarters to press the matter, subsequently explained that Syria, according to the French conception, included Palestine.

The Greeks would gain Smyrna—against which the Italians protested—and Great Britain asked first for small benefits and then for far-reaching territorial acquisitions. On March 12, 1925, Sir George Buchanan handed Sazonov a memorandum which accepted Russia's proposal for the acquisition of Constantinople and the Straits and the territory on both shores of the waterway, but in a second memorandum submitted on the same day, the British Government pointed out that this assent "involves a complete reversal of the traditional policy of His Majesty's Government and is in direct contradiction to the opinions and sentiments which at one time universally held in England and which have still by no means died out." Sir Edward Grey urged, in consideration of these circumstances, that Constantinople be declared an open port for the transit of goods and that the Straits be always open to mercantile vessels. The British Foreign Office likewise presented territorial demands: that the Moslem Holy Places and Arabia be constituted an independent Mohammedan dominion, and furthermore, that the neutral zone in Persia be converted into a British zone.

But since these territorial bargains might make it difficult to maintain the public impression that the Allies

[9] Copied by the writer from the copy in the archives of the Czarist Ministry of Foreign Affairs.

were fighting against imperialism and for the safety of world democracy, Sir Edward felt that "it is most desirable that the understanding now arrived at between the Russian, French and British Governments should remain secret."[1]

The Petrograd diplomats consented with alacrity to Grey's request for secrecy and to the extension of the British "sphere of influence" in Persia so as to include the neutral zone, merely adding the condition that Ispahan and Jezd be joined to the Russian sphere.

These territorial exchanges, however, paled in significance compared with the real compensation Britain and France expected as reward for their delivery of Constantinople and the Straits to Russia. London and Paris aimed at nothing less than the division of Turkey's empire in Asia, and before long (February 1916) Sir Mark Sykes and M. Picot, the former French consul in Beirut, were in Petrograd explaining to the Russian Government the partition of Turkey's Arab domains which, later adopted and outlined in the Sykes-Picot Treaty, formed the basis for the decisions of the Paris Peace Conferences.

**SOVIET RUSSIA AND THE STRAITS** When the Czar abdicated and was supplanted by the Provisional Government, Miliukov, the new Foreign Minister, indignantly denied that the republic would surrender any of the privileges granted it by the secret agreement with Britain and France with respect to Constantinople and the Straits. He considered them to conform to the "life interests of Russia."[2]

The overthrow of Kerensky by the Bolsheviks scrapped all these secret understandings. "Constantinople must remain in the hands of the Moslems," said a proclamation issued over the signatures of Lenin and Stalin on December 7, 1917—exactly one month after the Communist coup d'état. This sentiment, repeated subsequently on numerous occasions, was fundamental to Soviet foreign policy. The Bolsheviks not only renounced all claims on the Turkish capital, Turkish waters, and Turkish territory in both Europe and Asia, but actually pursued a policy

[1] Copy supplied to the writer from the archives of the Czarist Ministry of Foreign Affairs.
[2] E. A. Adamov; *Constantinople and the Straits,* I, 479.

of friendship towards Turkey calculated to prevent the Powers from consummating that partition which London, Paris, and Petrograd had secretly agreed upon.

The natural and political geography of the Black Sea and the Straits was left unchanged by the revolution of November, 1917. Yet the Bolsheviks felt that the "life interests of Russia" no longer required the extension of Russian territory to the edge of the Mediterranean.

The Bolsheviks had enough trouble and enough territory. Nicholas II wished to guarantee his battle fleet free passage through the Dardanelles for purposes which can have been only aggressive. The Communists wanted to close the Straits to prevent the aggression of others.

As a measure against Czarist expansion, Great Britain, and other Powers too, had wished to close the Straits to Russia. Now, when Russia was unable and unwilling to expand, they advocated open Straits. Lord Curzon, in fact, admitted at the Lausanne Conference that, "The respective policies of Europe and Russia have now been reversed."[3] Foreign relations are never static. They depend to a great extent on geography, but very much on economic policies, on modified ratios of military strength, and on new conceptions of the nature of the "life interests" of a country.

At the time of the Lausanne Conference, England believed that Soviet Russia was so weak and so unlikely to build a strong navy that open Straits would not possibly tempt the Bolsheviks to venture out into the Mediterranean, but would, given the proper situation, enable Great Britain to penetrate into the Black Sea without violating international conventions or the neutrality of Turkey.

Soviet Russia, on the other hand, was sincerely gratified by the hostility of Turkey towards the Entente and therefore drew closer to Ankara in much the same way as a parallel feeling in Germany created a bond between Moscow and Berlin.

**GEORGE CHICHERIN v. GEORGE CURZON** "In M. Chicherin," says the *Manchester Guardian,* "he [Cur-

[3] *Lausanne Conference on Near Eastern Affairs.* 1922–3. British Blue Book. Records of the Proceedings and Draft Terms of Peace. (London, 1923). Cmd. 1814. p. 139.

zon] for the first time met a foeman whose rapier was sharper and quicker than his own."

The classic struggle between Chicherin and Curzon took place at the Lausanne Conference which met in 1922–3 to substitute for the Treaty of Sèvres a new agreement based on Kemal's smashing victory over the Greeks. Chicherin was at his best. His brilliance and deftness of argument and his lightning repartee in all Western tongues astonished the conference and the world that watched it. Equalled only by Curzon among post-war statesmen in his command of the historical, ethnographical and geographical facts of the situation under discussion, Chicherin enjoyed the advantage of humor and of impersonal approach.

Curzon's personal and political sensitiveness made him especially vulnerable. He resented most the blow which he could not immediately return twofold. The very presence of Chicherin provoked the first British delegate at Lausanne. Curzon could assume no cultural superiority vis-à-vis the commissar. But Chicherin, more perhaps than any plenipotentiary Russia might have sent, personified everything he detested in Bolshevism as well as everything he hated in Russia. Chicherin, to Curzon, stood for Communist doctrine and the history of Russia—a combination which acted like a red rag on a bull.

Curzon felt, moreover, that Soviet Russia separated him from an agreement with the Turks. He had conceived of Lausanne as one of the greatest triumphs of his career. It would bring him the office of Prime Minister.[4] It would make him the first Englishman to be Viceroy of India and Premier of England. This double distinction, Curzon's biographer explains with much pathetic detail, was the outstanding ambition of his life. He dreamed, wrote and spoke of it. Everything he did centered around it. And here was Chicherin preventing him from forcing the easy submission of the Turks, from winning the enthusiastic praise of the British Press—he was peculiarly susceptible to unfavorable criticism—and from concluding a treaty with Turkey which he hoped would unlock the doors to the highest honor his King and country could grant. In

[4] The Earl of Ronaldshay: *The Life of Lord Curzon, being the Authorized Biography of George Nathaniel Marquess Curzon of Kedleston, K.G.*, London, 1928. III, 328.

the circumstances it would have been only too human to hate.

If Chicherin distressed Curzon, Curzon indubitably irritated the Turks. The British Foreign Secretary wished to sign the death warrant of Turkey in Europe. "For nearly five centuries," he had written, "the presence of the Turk in Europe has been the source of distraction, intrigue, and corruption in European politics." Curzon therefore proposed "the ejection of the Turks from Europe and the establishment of a much-reduced but compact and homogeneous Turkish state in Asia Minor."[5] Constantinople would then be brought under "some form of international authority."

But though, in his opinion, it was "inevitable and desirable" "that the Turk should be deprived of Constantinople," he did not agree that "the fugitives are to be kicked from pillar to post and that there is to be practically no Turkish Empire and probably no Caliphate at all." Such radical changes, the ex-Viceroy feared, would kindle most dangerous Moslem passions and "sullen resentment which may easily burst into savage frenzy." Curzon was thinking of the 70,000,000 Mohammedans in India, and of the faithful in Afghanistan, Egypt, and Arabia. The Empire always took first place in his mind. Therefore, while he would have excluded the Turks from the European continent, he did not wish to deal too severely with them in Asia. Britain having taken her share of the Turkish Empire, Curzon wanted the Greeks and Italians to leave the remainder intact.

Curzon found support in Lord Balfour, and in Lloyd George, who would only have urged the Greeks and the Italians to take more of Asiatic Turkey than Curzon thought expedient in view of Islam's possible disaffection. Nevertheless, a British Cabinet meeting of January 6, 1920, rejected the plan of expelling the Turks from Constantinople. They preferred a "respectable and docile Turkish Government at Constantinople, preserved from its hereditary vices by a military cordon of the Powers."[6] Curzon called this a "chimera," but it was the policy he consented to effect at the Lausanne Conference.

The Turkish situation, essentially, thrust Lloyd George

[5] *Ibid.*, III, 262.
[6] *Ibid.*, p. 270

out of office. "The Prime Minister," Curzon wrote to his wife, "is as convinced a Venizelist and phil-Hellene as ever." Lloyd George encouraged the Greeks to land in Smyrna and furnished Athens with the moral support and material aid for its war against Kemal Pasha. France, on the other hand, supported Turkey. Yet Curzon had persuaded Poincaré to work hand in hand with the British at the meeting in Lausanne. At the Lord Mayor's banquet on November 9, 1922, Curzon delicately linked reparations with the Near East and hinted at his agreement with the French Premier.

**THE LAUSANNE CONFERENCE** But for the change in Poincaré's attitude achieved by Curzon, the Lausanne Conference might have witnessed the strange spectacle of a resurgent Turkey, reinforced by France and Soviet Russia, facing an England in comparative diplomatic isolation. For with Paris leaning sympathetically towards Kemal, Signor Mussolini, then only recently risen to prominence, would scarcely have sided with Curzon.

The conference opened in Lausanne on November 20, 1922; Curzon expected that the deliberations would last only two or three weeks. The prospect did not charm the French. They chose to complicate the discussions and retard their progress until the occupation of the Ruhr Basin in January. During that period the French, their slightly obstructive tactics notwithstanding, put great store on common action with Lord Curzon. Thereafter, too, Anglo-French co-operation continued, the French delegation even going to the length of permitting the Mosul problem to become a purely Turko-British affair, yet Poincaré's course zigzagged wildly on one or two occasions.

The Turkish delegation, seconded by the representatives of Soviet Russia, Soviet Ukraine, and Soviet Georgia, generally faced the united opposition of Great Britain, France, Italy, Japan, Rumania, Greece, and, at times, of Yugoslavia. Mr. Child, in his capacity of neutral United States observer, undoubtedly strengthened the hand of Ismet Pasha in the matter of Mosul where the American Admiral Chester held concession rights, but agreed with the Allies on the Straits and on those cognate issues which concerned Russia.

**THE SOVIET STAND AT LAUSANNE** The attitude of the French Government and the decision of the British Cabinet made it a foregone conclusion that Lord Curzon would not insist on the expulsion of the Turks from Constantinople. Kemal might have desired more; the closing of the Dardanelles, for instance, and the fortification of the Straits zone. But Turkey had been at war for twelve years and was exhausted. The defeat of the Greeks had required a tremendous effort. Insistence on Turkey's maximum demands would have involved her in hostilities with the Allies, and Kemal felt that his movement was too Asiatic and peasant to arouse any enthusiasm for a question which, after all, impressed villagers from the Anatolian plateau as distant and somewhat academic. Constantinople had ceased to be the actual capital of the country, and it was no longer looked upon as the religious or spiritual or commercial center. The nationalists did not wish to lose the city, but complete control over the Straits no longer represented a sine qua non. There is indeed a suspicion that even before the Lausanne Conference convened, Turkey promised the Allies to open the Straits. The battle of the Straits would therefore be fought between Russia and Britain.

It developed on the Russians at Lausanne, therefore, to be "more Turkish than the Turks," and Chicherin, actually, defended Turkish sovereignty over the Straits with greater zeal than Ismet Pasha. The only guarantee of the safety of the Caucasus, the Crimea, and the Ukraine was the closing of the Straits. Chicherin accordingly informed the Territorial and Military Commission of the Lausanne Conference on December 4, 1922, that, in Soviet Russia's opinion, "the Dardanelles and the Bosphorus must be permanently closed both in peace and in war to warships, armed vessels and military aircraft of all countries except Turkey."[7]

The chief Bolshevik delegate contended that the closing of the Straits would grant equality on all nations, "whereas the opening of the Straits to warships would confer a preponderant position on the strongest sea Power." Russia, he declared, "had liberated all the States of the Medi-

[7] *Lausanne Conference on Near Eastern Affairs, 1922–3*. British Blue Book. (London, 1923). Cmd. 1814. p. 129. All subsequent quotations from the proceedings of the Conference sessions are taken from this volume.

terranean from the threat of the century-old ambitions of Tsarism; but it was never her intention to acquiesce in a solution of the Straits problem aimed directly against her own safety." That her safety could be menaced, he explained, was clear from the progress of the Civil War; there would never have been a serious Denikin or Wrangel movement had the Straits remained closed to Allied warships.

"Russia is at the beginning of a new era," Chicherin pleaded, "and we wish to start this by creating stable conditions of peace around us, whereas you," he charged, "wish to put us in a situation which will force us to arm."

But Lord Curzon's program included likewise the demilitarization of the Straits and of the territory bordering them. Ismet Pasha, who had not objected to the opening of the Straits, raised a mild protest against this measure; it "amounts to leaving the most vulnerable and important districts of Turkey defenseless and at the mercy of a sudden attack," he said. "None of the Powers represented at this conference is deprived of the right to defend her capital." The treaty draft, as introduced by Curzon, would take that right from Turkey.

Demilitarization would confirm the freedom of the Straits which, Trotzky told a London *Observer* correspondent, "is nothing but a military dictatorship of the Black Sea for the country possessing the biggest fleet." The Panama Canal, on the other hand, was strongly fortified, the Russians submitted; likewise Gibraltar; and the Suez Canal, technically under the control of an international commission, was guarded only by the British who justified their protectorate over Egypt on the ground of its defense.

"Peace," Chicherin propounded, "is consolidated by the separation of conflicting forces." By converting the Straits into a strong military barrier between Russia and England which Russia promised to respect ("Russia is ready to undertake of her own free will not to send her Black Sea fleet into the Mediterranean") the cause of peace would be well served. Of course, Chicherin affirmed, "the ideal solution would be to put a stop to all naval armaments on every sea. But in the present situation the only possible compromise between the conflicting interests is for Turkey, as sovereign, to close the Straits to warships."

The Allies were willing to grant certain small concessions to Turkey, which, Russia argued, were designed to drive a wedge between the Turkish and Muscovite delegations. They agreed, for instance, to limit the time any warship might spend in the Straits to the twenty-four hours required for passage. This, the Soviet plenipotentiaries submitted, was proof, if proof were needed, that the proposed Straits regime was designed more with a view to giving foreign fleets access to Russian coasts than to menace Turkish territory. A second concession would permit Turkey to fortify the southern shore of the Sea of Marmora from which ships passing through the center of the waterway could not be shelled. Other Turkish demands were summarily rejected, although Lord Curzon did assure Ismet Pasha that if he wished to guarantee his country's territorial integrity he had only to join the League of Nations—whereupon Chicherin referred to Vilna. "The impotence of the League," the commissar commented, "has become proverbial."

**THE ALLIED POSITION** The Allies advanced two reasons for open Straits: the necessity of safeguarding the Black Sea nations—Bulgaria and Rumania—against Russian attacks, and their obligations to protect commercial vessels in the Black Sea.

"It is apparently forgotten," Chicherin retorted, "that Bulgaria had been deprived of all her means of defense on land and sea by a treaty to which Russia was not a party—a treaty which she will never recognize." (The Treaty of Neuilly.) If the Allies were so solicitous for Bulgaria's safety, Chicherin hinted, why did they rob her of the means of self-protection? "As to Rumania, has she been Russia's neighbor since yesterday only?" Chicherin inquired rhetorically. Before the War, "she never protested against the regime of the closing of the Straits." Soviet Russia's relations to Rumania, moreover, are governed by what happens on land. Russia has no aggressive intentions against Rumania; but if she had, Rumania would prepare to defend herself by means of arrangements on land which are well known to us." (The commissar probably referred to Bucharest's alliances with Poland and France.)

To Curzon's second reason Chicherin replied that the same disadvantages to foreign commerce in the Black Sea existed before the War when Great Britain had always demanded closed Straits, and that piracy was practically unknown on the Black Sea since Wrangel quitted its waters. Nevertheless, and in view of the general desire that warships perform peaceful missions in the Black Sea, the Russians agreed to give the Turkish Government "the right to permit the passage of light war vessels in individual cases and for definite purposes but on no account with a military object."

This was inadmissible. The Allies desired the permanent privilege of entering the Black Sea, no matter what the purpose. They objected to any control whatsoever.

The Allies proposed that in time of peace and in time of war, Turkey being neutral, the maximum naval strength each Power might send into the Black Sea was not to exceed the Black Sea fleet of the largest Black Sea Power—Russia. Turkey suggested modifications: that in time of peace "the total force of foreign fleets passing through the Straits at the same time must not exceed the force of the Turkish fleet" in the Straits; that in time of war the provision of the Allies would remain, but "the warships of one belligerent Power may not enter the Straits before the warships of the other belligerent Power shall have quitted the Straits and the Sea of Marmora." For the Russians contended that if each Power sent in a fleet not larger than the Russian, and if the Soviet naval strength in the Black Sea equalled say 30,000 tons, then Britan could send in 30,000 tons, France 30,000 tons, Italy 30,000 tons and so on ad infinitum, with the result that the foreign forces might triple or quadruple the Russian. The Turkish amendment would have made the Black Sea accessible to the warships of only one foreign nation at a time.

Curzon, however, pronounced the Turkish attempt to "lump the ships of all Powers together" . . . "a quite impracticable arrangement." Nor did the Allies accept Turkey's protests against the flight of military aircraft over the Straits.

**TURKEY ACCEPTS, BUT THE CONFERENCE BREAKS UP** One easily intelligible consideration actuated the Allies at Lausanne. M. Barrere, the chief French delegate, emphasized it when he referred to the Anglo-French defeats at Gallipoli during the World War; "on the day of their victory," he said, "the Allies resolved that the dangers of this situation must never be allowed to recur." Militarized, closed Straits had handicapped the Entente in fighting Germany, Austro-Hungary and Turkey; they could prove an obstacle again. Now the Allies had the power to force a change. Their fleets were anchored in the Straits. Their troops held Constantinople. The Turks could not oppose military force to this force, nor could the Bolsheviks.

Under the circumstances, the Turks acquiesced to the Allied propositions with few modifications.

The difficulty arose as a result of disagreements on questions which involved Soviet Russia less directly—on Greek reparations, and capitulations. Even on the Mosul question a compromise formula was reached postponing the decision for a year. Nevertheless, the Turkish delegation, having admitted defeat in all else, stood its ground stubbornly in the question of the legal position of foreigners and on capitulation generally. Curzon threatened Turkey with war as he had on several previous occasions during the conference. He brought the Turkish Angora representatives to his hotel room on February 4 and warned that "if within the next two hours we do not conclude peace, there will be no peace." Curzon's train was waiting. "Did it mean that Allied and Turkish soldiers would begin fighting again?" the British Foreign Secretary asked. But the suave Ismet was "calm and certain." He had learned that Poincaré did not stand solidly behind Curzon. "He knew what war meant," he said, "but Turkey could not be deprived of her economic and judicial liberty." No further concessions could be expected from Turkey.

The French, Italian, and British plenipotentiaries argued, cajoled, threatened. But at 7.45 P.M. Ismet Pasha and Riza Nur "rose and took their leave," and this made it possible for Lord Curzon to be in his train "soon after nine o'clock."

Chicherin had seen Ismet Pasha practically every day during this period. In Chicherin's view, a break would only strengthen Turkey's position. He felt that in case of war, France would not fight by the side of England. In the end, when rupture brought greater benefits, Ismet agreed that Chicherin's counsel had been wise—and helpful. He never forgot.

## MOSCOW SUBSCRIBES AN OBJECTIONABLE PACT

The conference thus closed without any decision on the future regime of the Straits. In April, however, there was a resumption of the negotiations with Turkey. Vatzlav Vorovsky, the Soviet political envoy in Rome, protested Russia's title to participate in the discussions regarding the still undetermined question of the Straits, and on April 27 he himself, accompanied by two attachés, arrived in Lausanne to assert his country's rights.

Vorovsky was seated at the dinner-table in the restaurant of his hotel on the evening of May 10 when a counter-revolutionary named Conradi entered, fired, and killed the envoy and wounded both his companions.

The Allies were somewhat stirred by this incident, but continued to deny Russia the privilege of debating the terms of the Straits convention. They did, however, invite Moscow to sign the finished document.

The treaty was finally signed by all the Allied Powers and Turkey in Lausanne on July 24. Jordansky, Vorovsky's successor, appended his signature on behalf of the Soviet republics on August 14, 1923, in Rome.

The convention[8] contained all the features and regulations which Chicherin had fought during the Lausanne Conference. In time of peace, complete freedom of navigation was stipulated by day or night, under any flag, with any kind of cargo and without any formalities, or tax, or charge. Even pilotage remained optional. The same conditions would maintain in time of war, Turkey being neutral. In such a situation, Turkey might not interfere with navigation through the Straits, "the waters of which, and the air above which, must remain entirely free" to merchant vessels of all kinds.

Should Turkey become a belligerent she would exercise all the rights of a belligerent under international law without, however, impeding the passage of neutral commercial craft.

Warships, too, must, in time of peace, be accorded complete freedom of passage through the Straits "by day and night, under any flag, without any formalities, or tax or charge whatever," but no single foreign Power could send into the Black Sea a force exceeding that of

[8] *Treaty of Peace with Turkey, and other Instruments signed at Lausanne on July 24, 1923.* British Blue Book. Cmd. 1929. (London, 1923). pp. 109ff.

the most powerful fleet of the littoral Powers of the Black Sea (Soviet Russia)—yet, even if all the Black Sea nations disarmed completely, the Powers could still dispatch into the Black Sea three or less ships, none of which would exceed 10,000 tons.

In time of war, Turkey being a neutral, warships and commercial vessels would be allowed to pass unhindered, and if Turkey were a belligerent, the ships of neutral nations would not be interfered with by Turkey. Submarines must at all times pass through the Straits on the surface. Warships would under no condition remain in the Dardanelles and the Bosphorus longer than was required to traverse them.

The Straits, according to the convention of July 24, 1923, were demilitarized. "The Straits" applies to the waters of the Dardanelles and the Bosphorus, the islands situated in them, in the Sea of Marmora (except the island of Emir Ali Adasi), and Samothrace, Lemnos, Imbros, Tenedos, and Rabbit Islands in the Ægean Sea, and the shores of the Dardanelles, including the Peninsula of Gallipoli, and a strip of territory about fifteen kilometers wide on either side of the Bosphorus (including Constantinople). The Turkish Government, nevertheless, was authorized to maintain a garrison of 12,000 men in the neighborhood of Constantinople as well as an arsenal and naval base.

A commission consisting of representatives of the signatory Powers would supervise the regime thus provided for.

The arrangement violated Soviet sentiments and principles—as it did Turkey's, no doubt. But if hard circumstances compelled Ankara to sign, and if the roles of the diplomatic game made acceptance of the Allied terms unavoidable, no such factors operated to influence Moscow's decision. The Bolsheviks might have refrained from approving principles and regulations which did violence to every one of their policies, declarations and interests. The opponents of signing were not few in Soviet circles. But Russia subscribed to the Straits convention partly because this would be the first international instrument to bear her name and would thus give her a recognized political status in world politics, and, partly, because, with all its limitations and prejudiced position, the International Commission would still exercise some jurisdiction over the Straits.

Our refusal to participate in it [ran the official Bolshevik explanation][9] can only do harm, and will, in any case, rob us of the possibility to control the acts of other Powers, anticipate abuses, demand reforms, and, when necessary, appeal to the entire world in defense of our own and Turkish interests.

Yet despite such convincing argumentation the Soviet Government refused in the end to enter the International Commission or to ratify the Lausanne Straits Convention.

**ANGLO-RUSSIAN RIVALRY AT LAUSANNE** The Bolsheviks frequently exaggerate the role they play in a given international situation. Thus, with respect to Lausanne, they argued that Lord Curzon's Straits program was directed against them. It was also directed against Turkey. It robbed Turkey of prerogatives she had exercised before the World War when she was stronger and bigger. Turkey ceased to be sovereign in the waterway that connects the Ægean and Black Seas.

Chicherin has written that the gigantic forces of England were not thrown against Turkey after the February rupture of the Lausanne Conference "because of Soviet Russia."[1] But just on the eve of that break Poincaré wired an encouraging message to Ankara which to Lord Curzon was very embarrassing. Paris, now that her legions sat securely in the Ruhr, once more thought of a separate pact with Kemal. The British were distressed and became less bellicose.

Moreover, a war against Turkey in 1923 might have thrown India and the whole Moslem world into convulsions. Here Soviet Russia's role might have proven important. The fear of what Moscow could do in such an eventuality probably sobered Lord Curzon who, judging from his mood on the night of February 4, when Ismet Pasha frigidly defied him, would have been only too ready to order the Mediterranean fleet to Smyrna. Bolshevik prestige with Islam was then very high. For if Great Britain, before the War, won sympathy among Mohammedans by emphasizing the evils of Czarist oppression, she put a similar weapon into defter hands after the Communist revolution. A war against Turkey might therefore have shaken the British Empire.

[9] *Annual Report of the Commissariat of Foreign Affairs for the Year 1923.* (Moscow, 1924).

[1] *International Life.* (Official Journal of the Commissariat of Foreign Affairs.) (Moscow, 1923). No. 2.

In the event of Anglo-Turkish hostilities, England would have stood alone. For neither Poincaré nor Mussolini were then prepared to fight Britain's battles in the Near and Middle East even though they did on occasion support her diplomatic policies. Had Turkey been stronger or had the Bolsheviks taken the grave responsibility of interrupting Russia's economic reconstruction by a war that may have been world-wide, the Straits regime would perhaps have undergone modification. But London, Moscow, and Ankara fought shy of activity, and as a result, the passive weight of Britain won the day.

Although the situation was somewhat more complicated than the Russians supposed, their presence at Lausanne no doubt interfered with Lord Curzon's management of the conference. They strengthened the Turks morally and inspired them to make not a few of their cleverest moves. Curzon resented this.

And, although the Lausanne Straits convention brought innumerable disadvantages to Turkey's position, the Bolsheviks could with reason contend that it was designed with a view to their detriment. "There is no gain to us in this" [the British Straits program.—L.F.], wrote the *Manchester Guardian* on December 21, 1922, "beyond the possibility of attacking the southern coast of Russia if we should be at war with her." Liberal opinion in Britain wished to dull the point of the spearhead aimed against Russia, for "Russia in this matter," the *Manchester Guardian* declared, "matters a good deal more than Turkey. . . . On any large view our relations with Russia matter far more than our relations with Turkey and it would have been infinitely worth while to explore the possibility of an agreement."

A few days later the same newspaper complained that Curzon never tried to come to an understanding with Russia or to treat her envoys at Lausanne "with the sort of courtesy which was never denied them at Genoa." England's diplomats, the *Guardian* affirmed in its issue of January 10, 1923, "still regard the power of bombarding Odessa as more important than a peace with Russia which would relieve us for many a long day and perhaps for ever of any such necessity. . . . The primary means to peace"—the editorial continued, echoing the sentiments of the Lloyd George party—"is a rational agreement with Russia."

Curzon, however, had wider interests and more far-reaching aims than the mere preparation of the bombardment of Odessa or some other Russian Black Sea port. He was not concerned with bridging the difference between the Empire and Bolshevism.

During the Lausanne Conference a highly interesting interview took place between Lord Curzon and Chicherin. On one occasion, the two statesmen met in the ante-rooms of the conference hall. They shook hands and Curzon expressed the hope that they might see one another again. It had not occurred to the commissar that this constituted an invitation, but it did, and Mr. Armstrong, a British business man who brought this information, subsequently arranged an interview. Sir William Tyrrell was the only other person present.

Curzon talked to Chicherin in the same tone the ex-Viceroy had adopted towards Ismet Pasha. Communist propaganda, he said, could not be tolerated. Chicherin referred to anti-Soviet acts and statements by British representatives. Curzon denied the fact. Thereupon the Russian proceeded to explain that the Bolsheviks were prepared to guarantee that the Soviet Government would indulge in no propaganda hostile to Great Britain, and that no Soviet agents would engage in anti-British activities abroad. But the Soviet Government, he submitted, could not accept responsibility for every person who stood up in some corner of the world and criticized England.

Curzon, in reply, made a significant statement. "If an agreement," he said, "meant that there would be only 50 per cent Bolshevik propaganda instead of 100 per cent, no Minister of the Crown would accept it."

Curzon rejected a half-solution though he could not have a whole one. Subsequently, after his famous ultimatum of May, 1923, he himself submitted to the Soviets a new formula which, Chicherin told me, "embodied in its mutual pledge no more than my formula at Lausanne."

# 13

# ANGLO-RUSSIAN RIVALRY IN CENTRAL ASIA

HATRED for Russia—and love of India—were the inspiring passions of Curzon's career. While yet a *Times* correspondent and a plain M.P., he styled Russia "the mammon of unrighteousness."[1] The monumental literary works of his early manhood (*Russia in Central Asia* and *Persia and the Persian Question*) reveal a fear of the Colossus of the North and abhorrence for the "bear that walks like a man" which demonstrably determined his policy as Viceroy of India and Foreign Secretary of England. Spiritually he lived in Central Asia.

> Turkestan, Afghanistan, Transcaspia, Persia, [he wrote in the introduction to his *Persia*] to me . . . they are the pieces of a chessboard upon which is being played out a game for the dominion of the world. . . .

The struggle he saw in Asia involved the two greatest empires of the world—Russia and Britain. The prize was India. "Without India the British Empire could not exist. The possession of India is the inalienable badge of sovereignty in the eastern hemisphere."

That his anxiety for the safety of India was more than a hallucination is clear from the undisguised declarations and deeds of Czarism. "The stronger Russia is in Central

[1] George N. Curzon: *Persia and the Persian Question* (London, 1892). I, 221.

Asia," affirmed the famous Skobelev, "the weaker England is in India and the more conciliatory she will be in Europe."

Pre-war Russia kept alive the threat of invading India largely as a means of exerting pressure on Britain in Europe. France influenced St. Petersburg in the same direction.

Russian statesmen knew that India could be conquered, but never held. Only one invader had remained to rule; the others were too happy to leave with their loot before army dissension and Hindustani disaffection undermined their strength. Even the staunchest Czarist imperialist, therefore, could never have dreamt of making India a Czarist province. At best, it might be taken from Britain and left to its fate.

Her own industrial development was so weak in the seventies and eighties of the nineteenth century that Russia could not have exported heavily to India even had political and geographic conditions been propitious, and in the nineties when industrialization commenced, the advance towards India ceased. Economic motives played a minor role in Russia's dream of Indian conquest.

Czarism sought to grow longitudinally and latitudinally. It tried to acquire new territories while keeping their inhabitants in a state of primitive-agricultural poverty. The law which requires growth of every living thing made it incumbent on Czarism to register new conquests. If these gave Russia cotton and semi-tropical fruits as in Turkestan, or offered employment to a large standing army, sinecures to the scions of the nobility, and larger holdings to the landowning class, the conquests were doubly and triply welcome.

But Russia's motives with respect to India were largely negative. Germany, France, Japan, and Russia have at one time or another in their history harbored designs against India in an effort to destroy Great Britain's economic prowess by robbing her factories of 300,000,000 prospective buyers and her shipping of a far-flung Asiatic commerce. If any of these nations proposed subsequently to exploit India themselves, that intention was secondary to the main wish to disrupt the British Empire.

The fall of England would have given Czarist Russia that which she coveted more than all else: new territories and an exit to warm waters. History had established the principle that Russia's growth in Europe would not be tolerated. In Asia she could attempt to register conquests where she met minimum resistance; if the path to the Near East was closed, the forward push would be in the direction of Afghanistan or Manchuria; when Central Asiatic developments stagnated, as in 1895, St. Petersburg concentrated on the Pacific sphere, and when the Russo-Japanese War called a halt in that region too, compensatory pressure in the direction of Afghanistan became so likely that Great Britain pressed more than ever for the conclusion of the truce of August 31, 1907. Thus held fast in Manchuria and Turkestan, Russia tried the third exit—the Near East, and in 1908 Izvolsky started secret negotiations for the acquisition of the Straits.

Between Russia and the fulfilment of her expansionist dreams stood a wall that was England. For decades, Czarism kept tapping at the wall to find the weakest spot. She tried the Near East, the Middle East, the Far East, and found the wall uniformly strong.

Czarism's failure to assert itself in even one of its three possible lines of expansion suggests an important cause of its ultimate disappearance from the historic scene.

**CURZON'S BUFFER STATES** Long before the 1917 revolution, Curzon advocated the erection of buffer States between Russian Turkestan and India so as to diminish the threat of a Slav thrust at the keystone of the Empire. These buffers were Afghanistan and Persia.

The struggle for supremacy in Persia and Afghanistan fills many lively pages of Russo-British relations during the nineteenth century. It is probably correct to say that Russia was the greater offender. England was engaged in consolidating her position within India proper, in subduing recalcitrant sections, suppressing great and small mutinies, and in extending her influence to the natural borders of the country. Russia sought to exploit this preoccupation to establish for herself positions in the buffer States, and particularly in Afghanistan. England could not be expected to look on with equanimity. No Power bent on the political and economic domination of so rich a colony as India could permit a rival, who made no secret of his unfriendly designs, to gain a strong foothold on the very borders of India.

The fear that Czarist Russia would dominate Afghanistan forced Great Britain to try to bring that backward country under her own influence. The endeavor was crowned with relative success after the second Afghan War of 1878–9.

The war gave Great Britain control of Afghan foreign affairs and of the tribes on the Afghan-Indian frontier. The passes leading from Peshawar to Afghanistan were transferred to British India. A British Resident was appointed for Kabul.[3]

A few months later the Resident was murdered. The war reopened. The British occupied the greater part of Afghanistan and appointed their own candidate, Abdur Rahman, as emir with an annual subsidy of 120,000 pounds sterling.

When Curzon published *Persia* in 1892 he identified British with Afghan interests. "British, i.e. Afghan" interests, he wrote, in exactly the same way as he referred to "British, i.e. Indian" interests. Afghanistan was considered a British colony. The emir even undertook military expeditions northward into Russian territory and attempted the conquest of the Pamirs while the British pursued the same purpose from Northern India and Chinese Turkestan. Afghan-British units occasionally met Russian troops in bloody contest on the "roof of the world" and the danger existed that the confiict would not remain localized.

In 1895, however, a delimitation of the Pamir boundary took place which assigned to Afghanistan a tiny tongue of land 15 to 30 kilometers wide between Russia and India so that the two countries might never become contiguous.

This agreement, as well as Russia's acquiescence in England's domination in Afghanistan, point to the lost confidence of Czarism in its ability to overcome British resistance. England, by that time, had so fortified herself in India, and her protectorate in Afghanistan was so secure, that it would have required a powerful army even to attempt a march on India or any advance in her direction. All the conquerors of antiquity met difficulties en route to India, but the moment they reached the Khyber Pass the territory across the Indus lay helpless at their feet. India was weak, disunited, passive. With the coming of

[3] Captain Gervais Lyons: *Afghanistan: the Buffer State. Great Britain and Russia in Central Asia* (London, 1910).

the British, however, a radical change intervened. In the twenty centuries between Alexander of Macedonia and Nadir Shah twenty invading armies marched over Indian soil. But since 1738 the forces of no hostile Power have as much as threatened India.

St. Petersburg's acceptance, in 1895, of the new Pamir frontier which set a limit to Russian expansion is to be attributed not only to Russia's weakness but to the diversion of her interests towards the Far East, where the Chinese-Japanese War of 1895 and events leading to the Boxer uprising of 1900 encouraged Czarism's hopes of winning new laurels on the Pacific. Work had begun on the Trans-Siberian Railway which was conceived as a link with distant markets and with possible territorial gains. In 1898 Russia obtained the Port Arthur lease. A period of foreign pressure on China now dawned through which, with the assistance freely offered by Kaiser Wilhelm, Russia expected to come into her own. Nicholas II therefore accepted the status quo in Central Asia and directed his attention further east.

Russia's adventures in Manchuria and Mongolia brought her into conflict with Japan and provoked the war of 1905 which checked her growth in the Pacific theater. The war was followed by a menacing internal revolution. The resulting weakness enabled England to press for the legalization of the status quo in Central Asia. Russia might utilize her energy, drained though it was, to renew the rivalry in Turkestan, Afghanistan, and Persia. London, moreover, needed allies for the world-rocking struggle with Germany then already casting its shadow before.

The interplay of these circumstances produced the treaty of August 31, 1907, signed in St. Petersburg by Sir Arthur Nicholson for His Majesty's Government and by Izvolsky on behalf of the Czar. In it the Russians "engaged that all their political relations with Afghanistan shall be conducted through the intermediary of His Britannic Majesty's Government; they further engage not to send any agents into Afghanistan." England, on the other hand, promised not to interfere in the internal affairs of Afghanistan or to annex any part of its territory.

The treaty, furthermore, admitted the sovereignty of China over Tibet and both contracting parties pledged themselves to refrain from sending representatives to Lhasa, but London recognized Russia's right to trade with

Tibet and thus, by implication, her special position in Chinese Turkestan on the borders of the Indian province of Kashmir.

With respect to Persia, a Russian sphere of influence was created in the north, a British sphere in the south, a neutral sphere between them. Hereby Czarism renounced its dream of reaching the Persian Gulf.

A period of passive rivalry now dawned during which Great Britain enjoyed the advantage of bigger financial and commercial resources, better diplomacy, and the presence of an armed force in India stronger and more mobile than the Czar's army in Turkestan.

During the decade that intervened between the ratification of this treaty and the outbreak of the Bolshevik revolution, the tug-of-war continued for domination over the Shah's Government and over Afghanistan. Russia had been reduced to a more distant threat. Nevertheless, the British looked askance at the extension of Turkestan and Caucasian railways to the Afghan and Persian boundaries, and would on no account permit the building of railroads by Russia in either of the buffer States. The Czarist State, which would have welcomed railroads in Afghanistan, strenuously objected to the granting of a construction contract in Persia to British subjects or to the nationals of a power friendly to Great Britain.

Thus the effect of Anglo-Russian rivalry in Central Asia was to confirm both buffer States in their backwardness, poverty, and dependence.

**CHANGED STATUS** With the advent of the Soviet revolution the black threat that had hung over these States from the north disappeared.

Great Britain took advantage of the new situation to occupy all of Persia in 1919 and use it as a base for operations against the Bolsheviks in the Caucasus and Turkestan. But in the same year, the disloyalty of the Anglo-Indian army, the unsettled state of affairs in India, the Pan-Islamic agitation in the Moslem world which England necessarily feared, and the influence of the Bolshevik upheaval, afforded a favorable conjuncture for the seizure of power by Amanullah Khan, the leader of the Young Afghans and Pan-Islamists—and the assertion of Afghanistan's independence.

The existence of the Soviet State encouraged the growth

of nationalist movements in Persia under the leadership of Riza Khan and in Afghanistan under Amanullah Khan. Just as the political and social influences of the French Revolution overleapt boundaries and ultimately made themselves felt in different parts of the world, so the establishment of Bolshevism in Russia produced very apparent effects on the history of numerous Eastern peoples. The granting of cultural, political and economic autonomy to the national minorities in Russia and the Kremlin's sermons on the right of Eastern peoples to national self-determination, provoked in those peoples a natural yearning for these privileges.

The Soviet-Persian Treaty of February 26, 1921, laid the foundation of a cordial relationship between Moscow and Teheran. Factors tending to complicate and cloud Russo-Persian affairs nevertheless remained. Red troops still occupied the Persian province of Ghilan, and British influence had not completely disappeared.

Moscow wavered, torn between two desires. The British Empire shook with dissension in Ireland, India, Egypt. There were indications that London would be forced to shorten the imperial line of communication by withdrawing its troops from Persia in the direction of Iraq which was itself in a disturbed state. The Bolsheviks saw a golden opportunity. Lenin weighed the plan of "sovietizing" Khorosan but was quickly dissuaded. Other Communists urged military penetration into Persia, using Ghilan as a base.

The treaty of February 26, 1921, made the evacuation of Russian troops contingent on the departure of the British forces in Persia. The weakened position of the British prevented the control of all Persia. Their alternative appeared at the time to be a division of Persia similar in effect to that outlined in the Czarist agreement of 1907. British policy, accordingly, inclined to favor the continued stay of Red battalions in Northern Persia. It would, by the indirect implication of the treaty of February 26, 1921, permit them to prolong their own occupation.

Sir Percy Lorraine, the British minister in Teheran, now hinted to Theodore Rothstein, the Soviet envoy, that the Soviets and England divide Persia into spheres of influence after the time-honored pre-revolutionary practice. Rothstein ignored the offer.

Rothstein had dissipated any thought in the minds of prominent Persians that he favored an imported revolution of the Socialist kind. When, in 1921, the Teheran authorities sought to prevent his entrance into the country and later into the capital on the ground that his mission was to foment revolution, he protested that if the Soviet Government really intended to precipitate a revolution it would have sent Budenny with his cavalry instead of himself—who came armed with Curzon's *Persia* as his Baedeker and Soviet declarations as his political guides. Subsequently, Zi ed Din, the Premier, responsible for the delay in Rothstein's arrival, fled to Bagdad in a British automobile.

The influence of the British had not been completely eclipsed. They sat securely in the south, where the Anglo-Persian Oil Company, a creature of the British Government, operated an invaluable petroleum concession. Its royalties to Teheran covered one-fourth to one-third of the annual expenditures of the Persian State. British officers, moreover, still held posts in the Persian Army, and great feudal khans, especially in Luristan, Kurdistan, and Southern Arabia were continually made aware of the special interest of the British in their territories.

Riza Khan's first task was the organization of a loyal national army with which he could break the power of the khans who resisted the central government, refused to pay taxes, or to approve of his reforms. Neither Zi ed Din nor his successor were exactly anti-British. The Medjlis had strongly feudal inclinations. Nevertheless, Riza introduced his militant nationalism.

In 1921 he dismissed the British and Swedish instructors of the Persian Army and disbanded and disarmed the South Persian Rifles who had been an undisguised British weapon. The result was a rich crop of feudal insurrections during 1922 and even 1923 in Ghilan and Khorosan in the north, in Luristan and Kurdistan—these he quickly suppressed with merciless ruthlessness—and in Arabistan and the Bakhtiari region where the sheiks and khans, grown rich on subsidies of the Anglo-Persian Oil Company and well supplied with foreign arms, were able to force Riza Khan to negotiate with them. Before the end of 1923, however, the War Minister had forced even the recalcitrant South to pay taxes and to contribute recruits to his battalions. The economic power of feudalism was not broken but it bowed to the military dictator; he had crushed its political omnipotence.

"Lost influence in Persia," read a London *Times* headline on August 21, 1923, over an article which declared: "It is an unfortunate but undeniable fact that the British are unpopular in Persia at present . . ." And popularity of the Soviets grew in proportion to the unpopularity of the British.

On October 29, 1923, Riza Khan became Prime Minister. The whole country hailed him as its national hero. He had united the nation and asserted the authority of the central government throughout the land. The future held defiance and difficulties in store for him, but Persia's national independence could no longer be questioned by the foreign or domestic foe. Early in 1924 the new Medjlis convened; Riza's words became its laws.

As the power behind the throne in 1922 and 1923, Riza Khan was far greater than the figure on it in 1925. He had conquered under the sign of nationalism and centralization; both were products of necessity and echoes of the revolution in the vast State of the north.

During this period Soviet-Persian diplomatic relations remained undisturbed, and Soviet commercial contacts—especially with North Persia and Teheran, whose export, import and transit trade depend on Russia—continued to develop.

**SOVIET-AFGHANISTAN RELATIONS. 1921–3** The tug-of-war between British and Soviet influence developed in Afghanistan as well, and ran parallel with Amanullah's attempt to mold a group of warlike tribes into a united nation. But Afghanistan's economic development lags behind that of Persia. Its bourgeoisie is younger and weaker. Its resources are fewer. Britain's strategic position with respect to Afghanistan, moreover, is far more favorable than in the case of Persia. Above all else, Afghanistan's destiny was determined by the fact of its neighborly proximity to British India.

Having won independence in 1919, Afghanistan was free to enter into a political treaty with the Soviets, which was signed on February 28, 1921. England could not, in view of her preoccupation with problems of empire, prevent the conclusion of this agreement, but she sought, in 1921, 1922, and 1923, to obstruct its operation.

The treaty entitled Soviet Russia to establish consulates in Herat, Meimen, Mazar-i-Sharif, Kandahar, and Ghazni. On November 21, 1921, however, Raskolnikov, the Soviet minister in Kabul, informed the Afghan Foreign Office that Moscow would temporarily refrain from opening consulates in Kandahar and Ghazni in order not to embarrass the Afghan Government. The embarrassment would have arisen from British India's opposition to the settlement of a Soviet official near the Indian border.

Amanullah felt keenly the effect of Great Britain's special interest in the Northwest Frontier region and of the new "Forward Policy" which was introduced after Afghanistan obtained her independence. The Anglo-Afghan War of 1919 had thrown the tribes of the North-West Frontier into a turmoil that lasted long after peace was officially declared, and the process of pacification cost the British more than any other similar enterprise in the history of their rule in India. To prevent a recurrence of that situation and as a prophylactic against repercussions of Afghan independence in India, British India sent the regular army into the Northwest Frontier—nominally independent under the Sir Mortimer Durand agreement of 1893—and proceeded, in 1921, to construct a railway through the Khyber Pass and motor roads in the direction of Kabul. At the same time, the pacification of Waziristan went on apace.

The corollary of greater firmness in British policy towards the warlike tribes of the Northwest Frontier was greater British firmness in relation to Afghanistan and increased resistance to Soviet influence at Kabul.

The Soviet-Afghan Treaty of February 28, 1921, provided not only for Russian consulates in Kandahar and Ghazni, but also for the "granting of financial and other material aid to Afghanistan by the Government of the Russian Socialist Federated Soviet Republic." The British tried to obstruct the execution of this provision.

During 1921 and the early part of 1922, British efforts to cloud the horizon of Soviet-Afghan relations received support from the circumstance of Afghan sympathy and aid for Enver Pasha's adventures in Bokhara. The Kabul Government even undertook military measures calculated to comfort the anti-Soviet insurgents. But when Enver disappeared, Russo-Afghan affairs returned to their normally smooth course. Towards the end of 1922, Russian engineers commenced preliminary surveys for the construction of a telegraph line from Kushk on the Turkestan-Afghan border to Kandahar and Kabul. And in December, Kabul suggested that the Soviet Republic might fulfil the promise of "financial and other material aid."

The year 1923 found all of Afghanistan stirred by British military activities in the Northwest Frontier province. Amanullah could only suffer from an improvement of Britain's position in Waziristan.

A Turkish mission had previously arrived in Kabul to train Amanullah's new army. Afghanistan's policy became more active. The Moslems of India, and the Hindus too, were in a black mood. Russia welcomed the new developments.

England fought back. Air bombing in Waziristan was one of her weapons. The stopping of munitions purchased by Afghanistan in Italy and Germany was another. The Curzon ultimatum was yet another.

# 14

# THE CURZON ULTIMATUM

CURZON's ten-day ultimatum of May 2, 1923, rested on British displeasure with the situation in Central Asia. The other subjects it discussed were of very minor importance. The seemingly important question of debts and confiscated private property was not as much as alluded to. Yet the disappointment of British business quarters with the results of the Anglo-Russian Trade Agreement of March 16, 1921, undoubtedly played a role in the submission of the ultimatum.

The British had supposed that the New Economic Policy signalized the scrapping of Communism, the reintroduction of private capitalism, and therefore readmission of foreign capital into Russia on easy terms. They had assumed that the Soviet Government would not defend its original principles in the matter of concessions, compensation, and foreign trade. But Genoa and The Hague created a contrary impression, and the following year confirmed the belief that the Bolsheviks would avoid far-reaching compromises.

**THE URQUHART CONCESSION** The Urquhart concession episode offered concrete proof of the Soviet's intransigent attitude towards foreign capital. Throughout 1921, Urquhart had conducted negotiations with Communist officials in London and Moscow with a view to the return of his vast holdings in Siberia. He was present in Genoa and The Hague, and as the latter conference failed, he expected to benefit from the Bolshevik desire to break the hostile Allied front by signing separate agreements with States and private groups. Actually, negotiations between Krassin and Urquhart now entered their final stage, and on September 9, 1922, they signed the concession contract in Berlin.

But Moscow's ratification was required. Lenin changed his mind three times: first he approved, then he disapproved, then he approved, and in the end he laid his veto on the agreement. The Soviet Press announced the final rejection of the concession on October 7, 1922. From an economic point of view, the papers said, the concession was not favorable to Soviet interests. It had been considered largely as a means of winning the goodwill of the British Government and of strengthening the rapprochement begun in Genoa and The Hague. But British policy in the Greco-Turkish situation and London's attempt to bar Russia from Lausanne indicated that Downing Street would persist in its hostility towards the Soviet regime despite the signing of the Urquhart contract.

This official reason received most prominence in Bolshevik editorials. Yet the industrial patriotism of Soviet engineers and economists who believed that they could operate Urquhart's former properties without him influenced the deliberations. And Urquhart's insistence on compensation for minerals taken from his holdings during the Civil War and for damages wrought in that chaotic period provoked the opposition of many Bolshevik elements who did not wish to establish a precedent which would reinforce the compensation claims of other former owners and entitle the Germans to make similar demands under the Rapallo Treaty. The same difficulty complicated conversations between Urquhart and the Soviets after the rejection of the 1922 agreement. Mr. Urquhart insisted on compensation even as late as 1928 and 1929, when he approached Bolshevik representatives in Paris.

Urquhart believed that the Curzon ultimatum should have presented demands for compensation and for payment of debts. "They are the pivot of Anglo-Russian relations," he wrote in a letter to the London *Times* of May 26, 1923. Nevertheless, he regarded the ultimatum as "the first touch of sense and firmness we have imported into our diplomatic dealings" with Russia. He thus set his stamp of approval upon Curzon's policy and indirectly criticized Lloyd George's, forgetting that the Bolsheviks might not have rejected his concession had they expected a continuation of the relatively conciliatory policy of Lloyd George.

**THE PRELIMINARY BARRAGE** The Curzon ultimatum, significantly, omitted any reference to the principles for which Lloyd George had fought in the Genoa and Hague periods. Nor did it argue the claims of Urquhart and the Association of British Creditors he had organized. The diplomatic barrage which preceded the Curzon ultimatum dealt neither with economics nor with politics—but with anti-religious persecution.

In March, 1923, Cardinal Cieplak, Monsignor Butkevich, and a number of priests of the Polish Roman Catholic Church in Russia were brought to trial in Moscow on the charge of espionage and other treasonous activities during the Civil and Russo-Polish Wars.

On March 27 Cardinal Cieplak was sentenced to ten years' imprisonment and Mgr. Butkevich to death. Protests poured in from every corner of the world, from Catholics, Episcopalians, Protestants, Jews, Moslems, etc. The Polish Government undertook a diplomatic démarche, and on March 30 Mr. R. M. Hodgson, England's official representative in Moscow, acting under instructions from Curzon, made "an earnest and final appeal for a stay of execution," which, his note assured, "cannot fail to produce throughout the civilized world a feeling of horror and indignation."

Moscow replied the very next day, but, in a premeditated and unwise effort to offend, the rejoinder bore the signature not of Chicherin or Litvinov but of Gregory Weinstein, the chief of the Anglo-American section of the Commissariat of Foreign Affairs. The contents of the note, however, aroused more indignation than this slight. It pointed out that

> Russia, being an independent country and a sovereign State, has the undeniable right of passing sentences in conformity with its own legislation on people breaking the law of the country, and that every attempt from outside to interfere with this right and to protect spies and traitors in Russia is an unfriendly act and a renewal of the intervention which has been successfully repulsed by the Russian people.

Not content with this sternly-worded restatement of an accepted principle, Moscow touched England roughly on what, at the moment, was her sorest wound: Ireland. The Black and Tans were engaged in the unpleasant task of taming the wearers of the Shamrock and did not hesitate to adopt some rather doubtful means of achieving that end.

The Weinstein message referred therefore to the

> hypocritical intervention of the British Government which is responsible for the assassination in cold blood of political prisoners in Ireland, where 14,000 men, women and young girls are treated in a barbarous and inhuman fashion. . . . If similar facts which have taken place under British rule in India and Egypt are taken into consideration, it is hardly possible to regard an appeal, in the name of humanity and sacredness of life, from the British Government as very convincing.[1]
>
> In bourgeois diplomacy but particularly in British diplomacy, [wrote *Izvestia*] when it is written Butkevich you must read oil, when it is written Cieplak you must read Russian fisheries, and when they say Tikhon they mean British interests in the East.

Poland protested in the name of humanity: "Hypocrisy," the Bolsheviks replied. "Do they not persecute the Greek Catholic Church in Poland? Did they not provoke the war of 1920 which cost thousands of lives?" France protested in the name of civilization; "Hypocrisy," they replied. "Did she not invade the peaceful Ruhr and use colored Colonials in order to add insult to injury?" England protested in the name of the "affronted moral sentiment of mankind"; "Amritsar," they shouted back, "Black and Tans."

Unmindful of all foreign appeals, the Soviet Government denied clemency to Butkevich or commutation of sentence to Cieplak. The Archbishop was released less than a year after the trial and permitted to journey to Rome.

The British Government refused to accept Mr. Weinstein's offensive note, whereupon he signed another in which the Soviet Government reiterated the hope that Great Britain would in the future "refrain from attempts of any kind at interfering in the internal affairs of the Soviet Republic."[2]

**THE ULTIMATUM** A month after the Weinstein notes

[1] *Correspondence between his Majesty's Government and the Soviet Government respecting the Relations between the Two Governments.* British White Book. Cmd. 1869 (London, 1923).

[2] *Ibid.*

episode, Mr. Hodgson placed the Curzon ultimatum in the hands of the Commissariat of Foreign Affairs. "The tone and character" of those notes, read the ultimatum, had induced the British Government to examine whether "it is desirable, or indeed possible, that the relations between the two Governments should remain any longer upon so anomalous and indeed unprecedented a footing."

Commerce with India was far greater concern to Curzon than trade with Russia. He attached little importance to the Anglo-Russian Agreement of 1921. Its cancellation might, he thought, give England freedom of action. For it is clear from the contents and spirit of his ultimatum that he wanted or expected a break. The Weinstein notes may have encouraged his hope that the ultimatum would produce the effect he desired. If Moscow replied in the rude manner of the Weinstein communications, British public opinion would be aroused and the Foreign Office would feel justified in severing relations.

The bulk of his ultimatum dealt with alleged Russian "pernicious activities" in Persia, Afghanistan, and India. "Upon unimpeachable authority," the British Government had information that would fill many pages. "Such a narrative would doubtless provoke, as it did before, an indignant denial from the Soviet Government with allegation as to false information and spurious documents." His Majesty's Government therefore "have no intention to embark upon any such controversy."

Curzon stated that the British knew the exact sums sent by Moscow to Shumiatsky, the Soviet minister in Teheran, that they had "seen the instructions that have passed between him and his superiors and between him and his subordinate agents," and he quoted from a telegram to the Commissariat of Foreign Affairs in which Shumiatsky is purported to have requested funds for anti-British work in North Persia.

Raskolnikov, the Soviet minister in Kabul, was the subject of a more vehement attack. "He had distinguished himself by exceptional zeal," Curzon declared, in conducting activity against the British in Afghanistan and among the tribes on the North-West Frontier.

The Russian Commissariat of Foreign Affairs, [read the ultimatum] will no doubt recognize the following communication dated the 21st February, 1923, which they received from M.

Raskolnikov: "I am making arrangements for giving help to Waziristan, probably to the extent of the outlay of 3,000 roubles and ten boxes of cartridges."

Curzon then cited a number of documents he declared to have in his possession which offered proof of Soviet arms shipments to India, of Communist contacts with revolutionary Hindus, and of heavy subsidies from the Third International (Comintern) to the Indian and British Communist parties.

These were but a "few selected examples" which testified that the Soviets had consistently flouted the non-propaganda pledge of the Anglo-Russian Agreement. "Unless," therefore, "such acts are repudiated and apologized for, and unless the officials who have been responsible for them are disowned and recalled from the scene of their maleficent labors," the agreement would be discontinued.

Further, the ultimatum discussed "a series of outrages inflicted upon British subjects in the past few years," the most conspicuous of which were the murder of Mr. C. F. Davison, in January, 1920, and the arrest and imprisonment of Mrs. Sten Harding on the charge of espionage. "His Majesty's Government are unable to allow the matter to be trifled with any longer." Curzon demanded "equitable compensation" and noted incidentally that these were not the only personal claims.

Followed the question of the British trawlers off the coast of Murmansk. The Soviet Government had extended the regular, international three-mile limit to a twelve-mile limit on her Arctic seaboard. British trawlers nevertheless continued to fish within the territorial zone. The Red Navy endeavored, accordingly, to interfere with their operations, and Curzon charged that the result had been the sinking of the *Magneta,* the confiscation of the *St. Hubert,* and the seizure of the *James Johnson*. The British Government insisted on compensation, release, and a promise of non-interference with fishing outside the three-mile limit.

The final ultimative British demand was the withdrawal of the two Weinstein notes.

**THE IMPRESSION IN RUSSIA** The Curzon ultimatum reached the Soviet authorities on May 8 and produced a painful impression. The question of propaganda and anti-British activities in the Middle East had been the subject of a long correspondence. There had been no new or unexpected developments in the recent past to prepare the Bolsheviks for London's threat of a rupture of relations.

Davison was killed in 1920, Mrs. Harding incarcerated soon after, and the exchange of notes had continued for years.

Moscow did not believe the trawler issue serious enough to justify drastic English action. Moreover, that problem too had been weighed in unfinished negotiations. Did Curzon then intend to force a break because of the Weinstein notes? the Bolsheviks wondered.

Alarmists saw the menace of a new intervention or of an international war. Britain, said the Press, wished to kill Russian economic reconstruction in the bud. England, Chicherin declared at a public protest meeting in Moscow, thought the illness of Lenin presented a favorable moment for the overthrow of the Soviets.

Meanwhile the statesmen deliberated calmly in the Kremlin. The temper of Curzon's note and the fact that it was a ten-day ultimatum made it clear that London could no longer be trifled with. If Russia permitted a break, Poland and Rumania, it was said, would be encouraged, and Europe, already disturbed by the Ruhr invasion, might conceivably burst into flames. But the Bolsheviks could not afford a war. They did not want to fight. "Cursed be any one in this country who favors hostilities or a future war," Trotzky declared. "We will not take a single step or say a single word that could make the situation more acute or close the path to a peaceful situation through negotiations. We want peace most and above all," the Commissar of War affirmed.

Communist councils decided to return the soft answer that turneth away wrath. "He [Curzon]," Trotzky said at a meeting on June 19, "cooked [couched] his note in strong phraseology hoping to receive a sharp answer that would insult the English Philistines and thus arouse public opinion against us." But "we understand this clumsy trap."

Some Soviet leaders, moreover, had been distressed by the obvious crudity of the Weinstein notes. And while all Bolsheviks agreed that in principle Russia was within her rights in urging that the longer range of modern guns justified the widening of the three-mile into a twelve-mile limit, some nevertheless submitted that she could not well put the change into practice upon the basis of her own unilateral declaration, even if Great Britain had set a precedent for such action by establishing a twenty-mile limit around Ceylon in order to protect the island's pearl fisheries.

The Russians believed, however, that Curzon's demands for compensation to Mrs. Harding and Mr. Davison's family were entirely unreasonable. "We must wonder," Trotzky said sarcastically, "at Curzon's moderate claims. We must wonder that he does not insist on pensions for the families of those fifteen British soldiers who died throwing Russian workers into the ice and robbing Russian forests." Thousands of Russians, the papers stated, had been killed as a result of British intervention. Mr. Davison, they affirmed, was a spy and belonged to the secret service organization of Paul Dukes. He had been killed in January, 1920, when England and Russia were engaged in actual warfare. The arrest of Mrs. Sten Harding belonged to the same period, and she had been detained, the Bolsheviks contended, on the charge of espionage and on the basis of information supplied by Miss Margaret Harrison, an American journalist.

Finally, the Soviet leaders insisted that the accusations respecting anti-British acts in Central Asia lacked all foundation. "They dream of secret agents," Chicherin told a Moscow audience on May 12, "when they are faced with the effects of an historical process." Curzon's ultimatum, he continued, was "a collection of false charges." The "quotations concerning Persia were entirely invented." Curzon's demand for the recall of Russia's ministers from Teheran and Kabul was "unheard of."

The Bolsheviks, nevertheless, feared the political and economic consequences of a break to such an extent that they decided to do what was not consonant with right and national honor. They would satisfy claims which, in their opinion, had not the remotest justification. They would accede to demands which they thought were exorbitant. They bowed to a stronger force and proceeded on considerations of expediency. "Our relations to capitalist countries," Trotzky had told an interviewer, "are based on expediency. Our only aim is to secure peace and normal economic relations." If peace and Bolshevik reconstruction required the acceptance of a humiliating defeat, Moscow did not hesitate.

**THE RUSSIAN REPLY**[3] Mr. Hodgson received the Soviet reply on May 13, just five days after he presented Curzon's ultimatum to the Commissariat of Foreign Affairs.

The ultimatum, read the cabled version of the rejoinder, "was for Soviet Government greatest surprise on account of its sharp and unjustified hostility." After a reminder to British commercial interests of the growing importance of Russian trade—indirectly an appeal to them to frustrate Curzon's efforts toward a scrapping of the commercial agreement—the Soviet reply, which was written by Trotzky, proceeded to elaborate on British hostility towards Soviet Russia in the questions of the Straits, Eastern Galicia, Memel, Bessarabia, etc.

But this was not all. The Russian Government

> has plenty of reports and documents pointing to intense activity of agents of British Government against interests of republics in Caucasus and in particular in localities bordering on Central Asian parts of Soviet republics, to support given to bandit and Bassi (Basmachi) movement in Turkestan and Eastern Bokhara, to assistance given by British consul to White Guard in recruiting officers and sending them to Vladivostok during its occupation by Whites.

One of these charges subsequently found corroboration from the British officer who supervised anti-Soviet moves in Central Asia. Lieutenant-Colonel P. T. Etherton, the British Resident and Consul in Kashgar, Chinese Turkestan, admits in his *In the Heart of Asia,* published in London in 1925, that he intrigued against the Bolsheviks in Turkestan, that he assisted the Emir of Bokhara, that in fact the purpose of his mission was subversive activities against the Communists—and that he continued his work after the signing of the Anglo-Russian Trade Agreement. Some of the documents referred to in Moscow's reply to Curzon dealt with Etherton's work.

"Similar material," the Soviet note submitted, "is at the

[3] *Reply of the Soviet Government to His Majesty's Government respecting the Relations between the Two Governments.* British White Paper. (London, 1923). Cmd. 1874.

disposal of all Governments, and if they use them for creating conflicts and as a foundation for protests, then friendly relations between any two Governments could hardly exist."

The note then attempted to explain that Great Britain misunderstood Soviet policy in the East which consisted of establishing friendly contacts with independent nations. Surely the British do not expect that "the Russian Republic should have no policy of its own in the East, but should everywhere support English aspirations."

On the most important issue raised in the Curzon ultimatum, therefore—on the question of Soviet activity in Central Asia—Moscow gave the British Foreign Office no satisfaction.

Moscow, however, agreed to pay compensation to Mrs. Harding and to the family of Mr. Davison. The note, nevertheless, named Russians for whose death the British were responsible and protested that during the intervention "an immeasurably greater number of Russian citizens suffered both physically and materially from actions of English authorities in north and south Soviet republics and in sphere of English influence."

The Russians likewise satisfied Curzon's demands respecting trawlers. And the two Weinstein notes "can . . . be considered as non-existing."

**ANTI-CLIMAX** The Soviet reply had a good press in Great Britain. The fact that it met the British on three of the four issues raised by the ultimatum offered effective ammunition to the English opponents of a break. The Conservative thesis that the Russians could not be budged from their intransigeant position had been weakened. Relations, the Liberals argued, opened the way to diplomatic gives and takes; a rupture gave the Bolsheviks a free hand and robbed London of the possibility of exerting pressure on Moscow. Business men, moreover, feared the loss of the Russian market. For although the high hopes of some had been disappointed, the business turnover of the two countries, which amounted to 4,876,000 pounds sterling in 1921, rose to 11,760,000 pounds sterling in 1922,[4] and thus inspired hopes of rapid progress. The bondholders and concession seekers may have felt that

[4] *Statesmen's Yearbook,* 1925, p. 1259.

Curzon's tactics would force the submission of the Bolsheviks, and therefore welcomed it. Yet it is doubtful whether they desired an irrevocable rupture which, obviously, could yield them nothing but lost opportunities. The commercial interests certainly had nothing to gain from a severing of relations, and the Bolsheviks' "soft answer" enabled them to argue their case with greater cogency. Labor too opposed the nullification of the Anglo-Russian Trade Agreement, and the cumulative weight of all these influences was not without its effect on the Baldwin Government of 1923.

The break, moreover, would have come in May or June—just at the time when the French invasion of the Ruhr and the devaluation of German currency threatened to draw Germany to the brink of a national upheaval which would throw all Europe into turmoil. The interruption of Anglo-Russian relations would further prejudice the continental situation in favor of social disturbances. Cooler heads in London accordingly advised against any too brusque move that would antagonize Russia. Moreover, even the Conservative Press could not explain, objectively and analytically, how England might benefit from a rupture.

Accordingly, the British answer to the Russian note was couched in far more gentle phraseology than the original ultimatum. It admitted that three of the issues "have now been removed from the arena of controversy." But there remained "the all-important question of hostile propaganda."

After a further exchange of memoranda,[5] however, both Governments agreed to sign a formula respecting propaganda which was somewhat more precise than the first article of the Anglo-Russian Trade Agreement, and Moscow, while protesting that no third Power was entitled to interfere in the relations between two states, nevertheless recalled Raskolnikov from Kabul but kept Shumiatsky in Teheran. A British note of June 13 therefore declared the correspondence closed, and on the same day Curzon wrote to Lord Crewe saying, "I think I may claim to have won a considerable victory over the Soviet Government, and I expect them to behave with more circum-

[5] British Blue Book. Cmd. 2895. Also, *Anglo-Russian Relations (1921–7.)* Notes and Documents. Moscow, 1927 Official publication of the Commissariat of Foreign Affairs.

spection for some time to come." The Bolsheviks, too, congratulated themselves: they had prevented a crisis and the accompanying dislocation of trade and industry; they had obviated even the remote possibility of renewed intervention.

# 15

# RUHR, RUSSIA, AND REVOLUTION

THOUSANDS of workers marched through the streets of Moscow on January 15, 1923, demonstrating against the French occupation of the Ruhr a few days previously. "Down with Imperialist Slaughter," their placards read: "Down with French Imperialism." Bukharin and other Bolshevik leaders addressed meetings that afternoon protesting against the use of Poincaré's "800,000 arguments in the form of 800,000 soldiers" for the purpose of "enslaving Germany."

Two days prior to this popular outburst, the Commissariat of Foreign Affairs issued an appeal to the nations of the earth which declared the action of the French Government "a crime." The Bolsheviks considered the occupation of the Ruhr an illegal attempt to suppress the independence of Germany, and a natural result of the spirit in which the Versailles Treaty was drafted. "Our sympathy is with Germany, as it is with any oppressed nation," Litvinov told the *Manchester Guardian* correspondent on January 27.

Chicherin stated[1] that the "Ruhr adventure had administered a shock to the political and economic life of all Europe and thus brought a great harm upon the Soviet republics which require economic relations with other countries. . . ."

Moscow saw in Germany a barrier against the aggression of France. "The complete domination of Germany," *Izvestia* therefore suggested, "is a sharp threat to Soviet

[1] *Pravda,* February 15, 1923.

Russia. It would make French imperialism our immediate neighbor." It would give Poincaré control over the territory from the Seine to the Rhine, from the Rhine to the Vistula, and—Poland being an ally of France—from the Vistula to the Soviet frontier. Accordingly, said *Izvestia,* "the political balance in Eastern Europe will depend on the position assumed by Poland in the coming conflict."[2]

The Moscow *Pravda* echoed the same official view.

"It is necessary to watch events in Poland closely," read an editorial on January 19. "Poland long ago coveted poorly-protected sections of Germany. . . . If the Polish bourgeois will follow the example of his French patron a European upheaval is inevitable. On the Polish Government rests a heavy responsibility."

**POLISH AND CZECH POLICIES TOWARD GERMAN REVOLUTION** These and similar published statements were intended as direct intimations to Warsaw that Russia would not tolerate Polish military moves against Germany. With the French in the Ruhr and Rhineland, and the Poles in East Prussia and German Upper Silesia, Germany's unity would be ruined, German economic cooperation with Russia precluded. And the danger existed that a grand French sweep through Germany into Poland would gather too much momentum en route to stop before it reached Moscow. *Izvestia* therefore warned that "if, on some excuse, the Polish imperialists find the moment suitable for military action, the Soviet Government, notwithstanding its desire for peace, will not be able to allow the Polish imperialists freedom of action. . . ."

French and Polish policies towards the German situation caused alarm in Moscow. In the latter half of 1923, Roman Knoll, then Polish chargé d'affaires in Moscow and subsequently a member of the Polish Cabinet, came to Radek and declared that his Government would not interfere with a Communist Germany provided Poland could annex East Prussia. Chicherin was informed, and in a subsequent interview with Knoll the commissar several times reiterated his belief that neither France nor Poland would violate German soil. The belief was in truth merely a hope, and the hope was not a very firm one, for, apart from Knoll's intimations to Radek, Moscow disposed of very positive information that Czecho-Slovakia too was

[2] *Izvestia,* January 21, 1923.

considering the possible results of sovietization in Germany. The cautious and almost simultaneous démarches in Moscow by representatives of Poland and Czecho-Slovakia aroused a suspicion among Russians that France would connive at the establishment of a German Communist regime in the expectation that economic collapse and territorial disintegration might follow.

Soviet Russia's role in the Ruhr conflict consisted, therefore, in paralyzing Poland by the threat of moving the Red Army. At a time when separatist movements were rife in Bavaria, the Rhineland, and the Palatinate, when the foreign invader had seized the heart of Germany's coal and metallurgical industry, when, moreover, financial difficulties and economic crises multiplied with lightning speed, the Bolsheviks saved the situation for Germany by keeping her eastern neighbor in inactivity.

In this mood, the *Pravda* hinted to Wilhelmstrasse on January 11, 1923, that "only a closer economic and political contact with Russia will strengthen the position of the present German Government."

Such sentiments moved the Soviet Press and the Soviet leaders throughout the first five or six months that followed the invasion of the Ruhr. The attitude still prevailed in May when the Curzon ultimatum thoroughly frightened the Bolsheviks and led them to believe that the British Foreign Office's stern note was merely the forerunner of more concrete anti-Soviet measures which events on the Rhine seemed to favor. Moscow's reply to Curzon would never have been so meek had the Bolsheviks expected or planned a Red revolution in Germany at that juncture.

On March 22, as a matter of fact, Radek hurled his scintillating literary lance at Poland once more, and, dissecting statements carried to Moscow regarding a Polish mobilization and a French loan of 400,000,000 francs for this purpose, repeated the hint of Russia's intimate relation to such an eventuality.

During all this time, diplomatic and trade relations between Soviet Russia and Germany continued undisturbed. The sense of mutual interests and common enemies, and the political benefits and commercial gains that had accrued to both sides as a result of the favorable beginnings made in 1922, tended to cement the friendship reflected in and reinforced by the Rapallo Treaty. German business with Russia increased.

Much of the credit for the smooth course of German-Russian relations in 1922 and 1923, as well as in subsequent years, belongs to Count Brockdorff-Rantzau, the Wilhelmstrasse's ambassador in Moscow. A man of high culture, wide political experience, and deep psychological understanding, he not only established warm personal ties with Chicherin and other Soviet leaders, but knew how to bridge the gap between his own capitalist country and Bolshevik Russia. Though the task of dovetailing was difficult, he proved that it could be done. He alone, of all the official envoys sent by foreign States to Red Moscow, rose above the small physical discomforts, the social deprivations, and the innumerable irritations incident to life in the Communist capital, and saw the possibilities of relations with Bolshevism in the light of his broad political horizon.

Rantzau owed his success in no small measure to his extraordinary position. Originally suggested for the appointment by President Ebert, who was under obligations to him, he accepted his mission to Moscow with the assurance that he could, if it proved necessary, appeal to the Reichspresident over the head of the Ministry of Foreign Affairs. He made more use of this arrangement after Hindenburg came to office than during the incumbency of Ebert.

The strongest and most lasting impression of Count Rantzau's political life was probably given him by the Versailles Peace Conference. Representative of a defeated, humiliated nation, he appeared in the Hall of Mirrors in Versailles on May 7, 1919, to receive a neatly-bound copy of the Paris treaty from the hands of Clemenceau.

The ceremony was solemn and important. Clemenceau addressed the delegates and called on Rantzau. The German remained seated. Colonel House suggests that he may have been too nervous to stand. The Count was certainly white and shaken. "It is demanded of us," he said, "that we confess ourselves the sole guilty ones in the war. Such a confession would be a lie in my mouth. . . . During the last fifty years the imperialism of all European States has poisoned the international situation. The policies of revenge, of expansion, and disregard of the self-determination of nations brought about the sickness of Europe which saw its crisis in the World War."

That historic scene in Versailles imprinted itself indelibly on Rantzau's sensitive personality. He could see no salvation for Germany from the West, from those Powers whose representatives gazed at him as he accepted the peace treaty which he regarded as cruel and unjust. Inevitably, he turned to Russia. From the East, from the nation which was as anti-Versailles as Germany, his fatherland could obtain the political strength required to resist the pressure of the Allies. He believed, likewise, in the great business potentialities of Russia and in the possibilities they offered to Germany.

Guided by these views, Rantzau succeeded in establishing a modus vivendi with the Bolsheviks which produced appreciable results in 1922 and the first half of 1923. The moral support Moscow gave Germany in the Ruhr crisis and its very concrete aid in the form of periodic warnings to Poland would have been inconceivable had Rantzau failed in his mission.

**RUSSIA AND REVOLUTION IN GERMANY** The blow delivered by the French on the Ruhr struck the entire German people. The Cuno Cabinet encouraged the Ruhr industrialists to practice passive resistance against the invaders and subsidized them to the extent of several hundred million gold marks for the purpose. As a result of this and contributing circumstances the mark began to fall catastrophically, thus not only dislocating manufacturing, commercial, municipal, and communal undertakings but introducing a fiscal inflation which rapidly impoverished the small rentiers of the petty bourgeois class, reduced the standard of living of State officials, teachers, the intelligentsia, and workers to the minimum of malnutrition, and put a premium on valuta speculation which demoralized business and large sections of the population.

This complex of intolerable conditions stimulated the growth of Communism among the workers and Fascism at the other extreme, while ambitious generals, misguided intellectuals, Nationalist-Monarchist leaders, and the French saw in the situation an opportunity to build up separatist movements and thus break up the Reich.

In the Ruhr, the working-men were caught between two fires: their employers refused to grant wage increases and even, at times, to pay wages at all, yet appealed to their patriotism to resist the French and co-operate with capital. The occupational authorities, on the other hand, suppressed their strikes, prohibited their meetings, proscribed their propaganda, and arrested their leaders. A proletarian struggle therefore developed "against Poincaré on the Rhine and Cuno on the Spree."

Both the Left and Right elements in Germany felt the urge to decisive measures. Late in September, the Conservatives started trouble in Bavaria; on October 1, a Fascist putsch took place at Kuestrin which, had it worked according to plan, would have marched on Berlin with the help of the Reichswehr. In the latter part of October, Hitler, Ludendorff, von Kahr and von Lossow, staged a putsch in Munich, and during the same period, loyal German troops were engaged in fighting down separatist attempts in the Rhineland and other parts of the country.

The same wave of unrest and dissatisfaction which inspired the Rights to action, stirred the workers to seek a radical solution of their problems. In August, the German Communists called a general strike, and in the same month a number of cities witnessed serious food riots. During September, bloody battles took place between the police and hungry strikers and unemployed poor. The situation had become highly explosive.

On October 11, Left Social Democrats and Communists formed a Cabinet in Saxony with Zeigner as Premier. Two days later, the Reichstag granted the Federal Government extraordinary powers to cope with the unrest that had now become general. This move, ironically or logically, was followed by sanguine clashes with the authorities. The 15th and 16th saw food disturbances in Western Germany, the Rhineland, and Berlin, where haggard housewives, weary working-men and boys and girls threw themselves on the police; a few days later there was fighting in Munich, and in the Palatinate and Rhineland with pro-French separatists.

The climax of this incipient civil war was enacted in Hamburg. Here, on October 23, the working-men, led by German Communists who, in turn, had been encouraged and advised by Comintern agents sent from Moscow, opened a battle which they conceived as the beginning of the German revolution. Barricades were erected. The

Communists fought with clubs, war-time rifles, revolvers, but also with high-powered guns and armored vehicles. The State directed the regular army and large police forces against the revolutionists. On the 24th two cruisers approached the scene of fighting. That same day, Soviets were proclaimed and actually seized control of some of the precincts of Hamburg.

But the working-men were too poorly organized. The bulk of the trade unionists still adhered to the moderate, anti-Communist Social Democrats who, on October 6, had joined the Stresemann Cabinet and lent their influence to the suppression not only of the Hamburg uprising but of the Radical Government in Saxony. Hamburg, moreover, remained an isolated episode; no parallel upheavals occurred in other cities; no general strike accompanied it. The authorities were therefore able to concentrate against the Communists and to liquidate their abortive attempt three days after its commencement.

Moscow watched these events with interest and concern. Both the Soviet Government and the Communist International would have welcomed a revolution in Germany. But while the Comintern participated actively in the preparations for the upheaval, the Soviet State waited in the background for developments.

**THE SOVIET GOVERNMENT AND THE COMINTERN** The roles of the Comintern and Soviet Government in such a situation might be defined as follows: the Communist International is the organizer of revolutions. The business of the Soviet Government is to safeguard the interests of the revolution in Russia and of already established revolutions abroad. It goes almost without saying that the Soviet Government of Russia would be strengthened in its international position by the creation of another soviet regime and that it would support such a regime to the extent of its power in much the same way as France, for instance, sees in Poland a pillar of strength, and therefore has in the past granted loans to Warsaw for military and construction purposes.

A Soviet regime in Germany, or in South Africa, or in Siam would, moreover, adhere to the Soviet Union which, officially called into existence on July 6, 1923, is based on the theory that not only the soviet republics founded on the territory of the former Czarist empire, but soviet states organized at any time in the future and in any corner of the world could, and, presumably, would become members of that Union.

Even the Comintern, however, was not convinced that the time to strike had arrived. Radek was accordingly sent to Germany to study the facts and to decide whether the potential revolutionary situation warranted immediate action.

In the event of a seizure of power, the German Communists would be faced with two dangers: foreign blockade and starvation, and foreign intervention. The Soviet Government could not raise the blockade by the use of its navy, but it could send bread to Germany. It could not prevent France from seizing more German territory but it could guarantee Poland's passivity and hope that national, even bourgeois resentment against French aggression might react favorably on the Communist regime.

With a view to possible bread shipments to Germany, and to securing the neutrality of Poland, the Soviet Government accordingly undertook a well-planned diplomatic démarche in August, 1923, when it instructed Victor Kopp to sound the foreign offices of the Baltic States and Poland.

These countries had entertained what was probably a very genuine fear that the Red Army would be ordered to Germany across their frontiers to assist a Communist Government in Berlin. "Such thoughts, in that absolute form, we actually did not have," wrote the Commissariat of Foreign Affairs. But, "the only thing that could have compelled us to interrupt peaceful labor and take up arms was Polish interference in the revolutionary affairs of Germany."[3] If Poland promised to remain passive, Red Germany would be spared an additional enemy and Red Russia the necessity of going to war. Kopp therefore suggested that Soviet Russia and border states sign a treaty in which all parties would pledge themselves to neutrality towards Germany no matter what crisis arose. The proposed agreement would likewise grant free transit to Russian grain destined for Germany.

In Reval, Riga, and Kovno, says the Foreign Commissariat's report for 1923, "the success of Comrade Kopp's mission, it seemed, exceeded all expectations." Even in

[3] *Annual Report of the Commissariat of Foreign Affairs for 1923.* (Moscow, 1923), pp. 41ff.

Warsaw "complete sympathy was expressed" for the idea. But difficulties were encountered as soon as the diplomats attempted to formulate the arrangement in a written protocol. Poland, says the official report, refused to sign, because of French pressure. The Baltic countries therefore hesitated, and Lithuania, which agreed in principle, would not sign alone. The talks, nevertheless, continued. In December, Riga suggested a conference to discuss the subject. Latvia and the other succession nations found the Soviet formula acceptable; objecting, however, to the procedure. Poland, on the contrary, proposed different terms and less binding pledges. But before the conversations on these issues had been concluded, the German bourgeois Government regained control of the internal situation, the Ruhr crisis became less threatening, indications multiplied in England and the United States that many influences desired a more peaceful solution of the reparations problem, and the prospects of the German revolution consequently grew dim.

The year 1924 introduced a relatively pacific atmosphere into Europe, and that fact plus the improvement of Russia's economic position opened a new era of more relations between Soviet Russia and the rest of the world.

# 16

# THE PASSING OF LENIN

THE YEAR 1924 began sadly for Soviet Russia. At 6.50 p.m. on January 21 Lenin died in Gorki, near Moscow. The nation, the Government, and the Communist Party lost its "leader, teacher, friend."

Lenin combined a mastery of general principles, not unusual—in less developed form—among Russians, with an unusually keen ability to grasp details. But perhaps the outstanding quality of his mind was its agility. He could smell the wind from afar and, like a seasoned captain, realistically trim his sail to it. Held within relatively narrow limits by the principles and morals in whose name he and his party made the revolution, Lenin nevertheless found sufficient room for maneuvering and for avoiding those rocks on which less gifted statesmen would have broken their ships—and their heads.

Most of the basic principles of Soviet foreign policy between 1917 and 1923 originated with Lenin, but, in the final analysis, with the Bolsheviks' conception of capitalism and imperialism. Lenin's tactics consisted in exploiting the contradictions between capitalist governments and within capitalist countries. When the German offensive threatened in 1918, he advised appealing for assistance to the "Franco-British imperialist brigands"; when Allied intervention commenced he weighed the possibility of German aid against the French and British. He tried to use the antagonism between Japan and the United States, and between England and France. His policy was to win the support of business elements within capitalist countries by offering them concessions and trade, and of proletarian elements abroad by emphasizing the necessity of defending the revolution.

This strategy of defense was perhaps the most marked characteristic of Lenin's foreign policy. It aimed to divide the forces of the enemy and weaken the united front against Bolshevism. It aimed, in like manner, to win time even at the expense of serious loss of territory or apparent loss of honor.

Lenin and Chicherin co-operated closely in the direction of foreign affairs.

> In the first years of our republic, [Chicherin wrote a few days after Lenin died][1] I spoke with Lenin over the telephone several times a day; some of these conversations were very long. Besides, we had private personal interviews and frequently I discussed with him all the details of current diplomatic affairs that were at all important. . . . In his conversations, Lenin always gave the most brilliant analysis of diplomatic conditions, and his advice—frequently he immediately drafted the text of a reply to the foreign Power—could serve as models of diplomatic art and agility.

Lenin could agree to compromises if they appeared necessary, but he was adamant when the situation required and permitted. Sometimes he would decide that "these demands are stupid" as he did after Count Mirbach's death when the Germans wished to send armed troops to Moscow. On such occasions, writes Chicherin, he waited for the result with "complete calm."

When the Allies had definitely decided on war against Bolshevism, Lenin, while directing both the military and diplomatic defensive, sought to refrain from any measure that might excessively antagonize the enemy. And throughout the era of intervention, according to Chicherin, Lenin insisted "on making peace proposals to our enemies. He never feared creating an impression of weakness by so doing. On the contrary, he regarded it as one of the finest means of applying pressure on the militant interventionism of Entente countries."

The invitation to attend the proposed conference in Prinkipo first gave Lenin the occasion to outline his policy of "appeal to the Entente in the name of economic advantages." We have Chicherin's authority for saying that

[1] *Izvestia,* January 30, 1924.

"this idea became one of the most outstanding in Lenin's foreign policy." In this connection, the Premier declared his readiness to recognize and pay the debts which an early decree had cancelled—a position he embodied in the document handed Mr. Bullitt for Woodrow Wilson. "Each word of the proposal to Bullitt was meticulously weighed by Lenin." But he set a time limit for its acceptance. "If they do not accept now," he said, "they will not receive such favorable terms next time." This, too, became a guiding principle for the Commissariat of Foreign Affairs: moderate offers made at the Hague Conference, for instance, were recalled a few months later, and concessions suggested in the early part of the revolution were subsequently withdrawn.

Lenin attached little importance to territorial losses or gains. When Finland insisted on Pechenga he forced the Soviet agreement through Government councils against the opposition of a number of prominent comrades. It was Lenin's idea to give Poland more than the Curzon Line granted her. He likewise insisted on demarcating a frontier favorable to Turkey.

One of the pillars of Lenin's foreign policy was friendship for the nations of Asia. The aim of the Soviet Government, he wrote, must be to "group around itself all the awakening peoples of the East and fight together with them against international imperialism." He advocated co-operation with Kemal Pasha and regularly interfered when more militant Bolsheviks tended to overlook the interests of a united, nationalistic Persia. He wrote personally to the King of Afghanistan, received numerous Moslem and Mongolian delegations, and frequently underlined the decisive importance of Chinese nationalist developments.

In 1921, Lenin's fatal sickness began to make itself felt, and more and more he delegated his tasks to others. In the realm of foreign affairs, his personal participation, Chicherin writes, "gave way to collective deliberations" in which the members of the pivotal Political Bureau (Politburo) of the party—Bukharin, Dzerzhinsky, Kamenev, Rykov, Stalin, Tomsky, Trotzky, and Zinoviev—consulted with spokesmen of the Commissariat of Foreign Affairs. Lenin, nevertheless, devoted his special attention to the Anglo-Russian Trade Agreement, to the treaty negotiations with Turkey, and to the negotiations with Hoover's A.R.A. and with the Nansen relief organization.

Illness now commenced to make ever-increasing inroads on Lenin's energy, and during the winter of 1921–2 he spent much time on the outskirts of Moscow, where his participation in affairs of State was necessarily intermittent. The Genoa Conference, however, called forth a series of memoranda which he sent into town and which formed the basis of the Russian delegation's offers and claims. Chicherin discussed with him the text of his speech at the opening session of the conference, and "when, in that connection, certain accusatory phrases were suggested in the spirit of our former declarations, Lenin wrote much to this effect: 'We don't need big words.' "

On one of the slips of paper Lenin directed from Gorki to Moscow for Chicherin's guidance, he wrote, "We go to Genoa not as Communists but as merchants." "They need trade," he added, "and we need trade." But if the conference brought no solution of outstanding problems, then the Soviets would take advantage of the differences in capitalist ranks and reach separate agreements with some of the conference nations. After Genoa, Lenin threw the weight of his inspired influence against the ratification of the Italian trade agreement which Chicherin negotiated there, and in October, 1922, he forced the rejection of the Urquhart concession against the will of the entire Politburo, which favored its approval.

Chicherin's last interview with Lenin took place in the autumn of 1922 on the eve of Lausanne. The lines of the Soviet mission's programme at that conference were discussed and fixed with "the lively participation of Lenin." Lenin's last contribution to Soviet foreign affairs took the form of instructions to the Bolshevik representatives at the Moscow Disarmament Conference in December, 1922. Thereafter, throughout the year 1923, his participation in domestic affairs and in foreign politics was reduced by illness almost to zero.

# 17

# SOVIET RUSSIA ENTERS THE COMITY OF NATIONS

THE DEATH of Lenin exploded a false theory about Soviet Russia: that the stability of the regime depended on its leader. It was now no longer possible to doubt at least the relative permanence of the Bolshevik Government.

At the beginning of 1924, Europe was sorely in need of peace. The invasion of the Ruhr had been barren of any favorable result, and the United States as well as important financial circles in England clamored for policies that would facilitate the unravelling of the reparations tangle. The Experts Commission which would hatch the Dawes idea into the Dawes Plan required for its labors an atmosphere of political relaxation in Europe.

Under the circumstances it became unwise and positively detrimental to hold Russia outside the pale and thus postpone the political pacification of Europe. These considerations appealed to two sets of statesmen in Europe: to realists, and to pacifists.

It is scarcely an accident, therefore, that Mussolini, the arch realist, and MacDonald, the pacifist, should have recognized the Soviet Union almost simultaneously, and that Herriot, another pacifist, followed their example later in the same year.

**SOVIET ECONOMIC CONDITIONS** Russia had reappeared on the world market as an exporter of grain and oil. Her foreign trade increased from 281,000,000 rubles (in pre-war prices) in 1923, to 548,000,000 rubles in 1924, and the foreign trade balance which was minus 15,000,000 rubles in 1923 grew to plus 132,000,000 rubles in 1924.[1] Favorable developments in industry and agriculture had preceded these significant developments, and the ruble, whose paper value in 1923 was expressed in astronomical figures, underwent stabilization early in 1924; the chervonetz, with a parity equal to the British pound, became the recognized monetary unit of the country. "Our Red Army, the chervonetz, and grain exports"—these, Chicherin declared on January 7, 1924, were the chief factors in strengthening the political situation of the Soviet Union.

Economic gains at home and political neutrality abroad even introduced an atmosphere of over-confidence in the Soviet capital. "No negotiations, no preliminary concessions on any questions," Litvinov insisted in an interview printed in *Izvestia* of February 14. "Recognition must be unconditional." This became the guiding principle of Soviet foreign policy. First the declaration of de jure recognition; then the two countries might discuss debts, trade, concessions. During this period, in fact, the Bolsheviks developed a new theory; that the foreign Powers must pay them for recognition, and on innumerable occasions, the Press and orators repeated Lenin's phrase to the effect that "they who arrive later will have to pay more." Moscow consented, however, to grant a "prize" to the country that first gave its de jure recognition, and strange as it may seem, a little race started between Italy and England for the reward.

During the Genoa Conference, a permanent trade agreement was hurriedly negotiated between the Soviet representatives and the Italian Government which, in the eyes of the Russians, offered practical benefits to Italy without giving Soviet Russia compensatory advantages. The agreement, moreover, was largely economic in character, withheld de jure recognition, and did not guarantee the safety of trade contracts. On these grounds, Lenin insisted on the rejection of the treaty, and the Council of People's Commissars duly vetoed the document on June 8, 1922.

The advent of Mussolini to power (October 30, 1922)

[1] Article by L. Krassin, Soviet Commissar of Foreign Trade, in the London *Daily Herald* of May 23, 1925.

seemed to hold no bright prospects in store for Soviet-Italian relations. Two days after the Duce's coup, in fact, a band of Fascists entered the Soviet trade headquarters in Rome, seized an Italian employee, and, dragging him to the staircase, severely wounded him with several revolver shots. This incident, however, was quickly settled by assurances on the part of the Ministry of Foreign Affairs.

Mussolini wished to free himself of petty prejudices. The problem of de jure recognition of the Soviet Union, he said, was "a fig leaf with which people tried to cover a concrete truth." And on November 30, 1923, he appeared in Parliament to make his famous declaration: "I recognize the Soviets."

But Mussolini asked a reward. "I demand a good trade treaty," he said. "I demand concessions for raw materials which Italy needs." The establishment of "cordial relations" with Russia would open the great Slav ways of communications and bring benefits to "our fatherland as well as to all other countries."

The Russians were pleased. They did not consider Mussolini's demands exorbitant. They knew that Mussolini would not show much interest in Czarist debts. They therefore agreed to offer Mussolini a "premium" if he recognized them first.

This unusual incentive stimulated the trade treaty negotiations that had commenced in September, 1923. Mussolini promised that they would now be completed within a fortnight. But Rome asked more than Moscow was prepared to grant, and the negotiations lasted longer than had been expected.

Meanwhile, national elections took place in Great Britain on December 6, 1923, and on January 23, 1924, the MacDonald Labor Cabinet came into office. MacDonald was pledged to de jure recognition of the Soviets. Now the race began. Litvinov sat in Moscow sending telegrams to Rakovsky, who was in touch with MacDonald, on the progress of negotiations in Rome, and to Jordansky, who was in touch with Mussolini, on the progress of events in London.

Mussolini suspected that ancient hatreds and the debt problem would delay British recognition. He accordingly pressed his maximum demands. But on February 2, MacDonald notified the Soviet Union Government of its de jure recognition. Mussolini was frantic. He argued that he had actually granted recognition in his address to Parliament of November 30, and the Soviets could scarcely dispute the fact, although formally no speech in a Chamber of Deputies is tantamount to a diplomatic step of international validity. The Russians, in the circumstances, did not deprive Mussolini of his "prize" but it was not as rich as it might have been. It consisted of a concession granting conditional transit through the Caucasus to Persia, special customs reductions, coastal shipping privileges, and other benefits. Who recognized Soviet Russia first, Italy or England, still remains an unsettled question which the pedants of the future may decide. Italy's formal recognition was granted on February 7.

Italy and the Soviet Union immediately exchanged ambassadors, and the trade and customs agreements went immediately into effect.

Under the Soviet monopoly of foreign trade, the Soviet Government itself, and not private Russian merchants, buy abroad everything the country needs. These purchases are made by an official trade organization operating in the capitals and larger cities of states with which the Soviet Union has established treaty relations. In view of the official character of these trading organizations, the Soviet Government consistently insisted on their receiving extra-territorial rights in common with diplomatic representatives. Germany, Czecho-Slovakia, etc., had written the trade delegations' extra-territoriality into registered agreements, while other nations granted de facto extra-territoriality. But Italy's negotiators resisted Soviet demands on the ground that a precedent might be set which France, England, etc., might wish to follow. Mussolini swept such objections aside. "You never were a Socialist," he said to the chairman of the Italian delegation. "If France becomes Soviet and institutes a monopoly of foreign trade it too may sue for trade extra-territoriality." The Soviet trade headquarters obtained the right, by the terms of the agreement, to use a code.

Geographical propinquity, sea connections, and the fact that under normal conditions Russia can sell Italy food and raw materials at cheap prices (oil for the Roman fleet, for instance) tended to foster good relations between the two countries.

In 1927, however, Mussolini's efforts in the Balkans,

which had commenced on a large scale in 1926, became the driving force of Italian foreign policy. Rome's hold on Albania became tantamount to colonial dominion, and its enmity toward Yugoslavia grew. Italy strove to dislodge France from her position in the Balkan Peninsula and would have been pleased to enlist the Soviets in support of her plans, but when efforts in this direction failed, an important treaty was concluded in the latter half of 1926 with Rumania as a result of several personal conferences between Mussolini and General Averescu. Rome gave Rumania a helping loan. Mussolini's recognition of Rumanian rule in Bessarabia followed on March 7, 1927. Rome was alive to the definite benefits that might be gained by aligning Rumania on its side through such a move which it knew would provoke resentment, some sharp editorials and a diplomatic protest from Moscow but nothing in the nature of practical Soviet reprisals. A dark cloud now descended over Italian-Russian relations.

British recognition of the Soviets pleased the Bolsheviks extremely; the Congress of Soviets which, by chance, was in session when Mr. MacDonald's telegram reached Moscow, applauded it. It disarmed international antagonism—at least temporarily.

The Labor Cabinet headed by Ramsay MacDonald made a sincere effort to bridge the financial and political chasm between the two States. Yet the good results were not at all proportional to the good will on both sides.

Recognition was unconditional. Yet it stipulated mutual non-interference in internal affairs, and made mention of the problems of debts and credits to settle which Moscow was invited to send delegates to a conference in London. Ambassadors were not appointed. The countries would, for the time being, be represented by chargés d'affaires. Great Britain appointed Mr. R. M. Hodgson, who had represented his Government with Kolchak; the Bolsheviks, Christian G. Rakovsky.

The failure to exchange ambassadors imparted to recognition a somewhat grudging and incomplete character. Rakovsky believed that the opposition originated with the King, who had not forgotten his blood relations with the murdered Czar. Later in the month of February, the Court's resistance was largely overcome. But MacDonald now resented the personal attacks levelled against him by

Communist leaders in Russia; his disinclination to appoint O'Grady, to whom he, according to reports, had rashly promised the post, likewise played a contributing role.

**BOLSHEVIK ATTITUDE TOWARD MACDONALD** The Bolsheviks harbor a sincere dislike for such "middle-of-the-road" Laborites and mild, sometimes non-Marxian Socialists of the MacDonald-Snowden-Clynes type. But MacDonald was the chief of a government with which they were trying to reach an understanding. They might have refrained at least temporarily from giving expression to their feelings. Such restraint, however, is unusual in the Communist world. The Bolsheviks often find it difficult to hold their tongues.

Though English de jure recognition was a "brave step," and though Rykov, who had succeeded Lenin as Premier, realized that "the transfer of power to the Labor Party will considerably facilitate an agreement,"[2] the Bolsheviks conducted a vituperative campaign against MacDonald. In a speech in Tiflis, Trotzky referred to the British Prime Minister as a "Christian Menshevik"—a term of deepest opprobium in Soviet Russia—and to MacDonald's policy as "Menshevism in action." The masses of the East, he added, saw no difference between Imperialists and the present British Government. Frequently, the Moscow Press caricatured the worthy Ramsay with a halo about his head, and one cartoon in *Pravda* so offended some English sentiments that the paper was barred from Britain. Trotzky especially outdid himself. "It is impossible to expect of MacDonald," he declared at Baku, "the leader of the Second International and an outstanding Menshevik, that on coming to power he would seize a broom and sweep the cockroaches from his monarchy." Zinoviev spoke in the same view. The Communists expected radical reforms from a British Labor Government. Would it not publish the secret pre-war and war treaties, abolish the House of Lords, tamper with the institution of monarchy, etc., etc.?

**THE IMPRESSION** Generally speaking, however, recognition had a good press in Russia, and also in England. *Izvestia* noted that it "broke the diplomatic blockade of the Soviet Union" and would perhaps cause America to

[2] *Izvestia,* May 10, 1924.

open diplomatic relations with Moscow. It relieved the Bolsheviks of considerable anxiety—they had never ceased fearing a resumption of foreign attacks. Now that seemed impossible.

In England, the extreme Conservative *Morning Post* regarded recognition a "leap in the dark" and Curzon believed it "a grave mistake," but in this attitude they stood almost alone. The Conservatives of the Garvin school warmly welcomed the measure. The Liberals unanimously supported it. The most interesting reaction came from the pen of Lloyd George, who divulged an unusually important secret in an article in the *Daily Chronicle* of February 16.

"The Labor Government," he wrote, "are quite justified in entering into separate negotiations with Russia. The separate action of France and Belgium in the Ruhr has dissolved the Entente, and Britain and Italy are no longer restrained by the bonds of alliance."

The four Western Powers had, when Lloyd George was yet in office, agreed not to undertake separate moves vis-à-vis Russia or Germany. It is perhaps not accidental, therefore, that Italian and British recognition came within five days of one another.

**BRITAIN'S BILL AND BOLSHEVIK CLAIMS** Recognition was a mere formal preliminary to the settlement of England's claims on Russia and Russia's on England. According to one authority of repute,[3] Russia's public debt to Great Britain equalled:

| | |
|---|---|
| Government and Railway bonds | $333,000,000 |
| Commercial investments | 261,000,000 |
| War debt | 2,766,000,000 |
| Total | $3,360,000,000 |

The Bolsheviks asked for reparation for damages done by British and British-supported forces in Russia during the Soviet Civil War. At Genoa, the Soviet delegation had presented counter-claims amounting approximately to 4,067,226,040 pounds sterling. Britain's share bulked very large. Rakovsky, in a memorandum to the Labor Government, which Ponsonby, MacDonald's Under-Secretary of State, pronounced "Vague and unsatisfactory," set

[3] Harvey E. Fisk: *The Inter-Ally Debts,* Bankers Trust Co. Publication.

it at approximately 2,000,000,000 pounds sterling. But no matter what the sum, the Bolsheviks insisted that their counter-claims for an indemnity be duly honored. "One million three hundred and fifty thousand human lives alone," Rakovsky affirmed at the May 15 session of the Anglo-Soviet conference, "were lost in the fight against intervention." Three thousand five hundred bridges were destroyed. Whole provinces were laid waste. "I repeat," Rakovsky continued, "that the question of British claims is insolubly connected with the Russian counter-claims."

History supplied a precedent. The Russians invariably cited the case of the privateer *Alabama,* which, though fitted out in England, did not belong to the British Government. Yet the Geneva Court of Arbitration, on September 14, 1872, ordered the British Government to pay the United States Government $15,500,000 for damages caused by the *Alabama* in helping the Confederacy against the North. Britain's action in Russia between 1918 and 1920 was more direct and more destructive.

Rakovsky stated, however, that

> the Soviet delegation does not consider the Soviet counter-claims as ranking against the whole mass of British claims but principally as ranking against the British war debt. The Soviet delegation fully understands that private British claimants must receive some satisfaction.

The Genoa Conference had given prominence to the principle that Entente war debts to Russia and Soviet counter-claims for interventionist and blockade damages cancel each other. But this involved the entire problem of Inter-Allied debts. If England wiped out Russia's war obligations when Russia was ruled by hostile Bolsheviks, France and Italy would demand a treatment at least as favorable. Ponsonby therefore urged on May 15, that the war debts and counter-claims "shall be reserved for discussion at a later date." Subsequently, Ponsonby announced in Parliament that both had been placed in "cold storage" and it was generally agreed that the British Government accepted the Soviet contention for cancellation. Since the French later adopted the same procedure, and in view of the fact that neither the Japanese nor the Italians have ever asked Mosow to pay the Czar's and Kerensky's war debts, there is reason to believe that the matter will not be raised in future negotiations between the Soviet Union and the Powers.

The Russians advanced a supplementary argument in favor of the annulment of war debts. Whereas France made loans to the Czar during the World War without any special guarantee, Lloyd George and Reginald McKenna, the British war-time Chancellors of the Exchequer, demanded the deposit of Russian gold as guarantee, and during the war, according to Harvey E. Fisk, no less than $331,000,000 of the Czarist yellow metal reserve was shipped to the British Empire by devious routes to avoid German submarines. To this must be added the British share of the 120,000,000 gold rubles paid by the Bolsheviks to the Germans under the supplementary Brest Litovsk treaties, transferred by the Germans to several Allied countries, and held by them in trust pending a settlement with a Russian government. Considering that the war obligations of continental nations to England and America were written down radically, the sum remaining to be funded by Soviet Russia would scarcely exceed by any appreciable amount the value of Russian gold held by British banks as war-time guarantees. If the Bolshevik counter-claims are then thrown into the scales, the war debt, as even Conservatives tacitly agreed, must be wiped from the slate.

There remained, however, the claims of private British bondholders and the demands of ex-property owners in Russia. These, and small personal losses by British subjects—bank deposits, salaries, jewelry, furniture, etc., totalling, according to the British, 26,000,000 pounds, formed the subject of the memorable Anglo-Soviet Conference which opened in London on April 14, 1924.

**THE BANKERS' MEMORANDUM** The day the conference opened, a memorandum was submitted to the British Government and Press above the signatures, among others, of Charles Addis and E. C. Grenfell of the Bank of England, Walter Leaf of the Westminster Bank, Reginald McKenna of the Midland Bank, J. Beaumont Pease of Lloyds Bank, and Lord Swaythling of S. Montague and Company.

The Bankers' Memorandum demanded (1) that the Bolsheviks recognize Russia's public and private debts, (2) that an equitable restitution of private property to foreigners be made; (3) that a proper civil code be brought into effective operation, independent courts of law created, and the sanctity of private contract again firmly established; (4) that the Soviet Government guarantee that in the future private property shall in all circumstances be free from confiscation by the State; (5) that British bankers, industrialists, and traders should be able to deal freely with similar private institutions in Russia; and (6) that the Bolsheviks abandon propaganda. The authors of the memorandum were renowned financiers and wise men. They knew that no Bolshevik government could accede to their program and live another day.

**THE ANGLO-SOVIET CONFERENCE**[4] The opening session of the conference, on April 14, consisted of an address of welcome by MacDonald and a reply by Rakovsky. A further meeting on the next day dealt with those Anglo-Russian treaties which had become obsolete or impossible and therefore required cancellation or modification. Sessions on April 16 and 24 were devoted to questions of procedure, old treaties, the organization of committees, and other technical and secondary matters. Both delegations were feeling their way and feeling themselves out. The meeting of May 15, however, came to grips with the real problem of war debts and counterclaims, and, finally, on May 20, private expropriated property came under discusion. Rakovsky had declared, on May 15, that "nationalization as a result of the revolution is legal and . . . we must refuse to pay for its consequences." Since the British would not accept this principle and since the Bolsheviks would not budge from it, the chief Soviet delegate therefore suggested that they try to reach a practical settlement. He now asked for information. What were the claims of former private property owners? Did they ask for concessions? The Bolsheviks realized that a refusal to consider the claims would make agreement impossible. For this reason, and not because they thought it right, they consented to listen to applications for compensation.

As to pre-war bonds, Rakovsky submitted this formula:

On condition of the conclusion, with the assistance of the

[4] The account given here follows the unpublished protocols.

British Government, of a long-term loan for productive purposes the Government of the Soviet Union agrees, in accordance with the amount of the loan and its conditions, to determine by agreement with the British Government a lump sum in order to cover the pre-war debts of Russia in relation to British subjects.

Speaking of pre-war Russia, Pasvolsky and Moulton say:[5] "She was an old country with a large existing foreign debt resulting from past wars and bad financial administration." The people did not want the Czar's wars and were not responsible for his bad administration—they merely suffered from it. Indeed, these authors explain that Russian railways were developed not to improve conditions ("The Russian bureaucrats were quite content with the feudal economic system of the country; they were not interested in internal development . . .") but in order to serve as securities for foreign borrowing.

Had the Soviets held fast to a dogmatic, theoretical position, they would have refused to pay pre-war debts or war debts. Such a policy in respect to peace-time obligations would have made normal economic relations with foreign lands too difficult and strained. Expediency demanded some settlement, and Moscow therefore proposed the following: Great Britain would give the Soviet Union a loan of, say, 50,000,000 pounds on which an annual interest of, say, 8 per cent would be paid. In Russia the interest on money was, say, 13 per cent. Moscow would devote the difference—or 5 per cent of 50,000,000 pounds—to satisfying the claims of the holders of pre-war bonds. One million pounds or more, depending on the volume of borrowing, would thus be available each year for that purpose.

A loan was the sine qua non of debt payment. "The central question is the loan," Rakovsky said in an interview with *Izvestia* on July 30.

**THE GOVERNMENT GUARANTEE OF A BOLSHEVIK LOAN** At the session of May 20, Ponsonby stated emphatically that "the British Government can in no way guarantee such a loan." MacDonald maintained that the Bolsheviks should negotiate directly with the City. He felt that the good will of the Government, not its guarantee,

[5] Leo Pasvolsky and Harold G. Moulton: *Russian Debts and Russian Reconstruction,* (New York, 1924), p. 38.

was required. But when Rakovsky went to the City, the quest was vain.

After several such meetings, Rakovsky and the Labor Government were convinced that the City would refuse a loan which lacked a State guarantee. The struggle now commenced to win MacDonald and his ministers for the guarantee. When Rakovsky left London for a hurried airplane trip to Moscow on July 26, 1924, the question still hung in the balance. En route he received a message from Ponsonby stating that the guarantee would be granted.

The decision to grant the guarantee followed a Cabinet session in the last week of July. Snowden persisted in his uncompromising opposition. He found support in J. H. Thomas, Lord Olivier, the Secretary of State for India, and—much to the surprise of many—in Colonel Josiah G. Wedgwood, who fought the project bitterly. When Ponsonby suggested a loan of 30,000,000 pounds, Snowden objected. But the Prime Minister and Henderson stood firmly by Ponsonby. Snowden, MacDonald submitted, looked at the problem from the narrow point of view of the Exchequer. But the pacification of Europe and the world were involved. The debate was long and bitter. Finally, however, the MacDonald-Ponsonby faction won the day.

## NEGOTIATIONS WITH THE BONDHOLDERS

Meanwhile, the Soviets negotiated directly with the British bondholders. Downing Street took the view that it would interfere in the issue between Soviet Russia and her creditors only if they could not agree without such mediation. And the bondholders themselves insisted on direct negotiations with the Bolsheviks.

The first meeting between Rakovsky and Scheinmann, and the representatives of the bondholders was held in the British Foreign Office on June 12.[6] Ponsonby and Gregory made non-committal introductory statements and departed. Sir George Marjoribanks, and Messrs. Crisp, Trotter, Cooper, and Cramp attended for the creditors. They refused to present a statement of their claims, but asked Rakovsky to make his offer. It was generally agreed that the total debt would suffer reduction. But how large was

[6] The summary of the proceedings of this and subsequent meetings was made by the writer from the unpublished protocols.

the total? The second meeting, held at 17 Moorgate Street on June 23, revolved around the same issue. Rakovsky showed a report handed him officially by the Board of Trade on May 1, according to which a Government registration of claims ending March 31, 1924, revealed a total of 39,023,165 pounds. This figure, Rakovsky added, approximated very closely that of the Czarist Ministry of Finance. Chairman Barnett, however, submitted that some holders might not yet have registered their bonds, and that the total stood between 50 and 60,000,000 pounds. He suggested that 50,000,000 pounds be accepted as the basis of discussion. But Rakovsky insisted on the Board of Trade sum, and then declared that the Soviets would, if they obtained a Government-guaranteed loan in England, pay 6,000,000 pounds or, roughly, 16 per cent of the whole. This, Rakovsky remarked, was more than three times the present market value of all the bonds held in Great Britain.

The third and final session of the conference with the bondholders met on June 27. The bondholders refused to accept Rakovsky's offer and refused, likewise, to make one of their own. Rakovsky accordingly declared that unless he heard from the bondholders within a few days, the bondholders' claims would be discussed in the official Anglo-Soviet conference without the bondholders. The private talks thus ended without result. But before the final close, Mr. Burtch-Crisp, a prominent bondholder, passed a pencilled note to Rakovsky which Rakovsky later showed the writer. It contained the Britisher's proposal for a settlement: "Amount outstanding," it read, "to be reduced to 50 per cent. Soviet will pay 2½ per cent on ½ of balance and the bondholders will give an option to Soviet to pay off principal at 50 per cent discount, i.e. 25 per cent of original sum." If the option were not exercised during five years, Mr. Crisp added, payments would be spread over a period of fifty years.

On this basis, a settlement might easily have been reached. Mr. Crisp, apparently, believed that he could mobilize 50 per cent of the bondholders for his solution—a belief which was reflected in the final treaty.

**THE BREAK** With the bondholders' claim reserved for the consideration of the inter-government conference, and with the guarantee accepted by the British Cabinet, the official discussions had reached their final stage. The decisive session took place on August 4. It lasted twenty hours and left the participants in a state of physical collapse. It ended with a sensational rupture. When the proceedings opened, Ponsonby stated: "At the earlier meetings, I repeated more than once that the Government could not undertake to guarantee a loan. That decision has been reversed . . ."

MacDonald's objection to the guarantee had threatened the success of the negotiations. His acceptance of it should have paved the way to a final settlement. The Russians, indeed, felt that an agreement was within reach. Both sides made compromises.

The draft of an important commercial treaty presented no difficulties. A fisheries convention was drawn up which gratified British fishing interests—the Bolsheviks dropped their claim to a twelve-mile territorial waters limit in the White Sea, Soviet fishers were given a measure of protection against the better equipped English trawlers, and an article was even introduced which provided for the arbitration of disputes by the University of Leyden. "This is the first arbitration treaty which the Soviet Government are entering into," Rakovsky declared. But the details of the arbitration procedure required careful probing—and the conference had been set the task of completing the treaties before it rose, so that MacDonald might present them to Parliament before the recess. Owing to the haste, the arbitration clause was therefore eliminated from the fisheries agreement.[7]

Only two problems now remained outstanding: bonds and nationalized private property. Rakovsky argued that since direct negotiations with the bondholders had been fruitless, the British Government must interfere. He did not expect the Government to negotiate with the bondholders; that was Moscow's affair. But the British Government would represent the nation, and when an agreement had been reached with at least half of the claimants, the Government would regard the settlement as legal and satisfactory. This Ponsonby accepted and it was written into Article 6 of the draft General Treaty.[8]

[7] For text, see British White Paper, Russia No. 4 (1924), *General Treaty between Great Britain and Northern Ireland and the Union of Soviet Socialist Republics*. (London, 1924). Cmd. 2260. pp. 4 ff.

[8] *Ibid.*, pp. 10ff.

Article 7 "reserved for discussion at a later date" all claims in respect of British war loans to Russia, Russian gold deposited in England by the Czarist Government in the course of the war or by Germany under the Brest Litovsk treaties, Czarist and Kerensky non-war debts, and Bolshevik counter-claims.

Articles 8 and 9 provided for the settlement of petty claims of British nationals by the payment of a lump sum by Moscow to the British Government for distribution among the claimants.

Now the session, having found an acceptable formula for the solution of the bondholders issue, attacked the problem of private property. The Genoa and Hague conferences had foundered on this rock. Much of the foreign opposition to the Soviet Government found inspiration and support in industrialists whose properties were sequestrated. Urquhart had welcomed the Curzon ultimatum and perhaps helped to create the atmosphere that made it possible. He had organized the Association of British Creditors of Russia which became a chief source of anti-Soviet agitation in England. Sir Henri Deterding, another dispossessed owner, sponsored the oil blockade against Russia in 1922 and 1923, and although he himself purchased petroleum from the official Soviet Naphtha Syndicate, he fought the sale of "stolen" Soviet oil with vehemence and persistence. Moreover, British ex-owners were not without their influence on the British Government—even on the Labor Government. The MacDonald Cabinet had in fact, as Ponsonby declared in the twenty-hour session on August 4, acceded to the Soviet demand for a loan guarantee only on condition that the article of the draft treaty referring to nationalized private property remain essentially unchanged.

Practically all the former owners had presented their claims to Rakovsky in London. One Englishwoman wished to call on the Soviet envoy and collect rent for the three years he had lived in her house in Kharkov while Prime Minister of the Ukraine. More serious demands came from the Lena Goldfields Company, Urquhart's Russo-Asiatic Corporation, etc. Deterding, however, never presented any demands for compensation or a concession. He wished merely to be reinstated in the ownership of his former plants.

The Soviet Government had decided that it would admit

either Urquhart or Lena Goldfields to Siberia, but not both. Rakovsky had received a favorable offer from the latter. "The directors of the Lena Goldfields, rightly or wrongly," Herbert Guedalla, chairman of the company, wrote in the *Morning Post* of May 12, 1925, "some time ago came to the conclusion that the recovery of the large losses of their shareholders in Russia by methods of Government diplomacy must be a very slow procedure. . . . We . . . approached the Soviet Government . . . they did not approach us. . . ." This letter reflected a business-like attitude and friendly relationship which could not but impress the Russians.

Progress was registered in discussions with other companies too, for the Soviet Government intended to grant a considerable number of concessions to former owners—not because it considered nationalization wrong, illegal or outlived, but, as Rakovsky stated at 3 P.M. on August 5, "because we believe the concessionaires will be valuable workers in Russia."

The Bolsheviks, however, could not satisfy all the former owners. A controversy developed on the topic of losses *v.* claims. The substitution of the word losses for claims would, Rakovsky warned, make the treaty entirely unacceptable. "We are under no obligation to pay losses," he affirmed. "But we are prepared to pay compensation" in the form of concessions or perhaps even cash. To pay reparations for losses would mean to recognize the illegality of nationalization, whereas to settle claims would merely permit the capitalists to return to Russia and be of service to the country.

Also, an important legal point was involved. In the Anglo-Russian Commercial Treaty of March 16, 1921, the Bolsheviks had accepted private British claims. Subsequently, in April, 1922, the Rapallo Treaty had been negotiated with Germany. Accordingly Scheinmann declared that "if this idea of the settlement for losses were adopted, then such claims could be presented not only by British but by all other nationals." A precedent would be set from which the Bolsheviks might suffer in future negotiations with France, America, etc.

Ponsonby thereupon explained that the British Government did not expect the Bolsheviks to pay all claims but only "valid" ones. The tired delegates now commenced to discuss the question of validity. Who would decide? Since the loan would be forthcoming only when, in the opinion of the British, sufficient progress had been made in the settlement of claims, the decision as to validity lay with Downing Street. Rakovsky suggested instead that only those claims be satisfied the justice of which had been recognized by the Soviet Government or by both governments.

It was now 7.15 in the morning. Perhaps, if the negotiators had had some sleep, an understanding might have been arrived at. Perhaps if Gregory of the Foreign Office had not suggested a break to Ponsonby at 4 A.M., none would have come. Perhaps a few minutes' talk between Ponsonby and MacDonald or between MacDonald and some Labor leaders might have sufficed to heal the breach. As it was, Ponsonby arose at 7.15 to announce that the treaty, unfortunately, could not be signed and the negotiations, therefore, "fall to the ground."

A Labor government and a Workers' and Peasants' government had split on a question involving the private property of expropriated capitalists. The position of Moscow was clear: it felt that nothing ought to be paid, but on purely utilitarian grounds it was ready to make and grant concessions. The British Government felt the pressure of the industrialists and the banks. To yield too much would endanger Labor's position in Parliament. MacDonald desired to have the whip hand. He asked that all the private property claims be satisfied, or at least, that it rest with Britain to determine which were valid.

**PATCHWORK BEHIND THE SCENES** That afternoon England was stirred. The Conservative Press rejoiced. Labor realized that, apart from the intrinsic significance of its failure to agree with the Russians, the collapse of the negotiations would probably involve the fall of the Cabinet.

First, Labor leaders prevailed on MacDonald to postpone the adjournment of Parliament to permit of one more attempt to heal the breach. The same evening, Rakovsky answered a summons to report on the negotiations before a special caucus of about twenty-five Labor M.P.'s. Commander Kenworthy, then still a Liberal, likewise attended.

Purcell, Morel, Wallhead, Lansbury, Maxton, and other Left trade unionists and M.P.'s consulted with Ponsonby and probably MacDonald, and the same evening brought to the chief of the Russian Delegation, who was waiting on the terrace of the House of Commons with a Labor M.P., the glad tidings that the negotiations would be resumed the next day, August 6. The next morning, in fact, Gregory brought a new Foreign Office formula which Rakovsky rejected because he regarded it as worse than the previously suggested solution. Within several hours, the Left leaders submitted to Rakovsky a third Foreign Office formula. This time, after consultation with his colleagues, he accepted.

That very day, August 6, the Anglo-Soviet conference met again. Ponsonby read the new draft of the disputed article on private property and Rakovsky immediately approved. It is characteristic of Rakovsky's interesting mind that when this great problem had been disposed of he raised for the second time the question of the tiny Island of Wrangel in the Arctic and drew from Ponsonby the definite statement that after consultation with the Canadian Government "His Majesty's Government lay no claims to the Island of Wrangel."

On August 10 the Anglo-Soviet General Treaty as well as the Commercial Treaty were signed by MacDonald and Ponsonby and by Rakovsky, Joffe, Radchenko, Scheinmann, and Tomsky.

Article 10 elaborated the procedure for the settlement of private property claims. Article 11 provided for a second treaty which would contain (1) conditions for the settlement of bondholders' claims, (2) the amount and method of payment of compensation for petty British losses, and (3) "an agreed settlement of property claims other than those directly settled by the Government of the Union of Soviet Socialist Republics." This was the formula on nationalized property reached after the break. Moscow would negotiate separately with the expropriated owners. Claims not satisfied by this method of private agreement would have to be settled according to the provisions contained in the second treaty. This was generally understood to mean that tribunals would be set up to adjudicate claims preferred by numerous governesses, teachers, and small property holders who had suffered through the revolution. But the larger, more important claims of Urquhart and firms of the same magnitude would be settled by direct negotiations and thus pave the way to the loan.

Only then would the second treaty be signed. And only after the second treaty was signed would the British Government "recommend Parliament to enable them to guarantee the interest and sinking fund of a loan to be issued by the Government of the Union of Soviet Socialist Republics." No amount was stated, nor were the conditions and terms.

**THE FALL OF MACDONALD** Powerful opposition soon developed to the treaties. Its spirit resembled that of the Bankers' Memorandum of the opening day of the Anglo-Soviet conference.

The treaties would lie on the table for twenty-one days before they could be ratified by Parliament. Since Labor controlled no majority the balance was held by the Liberals. On September 10 a former associate of Lloyd George informed Rakovsky by letter that "a considerable proportion of the Liberals will definitely vote against the ratification of the treaty and, of the balance, a considerable number will not vote at all." Lloyd George had always favored an economic settlement with Russia. He had written it on his banner in 1920, in 1921, at Genoa, and at The Hague. His position, in fact, had not changed in 1924. But the ex-Premier's eye was now on the domestic political scene. He preferred to risk an autumn election before Labor had made too long and too good a record in office. The polemic raged throughout September, and on October 2 the London *Daily Herald,* organ of Labor, carried a full-page headline: "Prepare for a General Election."

It so happened that during this period the Government withdrew the proceedings against John Ross Campbell, editor of the Communist *Workers' Weekly,* who had been charged with inciting the King's armed forces to mutiny. The Tories' and Liberals' motions of censure against the MacDonald Cabinet referred to this action, but it was no secret that the Campbell case merely served as a convenient excuse for burying the Government which had signed the Anglo-Soviet treaties.

No British money must go to build up Soviet Russia, the opposition's slogan read. But, complained the *Daily*

*Herald* on October 6, "if the Labor Government had proposed to spend fifty million pounds in crushing Russia there would not have been any talk of a General Election."

On October 8 the Government suffered defeat in the House of Commons, and MacDonald went to the King to ask for the dissolution of Parliament. National elections were scheduled for October 29.

**THE "ZINOVIEV" LETTER** In the midst of the short election campaign, the Press published the famous "Zinoviev" letter in which, among other things, the Third or Communist International gave instructions to the British Communist Party on its tactics in the election and, also, on the necessity of working within the British army with a view to "paralyse all the military preparations of the bourgeoisie."[8]

The letter when published caused an unprecedented storm of excitement in England, and undoubtedly determined the outcome of the elections. The smashing victory of the Conservatives would have been impossible without it. Neither the Tories nor the Liberals nor Labor denied for one second the effect of the "Zinoviev" letter in determining the constitution of the House of Commons from November, 1924, to June, 1929. It changed the nature of many seats—of at least 100 is the usual estimate.

Beginning with 1924, until as late as 1928, the "Zinoviev" letter was debated in Parliament, and frequent references are made to it in the press, in books, and in public documents. A Government lifted into office by such a "Red" letter was of necessity bound to an anti-Soviet policy. The document helped to determine the course of Anglo-Russian relations for half a decade.

A number of points can be made:

(1) The original of the "Zinoviev" letter has never been published and was never seen by British Government officials. Three or more copies circulated in Great Britain, but only an original would reveal mistakes in orthography, erasures, quality and watermark of paper from which it might be proved a forgery. Perhaps therefore the original was destroyed.

(2) The document contained internal evidence against its authenticity. The heading of the letter reads "Executive

[8] Full text in British Book. Cmd. 2895. (London, 1927), pp. 30 and 32.

Committee, Third Communist International, Presidium." But, as Rakovsky stated in his reply note to MacDonald, dated October 24[9]:

> In circulars of the Communist International (which may be seen in the press, for its activities are not concealed) it is never described as the 'Third Communist International'—for the simple reason that there never has been a First or Second Communist International. The signature [Rakovsky continues] is a similarly clumsy forgery. M. Zinoviev is made to sign himself as the 'President of the Presidium of the Executive Committee of Communist International,' whereas actually he is, and always signs himself officially as, 'President of the Executive Committee.'

The letter is also signed by "McManus" of the British Communist Party, whereas Communist International documents, as seen from one specimen which has been published,[1] bear the signature of "MacManus" as he signed himself in Russia. In England he was McManus and the deduction has been made that the forgers were insufficiently acquainted with Comintern documents to know the difference.

Finally, Mr. Thomas Marlowe, the editor of the *Daily Mail,* which first published the document, wrote a letter to the London *Observer* of March 4, 1928, wherein he explained that he had at the time received two copies of the "Zinoviev" communication; "The only important difference was that in one copy the name of McManus, to whom the letter was written, appeared immediately under the name of Zinoviev, as if McManus were the co-signatory." As the official British Blue Book published the letter, "McManus" is a co-signatory. But if the letter was addressed to McManus, it could not have been signed by him. In one of Mr. Marlowe's copies, McManus was made to be a signee, in another the recipient. The forger erred slightly.

(3) The Conservative Baldwin Government consistently refused to investigate the origin of the "Zinoviev" letter. It rejected an official Soviet offer to submit the question to arbitration. After Mr. Thomas Marlowe's letter appeared in the *Observer* on March 6, 1928, many

[9] Full text in British Blue Book. Cmd. 2895. (London, 1927). pp. 30 and 32.

[1] *The "Zinoviev" Letter, Report of Investigation by British Delegation to Russia for the Trades Union Congress General Council. November–December 1924,* (London, 1925), p. 10.

persons realized the necessity of an investigation, especially since Mr. Gregory of the Foreign Office had become implicated in the Francs Case and was suspected of illegal practices with a view to speculating on the fluctuations of French currency. Mr. Gregory was also said to have been responsible for the publication of the "Zinoviev" letter. "After the events of the week-end," wrote the most-Tory *Morning Post* on March 6, "one finds a growing feeling among Conservatives that the Government would be well advised to grant an investigation." "No reason," wrote *The Times* on March 7, "seems to exist why the demand should not be granted. . . . The refusal might conceivably confirm some lingering suspicion that the present Government . . . has something sinister to hide." "We fear an inquiry is necessary," declared the Conservative *Spectator* on March 10.

But the Government refused to institute an investigation.

In the course of a speech in the Ardwick Picture Theatre in Manchester on October 26, 1924, attended by the police and the press, McManus challenged the authorities to prosecute him. If he had in the "Zinoviev" letter urged the organization of subversive units in the British army, why did not the Government arrest him and bring him to trial? But the Baldwin Cabinet did not order his arrest.

(4) Rakovsky told the writer that an official of the Quai d'Orsay of international repute informed him that the "Zinoviev" letter was a Polish forgery.

(5) One careful investigation of the "Zinoviev" letter was made by a special British Trade Union Congress delegation consisting of Messrs. Ben Tillett, Grenfell, and Young, who possessed a knowledge of Russian and German, and considerable experience in intelligence work. The deputation went to Moscow and obtained permission from Zinoviev to examine the most secret archives of the Comintern, the file of the Comintern's correspondence with the British Communist Party, the daily ledger of outgoing correspondence ("There were many hundred entries in Russian and German, and wherever an entry could either directly or indirectly concern England the communication was asked for and produced from its proper place in the archives. It was impossible that this record, a large volume in many different handwritings bearing every

evidence of having been daily written up, could have been tampered with"), and a volume of the minutes of the Comintern from June to October, 1924. The deputation made copies of some documents. Its conclusions were as follows: The activities of the Comintern in respect to England "conformed to the international agreement as to propaganda." . . . "Before leaving, the deputation satisfied themselves that there was no other channel in the Comintern departments by which a letter signed by M. Zinoviev could have been either discussed, drafted or issued." . . . "This inspection convinced them [the deputation.—L.F.] as far as a negative can be proved, that no 'Red Letter' ever left the Comintern."[2]

After the investigation, Labor asked a similar examination of British Government files, or at least a court of inquiry into the "Zinoviev" letter affair. The request was denied.

MacDonald declared on March 19, 1928, that the letter

> was a deliberately planned and devised concoction of deceit, fitted artfully for the purpose of deceiving the public and to influence the Election. That it played a major part in the verdict, no one will deny. That it was a fraudulent one, few will dare to deny.

The "Zinoviev" letter created a sort of noblesse oblige for the Baldwin-Chamberlain Cabinet to indulge in that unconcealed, unbridled hostility towards the Soviet Union which continued till the rupture of Anglo-Soviet relations in May, 1927, and from then to the General Election in May, 1929.

*Royal Dutch* British recognition of Soviet Russia on February 2, 1924, was not without its effect on the Dutch Government, and on March 17, 1924, a delegation headed by a high official of The Hague Foreign Office arrived in Berlin to conduct negotiations with Krestinsky, the Soviet ambassador to Germany. After preliminary conversations in which the basis of political and commercial relations was discussed, the plenipotentiaries departed to report to their superiors, and on April 28 they returned to Berlin.

Holland had, before the revolution, been an important transit country for Russian exports. Rotterdam had

[2] *The "Zinoviev" Letter, Report of Investigation . . .*

handled large quantities of Russian goods and immigrants. Obviously, no outstanding territorial or political questions obstructed the resumption of normal relations between Holland and Soviet Russia. But the Russians unwisely refused to grant Holland most-favored-nation treatment. On this point the negotiations collapsed.

Both countries might have gained by normal relations. Certainly, neither country benefited from the rupture of the Berlin negotiations early in May, 1924.

*Belgium*[3] Acting probably under the effect of British recognition, Belgium took the initiative in May, 1924, and opened discussions with the Soviet Government. Baron Moncheur, the Belgian ambassador in London, called on Rakovsky and stated his government's views: it would establish diplomatic relations with Moscow provided the Bolsheviks accepted a formula for the satisfaction of debt claims in advance of de jure recognition. Rakovsky weighed the possibility of granting Belgium most-favored-nation treatment in the matter of debts. But after three or four meetings, Baron Moncheur discontinued the conversations. A pause of several months now intervened.

When Krassin came to Paris after French recognition of Russia in October, 1924, the Soviet trade headquarters in Paris, at the request of the Belgian authorities, established a branch in Brussels. The Belgians showed considerable interest in Russian trade. They desired to see Russian grain sold on the Antwerp market. They wanted to buy Russian oil, flax, and timber. But above all, they were concerned with their tremendous pre-revolutionary investments. Belgians had owned shipyards in Nikolaiev, steel mills, street-car factories, electric stations and machine shops in the Ukraine, and huge properties in the Don region. They had also bought Czarist bonds in considerable quantities.

In 1926, after Rakovsky was appointed ambassador to Paris, he once met Vandervelde, then Belgian Minister of Foreign Affairs, in the salon of Madame Menard-Dorian. Vandervelde informed Rakovsky that he favored de jure recognition of the Soviet Union but refrained from granting it because the internal political party situation did not permit. He nevertheless urged the conclusion of a trade agreement, and, accordingly, sent M. Tellier, an official

[3] The writer's information regarding Soviet relations with Belgium was given him by Rakovsky.

of the Belgian Foreign Office, to negotiate with Rakovsky. The conversations dragged on for months, but in 1927 they had practically drafted the complete text of a commercial treaty. Tellier, it was understood, would go to Moscow as trade commissioner. Yet they failed to agree on one cardinal issue: Rakovsky demanded a guarantee that Soviet goods shipped to Belgium would not be subject to confiscation by order of the courts or the Government. Tellier replied, however, that an arrangement of this kind would infringe on the liberty and independence of the judicial system. In vain did Rakovsky argue that Lloyd George had written such a condition into the Anglo-Soviet trade convention of March 16, 1921. Belgium would not concede the point. And since the possibility of confiscation might interfere with trade and cause the Soviet Government considerable losses, the negotiations ended with failure, and Paris withdrew the Soviet branch trade office from Brussels.

*Scandinavia* Norway, Sweden, Denmark, and Iceland were the first industrial countries to engage in trade with the Bolsheviks, and in 1920 Sweden accounted for 28.4 per cent of Soviet imports. It was through Sweden and at great expense that Krassin broke the Allies' gold blockade. Despite geographical propinquity, no incidents of any kind marred Soviet-Norwegian or Soviet-Swedish relations—except that on several occasions Moscow registered academic protests against Norway's sovereignty on the island of Spitzbergen. The heroic exploits of the Soviet icebreaker *Krassin* and of the Russian aviator Chukhnovsky in saving the crew of Nobile's expedition into the Arctic in 1928, and their efforts to save Roald Amundsen, aroused a wave of popular enthusiasm throughout Scandinavia for Soviet Russia which had a moral as well as political significance. Russian trawlers and fishers on more than one occasion rescued Norwegian sailors on the frozen seas; Scandinavian countries accordingly have a fine appreciation of the human qualities of the Russian. The high cultural standing of Soviet diplomatic representatives in Scandinavia—Kerzhentsev, Ossinsky, and Madame Kollontai, then the only woman minister in the world—likewise tended to facilitate cordial dealings.

Kerzhentsev, a literary critic, arrived in Stockholm as early as February 13, 1921, and commenced negotiations with Sweden, Norway, and Denmark. On September 2,

1921, a commercial treaty was signed with Norway which also regulated questions of political representation. He concluded a similar agreement with Sweden on March 1, 1922, but the then Branting Government controlled no majority in the Riksdag and the convention therefore remained unratified. The Soviet Government accordingly transferred many of its orders from Sweden to Norway.

Kerzhentsev likewise negotiated with Denmark, and in 1922 the draft commercial treaty was ready for signature. But inner political changes and the lobbying of Russian Whites and influential Frenchmen prevented the signing until April 23, 1923.

The Danish, Norwegian, and Swedish agreements contained non-propaganda clauses patterned after the provision in the Anglo-Russian trade convention of March 16, 1921, and recognized the Soviet Government as the only government of Russia.

British de jure recognition of the Soviet Union in February, 1924, quickly brought similar moves in Scandinavia. Norway granted Russia de jure recognition on February 13, 1924, just two days before Moscow interrupted the granting of most-favored-nation treatment, Sweden on March 15, 1924 (and on the same day signed a permanent commercial treaty which was ratified on May 3), and Denmark on June 18, 1924. Iceland recognized the Soviet Union on June 22, 1925, but the two Governments exchanged no diplomatic representatives and conducted their few formal affairs through the agency of Denmark.

Norway concluded a new commercial treaty with the Soviet Union on March 3, 1926, and subsequently the Bolshevik Government granted the most-favored-nation treatment to Scandinavian countries which previously had been denied them.

Some credit for the undisturbed course of Soviet-Scandinavian relations must of right be given to Dr. Nansen, explorer, humanitarian, and diplomat, and to the fruitful contacts between scientific and cultural institutions.

*Austria* By the terms of the Brest Litovsk Treaty, Austria, the mighty member of a victorious alliance, granted de jure recognition to a new and weak Soviet republic. Came the Armistice and the nullification of the treaty—but not of recognition, for although diplomatic relations may be interrupted, recognition, once given, cannot be annulled. Austria was shorn of her territories and her might. She became a third-rate Power with no voice in international councils and little influence in European politics and economics.

The raid on the Soviet Trade Delegation headquarters in Berlin in 1924 and Germany's resentment over the Don engineers' trial in 1928 introduced a perceptible coolness into Austria's attitude toward Russia, whereas the rupture of Anglo-Soviet relations in 1927, which so obviously effected the policies of certain lesser States to the Bolsheviks, left Austro-Russian relations unchanged. Austria's indifference to British, as well as French politics, and her orientation on Germany were thus, in a measure, a guarantee of normal relations with the Soviet Union, especially since the Social Democrats and the Clericals, her two largest parties, pursued an equally friendly policy towards Russia.

The first post-war contacts between Austria and Soviet Russia were established when Litvinov and Richter signed a convention for the exchange of prisoners in Copenhagen on July 5, 1920. A temporary agreement of December 7, 1921, provided for the resumption of political and trade relations; the Czarist Embassy in Vienna was surrendered to the Bolsheviks; and the representatives of the two countries were given diplomatic status. This agreement practically repeated the stipulations of the German-Russian trade convention of May 6, 1921.

Until 1926, Soviet imports from Austria consisted largely of agricultural machinery and scythes. In that year, however, the effect of the Bolshevik industrialization program began to make itself felt and Moscow commenced to manufacture these articles at home. The danger that the bottom might therefore fall out of Russian imports and the fact that Germany at this time was granting credits to Soviet Russia, induced the Austrian Government and the Viennese municipality to undertake the crediting of exports to Russia.

*Czecho-Slovakia* As early as 1920, when Lenin sent Krassin to Copenhagen, Beneš dispatched a telegram to Krassin offering to serve as middleman between the East and the West. Thereafter, in every possible circumstance, Beneš pursued the same tactics. He on various occasions tried to mediate between Rumania or Poland or France on the one hand and Russia on the other. He attempted it at the Genoa Conference, when Lloyd George said to Chicherin, "Who is Mr. Beneš?" This was the Welshman's method of disassociating himself in a given instance from persons he knew quite well. As the foreign minister of the greatest Slav state near Central Europe, Beneš would have enjoyed the position of link between two worlds, but neither the East nor the West availed itself of the good offices he volunteered. Nevertheless, he continued to sue for the role, and as late as 1928 he wished to bring Moscow into the League of Nations.

Acting under the impression of Soviet Russia's first appearance in the international arena at Genoa, Czecho-Slovakia entered into negotiations with Russia which closed with de facto recognition of the Soviet Republic. Litvinov settled all moot points with Girsa in one sitting of three and a half hours during the course of the conference, and their agreement was signed in Prague on June 5, 1922.[4] It provided for an exchange of representatives enjoying the usual diplomatic privileges, pledged Czecho-Slovakia not to recognize or enter into relations with any other party or group which pretended to be the government of Russia, and included a mutual non-propaganda clause. The Czecho-Slovak State likewise recognized the Soviet State monopoly of foreign trade and undertook to refrain from measures aimed against it.

So detailed and cordial an agreement of so political a nature was only one formal step from de jure recognition, yet such recognition was withheld.

Throughout 1923, Beneš, Czecho-Slovakia's Foreign Minister, kept a close watch over the relations of Western Europe towards Soviet Russia, and the moment a fair wind began to blow, indications multiplied that Prague would grant de jure recognition. Such signs disappeared the moment a sterner note was introduced into the attitude of the Great Powers to the Soviet Union.

The writer has it on the authority of the secretary of the Czecho-Slovak mission in Moscow that in January, 1924, Beneš asked him to inform Chicherin that Moscow would be recognized after France granted Russia recognition. In the spring of 1924 Beneš publicly declared that his Government would recognize the Soviet Republic de jure at the appropriate time, but despite Italian and British recognition in the early part of 1924 and French recogni-

[4] *International Politics of Modern Times.* Part III, pp. 1942–5.

tion in the latter half of 1924, Czecho-Slovak recognition was not forthcoming.

In larger problems of international politics Prague usually took its cue from Paris, and successful negotiations between France and Russia would very likely have induced Beneš to recognize the Soviet State de jure. But the failure of Rakovsky's negotiations on debts, and the collapse of the Herriot Cabinet permitted internal Czech problems to prevent the granting of recognition.

Czecho-Slovakia is a highly industrialized country. Yet Agrarians controlled more votes in her parliament than any other party and they were not interested in trade with the Bolsheviks. This fact deterred recognition.

Kramarsch, the leader of the National Democratic Party, was vehemently opposed to recognition, and though his party sent very few representatives to Parliament—13 in 1929—it formed part of the government coalition, and Kramarsch therefore made non-recognition a condition of his support of Beneš. Not all National Democrats, however, saw eye to eye with Kramarsch on this point, and the suspicion was frequently entertained in Czech quarters that Beneš used Kramarsch as an excuse for not doing what he himself disliked.

*The Balkans and the Bolsheviks* The "Balkanization" of Europe after the Versailles Peace deprived the Balkans of their privileged perch as the "powder magazine" of the Continent.

The World War broke up the Austro-Hungarian Empire whose annexations in the Balkan peninsula served as one of the chief causes of Balkan unrest. Turkey, after 1918 and particularly after 1922, became an almost totally Asiatic Power without that burning interest in the Balkans which provoked pre-war enmities. Czarist Russia was gone and with it Russia's designs on Constantinople, the Straits, and Pan-Slavism.

The importance of the Balkans fell.

Soviet Russia displayed even less than normal interest in Balkan affairs. In its internal organization, the Commissariat of Foreign Affairs treated them as a minor adjunct to its Anglo-Roman department, whereas in antebellum days they occupied St. Petersburg's maximum attention.

In each of the Balkan nations, the influence of one or the other Great Power is predominant and tends to determine foreign policy. Greek and Bulgarian relations towards the Soviet Union generally reflect Anglo-Russian relations; Yugoslavia conforms more or less closely to French policies vis-à-vis Moscow; while Rumania's attitude is the result of her own apparently insoluble boundary dispute with the Bolsheviks.

**"ALSACE-LORRAINE ON THE DNIEPER"** Bessarabia was the "Alsace-Lorraine on the Dnieper," the only Soviet irredenta. The Bolsheviks regarded the province as illegally annexed by Rumania, and Soviet maps showed Bessarabia within the boundary of the Soviet Union. Rumania, on the other hand, indicated no intention of surrendering the disputed territory. This impasse determines the character of Russo-Rumanian relations.

Rumania claims Bessarabia on the basis of its status prior to 1812. Moscow replies that Rumania, in the person of General Averescu, her Prime Minister, agreed on March 5, 1918, to return the province to Soviet Russia, and, at the instance of the Allied representatives, signed a proposal to that effect.[5] No mention was then made of the 1812 claim.[6]

The Kaiser, says Sazonov, promised Bessarabia to Rumania as a reward for entering the war on the side of the Central Powers. "Rumania wisely refused the dangerous gift."[7] Rumania, like Japan, did not recognize the Kerensky regime and prepared in 1917 to penetrate into Bessarabia. Events prevented the move. But in December and January, 1918, when the Bolsheviks were otherwise engaged, Rumania occupied Bessarabia. That occupation, Moscow contends, gives Rumania no title to ownership. Rumania, nevertheless, seeks to obtain international sanction for her annexation of Bessarabia. She failed at Versailles where the question was discussed on several occasions.

On October 28, 1920, however, Great Britain, France, Italy, Japan, and Rumania signed the Paris Protocol which

[5] See p. 51.

[6] E. A. Adamov: "The Bessarabian Question in Russo-Rumanian Relations," in Nos. 6 and 7 of *International Life* (official organ of the Commissariat of Foreign Affairs), gives a history of Bessarabia's role in the pre-war relations between Russia and Rumania.

[7] S. O. Sazonov: *Sechs Schwere Jahre* (Berlin, 1922). *Fateful Years.* (New York, 1928).

declared Bessarabia Rumanian property.[8] The Protocol acquires legality only after ratification by all its signatories. Great Britain ratified first on May 19, 1922.

Meanwhile, intermittent conversations proceeded between Rumania and Russia. In 1921, Karakhan, then Soviet minister to Poland, held several conferences on the subject of Bessarabia with Filaliti, the Rumanian minister in Warsaw. During these, Karakhan offered to recognize Rumanian suzerainty in Bessarabia if Bucharest relinquished its claim to the gold deposited during the war in Moscow. The Soviet suggestion was first made by Trotzky and although numerous Bolsheviks, particularly the Ukrainian Party, opposed, Karakhan received instructions to advance the offer. Take Jonescu, the Rumanian foreign minister, fought it vehemently. Averescu, the Premier, favored it. They summoned Bratianu to mediate. But Bratianu's view was less weighty than that of the Quai d'Orsay. In Europe, at that time, the stability and permanency of the Soviet State was not generally accepted, and a settlement with the Bolsheviks therefore did not appear to warrant any sacrifice.

In 1922, the Soviet summons to Bucharest to attend the Moscow Disarmament Conference offered the invited Power an opportunity to demand Russian acceptance of Bessarabia's changed political status as a condition of her participation. Moscow replied that the purpose of the conference was the reduction of armaments and not the delimitation of frontiers. In 1923, efforts to conclude a Russo-Rumanian trade treaty foundered on the unsettled problem of Bessarabia, and both sides therefore agreed to convene a special conference at Vienna.

The Vienna conference was scheduled to meet on March 27, 1924. On March 11, the Poincaré Government announced the ratification of the Paris Protocol of October 28, 1920.[9] This move pre-determined the fate of the conference. Such support from France on the eve of discussions with the Bolsheviks would scarcely make Rumania more likely to yield to Russian arguments.

Krestinsky, the chief of the Soviet delegation to the Vienna Conference, argued that Bessarabia could not have

[8] Antony Babel: *La Bessarabie* (Paris, 1926).

[9] *Journal Officiel de la République Française. Debats Parlementaires.* March 11, 1924.

belonged to Rumania in 1812 since Rumania began her national life several decades after that date. In 1918, moreover, Rumania had declared that her occupation was temporary, and on March 5, 1918, he added, she agreed to evacuate within two months.

But Soviet Russia, Krestinsky contended, would not rest her case on the historic claim of Bessarabia's previous adherence to the Czarist Empire. In conformance with the principle of self-determination to which Bolshevik and bourgeois did homage, Russia suggested that the Bessarabians decide for themselves: did they wish to remain with Rumania, did they wish to join the Soviet Union, or would they set up an independent state? Krestinsky proposed a plebiscite in which the population of Bessarabia could decide its future political status.

> If the Rumanian Government [Krestinsky urged] were convinced, if it thought that the predominant majority of the inhabitants of Bessarabia honestly regard themselves Rumanians and desire the inclusion of Bessarabia in the Rumanian state, the Rumanian Government would have no reason to fear the results of a plebiscite or to refuse to arrange one.[1]

Rumania rejected the plebiscite. "The Rumanian Government," read the Bucharest delegation's declaration, "rejects the plebiscite if only because the acceptance of the plebiscite proposal would provoke differences among the Allies which had recognized the adherence of Bessarabia to Rumania."

The Vienna Conference thus ended in complete failure.

During the latter half of 1926 important negotiations proceeded between Rumania and Italy, and Leo Kamenev, the Soviet ambassador to Rome, found it necessary to protest against any possible decision regarding Bessarabia. The Italian-Rumanian Treaty of September 16, 1926, accordingly contained no published provision on the question of the "Alsace-Lorraine on the Dnieper."

Rome finally informed the Soviet Government of its ratification of the Paris Protocol on March 7, 1927, just a week before Chamberlain, in an interview at Geneva, characterized the relations between England and Russia in one word: "Bad." The tension between Moscow and London, in fact, encouraged anti-Russian moves on the

[1] The unpublished protocols of the Vienna Conference were seen by the writer in the Commissariat of Foreign Affairs.

part of other countries. The Belgrade Press and newspapers elsewhere on the European continent actually declared that Mussolini's approval of the status quo in Bessarabia was conceived as a favor to Great Britain. The London *Daily Telegraph* deemed it wise to deny that Italy had acted under British pressure, yet French dailies blamed both Chamberlain and Mussolini for the ratification—this though France had given her assent three years previously. France saw in Mussolini's rapprochement with Rumania a danger to her standing vis-à-vis the Little Entente.

On March 10, 1927, the *Manchester Guardian* declared that "a legal title to Russian territory without Russian assent is surely unthinkable." This matter is important for, as the newspaper continues, "only a de jure frontier can be the subject of aggression such as would compel League intervention." If Bessarabia had been de jure a part of Rumania, the League of Nations, under Article X of its covenant, would have been warranted in undertaking sanctions against any nation that sought to invade Bessarabia and wrest it from Rumanian domination. A Soviet invasion of Bessarabia would not have infringed a single international treaty.

The Bolsheviks, however, had no intention of seizing Bessarabia. Such violence on their part would have been madness except in the event of war or widespread revolution. On the other hand, they saw no compelling reason to renounce rights to territory which they considered their own. Meanwhile, the Rumanian gold fund, Queen Marie's jewels and the Rumanian archives transferred to Moscow during the war, were intact in Russia.

**YUGOSLAVIA** Nothing of moment occurred in Yugoslav-Soviet relations until the summer of 1924, when Stephan Radich, the leader of the Croation peasant movement, visited Moscow, where the writer enjoyed his absorbing conversation for many hours. Educated in Russia, and attracted by the Bolsheviks' agrarian principles, Radich made no effort to conceal his warm sympathy for the Soviet regime. The Bolsheviks received him cordially and entertained him as their guest.

But Radich wanted the Bolsheviks to recognize the independence of Croatia, and presented Chicherin with a draft convention embodying such a move. Chicherin replied that although the Soviet Government sympathized with the aspiration of struggling national minorities, it could not interfere in the internal affairs of foreign countries. Radich felt disappointed. He returned to Zagreb a disillusioned man and before long he had executed that volte face and reconciliation with the Serbs which was quickly ended by the assassin's bullet.

After Radich's visit to Moscow, Yugoslav-Soviet relations became colder than ever. Premier Pachich suspected the infiltration of Russian influence to complicate the already complicated Serb-Croat problem.

On December 17, 1925, Chicherin and Tewfik-Rushdi Bey signed a Soviet-Turkish neutrality pact in Paris. Shortly afterwards, the same Turkish diplomat signed a Yugoslav-Turkish treaty. One link was missing to complete the circle: a Soviet-Yugoslav agreement. Rushdi Bey tried hard to persuade Belgrade to make the move, and, whether to please him or in a sincere desire to effect a settlement, Yugoslavia opened informal conversations with Krestinsky in Berlin.

In December, 1925, Briand informed Rakovsky that Yugoslavia and Czecho-Slovakia had decided to recognize the Soviet Union de jure. By volunteering such information, the French minister wished to testify to his friendly attitude towards Moscow. Nevertheless, recognition was not forthcoming. During the summer of 1926 Pachich, the Yugoslav Premier, who was on vacation in Carlsbad, expressed readiness to meet Litvinov who was taking a cure in Marienbad. Litvinov assented, but the statesmen never met.

**THE GREEK REPUBLIC** Soviet Russia's partiality for Turkey in her war with Greece did not tend to dispose Athens favorably towards Moscow. But in 1924 the Greek Monarchy fell, and, acting under the impression of British and Italian de jure recognition of the Soviet Union, the new republic granted Moscow unconditional recognition on March 8, 1924.

Before long, the Bolsheviks established trade headquarters in Athens, which enjoyed actual extra-territoriality despite the absence of an understanding on the question. Negotiations, however, proceeded at snail's pace. Only on July 20, 1926, after a military insurrection had raised Pangalos to the post of Dictator, could the commercial agreement be signed. It granted Greece most-favored-nation treatment, provided for shipping facilities to the Greek merchant marine, gave the Soviet trade headquarters de jure extra-territoriality, and regulated customs duties and harbor fees. Greece, however, witheld ratification.

Toward the beginning of 1927, the Pangalos regime collapsed and was succeeded by a constitutional government. The new Cabinet felt keenly the traditional British friendship towards Greece and its action in foreign affairs closely copied London's. The Soviet minister in Athens was accordingly informed on April 14, 1927—on the eve of the Anglo-Soviet rupture—that it considered the treaty signed under Pangalos one-sided. Moscow agreed to revision, but numerous conferences achieved no concrete results and on June 22, 1928, Parliament rejected the treaty of July 20, 1926. Relations, however, remained unchanged.

In August, 1928, a Venizelos government came to power which immediately proposed the renewal of negotiations. These opened in Athens on October 29, 1928. The treaty was signed in Athens on June 11, 1929.

**BULGARIA** During the regime of Stambuliisky, the radical peasant leader, Soviet Russia and Bulgaria were on friendly terms. But in June, 1923, reactionary circles, encouraged by foreign interests, raised an insurrection against Stambuliisky in the course of which he was killed. Immediately after the coup, the Soviet Red Cross Mission delegated to repatriate Russian refugees in Bulgaria was arrested. One member was killed and all the others subjected to maltreatment. The Bolsheviks thereupon withdrew the mission and declared that no relations of any kind would be established until the Bulgarian Government made amends for its rough handling of the delegates and the refugees.

**ALBANIA** On July 6, 1924, the Albanian minister in Rome informed the Soviet ambassador of his Government's de jure recognition of the Soviet Union. The initiative was Fan Noli's, the head of the new Albanian Government. Fan Noli, a Catholic priest, graduate of Harvard University, and man of culture, harbored a special interest in Soviet affairs and in 1927 attended an international congress in Moscow of the "Friends of the Soviet Union."

In November the Soviets appointed a minister to Tirana. His arrival in the Albanian capital, however, coincided with Achmed Zogu's insurrection against Fan Noli, and the authorities deemed it wiser that Krakovetzky take his leave. The uprising was successful, and the Zogu regime never resumed relations with Russia.

*Polish Federalism, The Baltic Bloc, and the Bolsheviks* Seven years had passed since the end of the World War, and four and a half years since the end of the Polish War. Yet the two neighbors had not even established regular postal and railway connections. In March, 1925, these were provided for. Trade began to grow, and in May direct freight facilities were made available. During the next month a Polish trade delegation visited Moscow and in August a bi-lateral commission was organized to adjudicate border difficulties.

Relations, of course, scarcely resembled friendship but so much improvement had taken place that Chicherin felt disposed to spend four days in Warsaw en route to Germany. (On subsequent trips, whether for political or other considerations, he always avoided the Polish capital.) Between September 26 and 30, on the eve of Locarno, Chicherin saw Count Skrzynski and other Polish statesmen and discussed a Soviet proposal for a guarantee and nonaggression pact, as well as large questions of European politics.

Although the negotiations on this subject made relatively little progress, relations were not disturbed, and in January, 1926, a group of Polish parliamentarians travelled through the Soviet Union.

Very soon, however, Pilsudski's coup d'état of May, 1926, began to cast its shadow ahead. Poland had suffered a crop failure in 1924 which forced her to accept a $35,000,000 loan from the American banking house of Dillon, Read and Co. for food purchases in the United States. The bonds were difficult to sell and the whole operation reflected a lack of confidence in Polish economy which was more than justified by the collapse of the zloty, the suicidal Polish-German tariff war which the Poles initiated in the autumn of 1925, and the general depression in trade and industry.

It is probably correct to affirm that in the early part of 1926, all classes of the Polish populations yearned for a change. The return of Pilsudski to power seemed inevitable. In foreign affairs the coming upheaval announced itself by the renewal of the Polish-Rumanian alliance of 1921 which was directed against Russia, and the activization, in April, of Poland's old Baltic policy. On May 1 came Marshal Pilsudski's coup; street-shooting, the patrolling of the city by armored tanks, the cleansing of the army.

The Pilsudski coup marked a break with the Skrzynski policy towards Soviet Russia, and overt hostility now replaced attempts at settlement.

*The Vatican and the Kremlin* When Pius XI ascended the throne in 1922 he was presented with the opportunity of achieving the greatest Papal conquest in modern times: he could break up the Greek Catholic Church and convert ninety million Eastern Orthodox Christians to Roman Catholicism. The separation of Church from State in Russia after the Bolshevik revolution had weakened Greek Orthodoxy and Communist campaigns against the Church, specifically against the solidly and bitterly anti-Bolshevik Greek Church which represented one of the chief organized opponents of the new regime, appeared to made Rome's task easier. Italian papers of the day published cartoons showing the Holy See in the act of granting its blessing to Bolshevik efforts against Greek Catholicism.

The Polish Roman Catholic clergy obstructed the Pope's policy which would succeed only at their expense. A Bolshevik understanding with the Vatican was possible if the Holy Father consented to strip the Roman Church in Russia of its Polish influence and leadership, yet even then Moscow would never sign a concordat or agreement with the Pope. The Bolsheviks merely offered to submit to the Vatican's examination a Commissariat of Justice circular regarding the status of the Catholic Church in the Soviet Union.

Father Edmund A. Walsh, of Georgetown University, Washington, D.C., who was the Curia's official delegate to Moscow, directly told Chicherin that two tendencies existed at the Vatican: one led by the Pope which aimed at a compromise with the Bolsheviks and to win over a vast multitude of simple-minded followers; the other represented by Walsh himself whose program was a strugle with Bolshevism.

The Bolsheviks expected the Holy Father to dominate.

In 1922 and 1923 they had not yet been recognized by the major Powers. Normal relations with the Vatican could bring them certain benefits in Catholic countries and with Catholic parties in other countries. Such advantages are not to be overlooked by the makers of a realistic foreign policy. Moreover, the triumph of Roman Catholicism in Russia would be won at the expense of Greek Catholicism and of Polish prestige—results the Soviets were ready to facilitate. Years would elapse before Roman Catholicism became a menace and then Moscow could cope with it. In like manner, the Bolsheviks encouraged reformistic schisms in the Greek Catholic Church as well as independent sects. The purpose was to destroy the solid phalanx of Greek Catholicism.

During the Genoa Conference in 1922, Chicherin found himself seated opposite the Archbishop of Genoa at a small dinner given by the King of Italy aboard the cruiser *Dante Alighieri*. The Archbishop inquired about the condition of Catholics in Soviet Russia. Thereupon Chicherin elaborated on the advantages of separation of Church from State, in Russia in particular, and throughout the world generally. Separation, the Bolsheviks believed, should arouse no serious objections among Roman Catholics. Chicherin's remarks reflected this view. Archbishop Signori listened with rapt attention, then he rose, clinked his wineglass to Chicherin's, and said, "I thoroughly agree with you." The Archbishop's view was not that of the Vatican as a whole, yet important influences within the walls of the Curia felt that at least in Russia the new status might prove of practical benefit.

Father Walsh constituted the chief obstacle to the successful consummation of the Pope's plan. The Bolsheviks found him "most objectionable, proud, and inclined to make a terrible scandal out of every little issue." He had come to Russia in 1922 to administer relief in Russia on behalf of world Catholic organizations, and to act as the Vatican's plenipotentiary. His implacable and undisguised enmity soon caused difficulties. First he demanded that his food shipments for the famine sufferers be accompanied by foreign monks—mostly Italian. Then he proposed a method of money transmittances from foreign countries to Russia and from Russia abroad which the Bolsheviks interpreted as an effort to establish financial contacts between Roman Catholicism in the Soviet Union and the White emigrés in Europe. The bitterest feud arose over the question of church property. The Bolsheviks, having nationalized all property in Russia, nationalized the churches, but were willing to grant them to religious communities for use. This was an issue on which Roman Catholicism had fought unyieldingly through the ages. The Church is sacred and remains sacred and in the hands of the faithful for ever, is Rome's principle. The stand of the Petrograd Catholics had become particularly unrelenting, and the Bolsheviks finally agreed on a formula, limited in time and to Petrograd, which settled the conflict. But Father Walsh, the Bolsheviks declare, immediately informed the Vatican that this formula applied to all Russia so that when Jordansky arrived in Rome to negotiate with Macchi-Venturi, Cardinal Ledochovski's assistant in the Jesuit Order, he was told that the problem no longer existed. He likewise learned that modifications suggested by Walsh to a draft Bolshevik agreement had been transmitted to Rome as accepted by Moscow. Here again, therefore, Father Macchi-Venturi appeared to be under the impression that all moot questions had been solved. The Jordansky-Venturi conferences accordingly proved abortive.

The prosecution of Archbishop Cepliak and Mgr. Butkevich in 1923, evoked an interesting demonstration of the Pope's position toward Russia. When the Roman Catholic priests were arrested and brought to trial, protests poured in from the entire world, and when the sentences were passed, a storm of anti-Bolshevik feeling swept through many countries. The Polish Government, the British Government, and innumerable church and secular organizations protested. But the incident provoked no fierce reaction on the part of the Pontiff himself.

In 1924 a change of attitude became noticeable in both camps. The Bolsheviks had obtained British, Italian, and French de jure recognition. Signs were not wanting that they would patch up a peace with Patriarch Tikhon. The Vatican, on the other hand, began to orient itself on the White emigration in Europe. A group of prominent Russian noble families living in exile had adopted Roman Catholicism, and the Curia, remembering that the nobility in Russia and even the Royal Family had at various times in history toyed with the idea of conversion to the Roman Church—see, for instance, the rumor that Alexander I had accepted Catholicism before death, and the practice of certain Russian circles to employ Catholic teachers (the Abbé in Pushkin's *Eugene Onegin* will be recalled)—changed its strategy and commenced to place its hope on political developments in Russia which would sweep away the Bolsheviks.

The Bolsheviks, nevertheless, had not despaired of an understanding with the Vatican on practical problems affecting the Roman Church in the Soviet Union. In 1925 Chicherin and Krestinsky handed Pacelli, the Papal Nuncio in Berlin, two documents—one outlining Soviet principles in Roman Catholic church matters, the other dealing concretely with the appointment of Bishops, the transmission of Vatican funds to the Russian Church, and education. In the matter of moneys and schools, there was a feeling that, if the Vatican respected Soviet laws—and nothing else could be expected—an accord would present no great difficulties. As to bishops, the Bolsheviks preferred a preliminary agreement on their part to the candidate. The Russians likewise objected to the publication in Russia of Papal Bulls and to uncensored communication between the hierarchy of the Russian Catholic Church and Rome.

The Vatican kept the Soviet documents for one year, and then returned a reply on three of the twelve or more questions involved. In 1927 Rome intimated that the Soviet proposal did not satisfy. The negotiations were never resumed.

*Spain and Latin America* Shortly after British de jure recognition of the Soviet Union, M. Solar, the Spanish minister in Berlin, met Krestinsky at a dinner especially arranged for this purpose by Baron von Maltzan and suggested an exchange of notes on recognition. The Russian ambassador naturally consented, but political conditions in Spain interfered with the move, and M. Solar's initiative was coldly received in Madrid. Subsequently, in 1927, at the time Spain introduced a national petroleum monopoly and signed a contract with the Naphtha Syndicate for the purchase of oil covering approximately 60 per cent of her annual requirements, another unsuccessful attempt was made to establish diplomatic relations between Moscow and Madrid.

Of Spain's American cousins, only Mexico and Uruguay maintained relations with the Soviet Union. Negotiations commenced with Mexican representatives in London and Berlin early in 1924, and on August 1, 1924, Mexico recognized the Soviet Union de jure and unconditionally. Normal and cordial relations continued. Mexican ministers in Moscow for several years usually showed some special interest in Soviet social legislation in rural districts, and the Bolshevik Press, although severely critical of "reformist" activities in Mexico, assumed a mildly friendly attitude towards her revolutionary tendencies. When President-elect Calles visited Berlin in 1924 he attended a banquet in his honor at the Soviet Embassy.

In January 1930 the Mexican government, to the surprise even of its own minister in Moscow, suddenly broke off diplomatic relations with the Soviet Union, on the ground of a hostile Communist demonstration before the Mexican legation in Washington.

*Arabia* Arabia is an outpost from which British imperialist policy can be observed; Moscow wishes the Arabs to see a friend and moral supporter in the Soviet Union; moreover the Bolsheviks, despite their atheistic policies, cannot wholly ignore the spiritual bond that connects their millions of Moslem citizens with the holy places of Islam. Russia is one of the great Mohammedan countries. She has intimate relations with Turkey and Afghanistan.

When King Hussein declared himself Caliph on March 6, 1924, he sent a telegram to Chicherin announcing the fact, and on August 6, 1924, normal diplomatic relations were established with the arrival of a Soviet agent in Jedda. Prince Lotfallah visited Moscow in the same year on behalf of the Sheriffian dynasty.

In 1925 Ibn Saud, the Wahabite ruler of the Nejd, undertook a crusade against King Ali, Hussein's son and successor, and finally set up his own Government in Arabia. On the capture of Jedda, December 22, 1925, Ibn Saud addressed a letter to Hakimov, the Soviet consul, thanking the Soviet for their neutrality in his struggle against Ali. Later, in February 1926, Ibn Saud assumed the titles of King of Hedjas and Sultan of Nejd. Moscow recognized him in these titles on February 16, for which the new monarch wrote a warm letter of thanks.

A dispute now developed in the Moslem world between those followers of the Prophet who accepted Ibn Saud's suzerainty over Mecca and Medina and another section, supported by the Egyptian priesthood and probably Great Britan at one time, which favored a rival candidate. In July, 1926, Ibn Saud convened an All-Moslem congress in Mecca while his opponents prepared to summon a similar meeting in Cairo. The Bolsheviks allowed the Chief Ecclesiastical Directorate of the Mohammedan Church in Russia with headquarters in Ufa to send a strong delegation to the Mecca assembly, and thus contributed to the reinforcement of Ibn Saud's position in the Moslem world. Moscow sought in this and other ways to remind the Arabs of the existence of a big, anti-imperialist Power.

**CZARISM IN CHINA** Japan's awakening, after Commodore Perry sounded the réveille call in 1854, Russia's expansion to Vladivostok in 1861, and the consolidation of the German Empire in 1871, introduced the modern period of foreign aggrandizement in China. Powerless before superior armaments, China remained passive while the civilized nations of the East and West tore tremendous territories from her mammoth hulk. France seized Annam, England took Burma, and Japan made ready to occupy Formosa and Korea.

In 1894, however, China roused herself to resistance against the Mikado. Her effort ended with defeat and the conclusion of the humiliating Treaty of Shimonoseki the following year.

By the terms of the treaty, China ceded the Liaotung Peninsula, Formosa and the Pescadores to Japan and acknowledged the independence of Korea. She also agreed to pay an indemnity.

But Russia had coveted Port Arthur at the tip of the Liaotung Peninsula. St. Petersburg, moreover, could not permit so marked an improvement of Japan's position on the Asiatic mainland. Count Witte, the exponent of Far Eastern expansion and the builder of the Trans-Siberian Railway, accordingly insisted on the necessity of thwarting the execution of the peace treaty[2] of Shimonoseki.

St. Petersburg's move was opposed by the British Government, but supported by France and Germany. Japan therefore renounced her claim to Liaotung and

[2] *The Memoirs of Count Witte.* (London, 1921), p. 83.

Port Arthur. Simultaneously, Russia guaranteed a large French private loan to China. The operations of this loan required the organization of the Russo-Chinese Bank.

Russia expected her quid pro quo. Witte had constructed the Trans-Siberian Railway as far as Transbaikalia. What would be its further course? Witte "conceived the idea of building the road straight across Chinese territory . . . to Vladivostok." The Chinese route, he reckoned, was 514 versts shorter than the distance from Transbaikalia across Russian territory to the Pacific, and would, moreover, put Russia in a strategic position to occupy Northern and Southern Manchuria and Outer Mongolia, and to check Japan on the Asiatic continent.

Nicholas II was about to mount the throne. China had been invited, and agreed to send its highest dignitary, Li Hung Chang, to attend the ceremonies. He arrived in St. Petersburg in April, 1896.

Amid the festivities and bloodshed which accompanied the coronation of the youthful monarch, Li Hung Chang and Witte negotiated secretly about a Sino-Russian alliance. The two countries obliged themselves to defend each other against Japanese attack, and China granted Russia the permission to build a railway from Chita to Vladivostok on Chinese soil.

Li Hung Chang, however, would under no pressure consent that the Russian State officially own or operate the road. He wished to be spared the odium of bartering away Chinese sovereignty and to anticipate Japanese opposition. Witte therefore organized the Chinese Eastern Railway Company with Government funds. Li agreed to grant the concession to the Russo-Chinese (later Russo-Asiatic) Bank which, by an agreement with Witte, ceded its formal, fictitious concession to the Chinese Eastern Railway Company, a creature of the Czarist exchequer.

The Russian Government would construct the line; the Chinese Eastern Railway Company would own and operate it on the basis of rights transmitted to it by the Russo-Chinese Bank which had come into possession of these rights for a formal moment. The Bank's concession contract, Witte writes, "was drawn up under my instructions by the Assistant Minister of Finance, Piotr Mikhailovich Romanov, in consultation with the Chinese Minister in St. Petersburg. . . ." Despite careful deception, the Chinese

Eastern Railway was clearly the property of the Russian State, and the agreement moreover provided that only Russian and Chinese subjects could hold its shares.[3]

On July 1, 1903, the road was ready for exploitation. According to official accounts,[4] the cost of building, including the South Manchurian spur to Dairen, amounted to $223,332,502 in gold—paid from the treasury of the Czar.

At the close of the Russo-Japanese War, Russia ceded the South Manchurian section of the line, from Kwangchentze to Dairen (475 miles) to Japan. South Manchuria became a Japanese "sphere of influence." North Manchuria remained a Russian "sphere of influence." This substantially was the situation when the Czarist Government fell.

Russian events in 1917 and 1918 disorganized traffic and introduced chaos on the Chinese Eastern Railway. In the summer of 1918, Japan, in pursuance of the Japanese-Chinese Military Agreement of March 25, 1918, seized the Chinese Eastern Railway and the Trans-Siberian Railway as far as Chita. General Horvath and Ataman Semenov acted on behalf of Tokyo in operating the lines and subduing the surrounding districts.

Such an arrangement being prejudicial to American Far-Eastern interests, Washington proposed that a commission headed by John F. Stevens undertake the management of the railways. Japan objected. The United States insisted. The resulting situation even bore within it a menace of war until, on January 8, 1919, an agreement was drawn up naming Stevens the chairman of a technical board to manage the lines. The Chinese Eastern Railway would be guarded officially by China, but actually by Japanese. Endless friction developed between the American director and the Japanese military, and ultimately Stevens retired. For a brief period, the Chinese Government now took over the railway, but direct control and management were vested in the same Russian Whites who dominated the situation throughout the Civil War. This anomalous state of affairs required regulation when Soviet Russia returned to the Far-Eastern scene in 1923.

[3] The full text of the contract between Russia and China for the construction of the railway will be found in pp. 13ff. of *Manchuria, Treaties and Agreements*. A Carnegie Endowment Publication. (Washington, 1921).

[4] *North Manchuria and the Chinese Eastern Railway*. Official Publication of the Chinese Eastern Railway. (Harbin, China, 1924).

**OUTER MONGOLIA AND RUSSIA** Mongolia presented another stumbling-block to the resumption of Sino-Soviet relations. It was a question which exposed the Soviet Government to the charge of "Red Imperialism."

From the beginning of the twentieth century, Mongolia objected actively to Chinese rule. The Mongolian princes desired to wield power themselves without the aid of Chinese bureaucrats or of Chinese taxation. This circumstance "drove the Mongolian princes still deeper into the camp of the Russians,"[5] while the nomads of the vast country frequently crossed over into Czarist territory to escape the financial burdens imposed by Peking.

Chinese rule brought real hardships. The Chinese discouraged trade, handicrafts, and agriculture by Mongols in Mongolia, while engaging in these pursuits themselves, and sought to keep the country primitive, wild, and devoted exclusively to herding. The Mongols were taught the sinfulness of "opening the breast of the earth" in order to cultivate it, and in this respect the Buddhist hierarchy supported the Chinese. The Buddhist Church, insensitive to the economic realities of the situation and intent merely on maintaining intact its almost absolute domination over Mongolia, was anxious not to separate Outer Mongolia from China but to unite Outer with Inner Mongolia and thus extend its sphere of influence into a richer region. This circumstance offset domestic and local efforts in the direction of Mongolian autonomy.

The Mongolian movement toward secession and independence from China received a set-back when the Manchus exploited Russia's preoccupation with Japan in 1904–5 to strengthen their hold on the vast semi-desert state. In 1908 they reinforced their garrison in Urga and at the same time began intensive colonization of Chinese along the Kalgan-Urga caravan route.

Early in 1911 a Mongolian deputation traveled to St. Petersburg to petition the Czar for aid in throwing off the yoke of the Celestial Empire.[6] The Russian Government instructed its Minister in Peking to make remonstrances to the Chinese authorities, gave arms to the Mongolians, and intimated that they "could depend on the support of Russia in their struggle for autonomy."

The fall of the Manchus in 1911 gave Russia an

[5] Georg Cleinow: *Neu-Sibirien*, (Berlin, 1928), p. 75.
[6] *Ibid.*, p. 77.

opportunity of winning China's recognition of Outer Mongolia's nominal autonomy. Chicherin, who examined the archive of Korostowetz, then Czarist minister in Peking, tells the writer that the Czar refused to recognize the new Chinese republic except on condition of Mongolian autonomy, and China therefore forced Urga to accept that status against the wishes of the Buddhist Church.

Sazonov, however, did not wish to antagonize China for the sake of Mongolian independence. He therefore proposed to bridge the gap between the mother country and the intractable daughter, and, while safeguarding Russian commercial interests in Mongolia, to heal the breach between Urga and Peking.

On May 25, 1915, after protracted negotiations, a tripartite agreement was signed which granted Mongolia considerable autonomy, withdrew Chinese troops from Mongolian territory, and guaranteed Mongolia against forced Chinese colonization. The "Living Buddha" became the chief of the new buffer between Russia and China. Actually, however, power was vested in the Russian Resident.

The Russian Resident in Urga exercised great influence over Mongolian affairs, and, through Mongolia, furthered Russian expansion towards Tibet, and towards Tannu-Tuva, a No-Man's Land with neither a Russian nor a Mongolian administration but gravitating, by reason of trade and nomad migrations, to Siberia.

Still further to the west along the Siberian-Mongolian frontier, Czarist Russia sought to obtain a foothold in the furthermost province of China—in Sinkiang or Chinese Turkestan whose importance as a commercial possibility and as a neighbor of India, Tibet and Russian Turkestan St. Petersburg vividly appreciated.

It is 4,300 kilometers from Tihwa or Urumchi, the capital of Chinese Turkestan, to Peking, and the only route is by cart to Semipalatinsk and thence, via the Trans-Siberian Railway, to China. Sinkiang exports—cattle, wool, and cotton—were eagerly bought by Russia. China had no need of them. Nor could China supply the province with the articles it wished to import: sugar, matches, textiles, kerosenes, iron goods, etc. Chinese Turkestan, moreover, is three-quarters Turanian: Uzbeks, Kirghizi, and Cossacks, whose blood-cousins and Moslem co-religionists live near-by just across the Russian frontier.

Chinese authority never became firmly established in Sinkiang. Its trade with the rest of China, as well as with India and Afghanistan, which likewise abut on it, was almost negligible, whereas the turnover with Russia amounted in 1913 to some 20,000,000 gold rubles.

Sinkiang, larger probably in extent than Germany, France, Italy, and England combined, thus constituted a strong attraction for business and imperialist circles in Czarist Russia; documents indicate that St. Petersburg seriously intended, on the very eve of the World War, to appropriate that part of the province co-terminous with Tannu-Tuva and Mongolia while refraining from touching the section around the city of Kashgar because of its special interest to British India and Afghanistan.

The Bolshevik Revolution overnight destroyed Russia's position in Chinese Turkestan, in Tannu-Tuva, and in Outer Mongolia. Russia, in fact, ceased to play a role in Far-Eastern politics. Kolchak, Semenov, Kalmikov, General Horvath, and the Japanese prevented any physical contact between Bolshevism and China, and in Sinkiang, British missions easily took advantage of the situation to exterminate any vestige of Russian prestige. At Kashgar, as Lord Balfour admitted during the Washington Disarmament Conference, England even erected a wireless telegraph station for anti-Bolshevik propaganda.

Japanese agents, preaching the doctrine of "Asia for Asiatics," of Pan-Mongolism or of Pan-Islamism wherever that was necessary, penetrated into Chinese and Russian Turkestan, into Tannu-Tuva, and into Mongolia, while China attempted to reassert her authority over Urga. The advent of Bolshevism and the Red-White Civil War had thrown the whole vast continent into a turmoil and in the chaos only one thing seemed certain: that Russia would never reoccupy her former position in the buffer lands which separated her from China.

**BARON UNGERN-STERNBERG** Early in 1920, however, the Red Army smashed Kolchak. The remnants of his forces fled south and east into Chinese Turkestan, Mongolia, Manchuria, and China, where, after various adventures in which many starved or froze to death, the stragglers reached the Pacific coast and volunteered for mercenary service in the Chinese civil war. One of them, a Pole named Ossendowski, has left a vivid, highly colored record of his experiences.

General Baron Ungern von Sternberg found himself, after Kolchak's collapse, with a small band of homeless, hopeless warriors on the borders of Outer Mongolia. He was an interesting figure and bore an interesting philosophy.[7]

Ungern-Sternberg was half Russian, half Magyar. He had served in the Russian Navy, fought in the Russo-Japanese War and seen service in the World War. Fate left him stranded in 1920 on soil his conquering forefathers trod, for in him ran the blood of Batu, a grandson of Genghis Khan, who invaded Hungary and besieged Budapest in 1240.

Ungern's wife was a Manchurian princess. He himself was steeped in the lore of Buddhism. From it he took his mysticism and love of the East.

The elements of his credo were monarchy, anti-revolutionism, and anti-Westernism. "We aristocrats," he wrote to General Lu Chang-Kuu in May, 1921, "have only one thought, one purpose, one task—the restoration of kings." This goal limited him to no country; his internationalism is beyond dispute; he wished to reestablish the Central Empire to include Outer and Inner Mongolia to the edge of India, Manchuria, and Tibet. He wanted to see an Emperor in Peking and a Czar in St. Petersburg. "By the will of the All-High God," he proclaimed after capturing Urga in February, 1921, "it is given to me to help the ruler of Kiakhta, His Beatitude the Living Buddha, to overthrow the power of the Chinese revolutionists-Bolsheviks and carry out the task of uniting all the districts of Outer and Inner Mongolia into one great Mongolia." "As the earth cannot be without a heaven," he wrote, "so the nations cannot be without their kings."

I. J. Korostowetz, former Czarist minister in Peking,

[7] Baron Ungern-Sternberg's letters, some of which were composed by Ossendowski, are now in the Moscow archives. Some of them were published in the *Peking and Tientsin Times* and reprinted by the Special Delegation of the Far-Eastern Republic to the Washington Disarmament Conference: *Letters Captured from Baron Ungern in Mongolia,* (Washington, 1921); others are published in the *Journal of the Commissariat of Foreign Affairs.* Moscow, December 15, 1921.

calls Ungern "the terrible baron,"[8] and tells how the conqueror of Urga behaved after it succumbed to his attack. "Urga lived through a new period of horror," he writes. . . . "The Chinese and the revolutionaries were tortured. . . . Especially the Jews were mercilessly massacred, scarcely one of them being left alive."

Revolution was anathema to Ungern-Sternberg. "European culture," he believed, "has brought so much evil to the States of the East that it is time to take up the struggle with it and, united, inflict on it a lasting defeat." The West and the "putrid sciences of Europe" encouraged the plagues of socialism and revolution. He summoned the Mongols to a crusade on Europe—perhaps an appeal to the primitive instincts which sent Genghis and his sons to the gates of Moscow, Vienna, and Budapest.

Practically and immediately, Ungern worked with Japan against Soviet Russia. "Your Excellency," he informed General Lu Chang-Kuu, "is well aware of my hatred to revolutionaries wherever they may be, and therefore you will understand my readiness to aid in the task of restoring the monarchy under the general supervision of General Chang So-Lin." Ungern's contacts with Ataman Semenov, the Japanese puppet, were public property, and he received munitions and other material assistance from Manchuria. His slogans, "Asia for the Asiatics" and "Pan-Mongolism," recall the idealogical masquerades with which Japanese imperialism then adorned its aggressions deep in Asia.

After his conquest of Urga and his expulsion of the Chinese, Ungern laid his plans for an offensive into the Baikal region of Siberia. "Now," he informed General Lu Chang-Kuu, shortly after taking Urga, "all my strivings are centered on the North, where I will move in order quickly to enter Russian territory." For this purpose he courted Kirghiz princes. He expected to rally the Siberian Cossacks. "All Russia suffers," he wrote in 1921; "brother lifts up hand against brother, son against father, all have grown poor; they starve, and have forgotten God." The Russian people would rise, he believed, and he would be their savior.

[8] Iwan J. Korostowetz: *Von Cinggis Khan zur Sowjetrepublik,* (Berlin 1926), p. 310.

Ungern-Sternberg's star glittered for a brief day. He entered the Mongolian capital on February 3, 1921. Internal organization and executions occupied him completely for some time, but in May he assumed the offensive and marched in the direction of Verkhni-Udinsk and Lake Baikal. Success temporarily crowned his efforts against the weak Bolshevik forces in that region. Ungern had penetrated only 70 versts north of the Soviet frontier, however, when he encountered several fresh brigades of Budenny cavalry which had been rushed by rail from the West. The baron was beaten back, and on July 7 the Red Army undertook the pursuit and captured Urga.

Several weeks later, Ungern, reinforced with mobile lancers from Kobdo and other centers of Western Mongolia, again raised the war standard and got as far as Gusina Lake on Soviet soil, where he met decisive defeat. In the end of August, Ungern himself fell into Soviet hands, and after an interesting cross-examination, he was executed at Novo-Nikolaievsk.

**SOVIET RUSSIA AND MONGOLIA** The presence of Red troops in Mongolia (their number was estimated at 4,000 in Urga and 2,500 in Western Mongolia) relieved Mongolia from the danger of Russian Whites, thousands of whom still infested the region, and from the menace of Chinese invasion. The Bolsheviks adapted to Mongolia the method they had applied in the Russian village: the poor were stirred up against the rich, the plebians against the princes, and the Mongolians generally against the prerevolutionary Russian merchant class which none of the vicissitudes of civil war had been able to dislodge.

By suppressing the Chinese merchants, by eradicating the old Russian merchants, and by buying large quantities of wool in Mongolia, the Bolsheviks won the goodwill of Mongolian traders. The intelligentsia, to the extent that it exists, was grateful to the Soviets for a chance to participate in the new autonomous government. And the rich v. poor campaign did not achieve sufficient fundamental success to antagonize the princes. All sections of the Mongolian population felt grateful for the dismissal of the Chinese; the desire for autonomy was not new. Chinese taxes had disappeared with the Chinese bureaucrat, and no Russian had taken his place.

The influence of the Bolsheviks in Outer Mongolia caused considerable resentment in Peking, in Tokyo, and in Mukden. China had regarded herself Mongolia's master, Tokyo its potential suzerain, and Chang So-Lin had been appointed "Commissar of Mongolia" by a convention of tuchuns which met in Tientsin in April, 1921.

**EARLY ATTEMPTS AT SINO-SOVIET RELATIONS**

The Versailles Peace Conference of 1919 failed to dislodge the Japanese from the Shantung Province. Peking refused to sign the Peace Treaty. China stormed. Meetings of protest were held throughout the land; foreigners were assaulted, Japanese goods boycotted. Disillusionment with the capitalist Powers enveloped the vast land.

Into such a situation, the Soviet Government threw its first appeal to the Chinese people dated July 25, 1919. In it, Leo Karakhan, Assistant Commissar of Foreign Affairs, reviewed the events of 1918; Soviet Russia had offered in 1917 to annul all unequal treaties with China and all Czarist treaties with Japan. Negotiations to this end proceeded with a Chinese representative till March, 1918, when "the Allies suddenly seized the Peking Government by the throat, covered the Chinese mandarins and the Chinese Press with gold, and forced the Chinese Government to forgo all relations with the Russian Workers'-Peasants' state." Now, "in order to open its eyes," Moscow again appealed to the Chinese people. The Soviets renounced all the conquests of Czarism in China, Manchuria and other parts, as well as Russia's share in the Boxer indemnity and all the unequal privileges formerly enjoyed by Russian merchants in China. These changes, Karakhan suggested, could be written into a treaty which would abolish all acts of force and injustice.

This appeal, addressed to the Peking and Canton Governments, elicited no official response. Karakhan accordingly sent a more detailed note to the Chinese Foreign Minister on October 27, 1920. The note proposed: (1) to annul all pre-revolutionary treaties and to return without compensation everything seized from China by the Czarist Government and the Russian bourgeoisie; (2) to establish economic relations on the basis of most-favored-nation treatment; (3) to refuse capitulation privileges for

Russian citizens; (4) to reject payments under the Boxer Protocol; (5) to establish diplomatic and consular relations with China; and (6) to sign a special agreement regarding the use of the Chinese Eastern Railway.

Internal conditions and foreign influence prevented the Peking authorities from taking advantage of the Soviet offers. Unofficial relations were nevertheless established. China sent General Chang So-lin to Moscow, and the Bolsheviks delegated first Jurin, then Paikis—diplomats of third rank—and finally Adolf A. Joffe.

Mongolia and the Chinese Eastern Railway constituted the obstacles to a settlement. Peking demanded the evacuation of Mongolia and, in the question of the railway, responded to foreign pressure. An agreement between the Russo-Asiatic Bank and Peking on October 2, 1920,[9] had in effect recognized the French Bank's title to the Chinese Eastern Railway, although that title was clearly formal and fictitious. The agreement stated specifically that its purpose was to bridge over the period until China agreed on the future of the line with a recognized Russian Government, yet its net result was to surrender the railway to the de facto control of the Russian Whites. Neither the Peking nor the Manchurian Government could claim the Chinese Eastern Railway as its own. But they were not free to make a settlement with Moscow.

Joffe parleyed with the Peking ministers month on month. But the situation remained essentially unchanged except that the disappointment over the results of the Washington Disarmament Conference coming less than two years after the resentment against Versailles added to the momentum of the Chinese revolutionary movement whose sympathies were with Soviet Russia. Dr. Sun Yat-sen had established himself in Canton, and a parliament in that city elected him President of China on April 7, 1921. And although in August of the following year General Chen Chiung-ming forced Dr. Sun to quit Canton, the old revolutionary leader represented a real moral force and a potential governmental power which, to the discerning, was of infinitely greater significance than Peking whose authority scarcely reached outside its own walls.

Accordingly, A. A. Joffe met Dr. Sun in Shanghai during January, 1923, and on January 26 they issued a

[9] Full text with supplementary declarations in *Manchuria: Treaties and Agreements* (Washington. 1921), pp. 210ff.

joint statement. Dr. Sun declared that the Soviet system could not be introduced into China

> because the conditions do not exist here for the successful establishment of Communism or Socialism. Mr. Joffe absolutely agrees with this view and, furthermore, submits that the chief and immediate aim of China is the achievement of national union and national independence. Mr. Joffe informed Dr. Sun that in the solution of this great problem, China would find the warmest sympathy of the Russian people and could depend on the aid of Russia.

Dr. Sun agreed that Soviet Russia, China, and Chang So-lin would jointly determine the disposition to be made of the Chinese Eastern Railway. Moreover,

> Mr. Joffe affirmed categorically to Sun Yat-sen (who expressed complete satisfaction on this point) that the present Russian Government has not and never had the intention of carrying out an imperialist policy in Outer Mongolia or to force it to separate from China.[1]

A few days later, Joffe proceeded to Tokyo on the invitation of Viscount Goto, then the mayor of that city, where he conducted negotiations with unofficial delegates of the Japanese Government with a view to the reestablishment of relations.

Joffe's agreement with Dr. Sun and his negotiations in Tokyo exerted an indirect but very potent pressure on the Peking Government. The union of the Far-Eastern Republic with the Soviet Federation, confirmed by a Moscow decree dated November 15, 1922, gave the Bolsheviks a common frontier with Manchuria. These factors plus the rising tide of revolution convinced the Central Chinese Government in Peking as well as Mukden of the necessity of regulating their relations to the new Russia. Russia had resumed her position in the Far East. Objectively the way was thus well prepared for Karakhan, who, in view of the severe illness of Joffe, received an appointment in June, 1923, as Soviet plenipotentiary to China and Japan.

**KARAKHAN'S TRIUMPHAL ENTRY** *The North China Star* declared at the time that the arrival of Karakhan in China was of greater significance than that

[1] Translated from the fortnightly bulletin of the Soviet political representation in Peking, February 1–15, 1923, now in the archives of the Commissariat of Foreign Affairs.

of any diplomat in the last ten years. His progress through Manchuria was a triumphal procession. Everywhere he was fêted and applauded as the author of the famous declaration of July 25, 1919, and October 27, 1920.

Karakhan subsequently told the writer that he went to China with two objects: to negotiate an equal treaty and to fight imperialism. Wherever he went, later even in the presence of the diplomatic corps, he preached revolutionary nationalism and anti-imperialism. At a banquet in Manchuria before he reached Peking he said: "If once again foreign hands will interfere in our mutual affairs we must mercilessly cut off those hands."

Such words from the envoy of a Great Power were a novelty in Chinese life. Karakhan began to be looked upon as a guarantee of Chinese revolutionary success.

When he passed through Harbin, the Russian colony met him with enthusiasm. To them he represented the return of Russia to the Far East, and patriotism inspired feelings which temporarily drove anti-Bolshevism under cover. The intellectuals in Harbin, led by people like Ustralov, gave Karakhan their good will and later did what little they could to improve his position.

Karakhan halted in Mukden to parley with Chang So-lin. The ruler of Manchuria was impressed by the expulsion of the Japanese from the Maritime Provinces. Japan, he knew, could not oppose the return of the Chinese Eastern Railway to Soviet Russia. Such a stand would, by direct implication, recognize the title of the Russo-Asiatic Bank which might then dispute the Czar's right, in 1906, to transfer the South Manchurian section of the Chinese Eastern Railway to Japan.

Karakhan's visit to Chang no doubt flattered the tuchun, while the readiness of Moscow to treat with him as the de facto master of the road strengthened his position. But since he himself had designs on Peking he could not completely undermine its authority nor could Karakhan negotiate a final settlement with Mukden before even he had set eyes on Peking. Nevertheless, the general lines of an agreement were determined in several interviews between the general and the diplomat, and Chang So-lin pledged himself to execute the treaty once it was negotiated. Such points as equality in the administration of the line were accepted in principle.

**KARAKHAN NEGOTIATES** Karakhan had established relations with Chang So-lin. On September 7, five days after his arrival in Peking, Feng Yu-hsiang, "the Christian General," then one of the lieutenants of Wu Pei-fu, the ruler of Peking, gave a banquet in honor of Karakhan at which Dr. C. T. Wang, delegated by the Chinese Foreign Office to negotiate with Russia, attended. The next day Karakhan wrote in cordial tone to Dr. Sun Yat-sen. He thus fought on a series of Chinese fronts in order to win maximum support and maximum insurance against failure.

Karakhan first demanded unconditional de jure recognition for the Soviet Union, after which all outstanding problems could be solved in diplomatic conferences. But China stubbornly refused.

Negotiations accordingly commenced between Karakhan and Dr. Wang. No difficulties were encountered on a number of important questions: the Soviet Government would not accept Boxer payments, it returned the Russian concessions in Tientsin and Hankow, and renounced all extra-territorial privileges in China. These terms won the Soviets wide popular acclaim, for Karakhan spent much of his time addressing Chinese audiences on the benefits of national revolution (he was opposed, he told me, to the "sovietization of China"), on Moscow's willing concessions to Peking, and on the likelihood that an equal treaty with the Soviet Union would add momentum to the movement for scrapping all unequal treaties with the Western Powers and Japan.

Even the question of the Chinese Eastern Railway offered little obstruction to an agreement. In fact, important Chinese circles considered the Soviet position in the matter a decided gain for China: it recognized China's right immediately to share in the administration of the line and ultimately to acquire it.

Mongolia presented greater difficulties. Dr. Wang invited the Russians to evacuate; Karakhan retorted that they were there by consent of the Mongolian Government.

When Karakhan arrived in Peking he declared in unmistakable language that the Soviet Government regarded Mongolia a part of the Chinese Republic; the exact relationship between China and Mongolia, he said, must be fixed by direct negotiations. To this end, Mongolia sent Japon Danzan to Peking early in 1924.

In his final negotiations with Dr. Wang, Karakhan stated that Soviet Russia would recognize Chinese suzerainty in Outer Mongolia, and agreed to name the date of evacuation.

The settlement, after months of negotiations, was now complete, and at eight o'clock on the morning of March 14, 1924, Dr. Wang and Leo M. Karakhan attached their signatures to a treaty which recognized the Soviet Government de jure and embodied all the points of agreement.

## THE POWERS VETO CHINESE INDEPENDENCE

Italian and British recognition of the Soviet Union early in 1924 had reduced the likelihood of open diplomatic interference by those countries against a Sino-Soviet understanding. But France, the United States and Japan remained.

With the Chinese public mind aroused against unequal treaties, the conclusion of the first equal political treaty might prove a dangerous precedent. To the Powers, Karakhan was an uncanny figure, and his treaty with Dr. Wang a threatening example of what the future had in store if they did not uproot the evil in good season.

Since objection to an equal treaty and to the return of concessions could not, however, form the basis of legitimate complaint, the dissenting nations protested their interests in the Chinese Eastern Railway.

> Sino-French correspondence (on this subject) had taken place during March and April. France apparently advanced the claim that the Russo-Asiatic Bank had been placed under French protection in consequence of the disturbances in Russia, and that protest would be made against alterations in the road's existing management.[2]

A second French note claimed for France the returned Russian concession in Hankow, and, in confirmation of this policy, the French consul-general in Hankow informed the local authorities early in July that the Sino-Soviet treaty notwithstanding, no change in the status of the former Russian concession would be permitted without

[2] Bulletin *The Chinese Eastern Railway,* Foreign Policy Association, Information Service. New York, February 27, 1926.

the consent of France. In Northern Manchuria and in Hankow, France regarded herself as the rightful heir of Czarism.

On May 3, 1924, Professor Shurman, the American minister in Peking, likewise delivered a note of protest to Dr. Wellington Koo, Chief of the Chinese Foreign Office, in which "China was warned against entering any unilateral agreement which would invalidate foreign interests.[3]

Japan is said to have made similar démarches against the Karakhan-Wang agreement of March.

French, American, and Japanese representations caused the Chinese Foreign Ministry to disavow the signature of Dr. Wang, its delegate, and to declare the treaty of March 14, 1924, non-existent.

**CHINA'S FIRST EQUAL TREATY** When Peking repudiated Wang's signature, Karakhan published the treaty text. The effect was tremendous. People saw that it was not only an equal treaty—it was an unequal treaty; China received more than she gave. Karakhan likewise negotiated openly with Yoshizava, the Japanese minister in Peking, on the resumption of relations with Tokyo, in the hope that the Powers would be misled into believing that simultaneous negotiations were not proceeding with the Chinese. And while he discussed the treaty in secret with Wellington Koo, Karakhan devoted much attention to the parallel negotiations with Chang So-lin regarding the Chinese Eastern Railway. After Karakhan's initial visit to Manchuria, Davtyan had continued the conversations with Mukden. When the Karakhan-Wang agreement was rejected, M. M. Borodin took up the negotiations with Chang So-lin and, after about ten weeks, the tuchun was ready to sign.

The threat of a separate agreement with Mukden on the most important Soviet-Chinese problem convinced Koo that the treaty with Moscow could no longer be postponed. Pressure was also exerted by Wu and Feng. Negotiations, accordingly, recommenced on March 20, at the request of Wellington Koo who, nevertheless, asked Karakhan to keep the fact a deep secret. He feared the interference of the Powers and told Karakhan so frankly. Indeed, the treaty was concluded without the knowledge

[3] *Ibid.*

of the highest officials in the Chinese Foreign Office. When everything had been settled, Karakhan came to the Foreign Office on May 31, and only after some leading Chinese officials were summoned into the chamber where the signing was about to take place did they learn of the nature of the ceremony.

The new treaty differed from the Karakhan-Wang agreement in unessential details. The only important change was an increase of Russian rights in the Boxer indemnity commission.

By the terms of the treaty, normal diplomatic and consular relations were provided for, the Chinese Government promised to transfer to the Soviet Union the buildings of the Czarist legation and consulates, both parties agreed to summon a conference within one month to give detailed content to the solutions which the treaty outlined. The Soviet Union canceled all special pre-revolutionary privileges, treaties, etc., and China undertook not to grant these privileges or concessions to a third party. The Soviet Government "recognized that Outer Mongolia is an integral part of the Chinese Republic and respects the sovereignty of China there" and declared its readiness to evacuate the Red forces from Outer Mongolia as soon as the conference fixed the date. Both Governments affirmed their intention of refraining from propaganda against one another. Peking and Moscow asserted that

> the Chinese Eastern Railway is a purely commercial enterprise and that therefore all non-commercial rights formerly exercised by Russia in the railway zone—administration of justice, military administration, policing, municipal management, taxation and land ownership—were transferred to the Chinese authorities.

The Soviet Union agreed to the purchase of the Chinese Eastern Railway by the Chinese Government with Chinese capital, and both States solemnly stated that all matters affecting the line would be determined by themselves only "without the participation of a third party or parties." The Soviet Government renounced Russia's share in the Boxer indemnity.

A special declaration applied Russia's share in the Boxer payments to Chinese education and provided for a commission consisting of two Chinese and one Russian to administer the fund. The Commission's decision must be unanimous.

**KARAKHAN AND THE PEKING DIPLOMATIC CORPS** The signature of the Sino-Soviet Treaty was not accepted as final by the Powers. They continued their protests and pressure until June 16 when China declared in identical notes to the United States, Japan, and France that China and the Soviet Union alone would deal with the Chinese Eastern Railway. Then the diplomats began to work on Chang So-lin.

On the day after the identical notes were delivered, Karakhan informed Wellington Koo that Moscow desired to appoint an ambassador instead of a minister to Peking. The fact that none of the Powers appointed ambassadors to the Chinese capital had always been interpreted by China as a studied offense and a badge of the un-sovereign character of the Chinese Government. So large and important a country as China would of course have received full-fledged ambassadors had she not been subjected to the humiliation of capitulations, foreign territorial concessions, etc. The Soviet announcement of Karakhan's designation as ambassador endeared him and his Government to the Chinese nationalists as no other single act. It was good politics and excellent psychology.

**AGREEMENT WITH MUKDEN** Meanwhile, Karakhan had been directing negotiations with Chang So-lin on the Chinese Eastern Railway. Peking actually had no jurisdiction in Manchuria, and an agreement with Wellington Koo remained a scrap of paper until confirmed by the de facto master of the railway zone. On September 20, 1924, an agreement[4] was signed between Chang So-lin and the Soviet Government which differed in few essentials from the Karakhan-Koo Treaty of May 31 except that it permitted China to acquire the road at the end of sixty years instead of eighty according to the Peking Pact. To the Bolsheviks the practical distinction between sixty and eighty years was almost nil. The Bolsheviks felt that in less than fifty years a strong united or federated China would permit Russia unhampered transit through North Manchuria to the Pacific without Soviet ownership of the line.

[4] Published in English and in Russian in an official Soviet publication, *Collection of Laws and Institutions* (August 16, 1927, No. 32, Part 2, pp. 732ff. and in French in *Le Probleme du Chemin de Fer Chinois de l'Est,* by Dr. Houng Tchang-sin (Paris, 1926).

**THE REGIME ON THE C.E.R.** The Mukden-Moscow agreement regarding the Chinese Eastern Railway provided that "China shall enter gratis into the possession of the said Railway and its appurtenant properties" at the expiration of sixty years from the date of the signing of the original Russian-Chinese contract, in other words, on September 8, 1956. "The question of the further reduction of the said time-limit may be discussed" with the consent of both contracting parties. The Chinese Government, however, enjoys the right to redeem the road before 1956 "with Chinese capital at a fair price."

A board of directors was provided for, consisting of five members appointed by the Soviet Union and five by China. All decisions of the board must have the approval of at least six members—in other words, of at least one citizen of the other country. The president of the board was to be a Chinese. When the board of directors could not agree, the subject of disagreement was to be referred to the two governments for diplomatic discussion.

In the highly important Board of Auditors, the Soviet Union had three members, China two; the chairman was a Chinese. The manager of the road was a Russian. He and one Russian and one Chinese assistant were to be appointed by the board of directors and confirmed by their respective Governments.

If the chief of any given department was a Russian, his assistant would be a Chinese, and vice versa.

Half of the personnel on the road was to be of Soviet citizenship, half of Chinese.

The Moscow-Mukden settlement further regulated the problem of shipping on the Sungari and Amur rivers on a basis of "equality and reciprocity," and guaranteed the respective signatories against hostile propaganda.

The Chinese Eastern Railway, operating under the agreement of September 20, 1924, contributed considerably to the economic development of North Manchuria. The profit from the exploitation of the road amounted, according to official figures, to 15,600,000 gold rubles in 1924; 24,100,100 in 1925; 28,200,000 in 1926; 20,700,000 in 1927; and 12,100,000 in 1928. After the reduction of special expenditures, amortization, etc., the net income was divided equally between Moscow and Mukden.

**THE AFTER EFFECTS** Several days after the Sino-Soviet Treaty of May 31, 1924, was concluded, Karakhan received a message of congratulation from Hu Ao-tung in the name of 181 members of the Chinese Parliament. The agreement, they said, represented a "victory over international imperialism." Further, they expressed the hope that the two nations "will go hand in hand . . . and force world diplomacy to open a new era." At a celebration on June 9 in the Peking University, Karakhan closed his remarks with the words "Long live the brotherhood of the peoples of China and the Soviet Union. Long live China, independent and free from imperialism." On a similar occasion during the same week, Wellington Koo said, "Up till now it was not the Chinese Government that drew up the treaties with other Powers; they were forced on China from the outside. But it is quite different in the present case."

The Chinese had taken heart. In 1922 Chicherin had declared that China and the Soviet Union were natural allies. And there is no doubt that the impression created by the new treaty and its affirmation of Russia's sympathy for China in the struggle with the foreign Powers acted as powerful stimuli to the Chinese revolutionary movement which made history between 1924 and 1927.

Red in China goes with a wedding. At one festive function following the signing of the May 31 treaty, the counsellor of the Chinese Foreign Office said: "We are celebrating to-day the wedding of China and Soviet Russia. . . ."

*Japan and the Soviet Union* The Sino-Soviet Treaty hastened the assumption of relations between Japan and the Soviet Union. A series of other important events contributed to the same end: The catastrophic earthquake of September, 1923, weakened Japan financially and economically. She needed undisturbed peace. She could no longer pursue imperialist designs in Siberia. Apart from the fact that Chinese revolutionary developments demanded more attention. Tokyo could not afford the heavy expenditures necessary if hositility toward Moscow continued.

On April 17, 1924, the United States Senate approved the Anti-Japanese immigration bill despite the protests of Secretary Hughes. The new law offended Japan's national honor and damaged her material interests. The economic possibilities thus lost in California might, however, be found in Siberia. This American measure did much to throw Japan into the arms of the Soviet Union.

Japanese-American enmity was at its height after the Washington Disarmament Conference of 1921–2 and the anti-Immigration law of 1924. The bonds with London which the cancellation, at American insistence, of the Anglo-Japanese alliance had severed were not yet resumed. The construction of the great British naval base at Singapore caused concern in Tokyo. The United States and England worked hand in hand in a number of important fields. Japan felt isolated. Symptomatic rumors of a Franco-Japanese bloc appeared in the press. The fact that the Bolsheviks too, after years of idle expectation, now felt disillusioned about friendship with the United States, created the tie of similar psychological positions.

These changes strengthened the opposition in Japanese politics. The control of the military and naval clique was not broken but its authority began to be questioned. The national elections of May, 1924, ended with an opposition victory which testified to popular displeasure with the policy of undisguised aggression against Soviet Russia.

All these circumstances compelled the Japanese Government to regulate its relations with the Soviet Union. The final treaty was negotiated in Peking between Karakhan and Yoshizava and signed by them on January 20, 1925. It brought to a close a series of conferences which began in August, 1921.

**THE RUSSO-JAPANESE DIPLOMATIC WAR. DAIREN** Japan's role on the Asiatic mainland was perhaps the decisive factor in the Far-Eastern situation. Nothing so well illustrates Japan's political philosophy and her practical strategy in foreign affairs as her diplomatic maneuvers vis-à-vis Russia between 1921 and 1925. These took the form of prolonged and animated conferences, and disclose the temper of the Japanese mind, its attractively frank opportunism, its submission to realities, and its desire to hold too long to temporary gains on the false assumption that the longer the delay the greater the price of redemption. The first two of these conferences—in Dairen from August, 1921, to April, 1922, in Chang-Chun in 1922—ended in complete failure.

Time was on the side of Russia. Japan, anxious to put her politics on a peace-time footing, could not well continue the occupation of Siberia endlessly against the will of United States, of the Far-Eastern Republic (F.E.R.), and of Moscow. On June 19, 1922, Baron Uchida, the Japanese Foreign Minister, was still insisting that Japan could not withdraw her troops because of the necessity of protecting Japanese lives and property. Four days later, the new Kato Cabinet ordered the retirement of the Japanese occupation army from the Maritime Provinces. A few months earlier, at the Dairen Conference, Russia would have paid a high price for this victory.

The evacuation of Japanese troops from the Maritime Provinces commenced on September 3, and on the morrow a Japanese-Russian-F.E.R. Conference assembled at Chang-Chun, a station on the South Manchurian Railway, to discuss future relations and the evacuation of Northern Sakhalin. No agreement could be reached.

**JOFFE, GOTO, AND KAWAKAMI** Japan completed the evacuation of the Amur and Maritime Province in October, and on the 25th of that month F.E.R. troops entered Vladivostok. November 14, Chita requested admission into the Soviet Union; by a decree of the 15th the request was granted.

After meeting Dr. Sun Yat-sen early in the year, Joffe accepted an official invitation from Viscount Goto, the Mayor of Tokyo, to come to Japan for a cure. Goto, one of the Nippon's most influential statesmen, had always been a protagonist of Russian-Japanese co-operation. He wished to use the presence of Joffe to press his policy.

Joffe's conversations, until April 24, 1923, were altogether unofficial and unbinding. But on that day, Goto informed Joffe that

> the Japanese Government on April 20 apparently decided that it was prepared to enter a third Russo-Japanese conference on condition of the preliminary solution of two questions, (1) Nikolaievsk massacre, (2) Sakhalin, and that the Japanese Government prefers to solve the Sakhalin question by means of the purchase of Northern Sakhalin.

Joffe countered with his preliminary conditions: (1) equality in the negotiations, (2) fixing date of evacuation of Northern Sakhalin, (3) de jure recognition.

On May 6 Goto wrote Joffe explaining that the Tokyo Cabinet further desired Russian recognition of old debts to Japan, reparations for Japanese losses during the revolution, and recognition of all former treaties.

Joffe replied on May 10. The Soviet Government, he said, categorically refuses to recognize old debts, satisfy private claims, or recognize old treaties. "Russia," he added, "expresses deep regret over the unfortunate events in Nikolaievsk in March, 1920, and recognizes its material responsibility for them." Japan must, however, offer a similar expression with respect to similar events in Russia. Japan's financial claims would cancel Russian claims. Russia, Joffe declared, could sell Northern Sakhalin only at a very high price; he therefore suggested the formation of a mixed Russo-Japanese company to exploit the oil- and coal-bearing lands and the forests of Northern Sakhalin. Japan, finally, must evacuate the upper half of Sakhalin island.

Japan felt that unofficial negotiations between unofficial persons had now accomplished as much as they could. She accordingly suggested unofficial negotiations between official persons, and Joffe and Toshitsume Kawakami received corresponding authorization from their respective States. They held twelve meetings. What follows is from the official protocols and from Kawakami's detailed summary of the negotiations which he compiled and sent to Joffe on August 3, 1923.

Japan wished to buy Northern Sakhalin for 150,000,000 yen. Instead of refusing outright, Joffe asked 1,000,000,000 gold rubles, and later, quite arbitrarily, 1,500,000,000 gold rubles. At the session of June 29, one day after the opening of the conference, Kawakami therefore inquired whether the Russian Government agreed to grant Japan concessions in Northern Sakhalin.

*Session of June 30.*—Kawakami demanded payment of Japanese claims for losses in Nikolaievsk between March 12 and May 27, 1920.

> Joffe declared that if the question is put in this manner he will immediately close the negotiations. The attempt to make the occupation of North Sakhalin a guarantee for the solution of the Nikolaievsk question was the cause of the rupture of the Chang-Chun Conference. Mr. Joffe continues without change to present his former view that the occupation of Russian territory as a guarantee of the solution of any question is absolutely inadmissible.

Kawakami explained that Japan does not ask a blanket concession for all Northern Sakhalin, but a series of separate concessions.

*Session of July 2.*—Kawakami declared that in his personal opinion Japan would not evacuate Northern Sakhalin before the opening of an official conference. Japan, he said, proposed concessions as an alternative to sale.

*Session of July 9.*—Kawakami stated that the draft which Joffe had presented of his Government's regrets over the Nikolaievsk events had made a good impression on the Japanese Government which, nevertheless, insisted on its own draft. The Japanese delegate announced that the question of Nikolaievsk claims would be settled in a manner satisfactory to Russia, but asked a hasty solution of the Sakhalin problem. Joffe affirmed that the Sakhalin concession could easily be settled. Kawakami suggested that Japan be granted a fifty-five to ninety-nine-year lease to the oil, coal, and forest resources of Northern Sakhalin. These, in turn, would be transferred by the Japanese Government to a Japanese company.

*Sessions of July 13, July 18, and July 20* were devoted almost exclusively to debating the draft of Russia's official regrets over the Nikolaievsk occurrences.

*Session of July 24.*—Kawakami declared he had failed to convince Count Uchida to accept Joffe's draft.

*Session of July 31.*—Joffe announced that he had received instructions from his Government to discontinue the unofficial negotiations and to commence official conferences if Japan voluntarily announced in advance her intention of evacuating Northern Sakhalin.

Japan refused and the conference was suspended.

**KARAKHAN AND YOSHIZAVA** After these failures, Russia and Japan remained as far as ever from agreement and de jure recognition. But then came the earthquake of September, 1923, the anti-immigration bill in Washington of April, 1924, and the formation of international political constellations unfavorable to Nippon. Japanese fishing interests demanded a settlement that would enable them to bring sea food to their country from Kamchatka and other parts of the Soviet coast. Japanese coal and oil companies urged an agreement that would enable them to exploit the riches of Northern Sakhalin on a permanent contractual basis. Day by day, Soviet Russia grew stronger. Her international position improved, and statesmen in Tokyo were beginning to feel that the longer the bargain was delayed the worse it would be. Objectively, in fact, Japan certainly lost very much by signing a treaty with Moscow in January, 1925, instead of in 1922 or 1923. She gained nothing from the delay except heavy military expenditures, resentment in Russia, and the reinforcement of the opposition at home.

Karakhan made advances to Yoshizava, the Japanese minister in Peking, as soon as he arrived in China in September, 1924. Yet it was not until May 15, 1924, that the Soviet and Japanese delegations in Peking exchanged credentials.

The only real issue was Northern Sakhalin. Regrets over the Nikolaievsk events were needed by the Japanese Government for the sake of prestige and to justify the claim that it had occupied Sakhalin to avenge the so-called Nikolaievsk massacre which, the Bolsheviks declared, took place when the Red Army had not yet advanced within hundreds of miles of the town, but for which Moscow would apologize because it attached no importance to formal matters of "national honor" and because it was anxious to establish normal relations with Japan.

Northern Sakhalin was an economic necessity to Japan. Japan was a big and growing industrial and military power. She needed petroleum and coal for her factories, army, navy, and shipping. But her own petrol wells yielded no more than one-third of national requirements, and the supplementing of the supply by purchases from the United States, or even from the Dutch East Indies, Burma, and Persia, had its obvious political and economic disadvantages.[5] Tokyo had accordingly long cast a covetous glance at unprotected Russian Sakhalin, and in 1920 the opportunity presented itself. Now, in 1924, the shifting of positions on the international stage precluded the retention of the occupied territory. Nevertheless, Japan intended to exact the highest possible price for the surrender of her de facto possession. Unable to buy the territory, she wished to acquire exclusive rights to everything it contained.

Debts rarely formed the subject of discussion between Karakhan and Yoshizava. Both felt that they represented little live interest. Nor did Japan's demand for the recognition of all old treaties obstruct the negotiations. Mos-

[5] For more detailed treatment of this subject, see *Oil Imperialism*, by Louis Fischer. (London, 1926). Chapter VII, "The United States, Japan, and Russia."

cow rejected the general demand but consented with some reservations to recognize the Portsmouth Treaty by which, after the end of the Russo-Japanese War, Japan acquired far-reaching territorial, economic and political advantages. Tokyo no longer even insisted on an official apology for the Nikolaievsk events. The only issue remained Northern Sakhalin.

Negotiations dragged out for months, and Moscow gained the impression that Japan was "sparring for time" until unfavorable weather conditions in frozen Sakhalin would prevent evacuation for another year. Meanwhile, so the Soviet version ran, Japan speculated that some sad turn in Russian foreign relations might enable Tokyo to strike a better bargain.

On July 11, 1924, Yoshizava undertook the long trip to Northern Sakhalin. Officially, he would examine personally the possibilities of evacuation. But Karakhan believed that Japan was procrastinating. He aired his thoughts in a letter to Dr. Sun Yat-sen.

> Japan [the Soviet ambassador wrote] is manifesting irresoluteness and is wavering. On the one hand, they will not climb down from their claims, while on the other they are afraid of insisting on them resolutely for they know that in such an event the negotiations will be broken up. And so they prefer to drag on, ever deferring the decisive moment. A short-sighted policy indeed, for every day will accrue to our benefit, not to the Japanese.[6]

Yoshizava returned from Sakhalin on August 4, and on the next day he was closeted with Karakhan for four hours. The following day they met again, after which Karakhan stated to journalists that "we are now further from agreement than ever." He explained why in an interview which appeared in the Moscow *Izvestia* of October 10.

> During the last few days, [he said] the Soviet Government declared its readiness to give Japan enormous concessions . . . forty per cent of all oilfields in Northern Sakhalin. . . . But Japan insists on our giving her eight districts of her own choice and which, before the Japanese occupation, were almost the only ones containing oil. . . . Japan offers to pay the Soviet

[6] The Dr. Sun-Karakhan correspondence, much of which will be quoted in chapters that follow, was obtained by the writer from Karakhan's personal and secret files.

Union a 5 to 15 per cent royalty on petroleum production. . . . We insist on 10 per cent, rising to a maximum of 15 per cent with rising production.

**SAKHALIN OIL CONCESSION** Instead of an official declaration, Karakhan expressed his personal regrets over the events in Nikolaievsk; the Japanese Government pledged itself by the terms of the treaty to commence evacuation of Northern Sakhalin as soon as climatic conditions permitted and to complete it by May 15, 1925. On these preliminary conditions, the Soviet Government promised, in Protocol B attached to the treaty, to grant Japan oil and coal concessions in Soviet Sakhalin within five months after the complete withdrawal of the Japanese forces.

By the stipulations of the treaty, amplified by the detailed concessions contracts signed in Moscow on December 14, 1925, Japanese companies nominated by the Japanese Government obtained the legal right to mine petroleum on 50 per cent of the oil-bearing lands exploited by the Japanese during the occupation, and to conduct explorations on additional 1000 square versts of territory on the eastern shore of Northern Sakhalin. The Soviet Government might grant the remaining half of the petroliferous districts to other foreign concessionaries; in which case, however, Japanese companies must receive equal opportunities to enter bids.

Instead of fifty-five to ninety-nine years as the Japanese had urged, both the oil and coal concessions were for a period of from forty to fifty years.

In addition to an annual rental of 4 per cent of production, the concessionaires paid the Soviet Government a 5 per cent royalty on a total annual oil production of 30,000 metric tons or less. For every added 10,000 metric tons the royalty rose 0.25 per cent until a yearly output of 430,000 tons was reached, after which a 15 per cent royalty was to be collected. The concessionaire paid the Soviet Government a money fee equal to forty-five per cent of the value of all gusher oil and a royalty on gas varying from 10 to 35 per cent according to petrol content.

The royalty on coal production varied from 5 to 8 per cent.

Soviet labor laws were to be obeyed; 50 per cent of the technical staff and 75 per cent of the unskilled workers were to be of Soviet citizenship.

Japanese oil production in Northern Sakhalin yielded, according to official figures, 8,400 tons in 1923–4, 11,870 tons in 1924–5, 16,261 tons in 1925–6, 59,838 tons in 1926–7, and 92,012 tons in 1927–8. About 85 per cent of the coal mined was exported to Japan.

*U.S.A. and U.S.S.R.* In their somewhat schematic approach to American foreign policy, and in their ignorance of American psychology and conditions—for few leading Bolsheviks knew the United States—the Moscow statesmen believed that a rapprochement between themselves and Tokyo would frighten Washington into adopting a less hostile attitude to the Soviet Union. They were mistaken. The United States pursued the same tactics of consistent enmity.

The Bolsheviks welcomed the announcement in January, 1925, of Charles E. Hughes's retirement from the State Department as from March 4. Hughes was their *bête noire* whose caricatures were as popular in the Soviet Press between 1922 and 1925 as Austen Chamberlain's in a later day. They drew encouragement from his resignation, little realizing the continuity of United States foreign policy under different Secretaries of State and in successive administrations.

**RUSSIA'S FINANCIAL OBLIGATIONS TO AMERICAN GOVERNMENT** There was no prewar Russian debt to the United States Government. But during the World War, the United States Treasury opened a credit to the Provisional Kerensky government. On November 13, 1917, six days after the Bolsheviks came to power, the sum drawn amounted to $187,729,750. It was drawn by Kerensky to fight the World War. The Bolsheviks never took anything from the United States Treasury. The war materials bought with American money went, in part, to Kolchak and other enemies of the Soviet regime. Part of the American funds were spent by the Kerensky ambassador Boris Bakhmetiev in supporting anti-Bolshevik efforts in the United States and Europe. Now this sum is regarded as a Bolshevik debt to the United States. The irony becomes more striking when one remembers that long after the fall of Kerensky, Bakhmetiev shipped ammunition purchased with United States Government credits to Black Sea and Pacific ports for use against the Red Army.

Together with several negligible items, the total American Government claim on Russia is $192,601,297, on which approximately $96,000,000 in interest had accumulated by the middle of 1929.[7] (Interest amounts at the rate of approximately $8,000,000 annually.)

**CZARIST DEBTS TO U.S. BANKS** In addition to this government-to-government war debt, Russia borrowed during the war from American financial institutions. Prior to America's entry into the World War, the National City Bank or syndicates headed by it granted the Imperial Government a $5,000,000 credit in 1914, $50,000,000 and $25,000,000 in 1916, and $11,000,000 in 1917, thus making Russia's private war debt to the United States $91,000,000 without interest.[8]

The total Russian war debt to American citizens and to the American Government, without interest, amounts therefore to $91,000,000 plus $188,000,000 or approximately $279,000,000.[9]

To this sum must be added $10,000,000 which is the extent of Russian Government borrowing from American banks before the war. Accordingly, Russia's public debt, war and pre-war, to the American Government and American banks, equals $289,000,000, without interest.

**PRIVATE PROPERTY CLAIMS** There are also American private property claims. These, naturally, permit of no final estimate. A Soviet publication puts the figure at $61,000,000.[1] One American estimate goes as high as $300,000,000. The largest of American companies which operated in pre-war Russia, the International Harvester Company, has apparently written its Russian assets off its books as a permanent loss—it pays no income tax on them—and is selling agricultural machinery to the Soviet Government on long-term credit. Other concerns, like the General Electric Company, the Standard Oil of New York and the Vacuum Oil Company, whose Russian properties

[7] New York *Current History,* February 1926, p. 628.

[8] Harvey E. Fisk: *The Inter-Ally Debts,* Bankers Trust Company Publications. (New York-Paris, 1924), p. 145.

[9] *Ibid.,* p. 111.

[1] *Ibid.,* p. 298.

suffered nationalization, have probably forgone their claims on the Soviet State and are doing business with it.

The Singer Manufacturing Company had invested approximately $25,000,000 in Czarist Russia. But in this case it is questionable whether any government can be held responsible for the sewing machines sold to the remotest villages of the empire (one sees them up in the heights of the Caucasus) on instalment plan and not paid for on account of war, revolution and other force majeure. Further claims, amounting to $250,000 each, could be presented by the Otis Elevating Company, the Babcock and Wilson Corporation, the New York Life Insurance Society, and the Equitable Life Assurance Company.

American property in Russia was never officially nationalized. In the summer of 1918 Soviet Russia and Germany were engaged in negotiating the supplementary treaties provided for in the Brest Litovsk Treaty and ultimately signed in August. The Germans demanded compensation for damages done to the property of their nationals during the World War, and it was generally assumed that the Bolsheviks could only acquiesce. Many foreign and Russian property-holders immediately commenced transferring their titles to German citizens in the hope that they too would receive indemnification under the terms of the forthcoming agreement. To cope with this situation the Soviet Government hurriedly issued its Nationalization Decree on June 28. But at that time, Colonel Robins was conducting negotiations with Lenin regarding American economic assistance, and Lenin accordingly agreed that American property would be exempt from the rulings of the new act. Subsequently, the Russians took over American plants because they were not being operated, and in the case of the Harvester Company's factory at Lubertsi, Moscow several times urged the owners to return before it actually assumed possession of the works. Legally, therefore, American property is in a different category from that of other foreigners—a point which may have tremendous bearing on a future settlement.

Clearly, the private claims of Americans were neither large nor serious, and could not constitute an obstacle to normal relations.

Japan had consistently ignored a Russian public war debt amounting to 233,337,000 gold rubles, according to the Bolsheviks, or $152,000,000 according to a Bankers Trust Company compilation. Italy had never raised the question of a similar war-time liability of 60,000,000 rubles. The Germans, in the Rapallo Treaty, cancelled their claims against Russia. In the MacDonald-Rakovsky treaty of 1924, England's immense war credits to Russia were "placed on cold storage." France, too, showed a readiness to forget war debts. The United States Government debt, which is almost a World War debt, should therefore present no difficulties.

As against American claims on Russia, the Bolsheviks have counter-claims on the United States Government. American troops intervened in Russia and fought against the Red Army. American expeditionary forces in Murmansk, Archangel, and Siberia demonstrably caused damage to Russian property and were responsible for the loss of Russian lives. The intervention took place without a declaration of war. It was not undertaken for American national defense. Its illegality was not open to dispute.

The sum of Soviet counter-claims against the United States is not known. Since the Americans always constituted component parts of international expeditions their total would indeed be difficult to compute. But it doubtless ran into tens of millions of dollars.

At the Genoa Conference and in the Anglo-Russian negotiations of 1924 it was implicitly agreed that the Bolsheviks would drop their counter-claims if the other countries dropped their World War government-to-government debts. The Kerensky debt was a war debt. If it were cancelled by Soviet counter-claims, the total of official American financial claims on the Soviet Union would be ridiculously small.

**COMMUNIST PROPAGANDA** Before Mr. Dwight Morrow went to Mexico City as Coolidge's ambassador, high State Department officials had convinced him that the Russian Bolsheviks were conducting propaganda in Mexico. After a few months' experience at his post he knew this was not so. Mr. Frank B. Kellogg likewise believed that Moscow sent $200,000 to Sandino in Nicaragua. But it is over-simplification to explain revolts against one's authority by outside influence.

The United States is the world's most prosperous nation. Its working class is the most conservative. Its Communist

Party is proportionately the smallest. The Russians would be fools to expect a revolution in the United States or to waste money in fostering one. There is no proof that they do. "Revolutions are not carried in suitcases," Karl Radek once said to the writer. "Revolutions cannot be imported. They grow." Agitators reap only in fruitful soil. They find American fields quite barren.

*Unchanging France* In 1922 French policy, supported by American influences, torpedoed the Genoa and Hague Conferences. Poincaré wished at all costs to prevent a rapprochement between England and Russia. Correspondingly, Poincaré exchanged cordial telegrams with Chicherin just when the Curzon ultimatum crisis was at its height in 1923, and promised to return the Russian fleet surrendered to France by Wrangel. Poincaré mentioned this in an interview with Chicherin in 1927. The French Premier had intended the move as a demonstration; it represented an attempt to erect a barrier between London and Moscow. Yet in 1922 Poincaré pronounced his blessing over an anti-Soviet grouping of world oil companies formed in Paris, and the entente of sympathies which had grown up at Genoa between Deterding and Paris continued to bear the fruit of hostility to Bolshevik Russia.

Poincaré had inherited an impossible Chamber with a liberal sprinkling of war heroes, aces, and pilots who prejudiced the situation against normal relations with the Soviets. The Bloc Nationale dominated the scene, and it detested the new Russia.

French antagonism to Moscow found numerous expressions in 1924. In March, Paris ratified the Paris Protocol which assigned Bessarabia to Rumania; at the same time and until July, the French Government sought to obstruct the Russo-Chinese Treaty.

The most revealing French anti-Soviet measure during 1924, however, was Poincaré's attempt to interfere in the Anglo-Soviet Treaty negotiations. Speaking in the French Senate on April 9 in reply to de Monzie, Poincaré said:

> On February 16th [a fortnight after British recognition. –L.F.] I sent a note to the British ambassador. . . . The nature of a treaty which would regulate the controversial questions concerning British subjects who have interests in Russia would necessarily affect the fate of French interests in that country. . . . As far as debts are concerned there is a moral and material solidarity among all foreign creditors. Most-favored treat-

ment applied to some of them would damage the interests of others. . . . We believe to be within our rights in asking the British Government to take account of this situation in the coming negotiations.[2]

Two days after the negotiations commenced, it was stated politely, in the indirect language of diplomacy, that the French ambassador "Comte de St. Aulaire was instructed not to refuse such an invitation if given."[3] The *Guardian* disapproved, as did the MacDonald Cabinet. "The Anglo-Russian conference is a private affair," wrote the paper, and added,

> Historically it is a commonplace that the Genoa and Hague Conferences . . . failed precisely because France refused her cooperation, and the present position, in which the several Allies make their own individual arrangements with Russia, is primarily the result of French diplomacy.

Here the traditional French policy of "parallel lines" and "common action" vis-à-vis the Russian debt situation had again come into evidence. Poincaré realized that MacDonald might now negotiate a debt-paying convention with the Kremlin which would, necessarily, make the French bondholders more persistent in their demand for a similar accord. He accordingly wished to enter into the MacDonald-Rakovsky talks. It would be the best means of curbing the exuberance of the Labor Cabinet for an agreement. "France," said Rakovsky, "tried to participate in the Anglo-Soviet talks with the purpose of changing London into a second Genoa."[4]

Poincaré's advances were repulsed, but the press at the time occasionally hinted at French and American démarches in London during the Anglo-Soviet Conference. How far they determined its outcome is not known.

On June 14, 1924, an Herriot Cabinet came into office; the Left Bloc had carried off a victory in the National elections. Poincaré was defeated. But although President Millerand left his post as a result, the Radical swing was not sufficiently strong to put Painlevé in his place. Doumergue succeeded Millerand; the Conservatives had not suffered complete failure. This indecisiveness of Herriot's triumph was reflected in his relations toward Moscow.

[2] Paris *Temps,* April 11, 1924.
[3] *Manchester Guardian,* April 11, 1924.
[4] Paris *L'Humanité,* May 3, 1924.

The Radicals did not want enmity, but they could not establish friendship.

**HERRIOT AND SOVIET RUSSIA** Herriot, Mayor of Lyon, had visited Russia in 1922 as guest of the Soviet Government. On his return to France, he opened a spirited campaign for de jure recognition of the Soviet Government. In August, 1923, Senator de Monzie appeared in Moscow and subsequently seconded Herriot's efforts toward a rapprochement with the Bolsheviks. Yet the Herriot Cabinet's declaration of policy contained only a short equivocal paragraph on Soviet recognition—and recognition was withheld until October 28, 1924, four and a half months after Herriot became Premier.

Rakovsky saw Herriot in London in the latter part of June, 1924. The French Prime Minister promised the return of the Russian fleet taken by Baron Wrangel from the Black Sea and interned in Bizerta, Tunis. He also promised recognition—but why the hurry, he asked. The end of July or the middle of August would be a more propitious period. Herriot was not quite certain of the reception de jure recognition of the Soviets would receive in the French Parliament. He wished to wait until the Senate and Chamber rose for summer vacation. But before recognition could be granted, Herriot declared, his Government required some guarantee for the French holders of pre-war Russian bonds.

Opposition to Soviet recognition likewise came from the French Socialists, especially from Renaudel, who frequently pleaded with Herriot on behalf of the deposed Menshevik Government of Georgia which had established itself in Paris and obtained a kind of semi-official status there.

In September and October progress was registered, and in the middle of October, de Monzie went to Dover to discuss with Rakovsky the text and terms of the French announcement of recognition. The Quai d'Orsay had proposed to omit "de jure" from the note. Rakovsky insisted and won. He made certain that ambassadors would be exchanged instead of chargé d'affaires as England had done and as some French circles intended. He likewise ironed out the problem of Georgia. In a private letter dated October 25, de Monzie made all these concessions to

Rakovsky, and the next day he wired the drafted French note to Rakovsky for approval.

During the same conversations and written correspondence, de Monzie asked Rakovsky whether Moscow would agree to accept Jean Herbette, of the Paris *Temps,* as ambassador. Herriot had probably planned to send de Monzie as envoy. But after Rakovsky gave his written approval of Herbette, the Premier had been anticipated.

On October 28 Herriot addressed a telegram to Premier Rykov and Chicherin notifying them of the fact of de jure recognition, suggesting the exchange of ambassadors, and expressing the wish that delegates be appointed to discuss economic issues.[5]

French recognition was granted on the eve of the victory of the Conservatives in the British General Election, and a few days after the publication of the "Zinoviev" letter. This was partly coincidental. But Herriot and de Monzie probably felt that if they delayed any longer, the international situation might have made it more difficult to establish relations with Moscow. Herriot, moreover, hoped to strengthen the moral position of MacDonald and thus reinforce his own.

The Soviet Government immediately designated L. B. Krassin, theretofore Commissar of Foreign Trade, its ambassador to Paris, while France sent Herbette.

**FRANCO-SOVIET PROSPECTS** France needed the antebellum Franco-Russian entente as a check on the Kaiser's power and because it opened a rich field for French capital in Russia. The Czar wanted the union because it introduced into his country vast billions which, if not always wisely and profitably invested, at least served as political mortar.

Without the aid of Czarist Russia, France might have been crushed. Russian assistance meant life and safety to the Third Republic. The Armistice and the Peace, however, introduced fundamental changes. It created a new Poland to check Germany. Poland became the stoutest pillar of the French continental system. And, as between Poland and Soviet Russia, Paris preferred the former al-

[5] Exchange of telegrams, see *L'Europe Nouvelle* (Paris, November 1, 1924), and (Russian text) *International Politics,* by Kluchnikov and Sabanin (Moscow, 1928, III, 329–30).

though on several occasions attractive offers were made to the Bolsheviks. Germany, moreover, had been deprived of valuable territories, shorn of her army and fleet, separated from rich sources of raw materials, and subjected to foreign control. France had less to fear. To the extent that the menace continued, Poland was more trusted a partner than Bolshevik Russia. Czarist Russia and Republican Poland would consent to secret combinations, political pacts, etc. But the Communists were undependable.

On the financial side, France could no longer export tremendous sums of gold francs, and the new economic regime in the Soviet Republic no longer allowed free rein to foreign investments.

The special circumstances which favored Franco-Russian friendship before the revolution had largely disappeared.

Painlevé once said to Chicherin that although France now could be of more help to Russia than Russia to France, a reversal of circumstances may some day set in. Soviet insistence that Moscow will always be found on the side of the weaker encourages such expectations. And, although all these hopes and plans require antecedent developments in Europe and especially in Russia, even the beginnings of which are not yet visible, they undoubtedly operated during a short period—between 1924 and 1926—to improve relations between Moscow and Paris. It was a vague, indecisive improvement. But the conception of a future Russia that could be of more use to France than Poland always hovers in the background of Franco-Soviet relations.

**POLITICS AND DEBTS** From 1919 to 1924 France's opposition to a Soviet debt settlement gave her a free hand against Moscow in military and diplomatic matters. In 1919 and 1920 French leaders repeatedly declared that they would "enter no contract with crime," and several even promised that France would never recognize the Bolsheviks. The rejection of Russian debt-payment offers in 1919 and 1920 was not dictated by the interests of the French peasantry and petty bourgeoisie who held Czarist bonds. Poincaré's tactics at Genoa and The Hague reflected equally little interest in the purses of small bondholders, but gave evidence of his concern for the former private property owners of France and other nations.

The problem of Russia's foreign obligations divided into the question of loans, credits, etc., and of confiscated private property. An agreement on debts presented fewer difficulties. The Bolsheviks, however, were not prepared to restitute property. This had been the stumbling-block in all economic discussions between Moscow and capitalist states. This explains why, once negotiations with the United States were initiated, a settlement was relatively easy. The original declaration of debt repudiation remains, yet practically it has been cancelled by numerous Soviet offers to recognize and pay. Here expediency governs the situation. But nationalization is fundamental to the Soviet system. The Bolsheviks would not permit the return of all the former owners. Emphasis on private property, therefore, has in the past and must in the future obstruct a settlement.

The absence of immediate political possibilities and the difficulties of a financial settlement reduced Herriot's de jure recognition of the Soviet Union to a minor event in France although it was loudly acclaimed in Moscow. But the Bolsheviks, too, realized that the road to an economic agreement would be long and rocky. Chicherin in a speech quoted by *Izvestia* of November 12, 1924, declared that "without a loan we will not satisfy any claims" from France. He knew, however, how little exportable capital France then disposed of. The Commissar accordingly suggested that Russia was prepared to grant concessions to French citizens. And where would they find the money for such enterprises?

Soon Ambassador Krassin became convinced that there would be no loan. "There can be no question of it at present," he said to the *Quotidien* of December 5, yet loan negotiations subsequently made some progress.

The defeat of MacDonald in October, 1924, prejudiced Herriot's attempt to agree with Soviet Russia. A new British Cabinet had been swept into power on the strength of its anti-Soviet platform. France could not remain indifferent to the change. Early in December, Mr. Austen Chamberlain, the new British Foreign Secretary, visited the French Premier in Paris. They reached an understanding on a number of important problems. "With respect to Soviet Russia," said the official communiqué, "it was agreed that both governments should practice a common policy." Measures must be undertaken, they decided, to combat Bolshevik propaganda in Europe and the colonies.[6]

For France and Britain to carry out a "common policy" towards Russia meant that Herriot had adopted the policy of Chamberlain and Churchill.

During several years, Poincaré endeavored to establish a united Franco-British front vis-à-vis the Bolsheviks. He failed. But where he had failed, Chamberlain succeeded.

The Chamberlain-Herriot interview marked a milestone in European history; it turned the first spade for Locarno. On December 7, 1924, the *Matin* published a statement which seems too prophetic to be less than official:

> We must, say the British, anticipate a situation when it will be necessary to break with the Soviets and exert pressure on them. Russia has become the Soviet Union, which means that she is militarily less powerful than Czarist Russia but she is more dangerous on account of the contagion of her doctrines. . . . Lloyd George and MacDonald thought that the Soviets could be trusted. The new minister [Mr. Austen Chamberlain. —L.F.] does not think so. He does not propose to declare war, but he considers them as an enemy most to be feared in many parts of the world.

Chamberlain and Herriot agreed on many international questions. They discussed Turkey, North African questions —Morocco and Egypt, the Near East, the Mediterranean; there was a quid pro quo on a wide front. Chamberlain offered aid to France in the German theater. And then the *Matin,* having explained the situation with respect to Moscow, adds,

> It is logical therefore, that in offering this alliance against Germany which he [Chamberlain.—L.F.] does not think he need fear, he asks for the support of France against the adversary who worries him in his possessions in Africa and Asia.

Britain would side with France in Central Europe if France endorsed London's Russian policy. But in 1925, after the adoption of the Dawes Plan and when Europe entered upon economic stabilization, an alliance against Germany appeared crude. It would give France much and England very little. A statesman like Chamberlain preferred an alliance with Germany which would allay the fears of France and permit Germany as well as France to join England against Russia. This was the germ idea of Locarno. Apart from French opposition to such a

[6] *Quotidien,* December 6, 1924.

British plan, everything depended on the attitude of Germany and on her loyalty to the Rapallo Treaty. Downing Street accordingly turned its attention to the Wilhelmstrasse's relations with the Kremlin.

# 18

# LOCARNO OR RAPALLO?

At Locarno Russia . . . takes no part. But Russia is more likely to influence the ultimate result, if not the actual conditions, of a Pact than more than one of the Governments represented at the Conference.—Robert Crozier Long in *The Fortnightly Review,* November, 1925.

BEGINNING with the World War Armistice, Germany felt that in foreign affairs she must depend on England's aid against the designs of France. The Wilhelmstrasse oriented itself on England. The Rapallo Treaty represented only the dawn of a change, yet when Lloyd George raised his storm against it, Walther Rathenau asked the Bolsheviks to let the treaty fall. Wirth and Rantzau, on the other hand, regarded a purely Western orientation, and that on Great Britain alone, as unhealthy. Yet the fear of England remained, and when, early in 1923, Chicherin explained to Chancellor Cuno, Foreign Minister Rosenberg, and Maltzan at a luncheon in Berlin that it might be to Germany's advantage to co-operate with Russia in Turkey, Persia, and Afghanistan, Maltzan said, "Yes, but not against England." Even Maltzan, therefore, felt the necessity of first considering London's sensibilities.

The invasion of the Ruhr opened a new page. Curzon had not been able to prevent the French occupation. Certain circles at Berlin even suspected that Downing Street did not wish to ruffle Poincaré for the sake of German good will. It became clear that German foreign policy could not neglect the possibilities of better relations with France.

**THE DAWES PLAN AND THE LEAGUE** The Dawes Plan went into effect on September 1, 1924. On September 23, 1924, the German Foreign Office sent identical memoranda to ten governments in which it stated that "The German Government believes that now, especially after the proceedings and result of the London (Dawes) Conference, the basis exists for fruitful co-operation in the League of Nations."[1] A definite application for membership was made on December 12, 1924. The Dawes Plan signified the desire of France and England to collect reparations rationally. The effect was a greater readiness on the part of Germany to co-operate with the League and with France.

Late in September, 1924, Germany asked to enter the League. Early in December, Herriot and Chamberlain met in Paris and decided on a "common front toward Russia" and the co-ordination of policies with respect to Germany. As an outgrowth of this understanding, "in the early part of 1925 . . . the old discussions for an Anglo-French Treaty of Guarantee which had figured both in 1919 and again in 1922 during the ill-fated Conference at Cannes reappeared." In the three-power pact proposed, "Great Britain would guarantee to France and Belgium the inviolability of such territories as had been vested in those countries by the Treaty of Versailles."[2]

The new pact would reinforce the Treaty of Versailles. Nevertheless, Germany offered to join it.

Germany's offer of February 9, 1925, to join the Guarantee Pact has been styled "spontaneous," and yet, according to Professor Alexander, "Lord D'Abernon was no doubt partly responsible." Lord D'Abernon, the British ambassador in Berlin, earned the title of "The Father of Locarno." There is indeed every reason to assert that the German suggestion followed a friendly intimation on his part that it would be welcomed in London. D'Abernon found valiant support in Herr von Schubert, Stresemann's Anglophile State-Secretary.

The Bolsheviks believed that the Locarno Pacts were directed against the Soviet Union. "The entire guarantee pact policy of England," Chicherin stated in an interview with M. Mueller-Jabusch of the *Berliner Tageblatt* on October 2, 1925—on the eve of Locarno—"is an integral part of her basic anti-Soviet activity. For this reason we note

[1] First published by the *Berliner Tageblatt* on September 23, 1925.

[2] F. Alexander: *From Paris to Locarno and After* (London, 1928), p. 105.

with increasing concern how Germany more and more enters the wake of British plans." Great Britain, he said, looks on Germany as a "chess-piece in her diplomatic game" against the Soviet Union.

**BRITISH REBUFFS TO THE BOLSHEVIKS** "Not once but many times," Chicherin declared in the same interview, "we proposed to England to examine our points of dispute diplomatically or at a conference. England refused . . ."

The Baldwin-Chamberlain Government, helped into office by the "Zinoviev" letter, scrapped the Anglo-Soviet treaty signed by MacDonald and Rakovsky, and rejected any suggestion to modify it or renew negotiations or to appoint an ambassador to Moscow.

Speaking on March 4, 1925, in Tiflis at a session of the Central Executive Committee of the Soviet Union, Chicherin announced that he was ready for negotiations with England. A reference to this speech during the Parliamentary question hour on March 11, 1925, found the Ministerial bench consistently unconciliatory. In fact, Cabinet members were indulging in attacks on Russia. Sir William Johnson-Hicks, for instance, stated in an address on March 9 that "Bolshevism had laid Russia in ruins, and declared endless war on the rest of the world."[3] Winston S. Churchill, Chancellor of the Exchequer, in a speech on November 28, 1925, referred to the "dark power of Moscow" where "we had what we had never had before, a band of cosmopolitan conspirators gathered from the underworlds of the great cities of Europe and America."[4] Lord Birkenhead had put it on June 20, "a junta of assassins and plunderers."[5]

Towards the middle of 1925 British official circles commenced to be distressed by the Chinese revolutionary situation, and accusations against Soviet activity multiplied. In the House of Commons veiled hints were heard of the possibility of serious developments in Anglo-Soviet relations.

**THE PACT "BECAUSE OF RUSSIA"** While the discussions leading to the system of Locarno were in progress,

[3] *Morning Post,* March 10, 1925.
[4] *Morning Post,* November 30, 1925.
[5] *Ibid.,* June 22, 1925.

the *Chicago Tribune* published what purported to be a secret memorandum setting forth His Majesty's Government's views on European security. A few months later, May 10, 1925, the New York *World* reprinted the document. The next day Ramsay MacDonald questioned Austen Chamberlain about it. The Foreign Secretary did not deny its authenticity. He merely stated that it had not been circulated by his department, but it was clear from his careful statement that the memorandum was official. The *Survey of International Affairs* for 1925, published by the Royal Institute of International Affairs—a well-connected British body—likewise reviews the contents of the paper without, however, making direct reference to it.[6] Although Chamberlain assured Stresemann and Briand at Locarno in October, 1925, that he knew nothing about the memorandum, the chancellories of Europe regarded the document as bona fide.

The British Government memorandum began with Russia.

> Europe [it read] to-day is divided into three main elements, namely, the victors, the vanquished, and Russia.
>
> The Russian problem, that incessant though shapeless menace, can be stated only as a problem; it is impossible to foresee what effect the development of Russia will have on the future stability of Europe. . . . Russia is not, therefore, in a sense, a factor of stability; she is, indeed, the most menacing of our uncertainties, and it must be in spite of Russia, perhaps even because of Russia, that a policy of security must be framed.

It is not without significance that "Augur," a name that veils M. Poliakov, an anti-Bolshevik Russian who was considered by many a mouthpiece of the British Foreign Office, wrote in almost similar style in the *Fortnightly Review* of May, 1925. "European security," he declared, "must be found without Russia and perhaps against her." Chamberlain made it "because of Russia"; "Augur"—"against her." In his *Germany in Europe* (London, June, 1927, p. 12) Augur quotes verbatim from the British Memorandum without using quotation marks.

**THE POSITION OF FRANCE** France, unlike England, did not always wish to exclude Russia from her political combinations. Herriot had recognized the Soviet Union in October, 1924. He and de Monzie, and after he resigned

[6] *Op. cit.*, pp. 7–8.

on April 10, 1925, Premier Painlevé and Foreign Minister Briand likewise attempted a political rapprochement with Moscow. French statesmen hinted to Rakovsky on several occasions that their interest in Poland was as an ally against Germany but not against Russia. In this respect, France had executed a volte face after 1921. Until then she did not believe in the permanence of the Soviet regime. But after the defeat of Poincaré's Ruhr policy and the gradual evolution of England's policy of better relations with Germany which culminated in the Dawes Plan and Locarno, France looked for new friends on the Continent.

Poincaré was opposed to Locarno. It would, he believed, make England the arbiter between Germany and France and strengthen Germany while hampering French freedom of action. The parlous state of the French Treasury showed the Quai d'Orsay the wisdom of an agreement with Germany but not on British terms. Briand knew and in private conversation made no secret of his view that Locarno was an instrument of British foreign policy, while Caillaux, in office and as an outsider, inclined to the idea of a continental bloc between France, Germany and the Soviet Union.

The German pact proposal, British in inspiration and philosophy, won sharp disapproval in France. For the pact promised to secure France's eastern frontier against aggression, but not Poland's western frontier. France, says the *Survey of International Affairs,* 1925, "was ready to reject the German offer altogether, unless Great Britain consented to extend her proffered guarantee to the East." Chamberlain did not consent, while Germany would agree to the Versailles frontier in the Rhineland, but as to Poland she offered only to submit to arbitration all questions of dispute. She would not go to war to modify her boundary with Poland, yet she did not despair of changing it by peaceful means.[7]

On the West, Germany bowed to superior force. France, Germany knew, would never relinquish Alsace and Lorraine. Lorraine, moreover, was extremely important to Rhenish industry and economic co-operation required a preliminary burying of political swords.

[7] For the complete text of the Locarno Treaties see *Survey of International Affairs,* 1925, by C. A. Macartney and others. (London, 1928). Vol. II, Appendix 1.

Eastern problems, on the other hand, aroused stronger feelings. The corridor cut off East Prussia completely from the Fatherland. Danzig, the Germans argued, was a German city. Upper Silesia had been divided unfairly and in defiance of the plebiscite. All Germany vehemently opposed any solution involving permanent renunciation of these territories.

For this very reason, France endeavored all the more to obtain a German guarantee for Poland. Poland constituted part of the French system of continental defense. France could defend herself with facility against a disarmed and weakened Germany without British assistance. But even the small Reichswehr might prove a worthy foe of the Polish army—especially with Russia an unknown quantity.

**GERMANY'S DIFFICULT SITUATION** For the purpose of rushing to Poland's side in the event of aggression, France required the right of troop-transit through Germany. But Germany objected strenuously to such an arrangement. If she joined the League, Germany argued in her December 12 note to the League, and accepted without reservations Article 16 of the Covenant, then "in the majority of conceivable cases, Germany will be so to speak predestined to be the scene of European wars." Being partially disarmed, "Germany, unlike other members of the League, will not be in a position to take part in any coercive measure" or sanctions under Article 16. The Wilhelmstrasse therefore urged that "should international conflicts arise, Germany ought to be at liberty to determine how far she will take an active part in them."

On the ground of these reservations, and owing largely to the opposition of France, the League Council in March, 1925, rejected Germany's application for entrance into the League of Nations.

German public opinion resented the offense. It aggravated an already tense situation. On January 10, 1925, the Allies, if they wished to remain loyal to the Treaty of Versailles and fulfil its conditions, should have evacuated the Cologne zone. But France "was in any case determined that Cologne should not be evacuated before another and not less real guarantee for her security had been found."[8] The country which insisted most on obedience to

[8] *Ibid.*, Vol. II, p. 32.

the letter of the Peace treaties, the Germans commented, violated it when it suited her purpose. The French explanation, which Germany rejected, was Germany's failure to comply with all the Allied disarmament requirements.

After this bitter disappointment in January came the slight of non-admission into the League in March. The election on April 26 of Field-Marshal von Hindenburg as President of the Reich encouraged anti-German sentiments in France, Poland, and Czecho-Slovakia, and gave heart, for a time, to the German Nationalists who opposed Stresemann's policy of treaty and reparations fulfilment.

On the other hand, Stresemann hoped that his pact policy would achieve the belated evacuation of the Cologne zone, and prevent another Ruhr invasion. League membership, even if won at a sacrifice of larger national interests, would give Germany security against arbitrary punitive measures by the Allies. It would enable German statesmen to participate in the private discussions that habitually accompany the open diplomacy of League sessions and also give them an opportunity of making propaganda for their colonial aspirations, disarmament principles, etc.

But it was the Dawes Plan which brought the evacuation of the Ruhr. It was the Dawes experts who insisted on the territorial integrity and inviolability of Germany. In subsequent years, France and other Powers, when they respected German sovereignty, did so because any other course would have upset reparations payments, antagonized America, and thrown the whole international financial system out of gear. It was the Dawes Plan, likewise, which assured Germany of foreign credits and loans. The authors of the Plan knew as an elemental truth that it was unworkable unless Germany received outside financial assistance, and in fact this assistance began to come immediately after September 1, 1924—and before Locarno.

The Dawes Plan was Germany's security pact, not Locarno.

**BOLSHEVIK EFFORTS AGAINST LOCARNO** Germany was exposed to British pressure to accept guarantee pacts and to Bolshevik pressure to reject them. Moscow made it a question of "Rapallo or Locarno." If Stressmann signed at Locarno he would overthrow the policy inaugurated in Rapallo. Since the pact was a British product, necessary to Chamberlain "perhaps even because of Russia," Germany's adherence to them, the Soviets declared, threatened the cordial character of Russo-German relations.

The Bolshevik view found whole-hearted support in Count Brockdorff-Rantzau, the German ambassador to Moscow. Despite annoying incidents in the relations between the two countries—the trial of the three German students in 1925, for instance—Rantzau remained loyal to his pro-Russian policy. An unusual situation thus arose in which the Soviet Union and the German envoy accredited to it stood united against the German Government. When the document is published, the world will know how long and fiercely Rantzau fought Stresemann's pro-Pact and pro-League policy. As a mark of protest, in fact, he even tendered his resignation. Strong pressure was brought to bear on the ambassador and the matter was guarded in deep secret. Finally, President Hindenburg succeeded in persuading Rantzau to withdraw his resignation.

The Bolsheviks realized that Germany's adhesion to the League was inevitable. In fact, some saw the advantages of Germany's entrance. Germany would prevent unanimity at Geneva, they maintained, if the Powers should intrigue against Russia. Other Soviet statesmen did not go so far, but none of them believed it possible to prevent Berlin from going to Geneva. Moscow, however, did object strenuously to Article 16 of the League Covenant which granted League Powers the right of troop transit over German territory. If Germany entered the League unconditionally—that is, without reservations as to Articles 16 and 17 of the Covenant, Chicherin said in Warsaw,[9] it will be a very serious matter.

In Berlin a few days later, the commissar explained that these articles "are the means by which Germany could be forced to participate in a coalition against Russia."[1] The entrance of Germany into the League would open the geographical and political door to an attack on the Soviet Union.

In Berlin Stresemann tried to reassure Chicherin—and approved the Soviet-German trade treaty. On October 5, the day the Pact negotiations commenced, the German

[9] *Berliner Tageblatt,* September 29, 1925.
[1] *Ibid.,* October 2, 1925.

Foreign Minister denied to press representatives in Locarno that his country had adopted a Western orientation. Germany, he declared, desired friendly relations with Russia as well as with Western Powers. For her, neither an all-Western or all-Eastern orientation was feasible.[2]

Herr Stresemann undoubtedly spoke the truth. Given her geographical position, and her financial, political and military dependence on the Allies, an orientation on the West to the exclusion of Russia would have been suicide for Germany.

**GERMANY'S STAKE IN RUSSIA** Germany could not in 1925 forgo the advantage of friendly relations with Soviet Russia. The influence of Brockdorff-Rantzau, of the Nationalists, of the East Prussians, and of the East-oriented Democrats, Centrists and Industrialists, did not permit it. But considerations of sober politics likewise made a purely western orientation dangerous. Germans recalled the Ruhr situation in which the Bolshevik attitude kept Poland from taking Danzig and German Upper Silesia. Moreover, an estrangement between Berlin and Moscow must open the way to an attempt at a Franco-Soviet settlement—as it did after Locarno. Germany, likewise, could ill afford the loss of Soviet business. Another important factor operated to keep the two countries together. Moscow and Berlin had entered into an arrangement for the exchange of military experience, army experts, and munitions. Germany lived under Allied military control. In Russia she could do what she was not then permitted to do at home. Perhaps the most decisive consideration against the alienation of the Bolsheviks was an appreciation of the favorable repercussion of Rapallo on the Allied attitude towards Berlin. Locarno was another illustration in point. Chicherin's statements and activities in Warsaw and Berlin strengthened the hand of Stresemann in Locarno. Exposed to the pressure of Bolshevik diplomacy, Germany could appeal for greater concessions from the Entente. If Germany did not keep alive the passive threat that hostility from the West would throw her into the arms of Russia, the West would scarcely accord Germany friendly treatment. For fundamentally,

[2] *Ibid.*, October 5, 1925.

as the Anglo-French naval compromise of 1928 showed, England is still Germany's great commercial rival and France has no warm sentiments for the German. The fear of a Russo-German bloc helps to determine French and British policies towards the Wilhelmstrasse. That this is undeniable in the case of England even the political schoolboy understands, and a noted Russian once said to me: "The chief reason why Herbette [the French ambassador] remains in Moscow is to watch Soviet-German relations." If Germany were to sever her relations with Russia she would be at the mercy of changes in Allied policy. To antagonize Russia would be almost as fatal a mistake for Germany as the failure to win her before the World War.

Bismarck, in his efforts to preserve the strength of the Reich and the peace of Europe, worked untiringly to retain the friendship of Russia, and succeeded even in bringing Austro-Hungary and Russia into the League of Three Emperors despite their rivalry in the Balkans. When the Kaiser and Bismarck's pre-war successors discarded his policy they were writing the Treaty of Versailles of 1919.

**ARTICLE SIXTEEN** Germany of course appreciated the importance of maintaining intact their good relations with the Soviet Union. But Locarno was predicated on Germany's entrance into the League, and League members, under Article 16, are obliged to "take the necessary steps to afford passage through their territory to the forces of any of the Members of the League which are co-operating to protect the Covenant of the League." If Poland attacked the Bolsheviks, France might wish to aid her as she did in 1920 and might—for aggression and defense may easily be confused—mobilize the League in Poland's behalf. In 1920, writes Professor A. Mendelssohn-Bartholdi,[3] France offered to hasten Germany's entrance into the League if Berlin opened her border to a French army en route to Poland. Germany refused, but as a League member—and unless she made reservations to Article 16—she would be pledged to permit the passage of French troops or British or Belgian troops. Germany herself objected to the article because she was disarmed

[3] *Europaeische Gespraeche.* Berlin monthly. June, 1928, p. 15.

and would be helpless with a foreign army on her soil.

The hottest battle at Locarno centered around Article 16. In the early phase of the conference it was the chief subject of discussion, and several times during the first six days the negotiations appeared to be on the verge of a break. On two celebrated and stormy occasions Briand and Stresemann engaged in brilliant word battles. France insisted that Germany enter the League unconditionally. But Germany was adamant. At the last session, during the much-advertised trip of the "Orange Blossom" over the waters of the Lago Maggiore, Stresemann categorically declared that Germany rejected the troop transit right inherent in Article 16. Vandervelde then spoke against it. Chamberlain, assuming the role of impartial arbiter, thereupon stated that the transit right did not exist. Briand remained silent. Finally a settlement was reached. This was the agreement which made the Locarno pacts possible.

The Powers, in accordance with this settlement, signed a collective note stating their understanding of Article 16—an understanding which has itself become the subject of conflicting interpretations.

> Each state member of the League [read the note] is bound to co-operate loyally and effectively in support of the Covenant and in resistance to any act of aggression to an extent which is compatible with its military situation and takes its geographical position into account.

It is obvious that no French or British general will march an army through Germany without her consent. Such a lengthening of the line in hostile territory would probably be fatal to the purpose of the expedition. The decision, undoubtedly, lies with Germany.

Stresemann several times officially assured Chicherin that Germany had never accepted any obligation under the League Covenant to grant troop-transit rights. But in a given situation, the Versailles Powers might conceivably allow Germany to increase her army and military equipment so that foreign forces in transit would not become a domestic danger. Such permission to arm would win loud acclaim in certain German circles and might persuade the government to visa the passage of an army engaged in League sanctions. Or the Allies would make financial concessions to Germany. Or, Germany would be subjected to irresistible moral pressure. Assume that Russia and Poland are at war. The war would be advertised as a struggle for European civilization against the onslaughts of Bolshevism and Asia. Poland would be made out the last bulwark against World Revolution. If England and France wanted Germany to participate in such a conflict, Germany could scarcely resist even though it involved support to Poland, the occupant of pre-war German soil. Germany could scarcely afford the odium of sabotaging the interests of the capitalist world.

**THE BERLIN TREATY** The Berlin Treaty between Germany and the Soviet Union published on April 24, 1926, was a reply to Article 16. The initiative belonged to the Bolsheviks and the earliest conversations took place in December, 1924, immediately after Germany informed Moscow of her application for League membership. Yet even this initiative had a preliminary history. Kopp of the Commissariat of Foreign Affairs saw Baron von Maltzan in Berlin during the summer of 1924 and apparently threw out some vague hints which were misinterpreted and led to German soundings on the question of Poland. Moscow, however, declined an understanding on this narrow basis and proposed a general treaty concerning the most important problems of Soviet-German relations. The Bolsheviks would have preferred an anti-League of Nations treaty similar in design if not in text to the treaty with Turkey signed in December, 1925. That agreement pledged each party "not to participate in any union or agreement of a political nature with one or several third parties directed against the other contracting party . . . and not to participate in any hostile act on the part of one or several Powers directed against the other contracting party."

"Political nature," said a separate protocol, included all possible financial and economic agreements.[4]

This was the full Russian reply to the threat of League sanctions under Article 16. The Soviet-Turkish Treaty practically barred Turkey's entry into the Geneva body.

Since Stresemann had already made application for entrance into the League and was bent on gaining admission, a treaty containing any such clause was unacceptable. Nevertheless, a less far-reaching accord to

[4] London *Times,* December 23, 1925.

reassure the Bolsheviks of Germany's continued cordiality met with no serious objection in Berlin. The Right, moreover, fought Locarno and supported the idea of a new agreement with Moscow. The negotiations for this treaty proceeded parallel with the Locarno discussions, and at times occupied the Wilhelmstrasse as much as or more than the preliminary pact negotiations.

A mere platitudinous expression of friendship satisfied neither Rantzau nor Chicherin nor Litvinov. When, in March, 1925, the League of Nations rejected Germany's application, Moscow regarded the time opportune and struck while German national resentment was hot. Stresemann sent a long telegram to Rantzau in the middle of March outlining his views. But despite the rebuff administered by the Powers at Geneva, there was still no inclination in Berlin to accept the Russian suggestion of an anti-League convention. In May, therefore, Rantzau arrived in Berlin. Herr Gaus, the legal expert of the German Foreign Office, now drafted a treaty which embodied Stresemann's policy but made few concessions to the Easterners' wishes.

It was at this juncture that Rantzau submitted his resignation. He felt that he and his policy—the policy of Rapallo—had been disavowed, and that he would serve his country best by demonstratively quitting his post as a protest against what he considered a dangerous reorientation of Germany's foreign relations.

After almost two months of heated battles in closed council chambers, Rantzau, acting largely at Hindenburg's urgent wish, withdrew his resignation, and on June 25 left Berlin for Moscow in the company of Dr. Herbert von Dirksen, later his successor as ambassador to Russia. They took with them a modified draft treaty of which Rantzau disapproved. Dirksen presented it to Chicherin in the presence of Krestinsky and Rantzau, and discussed the problem on several occasions with the commissar, but six weeks in Moscow gave him a confirmed impression of Bolshevik displeasure with Berlin's proposal.

Although Dirksen, during his stay, arranged the basis of the 100,000,000-mark bank credit to Russia, and helped to give the trade treaty negotiations that political turn which assured their ultimate success, the Soviet Government remained resentful of Germany's Locarno venture and opposed to her efforts to enter the League.

Chicherin's visit to Berlin early in October marks the next phase of the treaty discussions. During these few eventful days, Stresemann and Chicherin had some tense moments together—usually deep into the night. They conferred until an hour before the German delegation's train left for Locarno. The Foreign Minister was drowned in work preparatory to the Locarno conferences. The Foreign Commissar argued and argued.

Germany could not yield to Russia's demand but the underlying thoughts of the Berlin Treaty as it saw the light in April, 1926, were finally agreed upon in those nocturnal meetings. And, although the version is incorrect that the text was then initialled there is no doubt that Stresemann gave a definite undertaking to Chicherin not to accept Locarno or enter the League without previous modification of Article 16.

Berlin wanted no repetition of the Rapallo scandal. The publication of an agreement with Moscow on the eve of the German delegation's departure for Locarno to sign pacts with the Allies would not have been improper but it was sure to raise a storm of Western protest. Throughout 1926 the Germans tried to postpone the final conclusion of a treaty with the Bolsheviks. They wished to wait until Germany entered the League.

The Guarantee Pacts were accepted in Locarno in the middle of October. Immediately Count Rantzau handed in his resignation a second time, and again to President Hindenburg; by virtue of the special circumstances of his appointment, he considered himself directly responsible not to the Foreign Office but to the chief officer of the Reich. But to let Rantzau go at this juncture would have been tantamount to a public announcement that Germany's attitude towards the Soviet Government had indeed cooled. This would have weakened Berlin's position vis-à-vis the West, strengthened the Right opposition at home, and antagonized Moscow—which was not in Germany's interest. Again the struggle commenced along a wide front to persuade Rantzau to remain, and while the conversations proceeded more and more concessions were naturally made to Moscow's and Rantzau's point of view on the Berlin Treaty.

Finally, through the repeated intervention of Hindenburg, Rantzau again withdrew his resignation, yet Stresemann insisted on negotiations in Berlin rather than Moscow. Berlin wished to determine the date of signature.

The time element was important. Locarno did not become effective until Germany entered the League. Yet despite intialing of the pacts in October and their signature amidst many affirmations of brotherly love in London on December 1, the League Council once again shut its doors in Germany's face at its March 1926 sessions. Some argue that France wished to weaken the significance of Germany's acceptance into the League Council by simultaneously winning a permanent seat for Poland. Others may say that France attempted to organize a Latin bloc and with the aid of its members, Spain and Brazil, and of Poland, keep Germany out of the Council and therefore the League. That France and Sir Austen Chamberlain encouraged Poland's claims is not open to doubt. But whatever the cause, Germany's second rebuff at Geneva—this time a personal rebuff too, for Berlin's delegates had arrived in the League town on the unquestioned assumption that admission was a mere formality—aroused bitter resentment in Germany. Rantzau regarded it an indirect vindication of his policy.

At this juncture, and acting under the impression of League rejection, the German Foreign Office discontinued its procrastinating tactics towards the Berlin Treaty and quickly concluded it. The question of neutrality occupied special attention. In November, 1925, Chancellor Luther had assured Chicherin that Germany's adherence to the League would never force her out of her position of neutrality. Luther, even more than Stresemann, favored unconditional neutrality. But the legal experts raised objections, on the ground that such a stand was incompatible with the League Covenant. The Russians, on the other hand, endeavored to widen the conception of neutrality to include not only cases of unprovoked attack but any attack, for the question of "provocation" introduced the danger of formalistic interpretations and delays. If the Soviet Union were attacked, it was necessary that German neutrality follow immediately and automatically, otherwise the tedious investigation, at a moment of crisis, of the issue of "provoked or not provoked" might result in lack of clarity and encourage the enemies of Russia to court German support. The treaty however provided that the second party remains neutral only if the first should be attacked "in spite of its peaceful attitude." Yet the accompanying Stresemann note stated unequivocally that Germany and not the League would decide whether Russia had been peaceful or whether she was the aggressor.

The treaty and the appended protocols were submitted to London and Paris early in April in the expectation that in the natural course of diplomatic events they would leak out into the press and thus justify publication before Germany's admission to the League. On April 14 the London *Times* duly published the first news regarding the Soviet-German agreement and on April 24, accordingly, the Berlin Treaty was officially signed by Stresemann and Krestinsky.[5]

The Berlin Treaty was intended as a German assurance to Moscow that Locarno did not signify a purely Western orientation on the part of Germany. The Paris *Temps,* therefore, considered it a victory for Soviet diplomacy, and wondered why Stresemann and Luther had not waited a few months longer, after having waited half a year, till Germany entered the League. The English Press was more restrained but no less displeased, and Downing Street asked the Wilhelmstrasse for more information. In general, France objected with greater firmness than England, and secret clauses were suspected in many quarters. The final publication of the Treaty and appended papers laid the storm.

The Soviet-German Re-Assurance Treaty of April 24, 1926, reaffirmed the Rapallo Treaty as the basis of the two countries' mutual relations, and enjoined them to neutrality in case of attack by a third Power or Powers. Each nation undertook not to adhere to hostile coalitions or economic or financial boycotts organized against the other in time of war or peace.

This would have been satisfactory. But the accompanying Stresemann note, while declaring that Germany would resist within the League any measures directed wholly against the Soviet Union, nevertheless stated that her relations to Russia could not suffer from her loyal fulfilment of her duties as League member, including even the sanction foreseen by Articles 16 and 17. Only Germany, it said, would decide whether Russia was the ag-

[5] Text, London *Times,* April 27, 1926.

gressor in a given military situation, and the decision of the League to undertake sanctions would not necessarily bind Germany. It was subsequently intimated to Moscow that even if Germany regarded the Bolsheviks as aggressors she might still plead neutrality on the ground of her geographical and economic positions.

Germany's position in the League was unique in that she made reservations to the sanctions articles of its covenant. She did this to demonstrate her cordiality towards Moscow. But these reservations and the Berlin Treaty into which they were written may become a scrap of paper, like so many other well-intentioned documents before it.

**THE PERMANENT VALUE OF LOCARNO** Germany's orientation after Locarno was not completely Western, but it was more Western than it had been. Objective circumstances demanded such a shifting of emphasis. Nevertheless, the price Germany paid for Locarno was exorbitant. The Wilhelmstrasse made the mistake of under-estimating American influence in Europe.

Germany's leaders realized this truth a few years later—after the publication of the Anglo-French naval compromise in the summer of 1928. Locarno had brought them no real friendship with France or England, nor the evacuation of the Rhineland, nor alleviation of reparations burden, nor mandates, nor colonies, nor equality in the secret council of the Great Powers. It would have been better to play the game with America, and, to the extent that America's aloofness prevented her concrete aid to Germany in the solution of many immediate problems, to play the game with France too. By Locarno, Germany appointed England arbiter between herself and France. A year later, after Thoiry, England used that position to obstruct a rapprochement with France which Germany desired.

A more Western orientation after the Dawes Plan was a necessity for Germany. But Germany need not have entered the British orbit. She realized the error only too soon. In 1925: Locarno. In 1926: Thoiry, that is, an attempt at a Franco-German rapprochement. If France wished to evacuate the Rhineland, England could not prevent it. If France did not wish to evacuate the

Rhineland, England could not force it. Reparations too depend more on France than on England. Berlin chose England and Locarno, but they gave her no practical results.

Locarno plus disarmament might have been an achievement. Locarno without disarmament was a maneuver.

# 19

## ANTI-LOCARNO

LOCARNO limited the sphere of activity of Soviet foreign diplomacy. It left Russia an approach only to Turkey, Lithuania—and, in part, to France. By narrowing the possibilities in the West, it put a premium on Bolshevik efforts in Asia.

Turkey offered the best opportunity of an anti-Locarno demonstration. Soviet-Turkish friendship, born in the period of close military collaboration against the Greeks, and tempered in the crucible of Turkey's revolutionary resurgence, remained undiminished as years passed. Petty incidents and the unavoidable friction of international affairs did not weaken it.

Britain was Turkey's great enemy. Here Turk and Tartar met on common ground.

Two months after Locarno, Europe's statesmen again met in Geneva where the League of Nations, on December 15, yielded to British insistence and granted Mosul to Iraq. Before the ink of the decision had yet dried, Chicherin and Tewfik Rushdi Bey, the Turkish Minister of Foreign Affairs, signed a treaty of friendship and neutrality in Paris. The time of its conclusion, and the feelings which animated the contracting parties were more significant than its text. "The treaty signed in Paris," said *Izvestia* on December 24, 1925, "is an anti-Locarno act in the sense that it is concluded for peace and not for war."

The December 17 treaty of friendship and neutrality was concluded for a period of three years but was renewable thereafter,[1] and consisted of only two short

[1] It was renewed by Karakhan in Ankara on December 17, 1929.

paragraphs: one enjoining neutrality, the other pledging each party not to attack the other and not to enter into blocs or coalitions, or agreements, or financial or economic combinations with third Powers aimed against the other.

By implication, since the League of Nations could, in the event of sanction, become a hostile coalition, Turkey and the Soviet Union hereby undertook not to seek membership in the League. Bolshevik opposition to the Geneva body needed no such strengthening. Turkey, however, had been subjected to considerable foreign influence to join the League of Nations. Throughout 1926 for instance, English politicians constantly brought home to Ankara the urgency of applying for membership. It would, they submitted, guarantee Turkey against Italian aggression and against Greek designs. Financial measures which amounted to an economic boycott were likewise calculated to impress the Kemalists with the desirability of shifting the center of attention of their foreign policy from Moscow to London. These efforts required a countermaneuver, and, late in 1926, a Turkish squadron brought Tewfik Rushdi Bey to Odessa where he conferred with Chicherin. Fresh from this meeting, the commissar came to Berlin where, on December 4, he told the writer that "Odessa was a demonstration." It reaffirmed the position taken by the two governments in Paris just a year before and permitted the statesmen to exchange opinions on the common sources of political dangers which threatened their interests. Chicherin and Rushdi Bey discussed the whole field of politics, but devoted special attention to three subjects: a commercial treaty, the League of Nations, and most important, Italy. Before they parted the commissar was able to present for Kemal Pasha's perusal a written statement assuring him that Moscow would do nothing calculated to damage Turkish interests in the Balkans. Subsequently Ankara stated officially that it would not enter the League unless given a permanent seat on the League Council. Since this demand could not possibly be met, insistence on it was tantamount to a refusal to accept League membership.

Turkey, Kemal said, "must cease to be a land of sheiks and dervishes." He would abolish the fez. He would make Nationalist Turkey in Asia more European than the Sultan's Turkey in Europe.

More than treaty bonds, it has been the parallelism of their revolutionary social tasks and the similarity of Western hostility towards them that kept Russia and Turkey in unbroken friendship throughout the trying years after Locarno.

# 20

# BRIGHT RAYS IN FRANCE

GEORGE CHICHERIN went from Warsaw late in September, 1925, to Berlin on the eve of the German delegation's departure for Locarno, to Paris where he met Briand after his return from Locarno.

The French Foreign Minister was neither enamored of nor filled with the "spirit of Locarno." He regarded it as a defeat and so did Poincaré and enough French politicians to endanger for a moment his tenure of office. Briand therefore felt constrained to paint Locarno a great moral triumph of world diplomacy, and by defending it and clothing it in the fiery flame of his oratory, to fortify his own position. Yet the new situation in Europe required French retrenchment in international politics. Chicherin would not have visited Paris had he thought this not the case.

In November, 1925, Rakovsky was transferred from London to Paris. France would become the center of Soviet diplomatic activity. "There is apparently a good deal more behind Mr. Rakovsky's appointment as Soviet ambassador to Paris than is generally believed," wrote the diplomatic correspondent of the London *Daily Telegraph* on November 3.

Rakovsky was the perfect diplomat and perfect gentleman, and he knew France. He had studied there and practiced medicine in Provence. In England he had won the sympathy and assistance of wide Labor circles, of Liberals and even of forward-looking Conservatives. In France he soon found a welcome in influential society and with numerous officials and journalists who subsequently helped him in difficult moments.

One problem that had worried Rakovsky in Britain caused him no concern in France: propaganda. Phillipe Berthelot, the Political Director of the Quai d'Orsay, once said to Rakovsky that France need fear revolution only in case of hunger or defeat in war.

**THE BOLSHEVIKS AND THE LEAGUE** In the first meeting between the new ambassador and Briand, the latter began by discussing relations with the United States and then urged the Soviet Union to seek admission to the League of Nations. Poincaré who was a power to be reckoned with in or out of office, and even Briand, were violently anti-American at the time on account of the debt question. Paris toyed with the idea of European solidarity in Inter-Allied debt problems. Briand believed in the League. He saw possibilities of making it a continental instrument against the United States and England. It seemed inevitable, moreover, that Germany would win a seat in the League Council and that Poland would not. Briand therefore wanted Moscow to straighten the balance. He reverted to this subject on more than one occasion.

Understanding of Bolshevik psychology was a rare thing in the Europe of 1926. French statesmen believed that the revolutionary character of Soviet foreign policy would gradually evaporate and that a few years in the League would "tame" the boisterous extremists and make them see the practical advantages of international combinations, diplomatic give and take, etc. Except on this assumption, Russian membership in the League Council, whose decisions must be unanimous, would have ruined or at least paralyzed the League. This is one of the reasons why Italy favored Soviet adherence to the Geneva body. But Briand, who wished the League to prosper, could only have conceived of it as a reformatory for Soviet statesmen and a school in practical politics. Even Austen Chamberlain once urged the Soviet Union to join the League, and Germany, until she saw the case was hopeless, sounded Moscow on the matter times without number.

The Bolsheviks remained unalterably anti-League. In 1924 Rakovsky stated during the Anglo-Russian conference that Moscow would be prepared to send an observer to Geneva "but this step must not be understood as the first step towards membership of the League of Nations." Russia even selected its representative for this post, Alexandra Kollontai, and had the first MacDonald Cabinet not fallen she might have undertaken her duties. Yet the hostile attitude of the Soviet Union toward the League was left unshaken.

The Soviet Union suspected that it would be isolated in the Council chambers of the League and subjected to pressure to accept decisions against its interests. Russia would again become an object of Western bargaining and offers. But she had every desire to avoid entangling alliances, coalitions, blocs, etc. Professor Fay in his brilliant work on the *Origins of the World War* proves conclusively that alliances make for greater armaments and these for universal war.[1] But the Bolsheviks expected to remain passive in the next Armageddon and to reap the economic and revolutionary benefits of neutrality. They would negotiate with all Powers and offer advantages to some, but their broadest policy would be aloofness. This, to be sure, was in part a product of the antagonism of the Powers who did not particularly want Russia within their innermost circle.But even in 1926, when that was not altogether the case, Moscow held back from diplomatic combinations with the capitalist world.

In 1926 Briand realized that Germany would take her seat in the League Council under the ægis of Britain. French control in the League seemed to be threatened. Locarno had somewhat disturbed the French political system on the continent. The Quai d'Orsay, and particularly Briand, accordingly investigated possibilities of winning new friends in Europe. Germany could be lured from the side of England and Russia might be ranged by the side of France. The debt negotiations with Moscow in 1926, and the Franco-German economic rapprochement of the same year over which Stresemann and Briand sought unsuccessfully to build a political roof at Thoiry, fall within this pattern.

The French Exchequer, moreover, was empty and the franc fell to catastrophic depths. Political and economic considerations prejudiced the situation in favor of a debt settlement with Russia.

[1] Sidney B. Fay: *The Origins of the World War,* (New York, 1929). See especially Vol. I, "Before Sarajevo. The Underlying Causes of the War."

**FRANCO-SOVIET DEBT CONFERENCE** The Franco-Soviet Conference opened on February 25, 1926, with a speech of welcome by Premier Briand, and after a number of sessions in which general principles arose for discussion, Rakovsky, on April 14, laid a definite Soviet proposal before the conference. The Soviet Government would pay 62 annuities averaging 40,000,000 gold francs each, the assumption being that the total debt was reduced 25 per cent to correspond with the post-war reduction of Russian territory, that the credit problem would be satisfactorily solved, and that a partial moratorium would be granted so that full payments commenced only at the end of the third year.

The French delegation accepted the 25 per cent debt reduction and was not in principle opposed to the Soviet offer of payments, but it refused to relate credits to debts. At the very session, however, at which de Monzie raised this objection—June 7—the Soviet delegation submitted a memorandum in which it presented the case for a credit of $225,000,000 to be paid in three years; two-thirds to be used for the purchase of French goods; $75,-000,000 would be received in cash.

Shortly afterwards, on June 15, the Briand-Peret Cabinet fell, and on the 23rd a new Ministry emerged with Briand as Premier and Foreign Minister and Caillaux as Finance Minister.

**BRIAND, CAILLAUX, AND RAKOVSKY AT LUNCH** Rakovsky first made the acquaintance of Caillaux at the official stand during the parade of July 14. The next day they and Briand met for a long luncheon in which they discussed all current Franco-Soviet problems. They dealt, in this connection, with the Bizerta fleet.

When the Germans occupied the Ukraine and the Crimea after Brest Litovsk, the Russian fleet in the Black Sea was in danger of capture. Raskolnikov therefore hastened to Novorossisk to carry out the scuttling of the dreadnoughts, destroyers, etc., docked there. He succeeded only partially, and his exploit may later have suggested "Scapa Flow" to the Germans, but a large flotilla escaped under its Czarist commanders and surrendered to the Germans in the Crimea.

When Wrangel entrenched himself in the Crimea in 1920, this fleet fell into his hands. After his defeat by the Red Army, he took these vessels—over one hundred in number—to Constantinople and other ports, and ultimately delivered them to the French Government which interned them in Bizerta, Tunis.

Herriot had promised to return the fleet when he saw Rakovsky in London in June, 1924. On March 4, 1925, Austen Chamberlain stated in the House of Commons that "Before recognizing the Soviet Government, the French Government informed His Majesty's Government that recognition would entail the handing over of these vessels." But, he explained, "the ships are still at Bizerta."

At the Briand-Caillaux-Rakovsky luncheon this issue was touched upon and Briand again promised to return the fleet to the Bolsheviks. Subsequently, in response to Rumanian protestations, France urged Moscow to move only part of the ships to the Black Sea and the rest to the Baltic. But although Russia agreed, the fleet remained at Bizerta.

The statesmen devoted most of their after-luncheon talk to financial matters. The war debt played only a minor role in the negotiations with France. The French were calling the Americans "Shylocks" for insisting on the funding of loans which had been spent to defeat a common enemy. They could not well demand of the Bolsheviks that they repay loans contracted by the Czar in the struggle against Germany. Rakovsky told Caillaux frankly that Russia would not pay war debts. If the Bolsheviks had claimed Russia's recognized share in German reparations instead of renouncing them, he declared, France would have lost more than through the Soviet debt repudiation.

Eugene Lautier, editor of *L'Homme Libre,* once asked in the Quai d'Orsay how much French independence was worth. "What!" came the indignant answer, "It cannot be bought." Well, he said, had Russia not thrown her army masses into the fight during 1914 and 1915, Paris would surely have been taken. The billions France gave Russia, he submitted, saved France from slavery.

Pre-war debts, however, constituted another category, and, for reasons of expediency, the Bolsheviks consented to partial repayment on certain conditions. Rakovsky knew the perilous state of French finances. He proposed therefore to organize a bank with a basic capital of approximately 100,000,000 francs which would enjoy the support of both governments. The French had in their possession $8,000,000 in gold paid by the Soviets to Germany under the Brest Treaty and transferred by Germany to the Allies pending a settlement with Russia. Rakovsky agreed to postpone the question of the ownership of the gold and permit its use for the founding of the bank. The idea appealed to Caillaux. As Rakovsky developed his plan, Caillaux asked whether they might not reach an understanding regarding oil. The problem of a state petroleum monopoly was then an acute French political issue. Moscow could sign a long-term contract to supply France with oil. The proceeds from the sale would be collected by the bank and serve to repay French credits to Russia.

**THE HISTORY OF A DEBT AGREEMENT**[2] Rakovsky went from lunch to the Soviet Embassy, where, with de Monzie, and in de Monzie's almost illegible handwriting, a preliminary debt agreement was drafted. A "financial institution" or bank would collect Russia's debt payments and be the channel through which French credits would be granted to the Soviets. It would likewise function as a clearing house for transactions growing out of Franco-Soviet commercial relationships.

By the terms of the draft agreement "The French delegation accepted the figure proposed by the Soviet delegation," that is 62 annuities of 60,000,000 gold francs each, and while rejecting the Soviet thesis of the organic connection between debt payments and credits, undertook to examine sympathetically the Russian demand for credits totalling $225,000,000.

But opposition developed within the French delegation against its chairman's draft proposal, and a modified "final protocol" was therefore drawn up on the next day, July 16, and accepted by de Monize at 5 P.M. It, as well as a counter-draft worked out by the French on the 17th stated that the Soviet offer of payment had been approved. Neither protocol altered anything with regard to the bank or credit. "The French delegation," read a paragraph in both drafts, "accepts the figure proposed by the Soviet delegation considering that it guarantees the 25 per cent of the debt which was the basis of its [the French delegation's.—L. F.] original demand for 75 millions." On the afternoon of the 16th, however, Berthelot, the Political

[2] The writer has seen all the pertinent archive documents.

Director of the Quai d'Orsay, telephoned to say that, despite amendments, Briand objected to the text of the agreement and insisted that the return of the Bizerta fleet must be made dependent on a settlement of all the questions discussed at the luncheon of the 15th. Rakovsky gained the impression that Berthelot acted as much on behalf of Poincaré as of Briand. In fact, Berthelot subsequently told Rakovsky that Poincaré had obstructed a settlement. Generally speaking, the Russian problem had now probably become an object of bargaining in the highly complicated larger political situation.

On July 17 Herriot, President of the Chamber of Deputies, stepped down from the presidential tribune to attack the Briand-Caillaux Cabinet. His success was greater than he may have wished, for the Ministry fell and the Mayor of Lyon once more received a commission to form a government.

Meanwhile, Rakovsky, faced with a rejection of de Monzie's draft agreement, flew to Moscow to attend an important plenary meeting of the Communist Party's Central Committee—the one during which Dzerzhinsky died. At the airport a telegram was handed to him. I am now Minister of Finance in a new Herriot Cabinet, de Monzie wired in effect. Come back and I will push through our draft. When de Monzie became minister, he looked into the French Treasury and found only 60,000,000 francs. His public announcement of the circumstance produced a financial and political crisis. If the Bolsheviks would immediately pay him a few millions—and they were not disinclined to do so—the situation might be saved.

Rakovsky rushed back to Paris in answer to de Monzie's summons, but on the day of his arrival, on August 2, Herriot's two-day Cabinet had been overthrown. Two days later Poincaré's "Cabinet of Premiers" came into office.

**POINCARÉ'S OPPOSITION** For Poincaré, the Russian debt solution as an aid to French official solvency had no attraction. His several predecessors in the Finance Ministry did not wish to increase taxation or had no time to undertake radical cures of the franc and the budget. He intended making thorough reforms.

With the advent of Poincaré, the de Monzie-Rakovsky draft agreement lost its validity. Even previously to his formation of the government, Poincaré had thrown his influence against de Monzie. And the new Premier wished to take the discussions out of the hands of the delegation and transfer them to the Finance Ministry under his immediate supervision.

Briand, Poincaré's Foreign Minister, was pledged to a Russian settlement and to the return of the Bizerta fleet. To avoid an embarrassing situation, therefore, he gave Rakovsky the presumably friendly advice to see Poincaré often. But Poincaré remained indisposed to deal conclusively with the Soviet debt problem.

Poincaré's policy with respect to the Soviet debt had always demanded international solidarity, that is, parallel procedure with Great Britain. But Anglo-Soviet negotiations had not been resumed after the defeat of MacDonald. Indeed, Anglo-Soviet relations grew alarmingly critical in the summer of 1926, and Poincaré was very sensible to such a situation across the Channel.

Poincaré never showed any desire to reach an agreement on financial matters with Moscow. He could have had an agreement with the Bolsheviks on debts which was satisfactory to the thousands of petty bondholders. But Moscow was not as prepared to meet the wishes of the big former owners of nationalized property who had the ear of Poincaré. And Poincaré naturally dominated French political life completely. A new phase in Franco-Soviet relations now commenced in which even the warmest protagonists of a rapprochement with Russia gradually identified themselves with the traditional French policy of parallel action and united front vis-à-vis the Bolsheviks. After a semester of bright prospects—from December, 1925, to July, 1926—Franco-Soviet relations returned to their normal level of coldness and distance.

# 21

# DARK CLOUDS OVER LONDON

LITVINOV AND RAKOVSKY paid a visit to Lord D'Abernon in Berlin during the latter half of 1925 and reassured him of Moscow's readiness to enter into negotiations and more friendly relations with England. They received no encouragement.

When Chicherin came to Paris in November, 1925, an attempt was made to elicit an invitation for him from London. But Chamberlain refused to invite the commissar directly. He only "authorized M. Briand to let M. Chicherin know that if he desired an interview, I should not refuse it."[1] In fact, however, Briand never spoke to Chicherin of the matter. Chicherin saw Briand twice during this period, once before and once after the signing of the Locarno Pacts in London.

Again and again, the British Foreign Office gave evidence of its disinclination to open parleys with the Soviets. Litvinov addressed the Central Executive Committee in Moscow on April 25, 1926, and declared his Government's willingness to renew negotiations with Great Britain "with a view to finding a way out of the present deadlock." But when Ponsonby called the Baldwin Cabinet's attention to this assertion, the House of Commons merely heard the oft-repeated formula that if Moscow made proposals "we are prepared to consider them."

Winston Churchill, Lord Birkenhead, Mr. Amery (the Secretary of State for Colonies), and Sir William Joynson-

[1] British Blue Book. *Russia, No.* 3 (1927). (London, 1927). Cmd. 2895, p. 43.

Hicks left no stone unturned to achieve a rupture of relations with Russia in 1926. Prime Minister Baldwin and Austen Chamberlain occupied a more moderate position and attempted, with only temporary success, to check the extremist Die-Hards.

Though Chamberlain's endeavor was to restrain the Die-Hards, he felt their pressure and admitted in a letter to his chargé d'affaires in Moscow dated November 5, 1925, that "It was of course true that I had not encouraged M. Rakovsky to enter into new negotiations with me."[2]

**THE BRITISH STRIKE** While Anglo-Soviet relations remained in their delicate state, the General Strike and the miners' strike broke out in Great Britain in May, 1926.

The General Strike surprised and then thrilled the Bolsheviks. If it lasted long enough, they thought, capitalist government in Britain would be doomed. Some Communists in Russia saw the imminent coming of a Soviet revolution in England, and even when the General Strike collapsed, the struggle of the miners impressed them with its herioc and serious aspects.

In respect to the British labor movement, the feeling of intimacy on the part of the Russian trade unions was especially strong because it had been nurtured by close co-operation in international questions which took organization form in the Anglo-Russian Trade Union Committee. The English trade unions and British Laborites had helped Rakovsky in his negotiations with MacDonald and had, during the Civil War and thereafter, lent themselves to pro-Soviet demonstrations. Within the conservative Amsterdam Trade Union International they usually defended the Soviet Union against the bitter attacks of Mensheviks and other anti-Communists.

When the General Strike shook a startled world, the Soviet Union hung on the telegraph wire waiting with tense impatience for every tiny item of news. And when, having been betrayed by British Labor leaders, as the Bolsheviks put it, the miners decided to carry on the struggle and did so for many long, hungry months, millions of rubles poured into the trade union treasury for the miners' organization, not only to feed the needy but to finance the struggle. Those who were in Russia at the

[2] British Blue Book. Cmd. 2895.

time—even cynical bourgeois journalists—testified in their letters and dispatches to the spontaneity with which contributions to the British miners' fund were made in every city and hamlet throughout the Soviet Union. To be sure, agitation accompanied the collection campaign, but the liberal response was due to a genuine interest fed by detailed newspaper messages.

In May, the Presidium of the Council of Trade Unions sent from its treasury 250,000 rubles and again 2,000,000 rubles. Local trade unions made contributions in the form of one day's wages of each worker or, as the strike progressed, 0.5 per cent of their wages per month. Collections were also made in theaters, concerts, and other public gatherings. Between May 22 and June 17, according to Sir W. Joynson-Hicks's statement in Parliament on June 17, the All-Russian Central Council of Trade Unions forwarded to the strikers four remittances totalling 380,128 pounds sterling. At the same time, contributions of much smaller dimensions arrived from other parts of the world, notably America and Germany.

Before these sums could be transferred in foreign currency by the Russian trade unions to England, the special permission of the Soviet Government was necessary. The Government granted the permission. The British Foreign Office protested on June 12 in a note to M. Rosengolz, the Soviet chargé d'affaires, against this act. Rosengolz replied on the 16th that his Government "could not prohibit the trade unions, comprising millions of workers of Soviet Russia, from sending money abroad in aid of trade unions of another country."

Herewith the diplomatic correspondence ceased. The Bolsheviks argued that the Soviet Government merely granted the formal permission for the transfer in view of the fact that no foreign currency could be exported without official sanction. Technically, the Soviet Government's position remained impregnable.

But Conservative circles now began to hint that the Soviet Government itself had given of its funds to the striking miners. This Mr. Rosengolz denied emphatically in an interview to the British Press of June 17,[3] and even Joynson-Hicks, who discussed the subject on that same day in Parliament, did not affirm unequivocally that the Soviet Government had contributed. He merely identified

[3] See, for instance, *Manchester Guardian.*

the Russian trade unions with the Soviet Government. The charge that the Soviet Government or any of its branches gave money to help the strike was never officially levelled. On the other hand, British Labor leaders, among them Robert Williams and Mr. Citrine, pointed out that the transmission of funds by the workers of one country to the strikers of another was a time-honored practice in which the British trade unions had engaged on previous occasions without interference from their Governments or any other government. Robert Williams accordingly asked "why Russia has been singled out for attack." He suspected that "there are forces more anxious to make political capital out of the incident of the dispatch of trade union money than anything else."[4]

**DIE-HARD ATTEMPTS TO PROVOKE A RUPTURE**

The General Strike released considerable capitalist animosity aginst the Bolsheviks. Russia had offered the British workers a bad example, and now she offered them money. Few distinguished between the Russian trade unions and the Soviet Government. In spirit, principle and intention, the bourgeoisie contended, they were one. The Government, the trade unions, the Comintern—all regarded the strikes as milestones on the road to the English revolution.

The Die-Hards exploited these widespread sentiments and sought, by a concerted plan, to precipitate a rupture of diplomatic and commercial relations with the Soviet Union. Churchill and Birkenhead both made violent anti-Soviet speeches on June 19.

Birkenhead declared that the money to the miners had come from the Soviet Government and hinted at the possibility of dismissing the Soviet chargé d'affaires while maintaining commercial relations intact.[5]

Churchill was more explicit. "I have always thought the United States policy towards Bolshevik Russia a right one," he admitted. That is: do business without diplomatic relations and without a trade agreement. The Russian Bolsheviks, declared the Chancellor of the Exchequer, were "miscreants." Russia, he affirmed, was "an ignorant slave State." The Bolsheviks believed that "the same sort

[4] *Some Documents concerning the Campaign against the Help Rendered by the Russian Workers to the British Strikers.* Pamphlet published by the Anglo-Russian Parliamentary Committee. (London, 1926).
[5] *Daily Mail,* June 21, 1926.

of stuff with which they bamboozled their own muzhiks would suit Britain."

Churchill went further and made a definite suggestion. "Personally," he said, "I hope to see the day when either there will be civilized Government in Russia, or we shall have ended the present pretense of friendly relations with men who are seeking our overthrow."[6]

As part of the Die-Hard maneuver for a rupture of relations, Sir W. Joynson-Hicks presented to the House of Commons a "Red" Blue Book three days after the Birkenhead-Churchill speeches. These *Communist Papers*[7] were seized during the arrest of British Communist leaders and a search of their headquarters in October, 1925. Now, nine months later, this purely internal matter of minor significance was brought out of the files to serve foreign political purposes.

But Lloyd George laughed it out of court.

> Well, now, [Lloyd George said] I thought really that at last the Home Secretary had dug something out. He has been very active. He evidently came to the conclusions before he got his evidence. That happens sometimes in politics. I will read some of this document. I think it is a very remarkable document, but it is a document that, if anything, vindicates the Labor Party. What is it? Here is the correspondence which is supposed by some of my hon. friends here to justify the breaking off of diplomatic relations with this great country on the ground that that country is spending unlimited gold to overthrow our institutions. In the first place the complaint throughout is that the gold is very limited. Here are letters from the Communist Party getting unlimited gold to say that they are running into debt because they owe £14. . . . Another of these gentlemen who is receiving this stream of gold complains that he has not got a stenographer. He says that he has to turn the office boy on to copying his letters. He says the arrears of his correspondence are so great that he cannot go out to address meetings. So he applies for a typist. He does not ask for poison gas, machine guns, rifles—only one poor typist. And this is the Russian gold that is pouring into the coffers of the Communist Party. . . . Here is another great phrase: 'We must adopt merciless measures.' What to do? To overthrow the Government, to overthrow the British Empire? No, 'We must adopt merciless measures to fight the Labor Party.' Here is a long list of the activities for which the Russian gold is to be used. First in the list is:

[6] *Daily Telegraph* and *Times*, June 21, 1926.
[7] British Blue Book. *Communist Papers*. (London, 1926). Cmd. 2682.

'Sharp criticism in principle of the conduct of the MacDonald Government.'

'A bitter fight should be carried on against MacDonald's policy. . . .'

'Active agitation should be conducted against . . .' What? 'The I.L.P.' [Independent Labor Party.]

Was there ever a more ridiculous Blue Book? And this is the basis? We have had a description of what they are going to do. They are going to subvert the whole of British society; the bourgeoisie is to disappear—not merely the capitalists but the *petit bourgeoisie;* the British Empire is to be wiped out—by funds that cannot provide one stenographer! Trade which runs into millions—£34,000,000 last year, and it will be more when we take what we want in the way of timber and other essential commodities from Russia—trade which is growing year by year, is to be thrown away for this miserable abortion of a book![8]

Austen Chamberlain told Rakovsky in November, 1925, that "though we had ample ground on which to base a rupture of relations with the Soviet Government . . . I desired, if possible, to avoid rupture."[9] He repeated these same words at Rosengolz on July 13, 1926, except that the "if possible" seemed to him in greater doubt.[1] Yet despite the resentment among non-working-class elements in England aroused by Russian aid to the miners, relations were not broken off. The resistance of business circles interested in trade with the Soviet Union only partially explains the British Government's policy of postponement. Political considerations probably played a great role: in April, 1926, Russia and Germany had signed the Berlin Treaty. London was first stunned, then anxious to wait and see what real practical significance that agreement would have. Moreover, in June and July, the very months in which the Baldwin Cabinet weighed the possibility of a rupture and some ministers tried to hasten it, the Franco-Soviet debt negotiations appeared to be on the eve of a successful conclusion. Under the circumstances, Chamberlain and the more moderate politicians felt that to throw the Bolsheviks over might help them and the Continental Powers to establish a closer community of

[8] Official Reports. Parliamentary Debates: House of Commons. June 25, 1926. Vol. 197, No. 90.

[9] British Blue Book, Cmd. 2895. (London, 1927), p. 40.

[1] *Ibid.*, p. 45.

interests. In some Conservative quarters it was still hoped that the Bolsheviks might reform, or that they could be restrained in their revolution activity in China by the existence of diplomatic relations with Great Britain. Only when Chinese revolutionary developments proved the vanity of this hope did the Die-Hards succeed in overcoming the last resistance to a break with Moscow.

# 22

# MOSCOW AND THE CHINESE REVOLUTION

DR. SUN YAT-SEN, the father of the Chinese Nationalist Revolution, made his last public utterance on November 28, 1924, at the Tokyo Pan-Asiatic Congress. Speaking of the Soviet Union, he said:

> Russia believes in benevolence and righteousness, not in force and utilitarianism. She is an exponent of justice, and does not believe in the principle that a minority should oppress a majority. Naturally, Russia comes to link hands with the Asiatics and breaks her family ties with the West. The Europeans, fearing that the Russians may succeed in carrying out these new principles, heap condemnations upon her as a rebel against the civilized world.

The Chinese believed that no imperialists would join them in the war against imperialism. Therefore they sought comfort in Moscow. Americans once asked Sun Yat-sen what was Borodin's real name. "His name is Lafayette," he replied.

"The Russian policy of the Kuomintang," writes T. C. Woo, formerly of the Hankow Foreign Office, "is one of the three cardinal policies laid down by Dr. Sun as the sure means of realizing the Nationalist Revolution."[1] The Chinese people, he says, "see in the success of the Russian Revolution perhaps a way out for their own problem."

Conditions in China and Russia prevented collaboration immediately after 1917, but in January, 1923, Dr. Sun

[1] T. C. Woo: *The Kuomintang and the Future of the Chinese Revolution*, (London, 1928), p. 120. On this question see also Wong Ching-wai: *China and the Nations*, (London, 1927), pp. 124 ff.

and Adolf A. Joffe met in Shanghai and, before issuing a joint communiqué, discussed the basis of revolutionary co-operation.

In August, 1923, Dr. Sun sent General Chiang Kai-shek, his Chief-of-Staff and confidential agent, to Moscow with letters of introduction to Lenin, Trotzky, and Chicherin. He was dispatched to discuss "ways and means whereby our friends there can assist in my work in this country." Chiang had received authorization to plead for military assistance from the Soviets.

When Karakhan succeeded Joffe in Peking, he immediately took up the thread with Canton, and on September 8, 1923, wrote to Dr. Sun explaining the anti-imperialist character of his mission. "I count on your support, Dr. Sun, old friend of new Russia, in my responsible task of establishing close contact between our two peoples."

Later in the month of September, Michael M. Borodin, a veteran member of the Russian Communist Party, received his appointment to the Canton Kuomintang Government.

## SOVIET POLICY TOWARD THE KUOMINTANG

On the basis of material made available to the writer, it is easy to trace Moscow's policy towards the Chinese nationalist movement at this stage of Chinese events

Chicherin wrote in English to Dr. Sun Yat-sen on December 4, 1923, after several conversations with the Chiang Kai-shek delegation.

> We think that the fundamental aim of the Kuomintang Party [declared the commissar] is to build up a great powerful movement of the Chinese people and that therefore propaganda and organization on the biggest scale are its first necessities. Our example was significant: our military activities were successful because a long series of years had elapsed during which we organized and organized and instructed our followers, building up in this way a great organized party throughout the whole land, a party capable of vanquishing all its adversaries. The whole Chinese nation must see the difference between the Kuomintang, a popular organized mass party, and the military dictators of the various parts of China.

Obviously the Russian stressed the advisability of slow, painful organizational activity among civilians, and held out the example of the Bolsheviks, whose military victory only followed a "long series of years" of party preparation. Nor did Chicherin believe that military aid supplied by Russia through Mongolia would solve the problems of Chinese nationalism. He suggested that they "must continue our exchange of ideas and discuss the matter further. When we reach a full agreement, everything will go on much better." Moscow was in no hurry.

Karakhan wrote to Sun Yat-sen in the same vein on January 7, 1924. "To make millions of Chinese people your followers," he said. . . . "Therein lies the main task before your party." He also attached "paramount importance to your decision to carry out the land decree," and called it "your main lever" of mobilizing popular support. "Literally and allegorically speaking, the ground will be taken from under your enemies' feet . . . but for this very reason the Kuomintang will feel itself on firm ground." If a certain section of the Kuomintang objects, cast them out, Karakhan advised. The Bolsheviks too expelled their faint-hearted. Untiringly, the Russians gave Canton the benefit of their own experience. Above all, Karakhan emphasized, strengthen the Kuomintang. "The army may be defeated; not the party."

**BORODIN IN CANTON** Borodin arrived in Canton in September, 1923. The situation was not a heartening one. An army of 200,000 paid allegiance to a large number of self-seeking militarists whose sympathies were not with the Kuomintang. The workers were divided, the peasants asleep, and the Kuomintang Party a little-frequented office. Dr. Sun sat on the island of Honam in the Canton harbor, a sick and broken man.

Before long Borodin became the "instructor and reorganizer" of the Kuomintang. In effect, this meant that he had been placed in supreme command.

**BORODIN'S PROGRAM** In November, 1923, soon after Borodin's arrival, Chen Chiung-ming threatened to take Canton from the Kuomintang. Borodin gave his interpretation of this development to the Kuomintang executive committee on November 13. The party had given no land to the peasants and satisfied none of its demands. Therefore the peasantry refused to feed the revolutionary demands. The party had paid no attention to the legitimate grievances of the proletariat. Therefore the workers refused to go to or stay at the front. What were they fighting for? Kuomintang deeds must answer the question, Borodin said in effect. He accordingly proposed the immediate promulgation of two decrees and one manifesto. They must allow peasant communities to confiscate landlords' holdings with or without compensation, and to collect land rent and distribute it according to their own discretion. The second document must grant labor the eight-hour day, a minimum wage, and other minimum rights. In a manifesto to the petty bourgeoisie, moreover, these gains for the working masses would be explained as its own gains too. The higher the living standard of the producing population, the better trade.

The three measures, Borodin declared, would make the Kuomintang a popular, nationalist party capable of pretending at least to being the socialist party which it called itself.

Chen Chiung-ming's army stood outside the city. Deserters from the Kuomintang front filled Canton. The executive committee was in somewhat of a panic and adopted all Borodin's suggestions unanimously. Forthwith, a tremendous propaganda apparatus was set into motion to acquaint the workers and peasants with the new decisions. The effect on the front was immediate and revolutionary. But when the menace had been removed, Kuomintang leaders began to waver. Some of the very men who had voted for the decrees went to Dr. Sun to sabotage their enactment into law.

Borodin went to see Dr. Sun on the island of Honam on November 16. The doctor began by explaining his interest in Russo-Japanese relations. It was his way of saying that he did not wish Moscow to be offended by Kuomintang lapses. But what of the three measures? He had no objection against the manifesto to the petty bourgeoisie, nor to labor reforms. But strong opposition had asserted itself in Kuomintang circles against the land measures.

Borodin cautioned the old leader of the unfortunate impression of the Kuomintang's failure to redeem its promise. Men had gone to the front inspired by that pledge. They would feel themselves deceived. What would all China, the labor world, what would Moscow think? Some pointed though polite sentences were exchanged. Dr. Sun may have suspected that Borodin wished to leave.

Dr. Sun bargained with Borodin. Finally they struck

a compromise—the best under the circumstances. Two land decrees would be promulgated: one reducing land rent 25 per cent, the other providing for the establishment of peasant unions. The first was never put into practice. But to the second Borodin attached supreme importance. It opened the way to the organization of the peasantry on radical lines.

This episode threw a bright light on the politics of the Kuomintang leaders and on their hesitation in the face of revolutionary innovations of far-reaching economic importance. The Kuomintang was enmeshed in feudal influences; its roots were in the bourgeoisie. Obviously, no Soviet or socialist revolution could be attempted.

The first Kuomintang congress took place in January, 1924. Borodin wrote the program which, with few corrections, that initial congress adopted—and he permitted it to guide his activities through several years. The party had been reorganized, and a strict system of discipline introduced striving to make every member conscious, active, and responsible. Borodin now gave it its declaration of principles: a national, democratic, liberal, modern, forward-looking program which was neither Communism nor Socialism.

The program shows concern for the merchants, intellectuals, industrialists, workers and peasants. But, "although one cannot be opposed to a merchant government as such, our demand is that the masses of the people will organize the government themselves, to represent the interests of the whole people, and not confined to those of the merchant class." Class suffrage based on property qualifications must be abolished but universal suffrage was not approved. Only those "who are really loyal to anti-imperialism" will enjoy all rights and privileges. There would be indirect and direct popular authority—that is, elections, plus the initiative, referendum and recall. Such a system would "supplement the shortcomings" of representative government and "rectify the evils of a purely elective system." Freedom of association, speech, publication, domicile, and belief were guaranteed.

Borodin entertained no illusions as to the disciplinary perfection and ideological homogeneity which a multi-class party like the Kuomintang could achieve. Nevertheless, he desired the axis of the whole governmental system to be the party—as in Soviet Russia. "The party must be the central organ of control of the political power," he wrote.

Borodin interpreted Sun Yat-sen's third principle as requiring "the equalization of land" and "the control of capital." But not wholesale nationalization of land, and not nationalization with compensation as in Russia. Borodin here made a concession to Dr. Sun's single-tax philosophy and wrote into it, as a compromise, this plank: "Private landowners shall declare its [the land's] value to the Government, which shall tax it according to the value so declared with the option of buying it at that price in case of necessity." This was an astute device for obtaining honest declarations. If the landowner stated a high land value he could be taxed heavily; if he gave a low estimate he would cheat himself when it came to selling his farm. Landless peasants must receive grants from the State and government credits from rural banks.

The essence of control of industry demands that "private industries, whether of the Chinese or of the foreign nationals, which are either of a monopolistic nature or are beyond the capacity of private individuals to develop, such as banking, railways, and navigation, shall be undertaken by the State"—but not a word about expropriation. The State must provide remedies for unemployment, and introduce a labor code to improve the status of workers. The support of the aged, the training and education of the young, the care of the sick and disabled likewise fell within the compass of Dr. Sun's principle of "People's livelihood." Sun Yat-sen himself sometimes called it socialism.

Borodin's program outlined a vigorous foreign policy. Unequal treaties, foreign concessions, extra-territoriality, foreign control of customs "should be cancelled." Other treaties, disadvantageous to China, "shall be revised." Foreign loans of China would be "guaranteed and paid" but in such a manner as shall not cause political and industrial damages to the country.

The Committee appointed by the Congress to draft this program consisted of Wong Ching-wei, Hu Han-min, Tai Chi-tao, Lao Chun-kai, and Borodin. Hu Han-min opposed Borodin's views, Tai Chi-tao occupied a central position, but Dr. Sun supported the Russian. The program was clearly a victory of the Left. It was based on three principles accepted by Sun Yat-sen: (1) Co-operation with Soviet Russia and the Chinese Communist Party, (2) Anti-Imperialism, and (3) A Workers' and Peasants' program. Around this formula Borodin wrote the entire declaration.

Borodin thus grafted Bolshevik determination on Chinese indifference, and the Soviet civilian method on Chinese military tendencies. Without Russian influence, without Moscow's doctrine of "the party first," Canton might well have become only another center of militaristic activity. Canton's army victories would have been mere territorial conquests devoid of revolutionary significance. This, indeed, has been and is China's chief problem: to deprive the generals of supreme power and subject them to civilian, democratic control.

One of Borodin's services to the cause of the Chinese revolution was the organization, early in 1924, of the military training academy at Whampoa in the Canton harbor. It became the cadre of the army which later conquered half of China. Russian officers assisted in the task, and the Soviet Government advanced 3,000,000 rubles for its early running expenses.

During the first year of his stay in the province of Kwantung, Borodin's energies were engaged in two directions: to prevent the northern drive on which so many leaders insisted and to establish a strong government in Canton. The Kuomintang had no power even in the city. Its authority was contested first by the compradores, and then by a large army from the southern province of Yunnan, which had marched through Kwangsi and made itself at home in Kwantung. The compradores, those peculiar products of a peculiar Chinese situation, were the go-betweens for foreign firms. In Canton, they represented the British colony on the island of Hongkong. From Hongkong came their political ideas and their class sympathies. They naturally opposed the Kuomintang. In October, 1924, they rebelled against Sun Yat-sen and threatened to become a government within a government. At Borodin's suggestion a special council was set up to combat the compradores; Dr. Sun named Chiang Kai-shek, Borodin, and Wong Ching-wei among its members. An assault was arranged on the richest section of the city, the stronghold of the compradores. Artillery was brought into play. Fires broke out. Bloody street fighting proved necessary. In the end the compradore volunteers were defeated and disarmed; their leaders fled to Hongkong.

The Kuomintang undertook no repressive measures against the compradores. Instead, a conciliatory manifesto promised milder taxation to the bourgeoisie, which feared Bolshevism in the Kuomintang. Yet parallel with this development, trade unions were organized among laborers, and peasant organizations sprang up which demanded land.

Dr. Sun, smitten with a fatal illness, left for Peking at the end of 1924. But the Kuomintang still maintained headquarters on Honam island. In June, 1925, however, the Cantonese forces crushed, decimated, and expelled the Yunnan army in Canton. And as the Kuomintang leaders approached the city in a barge, the Russians felt that in two years the national revolution would reach Peking.

**THE GREAT STRIKE** With the victory over the Yunnanese troops and the destruction of the political power of the Canton compradores, the Kwantung bourgeoisie began to look to the Kuomintang for leadership and protection. Its allies were the old nationalist leaders of the type of Hu Han-min and those Cantonese militarists whose first concern was not the revolution but their own control of the rich Kwantung province.

Against this Right bloc stood the Left Kuomintang or People's Socialists and the Chinese Communists who worked together within the Kuomintang to carry out the Kuomintang's program of January, 1924. They organized trade and peasant unions and conducted vigorous revolutionary propaganda throughout the province and in the army. Those departments of the Kuomintang Party and the Canton Government which dealt with labor or rural economic problems were usually placed under the charge of Chinese Communists.

General Chiang Kai-shek, Commander of the Whampoa Military Academy, sided with the Left Kuomintang and countenanced, somewhat reluctantly, the gradual weeding-out of conservative Kuomintang leaders during 1924 and 1925.

The struggle between Right and Left had commenced. But although it was fated to split the Kuomintang and paralyze revolutionary effort for a period of years, the chasm in 1925 was neither wide nor deep enough to prevent both factions from collaboration in the same organization.

Events in 1925, especially the Hongkong strike, strengthened the revolutionary tendency. On May 30, 1925, Chinese students and other demonstrators in the Shanghai International Settlement were fired on by European police. Twelve Chinese were killed; seventeen wounded.[2] This "bloody baptism" galvanized the forces of revolution. The shots rang through the length and breadth of the vast country. Nation-wide protest demonstrations took place and in Shanghai a tremendous general strike was called. British and Japanese goods suffered from a watertight boycott.

A three days' strike was proclaimed in Canton as a protest against the Shanghai shooting incident. On the third day, a demonstration of many thousands passed the British and French concessions on the island of Shameen. The Chinese did not enter the concessions. The marchers, with very few exceptions, had gone beyond the island and had their back to it when British and French forces in Shameen poured several heavy volleys into the receding demonstration killing thirty-seven and wounding several hundred. The British officially claim that they fired in reply to a shot from the rear of the procession. The Chinese dispute the fact.

The "Massacre of Shameen" fanned Cantonese anger. A spontaneous strike broke out against the British colony of Hongkong. One hundred thousand workers withdrew from Hongkong to Canton, leaving the export warehouses, industries and foreign inhabitants without Chinese laborers and servants. Pickets prevented British vessels or all vessels that had touched Hongkong from entering the Pearl River to come up to Canton. Hongkong, the British "Pearl of the East," lay moribund. British trade suffered. For sixteen whole months the vigilance of the pickets and the strikers continued without relaxations.

The Hongkong strike, Borodin said,[3]

> was really not an economic strike. It was the quintessence of the anti-imperialist movement and the most militant expression of that movement. That it concentrated on Great Britain was not a matter of specific policy but resulted from the fact that Hong-

[2] C. A. Macartney and Others: *Survey of International Affairs, 1925,* (London, 1928). II, 382.

[3] To the author.

kong was its immediate object. Had it been Formosa or the Philippines it would have been directed against Japan or America. It was a political strike pure and simple.

The strike grew out of political resentment against England. Its direct organizers were the Sailors' Union and the Chinese Communist Party (C.C.P.). But even the bourgeoisie helped. The Central Kuomintang bank in Canton made financial contributions to the picket funds. Rich Chinese in Singapore, the United States and other foreign countries sent enormous sums, and T. V. Soong, the Kwantung Minister of Finance, paid out $15,000 silver daily for the maintenance of the strikers.

Canton, in fact all of Kwantung, Swatow, the southern part of Hunan, and at least a part of Kwangsi gravitate economically towards Hongkong. It is their point of contact with the outside world—and with foreign imperialism. "You have no idea," Borodin once said to me, "to what extent Hongkong has permeated every nook and corner of South China. Hongkong is like a tremendous spider with its tentacles spread out to all parts of Kwantung, Kwangsi, etc."

Thousands of Chinese who do business in Canton live under British protection in Hongkong. They keep their money in Hongkong—and Hongkong, Borodin explains, even maintains its own bandit organization in Canton to persuade Kwantungese to deposit their earnings in the British banks of the colony. Canton is on the Pearl River but has no port. Its quality rice, silk, fruit, etc., goes abroad through Hongkong; it imports through the same city. Kwantung and bordering provinces are the economic thralls of the little British island metropolis.

The compradores thrive in this situation, but the petty bourgeoisie suffers from it; its growth is hampered by it. Therefore the Canton petty bourgeoisie aided the anti-Hongkong strike.

Hongkong was being ruined. The fabulously rich British colony languished. Its enterprises locked their doors. Its docks lay empty. Its workers had deserted. The Hongkong proletariat was organized and class-conscious. "They came over en masse to Canton," Borodin says, "and did wonders. Brave, disciplined fellows, they forced even their yellow leaders into the fight."

But although Hongkong faced ruin, Canton suffered too. The first effect of the strike was to transfer much trade to Canton. The city and the province prospered. The Kuomintang treasury, empty before the boycott, bulged with wealth during the first period. Kwantung won respect for its own currency—and for its determination and might.

Soon, however, the dislocation of business began to exert its deleterious effect on Canton. Moreover, the struggle was unequal. The struggle, according to Borodin, was between the British Empire and Canton. But the base of the anti-imperialist conflict was too narrow and the base of the imperialists too broad.

> Imperialism [he declared] either had to capitulate to China —for those 100,000 strikers represented the best interests of China—or China acknowledge defeat. Since, however, defeat could not be countenanced, it became necessary to terminate the battle in this corner in order to start out with greater vigor to fight imperialism throughout China—on the wider base.

This view of the Hongkong strike helped Borodin to decide in favor of the Northern Kuomintang Expedition to the Yangtse River. He had previously opposed it.

The Northern Expedition commenced in June, 1926. The strike continued till October 10, 1926.

**LEFT v. RIGHT** The presence of 100,000 Hongkong workers in Canton constituted a drain on the Kuomintang treasury and an influence for radicalism. Fifty thousand were sent to rural centers where they became nuclei of revolutionary propaganda. The other 50,000 remained in Canton and divided their time between picketing and regular courses in what the Russians call "Politgramota"—political theory and revolutionary tactics.

The bourgeoisie, however, did not look with complacency on the fortification of Left Kuomintang-Communist influence in Kwantung. The Hongkong strike was two months old when Lao Chun-hai, Dr. Sun's trusted friend, chief of the Workers' and Peasants' Section of the Kuomintang Party, and Political Commissar of the Whampoa Academy, was murdered—on August 20, 1925.

> This murder [Borodin contended] signified that the Cantonese generals who had helped to drive out the Yunnanese mercenaries intended to contest the victory with the Kuomintang, that the bourgeoisie and the landlords wished to contest the supremacy of the Left tendency, and that Hongkong had taken action to undermine the strike.

All these elements lay behind this political murder, he believed, and Hu Han-min, of the reactionary Kuomintang wing, was directly implicated in it. Chiang Kai-shek, an intimate friend of Lao Chun-kai, was convinced of Hu's guilt.

Apprehension lest anti-revolutionary forces would act quickly convinced Borodin of the necessity of decisive measures. He therefore proposed that the Central Committee of the Kuomintang appoint a committee of three with dictatorial powers. Hu Han-min, the chairman of the highest Political Bureau of the party, signed the order creating the body, but he himself was left out. And shortly afterwards Canton exiled him to Moscow.

The dictatorial triumvirate consisted of Chiang Kai-shek, the commander of the Whampoa school, Wong Ching-wei, who succeeded Lao as its political commissar, and Su Sun-chi, commander of the Cantonese army, whose chief desire centered on dominating Kwantung rather than on the national revolution.

The business of the triumvirate, as Borodin conceived it, was to defeat this Cantonese army. Su Sun-chi's role as one of the triumvirs disguised the maneuver and signified that the entire Canton army would not, as yet, suffer demolition.

The triumvirate's first move was to attack Canton units lying in the town. Su Sun-chi offered counsels of peace, but he could not help himself. He knew the next move would be directed against him. At a given signal, loyal Whampoa troops took the offensive. For a day and night, Canton echoed to rifle and machine-gun firing and the explosion of grenades. Chiang Kai-shek had military equipment from the Norwegian steamer *Hav* (whose cargo, originally ordered by the Cantonese compradores and merchants volunteers, was seized by the Kuomintang), and also from Soviet sources. After a day's fighting, the 15,000 Whampoa cadets succeeded in disarming 12,000 Cantonese soldiers. Hongkong workers assisted in the task.

Thereafter, until it reached the Yangtse, the Kuomintang Party, and the Chinese Nationalist movement, operated under radical control. Indeed, at the second party congress in January, 1926, the Canton Chamber of Commerce, stronghold of the merchant middle class, submitted a long declaration which closed with the words: "Long Live the World Revolution."

Chinese Communists and Soviet military advisers occupied pivotal positions in the Whampoa school and in the reorganized Kuomintang army, while Left influences dominated the Government's policy.

Nevertheless, no radical reforms were introduced in South China. The Kuomintang was incapable of carrying through an agrarian revolution. That would have been tantamount to its resignation in favor of the Communists. Nor could the Kuomintang, in view of its mixed class composition, undertake the confiscation of private property.

The more pro-Communist the political control in Canton became the greater became the resistance which the bourgeoisie offered to the Left program, and the clearer it became to Borodin that Kwantung was too limited a sphere in which to carry out a national revolution.

Borodin has been accused by the Trotzky opposition in the Soviet Union of obstructing the sovietization of South China. These Trotzkyists, he replied, who insist that Socialism cannot be built in one country—in Russia—how can they argue that Communism is possible in only one part of one country, and especially when that country, China, is more backward than Russia? Canton itself boasts only of a weak organized proletariat, and its more advanced workers, the mechanics, are the aristocrats of labor and anti-revolutionary. Moreover, said Borodin, "no theory of revolution had developed in China as in Russia. Theory is the prime requisite of revolution. China had not a single pamphlet on the agrarian question. The character of Chinese economy was neither known nor understood."

"We could have seized power in Canton," Borodin said, "but we could not have held it. We would have gone down in a sea of blood. We would have tried it if we had had a 25 per cent chance of existing for one year."

The Left held control in Kwantung, but it was powerless to effect a social revolution. The Right watched jealously for an opportunity to assert itself. It tolerated radical domination as long as nothing fundamentally radical was undertaken; meanwhile it gathered strength.

**BORODIN DECIDED FOR THE NORTHERN EXPEDITION** Three factors ultimately combined to persuade Borodin of the wisdom of a Northern Expedition. In the first place, Wu Pei-fu made steady progress southward and commenced to threaten territory bordering on the Kuomintang's sphere of control. But this was a minor consideration; Wu might have been beaten back in a war of defense. The second influence was the obvious impossibility of defeating imperialism by such weapons as the Hongkong strike. "The base of the anti-imperialist fight must be widened," Borodin told his followers in Canton. Finally, Borodin felt that if they remained much longer in Kwantung, an armed struggle would ensue between the Left consisting of the radical Kuomintang and the C.C.P., and, on the other hand, the Right or bourgeoisie. In that struggle, he knew, both would be defeated and only the Canton militarists would gain.

In March, 1926, the Trotzky opposition in Moscow began to demand a more revolutionary and purely Communist policy in Canton. "An open struggle with the [Chinese] bourgeoisie, not an alliance with it," one of its secret circulars insisted. The Stalin majority resisted this effort, but the Russian opposition was not without friends in the C.C.P., especially in the Shanghai headquarters. A Northern Expedition would prevent precipitate action.

Convinced of the necessity of a Northern Expedition of the Nationalist forces, Borodin went immediately to Peking to confer with Feng Yu-hsiang, the "Christian general." Chiang Kai-shek had been apprised of the purpose of Borodin's trip and gave the Russian a bodyguard of six Whampoa cadets. They traveled in secret from Canton to Tientsin by boat, and incognito from Tientsin to Peking, through an area bristling with foreign armed forces.

**BORODIN AND FENG YU-HSIANG** Borodin had met Feng once before. Towards the end of 1924, the Russian came to Peking with Dr. Sun and Wong Ching-wei. Feng held Peking and lived in the Western Hills outside the city. Wong then wrote a letter to the general suggesting a meeting with Borodin; Dr. Sun wished Kuomintang influence brought to Feng and sent a Russian Bolshevik. But Feng wrote back that they were having rather windy weather in the hills—which was Chinese for saying that Borodin might wait.

Within a few weeks, however, Feng's position grew worse. The diplomatic corps in Peking distrusted him, and he retired to Kalgan, where Borodin came to see him.

Feng held the North-West and his back was to Outer Mongolia and Soviet territory. Borodin told him that though his army was the best in China it would not stand its ground in a battle with a nationalist force. Feng was filling his men with love of God and other abstract feelings which killed nationalism; the Bible and Sun Yat-senism conflicted, Borodin preached.

Feng offered resistance. The Canton generals, he declared, robbed the people—and Borodin could make no denial; he, Feng, helped the population, put up baths for his soldiers, was building a modern city at Kalgan, fought opium, and introduced reforms. He explained the "miracle" by which he had come to believe in God, and the manner in which missionaries worked on his sentiments.

Feng was a difficult quarry. He evaded the hunter, argued deftly, talked for hours about himself, his past, his thoughts. But this was philanthropy, Borodin explained. He might, by such methods, benefit one province or one army, but all China needed salvation. That could be achieved only with a national ideal and a national program calling for the unification of China. Feng listened. His imagination, and perhaps ambition, were stirred.

Feng and Borodin warmed to their subject. The general ordered food—at first the lean food of the Christian hermit, but as he began to think in unison with Borodin, meat and other substantial viands, which both big men enjoyed better, were served. They had spent twenty-four hours together now. They went to bed in the same room, and then Feng summoned his generals. Borodin talked to them at length, all the time combating missionary influence and missionary ideas. Twenty more hours passed.

In the end, Feng did not join the Kuomintang, but he agreed to permit Kuomintang propagandists to enter his army and agitate for the new nationalism. Back in Canton, Borodin took special pains to train these agitators in the right spirit and to furnish them with the necessary arguments and tact. Thereafter, during 1925, officers, propagandists, and messengers went regularly from Canton to Feng's headquarters.

Early in 1926, Borodin came north once more to win Feng for the Northern Expedition. Borodin's goal was now a more definite one. He wanted Feng to declare himself in favor of the Northern Expedition, to announce himself leader of its northern section, and to join the

Kuomintang. Feng must enter politics, Borodin demanded, overthrow the Peking Government of foreign puppets which he had tolerated, and establish a Kuomintang Cabinet. Then, supported by the moral forces thus released, he could hold on till the Cantonese reached Peking.

Feng hesitated; his generals opposed. They were faced with an Allied ultimatum to give up the Taku forts near Tientsin. The answer, Borodin urged, must be his identification with the Kuomintang. But Feng accepted the ultimatum on March 18 and on the same day, forty students who participated in a demonstration against the surrender were shot in the capital.

Feng now adopted a typically Chinese attitude of indecision and "waiting till the clouds blow over." He retired, unaccompanied, to Urga. From there he went to Moscow to sue for more military and financial assistance. He had received it from the Bolsheviks since his Peking coup in October, 1924.

**CHIANG KAI-SHEK'S COUPS** While Borodin was absent in the North, Chiang Kai-shek executed his famous "coup against the Russians" in Canton, on March 20, 1926.

Chiang had watched with increasing concern the aggrandizement of power by the Left-Kuomintang-Communist bloc. The Kwantung bourgeoisie was subdued, and accepted the radical leadership meekly but bided its time in the expectation of a better day. Until the second Kuomintang congress in January, 1926, the bourgeoisie and Chiang Kai-shek tolerated their position and, without arousing the ire of the Lefts, sought to fortify it. But the undisguised near-Communist coloration of the second congress and the advancing Communization of the Canton Government made the Right somewhat panicky. If they did not act soon, if the Hongkong strike continued to weaken the Canton bourgeoisie while buttressing the control, morale, and self-confidence of the workers, if, moreover, the Northern Expedition set out under such auspices, the Right would be reduced to impotence and Chiang Kai-shek to a subordinate role.

Chiang was hampered by the civilian political commissar at the Whampoa Academy, who, following the Russian pattern, checked the work of the military chief. At one time, every order of the commander required the countersignature of the commissar. Lao Chun-kai, the first Whampoa Political Commissar, was murdered in August, 1925. Chiang's coup on March 20, 1926, was designed to overthrow Wong Ching-wei, Lao's successor, who led the Left Kuomintang and championed close co-operation with the C.C.P. and the Russians.

On the day of the coup Chiang's troops surrounded the premises occupied by the Kuomintang's Russian military advisers and of the Hongkong strike committee, arrested Chinese communists, detained radical Kuomintang members, and undertook more subtle measures to ensure his control of the Government. Canton immediately proposed to Hongkong to terminate the strike.

But Chiang apparently was frightened by his own action and its success, and sent his secretary, Shao Li-tsi, posthaste to Peking with a humble letter begging Borodin to return south without delay.

Meanwhile, Feng had lost Tientsin and Peking, and when Borodin and his bodyguard tried to steal through from the capital to Tientsin they were shot at and forced to turn back. Borodin now hastened to Urga where he once again met Feng in sulking retirement. The Russian then proceeded via Siberia to Vladivostok, and thence, by ship, to Canton.

The entire Kuomintang Navy—such as it was—greeted him as his vessel approached. Chiang Kai-shek, who took part in this welcome, overflowed with apologies and explanations. He complained that the C.C.P. had gained too much control. He did not object to co-operation with Soviet Russia. But the C.C.P. attempted to dominate him and the Kuomintang. Wong Ching-wei had rejected all his proposals. The immediate cause of the coup, he affirmed, was a Communist plot to kidnap him.

Chiang was becoming a militarist like all the other Chinese tuchuns, Borodin charged. If that were indeed the case, he retorted, he would retire and go to Moscow to learn and absorb the proper spirit. What, he asked of Borodin, must he do?

"Prepare for the Northern Expedition," Borodin replied.

Before the final decision to march north was taken, however, Borodin wished to repair some of the damage done by the coup of March 20. Chiang Kia-shek, therefore, engineered a second coup on April 25, this time against the Right. Extreme reactionary Kuomintangists were arrested, exiled, or removed from positions of trust. Others, like C. C. Wu, later Chinese minister in Washington, escaped and went into temporary hiding.

Why, having made his first coup against the Russians, did Chiang Kai-shek summon back Borodin? Why was he so contrite in Borodin's presence? Because he knew he faced defeat if he undertook to eliminate Left influence completely. He helped to make the second coup of April 25 because he wished to refrain from provoking a rupture at that moment. He was on the defensive.

But why did not Borodin, the Left Kuomintang and the C.C.P. eliminate Chiang Kai-shek? Because they were too weak. They could turn back the clock slightly in their coup of April 25. They had mass sympathy. But in Canton they wielded insufficient forces to overcome Chiang and the bourgeoisie which supported him. Chiang would have blockaded Canton. Under these circumstances, a Red regime was doomed

Both sides knew that the struggle between them was inevitable. But rather than engage now in blood-letting from which only the Cantonese militarists could gain, they tacitly agreed to postpone the issue until they reached the Yangtse. The resolution to commence the Northern Expedition was adopted by the Kuomintang Central Committee on May 15. At that meeting the unexpressed sentiments of each faction amounted to this: "Gentlemen, we know we must fight one another. But we need a wider area. Let us delay the day of reckoning and meanwhile go forward to a common goal."

Karakhan, observing in Peking, counseled against a break with Chiang in Canton. Wait till you get to Peking, his advice ran. The Left Kuomintang and C.C.P. wished to reach Shanghai, Hankow, Hunan, and the Yangtse where they would find reinforcement in the proletariat and the poorer peasantry. The Right yearned to establish contacts with the rich bourgeoisie of Shanghai and with the foreign Powers which nested there.

**THE SOCIAL FORCES IN KWANTUNG** Five elements in South China supported the Northern Expedition:

(1) The Federalists,
(2) The militaristic armies,

(3) The bourgeoisie,
(4) The workers and peasants,
(5) The Left Kuomintang or People's Socialists.

Each of these groups had its own reason for participating in the Northern Expedition.

**CHINESE FEDERALISM** Chinese federalism is the basis of the division of China into foreign spheres of influence. The entrenchment of the several Powers in the treaty ports creates a prejudice in favor of disunity and a class of Chinese compradores whose livelihood depends on the unequal treaties. Each treaty port, or colony in the case of Hongkong, holds under its economic and frequently political hegemony a tremendous *hinterland*. And even when the ports or colonies belonged to the same Power their territories competed with one another, fought with one another, and refused to unite.

For this grave reason, the Russians in China, and with them the Kuomintang until its split, insisted that the country could not be united until treaty ports, unequal treaties and extra-territoriality were abolished.

Powers interested in certain spheres of influence in China had to oppose Chinese unity and adopt policies conducive to federalism. A nation like the United States, which had no well-defined sphere of influence in China and disposed of excess capital to invest in the natural wealth of the interior, or a country like the Soviet Union, which had no sphere of influence in China and wanted none, could afford to advocate Chinese unity, the abolition of unequal treaties and the suppression of militarism, the tuchuns, federalists, etc. But Japan and England had to oppose unification.

The federalists in Kwantung favored the Northern Expedition even though its aim was Chinese unification because they desired the Kuomintang to get out of their province. They were sceptical about the success of the Northern Expedition, but apart from that, they felt the financial burden of supporting a government which pretended to represent the nation and which involved them in a bitter struggle with England. Li Tin-sin, the chief tuchun of Canton, was therefore one of the most active organizers of the Northern Expedition. He knew that the moment the Kuomintang forces moved he would be free to rule and he knew that they could not control him from the Yangtse. Those very people who shouted loudest "Kwantung for the Kwantungese" gave loans and soldiers to the Kuomintang Army, for they remembered that Dr. Sun had always opposed Canton autonomy.

**EMIGRANT ARMIES** The Cantonese viewed the Northern Expedition with favor because it would also rid them of emigrant armies. Throughout China, but particularly in the lower half, military tuchuns defeated at home made a practice of seeking refuge in Kwantung. The province is extremely rich, and has plenty of food. The militarists, moreover, though miles removed from revolution and Kuomintang, nevertheless harbored a deep respect for Sun Yat-sen. As soon as they reached the borders of Kwangtung, these armed exiles would hoist the Kuomintang flag and announce that they had come not, God forbid, to live off the fat of the land, but to aid the Doctor in achieving his goal. By joining the Northern Expedition they would get nearer home or even reconquer their home. At any rate, they would obtain arms and an occupation.

**THE NATIONAL BOURGEOISIE** "Japan and Great Britan," the Russians said, "must oppose any force, be it communism, nationalism, American imperialism, which aspires to unite China. Their influence is threatened by each. But so long as British, Japanese, and American interests clash, and until the last can crush the others, the United States, acting through the Chinese national bourgeoisie, must fail to achieve Chinese unification." Japan and England would use every weapon at their command—marauding generals, or federalist tuchuns, or diplomatic pressure, or, if the danger became acute, an anti-American war to prevent the fortification of American influence in China. For this reason, the Bolsheviks submitted, the Americanization of China was impossible, and without America, Chiang Kai-shek or his successor, remained nothing more than an incident in Chinese social development. Alone, the embryonic Chinese bourgeoisie was too weak to unite China, and the moment it coalesced with the only imperialism—American—whose interest demanded unification, it antagonized America's two great imperialist rivals.

The French Revolution, and the Turkish Nationalist

Revolution of 1920, were opposed to feudalism and foreign coalitions and could, therefore, produce their Napoleon and Kemal Pasha. But Chiang could neither dissociate himself from his land-owning supporters nor defy all foreign Powers. Without them, he was impotent. With them, he became a tool.

The Chinese nationalist bourgeoisie was concentrated in Shanghai, Hankow, and a few other large cities. It was economically weak. It could not develop the resources of China alone, but it had graduated from the compradore stage and wished to invest its own capital in business enterprises outside the limits of the treaty ports. Unlike the petty bourgeoisie of most cities, the land owned by the Shanghai bourgeoisie, or by the national bourgeoisie of lesser metropoles, did not necessarily lie immediately outside the city. Its interests covered a wider territory. Because it wished to extend its influence and economic power to further provinces, it supported a strong central government which could establish order, protect ways of communication, abolish the likin, and collect customs. But since this bourgeoisie with national ambitions was too poor to invest heavily in the exploitation of the country's tremendous wealth, it favored co-operation with imperialistic countries that would not encourage federalism, provincial tuchuns, regional economy, and regional governments. The only country with such a policy was the United States.

In Canton, the national bourgeoisie hailed the Northern Expedition as its salvation. By moving towards the Yangtse it would come into contact with Shanghai, the great bourgeois center, and receive reinforcements. At the same time it would be prosecuting the task of evolving a nationalist and bourgeois China.

**THE LEFT KUOMINTANG** The Left Kuomintang was not merely Eugene Chen, Wong Ching-wei, and Mrs. Sun Yat-sen. They and their colleagues represented the large petty bourgeois class of local traders, small manufacturers, rich artisans, etc. This group was caught between two fires: if the national bourgeoisie triumphed, the department store and organized modern industry would ruin it; if the workers, peasants and sovietism won, their power would be wiped out.

The Left Kuomintang tolerated Communism, but never accepted it. Intellectually such people as Eugene

Chen saw that the future in China smiled on Communism. He had no objection if the next generation went Bolshevik. But many other Left Kuomintangists, tied to Shanghai by a thousand bonds of blood and business, could not whole-heartedly enter the Red ranks.

This petty bourgeois group went to Hankow with the Northern Expedition because it hoped the workers and peasants would help them to power without yearning for it themselves. But when peasant uprisings began in Hunan, and when Hubei workers prepared for uprisings, they realized their error and, with some notable exceptions, reverted sharply to a more conservative stand.

The Left Kuomintang feared the big bourgeoisie more than the Communists. It believed that China was not ready for socialism and that the Chinese would reject the Soviet system. Sovietism would be a violent rejection of the Chinese past, whereas the bourgeoisie with the help of foreign Powers, could easily set up a government. The Left Kuomintang aligned itself with the force whose prospects of complete success were, in its opinion, weakest. For this reason, it welcomed the increase of the workers' and peasants' factor in the nationalist revolution, regarding it as the best bar to the Shanghai bourgeoisie's victory. Yet one must not leave out of account the intellectual bias of the Left Kuomintang's leaders for radicalism and their boundless anti-imperialism which made them the bitter enemies of a bourgeoisie that compromised with foreign influence.

**THE PROLETARIAT** There were, roughly, 50,000,000 workers in China, the great majority of them artisans, coolies, and unqualified laborers who live in the interior where it was difficult to organize or propagandize them. The industrial proletariat numbered between one and a half and two and a half million. But in the textile factories most of the employees were women and children who were bound by backward traditions and customs, and generally made poor revolutionary material.

Nevertheless, beginning with 1923, the Bolsheviks in China and the C.C.P. registered considerable progress in labor organization. Communist nuclei, trade unions and peasant unions multiplied throughout the provinces where the Kuomintang held sway.

The C.C.P. took its instructions in larger matters of

policy from Comintern headquarters in Moscow. A meeting of the presidium of the Communist International Executive Committee on November 28, 1923, adopted a resolution in favor of C.C.P. co-operation with the Kuomintang, and of nationalization of land, reduction of land taxes, nationalization of foreign firms, industries, and banks, and of railways and waterways.

Three years later, on November 30, 1926, Stalin discussed the "Prospects of Revolution in China" at a session of the Chinese Commission of the Comintern and there defended against the Trotzky Opposition the thesis of continued collaboration within the Kuomintang. "The exit of Chinese Communists from the Kuomintang," he said, "would be the gravest error." He likewise denied the wisdom of organizing peasant soviets as governmental organs to dispute the rule of the Kuomintang Government. The C.C.P., he submitted, must work through the apparatus of the new state and form a bridge between that apparatus and the peasant masses with a view to helping the peasantry satisfy its demands either by the confiscation of landed estates, or by the reduction of taxes and rent.

Neither Stalin nor Borodin desired a break with the Kuomintang or any measures calculated to provoke a break. "The purpose of the Northern Expedition," Borodin states, "was not, in my mind, the establishment of a proletarian State, but the creation of conditions which would give an impetus to the mass movement." Moscow advocated a bloc between the workers, the peasants, the petty bourgeoisie and the bourgeoisie to prosecute the purposes of the national democratic revolution in China and to conduct the Northern Expedition.

**PLANS FOR THE NORTHERN EXPEDITION** As a preparation for the Northern Expedition, Borodin made a deep study of the Taiping Rebellion in 1850–65. The Taipings, he found, fell into the costly error of attacking the Manchus, the imperialists, and the rising bourgeoisie at the same time. Borodin believed that if Canton directed its offensive against Shanghai it would be guilty of a similar mistake. It would antagonize the imperialists, the northern militarists and the bourgeoisie, and suffer defeat. His plan accordingly was to keep away from the east, from Shanghai, Pukow, Shantung, and Tientsin, where they would come into conflict with Japan and England.

He did not want to be smashed on the Yangtse. He wanted to reach the Hankow proletariat while preventing the national bourgeoisie in the expedition from uniting with its allies in Shanghai. This decision was based on an over-estimation of the comfort Hankow would offer and an under-estimation of the difficulties to be met there. Nevertheless, it appeared the best of all alternatives, or rather the only alternative acceptable to the Left Kuomintang-C.C.P. bloc.

Within this political scheme, the Russian military advisers outlined the details of the offensive into the north. The chief of the Russian war experts was General Galen, otherwise known as Blücher, who had fought in the Soviet civil war on several fronts and was later commander of the Red forces in the Ukraine. With Galen were about fifteen Russian officers who assisted in the drafting of the plan of campaign and the commanding of the army. One hundred thousand troops participated in the Northern Expedition. This army was divided into ten corps, and a Russian held a responsible post in each corps.

Although Chiang Kai-shek acted as commander-in-chief of the Expedition, the plan of campaign was drafted without his intimate participation. His approval followed automatically.

No more than 20,000 men fought directly under Chiang. Borodin weighed the advisability of displacing him before the inception of the expedition, but then the next choice would be a Canton militarist. Moreover, such a step would have been the signal for that battle between the Right and Left which Borodin sought to avoid as long as possible. In Chiang's two corps, Communist influence was extremely strong. Whampoa was really a breeding place for radicals as well as for officers. Chiang might have been ejected, but therewith the break-up of the Northern Expedition would have become inevitable.

The army commanded by Chiang was the national Kuomintang Army built up around the Whampoa Academy. The remaining 80,000 represented re-organized and re-trained troops of the tuchuns of Kantung, Yunnan, Kwangsi, Hunan, and other provinces who joined the Expedition.

The Kuomintang Army left Kwantung for the Northern Expedition with very little ammunition. On the average, each soldier was supplied with no more than 75 to 100 rounds.

**FIGHTING BATTLES WITH PROPAGANDA** The Northern Expedition, however, paid as much attention to its posters as to its rifles. A political department numbering thousands accompanied the army. Originally organized in January, 1924, to train political workers for the army, it became, during the Expedition, a powerful weapon for the organization of the masses on a radical basis. Dan Yen-da, Wong Ching-wei's successor as Political Commissar of Whampoa, directed this huge propaganda apparatus and infused it with revolutionary ideas. He himself belonged to the Left and was sympathetic to the agrarian revolution, although he wavered when direct action was involved. His aides were Chinese and Russian Communists and Left Kuomintangists. A section of the department marched with each army corps, teaching and preaching. Every company, in fact, had its own agitation squad.

The moment the army occupied a new rural or urban center, the political department organized the civil population. The capture of a village meant the immediate establishment of a peasant union. In the cities, trade unions sprang up and Kuomintang members enrolled in thousands.

Military advance presented no difficulties in a region where the masses met the invader with ringing welcomes and offered their sons to swell the ranks.

A giant printing-press moved forward with the Expedition printing proclamations, posters, and newspapers. "The Northern Expedition," says Borodin, "was not an ordinary military campaign." It fought with political weapons after the manner of the Bolsheviks.

In every military and political aspect, the Northern Expedition showed the dominating influence of Soviet citizens and Soviet ideas.

**THE BREAK** The Northern Expedition met with little opposition. On July 13, 1926 Changsa in Hunan was taken; early in September the twin cities of Hankow and Hanyang fell, and the siege commenced of Wuchang where the Kuomintang troops led by Chang Fa-kwei displayed remarkable heroism scaling medieval walls and fighting well-entrenched defenders. The fortress held out for a month and then, cut off from the world, hungry, its morale undermined by propaganda within, it too succumbed. Therewith the Kuomintang banner was planted firmly on the Yangtse.

At the same time, another section of the expedition engaged and defeated Sun Chuang-fang's army in the Nanchang district. On November 5 the Cantonese took Kiukiang. Therewith the Kuomintang had asserted itself throughout Soviet China. But now began those internal difficulties which the experienced observer foresaw before the start of the Expedition.

Borodin remained in Canton till October and then, when the battle grew hot in Hubei province, he moved slowly northward, accompanied by Left Kuomintang leaders, making speeches and organizing unions.

It had been agreed in Canton that the seat of the new Government would be Hankow. But Chiang Kai-shek felt that he would be in the minority there and far from his social base in Shanghai. He accordingly remained in Nanchang, while Borodin, Eugene Chen, Minister of of Foreign Affairs, T. V. Soong, Minister of Finance, Su Chen, Minister of Justice, Mrs. Sun Yat-sen and others proceeded to Hankow.

At that time 65,000 troops were located in the Hankow area. Chiang had 35,000 within his jurisdiction. The Government's army was more reliable, better trained, and more revolutionary.

At Nanchang, Chiang Kai-shek felt the warm, comforting breezes from the bourgeois center of Shanghai and from its International Settlement. But the Left met disappointment in Hankow. They had gone there to seek support in the industrial proletariat. After tremendous exertions, they reached the goal only to find that it had disappeared. Hankow was an illusion. The capitalists closed down the factories; the bankers suspended operations; the shipping companies withdrew their vessels. Why did not the Kuomintang seize the factories? Because it had no raw materials. Even the supplies for the arsenal at Hanyang were obtained by smuggling or at exorbitant prices. Before the end of its lease of life in Hankow, the Government had to cope with famine and dire distress. The river, which could have been a stream of life, was converted into a death-ditch by the presence in it of innumerable foreign gunboats. To the outside world, Hankow boasted that "this junkyard won't scare us." Yet when armored cruisers lay at anchor 200 meters from Eugene Chen's Foreign Office and from Borodin's headquarters, Hankow's position was far from enviable. Those guns could have bombarded the city. But the Powers were satisfied to see Hankow wither under the effects of their blockade. They were content with stopping Hankow's rice and coal. They saved their shells for a crisis that never arrived.

Other difficulties aggravated the situation. Generals from up the river at Szechuan threatened to attack. Feng hung over them—an unknown quantity. Chiang Kai-shek had revolted against the party. And Chang So-lin, with a powerful army which he had trained for four years for the supreme struggle with Southern nationalism, was heading towards the Yangtse.

Hankow might have surmounted all these difficulties and proceeded on to Peking. For, despite the dissension, it defeated Chang So-lin. It could have kept Feng in order and forced him to obey. Economic problems would have been solved by a further advance northward and especially eastward. But the internal split interfered.

On January 3, 1927 the Kuomintang leaders in Hankow received a telegram from Chiang Kai-shek in Nanchang which demanded that the Central Committee of the party meet in Nanchang, in Chiang's G.H.Q. President Tan Yen-kai, members of the highest Political Bureau and of the Central Committee, the message continued, had stopped in Nanchang on their way up from Canton. Chiang kept them there. He wanted the Hankow leaders to come too, and to submit to the power he exercised in his own camp.

Hankow returned a decisive "No." Acceptance would have shifted the popular base of the Kuomintang from the Yangtse peasantry to the Shanghai bourgeoisie.

Twelve days later Chiang came to Hankow. The rupture was not yet so sharp as to make it dangerous to his person to appear among his opponents. Moreover, he wished to achieve by persuasion what he knew he could not attain by force. But success was so unlikely that he virtually escaped from the city.

During January and February, the Hankow Government conducted an intensive propaganda campaign against

Chiang Kai-shek. He was branded as a military dictator. He offended against the great precept of "the party ueber alles." He was only another tuchun. He served as the weapon of the imperialist and of the hated Shanghai bourgeoisie. And at the end of this period, the Central Committee, two-thirds of whose members were in Hankow, met in Hankow on March 10 and, in effect, anathematized Chiang. Therewith, the break became complete, official, and, even in Chinese conditions, difficult to heal. Nevertheless, open enmity was not proclaimed. Only in April, after Chiang had given a free hand to the long-sworded executioners who walked through the streets of Shanghai beheading workers and Communists in broad daylight, did Hankow issue an order for the generalissimo's arrest.

Meanwhile, Great Britan, Japan, and other countries continued to pour unprecedentedly large forces into Shanghai, and a large international fleet including airplane carriers and numerous cruisers concentrated in nearby waters for the declared purpose of defending the International Settlement. During the same period—February and March, 1927—the Cantonese force under Chiang Kai-shek pressed northward, and, operating on the basis of military plans drafted by Russians but executed without their help, took Nanking on March 24. Then occurred that famous bombardment at Nanking in which one or two foreigners were killed and which aroused so much diplomatic excitement and provoked the sending of so much additional foreign armament to China. Chiang Kai-shek officially expressed his regrets, attempted to negotiate a truce or an alliance with his chief military enemy, Sun Chuan-fang,[4] and permitted the massacre of trade-union leaders and radical Chinese in Shanghai. He proposed, in this manner, to placate the Powers.

While Northern anti-Kuomintang troops commenced to fill Shanghai in thousands, the workers, though poorly organized for such purposes, actually possessed themselves of the Chinese sections of the city. Nevertheless, they were powerless against the battalions of Chiang Kai-shek, who soon obtained de facto control of the great metropolis and, to reinforce that control, closed workers' organizations, suppressed strikes, and proscribed Communist activity.

[4] *Chronology of Events in China. 1911-7*. With a Foreword by Sir Frederick Whyte. (London, 1927), p. 35.

In Peking, likewise, reaction reared its head. Chang So-lin had proclaimed a crusade against Communists —which to him covered a multitude of sins and particularly all his enemies. One of his measures doubtless conceived to gladden the hearts of native and foreign anti-Soviet elements, was the arrest and incarceration under unusually gruesome conditions of Mrs. Borodin and a number of other Russians from the Soviet steamer *Pamiat Lenina*.[5] Another move of the same character, for the same purpose, and probably under the same inspiration, was his raid of the Soviet Embassy in Peking on April 6.

**HANKOW'S ALTERNATIVE** Meanwhile Chang's son, Chang Sueh-lyan, pushed south towards Hankow with a powerful, excellently equipped and foreign trained army.

Hankow faced a difficult choice. It had now acquired a reputation for "redness" which seemed to offer numerous generals, among them Feng Yu-hsiang, a pretext for hostility. But the victorious army of the Left Kuomintang still remained intact, and the big arsenal continued to pour out valuable munitions. Despite all economic hardships and internal bickering, the Left leaders in Hankow felt confident that they could defeat their enemies in turn. In what turn? That constituted the chief problem.

Should they first destroy Chiang Kai-shek? Or should they stop Chang So-lin? Chiang Kai-shek had only a small army. He still faced Northern militarist opposition. In the territory he held, strikes and workers' antagonism prevented stabilization. In fact, in March and April his immediate entourage expected his downfall daily. Chiang's own wife supplied Hankow with information, and the generalissimo himself contemplated suicide. Hankow therefore decided to march against Chang So-lin.

The world thought Hankow "Communist." But the Left Kuomintang ruled, and the Left Kuomintang was neither Bolshevik nor Socialist, and the generals who shared their condominium in Hankow certainly opposed everything Communist. All hostility and personal accounts notwithstanding, and despite the actual break, some ties with Chiang Kai-shek remained intact. He represented the national bourgeoisie; they the petty bourgeoisie. Chang So-lin, on the other hand, was the great feudal

[5] F. S. Borodina: *In The Dungeons of the Chinese Satraps* (Moscow 1928).

lord from a distant province. The Left Kuomintang had expected that Hankow would give them power. Instead they found that peasant uprisings and workers' revolts threatened on all sides. Some of them therefore wavered. Perhaps, if they first annihilated the Manchurian force which seemed to constitute an immediate physical menace, they could come to terms with Chiang Kai-shek. As victors, they would dictate better conditions of peace. Much divided Hankow from Nanking. But something drew them together. Consciously or unconsciously, this motive weighed heavily when Hankow made its decision to give battle first to the Manchurian Army in Honan. The plan was to defeat Chang So-lin, then turn right towards Nanking while permitting Feng to come out of the desert and occupy Peking. Feng would be Hankow's new ally.

The decisive struggle took place near Chumatien, 125 miles north-west of Hankow. Those observers who imagined Chinese warfare a series of friendly picnics in which the participants paid more attention to their umbrellas than to their guns, received a rude and enlightening shock. The affray lasted three days. Hankow lost 14,000 men. Its army fought heroically, taking tanks with rifles. In the end, Chang So-lin suffered defeat and retreated rapidly northward. But Hankow left the flower of its army, most of them Communists, on the field of battle. A victorious army was forced to retire to its base around Hankow.

Now Feng, however, instead of emerging from his famine-stricken provinces to take up the pursuit of Chang's army in the direction of Peking, occupied Loyang, highly strategic from a political and military standpoint, established contact with Nanking, and immediately began to play Chiang Kai-shek against Hankow. Feng thus became the arbiter of the situation on the Yangtse. His victory, as usual, was not of his own doing. He merely benefited from Hankow's error.

**FENG DICTATES** Exhausted by the blood-letting of the battle with Chang So-lin, weakened by economic troubles and the hostility of its own provincial generals, Hankow was in no position to clip Feng's wings. On the contrary, he expected that it do his bidding. But the exact relationship between Feng and Hankow remained unclear. He wanted Hankow. He wished to treat with

Nanking. The Right elements in Hankow, on the other hand, may have seen in him a natural ally against the Communists and other Left influences at home, while both Right and Left wished to have him as an ally against Chiang Kai-shek and Chang-So-lin.

The situation required clarification. Feng, after all, was a member of the Kuomintang. He had received material aid from Moscow, and during the Northern Expedition the Kuomintang Treasury made regular money transmissions to him. Then, however, his power was limited to the poor district of Inner Mongolia. Now he had become a decisive force. Would there be an alliance between Feng and Hankow, or a war? And if an alliance, with which Hankow would he conclude it—with the red, pink, or black Hankow?

To settle some of these questions, a conference convened on Feng's territory, in Chengchow. Thither came Chang Fa-kwei, the commander of the Kuomintang "Iron Army" which had taken Wuchang, Tang Shen-chi of the Hunan army, and a host of minor generals. Politicians too put in their appearance: Su Chen, Hankow's Minister of Justice and leader of the Left Kuomintang, Sun Fo, a son of Sun Yat-sen, Tan Yen-kai, the President of the Hankow Government, Wong Ching-wei, and others. General Galen was there too. Feng arrived last so that all the dignitaries might do him the honor of meeting him at the railway station. Borodin remained away, sick with fever and nursing a broken arm. Borodin, however, might have proceeded to Chengchow a few days later. But the Left Kuomintang objected; they feared that he would dominate the gathering and prevent them from winning Feng's support for a more moderate anti-mass policy. For the same reason, they forced Galen into the background of the conference.

The generals at the conference registered unanimity on one question: that the workers' and peasants' movement must be stemmed. The Northern Expedition had accomplished just what Borodin and Moscow expected of it—it opened wide the door to mass agitation, it galvanized mass disaffection, it led to peasants' organizations and increased trade-union activity. In January, the population of Hankow took the British concession, and at the same time, the Chinese of Kiukiang occupied the British concession of that town. The peasants were dangerously active. They had seized the premises of officers at the front; they arrested or even killed recruiting agents sent from the front; they cut off women's hair; they organized militant unions. In the armies too the soldiers began to assert themselves. Being predominantly peasants, the rank and file sympathized with the confiscation of land and the reduction of land rent. They sympathized with the Changsa peasant revolt in Hunan. But the military clique was feudal. The army officers were landlords or sons of landlords. They demanded that this peasant movement be stopped. They demanded that the workers be checked. Otherwise tuchunism, military control, and conservative policies would be doomed.

With this Feng Yu-hsiang agreed. His "Bolshevism" ran as deep as his "Christianity" of a former day. He, but specially his generals, disliked all those "Red Spear" movements that had sprung up in his own territory. The peasants were pushing up too rapidly and had begun to threaten the inviolable paradise of the generals.

Whatever the outward circumstances which made the Chengchow conference necessary, its real raison d'être was the danger of a rising mass movement. Under this sign, the Hankow generals could unite with Feng.

The Left Kuomintang leaders had proceeded to Chengchow to persuade Feng of the necessity of pursuing Chang So-lin and of beating Chiang Kai-shek. They told him of conditions in Hankow: no money, no arms, unemployment, generals displeased, peasants disaffected. They complained of the mass movement. Then of what good to Feng could Hankow be? He wanted funds and munitions from it.

The civilian Kuomintang leaders at Chengchow did not share the generals' view that the radical movement had to be suppressed, immediately and mercilessly. They stood in the middle of the road. They wished to win Feng as a balance against the Hankow military and then, with him, pursue a milder strategy than the Chinese Communists proposed.

The conference told Hankow's generals and Hankow's politicians that Feng would not co-operate with them against Chiang Kai-shek. If it suited his purpose he might march on Peking. But Peking in his hands would not mean a Kuomintang victory or even a Hankow victory.

Hankow, in other words, had nothing to give Feng.

Feng would give nothing to Hankow, except his moral disapproval of the workers' and peasants' movement. The conference adjourned amid protestations of union which masked dismal failure. It left Feng in his pivotal position of Yangtse arbiter with the whip over Hankow, but otherwise its military and political achievements were nil.

A week after the conference dispersed, Feng held a similar meeting with Chiang Kai-shek at Suchow. He was playing Hankow against Chiang, and Chiang against Hankow. Such tactics gave him authority without fighting —to Feng always the highest desideratum.

**THE TROTZKY OPPOSITION** Meanwhile, sharp differences of opinion had developed in Moscow on the correct revolutionary strategy to be pursued in China. The writer several times discussed the question with Karl Radek at the time, and subsequently published his notes on these conversations.[6] The Trotzky Opposition, to which Radek adhered especially as far as Chinese politics was concerned, demanded an out-and-out Communist policy in Hankow. The Stalin majority argued that to adopt a purely Bolshevik policy for China would be to fight Hankow, to throw over the Kuomintang, and to destroy the only element capable of defeating Chiang Kai-shek. "Hankow is a fiction," the Opposition replied. "Organize Soviets in its territory," they urged, "even if those Soviets defy the Hankow Central Government. Raise a Red Army. Arm the Workers." To the Trotzky Opposition, Hankow, though the seat of the Left Kuomintang, signified nothing more than the stronghold of reactionary generals. The Lefts were tolerated, but real power lay in the hands of the Hunan military and of Feng Yu-hsiang. "Undermine Hankow" therefore became their slogan. They entertained little hope of immediate success, but Trotzky, Zinoviev, Radek, and their comrades were convinced that the next wave of the Chinese revolution would be exclusively proletarian and peasant in character. The preparations, they believed, ought to commence immediately.

The Opposition's analysis of the Chinese situation contained many elements of wisdom. But its program was

[6] New York *Nation,* November 30, 1927.

all right only on paper and in Moscow, not in South China.

In Hankow 10,000 workers might have been armed. Against these, the generals controlled 75,000 troops. After splitting with Chiang, to split with the Left Kuomintang would have meant ruin. The Russians in Hankow considered the advisability of distributing arms among the proletariat so as to make it an independent support of a radical policy. But the Hanyang arsenal, the second largest in China, was held by Tang Shen-chi with a force of three army corps. Various generals claimed the arsenal's monthly output of 6,000 rifles and quarrelled about its distribution. To organize a Red Army would have meant to antagonize the generals, and to equip it would have been impossible. Hankow was cut off from Shanghai, while Feng separated it from Mongolia, the only other possible source of munitions.

Moreover, Borodin considered Hankow a part-way station in Peking. To provoke a war with the generals, who were extremely suspicious of radical measures, would have meant to end the Northern Expedition on the Yangtse, while the Left Kuomintang still hoped to destroy Chang So-lin and Chiang Kai-shek. To organize soviets would have meant to provoke a rupture with the Left Kuomintang or petty bourgeoisie, but in April, 1927, when the Opposition raised its slogan of "Soviets for China" the possibilities of collaboration with the Left Kuomintang had not yet been completely exhausted. Borodin's chief concern was to prolong the mass movement's lease of life. If he could succeed, soviets would come of themselves. In June, 1927, they would have been premature.

Borodin did the only thing possible under the circumstances; he increased the Communist nucleus of Chang Fa-kwei's "Iron Army." Borodin wished to make it the bulwark of the Left policy in Hankow and a balance against the military strength of the independent generals who had declared their allegiance to the Kuomintang in Canton and participated in the Northern Expedition, but whose fundamental aims were anti-Kuomintang, federalistic, and anti-proletarian.

The Hankow generals opposed Chiang Kai-shek because he was their territorial rival. The Left Kuomintang sought Chiang's scalp for another reason. Similarity of goal kept them together; divergence of essential purpose produced friction between them. The tuchun-generals appreciated the propelling abilities of nationalism. It inspired troops, enthused armies, and conquered provinces with little loss of ammunition or men. But when these same principles began to express themselves in peasant disaffection against landowners, and a demand for soldiers' rights in the armies, the generals preferred a bloc with Feng.

This struggle proceeded within the frame of economic privation, imperialist antagonism, and Nanking hostility. Such circumstances, the Russians in Hankow held, did not warrant the adoption of Trotzkyist proposals for a sharp turn to the left. A Communist coup, they contended, would weld together all the forces opposed to radical reforms. It would have required fighting against large, well-armed armies now united in a practical coalition with the Left Kuomintang. Not even the whole Left Kuomintang could be expected to support an attempt at the enthronement of Sovietism. Borodin therefore resisted the suggestions of the Trotzky Opposition.

But the Trotzky Opposition though numerically weak in the Russian Communist Party, was not without influence in Moscow and in the headquarters of the Communist Party of China. In Chinese affairs, Radek enjoyed the advantages of tremendous knowledge and special concentration.

**BORODIN'S DEPARTURE FROM CHINA** Nationalism had carried the Kuomintang banner victoriously from the banks of the Pearl River to the banks of the Yangtse. There, however, it became entangled in militaristic intrigue and mass unrest.

Foreign hostility and Chinese politics held the Expedition fast on the Yangtse. But Borodin, far from despairing, felt that the situation was pregnant with success. He felt so till the very end of his stay in China.

There were three alternatives. (1) To overthrow Tang Shen-chi and the reactionary Hankow generals by a coup d'état. From the military point of view the undertaking was not impossible, but it required long preparations and great expense. Feng could be neutralized in various ways. He probably would not have marched south to aid Tang Shen-chi. But even if he had chosen to act in this un-Fengesque style, he would represent no serious danger to Borodin's larger ends, for differences of opinion would have arisen between Feng and Tang, and numerous contributory circumstances would have made for a political situation in which the mass movement—the Communist chief concern—might flourish. But Galen had no enthusiasm for the task. Moreover, the Left Kuomintang, faced with a Communist coup, would have listed very sharply toward the generals. A coup would just mean a rupture with both Tang Shen-chi and Wong Ching-wei, and Borodin's plan consisted in holding on to both or, at worst, to break only with the generals.

(2) The second alternative followed this same idea of maintaining temporarily the bloc with both Hankow forces. Tang Shen-chi and Chang Fa-kwei, whose army was partly Left Kuomintang and largely Communist, were to march on Nanking. That they could defeat Chiang Kai-shek was not subject to the slightest doubt. Chiang himself subsequently admitted that his fate hung on a hair.

The Russians in Hankow entertained no illusions as to what would happen once Nanking had been taken. A wild conflict would ensue. The generals would try to loot in Shanghai, fight for customs control, and curry favor with the bourgeoisie and the imperialists. But whereas Chiang Kai-shek had come home when he took Nanking and its territory, Tang Shen-chi would be considered an intruder. Forces would rise up to demolish him. Thus two reactionary elements—Chiang and Tang—would be weakened, and the mass movement would be correspondingly strengthened. Simultaneously, the workers' and peasants' urge in the Hankow region would be relieved from crushing pressure.

(3) The third alternative contemplated a return to Canton together with the entire Left Kuomintang or the more radical section of it, and there, in Kwantung, recommence the revolutionary struggle. Dan Yen-da, Mrs. Sun Yat-sen, Eugene Chen, and many less prominent though equally important Left Kuomintang leaders would certainly have joined Borodin and the C.C.P. in returning to Canton. But Wong Ching-wei too would have had no better choice. At the Chengchow conference, Wong was ready to combine with Feng against the C.C.P. He wished, however, to remain on friendly terms with Soviet Russia and to retain the services of Borodin. But

when it had become manifest that Feng would not ally with the Left Kuomintang, Wong somewhat modified his policy and moved toward closer collaboration with Borodin and the C.C.P. He could not work with Tang Shen-chi and the other Hankow militarists. This being the case, and if the C.C.P. and the extreme wing of the Left Kuomintang went to Canton, Wong would have stood practically alone. Together with the C.C.P., he could play a role at Hankow and compete for control of the mass movement. Against its will, he could neither aspire to control nor check that movement, nor present himself to the generals as a real power. If, therefore, Borodin had decided on the Canton alternative, Wong and with him the solid center of the Left Kuomintang could only have joined—or fled from Hankow and politics. In fact, Wong left Hankow, and with T. V. Soong, Chang Fa-kwei and Li Chai-sum, formed a government at Canton in November, 1927. But against the C.C.P. and without them, he could not remain, and accordingly sailed to Germany in December.

In June, 1927, accordingly, the Russians in Hankow and their Chinese friends decided to march on Nanking with Tang Shen-chi and Chang Fa-kwei. At the same time, they kept in mind the third alternative, and Chang Fa-kwei's troops were actually so placed that they could easily have moved south to Canton. Everybody concerned in this on-to-Nanking venture preferred its success to the necessity of turning their backs on the Yangtse for Kwantung. But the Bolsheviks in Hankow did not regard the prospect of a new stay in Canton as disastrous or permanently injurious to their cause.

Chang Fa-kwei's "Iron Army" therefore advanced eastward in the direction of Nanchang-Nanking, while the troops of Tang Shen-chi followed close behind.

Until this time, Borodin's control over events had been considerable. Feng Yu-hsiang and Chiang Kai-shek had demanded that he leave China, but their wishes and their statements in this regard had very little to do with his final departure. He left the country largely because ultra-Lefts from Russia, acting under the inspiration of the Trotzky Opposition and in collaboration with Chinese Communists, took the situation out of his hands. He felt disavowed not by Hankow but by Moscow, and therefore relinquished his duties. Otherwise, no desire of Feng's or Chiang's could have prevented him from going to Canton or from fighting against Nanking.

Early in 1927 Borodin went to the mountain resort of Kuling. He desired to recuperate and to be near Nanchang, the center of Chang Fa-kwei's forces. At Kuling Borodin was the object of much Shanghai-newspaper and Chinese curiosity. What were his plans? Nobody thought of him as a leader about to quit and no one treated him as such. He was still "the great Bao Ti-sing," his prestige with the masses undiminished, his faith in ultimate victory unshattered. But in the third week of July he returned suddenly to Hankow and on the 20th he retired from political activity.

Thereafter in Hankow he lived in T. V. Soong's house. Every day Chinese leaders urged him to reverse his decision. On the 25th a meeting took place in Borodin's apartment where Left Kuomintang statesmen attempted for hours to persuade him to stay. On the 27th they accompanied him to the railway station at Hankow and again begged him to remain. Were they sincere? Doubtless. For without Borodin, that is, without the spirit of revolution and its highest Chinese expression—the C.C.P.—the Left Kuomintang was doomed to extinction. It actually became a nonentity shortly after Borodin's departure.

Borodin, however, refused to be swayed. Several ways were open to him. He chose the route through Feng Yu-hsiang's territory because he had no fear of Feng. The adventure of that trip through the Gobi Desert to Mongolia has been dramatically detailed by Anna Louise Strong.[7]

**THE BLOODY AFTERMATH** On August 1, a few days after Borodin's departure for Moscow, a Communist revolt broke out in the "Iron Army" at Nanchang. Its spiritual leaders were ultra-Lefts from Moscow; its immediate organizers Chinese Communists. Borodin would have opposed such a development. The insurrection was directed against Chang Fa-kwei, and its instigators arrested that general a day before its outbreak, but on the morrow they put him at liberty and thus enabled him to

[7] Anna Louise Strong: *China's Millions,* (New York, 1928).

organize opposition against the Communists. Fifteen thousand troops went with the C.C.P.; 10,000 with Chang Fa-kwei.

The directors of the coup now discarded both Borodin's alternatives: they did not proceed to Nanking. That had become impossible. They did not turn towards Canton where they might have mobilized some mass support. No military opposition could have prevented them from reaching that goal. Indeed, they defeated all the generals sent from Kwantung to retard their progress. Yet instead of marching on Canton, they directed their steps to Swatow right into the mouths of the imperialists. The coup antagonized Chang Fa-kwei and alienated Wong Ching-wei. It split the Left Kuomintang, or more correctly, it dispersed the Left Kuomintang—some, Mrs. Sun Yat-sen and Eugene Chen, going to Moscow, others to Paris, others into the camp of Chiang Kai-shek. This may have been what the ultra-Lefts desired. It was exactly what Borodin wished to avoid.

This change of direction marked the end of the Kuomintang phase of the Chinese revolution. Thereafter, the roles were divided between Chiang Kai-shek, Feng Yu-hsiang, and other provincial generals who made their peace with England, Japan, and America, or attempted to do so. The Kuomintang Party became subservient to a group of generals.

In the south, the Communist remnants of Chang Fa-kwei's army erred about achieving indifferent military success, but never establishing a real social base. Finally, in December, 1927, the ultra-Lefts responsible for the Nanchang coup precipitated a Communist coup in the city of Canton. Ill-prepared and poorly thought out, the attempt proved abortive and ended in the slaughter of some 2,000 Communists.

To be sure, the mass movement of workers and peasants did not die with the culmination of the adventure which opened on the Yangtse when the Communists struck against Chang Fa-kwei. It continued to grow in extent despite all repressions.

# 23

# THE BRITISH RUPTURE WITH RUSSIA

DIPLOMATIC RELATIONS between Great Britain and the Soviet Union came within a hair of complete rupture in the summer of 1926. At that time, Lord Balfour threw his influence and wisdom against such a move. Chamberlain too felt that a break with Moscow would militate against British political interests on the continent and release the Bolsheviks from any restraint they might have exercised in China in order to keep intact their relations with Downing Street. There was one question, furthermore, which the advocates of a rupture could not answer: What will be its benefits?

The person most active in urging a rupture of English diplomatic relations with Moscow was Commander Oliver Locker-Lampson, M.P. He advocated the measure in Parliament and in the press. But being a man of ambition and having fought with Denikin in the Russian Civil War, he attached little importance to the mere severance of diplomatic relations. This was only a stepping-stone to a greater goal—a war against the Bolsheviks. His collaborators were Sir Henri Deterding, President of the Royal Dutch-Shell Oil Company, and General von Hoffmann of Brest Litovsk fame.

Deterding bought oil from the Bolsheviks from 1922 to 1926, and again in 1929. But between 1926 and 1929, Soviet oil was to him "stolen" oil, and his magazines and newspapers conducted a virulent campaign against it and the Bolshevik regime. He used the Association of British Creditors as a weapon in this fight, and suspicion made him the financier and instigator of the Menshevik insurrection in Soviet Georgia in the fall of 1924. If he did not shrink from such action during MacDonald's term of office, the anti-Soviet bias of the Baldwin-Chamberlain Cabinet must certainly have encouraged him to redouble his machinations against Moscow.

Georgians in some way linked up with Deterding were charged in Germany with counterfeiting Soviet currency to finance anti-Bolshevik measures. General Hoffmann saw in Bolshevism "a danger to the orderly development of Europe." his wife wrote.[1] He tried repeatedly to win English and French political personalities for his scheme of uprooting the Soviet regime. In 1925, his wife states, he discussed it with Deterding in The Hague. In the summer of 1926, Deterding invited him to London where the general laid his plans for military intervention against the Bolsheviks before Commander Locker-Lampson. He wished, Mrs. Hoffmann writes, to interview Austen Chamberlain, but the Foreign Minister denied him the opportunity. Nevertheless, Hoffmann was asked, by whom his wife does not disclose, to prepare a memorandum on his plan for the British Foreign office. He proposed to exploit the ambitions of the Ukrainian émigré to separate Soviet Ukraine from the Soviet Federation and in Paris en route to London he conferred with their leaders. "In these Paris conversations," Frau Hoffmann declares, "General Hoffmann told the Ukrainians very frankly that he could co-operate with them only if he won Britain's interest for the whole problem."

Several months later, Locker-Lampson again asked Hoffmann to London, but the general was growing old, and he despaired of success.

The Locker-Lampson-Hoffmann-Deterding intrigue was part of the parallel British tendency to break with the Bolsheviks. Early in 1927 even the more moderate Conservative wing had been convinced of the inevitability of rupture. Differences of opinion remained only with respect to the expediency, the opportune moment, and the immediate provocation. In January, 1927, the Chinese seized the English concessions at Hankow and Kiukiang. The argument that diplomatic relations with Russia might check revolutionary developments in China

[1] Berlin *Vossische Zeitung,* February 2, 1929.

therewith lost its cogency. The disastrous decline of British trade with China and the unimpeded success of the Northern Expedition threatened further to undermine British influence in the Orient. It was time to act.

**PREPARATIONS FOR THE RUPTURE** The initial preliminary took the form of an official note dated February 23, 1927, sent to Mr. Rosengolz by Sir Austen Chamberlain.[2] The relations between the two governments, it said, "continue notoriously to be of an unsatisfactory nature." Despite repeated Soviet pledges to refrain from propaganda, it alleged, the Bolshevik leaders continued to defame, attack and offend the British Empire. The document proceeded to cite proof. Commissar of War Voroshilov was guilty of anti-British declarations. "Comrade Voroshilov," Appendix No. 2 quoted a Soviet Press report, "drew then a picture of the secret negotiations of English imperialism egging on the small States, its faithful hirelings, against the Soviet Union." Bukharin had indulged in a frank statement of Communist hopes in China, in India, and with respect to the British miners.

> During the great English strike, [the note cited] during the great Chinese revolution, our [Bolshevik] party–we can and dare assert this—has shown itself in the forefront. And we here declare that if history shall produce still greater tasks we will throw all our forces into the scale of world revolution and will fight to a victorious finish.

Chamberlain resented especially a "mendacious cartoon" of himself in the official *Izvestia* and the same paper's reproductions of numerous revolutionary utterances.

Therefore Chamberlain threatened "that a continuance of such acts as are here complained of" must sooner or later result in the abrogation of the Trade Agreement "and even the severance of ordinary diplomatic relations."

Maxim Litvinov, Assistant Commissar of Foreign Affairs, had his reply ready only three days later.[3] Its essence was contained in one sentence:

> It is impossible, really, [it read] to regard as anti-British propaganda an analysis and estimate of the foreign policy of the

[2] British Blue Book. *Russia No.* 3 (1927). *A Selection of Papers dealing with the Relations between His Majesty's Government and the Soviet Government, 1921–7.* (London, 1927). Cmd. 2895. pp. 45ff.

[3] *Ibid.*, pp. 64ff.

British Government and of its relation to the Soviet Union, or reasonings based on general principles on the part of [Bolshevik] party workers on the inevitability of the world revolution, on the significance of the national revolutionary movement in the East, much less still the idea expressed by the People's Commissary of Health [to which the British note had taken objection.—L.F.] respecting the significance of physical culture from the point of view of the revolutionary labor movement. . . .

Litvinov likewise declared that the non-propaganda pledge did not limit the freedom of the Bolsheviks to speak of England and English policy in their own press and meetings in any manner they pleased.

Litvinov had preferred firmness to mellowness. He met each British argument. He hinted that the Baldwin Cabinet had been lifted into power by the forged "Zinoviev" letter. He declared that threats to break off relations "cannot intimidate anyone at all in the Soviet Union." But if the British Government believes, he continued, that a rupture will benefit the British people or advance the cause of world peace, then "it, of course, will act accordingly, taking upon itself the full responsibility for the consequences arising therefrom."

This constituted an open challenge to Chamberlain to carry out his threat of the break. Moscow did not believe he would dare.

**ON THE EVE** Three factors contributed to fix the date of the break. On April 6 the Peking police raided the Soviet Embassy and found documents respecting Soviet revolutionary activity in China. This material supplied arguments to the Die-Hards and Conservatives, and the apparent success of the search may have suggested a similar measure in London.

Between May 4 and 27 the International Economic Conference, held under the auspices of the League of Nations, met in Geneva. The Soviet Union, which, through the mediation of Paul Scheffer of the *Berliner Tageblatt,* had satisfactorily settled its dispute with Switzerland arising out of the assassination, on Swiss soil, of Vorovsky, the Soviet envoy, sent a delegation headed by Ossinsky and Sokolnikov. These men established working contacts with the American delegation, and generally made so good an impression that rumors of large credits to the Bolsheviks began to multiply. Such a development, if of sufficient magnitude, might have been used to defeat the Die-Hard policy of a break with Russia. The Die-Hards accordingly began to object vehemently to further delay.

During the early months of 1927 negotiations proceeded between the Midland Bank in London and Soviet financiers with a view to a large credit. The arrangement was concluded several days before the Arcos Raid, but no final agreement had yet been signed. In the House of Commons on May 26, Sir E. Turton, to whom all speakers deferred for information on the question, stated that "The arrangement between the Midland Bank and the Russian Trade Delegation contemplated orders being given in this country for machinery and plant by Soviet trading organizations up to the amount of ten million pounds sterling." This stimulus to Anglo-Soviet commerce would have stimulated greater opposition to a rupture.

These happenings made the month of May, 1927, a fitting season for the Anglo-Soviet rupture. It was necessary to anticipate and prevent a favorable change in the Soviets' foreign political and economic position. In China, moreover, the split between Hankow and Chiang Kai-shek and the Generalissimo's alignment with the Shanghai pro-British bourgeoisie indicated that the revolution would be checked and moderated by inner conflicts. The absence of diplomatic relations with Moscow therefore represented less danger to the British position in China.

The Baldwin Cabinet, however, decided not to raid the Soviet Embassy in London. The order was given to raid the Soviet Trade Delegation and Arcos.

**THE ARCOS RAID** The facts of the Arcos Raid are clear, and accounts of it in the press of the several British parties, in the Russian papers, and in a Labor publication based on sworn evidence and official documents[4] differ in no important particulars.

On May 12, 1927, at 4.20 p.m., a large force of police and plain-clothes men entered the building of Arcos and the Soviet Trade Delegation at 49 Moorgate, London, and proceeded to search the premises and employees. An hour later, in response to persistent requests, they produced their warrant.

[4] *Raid on Arcos Ltd. and the Trade Delegation of the U.S.S.R. Facts and Documents*. Published by the Anglo-Russian Parliamentary Committee. London. May, 1927.

The police took possession of the telephone exchange, all exits and corridors, and detained the employees until late in the evening. They remained in supreme control of the building throughout the 12th, 13th, and until the 16th. Pneumatic drill machinery was brought to the premises to pry open strong rooms and steel boxes. The documents were examined on the spot with thoroughness and deliberation, and without haste. This search proceeded in the absence of Arcos and the Trade Delegation officials, and no list of the documents found or taken away was made in their presence. Among the women subjected to personal search were two possessing diplomatic passports which entitled them to immunity: the wife of M. Rosengolz, Soviet Chargé d'Affaires, and the wife of M. Shannin, the Financial Attaché of the Soviet Embassy.

The next day, the Soviet Embassy handed in an official note of protest. It stressed the illegality of the raid of the Soviet Trade Delegation. Arcos was a British company operating under British laws. Its stockholders were Soviet citizens. In the six years of its existence it had made purchases amounting to 100,000,000 pounds sterling and was the main channel for Anglo-Soviet trade. Nevertheless, Scotland Yard was under no obligation to consider the interests of British business when its authority was a warrant issued under instructions from Sir W. Joynson-Hicks, the Home Secretary. But the raid on the Soviet Trade Delegation presented another aspect. The Chairman of the Trade Delegation, Mr. Khinchuk, enjoyed immunity and diplomatic privileges by the terms of the Anglo-Russian Trade Agreement of March 16, 1921. Article V of that paper stipulated that the official trade agents "shall personally enjoy . . . immunity from arrest and search." In reply to a question in the House of Commons, on June 23, 1926, Mr. Locker-Lampson (not to be confused with Commander Locker-Lampson) had stated that "the Chairman of the Soviet Trade Delegation appointed under the terms of the Anglo-Russian Trade Agreement of 1921 is the only commercial agent of the Soviet Government who enjoys diplomatic immunity in this country." "Diplomatic immunity," in the interpretation of experts on international law, applied not only to his pockets but, what is important to such an official, to his papers, offices, and home. Moreover, he was "allowed to send and receive sealed bags," and to communicate with his government by telegraph and wireless in cypher.[5] His status, accordingly, resembled that of an ambassador or minister.

Scotland Yard's agents, led by Sir Wyndham Childs, spent most of their time breaking into Mr. Khinchuk's safe and strong rooms and in examining the documents it contained. They opened envelopes on his desk which contained sealed diplomatic mail he had not read, and in the absence of any Soviet official they studied the contents of those communications which, by international law, were immune.

But the British Government permitted no legal matters to interfere with the raid. Scotland Yard was given plenty of time—four days at least, and the detectives took away documents to peruse at their leisure.

**THE FRUITS OF THE SEARCH** Nevertheless, the search was barren of serious results. It disclosed nothing that had not been known before, and failed to produce the highly important War Office document, the rumored theft of which served as excuse for the raid. The official White Paper containing the documents found in the raid was thin evidence indeed, and led to no arrests or charges for illegal or subversive activities by Russian or British subjects.[6] "There is nothing to prove," said the *Manchester Guardian* on May 25, "that the [Trade] Delegation has done anything which a British Communist might not legally do nor anything worse than the things of which the British Government have before complained." The published documents were the personal correspondence of Arcos and Trade Delegation employees dealing with Communist Party activity. Similar material could be discovered in the private files of any active Communist anywhere in the world. It is data that probably went through the British mails or could have been forwarded through that medium without contravening the law. Some of the correspondence dealt with job-finding for unemployed British Communists—not on British vessels or in the British war fleet, but on Soviet merchant ships. Part of the paper treasure referred to Communist activities in connection with the "Minority Movement" in the Labor ranks of England—activities

[5] Article V. of the Trade Agreement.

[6] British White Paper. *Russia No. 2 (1927). Documents Illustrating the Hostile Activities of the Soviet Government and the Third International against Great Britain.* (London, 1927). Cmd. 2874.

known, public, and of too limited effect to seriously trouble MacDonald, much less Chamberlain.

Despite the sensational title of the official White Paper, there was nothing in the Arcos or Trade Delegation documents which it printed to prove hostile activity by the Soviet Government or even by the Communist International against the British Government or British Empire. Scotland Yard probably handled tons of letters in the offices it searched, and if this White Paper was the most incriminating dossier it could present to the public, its findings must have been very poor. To conceal the flimsiness of its evidence, the Government, in fact, included in the White Paper several documents not found in the raid, but obtained in a manner which Sir Austen Chamberlain, on being questioned in Parliament, refused to reveal. As Ramsay MacDonald said in the London *Daily Express* of May 25, "The Arcos Raid was pathetic—a tragic-comic melodrama, and official approval of such a thing shows merely weakness." In the House of Commons on May 26, Clynes, the leader of the Opposition, characterized the raid as "obviously a failure," and the White Paper "a bright, diverting, comic publication." The Labor and Liberal Press shared this view, and even the Conservative *Daily Express* aired unorthodox views on the subject.

**THE RUPTURE** On May 24 Premier Baldwin laid the Arcos, Trade Delegation, and other documents before the House of Commons, and stated that on this basis, and unless Parliament objected, the British Government would "terminate the Trade Agreement [of March 16, 1921], require the withdrawal of the Trade Delegation from London and recall the British Mission from Moscow."

Two days later, Parliament debated the subject. Chamberlain rose to justify the rupture. Lloyd George delivered the best speech in opposition.

> I think the Foreign Secretary has had his hands forced in regard to this breach of relations [he said]. In my judgment, I do not think the Foreign Secretary came to the conclusion before the Home Secretary acted that the time had arrived to have a rupture with the Soviet Union. . . . I do not think the time was well chosen. . . . I have listened to the Foreign Secretary with great care. He did not point out a single advantage that would be gained to this country by a rupture.

The reason why Chamberlain could point out no benefits of a break was perhaps anticipated by the *Daily Express* on May 25. "The break with her [Russia]," this Conservative organ suggested, "benefits nobody. It is one of those events in history that put back the clock for the nations concerned." Then why the break? Mr. Lloyd George hinted with no excess delicacy that Chamberlain had been forced by the Die-Hards to adopt his present position. "It may be simply," the *Manchester Guardian* of May 25 commented, "that the Government have once more surrendered to the continuing pressure of their own Die-Hards." Baldwin and Chamberlain, the newspaper intimated, could not disavow Sir W. Joynson-Hicks. It is even said, on good British authority, that Chamberlain nearly resigned after the Arcos raid out of protest against Joynson-Hicks' action. He had resisted Die-Hard pressure for many months during 1926. "In his heart," as the *Guardian* suggested, Chamberlain "still disapproves." This may explain the weakness of his arguments for the break.

In the debate on May 26 Lloyd George also examined the official reasons for the rupture. "What is the first charge brought by the Prime Minister in his document?" he asked. "It is espionage for the purpose of obtaining information about our Army and Navy. Are we not doing that?" he demanded of a House which listened with astonishment as a former Prime Minister, who knew well the ways of British Cabinets, revealed the inner processes of British government.

"If the War Office and Admiralty and the Air Force," he continued, "are not obtaining by every means every information about what is being done in other countries, they are neglecting the security of this country. . . . As for employing agents to stir up trouble, that is not a new experience of Governments to bring pressure on others," and he presented instances in British history when such tactics had been adopted.

Arthur Ponsonby, the virtual chief of the British Foreign Office under MacDonald, confirmed everything Lloyd George said, only in less polished language. "We must really face the facts," he urged, "when we are getting on our high moral horse, that forgery, theft, lying, bribery, and corruption exist in every Foreign Office and every Chancellory of the world." Murmurs passed through the House. The diplomatic gallery leaned forward.

Ponsonby continued: "I say that according to the recognized moral code our representatives abroad would be neglectful in their duty if they were not finding out secrets from the archives of those countries." To prove the charge, he asserted that "I have during my career seen a document which was taken from the archives of a foreign country."

All this was said by Lloyd George and Ponsonby on the assumption that Joynson-Hicks had not erred when he asserted that the highly secret War Office document "had left Arcos some days at all events before the search took place." He adduced no proof, however.

But the fact that the British Government engaged in spying, it was pointed out in Parliament, was obvious from the fact that it had in its possession and printed in the White Paper Soviet documents found neither in Arcos nor in the raided Peking Soviet Embassy.

The availability of these secret Soviet papers rather confirmed the *Manchester Guardian's* contention that "all states habitually use their diplomatic immunity to commit thefts of this kind [the reference is to the alleged purloining of the War Office document.—L. F.], and we probably have as many secret Russian documents as they have of ours."

By basing its policy of rupture on the Arcos raid, the British Government removed its real grievances from the limelight. Yet it had enough real grievances to build up a powerful case. In China, the Bolsheviks were in effect if not by direct intention damaging British interests and threatening British imperialism. Russian Communists gave support to the British miners in the hope that immediately or ultimately this action would do harm to the British capitalist state.

On May 26 Sir Austen Chamberlain informed the Soviet Government that diplomatic relations were severed. But in the same note, the Foreign Secretary stated that Arcos might remain to conduct legitimate business operations. Other Soviet commercial institutions, like the Naphtha Syndicate, likewise remained and continued to function for years after the rupture. What, then was the sense of the rupture? To placate irate British firms and to facilitate Russian trade, Joynson-Hicks, the extremist enemy of Soviet Russia, declared publicly that since de jure recognition of the Union had not been withdrawn, Soviet imports into Great Britain would not be subject to confiscation. The rupture, accordingly, was really a half-way measure. It tried not to ruin trade possibilities, but it did, and the record shows that it achieved little else that brought any benefit to England. The absence of relations continued so long because of inertia and because old men regard the reversal of a mistaken action injurious to their prestige.

The capitalist world is faced with two alternatives in respect to the Soviet Union: either it rises up to destroy it, or it becomes reconciled to its existence and makes the best of it. Russia cannot be ignored. The British Conservatives failed to realize how barren a negative policy must be.

# 24

# THE AFTER-EFFECTS OF THE BREAK WITH ENGLAND

*England* The history of Soviet relations with the Western world is a chain of reversals relieved by little triumphs and temporary victories. But no set-back was as serious and far-reaching as the rupture of Anglo-Soviet relations. British de jure recognition of Moscow had encouraged a series of similar moves by other Governments. Britain's severance of relations with Russia likewise served other Powers as an example.

At least one concrete after-effect of the break in England was direct and undeniable. Negotiations had taken place throughout 1927 between the Midland Bank and Soviet representatives for a large credit to facilitate Russian purchases of British textile machinery. The negotiations, opened on British initiative, were conducted by Allan Smith and, subsequently, Reginald MacKenna on the one hand, and Boyev and Khinchuk on the other. In May they reached a successful conclusion, and an arrangement providing for a one-year 10,000,000 pound sterling credit to the Soviet Government was confirmed in a letter of Boyev's dated May 9, 1927, and of MacKenna's dated May 11. But two days later Arcos and the Soviet Trade Delegation were raided, and immediately the credit agreement suffered practical cancellation, although well-informed persons stated privately at different times during the following years that the Bolsheviks might avail themselves of its benefits if they wished.

Trade with England became insecure and expensive for the Bolsheviks after the Arcos incident. No guarantee existed that similar raids would not be undertaken, that Soviet commercial secrets would not be intercepted, and that Russian business men would enjoy relatively unhindered entrance and egress. Credit and financing naturally became more costly, and the discounting of Russian bills sometimes absorbed unbelievably high sums. For purely practical considerations, therefore, the Soviet Government felt justified in transferring most of its normally British purchases to other countries, while political resentment and diplomatic hostility scarcely tended to encourage trade exchanges. As a result, Russian imports from England fell appreciably, although English imports from Russia continued at a higher level. Vis-à-vis the Soviet Union, therefore, the break brought Great Britain a larger passive trade balance. It constituted a blow to British exporters and manufacturers at a time when the British economic world, conscious of Britain's losses in overseas trade, strained every nerve to stimulate sales to foreign nations. The break, as Sir Herbert Samuel stated in a speech quoted in *The Times* of November 19, 1928, was a "measure more extreme than the occasion demanded, and one which has caused injury to some of the most important branches of our national trade."

Big concerns, to be sure, continued to trade with the Soviet Government, and the Co-operative Wholesale Society between 1927 and 1929 advanced millions of pounds to Siberian butter and dairying co-operatives. British imports of Caucasian oil increased above the pre-rupture level despite Deterding's "stolen" oil agitation. Nevertheless the general turnover suffered.

**SOVIET AND BRITISH LABOR** The diplomatic rupture between Russia and England produced a parallel break of relations between the Labor movements of the two countries. Beginning with the early period of intervention, an entente had sprung up between working-class organizations in Great Britain and Soviet Union which reached its highest flower during the Russo-Polish war crisis but continued to bear fruit immediately before and during MacDonald's term of office in 1924 when Rakovsky established warm personal ties with numerous British Labor leaders. After the emergence of the Baldwin-

Chamberlain Cabinet, Labor pursued its pro-Soviet tactics in Parliament, and persistently defended the Soviet Government on the platform and in the Press. Meanwhile, in 1925, an Anglo-Russian Trade Union Committee had been organized to coordinate some of the foreign political acts of the British and Russsian trade unions. British representatives obstructed anti-Bolshevik measures at congresses of the Second International and of the Amsterdam Trade Union International, Russians frequently visited London and British Laborites traveled to Moscow, and the bond grew stronger and thicker.

Then, in May, 1926, came the General Strike which certain less radical Labor Party leaders had supported with undisguised reluctance. The Soviet trade unions offered the General Council large sums of money to finance the strike. The General Council refused.

The defeat of the General and Miner strikes provoked a reaction against radicalism and against the Soviet Union. It likewise enabled the Government to pass the Trade Union Act which deprived trade unions of rights and privileges they had learned to regard important and sacred. It was scarcely a coincidence that the same Parliamentary session which authorized this act also voted the diplomatic break with the Soviet State, for the undermining of Labor influence and the aggressiveness of the Die-Hards partly explained both.

The dissolution of the Anglo-Russian Trade Union Committee and the divorce of the British Labor movement from the Russian together with the absence of diplomatic relations between Downing Street and the Kremlin, definitely estranged the two movements and even introduced notes of enmity. Labor M.P.s continued to champion the cause of good relations with the Soviets, yet a marked cooling-off had occurred.

**THE ACCOUNT** Labor ties weakened, trade diminished, while British Conservatives felt completely free after the rupture to indulge their hostility against the Bolsheviks. These after-effects of the Anglo-Soviet break exhaust the major disadvantages suffered by Russia in England. The Die-Hards had probably expected that the fulfilment of their highest desire would bring harm to the Bolshevik regime. They were disappointed.

*Germany and the Break* Soon after the severance

of Anglo-Soviet relations, a British royal personage drew aside a prominent German official at a famous English sporting event and suggested that, after England had broken off relations with the impossible Government in Moscow, Germany might follow Downing Street's example. Such pressure from such an unusual source required conviction to resist. Berlin was somewhat disturbed. Nevertheless, it refused to succumb.

At the June, 1927, session of the League Council in Geneva, the representatives of England, France, Germany, Belgium, Italy, and Japan met in secret meeting to discuss the Soviet problem. Briand, who presided, called on Sir Austen Chamberlain to present Downing Street's case for the break. The Foreign Secretary made a lengthy statement, laying stress on the danger of Bolshevik propaganda not only to Britain, but to all Europe and Asia as well. The suggestion was clear and direct. But Stresemann explained the basis of Germany's friendship for Soviet Russia, discussed the Russian internal situation, and expressed the opinion that the Bolsheviks were the only barrier to chaos. Briand agreed. Stresemann's reply reflected the intent of Chamberlain's appeal. But Germany declined to follow.

Soviet-German friendship lay embedded in a common antagonism to the Versailles system. To the extent that Locarno created an illusion that Versailles had been superseded, the friendship between Berlin and Moscow suffered. But in sober moments, the Wilhelmstrasse realized that Russia offered it many political advantages.

Commercially, too, Germany had much to seek in the Soviet Union. Soviet foreign trade is intimately related to Soviet foreign policy, and, all other things being equal, the political friend or neutral gets more business than the political enemy. Germany therefore occupied a favorable position in Soviet trade. She needed that trade. Borrowing in America might enable her to transfer Dawes Plan annuities, but in the long run Germany's capacity to pay reparations and to transfer them depended on her excess of exports over imports. Without colonies, with the United States raising the tariff, and with England a stubborn competitor, an active German foreign trade balance was extremely difficult of achievement. The Soviet Union, despite, or perhaps because of, industrialization, presented a promising field—only on condition of credits, however.

The German Government accordingly proposed to grant Moscow a 300,000,000 mark credit. The federal Reich would guarantee 35 per cent of this sum, the German States, Prussia, Saxony, etc., 25 per cent. The Wilhelmstrasse knew, of course, that the Bolsheviks had paid all their previous bills and would not default on any foreign credit. Nevertheless, its guarantee would facilitate financing and cheapen the cost of the credit.

The German industrialists welcomed the scheme enthusiastically. German political party leaders, including Social Democrats, expressed themselves warmly in favor of it, and German trade union leaders gave their support to a credit which promised to reduce unemployment. A law approving the Government guarantee passed through the Reichstag with practically no opposition.

But friction developed with the banks. Originally, Otto Wolff had informed the Russians that the banks asked a certain percentage of interest plus commission. Quite suddenly, however, the banks raised their interest demands. Long and unpleasant negotiations followed. The Russians gained the impression that no political motive actuated the banks. Nor had they succumbed to British influence against a credit. They simply regarded themselves in a monopoly position and sought to exploit it for their own financial profit and prestige. English and American financiers remained hostile, the German "D" bankers thought, and no other country would or could undertake such a venture. They therefore asked 13⅛ per cent interest and commission.

German Government and industrial circles resented the narrow viewpoint of the banks, and made no secret of the fact. The Bolsheviks fumed. To Moscow it was not merely a matter of reducing interest payments on the German credit by 1 per cent or 0.5 per cent, but rather of preventing the establishment of a high standard of interest for Soviet credits throughout the world. Moscow was then engaged in credit discussions with large financial institutions in other countries. It would only injure its credit and damage its purse by accepting exorbitant German demands. Stomoniakov therefore sought alternative solutions.

He first entered into contact with the "Laender" or provincial banks of Germany. He negotiated with the Prussian and Saxon State banks, and in Dresden agreement was practically complete when the Saxon Minister of Finance suggested that he wished to see how matters stood in Berlin. Therewith the negotiations ended and the Minister of Finance never returned to the subject. Subsequently it was learned that a well-known "D" bank had taken steps to prevent Saxony from entering into independent financing arrangements with Moscow. These same banks, furthermore, issued an order forbidding their branches and associates from undertaking the financing of any part of the Russian credit.[1]

The unrelenting hostility of the "D" banks forced Stomoniakov to search the horizon for non-German financing possibilities. He turned to W. A. Harriman and met a good reception.

**HARRIMAN AND BOLSHEVIK CREDITS** W. A. Harriman of New York had obtained a concession from the Soviet Government in 1925 to the rich manganese deposits at Chiaturi in Georgia. Moscow impressed him with its business-like approach, its broad commercial outlook, and its economic reliability. He expected that the concession would make him the dictator of the manganese world and open the path to wide co-operation with the Bolsheviks. Young, the heir to a rich imagination and large fortune, unhampered by petty business inhibitions or fears, possessed of vision and a wholesome sense of economic adventure, he had seen the wide potentialities of American investment in post-war Europe, and acquired properties in Germany, Poland, and Soviet Georgia. Stomoniakov's proposal appealed to him. Stomoniakov, Harriman, and Rossi, Harriman's European director, now opened intensive negotiations.

Since the German banks would in any event be forced to discount their Soviet acceptances in American, Dutch, and Swiss banks, Harriman proposed to issue bonds on the New York market to the sum of 300,000,000 marks. Sixty per cent of this four-year loan would be guaranteed by the German Government and by German industrialists, 40 per cent by the German industrialists and German

[1] Dr. B. Hahn: "Die deutsche Ausfallbürgschaft für Lieferungen nach Russland." *Ost-Europa.* (Berlin, 1925–6). Issue #10.

banks. The interest rate would be 6½ per cent, commission 1½ per cent maximum, and the German banks would receive 1 per cent commission on the entire loan for guaranteeing two-fifths of it. The total cost to the Russians, therefore, would be 9 per cent—a figure which was not subject to change during the four-year period.

The German banks opposed. The Deutsche Bank was incensed against Harriman because he had taken a concession for properties in the Chiaturi manganese field claimed by some of its richest clients. Moreover, the big German financial institution naturally felt disinclined to let slip from their hands and into the American market a large piece of business which normally belonged to them. Prestige too was involved. Doubts had also arisen as to whether a German Government guarantee did not conflict with the Dawes Plan system.

Unable to persuade the German banking world to accept his first plan of financing Soviet trade with Germany, W. A. Harriman presented a second scheme. Harriman would float the loan without the guarantee of the German banks and the German State. A German export company would be organized. Harriman undertook to grant this company a five-year loan of 150,000,000 to 300,000,000 marks at 9 per cent. The sum would reach the company through a trustee who might be the Reichsbank or a group of private banks. The Soviet bills of acceptance would be guaranteed by the German Government and by German banks.

The German Government approved. The German Reichskredit Gesellschaft participated in the negotiations with Harriman as the possible trustee. Hjalmar Schacht, the President of the Reichsbank, at first welcomed the plan.

Harriman had consulted American financiers. He knew that S. Parker Gilbert approved. Leading German politicians and businessmen were astonished at the conduct of the German banks and would have welcomed a successful issue of Stomoniakov's negotiations with Harriman. But many of these persons looked on the Harriman move as a maneuver calculated to make the "D" banks more tractable. When they discovered that the Russians intended the arrangement not as pressure but as a serious transaction, they disliked the passage to America of business which legitimately belonged to Germany.

Everything was settled. On May 6 W. A. Harriman informed Ministerial Director von Dirksen, then Chief of the Eastern Division of the German Foreign Office, that he had reached an agreement with the Bolsheviks, that he would organize a German company to issue the bonds in New York, and that the State Department, while not vetoing the proposition, had expressed no enthusiasm for it.

The German ambassador in Washington received instructions to be of service to Harriman and to support the loan in every possible manner. The German Government and German industrialists have always favored German-American business collaboration in Russia.

Later Felix M. Warburg of Kuhn, Loeb & Co., New York, informed Harriman of his willingness to facilitate the German credit transaction.

Harriman went to New York where the banking world gave its consent provided Washington approved. But in the national capital Secretary of Commerce Hoover objected. He expressed his well-known viewpoint against German-American collaboration in Soviet trade. If American banks wished to finance American exporters to Russia he would erect no obstacles. But why should American financiers advance credits to German producers? That would limit American exports. The State Department seized on the Department of Commerce's attitude and publicly announced its veto on the Harriman project. Harriman therefore dropped it.

**THE 300,000,000 MARK CREDIT** The Soviet Government was now thrown back on the German "D" banks. At this juncture the discount rate in Germany fell and, in addition, the banks, threatened with Premier Rykov's refusal to accept the credit, and subjected to political and economic pressure, assumed a more conciliatory attitude. They therefore agreed with the Soviets that the interest rate would equal the official discount rate at the time of the repayment of an instalment of the 300,000,000 mark credit, plus commission. Of the 300,000,000 marks, 180,000,000 marks represented a four-year credit for purchasing complete factory equipments and 120,000,000 marks a two-year credit for lighter industrial fixtures. The final agreement was signed early in July, 1926, after

Krestinsky and Dr. Curtius, Reich Minister of Public Economy, had reached an agreement about interest rates on June 26.

The Bolsheviks, looking back on this already exhausted credit, leveled four criticisms against it. The credit became operative on the day an order was given to a certain German firm, so that that firm, by postponing delivery, actually shortened the credit term and increased the rate of interest. The whole system of the 300,000,000 mark credit was cumbersome and expensive. Too little time was allowed from the granting of the credit to the date when all orders had to be placed. The credit was finally negotiated in July, 1926; December 31, 1926, was fixed as the last day for orders, so that in many cases specifications for whole electrical power stations and complicated equipment for entire plants had to be drafted in a few months. And finally, the German producers sometimes raised their prices and reduced their quality for the Russian purchaser.

The Germans likewise had their grievances. If the German system of crediting was cumbersome, the Soviet method of making purchases was highly bureaucratic, slow, undependable, and erratic. Moreover, the Germans argued that the Bolsheviks used the 300,000,000 marks to cover purchases they would have made in Germany even if it had not been arranged, whereas the Germans, it is said, intended that the credit apply to purchases supplementary to the normal trade.

Considerable mutual discontent notwithstanding, the 300,000,000 mark credit encouraged Soviet trade. In fact, the actual purchases amounted to 360,000,000 marks, and the Government raised its guarantee correspondingly. That neither Germany nor Russia was disappointed with the results of the guaranteed credit is clear. The German Government continued without any special agreement to guarantee the financing of Soviet imports from Germany. Furthermore, Germany took the initiative to offer the Bolsheviks another larger and longer credit in 1929.

**THE EFFECT OF THE RUPTURE** Several times after the Anglo-Soviet rupture, Herr von Kuehlmann, the Reich representative at Brest Litovsk, Arnold Rechberg, a rich industrialist, and, rumor has it, even Hjalmar Schacht, the President of the Reichsbank, intimated to Western states men their readiness to attempt to persuade the German Government to forsake its cordial attitude towards Moscow, if, as compensation, Germany received colonies, or reparations reductions, or other important advantages. The possibility of such a bargain probably brought Lord Birkenhead to Berlin in 1928 "to play golf." He made no secret in public and private utterances of anti-Bolshevik plans. In fact, he prophesied openly that the Soviet Government would fall within six months, and the Press asked what outside influence would achieve such a result. The Wilhelmstrasse was embarrassed by the reported efforts of the Kuehlmann-Rechberg group in 1927 and 1928 and in 1929 at the Young Plan conference in Paris, and fought against anti-Soviet tendencies at home and in international politics. Yet Germany began to feel her isolation as the only Great Power maintaining friendly relations with Moscow. Germans bewailed it in private conversations. It caused them considerable diplomatic discomfort. It was reflected in the work of some permanent German correspondents in Moscow. The Social Democrats took the opportunity it offered to agitate for a re-orientation of German foreign policy. At a meeting, for instance, of the Foreign Relations Committee of the Reichstag in the fall of 1927, Rudolf Hilferding, later Social Democratic Minister of Finance, launched a bitter attack against the Government's political and economic policy towards Russia, tried to prove that the Soviet Union was in a state of hopeless chaos, and contended that Poland offered wider trading possibilities than Russia.

In the very beginning of 1928 a slight improvement became noticeable. For one thing, the war scare had subsided and with it the curious fear in some German circles that the Soviet Government stood on the brink of destruction. The new atmosphere facilitated the opening of a Soviet-German economic conference in Berlin in February–March, 1928, to discuss legal and financial phases of trade. Even of themselves the talks were probably doomed to failure, but the arrest of three Germans in connection with the prosecution of the Don engineers (the Shakhti trial) torpedoed it. That unfortunate trial introduced what was perhaps the bleakest period in Soviet-German relations.

*Rakovsky's Recall* With the recall of Rakovsky at the request of the French Government in October, 1927, diplomatic relations between Russia and France came to an end for all practical purposes, and Rakovsky's successor had as little of importance to do in Paris as M. Herbette in Moscow. Poincaré in October, 1927, established the same de facto absence of relations as Baldwin in May, 1927, and only the form was different.

When Chicherin saw Poincaré in May, 1927, Poincaré said he did not expect there would be an agreement between them, but he did not desire a rupture. Poincaré, in general, did not wish to participate in hostile international combinations against the Soviets; on the other hand, he wanted no further negotiations and no activity that might improve relations with Moscow. He said to one person: "We will not separate from England, but we cannot follow her."

Rakovsky had to leave the Paris Soviet Embassy on account of his efforts to force the tempo of Franco-Russian debt negotiations. Poincaré opposed those efforts and sought to transfer the negotiations from the debt commission to the Ministry of Finance. Poincaré was Minister of Finance. The change would have meant burial.

### FRANCO-SOVIET DEBT NEGOTIATIONS IN 1927

Poincaré, even while out of office, had found it possible in July, 1926, to bring sufficient pressure to bear on Briand to prevent the ratification of the de Monzie-Rakovsky debt agreement. The Bolsheviks did not urge a renewal of conversations. The conclusion of the 300,000,000 mark German credit in July, 1926, and the prospect of serious credit negotiations with English banks inspired the Russians with confidence, so that when Mikoyan became Commissar of Trade in August, 1926, he proposed to let France wait.

But the Chamberlain threat of a rupture contained in his note to Moscow of February 23, 1927, impressed the Soviet Government with the immediate necessity of greater activity in Paris, and Rakovsky accordingly received instructions to resume the talks.

In the summer of 1926 the Soviet delegation had agreed to pay sixty-two annuities of 60,000,000 gold francs each. Two questions remained outstanding, however. France demanded that the full annuity commence immediately, whereas Moscow proposed a scale of progressions under which the standard annuity would not be reached for three years. France, secondly, insisted on most-favored-nation treatment in the matter of debts. This the Soviet Government had not seen fit to concede.

The negotiations between Rakovsky and de Monzie were renewed on March 19, 1927. On the 26th de Monzie wrote to the Bolshevik suggesting the abandonment of the Russian table of progressions.

In the early part of May, Rakovsky complied with this request and likewise accepted the French demand for most-favored-nation treatment. It would seem that the way to an agreement had been paved.

But Poincaré had never desired a debt settlement, and the rupture of Anglo-Soviet relations, which accounted for Rakovsky's important concessions to de Monzie's committee, made him more than ever opposed to a financial modus vivendi with the Bolsheviks.

Meanwhile, no plenary sessions of the Franco-Soviet debt conference had taken place since March 19. Rakovsky complained to de Monzie in a letter dated June 30. On July 26 the French chairman replied in a communication which disclosed the mainsprings of Poincaré's policy.

> It is true [wrote de Monzie] that the obligations accepted [by the Soviet Government.—L.F.] in respect of debts would considerably facilitate economic relations and develop them on a much larger scale. Nevertheless, we cannot leave out of consideration other phases of the question which belong to the fundamental elements of the general problem: the regulation of the inter-State debt, the settlement of the losses sustained by our citizens in the Soviet Union, an economic convention which must provide our enterprises and transactions with a guarantee without which development is scarcely conceivable. Yet some of these problems have never been discussed together.

"For the time being," de Monzie added, "we must appreciate and welcome the success achieved in the settlement of the debts." He hoped negotiations would not be interrupted by the summer vacation.

Several things are clear: the Bolsheviks had accepted all French debt demands and a settlement had been reached. But just when it had been reached, Poincaré raised new, extremely involved issues which "have never been discussed together" and which the French had not presented for deliberation during eighteen months of discussions.

Poincaré wanted no economic understanding, no debt

agreement, and no political rapprochement with the Bolsheviks. Under the circumstances, Rakovsky became a nuisance. For Rakovsky had influential and popular friends in high French circles. His attempts to hasten the tempo of debt negotiations embarrassed Poincaré. Rakovsky had injected this issue into French internal politics. It promised to become a subject of controversy in forthcoming French elections when the Left might use Poincaré's opposition to the debt settlement as an argument for the mobilization of peasant and petty bourgeois votes. In April, 1927, Rakovsky had published the contents of the actual debt settlement in the Paris *Oeuvre*. Poincaré never forgave him. The ambassador thereby gave a club to the Premier's political enemies, and they immediately proceeded to wield it without delicacy.

The Anglo-Soviet rupture encouraged anti-Soviet tendencies in Paris. In June French banks restricted the financing of Russian trade credits.

**THE CAMPAIGN FOR RAKOVSKY'S RECALL** An incident now intervened which afforded the French Government an opportunity to request the recall of Rakovsky. Early in August Rakovsky went to Moscow, partly on diplomatic business—de Monzie and Alphand had assured him that if he reduced Russia's credit demands to $120,000,000 an agreement could be reached—but largely to participate in the inter-party controversy between the Stalin majority and the Trotzky Opposition to which Rakovsky adhered.

In the course of the bitter struggle which raged around Trotzky's differences with the Central Committee of the Communist Party, the Opposition had been criticized for precipitating damaging splits and for attacking the party at a time when the severance of relations with Great Britain and accompanying phenomena confronted the Soviet Union with the danger of war.

Trotzky replied that even if war broke out he would not abandon his struggle against Stalin. He stated that his tactics would correspond to Clemenceau's at the beginning of the World War when the Germans stood 80 kilometers from Paris. Clemenceau opposed the then French Cabinet even in that critical hour and ultimately succeeded in overthrowing it, but his patriotism and his support of France against Germany were never in doubt. This Trotzky declaration provoked an even more vehement onslaught against the Opposition. It was submitted that in a war with foreign imperialism, which the Bolsheviks then thought imminent, Trotzky would attack the party in the rear, divide its forces, and thus contribute to a capitalist victory.

Trotzky and his associates felt called upon to meet this serious charge, and on August 9 they signed a declaration enunciating their views. They would, they said, stand by the Soviet Government and the party in the event of a conflict, and more than that, they would consider it their Communist duty to call on the soldiers of their bourgeois antagonists to desert and join the Red Army.

Rakovsky signed this declaration. L. B. Kamenev, the Soviet ambassador in Rome, likewise subscribed his name as a member of the Opposition. Mussolini passed over the matter lightly. He understood that the statement had been provoked by an internal party controversy and need not concern him as the head of a foreign government. It was natural, he must have thought to himself, that the Bolsheviks would pursue the same tactics in the coming war as the Allies had in their World War propaganda within and behind the enemy lines.

But a storm of protest arose in France. The Right Press fumed, and few undertook to defend Rakovsky's move. M. Herbette made representations in Moscow. An exchange of verbal notes and conversations ensued, "as a result of which," Chicherin wrote to Herbette on October 12,[2] "you, Mr. Ambassador, declared to me, on September 4, that your Government considered itself satisfied with the explanations given by me and that the incident may be considered closed." Briand made a public statement to the same effect.

Nevertheless, the agitation for Rakovsky's dismissal continued with undiminished vehemence. Sir Henri Deterding supplied the anti-Rakovsky Press with arguments and even more convincing material, whereas Gulbenkian, then an oil rival of Deterding's, offered *Le Soir* and other publications information calculated to embarrass Deterding. In political circles and even in editorials veiled or open hints were heard that the Royal Dutch was financing newspapers which maligned Rakovsky. From being

[2] For full text of note see *Soviet Review*. Washington, January, 1928.

a controversy to protect capitalism against Communist desertion appeals to bourgeois soldiers, the affair had developed into a rich feud between petroleum interests, with money flowing as freely as oil. Caillaux, Charles Baron, the Chairman of the Parliamentary Oil Commission, M. Margaine and other prominent Frenchmen had connected the France-Soviet debt settlement possibility with a federal French petroleum monopoly operating largely on naphtha purchased from the Soviet trust. In his opposition to a debt settlement, Poincaré therefore found enthusiastic support in the opponents of the oil monopoly.

Much of this episode is still hidden under the veil of Poincaré's time-honored differences with Briand. Apparently, the Foreign Minister wished to gloss over the difficulties. He had been responsible for the amicable solution of the incident connected with Rakovsky's signature of the Opposition declaration. But Poincaré continued the battle, and when Briand went to Geneva in September, 1927, the conflagration broke out anew.

The Press attack against Rakovsky recommenced with renewed vigor on September 4. In the second half of the month a Cabinet meeting took place without Briand, after which Havas announced that the Government would ask for Rakovsky's recall. Then the Quai d'Orsay denied the report, probably as a result of Briand's intervention from Geneva. On another occasion, Loucheur, a friend of Briand, stated for publication that Rakovsky must go. Then he issued a démenti. But soon they realized that the Right was exploiting the entire affair to make capital against the Left for the next elections. As in England, the Russian issue had become a factor in internal politics. Then the Left struck back.

The Press offensive against Rakovsky failed to abate. The objective was no longer the dismissal of the ambassador. Rakovsky's foes demanded the severance of all diplomatic relations with the Soviet Government. After the blow delivered by Chamberlain, a similar blow from Poincaré, together with pressure from both on lesser States, might have been disastrous to Moscow's diplomacy. Moscow accordingly opened a counter-offensive and cynically tried to buy off French opposition or to strengthen the French friends of cordial relations with Russia. In August, Rakovsky proposed a pact of mutual non-aggression and non-interference in domestic affairs. Briand at first approved, but subsequently he subordinated the French pact to a Soviet-Polish pact, which the Poles, however, agreed to negotiate only on condition of parallel Soviet pacts with the Baltic states—a condition Moscow could not accept. At the same time, Moscow agreed to concessions in the debt question. Accordingly, Rakovsky, on September 21, wrote to de Monzie and made the following offer: the Soviet Government would pay French bondholders 60,000,000 gold francs annually for the next sixty-two years and undertook to deposit 30,000,000 gold francs in France which could be distributed among the bondholders immediately after the ratification of the debt convention. Russia granted most-favored-nation treatment and dropped her scheme for progressive annuities. Instead of the $225,000,000 advance on which the Soviets had previously insisted, part of which was to have been in cash, the new offer asked $120,000,000 in six annual instalments, the entire sum to be spent for productive purposes, not, for instance, for the purchase of war material, and in orders to French industrial and commercial firms exclusively.

The French debt delegation headed by de Monzie received this Moscow offer favorably. It exceeded anything they had ever expected to extract from the Russians. They wished to sign immediately. De Monzie had urged Rakovsky to publish the facts in order to mobilize French public opinion in favor of it and thereby prevent its rejection.

But de Monzie had reckoned without Poincaré. The French Government accused Rakovsky of an irregularity in giving the Soviet proposal to the press. The rapid liquidation of the Rakovsky "Opposition declaration" incident had left the enemies of Briand displeased, their appetites unsated. Here a new opportunity offered itself. By publishing the offer, Rakovsky had committed his greatest cardinal sin: he had given a weapon into the hands of Poincaré's enemies. Herbette formally requested Rakovsky's recall on October 7.

Herbette's note of that date declared that the French Government's move was based on the circumstances that Rakovsky had appended his signature to the Opposition document advocating the suborning of foreign soldiers, and on Rakovsky's publication of his letter of September 21 to de Monzie outlining the new Soviet debt proposals. Chicherin's reply of October 12 asked why, after Herbette had announced his Government's satisfaction with Bolshevik explanations on the Opposition document, Paris now reverted to the subject. This "is perfectly incomprehensible," the commissar affirmed. Nor could Chicherin understand how the publication of a letter with the knowledge of de Monzie could make Rakovsky persona non grata to the French Government.

But although the reasons for Rakovsky's recall "are without a basis," as Chicherin wrote, he could not deny the French Government's formal right to demand the withdrawal of an ambassador unacceptable to it. Moscow therefore relieved Rakovsky of his duties and, shortly afterwards, appointed Dovgalevsky in his stead.

If the personality of Rakovsky had in truth prevented a debt agreement between France and the Soviet Union, his removal should have facilitated a settlement. It should have opened the road to the conclusion of a non-aggression pact. As a matter of fact, however, the debt and pact negotiations ended with Rakovsky's departure and were never resumed.

*Poland and the British Rupture* The tension in Anglo-Soviet relations culminating in the rupture of relations in May, 1927, had its direct effect on Polish policy towards Russia.

Pilsudski came to power in May, 1926, as the result of a coup d'état. Locarno had activized British policy on the Continent and English influence became a force more to be reckoned with. France had not been unseated from her position of friend and ally of the Polish Republic. Yet England was making a bid for closer contacts with Pilsudski. The Polish Foreign Minister Zaleski admitted to the writer on October 25 that relations with England had become warmer and that a possibility existed of further developments in the same direction. The bond would be a loan floated, for the most part, in London. Conversations to this end proceeded during the middle of 1926, but, owing to the condition of the Polish state apparatus, the budget, and the national economy, no bank wished to advance funds without concomitant control over customs, railways or federal budget. That privilege, however, Pilsudski refused to grant. And though Polish bankers and industrialists urged it, the dictator objected and won against the British, only to yield after a time to the Americans.

Economists whom the writer consulted at the time agreed that the sources of Polish ills were twofold: the army and the absence of normal relations with Germany and Russia.

Military expenditures in 1926 constituted 33 per cent of the Government's budget. But this did not include the costs of certain military academies paid for by the Ministry of Education, transportation of soldiers paid for by the Ministry of Communications, and the upkeep of a frontier guard of some 17,000 paid for by the Ministry of the Interior. If these outlays are included, members of the diplomatic corps agreed, the total would represent not 33 per cent but 45 per cent of federal expenses.

Asked why such a huge army expenditure was necessary, Polish officials moved to a wall map and indicated Poland's geographical position between two mighty neighbors, Germany and Russia, and exposed to the undying enmity of Lithuania which resented the loss of Vilna.

Pilsudski proclaimed that he wanted no foreign financial control and that he would conduct foreign affairs independently, that is, independently of France and England. This was true; but the plea of self-reliance also justified a large army. And that army, even the Western Powers feared, might involve Europe in war. They showed their apprehension when Lithuania and the Soviet Union signed a neutrality treaty of September 28, 1926.

**THE SOVIET–LITHUANIAN TREATY** Lithuania never reconciled herself to the loss of Vilna, her national capital. She was also apprehensive lest her stubborn attitude on this point justify the "colonel" clique around Pilsudski in provoking a war against her. Support for her difficult cause could come from Germany, whose help, however, was limited by her international position, and from the Soviet Union which refused to recognize Vilna as a part of Poland. In fact the Russian-Lithuanian peace treaty of July 12, 1920, recognized Vilna as a part of Lithuania, and Moscow reaffirmed that provision on September 28, 1926.[3] Moscow and Kovno agreed "under all cir-

[3] Kluchnikov and Sabanin: *International Politics, etc.,* III, 352–4. English text, *London Times,* also *Survey of International Affairs,* 1927, by A. J. Toynbee (London, 1929), p. 544.

cumstances" to respect the "sovereignty and territorial integrity and inviolability of one another"—territorial integrity as of July, 1920. Russia thus declared Vilna Lithuanian soil although it was actually under Polish domination. To be sure, the Bolsheviks could argue that the illegal seizure of a city did not constitute title nor did the plebiscite of January, 1922, held under Polish auspices. (The writer was in Vilna at the time.) Nevertheless, the recognition of Vilna as Lithuanian territory was an unfriendly act toward Poland, and the Poles interpreted it as such. So aroused, in fact, were Polish Government circles that France and England thought it advisable to warn Warsaw not to undertake military moves against Lithuania. The Powers wanted no European War.

Russia's sympathy with Lithuania in the Vilna question put her in a position to exercise influence in Kovno. Moscow used that advantage in 1928 when the uncompromising attitude of Lithuania's statesmen threatened to precipitate a violent and dangerous conflict with Poland.

In a note addressed to Chicherin on the day of the signature of the treaty, Lithuania declared, in substance, that her geographical position would require her to remain neutral in the event of League sanctions against the Soviet Union and then added a theoretical affirmation that the Soviet-Lithuanian treaty did not conflict with her obligations under the League Covenant.

The Soviet-Lithuanian Treaty pleased the Germans because, despite the burning desire of Kovno, it made no mention of Memel. The agreement, moreover, delivered almost a fatal blow to the Polish idea of a Baltic bloc which, as Herr Rauscher, the German minister in Warsaw said to the writer, was as much anti-German as anti-Russian. The Poles therefore believed, and M. Zalesky said so definitely in a conversation with the writer in Warsaw on October 21, 1926, that Count Brockdorff-Rantzau had inspired the Russians to negotiate the Soviet-Lithuanian Treaty, and that Schubert, of the German Foreign Office, deposited it with the League four or five days before its publication.

The immediate effect of the treaty was the opening of negotiations between Moscow and Latvia. In my discussion with Zalesky on October 21, he denied the fact when I mentioned it, but in a second interview four days later he reversed himself and declared, not without bitterness, that if Russia agreed with all the Baltic States separately Poland would feel released from her moral responsibility towards them and might then sign a separate pact with the Soviet Union.

In 1926 the Bolsheviks reckoned with the possibility of foreign attack. To guarantee themselves against this eventuality and in an effort to prevent the formation of a Baltic bloc, the Kremlin accordingly proposed to all Baltic States that they sign non-aggression pacts with Russia. The first of these treaties was negotiated with Lithuania in September, 1926. But the greatest danger threatened from the side of Poland, which had fought one war with Soviet Russia and harbored undisguised feelings of hostility towards the Red neighbor.

**SOVIET–POLISH DIFFICULTIES** Diplomatically Soviet-Polish relations were unfruitful and business remained at a miserable minimum. The industries of pre-war Russian Poland catered to the Russian and Siberian markets and many of Poland's factories, artisans and commercial houses depended completely for custom on her eastern neighbor. Since the revolution, however, little attention had been paid in Warsaw to trade possibilities with the Bolsheviks. M. Dolezal, Polish Assistant Minister of Industry and Trade, told the writer that whereas in 1913 Poland exported to Russia goods valued at one and a half billion gold francs, her sales to the Soviet Union in 1925 amounted to only nineteen million gold francs. This and Poland's almost uninterrupted tariff war with Germany were perhaps the chief causes of Poland's chronic economic crisis, of her bad trade balance, of her poor foreign credit situation, and of many of Mr. Dewey's difficulties as American Financial Adviser of the Polish State. "Russia has been neglected," Felix Mlynarski, the Vice-President of the Bank Polski told the writer in Warsaw in October, 1926, "and therefore the financial recovery of Poland is delayed. The moment Russia gets foreign capital and can buy more goods, Poland's problem is solved," the implication being that the best way of helping Poland was to give money to Russia.

Polish banks and industrialists (and the National Democrats) enthusiastically supported the establishment of more normal relations with Moscow, but Pilsudski was notoriously anti-Russian. It was the heritage of a life of patriotic struggle against the Czarist monarchy. Moreover, the Pilsudski regime represented the philosophy of the agrarianization of Poland—in which Mr. Dewey concurred—and although industries would benefit by regular commercial relations with Russia, the Polish village would suffer from new competition. Official Poland accordingly evaded further agreements with Moscow. When Polish statesmen were asked why they did not negotiate a treaty with the Soviet Union they mentioned the Riga accord. But that terminated a war. Even Mr. Stetson, the American minister in Warsaw, echoed the official Polish view and at the same time very naturally aired unrestrained anti-Soviet sentiments. The two went hand in hand. "If we made real peace with Russia," Professor Ashkenazi, at one time Polish representative to the League, said to the writer in Warsaw, "we would need only half our army." Yet he too declared that "we have the Riga Treaty and do not need a pact with Russia."

Zalesky likewise enumerated his arguments against the conclusion of a trade agreement. "No device has yet been found to serve as a basis for such a convention. Most-favored-nation treatment is of no avail in a country which has a monopoly of foreign trade and in which, therefore, customs duties mean nothing. Besides," the minister continued, "the Russians use their commercial relations for political purposes." These statements are not devoid of truth; nevertheless more than one country, Germany among them, conducted profitable business with the Bolsheviks on the basis of trade treaties, and after Zalesky made this analysis two of Poland's candidates for the Baltic bloc—Latvia and Estonia—concluded such agreements with Moscow.

**SOVIET–POLISH PACT NEGOTIATIONS** In accordance with Moscow's policy of securing her western frontier against aggression, Voikov, the Soviet minister in Warsaw, laid a draft neutrality and non-aggression pact before the Polish Foreign Office, August 24, 1926.

Poland's objection to a pact with Russia arose from fear that it would destroy forever Warsaw's chances of organizing a Baltic bloc. Rakovsky told the writer that from the beginning of his diplomatic activity in Paris he proposed a pact of non-aggression by which France and the Soviet Union would guarantee Poland's Eastern frontier, and France and Poland and the Soviet Union's Polish border. But the French replied that Warsaw rejected such an agreement. Rakovsky felt that the grounds for Poland's attitude were her special interests in Rumania and the Baltic states. Chicherin sketched a pact of neutrality to Poland when he visited the capital in September, 1925, on the eve of Locarno. Chicherin declares that Skrzynski was conciliatory, asking merely to be satisfied that the Baltic States would not be destroyed by Russia. In regard to Rumania, he submitted that Poland could not renounce her obligations. But when Zaleski succeeded Skrzynski he adumbrated a plan for a series of treaties between Russia and Poland and between Russia and the Baltic countries which, however, would be bound together by a common clause. Russia refused. Russia saw no reason why her negotiations with Poland should be mixed with her relations with the Baltic nations or why Poland should speak in the name of the Baltic nations.

These maneuvers and counter-moves consumed almost a year. "I feel," the Polish minister said to the writer some seven weeks after the Bolshevik pact proposal was made to him, "that it is inadvisable to make a separate pact with Russia, for she could then attack the Baltic States one by one, destroy them, and then prepare to attack us." The pact draft, however, provided that Poland would be released from her promise of non-aggression the moment Russia became the aggressor against a Baltic State or against any other Power. "Yes," Zaleski continued, "but who is to determine who the aggressor is. The League has been working on this question for eighteen months." "Poland is free to decide," I suggested on the basis of a study of the text. "That is not clear from the text," the minister affirmed. But if the draft did not state categorically that Poland would not be free to decide, Poland obviously retained freedom of action.

This, of course, was not the chief objection. Poland had her own policy toward the Baltic States. A pact with Moscow would frustrate it. She also had accepted obligations vis-à-vis Rumania. Zaleski explained to me that the Polish-Rumanian Treaty, renewed on March 26, 1926, guaranteed Rumanian sovereignty over Bessarabia. If Red troops entered Bessarabia, Poland would not be forced to march immediately, he said, but her duty to

Rumania was more direct than that of England or France which had also recognized Bucharest's title to Bessarabia. And this was only natural, the minister added, for if the Bolsheviks took Bessarabia Poland's flank would be exposed.

To meet this Polish objection, the Soviet Government, on May 14, 1927, suggested the text of a protocol to be signed simultaneously with the Pact in which the contracting parties

> took cognizance of all those agreements and conventions which have been concluded by one of the contracting parties with a third Power or group of Powers and the texts of which had been published in official publications at the time of the signing of the present treaty.[4]

That is, the Bolsheviks agreed to countenance the operation of Poland's obligations vis-à-vis Rumania even if they conflicted with the Pact. Poland would not, therefore, violate the Pact if she engaged in a war against the Soviet Union on the side of Rumania without having been attacked herself. Nevertheless, even this provision did not satisfy the Poles.

Rumania, the Baltics, and the worsening of Russia's relations with England and France in 1927 prevented the creation of an atmosphere in which a Soviet-Polish non-aggression accord could be negotiated. These and internal factors made for friction between the two countries.

Of internal problems, the Ukrainian question was perhaps the most important.

**POLAND AND SOVIET UKRAINE** According to the 1921 census, Poland had a population of 27,500,000 of whom 9,000,000 were not Poles. The most numerous of the national minorities, the Ukrainian, accounted for four of the nine million non-Poles. There were, in addition, 2,800,000 Jews, 1,200,000 Germans, and 1,000,000 White Russians.

The pronounced nationalistic and Polonification policy of the Pilsudski regime antagonized these minorities. On the other hand, the Ukrainians of East Galicia entertained ambitions in the direction of Soviet Ukraine, and in this point met Pilsudski on common ground. Petlura had made

[4] The texts of this protocol and of the Soviet draft pact were supplied to the writer from the archives of the Commissariat of Foreign Affairs.

an agreement with Pilsudski in 1920 on the eve of the Soviet-Polish war whereby the hetman recognized Polish suzerainty over the Ukrainian population of Polish East Galicia in return for the assurance that this territory would become a part of the Ukrainian member of the greater federated Poland to rise after a successful crusade against the Bolsheviks. Levitski, Petlura's minister in Copenhagen in 1920, had denounced the hetman for this move yet when the writer met Levitski in Lemberg in November, 1926, he not only held the Petlura banner high but stood on a purely Petlurist platform which was more anti-Semitic than anti-Polish. Despite a façade of hostility towards the Polish State, the Unda Party, headed by Levitski, was then engaged in negotiations with Pilsudski and later made a broad peace with Warsaw. Levitski said to me that in five years a war would break out in which the Soviet Ukrainians would rise against the Bolsheviks, join forces with the Ukrainians or Ruthenians in East Galicia and form an autonomous, democratic, nationalistic Ukrainian State. This scheme fitted in with Polish federalistic designs. Its chances of success were rated high in European chancellories. Poland's ambitions in the Ukraine served as a hindrance to normal Soviet-Polish diplomatic relations. This question, plus Poland's pledges to Rumania, plus Poland's plans for a Baltic bloc, plus the influence of Western Powers in Poland, militated against the conclusion of the Soviet-Polish pact of non-aggression and neutrality in 1926 and 1927. The talks nevertheless were dragged out so as to avoid the impression abroad that the Warsaw diplomats objected to a peace settlement with Russia.

While the conversations were proceeding, Voikov, the Soviet minister to Poland, was assassinated in Warsaw on June 7, 1927.

The murderer proved to be a young Russian emigré named Koverda, member of an anti-Bolshevik society operating in Poland. In notes delivered before the assassination Moscow had called the Polish Government's attention to the existence of such organizations and had insisted that Polish tolerance of them was no token of friendship for Russia. After the assassination the Commissariat of Foreign Affairs recalled these warnings, while the Soviet Press, in the white heat of anger, laid the crime at the door of the Polish Government.

The Voikov assassination formed the basis of a long and acrimonious diplomatic correspondence between Moscow and Warsaw. At one time, in fact, alarmists wished to see an embryo war in the controversy. The Soviets, in the end, received some satisfaction, but the atmosphere which the murder and the consequent controversy created was scarcely congenial to further pact negotiations. These, in fact, were discontinued after the death of Voikov.

Soviet-Polish relations long stood under the sign of the Voikov affair and before it was forgotten the same Russian emigré circles in Poland undertook similar attempts on the lives of other Soviet officials in Poland. Efforts to renew the pact negotiations therefore bore no fruit.

**PACTS WITH THE BALTICS** Simultaneously with the neutrality pact negotiations with Poland and Lithuania, the Soviet Government opened conversations to the same end with Latvia, Estonia and Finland.

Finland commenced negotiations in the autumn and discontinued them in November of 1926. The history of the Soviet-Estonian pact conference was similar and equally brief. Only Latvia's record was different.

Aralov, former Soviet ambassador to Turkey, went to Riga in the autumn of 1926 to open the negotiations, and on March 9, 1927, the pact was actually initialed by Russian and Latvian representatives. "League of Nation circles were thrown into confusion by this act," the *New York Times* correspondent wired from Geneva. It broke the "second lap in the League's Eastern front," he added. But why should a peaceful pact of non-aggression alarm the League?

Before final signature and ratification could take place, the more or less "Left" government of Premier Skuenek and Foreign Minister Cielens had been succeeded by a Latvian Cabinet unfriendly to Moscow. And in the same period came the interruption of Soviet relations with Great Britain after which the acceptance of a non-aggression pact with the Bolsheviks would have been interpreted in London as disrespectful. Even if Chamberlain never as much as hinted his opposition to an agreement with Moscow, the effect of open antagonism between Russia and England could not but call forth caution and coolness on the part of statesmen of minor Powers which were financially, morally, or politically dependent on Great Britain.

*The Soviets and Asia* The Anglo-Soviet rupture which affected so profoundly the relations of European Powers to Moscow, left Asia almost untouched—except in China, where British influence expressed itself in armaments and through internal Chinese forces. Before the break, during the period of tense hostility, and after it when all Europe reacted, the Soviet Government's diplomatic position in Turkey, Afghanistan, and Persia remained intact. Indeed, Bolshevism's formal political ties with these countries were reinforced by a treaty of friendship and neutrality with Turkey on December 17, 1925, of neutrality and mutual non-aggression with Afghanistan on August 31, 1926, and of guarantee and neutrality with Persia on October 1, 1927.

Turkey, Persia, Afghanistan, Mongolia, and China were not capitalistic states in the Western sense. They boasted no industrial or financial capitalist classes. The social and economic contradictions between them and the Soviet Union were therefore smaller and less important than between the intensely capitalistic West and Russia. Ethnologically Asiatic Russia merges into Russia's Asiatic neighbors, whereas a chasm of race, church, and culture divides the peoples of European Russia generally from Western Europe.

The basic friendship between Turkey, Afghanistan, and Persia and the Soviet Union did not, of course, preclude moments of friction and bad feeling. Quarrels and annoying incidents marred the relations even of allies to one another. Yet in respect to Russia and Turkey even such minor difficulties scarcely existed. Now and then small marauding bands crossed the frontier into the Caucasus, and smuggling parties went to and fro, but the final regulation of the Soviet-Turkish boundary in September, 1926, reduced such occurrences to a minimum. Politically, the spirit of the treaty of December 17, 1925, and of Chicherin's interview at Odessa with Rushdi Bey in November, 1926, continued to govern the relations between the two governments. When Kemal persecuted Turkish Communists, cries of protest went up in Moscow, but they merely scratched a hard surface.

The status of Soviet-Persian relations was not as exemplary. The establishment of the Pakhlevi dynasty on December 12, 1925, and the subsequent coronation of Riza Khan as Shah did not affect these relations favorably. As War Minister, Premier and nationalist consolidator of Persia, Riza had courted the support of the forward-looking, anti-feudal classes. He had suppressed the tribal chiefs who opposed his centralistic policies. His relations with Britain in this period were cold, with Russia warm. But when he took the throne, reactionary groups flocked to his side. He needed more money, he loved the monarchical ceremony. His dependence on the Medjlis grew, and the Medjlis was controlled by the landowners and the nobility whose political sympathies frequently lay with England.

The Bolsheviks, had they wished to interfere in internal Persian affairs, or had they foreseen developments, might have persuaded Riza to become President. Riza came to Rothstein, the Soviet envoy in Teheran in 1921, and on two occasions asked his advice about assuming the crown. Rothstein did not encourage him. The British did. The assumption by Riza of the throne, moreover, strengthened the Persian national government and therefore Persian independence. Persia had less to fear from foreign enemies of her independent status. She accordingly required less support from Russia.

Meanwhile British influence grew stronger in Persia at the expense not only of Russia, but of America as well. The Standard Oil and the Sinclair Oil Companies were gradually dislodged from the positions they had acquired in the Persian oil field, and that delicate but beautifully planned campaign commenced which ultimately resulted in the retirement of Dr. A. C. Millspaugh, the American Administrator General of Persia's finances—formerly the petroleum expert of the State Department.

Moscow, after Locarno and in view of its increasingly strained relations with London, was pursuing a pact-signing policy in the West and East. In Europe, Lithuania and Germany had agreed; in Asia, Turkey and Afghanistan. But Persia held back. Foreign and domestic influences served as obstructions.

First it was necessary to iron out trade difficulties, and the pact and commercial agreement negotiations therefore proceeded simultaneously. Finally, no less than six separate agreements were signed in Moscow on October

1, 1927: a non-aggression and neutrality pact,[5] a trade agreement, a customs convention, a fishing treaty, a contract regarding the port of Pakhlevi (Enzeli) and one for the use of piers, warehouses, and other equipment in the same city.

Apart from the pact, greatest importance attaches to the trade agreement. Until 1923 the Bolsheviks had attempted to conduct their business with Persia on the basis of the foreign trade monopoly. That system produced very unsatisfactory results; Persia was still a semi-capitalist country. Accordingly private Persian merchants received permission to buy and sell in the Soviet Union. The commercial convention of October 1, 1927, concluded for a trial period of two years, gave legal form to this arrangement, and provided for a so-called "netto-balance": Russia bought as much in Persia as Persia bought in Russia. The contingent established amounted to 50,000,000 rubles per year and therefore foresaw a total foreign trade turnover between the two countries of at least 100,000,000 rubles. In 1927–8, the turnover actually exceeded 140,000,000 rubles. No import licenses into the Soviet Union were required. Persian traders disposed of their goods in Russia, and with 90 per cent of the proceeds bought Soviet products. The 10 per cent remaining could be exported in foreign valuta to cover freight charges.

The agreement allowed Persia free transit to and from Europe. But the articles were enumerated. Since Russia sold sugar, textiles, matches, glassware, etc., these were not granted the right of transit. Goods not produced or manufactured in the Soviet Union passed through its territory to Persia customs-free.

At the time of the conclusion of the trade treaty, the pact and the accompanying instruments, however, the tension in Soviet-Persian relations immediately relaxed, while, contrariwise, Persia refused to permit the British imperial air route from London to Cairo to Karachi to pass over her territory and indicated a disinclination to tolerate capitulations any longer.

But Moscow closely observed Persia's relations with Turkey and Afghanistan. The Bolsheviks wished to see peace and friendship among these three states.

Differences existed between Persia and Afghanistan.

[5] *Soviet Union Review,* Washington, D.C., January, 1928.

Partly territorial along the Herat border, partly rooted in historical circumstances of long standing, they made for friction and misunderstanding. Moscow was not averse to offering its good services toward their removal. Late in 1927, a Persian-Afghan pact came into operation.

Further, an age-long boundary dispute existed between Persia and Turkey. Fluid ethnic and occupational conditions favored the passage of tribes to and from through the frontier zone, and acrimonious diplomatic controversies had frequently resulted. On April 22, 1926, these difficulties apparently found their solution in the conclusion of a Turko-Persian treaty of amity. Yet immediately the frontier became an area of unrest. The Turks accused the Persians of encouraging the warlike Kurds to engage in inroads on to Persian soil, while Teheran leveled similar charges against the Turks.

Moscow believed that Great Britain's policy at the time inclined towards the establishment of an independent or semi-autonomous Kurd state, or that the English, at any rate, were using the Kurds to further their own ends in the Near East, and to sow discord between Persia and Turkey. The Moscow *Izvestia* of October 6, 1927, charged that British gold was responsible for Kurd raids from Turkey into Persia and from Persia into Turkey. The Anatolian Press aired this view. Russians tried to bring this point home to both Turkish and Persian statesmen, and the Soviet Press warned against enmity between naturally kindred nations for which "a foreign imperialistic Power" bore responsibility. Towards the end of 1927 the Turkish-Persian quarrel had been settled, and Moscow accepted part of the credit.

A threadwork of pacts, treaties and one alliance now united the Soviet Union, Turkey, Persia and Afghanistan:

> Soviet-Turkish treaty, December 17, 1925,
> Turkish-Persian treaty, April 22, 1926,
> Soviet-Afghan treaty, August 31, 1926,
> Soviet-Persian treaty, October 1, 1927,
> Persian-Afghan treaty, November 28, 1927,

and the treaty of alliance between Afghanistan and Turkey which had been signed on February 19, 1921, and which still was of great practical and military significance.

It was contrary to one of the fundamental tenets of

Soviet foreign policy, however, to expand any of these bi-lateral engagements involving Russia into a triangular arrangement. Moscow, for instance, treasured its pacts of friendship and its warm diplomatic contacts with Turkey and Afghanistan, yet remained unalterably opposed to a tripartite Soviet-Turkish-Afghan treaty, or a Soviet-Afghan-Persian treaty.

The last links of the chain of pacts among Near Eastern countries and between them and the Soviet Union were forged after the Anglo-Soviet diplomatic rupture. That rupture, in fact, probably hastened the signature of the Soviet-Persian documents in October, 1927. The break brought Russia no loss of prestige in Western Asia. Chamberlain's "Bolshevik propaganda" charge meant nothing in that region and certainly frightened neither Kemal Pasha, nor Riza Shah, nor Amanullah Khan. Soviet organs emphasized that one of the chief causes of the break was Bolshevism's concern for the fate of the new democracies of the Near East and for the struggle of anti-imperialist China. These arguments did not fall on entirely deaf ears in Persia, Afghanistan and Turkey.

## THE CHINESE EASTERN RAILWAY CONFLICT

Chang So-lin, the Manchurian war lord, manifested most opposition to the Chinese Nationalist revolution and the firmest resistance to its military progress. He made and publicly proclaimed himself the champion of anti-Communism, and left nothing undone to infringe Soviet rights of ownership on the Chinese Eastern Railway which passed through the territory he dominated. On September 20, 1924, his Government had signed a treaty with the Soviet Government restoring Moscow to its possession of the line. Within a year, Chang proceeded to violate the terms of the contract.

Matters came to a head early in 1926 on account of Mukden's efforts to transport its troops on the C.E.R. free of cost. The Soviet officials of the railway resisted these attempts, and Chang So-lin, on January 21, accordingly ordered the arrest of M. Ivanov, the director-in-chief of the C.E.R., and of a large number of his co-workers. This actually constituted the transfer of the road into the hands of the Manchurian military authorities.

The very next day Moscow presented Chang So-lin with a three-day ultimatum. If Comrade Ivanov was not liberated and if the treaty status of the line was not restored within that short period, the Soviet Union would achieve those results through its own efforts. Chang So-lin complied immediately. An agreement, signed on January 24, provided for the resumption by Ivanov of his functions and the re-establishment of normal conditions in the management of the C.E.R.

Russia had won. But anxious to come to an amicable working arrangement with Chang So-lin, the Bolsheviks proposed a conference to discuss all controversial issues. The meeting opened in Mukden on May 26, 1926, with Serebyakov, a high Soviet official, as leader of the Russian delegation. Questions on the agenda included the privileges of trade unions of Soviet workers on Manchurian territory, Soviet schools in Manchuria, finances, etc. In the midst of the talks, however, Chang So-lin demanded on August 21 that all the vessels operated by the C.E.R. be handed over to him, and that its schools be placed under his direct jurisdiction. Chicherin protested, but Mukden disregarded it and on September 1 confiscated the C.E.R.'s ships on the Sungari River and dissolved the railway's department of education.

Subsequent efforts during 1926 and the early part of 1927 to settle these difficulties remained unfruitful.

Meanwhile, the Northern Expedition of the Cantonese continued to register signal progress, the Peking Government had been shorn of even any appearance of authority, and Chang So-lin dominated Manchuria as well as Peking and Tientsin.

**THE SOVIET EMBASSY RAID** Karakhan had returned to Moscow via Shanghai, because being accredited to a government that really did not exist appeared futile and wasteful. But the embassy continued to function, and in common with all diplomatic premises, to enjoy extra-territorial immunity. On April 6, 1927, Chinese soldiers and police entered the offices of the Soviet military attaché, the Soviet Dalbank, the Boxer Commission, and the Chinese Eastern Railway—all located within the Embassy compound—as well as the private apartments of embassy employees, and carried out a thorough search. Fifteen Russians were arrested. A large number of documents was taken away.

This coup had not been altogether without warning. Chang So-lin told foreign newspaper correspondents on March 27 that he "contemplated breaking off relations with the Soviet, and proposed to discuss the situation with the Foreign Ministers."[6] It is not recorded whether he carried out his intention of consulting the diplomatic corps, although nothing could have prevented it. He did ask the Foreign Ministers for permission to enter the Soviet Embassy grounds and to seize the Embassy's archives. The London *Times* of April 9 reported the Diplomatic Corps' protest to the Chinese Foreign Office on the ground that Chang So-lin had "exceeded the authority contained in the warrant of search granted by the Diplomatic Body."

After Chang had caused to be strangled seventeen of the Chinese apprehended in the Soviet Embassy, Chinese sources proceeded to publish Russian documents allegedly discovered in the course of the search. Some of these were authentic. They proved, what is now scarcely a secret, that the Chinese revolutionary movement had received material aid from Moscow. Canton and Feng were indeed the recipients of Soviet moneys and munitions which undoubtedly stimulated their activities and buttressed their forces.

On the day of the embassy raid, the Soviet consulate in Shanghai was surrounded by Chinese police and "White" Russian soldiers, and all persons entering or leaving it subjected to personal search. The next day, the headquarters of the Dalbank, the C.E.R., and the Soviet Mercantile Fleet in the French concession in Tientsin were searched with the consent of the concession authorities. On the tenth of April, the Soviet Government therefore withdrew its chargé d'affaires from Peking, thus breaking off diplomatic relations. Moscow, however, permitted its consulates in China to continue functioning.

The circumstance that the Soviet Embassy in Peking and the Soviet Consulate in Shanghai were searched on the same day further complicated the situation. Peking was dominated by Chang So-lin, Shanghai by Chiang

[6] *Chronology of Events in China: 1911–27*. With a Foreword by Sir F. Whyte. London, p. 33.

Kai-shek. Had they agreed on simultaneous and common anti-Soviet measures, or had those measures been inspired by the same foreign influence?

**THE FORMAL SINO–SOVIET RUPTURE** Meanwhile, the mass movement under Communist guidance assumed increasingly greater proportions in South and Central China, and Nanking's repressive measures became correspondingly more rigorous. The "White" Russian colony in Shanghai took special delight in agitating for anti-Soviet moves on the tenth anniversary of the Bolshevik revolution, and on November 7 a "White" Russian-armed unit attacked the Shanghai Soviet consulate.

Then, in connection with the Communist coup d'état in Canton on December 13, the Soviet consulate in that city was raided and its entire staff arrested. On the morrow, the Chinese executed six of these officials in the streets of the town.

Nanking, on the 14th of December, likewise informed the Soviet Government that it was severing relations with Russia. But no diplomatic relations had ever existed between Nanking and Moscow, nor did Moscow withdraw its consuls from China, nor did Nanking withdraw its legation or consulates from the Soviet Union. The declaration of the rupture was therefore nothing more than a gesture. The Bolsheviks allowed the Chinese minister in their capital to continue in his exercise of extra-territorial and all other usual diplomatic courtesies and to represent his country's interests actively. The protection of Soviet citizens in China, on the other hand, was undertaken by Germany. This anomalous and highly irregular position remained unchanged until July, 1929, when Chang So-lin's son followed the example of his ill-fated father and seized the Chinese Eastern Railway.

The rupture of Sino-Soviet diplomatic relations was the result of anti-Soviet developments in the Chinese revolution. When Chang So-lin offended Soviet Russia he was in effect aiming a shaft at the Nationalists. When Chiang Kai-shek severed non-existent relations with Moscow he really reacted to the ultra-left Communists' efforts in Canton and other localities.

# 25

# THE BOLSHEVIK WAR SCARE

BOLSHEVIKS often thought too primitively. They did not believe that the Die-Hards had severed relations with Moscow merely as a demonstration or to rid London of a Soviet Embassy. They saw a sinister, deeper purpose in the move. They were convinced that it would be followed by an armed British attack on the Soviet Union. They saw war in the nearest future.

The Die-Hards, according to Premier Rykov (in an address to the Moscow Soviet on June 1, 1927), wanted to anticipate the gradual eclipse of British capitalism by greater anti-socialism at home and firmer imperialism abroad. Great Britain, he indicated, desired to check her economic decline by securing a firmer foothold in imperial markets and in semi-colonial countries like China, and, furthermore, by reducing the wages and crushing the resistance of the working class. But in both these realms, Russia stood athwart the path. Russia advised and aided the Chinese revolutionary cause and offered moral support to radical thought and nationalist aspirations in the East, thus obstructing British success in the imperial field. For these reasons, it became imperative for England to strike at the source of her evils before she tackled their effects. This, Moscow considered, was the conscious or unconscious logic of the Anglo-Russian diplomatic rupture. And this logic, therefore, required further, more decisive steps in the same direction.

Bolshevik statesmen did not contend that a British army would march into Russia. "In conformance with the traditions of England's diplomacy," Rykov stated, "she has waged and will wage wars not with her own, but with strange hands." Stalin echoed the thought. "England always has preferred wars fought with the hands of others," he wrote. "And now and then, she has actually found fools to pick her chestnuts from the fire."

The Russians expected that the Baldwin Cabinet would avail itself of the services of Marshal Pilsudski and Marshal Chang So-lin.

"We refer," Stalin wrote in *Izvestia* on July 28, 1927, "not to some indefinite, vague 'danger' of a new war, but to the real and actual threat of a new war in general, and of a war against the Soviet Union in particular."

Stalin placed the blame for the raid on the Soviet Embassy in Peking upon Great Britain. A second link in the British anti-Soviet chain was the search of Arcos. The third was the assassination of Voikov "intended by its authors to play the role of Sarajevo and draw the Soviet Union into a war with Poland." In this it had failed, but further attempts would follow. "The entire international situation," Stalin continued, "all the facts in the field of the British Government's 'operations' against the Soviet Union, the fact that it organizes a financial blockade of the Soviet Union, that it conducts secret conferences with the Powers on a policy against the Soviet Union, that it subsidizes the emigrés' 'governments' of the Ukraine, Georgia, Azerbaijan, Armenia, etc., for the purpose of raising revolts in those states of the Soviet Union, that it finances groups of spies and terrorists to blow up bridges, set fire to factories, and terrorize Soviet Legations abroad—all this undoubtedly proves that the British Tory Government has definitely and concertedly undertaken to organize a war against the Soviet Union."

The writer arrived in Moscow towards the end of June, 1927, after a protracted stay in the West. On all sides, he was plied with the question, "When will the war break out?" In vain he tried to assure Communists and non-Communists that Europe did not want war, and did not seem to be on the verge of hostile operations. Moscow knew better. Moscow was panicky. Peasants throughout the country bought large quantities of salt, and hoarded their grain. A fully-developed war psychosis prevailed. War was salon talk, street-car talk, newspaper talk.

The Bolsheviks used the war scare against the Trotzky

Opposition. "Look at these traitors," they said in effect, "who undermine the party while the capitalists threaten from without."

When the summer and autumn of 1927 passed without the declaration of war, Communist certainty commenced to waver. Yet the Congress of Friends of Soviet Russia, meeting in Moscow on the tenth anniversary of the revolution, adopted a resolution in which it undertook "to fight against the war that threatens the Soviet Union from the capitalist world, and to discredit the intrigues of international diplomacy which is preparing that war."

For the Bolsheviks to have argued in 1927 that Great Britain was busily preparing for war against them was sheer nonsense. The fact that no war took place is sufficient to prove them wrong.

# 26

# SHALL THE WORLD DISARM?

THE RUSSIAN REVOLUTION, like the Chinese, and, in one sense, like the popular movements in India, was the expression of an elemental urge towards economic independence from the West. Independence required rapid industrialization.

The fall of Russian capitalism covered foreign capitalism in Russia with its debris. The Civil War and intervention completed the work of ruin, and when the hostilities closed in 1920, Russia thirsted for new industrial construction, new railways, and new possibilities of production in the city and the village. The Bolsheviks were now called upon to achieve with their own resources more than the Czarist regime had accomplished with a great measure of outside aid.

Quick industrialization in no wise represented a Bolshevik whim. Numerous circumstances made it a necessity, and one condition made it imperative: the Russian village was over-populated. It had regularly, for years and years, thrown forth masses of excess inhabitants into the towns. Only large-scale industrialization would supply them with employment.

Industrialization, then, is the paramount and the permanent concern of the Soviet Government. Peace permits of concentration on all-important domestic problems. Soviet anti-war slogans, therefore, are dictated first and foremost by self-interest rather than by idealism.

**THE MOTIVES OF SOVIET PEACE POLICY** The Bolsheviks knew that complete disarmament was a Utopia, and partial disarmament an ideal. They argued, in fact, that capitalist nations must maintain armies and navies. Yet Chicherin made a disarmament proposal at Genoa, in 1922, at the first international conference at which the Soviets were represented, and Litvinov another at the Moscow Disarmament Conference in December of the same year.

Stalin dilated on the dangers of war in *Izvestia* of July 28, 1927.

> What, then, must we do? [he asked] The Soviet Government must pursue, firmly and unwaveringly, its policy of peace and of peaceful relations notwithstanding all the provocative moves of our enemies, notwithstanding all the pin-pricks at our prestige. The provocateurs in the camp of the enemy taunt us and will taunt us that our policy of peace is the child of our weakness, of the weakness of our army. . . . We cannot and must not play into their hands. We must go our way, defending the cause of peace, demonstrating our will to peace, revealing the criminal designs of our enemies, and branding them as the protagonists of war.

"Revealing" and "branding" became leading Soviet occupations.

Europe was preoccupied with the Preliminary Disarmament Conference of the League of Nations. The Preparatory Commission for a Disarmament Conference had met three times in Geneva without evolving or presenting any suggestion, proposal, or thesis of even partial disarmament in any field. Russia had not participated because the Powers convoked the meetings in Geneva, although Moscow had no relations with Switzerland, and could dispatch no representatives to Switzerland on account of the assassination of the Soviet Ambassador Vorovsky on Swiss soil. In 1927 the conflict was settled through German mediation,[1] and in November, 1927, Maxim Litvinov, the Soviet Assistant Commissar of Foreign Affairs, appeared at the League seat to attend the Fourth Session of the League's Preparatory Commission.

**WHY DISARMAMENT?** "The Government of the Soviet Union," Litvinov announced on the eve of his first trip to Geneva, "has never concealed its mistrust of the readiness and ability of capitalist nations to destroy the

[1] For text of joint Soviet-Swiss declaration see *Izvestia,* April 16, 1927, and *Europaeische Gespraeche,* Berlin, July, 1927, p. 426.

system of war among peoples, and therefore to achieve disarmament."

The World War, he said, had strengthened that mistrust, and the post-Armistice record buttressed their conviction. The Geneva deliberations merely served to fortify the Bolshevik view that the bourgeois states would not disarm.

The Communists were ready to be convinced of their error. Litvinov referred to the scepticism of the official *Izvestia,* and of the Soviet delegation in an address to the Preliminary Commission at Geneva on March 22, 1928.

> It is up to the Commission itself, by the results of its activities, [he said] either to justify that scepticism or to give that newspaper the lie and to prove that it was wrong. The Soviet delegation will be the first to rejoice if the latter is the case.

Nothing the League Commission did afforded the Soviet delegation cause for rejoicing.

**LITVINOV'S FOURTEEN POINTS** Maxim Litvinov in the League capital was like a bull in a china shop. Theretofore, the League's Preparatory Commission on Disarmament had worked peacefully for two years listening to ringing appeals for disarmament, engaging in legal debates, interpreting clauses, phrases, and words of the League Covenant, receiving reports from military experts, referring reports back to sub-commissions, and sending reports to their governments. But Litvinov had no sooner arrived in Geneva than he presented for discussion a full, detailed draft convention for "immediate, complete, and general disarmament." In doing so, Litvinov indulged in a typical Bolshevik diatribe which could not but offend the Commission, its individual members, and the League as a whole.

With unabashed effrontery, Litvinov declared, in laying his draft before the Commission on November 30, 1927, that

> The Soviet Government is of the opinion it has always held, that under the capitalist system no ground exists for counting upon the removal of the causes which give rise to armed conflicts. Militarism and big navies are essentially natural consequences of the capitalistic system. By their very growth, they intensify existing contradictions, immensely accelerating and sharpening all hidden potential conflicts and inevitably convert these into armed clashes.

But the people of all countries want no "new imperialist wars." They want "to safeguard peace among nations." Therefore, the Soviet Government sent its delegation. "In doing so the Soviet Government demonstrates before the whole world its will to peace among nations and makes clear the real aspirations and true desires of the capitalist states in regard to disarmament."

His audience breathed heavily, but Litvinov continued unruffled: "Despite the fact that the World War was called the 'war to end wars,' the whole post-war history of international relations has been one of unintermittent and systematic increase of armed forces in the capitalist states and of a vast increase in the general burden of militarism, resting heavily on the shoulders of the working classes."

What the Commission had done was "of a purely decorative nature." Its methods evoked "endless and fruitless arguments on so-called military potentials" and afforded an opportunity for "the evasion of the fundamental and decisive question of the actual extent of disarmament." If this continued, Litvinov warned, "no curtailment of existing armaments will take place."

Litvinov then presented the Soviet alternative to these methods. He proposed[2]:

(1) The dissolution of all land, sea, and air forces and their prohibition in any concealed form whatsoever.

(2) The destruction of all weapons, military supplies, means of chemical warfare, and all other forms of armament, and means of destruction in possession of troops or military or general stores.

(3) The scrapping of all warships and military aircraft.

(4) The discontinuance of calling citizens for military training, either in armies or public organizations.

(5) Legislation for abolition of military service, either compulsory, voluntary or recruited.

(6) Legislation prohibiting the calling up of trained reserves.

(7) The destruction of fortresses and naval and air bases.

(8) The scrapping of plants for military purposes, and of installation for military industry in the general industrial establishments.

(9) The discontinuance of assigning funds for military purposes, both in state budgets, and in those of public organizations.

(10) The abolition of ministries of war, navy and military

[2] Complete Russian text, *Izvestia,* December 2, 1927; English translation, London *Daily Telegraph,* December 1, 1927; German translation, *Europaeische Gespraeche,* Berlin, January, 1928.

aviation, the dissolution of general staffs and all kinds of military administrations, departments, and institutions.

(11) The legislative prohibition of military propaganda and military training of the population, and of the education of the youth in the same spirit, either by state or by public organizations.

(12) The legislative prohibition to patent all kinds of armaments and means of destruction, with a view to the removal of the incentive for the invention of same.

(13) Legislation making the infringement of any of the above stipulations a grave crime against the state.

(14) The withdrawal or corresponding alteration of all legislative acts, both of a national and international scope, which are in contradiction to the above stipulations.

This whole program was to be carried out one year after its adoption. Litvinov wished in that time not only to abolish armaments, but to make the usual armament patriotism a "grave crime against the State." People demanding more cruisers, more airplanes, new army or navy appropriations, or private officers' training camps would be summoned to court and prosecuted as traitors.

However, if the "capitalist states reject the immediate actual abolition of standing armies," Moscow would propose that complete disarmament be carried out in gradual stages during a period of four years.

Litvinov then suggested that funds released from war budgets might be used for productive and educational purposes.

"This is our disarmament proposal," he said. "At first glance its radicalism, its wide sweep will seem to you complicated, difficult to realize, nay, even Utopian. But this is due to the fact that the subject is so new. It may be stated definitely that the question of general disarmament has never been taken up yet."

Even in the very polite surroundings of a League Commission meeting, most of the delegates refrained from applause when Litvinov at last sat down. Only the visitors testified that they had been impressed or entertained.

**THE LEAGUE FINDS AN ESCAPE** Litvinov's disarmament project struck the League like a thunderbolt and left it in want of good counsel. M. Jonkheer J. Loudon, the Dutch President of the Preparatory Commission, made an effort to postpone discussion indefinitely, but he met polite though firm objection from the Russian and accordingly opened the floor to the assembled delegates.

Long embarrassing moments followed. Nobody wished to speak. Finally, M. Paul-Boncour, the French Socialist-diplomat, mounted the rostrum. He had had no intention of addressing the gathering, he said.

"But in view of the absence of speakers, I do not feel it possible, if only out of courtesy to the Union of Soviet Socialist Republics, to pass over in silence the declaration made by their first delegate this morning."[3]

M. Paul-Boncour subjected the Soviet scheme to no examination. He merely stated that "it was too simple." He declared that disarmament and security were interdependent and that before the one could be undertaken the problems of the second must be solved. Beneš, Czecho-Slovakia's Foreign Minister, echoed the French delegate. It was accordingly quickly agreed to postpone discussion of Litvinov's Fourteen Points for three months—until March, 1928. Meanwhile, the Committee on Disarmament would bend its energies to a careful study of the question of security.

**SECURITY v. DISARMAMENT** This Committee met in Geneva on February 20. Various memoranda, reports, schedules, etc. were submitted. They found that no less than eighty-five treaties of conciliation and arbitration had been filed at League headquarters. They found pacts of nonaggression, of neutrality, of alliance. France had an alliance with Poland and Rumania, Poland with Rumania; France was the friend and protector of the Little Entente; France enjoyed a British guarantee against attack by virtue of the Locarno Treaty and by that instrument obtained promises of help or non-aggression from other Powers as well. But all these agreements, apparently, offered insufficient security to warrant disarmament.

The members of the League could ask for League assistance under Article 11 of the Covenant. By the terms of Articles 16 and 17 of the same document, the League could undertake military and economic sanctions against an aggressor-state. Apparently, this too was insufficient.

[3] Official League of Nations Publication. *Documents of the Preparatory Commission for the Disarmament Conference*. Series V. Minutes of the Fourth Session. (Geneva, 1928). Subsequent quotations from the proceedings are made from this and Series VI, Minutes of the Fifth Session.

The Kellogg Pact outlawing war was negotiated and solemnly signed. That also proved insufficient. League disarmament moved forward not one centimeter by reason of that Pact.

And yet the supporters of the Security thesis insisted that there must be more documents, agreements, treaties of conciliation and arbitration, of non-aggression and neutrality, of peace and friendship. All Europe was crossed and re-crossed by a complicated over-lapping system of such pacts, yet the Security seekers felt the need of further security before disarmament could be attempted.

When France wanted security against German revenge she disarmed Germany, and, as a guarantee aginst attack she kept Germany disarmed. Germany was a member of the League, Germany was a signatory of Locarno. Germany adhered to the Kellogg Pact. Yet France would not permit Germany any uncontrolled armaments. Because armaments are a menace.

The Soviet Government "regards complete and speedy disarmament as the most solid of guarantees of security." But the Soviet argument made little impression in Geneva.

## THE LEAGUE DISCUSSES LITVINOV'S PLAN

When the Fifth Session of the Preparatory Commission opened on March 15, President Loudon reported "very satisfactory" progress; "no fewer than six model treaties were drawn up," he said; "three deal with . . . arbitration and conciliation"; "three . . . deal more especially with security."

After devoting several days to matters arising out of this literary achievement, the Session, on March 19, proceeded to discuss Litvinov's proposal for immediate, complete and general disarmament. His proposal, now presented in the form of a Draft Convention,[4] differed, though in no essentials from the original reading. Disarmament was to be begun at once, but to be completed in quick stages stretched over a period of four years in such a manner that armies and navies became ineffective as war weapons within a year.

To be sure, Litvinov argued, it had been said that when armaments are abolished, nations, being incurably belli-

[4] Official League of Nations Publication. *Documents of the Preparatory Commission for the Disarmament Conference.* Series VI, Annex 2, p. 324.

cose, will rush at one another with sticks, penknives, and fists. This criticism was beneath criticism, he said. Stick bruises compare strangely with the effects of poison gas or airplane torpedoes. Litvinov then reiterated the Soviet standpoint on security as opposed to disarmament. He referred to petitions he had received from various organizations throughout the world supporting the Soviet proposals. He made light once more of the League's past record on disarmament; League organs "devoted over a hundred and twenty sessions—not sittings, mark you, but sessions—to this question of disarmament, on which one hundred and eleven resolutions have been passed by general assemblies of the League and the Council of the League alone." He wanted fewer resolutions, and a little action. He made a direct request for support from the American delegation whose government "is now publicly making a proposal for the prohibition of war." The outlawry of war, he reasoned, should make the weapons of war superfluous.

The only two delegations at all sympathetic to the Soviet proposals were the Turkish and German; Turkey out of friendship for Russia and gratitude for Soviet aid in her war with Greece; Germany for motives of her own. General von Seeckt had made it clear that Germany should of right increase her army. But in view of Germany's disarmament and in view of the disinclination of the Versailles Powers, and especially France, to moderate the treaty terms limiting Germany's armaments, the Wilhelmstrasse took pleasure in recalling that one of Woodrow Wilson's Fourteen Points which formed the basis of Germany's plea for the Armistice, contained a direct, definite provision for disarmament. Count Bernstorff, Berlin's chief delegate at Geneva, submitted that Germany's disarmament imposed an obligation on the Allies to disarm. That, in fact, was the assumption at Versailles.

Every other delegation entered objections. General de Marinia, Italy's representative, agreed that "this scheme is designed not only to do away with war in the future but also to efface it from history." Count Clauzel, the French delegate, found that Litvinov's proposal "is undoubtedly in keeping with the ideal we all have in view, namely the establishment of real peace with the least possible delay." Yet both, in short speeches, favored rejection for reasons of procedure and because their first business was security.

Lord Cushenden too agreed that "complete and general disarmament has been the ideal of mankind since the dawn of history, and . . . as a general proposition I certainly am in favor of it." But, "is it practicable?" The British delegate thought it was not, yet, being a practical person, Lord Cushenden took advantage of the opportunity offered by the discussion to indulge in an enumeration of his Conservative Government's grievances against the Bolsheviks: their interference in internal affairs, and their interest in revolution. Nevertheless, he was alone among the delegates to subject Litvinov's project to a serious and lengthy examination spiced, to be sure, with a delicate under-current of irony. In general, he felt that the Soviet scheme had too many faults to be applicable.

Most of the Commission members elaborated upon three fundamental objections to complete disarmament: (1) If all states disarmed, the large, industrialized states would be at an advantage in case of war when their factory equipment could quickly produce new weapons of destruction. (2) Security was a pre-requisite of disarmament since disarmament itself would not eliminate the possibility of conflicts. (3) Armaments must remain for civil, intra-national purposes such as quelling revolts, brigandage, strikes, etc.

Litvinov attempted to reply. How could even a highly industrialized country prepare for war, he asked, when according to his draft convention, war industries would be demolished? It took the United States twelve to twenty months to organize its war industry in the World War. Under the Versailles Treaty, war industries in Germany had been dismantled or rendered innocuous. "How much easier it would be to control war industry given the complete abolition of the corresponding means of production?"

Would his disarmament convention make the world secure against wars? No, Litvinov replied, not altogether. It does not "guarantee a just peace, does not destroy international distrust, does not point the way to the solution of international disputes—is not, in fact, a panacea." Litvinov had such a panacea—a proletarian, Communist revolution—but he could not recommend it, "for we know you would not entertain it for a moment." Meanwhile, however, one evil, the "Moloch of war" might be abolished.

As to the contention that his Fourteen Points infringed against the League Covenant—well, Litvinov advised, change the Covenant. "Man was not made for the Sabbath, but the Sabbath for man."

Finally, after days of brilliant debating on both sides, the President of the Commission submitted a resolution stating that most of its members considered the Soviet draft convention impracticable and could therefore not accept it as the basis of the Commission's work.

The very same day, March 23, Litvinov presented a brand-new set of proposals. If the Commission rejected complete disarmament, he offered them partial, gradual disarmament. It was a less-to-be-desired project than his first, but it represented a step in the direction of total disarmament. If its character was less radical, its fate would perhaps be less dismal.

The Soviet proposals for partial disarmament received no warmer welcome than the Soviet proposals for universal disarmament. During 1928 and 1929 the Preparatory Commission adopted neither. Nor did it convene the Disarmament Conference for which it was created. Litvinov and a staff several times traveled from Moscow to Geneva to attend its sessions, but each time their attitude towards it became more cynical—if that was indeed possible.

The amount of paper consumed in printing the Commission's proceedings became a standing joke in Moscow, as did the multitude of its resolutions. "The publications of the several organs of the League on disarmament," Premier Rykov told the Congress of Soviets in May, 1929, "cover 14,000 pages." "Laughter," reads the record. "They have eliminated not a single soldier, or gun, or cruiser, or cartridge, but they have managed to write 14,000 pages—what a tremendous quantity of paper and working energy to spoil." "Laughter," once more. Rykov then turned to the less mirth-provoking subject of World War victims. He read the statistics. He pictured the gruesome instruments of wholesale destruction at the front and in the rear which the next war would bring into play. He quoted Lloyd George on the terrible prospects of a future Armageddon. It would require decades to repair the damage of a second World War. Every worker and peasant must engrave that fact on his mind. The only solution was the overthrow of the forces responsible for uninterrupted war preparations, and the establishment of governments which would make disarmament a fact. That was Rykov's answer to Litvinov's failure at Geneva. The failure had been inevitable. Moscow knew that the Western world could not possibly adopt a Bolshevik disarmament proposal.

**THE RED ARMY** The strength of the Soviet army fluctuated as follows:

| | |
|---|---|
| 1920 | 3,538,000 |
| 1921 | 4,110,000 |
| 1922 | 1,590,000 |
| 1923 | 703,000 |
| 1924 | 562,000 |

The Red Navy was a ridiculously negligible factor. In 1926 the Soviet Union had a total tonnage of 128,900 tons, of which 25.2 per cent was depreciated.[5] Even the navies of Spain and Germany were larger.

Armies exist, presumably, to defend given territories and populations. The size of armies, therefore, should be in some ratio to the area of a country and the number of its inhabitants. For it is obvious that Holland will have less troops than France, Russia, or the United States.

| | | | | Approximate Number of Soldiers. | |
|---|---|---|---|---|---|
| | Area in square kilometers.[6] | Number of Inhabitants.[6] | Size of Army.[7] | Per 100 Kilometers. | Per 1,000 Inhabitants. |
| France | 550,986 | 40,743,000 | 673,000 | 120 | 16 |
| Great Britain | 230,616 | 44,114,000 | 197,000 | 80 | 4 |
| Italy | 310,090 | 40,548,000 | 248,000 | 70 | 6 |
| Poland | 388,279 | 29,589,000 | 270,000 | 70 | 9 |
| Rumania | 294,892 | 17,153,000 | 130,000 | 40 | 8 |
| Soviet Union | 4,202,300 | 112,105,000 | 563,000 | 13 | 5 |

[5] *The Europa Year-Book,* 1928. (London, 1928), p. 125.
[6] *Ibid.,* p. 4.
[7] *Ibid.,* p. 122.

# 27

# THE KELLOGG AND LITVINOV PACTS

In Moscow's view, the Kellogg Pact was the political expression of America's fast-growing economic influence in Europe and other parts of the globe. Through it Washington essayed to make the State Department the arbiter, or one of the chief arbiters, in future international disputes that concerned United States business interests abroad, and to check similar functions traditionally exercised by England or France. Economically, the remnant of America's "splendid isolation" disappeared with the World War. Politically, it breathed its last when Frank B. Kellogg put his golden pen to the "Multilateral Treaty for the Renunciation of War" in Paris on August 27, 1928.

The considerations which motivated Russia's participation in the Pact resemble, to an extent, those which brought Litvinov to Geneva. In fact, Litvinov was a staunch protagonist of adhesion, and contributed much toward finally overcoming the opposition of Chicherin and other prominent Soviet leaders whose attitude toward it was either hostile or indifferent.

The Soviet Union, conscious of its role as a Great Power, wished to be included in an international treaty of universal application. For Moscow no more cared to isolate itself than to be isolated by others. Isolation brought lack of understanding on both sides, and a greater likelihood of hostility.

**MOSCOW IS PRO-AMERICAN** The Bolsheviks, moreover, pinned their hopes on the United States. Not that they were sanguine about de jure recognition. Time and again Chicherin, Litvinov, and other Soviet statesmen told the writer in 1926 and 1927 that they no longer believed in the imminence of recognition, and one of them even said that he began to be bored by visitors who came with letters from prominent American politicians and raised the question of the terms of recognition. Nevertheless, Moscow had an intuitive feeling that sooner or later warm relations would be established with Washington.

The alarming state of Soviet foreign affairs in the spring of 1927 introduced a nervous note into Moscow's policy, and there was noticeable that anxiety to patch up Russia's relations with Europe which found expression in Ossinsky's, Sokolnikov's, and particularly Litvinov's trips to Geneva, in the retrenchment of the Soviets' diplomatic position in the Near and Middle East, and in a frank courting of American goodwill. But even apart from this circumstance, Soviet Russia had no anti-American interests. The European Continent may have wished to combine to resist United States tariff increases, or to vent its wrath against Washington's debt policy, or to defend its economic and political position against American encroachment. These matters concerned Russia little.

Capitalist Europe's relationship to the United States was that of debtor to creditor, of weaker to stronger, and repressed enmity was therefore inevitable. Briand once wanted to draw Moscow into a European united front against America. It was hopeless.

To be sure, the Communist theorist foresaw a day when capitalist America and Communist Russia would stand opposed to one another—the giants of a coming generation. But that eventuality was distant, and politics in 1930 was not made with 1980 in mind.

Apart from these speculations and expectations, very concrete considerations attracted the Soviets to the United States: the Bolsheviks preferred to trade with America.

**SOVIET-AMERICAN TRADE** In the summer of 1927 M. Mikoyan, the Soviet Commissar of Trade, told the writer that

after the break with Britain, contacts with the United States must become broader. . . . Our American purchases of oil equipment, coal-cutting and mining machinery, electrical appliances, automobiles, tractors, and agricultural machines, should increase year by year . . .

The Commissar added that he favored direct dealing with American firms in preference to trade through third nations. Here he stood on a common platform with Herbert Hoover.

There is much in common between the United States and the Soviet Union; vast natural wealth and great geographical expanses, the scope and scale of construction processes, and the vision of industrial leaders and their indifference to petty obstacles, traditions, and difficulties. Russia presented a parallel to the United States in its reconstruction period a decade or more after the American Civil War. Gigantic tasks, like the building of the tremendous power dam at Dnieperstroi—when completed in 1931, the second largest in the world—did not awe the Bolsheviks any more than a generation of American engineers stopped at the stupendous functions a growing country assigned to it between 1880 and 1914. A striking similarity of approach, psychology, pioneering spirit, and confidence characterized the builders of Soviet Russia and of America. The tasks were in many respects similar, and it is no accident that Mr. Hugh L. Cooper, an American engineer, was the Soviet Government's chief foreign consultant at Dnieperstroi. The Bolsheviks needed machines, turbines, and appliances, many of which were used and made only in the United States. The large American and Soviet farms had cognate mechanical requirements, and the Bolsheviks consequently bought few German tractors. More and more, Russia began to depend for technical assistance and engineering advice on the United States rather than on Germany and Britain. The Soviets were learning to make electrical equipment, to build power stations, to dig coal-mines, to mine oil, and to manufacture automobiles and auto-trucks after American methods and in accordance with technical aid contracts with large American firms.

The growth of American trade with the Bolsheviks has been marked:[1]

[1] *The Soviet Union: Facts, Descriptions, Statistics*. 1929. P. 162. Published by the Soviet Union Information Bureau, Washington, D. C.

| | Russian Exports to U.S.A. | Russian Imports from U.S.A. |
|---|---|---|
| | $ | $ |
| 1913 | 7,290,000 | 40,730,000 |
| 1923–4 | 4,377,500 | 49,955,000 |
| 1924–5 | 14,471,500 | 103,618,000 |
| 1925–6 | 15,810,000 | 62,881,500 |
| 1926–7 | 11,962,900 | 74,998,400 |
| 1927–8 | 14,368,500 | 96,717,000 |

The Chase National Bank and the Equitable Trust Company are outstanding examples of large American banking institutions which take a special interest in Soviet business. The Chase Bank helped to finance most of Russia's cotton purchases in the United States (these amounted to $54,300,000 in 1927–8), while the Equitable had watched the development of Soviet oil sales to American companies.

The Standard Oil Company of New York (Socony) bought Caucasian petrol after 1924, and its cousin, the Vacuum Oil, did likewise. On June 22, 1927, Socony signed an important contract with the Soviet Naphtha Syndicate for the sale of 100,000 tons of Russian oil annually over a period of five years for bunkering purposes in Trebizond, Port Said, and Colombo, Ceylon. This arrangement placed Socony in a position to compete successfully with British firms in the Near East and Indian markets, and consequently aroused the ire of Sir Henri Deterding, whose Press thereupon broke out into a campaign of renewed fury against "stolen" Soviet oil—the same oil which Deterding had bought and would again buy. The American newspaper and business world, however, sympathized with Socony and the Soviets, and arguments defending Moscow against Royal Dutch filled columns of metropolitan dailies.

Russo-American business ties were further cemented by a far more significant contract between the General Electric Company and the Soviet Government.

On October 9, 1928, the General Electric Company signed an agreement with the Amtorg (American Trading Corporation) on behalf of the Soviet Government granting chases were to stretch over a period of five years, credit the Soviet State credits aggregating $26,000,000. Purbecoming operative on the delivery of the General Electric

Company's equipment in New York and not, as in the case of the 300,000,000-mark German credit, on the day of the placing of the order. At no one time, it was said, would more than $16,000,000 be outstanding. No Soviet guarantees were attached to the credit, but it seemed that 25 per cent of each order was to be paid in cash. Repayments were distributed over five years.

This contract to furnish the Soviet electrical industry with part of the machinery and appurtenances for its vast expansion plans was negotiated by Clark Minor and S. A. Trone for G.E. and Saul G. Bron for the Russians. These men and their collaborators approached the problem without pettiness and in the same broad spirit as Owen D. Young, the chairman of G.E., with whom they were in contact.

Although the interest rate was higher than G.E. might have granted to another buyer, it was much lower than the Soviet Government had theretofore received elsewhere on long-term credits, and the method of financing guaranteed Moscow against high prices or excessive charges.

G.E. claimed to have undergone appreciable losses from the revolution. The conclusion of the $26,000,000 credit served to convince other corporations with similar records in Russia that their private claims need not constitute an obstacle to business operations with the Bolsheviks; it helped to convince statesmen that, in the event of United States de jure recognition of the Soviet Union, claims arising out of Soviet expropriation of American private property would be subject to equitable adjustment.

The G.E. agreement with Moscow made a deep impression in Germany, and even alarmed some German circles. The Allgemeine Elektrizitaets Gesellschaft (A.E.G.) had for some years done a flourishing business with Russia, and its president, Felix Deutsch, was one of Germany's staunchest pro-Russians. Now G.E., whose relations with the A.E.G. were rather intimate, had robbed the German electrical industry of an excellent customer. Herr Deutsch, it was said, attempted to dissuade G.E. from entering the Soviet field, but when he failed, German business realized better than ever the seriousness of American competition in Russia, and industrialists as well as statesmen in Berlin undertook to press with greater energy their case for German-American co-operation in the Soviet Union. The Bolsheviks did not favor this co-operation, but the greater obstacle was the tendency, best represented by President Hoover, which regarded such combination unnecessary and, for America, undesirable. It could, however, be achieved by indirect approach. The quick growth of American investments in German industry, and the amalgamation of important German industries with richer American concerns could prejudice the situation in favor of collaboration. But powerful forces continued to resist such a development.

Although many conditions favored American-Russian trade, several circumstances deterred it. Not all Soviet orders went to powerful trusts, and small business men, even some large firms, followed the same practice as in Germany of throwing their Soviet bills on a speculative discount market which charged exorbitant rates. Fundamentally the problem of financing Soviet trade had been no more solved in the United States than in Germany, for manufacturers' credit may facilitate commerce, but only banking credits can form a permanent healthy basis for it. American banks, however, did not grant Russia large long-term credits or loans. The Chase National Bank offered short-term credits for Soviet cotton orders, and Mr. Reeve Schley, the vice-president of that institution, had become known as an enthusiastic protagonist of Russian trade. Yet other important influences in the same institution were far from helpful.

One of the chief obstacles to proper American financing for the Soviet Union's American purchases was undoubtedly the National City Bank, whose opposition arose from its claims against the Czarist State for loans negotiated during the World War. Negotiations with a view to the removal of this difficulty commenced in New York in 1927. The discussions proceeded so successfully that Charles E. Mitchell, the president of the bank, together with Mr. Winston, formerly Assistant-Secretary of the United States Treasury, went to Paris where lengthy conferences took place between him and Rakovsky, Preobrazhensky, and Sokolnikov. Mitchell asked the Russians to accept indebtedness amounting to 25 per cent of the $91,000,000 he claimed, and to pay him 2½ per cent annual interest for sixty-two years. He would return the interest to the Soviets in the form of credits. But he promised no large, important credits. He merely indicated that through his efforts the American bankers' embargo on the discounting of Soviet bills would be lifted and that the cheapening of credits thus achieved would bring the Bolsheviks more than they would pay him. There was much to be said for his position. But the Russians regarded it as too vague. They wanted credits, and on September 19, 1927, the negotiations suddenly collapsed when Sokolnikov presented a demand for approximately $75,-000,000 in credits. Mitchell had intimated casually that credits would be forthcoming. The Bolsheviks, however, wanted a definite contract. Their policy throughout a decade had been: We give if you give. Perhaps Mitchell would change his mind after the debt agreement was signed, they might have thought. Perhaps the State Department would interfere. The State Department had interfered with Harriman. Moreover, what Moscow needed most was a loan. But Mitchell could not grant it without United States recognition of Russia, and only cynics would have suggested that Mr. Mitchell's influence with Washington was so potent as to effect recognition immediately after his claims had been satisfied.

On the one hand Moscow had Mitchell's inconclusive indications of assistance; on the other hand a debt agreement with him would have set an expensive precedent by encouraging German, British, and French demands for similar treatment.

**LITVINOV AND CHAMBERLAIN** These circumstances stood out prominently in the background of Soviet-German and Soviet-American affairs during the year 1928, and contribute to an understanding of Russia's policy in the Kellogg Pact. Despite the disgruntled attitude of German banks and business, and notwithstanding foreign pressure on Germany, the Wilhelmstrasse attempted to keep intact its friendly contacts with Moscow. Germany, in fact, remained the only Great Power in Europe whose diplomatic relations with Russia continued cordial.

Bolshevik efforts to smooth over their differences with England and France had ended in failure. Litvinov attempted to improve relations with Great Britain during his first visit to Geneva when he asked for an interview with Sir Austen Chamberlain after he had been assured, by a mediator, that his request would not be refused.

The meeting took place on December 5, 1927, and lasted an hour. The statesmen discussed one subject; propaganda and Comintern, and could reach no agreement. Litvinov pointed out that if the Soviet Government acted on Chamberlain's suggestion, it would have to cease being Communist. The Soviet Government, he argued, could not suppress the Comintern, nor could it prevent Soviet citizens or Soviet Government leaders from frankly speaking their views on developments in the capitalist world. Bolshevik analyses of the bourgeois economic situation or of revolutionary possibilities in Europe and Asia could not be banned at Moscow congresses. Communists had to think and express themselves as Communists. The Soviet Government, nevertheless, would gladly consent to abide by a mutual non-propaganda formula such as that of the abrogated Anglo-Soviet Trade Treaty. Perhaps modifications could be made.

At the end of the interview the statesmen agreed on the text of an innocuous communiqué which made it clear that their conversation had brought no good and would not be renewed.

At the same Disarmament Commission session (November–December, 1927) Litvinov saw Briand with a view to the re-establishment of more normal Franco-Soviet relations. But their discussions extended beyond these relatively narrow limits and dealt principally with affairs in Eastern Europe. Briand apparently[2] outlined the plan of an "Eastern Locarno" including frontier guarantees, neutrality obligations, and peace assurances between the Soviet Union, on the one hand, and Poland, Rumania, and the Baltic States on the other. France wanted a single agreement between Russia and all her European neighbors en bloc. Moscow, however, regarded this as a step towards the achievement of a united front against Bolshevism and the enthronement of Poland as the head of a Baltic-Rumanian entente directed against the Soviet Union.

**FRENCH IDEAS ABOUT SOVIET TRADE** At the same time, de Monzie and Clementel in France made propaganda for the idea of Franco-German business cooperation in the Soviet Union, and both these politicians visited Berlin in this connection. De Monzie likewise con-

[2] See Paris *Matin* and *Ere Nouvelle,* December 5, 1927.

tributed an article to the German Press on the same subject—an article which found an unfavorable echo in Moscow, for the moment such a plan is launched, the Bolsheviks begin to yell: "United front." De Monzie and Clementel, according to Professor Otto Hoetsch, one of Germany's best Russian experts,[3] wanted to divide a portion of Russia's foreign trade between France and Germany, and agree on prices, terms of delivery, etc. Such an agreement, Moscow feared, would, by ultimately establishing a monopoly, eliminate the possibility of ranging one seller against the other. In general, it would close a more or less free market. The Bolsheviks wished to distribute their dependence on the outside business world as widely as possible so that no one force or organization might be in a position to dictate terms.

A more friendly attempt was undertaken by M. Baron, the chairman of the Petrol Commission of the Chamber of Deputies, and M. Philippotaux, the chairman of the Commission for the Devastated Areas, both of whom requested Poincaré to initiate discussions with the Russians regarding the sale of oil to an official French petroleum monopoly. On January 13, 1928, Briand supported the proposition at a joint meeting of the Petroleum and Foreign Relations Commissions of the Chamber. Poincaré opposed. For a moment it had seemed as if Franco-Soviet relations might move from their congealed state. But they did not, either politically or economically. In fact the action of the Bank of France against the shipment of Soviet gold to New York in March, 1928, indicated that the old hostility had not moderated.

In like manner, Moscow's diplomatic position vis-à-vis Nanking and Mukden remained unsatisfactory, and only the visit to Moscow in January, 1928, of Viscount Goto, Japan's famous pro-Soviet statesman, justified a slightly brighter Bolshevik estimate of the Far-Eastern situation which Tokyo's suppression in April, 1928, of the Radical Japanese Labor and Peasants' Party did not nullify, for the Japanese Government usually chose to distinguish between Soviet policies and the irritating acts of Japanese Communists.

It would appear that in the circumstances of uninterrupted British, French, Polish, and Rumanian frigidity, and of an extremely unfavorable foreign political constel-

[3] *Osteuropa.* Berlin monthly. 1927–8, Issue #6, p. 437.

lation generally, Moscow would treasure and cultivate good relations with Germany. Quite the contrary was the case, for just at this juncture came the Shakhti trial.

**THE SHAKHTI TRIAL** In connection with the arrest, in February, 1928, of fifty or more Soviet engineers charged with counter-revolutionary activities in the Don coalfields, five German mechanics were taken into custody. Two were immediately released, because of insufficient evidence against them, and at the end of a long, highly sensational trial which opened on May 18, two others were acquitted and the third received a one-year sentence. Either innocence or expediency explains their good fortune. But the Government might have known the facts or adopted the same wise policy before the arrests.

The German Government took a strong stand on the matter. Stresemann felt that Moscow's action was particularly outrageous because a majority of the mechanics were employed by the A.E.G. whose president, Felix Deutsch, had always espoused the cause of friendly relations with Bolshevism, and was, in fact, one of the many "fathers" of the Rapallo Treaty.

Immediately the arrests, the imminence of which was known to Count Brockdorff-Rantzau, took place, the Wilhelmstrasse broke off the economic conference with Soviet representatives which had assembled in Berlin early in 1928 to regulate thorny problems of Russo-German trade. Stalin argued that the Germans suspended the conference for economic reasons, and merely used the Shakhti trial as an excuse. But the bitterness in Berlin was real, and Stresemann's position found an echo in an article by his public reflector, Baron Rheinbaben[4] which hinted that unless Moscow abandoned such methods as the Shakhti trial, a substitute for the Rapallo policy would have to be considered.

The entire incident, small though it might seem against a larger historical background, completely blackened the Soviet-German horizon in the spring and early summer of 1928, and the Soviet Union in that period had a worse press in Germany than at any other time in its existence. To be sure, the unsatisfactory state of German-Russian trade served as a convenient frame for popular feeling, and certain banking circles in Berlin and industrialist circles

[4] *Europaeische Gespraeche,* July, 1928.

in the Rhineland were suspected of exploiting the Shakhti trial to create an animus against the Bolsheviks. But no small share of the responsibility rested with the Bolsheviks themselves, and subsequently many of them were ready to admit it.

**GERMANY MEDIATES FOR MOSCOW IN THE KELLOGG PACT** Before the storm that raged around the Shakhti trial had subsided, the Kellogg Pact became the chief concern of the world's chancellories. Bolsheviks approached it with distrust and various degrees of hostility. But Germany wanted Russia to adhere.

President Kalinin, among others, alluded publicly to the Soviet view of the Kellogg Pact. He made a brief statement of the basic idea of the pact. "But this amounts to nothing," he commented. "Instead of a real abolition of war—some more talk." "Will the cause of peace be advanced a single meter?" he asked. "It will not," he answered. Then why do the nations do these things? he asked. To fool the workers and masses, he answered. To lull them into a feeling that war does not threaten, and thus dull the edge of popular protest against bigger armies and navies, and against imperialism. "This is the only purpose," Kalinin declared.

The Bolshevik position vis-à-vis the Kellogg Pact did not change even after they signed it.

> The Kellogg Pact [Prime Minister Rykov said in May, 1929,[5]] cannot be regarded as a preventive of war, because that document contains no real guarantee against war, and in particular, says nothing about disarmament or even the limitation of armaments.

"War," he said, "is the violation of all treaties," and when war came the Pact would go the way of other "scraps" of papers.

Then why did the Bolsheviks adhere to the Pact? Rykov frankly explained. Moscow wished to deprive the leaders of the "anti-Soviet bloc" of the formal possibility of an attack on the Soviet Union. Moreover, the Soviet Government agreed that, "with all its faults," the Kellogg Pact constituted a "moral obligation" and therefore "obstructed, to some small extent, the psychological preparation for war."

[5] *Izvestia,* May 23, 1929.

The Bolsheviks signed the Kellogg Pact because they wished to participate in any instrument which even remotely, in their opinion, conduced to peace. But the decision to adhere was preceded by a sharp struggle in Bolshevik ranks. Bukharin led the fight in favor of it; Chicherin against.

Chicherin objected to the Pact for the same reasons he objected to the League of Nations: it would open the way to outside dictation to Moscow. It would enable the Powers—as it almost did during the Chinese Eastern Railway crisis in 1929—to interfere in Russia's relations with other countries. Moreover, the opponents of the Kellogg Pact vehemently objected to the British and French reservations, more particularly the latter. These reservations, Bolsheviks declared, in effect, destroyed the efficacy of the Pact.

> There are certain regions of the world [Chamberlain had stated in a note to Washington dated May 19, 1928] the welfare and integrity of which constitute a special and vital interest for our peace and safety. . . . Their protection against attack is to the British Empire a measure of self-defense. It must be clearly understood that His Majesty's Government in Great Britain accept the new treaty upon the distinct understanding that it does not prejudice their freedom of action in this respect.

This Chamberlain note enunciated a British "Monroe Doctrine" without, however, even hinting at the areas included in England's special interest zone. Charles Trevelyan, M.P., asked in the House of Commons whether the "certain regions of the world" were Egypt, Afghanistan, China, and Mesopotamia. No answer was given. The world was ignorant of the location or extent of the territories to protect her interests in which England might go to war without violating the text of the Pact. Moreover, as Trevelyan commented, "The threat of the removal of large areas from the operation of the Pact remains indefinite and expandable at the whim of the British Government.[6] For, unless an unpublished understanding accompanied the Kellogg Pact, England might, in a moment of crisis, include Turkey, Persia, and Arabia, as well as China, Afghanistan, Egypt, and Mesopotamia among "those regions" which justified legal war on her part.

Chicherin was even more irritated by the French reser-

[6] *Europaeische Gespraeche,* August, 1928.

vations. He maintained that they gave universal application to Locarno, the League and to French alliances in Eastern Europe. He would even go so far as to say that the Pact made the League Covenant obligatory on the nations that signed it, and although Russia expressly stated that she rejected the reservations and was therefore not bound to them, other Powers, including America, had taken cognizance of them without demur.

These contentions carried weight with Moscow. Yet gradually a tendency in favor of adhesion took the upper hand: still another case of expediency worsting ideology.

The real difficulty was that Moscow had not been invited to negotiate or sign the Pact. This supplied the antagonists with ammunition. France, having originally proposed a bi-lateral treaty to Washington, was embarrassed by Kellogg's insistence on a multi-lateral agreement, and resisted every effort toward universality. America was indifferent to Russia's adhesion. In England there was opposition. For although General Smuts maintained that "it would be vain to organize for world-peace and leave out Russia," since she was "the greatest potential factor in the peace of Europe and Asia, probably for a century to come" the official attitude in London differed sharply. Chamberlain stated in his reply to Kellogg on May 19, 1928, that

> universality would, in any case, be difficult of attainment, and might even be inconvenient, for there are some states whose governments have not been universally recognized [Soviet Russia.—L.F.], and some which are scarcely in a position to ensure the maintenance of good order and security within their territories [China.—L.F.].

Only Germany wished the Soviet Union to become a partner to the Pact. Germany wished it when Moscow, Washington, Paris and London did not. As early as July 11, 1928, Herr von Schubert, the permanent chief of the German Foreign Office and at that time, in Stresemann's absence, the acting Foreign Minister, inquired informally of the American Government what its attitude would be if Russia were ready to accept the Pact. He had spoken to Krestinsky, the Soviet ambassador in Berlin, several weeks previously, and though the Russian had no instructions, knew, in fact, that his colleagues in Moscow were hostile, he nevertheless reacted favorably. Schubert felt that Soviet adhesion would be highly desirable.

Mr. Kellogg immediately replied that he did not want Russia to be one of the fifteen original signatories. But after the treaty went into effect, that is, after it had been signed and ratified by all parties, then the Soviet Union too might adhere.

Meanwhile, Schubert discussed the subject on several occasions with Krestinsky. Moscow gathered the utterly false impression that Schubert was acting on American instructions, and that he himself was rather lukewarm to Soviet adhesion while Washington favored it. Exactly the reverse was the case. Soviet statesmen, however, deduced from Schubert's feelers that Kellogg harbored some friendly intentions towards Russia. Their hope that the Pact might therefore form a bridge to America probably contributed appreciably toward Moscow's decision.

The Soviet Government now commenced to reconcile itself to adherence, and on July 27 Karakhan asked the German chargé d'affaires in Moscow whether the Union could join now or later, and whether reservations could be made by Powers which signed subsequent to the adhesion of the first fifteen signatories.

The next day Schubert, Litvinov, Krestinsky, Count Brockdorff-Rantzau, and Dr. von Dirksen met for luncheon in the Berlin Soviet Embassy to discuss Russia and the Pact.

It had become known that Spain had made application for a place among the original signatories. Krestinsky intimated that the Soviet Union was a Great Power. If Spain received an invitation to Paris, Russia had stronger claims. Litvinov inquired about reservations. Might Russia make reservations if she joined after the Pact's ratification? Schubert thought she could not. Litvinov made it clear that, in principle, the Soviet Government had no objection to adhesion, but the question of time and of reservations would affect its final decision.

Schubert carried away the impression that Moscow would, with some justice, be offended if Spain were invited and Russia snubbed. The Bolsheviks would be more likely to adhere now than after ratification. If Russia were excluded from the Pact, moreover, she would undoubtedly regard it as a weapon against her, as a phase of her diplomatic encirclement, and the opponents in Moscow of a more liberal foreign policy would be strengthened. German and American circles feared, on the other hand, that a Soviet delegate at the peaceful ceremony of signature in Paris might prove an embarrassment. He might propose difficult problems, open the question of disarmament and point out the ineffectiveness of the instrument they were that moment subscribing.

Germany would, nevertheless, have welcomed an invitation to Moscow to sign at Paris. But Kellogg rejected the idea, and Chamberlain and Briand too. The State Department, however, modified its attitude in one important respect: originally, Kellogg had stated that Russia would be permitted to adhere after ratification. Ratification was in fact delayed a whole year. But owing perhaps to Germany's interest in Soviet adhesion, Washington agreed that Russia become a party to the pact immediately after the signature in Paris, and before it went into effect.

Nevertheless, the invitation to Moscow remained outstanding, and Chicherin continued his opposition to Soviet adherence. His interview to the Soviet and Foreign Press on August 4 was charged with unbridled criticism of the Pact and its makers. Since last December, he said, the Powers had been discussing a pact to outlaw war. Yet it had never occurred to them to ask Russia's participation. Was it not patent, therefore, that the Pact was really "an instrument for the isolation of the Soviet Union and the struggle against Bolshevism"? The Powers had consented to renounce wars for national ends, but they simultaneously obtained universal sanction for their international alliances, colonial designs, and military treaties which made for world wars.

The Bolshevik supporters of Soviet adhesion subscribed to Chicherin's views but rejected his counsel. The Commissar for Foreign Affairs accordingly presented the only contention with a general appeal—and one that would relieve him of personal embarrassment in the event of adhesion. Moscow must participate in the preliminary negotiations, he argued. She could not sign unless she determined the character of the document. He put it in the astute form: "It is not yet too late," he said. "The Pact is not yet signed. Negotiations regarding its contents may still be conducted with the Soviet Government. . . . I can state that our Government is prepared to participate in these pourparlers." He hoped Moscow would not be invited to these pourparlers. Chicherin left it open to the Powers to deduce that in that event they would not sign. He was playing the prestige chord.

The Powers, however, wanted no Bolshevik at the signing ceremony in Paris. Kellogg did not wish to confront Chicherin or Litvinov. Nor did the nations desire to discuss the text of the Pact or its reservations with polemic-loving Communists. They were only ready to accept the Soviet Union as a partner to the Pact after everything had been settled.

**THE BOLSHEVIKS JOIN** On the very day the Kellogg Pact was signed in Paris, Jean Herbette, the French ambassador in Moscow, officially asked Litvinov whether the Soviet Union wished to adhere to the Pact. He asked in the name of his own Government and of the State Department. Mr. Kellogg, he affirmed, wished to limit the number of original signatories in order to hasten the consummation of the treaty, but early and subsequent adherents would be on the same footing. Herbette acted as intermediary for the United States Government. Litvinov asked for all official correspondence pertaining to the Pact.

Herbette called again two days later, on the 29th of August. The ambassador declared that he could receive no Soviet reservations. A little amusing dialogue ensued. Herbette explained that no interpretations or reservations were valid unless all the adherents accepted them. Litvinov repeated this statement. It meant that Russia could make reservations but that they would receive universal application only if all the Powers were asked and approved. No, Herbette replied, he could accept for transmission no Soviet reservations. Litvinov regarded this a contradiction. Herbette was acting for the State Department. He ought to bring the Soviet interpretations to Washington's attention. But Herbette insisted that he could accept only Moscow's act of adhesion. "And suppose I give you a negative reply?" Litvinov inquired. Herbette said he would accept it.

On the 31st Litvinov summoned Herbette to receive the Soviet Union's note of adherence.[7] Litvinov asked him to send it to Washington too. The document con-

[7] Soviet dailies for September 1, 1928, also *Der Kampf um den Frieden,* a collection of Soviet documents. Berlin, 1929, p. 232.

tained Moscow's criticism and Moscow's reservations. The most important Soviet reservation was the refusal to accept the British and French reservations. The Soviet Government, in particular, would not regard itself bound by the Chamberlain "Monroe Doctrine" respecting unnamed Asiatic neighbors of the Soviet Union. For the rest, the Bolsheviks reiterated that disarmament was the only effective guarantee of peace, and that the Pact, unless it provided for a limitation of the world's uninterrupted arming, would "remain a dead document without real content." Moscow saw in the Anglo-French naval Pact an immediate confirmation of this view.

**THE ANGLO-FRENCH NAVAL COMPROMISE** While the diplomatic exchanges preliminary to the Kellogg Pact still proceeded, enterprising newspaper correspondents published the fact of the conclusion of a secret naval agreement between England and France. The evidence was so incontrovertible that both governments soon admitted the truth of these reports. Reports gave the impression that the naval compromise revolved around military and air armaments as well as fleets, and America and Germany each considered it directed against her interests. A year later, Senator Borah wrote: "I do not know of anything which has had a more pronounced effect in the United States in late years, in giving an unfortunate impression, than this incident."[8] President Coolidge declared in an Armistice Day speech that the United States must build more cruisers in response.

The reaction in Germany was equally profound. Locarno had been scrapped, the newspapers announced. The naval compromise began to grow into an entente. Publications pointed to joint Anglo-French action in Bulgaria, and the Baltics, and to joint Anglo-French army maneuvers in the Rhineland. Germans found still other proofs. "We are isolated," they cried, and commenced to look about for a new orientation. Germany must no longer play the game of the big Powers at Geneva, the dailies pleaded. They must seek support in the Balkans, in South America. Theodore Wolf, editor of the *Berliner Tageblatt,* urged Stresemann to make advances to Rome.

Moscow reaped the benefit. Where is Locarno now? the enemies of Locarno in Moscow and Berlin asked.

[8] London *Time and Tide,* September 20, 1929.

"While for immediate purposes," a high official in the Wilhelmstrasse said to the writer at the time, "we must seek to mend our relations with France [he did not mention Great Britain.—L.F.], our orientation in the long run must be on America and Russia." And he was far from being an Easterner.

Berlin wanted to make a gesture to Moscow. So, on the very day Stresemann left for Paris to sign the Kellogg Pact, a note was rushed through the Foreign Office and Cabinet inviting Russia to resume the economic negotiations disrupted by the Shakhti trial. Several other irritating issues between the two countries were quickly removed—the matter of German correspondents in Moscow, for instance. At the same time, the fact that Schubert had mediated Soviet adhesion to the Kellogg Pact, though not fully appreciated because Moscow exaggerated American goodwill in the episode, helped to bring about a favorable feeling. The Shakhti atmosphere began to evaporate.

**THE LITVINOV PROTOCOL** The Soviet Union was the first Government to ratify the Kellogg Pact. It suspected that other countries would long delay ratification and that the multi-lateral agreement would therefore not become valid for an extended period during which Russia's neighbors might legally, so to speak, attack her. It occurred to the Bolsheviks, accordingly, to enter into an arrangement with Poland whereby the Kellogg Pact acquired immediate validity. This was the significance of the Litvinov Pact signed in Moscow on February 9, 1929, more than six months before the Kellogg Pact became international law.

Litvinov saw in the Kellogg Pact an opportunity to force Poland into a separate peace agreement with Moscow. This had been one of his arguments when the question of Soviet adhesion to the Kellogg Pact was still being debated in inner Bolshevik circles. Poland had signed the Kellogg Pact, he would say. The Soviet Union had signed the Kellogg Pact. Why not therefore make it immediately effective as far as Poland and the Soviet Union were concerned?

Poland had avoided the conclusion of a non-aggression treaty with Moscow partly on account of her policy vis-à-vis the Baltic States. Poland desired to align the

Baltic States on her side and to come to terms with Moscow only if the Baltic States and Poland constituted one united party and Russia the other. Moscow, on the contrary, aimed to destroy the possibility of a Baltic bloc.

Now on December 29, 1928, when Litvinov proposed his "hurry-up" pact to Warsaw, four months had passed since the Paris signing ceremony of the Kellogg Pact, and only Poland and Lithuania, of Russia's neighbors, had adhered to it formally. Litvinov could lay his protocol before these states only. Subsequently of course Finland, Latvia, and Estonia, Rumania and other states might join, but in the meantime Poland would be forced into a diplomatic act with Russia and without the Baltic countries.

One additional reason: Charles Dewey, American financial adviser to Poland, visited Moscow in the summer of 1928 and talked at length with Litvinov. Dewey's chief difficulties in Warsaw were budgetary. He found that 40 or 45 per cent of the budget went to the army. The Poles resisted reduction on the ground that they were continually threatened by Soviet aggression—and by Germany too, incidentally. Dewey wished to see for himself whether this alleged menace existed in fact. The Litvinov Protocol was intended to indicate that it did not.

Poland returned an equivocal reply to Litvinov's proposal, but stated that she would first discuss the suggested Protocol with the Baltic States. Warsaw also desired that Rumania, with whom Moscow had no diplomatic relations, be invited to consider the Protocol.

Numerous written and oral diplomatic exchanges followed. Russia accepted Rumania's participation, but Poland cleverly prolonged the discussions so that the Baltic States might find time to adhere to the Kellogg Pact. Certain individuals in the Soviet capital believed, however, that Poland's final decision to sign the Litvinov Protocol was not arrived at before influential American circles had emphatically urged such a move.

In the end, on February 9, Estonia, Latvia, Poland, Rumania, and the Soviet Union signed the Litvinov Protocol at an impressive ceremony in Moscow. Apart from the pact itself, the occasion was notable for Litvinov's announcement that while he welcomed the Rumanian delegate, Charles A. Davilla, on Soviet soil, his presence and his Government's adhesion to the Protocol in no wise changed Moscow's position towards the Bessarabian question.

Subsequently, Turkey, Persia, and the free city of Danzig added their signatures separately. Their adherence had not been on the original program, and was regarded as a Soviet victory, especially the adhesion of Danzig which gave to that city a status in international affairs as irritating to Poland as it was pleasing to Germany. Finland and Lithuania refused to sign.

The little maneuver that was the Litvinov Protocol brought some life into Soviet foreign affairs which, for a year, had been passive and negative. In 1927, Moscow received a number of very powerful blows—Britain, China, Poland, France—which it could not very well parry. The next year was spent as if in recovery and convalescence, with attempts at retrenchment here and there. Moscow became extremely introverted at this period, partly because of the effects of 1927, largely because home economic developments had entered a novel and more intensive phase. The Moscow *Izvestia,* mouthpiece of the Government, had between 1924 and 1927 probably averaged two or three leading articles on foreign politics each week. Now one in two weeks was more normal. Industrialization and preparations for the Five-Year Plan of national reconstruction absorbed all minds and every drop of enthusiasm.

And then came the fall of Amanullah.

# 28

## MOSCOW ENTERTAINS A KING

"THE SOCIALIST KING," Eastern papers called Amanullah. But Socialism and Afghanistan did not mix, and the term was applied loosely to denote a spirit of progress, extreme simplicity, unaffected democracy, and protest.

While visiting the Soviet Union, Amanullah on several occasions asked Karakhan about Peter the Great. Was he the Peter of Kabul? Afghanistan in 1928 did undoubtedly offer a certain analogy to Russia at the opening of the eighteenth century. Both were primitive and under-populated. Peter counted 14,000,000 inhabitants; Afghanistan boasted of 7,000,000. Peter, like Amanullah, had to create an army, develop industry, fix his country's star in the international firmament, and mold a national State.

But their characters differed widely. Peter possessed great will-power. Not Amanullah. Peter had energy and unbounded resourcefulness. He was a rough, simple man. In Holland he worked as a carpenter, in England at wharves. His hands were as callous as his rule. The Afghan Emir, to be sure, drove his own motor-car—much to the horror of the Shah of Persia—and got under it to repair punctures and breakages. But he never worked. He was a king par excellence. Peter evaded royal receptions and palaces on his several trips to Western Europe. Amanullah, when he arrived on Soviet territory, told Karakhan that he rejoiced to have reached a country where court ceremonies and stiff formalities might be dispensed with. And although he drank deeply of the luxury and pomp the West gave him, he spent considerable time in factories and workshops after the fashion of Peter.

Amanullah inherited neither the iron will of his mother nor the perverse profligacy of his father Habibullah. He became king by the grace of his mother, who hated the British and nursed Pan-Islamist dreams.

And then a struggle commenced between the influence of his domineering mother and that of his astute father-in-law. Queen Souriya's father was a modernist, a Westerner, a reformer. He wished to see his daughter's royal spouse in the role of Kemal. Mustapha Pasha was a strong figure; Amanullah was a feeble one. But Amanullah's true greatness lay in his ability gradually to discard, like Kemal, the old ideas of a Moslem empire, of Islam for the Islamites, and to take a sharp course towards modernization.

Like Peter, Amanullah defied the Church. But unlike the Czar, he formed no military-landlord caste that would support his innovations. He never succeeded in welding conflicting tribes into a national unit or in giving them a federal consciousness. At times he could rely on one tribe against the other, but never on one class against the other. And Amanullah, with all his fine plans for an industrialized country with its schools, factories, and conscripted army, possessed no constructive talent.

**THE BOLSHEVIK SUBSIDY** When Amanullah rose to power, Afghanistan for the first time achieved true independence in foreign affairs and complete internal sovereignty. Yet his father had received a big subsidy from Great Britain, and its withdrawal before other sources of revenue had been consolidated proved a hardship to his rule. The Soviet Government, accordingly, decided to grant him an annual subsidy of $500,000—a small sum, but important.

For two or three years Amanullah received his Bolshevik subsidy, sometimes in cash, sometimes in goods, sometimes in reduced volume. But in 1922 trouble started with the Basmachi in Soviet Bohkhara, and certain circles in Kabul supported the anti-Bolshevik uprising which Enver Pasha ultimately came to lead. Moscow was ill at ease. Some Communist leaders began to look at Amanullah as a "British puppet," and demanded the cancellation of the subsidy. But the passing of Enver and the suppression of the Basmachi soon relieved the tension between Moscow and Kabul, and a period of improved relations set in which lasted till the end of 1925. The subsidy arrears were paid, and the subsidy continued to be paid in gold, but more and more in goods, and more and more unpunctually.

In 1925 and 1926, however, Moscow began to count its gold and foreign currency with considerable niggardliness, and a disinclination made itself felt against financing Amanullah. Soviet leaders did not wish to part with even small sums that might advance the supreme task of economic reconstruction they had undertaken. Amanullah continued to receive a diminished subsidy in the form of armaments.

**AMANULLAH GOES TO EUROPE** Russo-Afghan relations remained friendly, and when Amanullah undertook his trip to Europe in 1928, no doubt existed in his mind that he wished to see the Soviet Union too. In fact, it was Russia, next to Turkey, that he probably wanted to see most of all.

His purpose in traveling to the West was obvious. He aimed to import ideas, equipment, men, and capital. The program of reform he contemplated for Afghanistan required greater resources than he could mobilize at home or obtain from politically interested foreign quarters without prejudicing his own freedom of action.

Amanullah had a natural curiosity about the West that had been lauded to him so much and which he was trying to imitate. He had never been outside the confines of Afghanistan. He wanted to see how high his country ranked with other Powers, and whether he could raise their estimation of it. He vowed to put Afghanistan on the world map.

**BRITISH DISPLEASURE** Whatever else it accomplished, Amanullah's trip did not improve his standing with the British. En route to London, Sir Percival Phillips, the *Daily Mail* correspondent who had accompanied the Padishah from India, asked him whether he was a friend of England. He could not say till he had spoken to Sir Austen Chamberlain, Amanullah replied. But neither his interview with the British Foreign Secretary nor his stay in London produced any favorable practical result or any friendly impression, and although the Emir undoubtedly carried away a feeling of Britain's wealth and military power, he could not envisage them as lending to the security or longevity of his own regime.

He had irritated the English. Leaving Kabul, he entered India amid popular jubilation. India received him as one of her own. He snubbed the British Viceroy. Lord Irwin snubbed him back. In Bombay, Amanullah preached in the great mosque and summoned the faithful to religious tolerance and peace with the Hindus.

In Cairo, Amanullah addressed Parliament, and praised Zaghlul Pasha, who hated the British. To a group of Indian students in the same city, he said: "I love India." Later, after his exile from Afghanistan, Souriya bore him a daughter whom he called "India." But the English are too sensitive about India to welcome such affection on the part of a neighbor-monarch.

During his stay in India, Amanullah appealed for Moslem-Hindu amity. He called Gandhi his "very, very great friend," and went out of his way to make a demonstration of friendship for Mrs. Gandhi. The British resented such encouragement to Indian national movements.

The *Bombay Chronicle* of June 26, 1928, quoted Kemal's address to Amanullah on freedom and national independence, and then added its own comment:

> India, [it said] that has suffered most for want of freedom and on which the sun of independence has yet to shine, may derive deep inspiration from the example and precept of Kemal Pasha . . . India, we hope, is not so dead as not to be stirred by the clarion call of Kemal Pasha and the lead of Turkey, Afghanistan, Persia, and, last but not least, China.

**AMANULLAH IN MOSCOW, ANKARA, AND TEHERAN** British dailies warned Amanullah when he was in London that he had best hasten home, as insurrections had broken out in his provinces. The report was premature. Other publications informed the Emir that the trip from Kabul to England had been very strenuous for his wife; he should not, therefore, take the long land route over Russia. But he decided he would. To omit the Soviet Union was obviously impossible.

Amanullah had got nothing in Britain, nor had the English from him. In Moscow, the simplicity of President

Kalinin, the expansiveness of War Commissar Voroshilov, the directness and learning of Foreign Commissar Chicherin, the engaging frankness of Karakhan who accompanied him throughout, impressed him. He saw an East that was yet of the West—his ideal for Afghanistan. Industrialization, science, art, sports, military prowess, the Lenin Institute—all were displayed to him. Kalinin made him a gift of two agricultural tractors of Soviet manufacture.

Amanullah, however, also wished to bring home from Moscow a commercial treaty. It would have been to the political advantage but the economic disadvantage of Russia. Therefore the Bolshevik statesmen refused it. His trip to Moscow, from this practical point of view, was a failure. Yet he saw the might, the extent, the energy of his great northern neighbor.

Most success attended Amanullah's sojourn in Turkey. Kemal won his heart. Mustapha Pasha's figure breathed force, dictatorial will, irresistible ruling power—everything Amanullah desired but did not possess. They signed a pact outlawing war: it was tantamount to a promise to co-operate. They discussed the impending Afghan reforms. "Do as I do," Kemal must have said. "If they refuse to remove their fezes, cut off the heads that wear them. The church will defy you. Make short shrift of it." Their problems were not dissimilar. Amanullah decided to adopt Kemal's tactics. He would show a strong arm and a firm will. In Russia they had counselled moderation. The effect of his conversations with Kemal was to override this Bolshevik caution.

Where Kemal grew fond of Amanullah, Riza learned to hate the Afghan king. To be sure, the Shah laid out a new public square in Enzeli in honor of Amanullah's arrival at that port, and another in Teheran. But in the capital, Amanullah drove his own motor-car to royal receptions, and walked through the streets unceremoniously. Souriya appeared unveiled before the eyes of strange males, and gave teas to liberal-minded women. Riza was a plebeian risen to kingship, and looked to strict etiquette to lend him the awing dignity of an ancient dynast. Amanullah, however, wore the crown gracefully because he wore it so infrequently.

The Shah and the Padishah rubbed each other the

wrong way. Yet Riza could not ignore the social significance of Amanullah's visit. During his stay, Persian women were permitted to be seen in public places with men other than their husbands. Women sang in amusement houses for the first time in history. The veil grew thinner, and began to smack less of Moslem *purdah* and more of Parisian chic. The Afghan Emirs' sojourn galvanized the moderns and antagonized the mullahs in Persia. The mullahs had originally asked Riza to refuse Amanullah an invitation. The Shah could venture no such offence. But before Amanullah quit Persian soil, he felt the bitterness of institutionalized Mohammedanism in Persia against him.

Amanullah wanted to play the part of the Great Emancipator of Islam's womanhood. Souriya helped. The clergy shuddered; the forces for progress took courage. And as Amanullah moved from capital to capital, the new spirit he personified leapt over boundaries with him. Socially, the result of the Emir's tour in the East was to correlate the movements for reform in Soviet Turkestan, Afghanistan, Turkey, and Persia.

When Amanullah finally drove into the Afghan town of Herat on June 22, 1928, he found the city decorated in Afghan, Turkish, Persian, and Soviet flags. He talked at gatherings of communal leaders. He stressed the reactionary role of the Moslem priesthood in stemming progress, and emphasized the necessity of feminine education. Home at last in Kabul, wildly acclaimed by tribal leaders, Amanullah in uniform and Souriya in Parisian frock and a light transparent gauze over her face, received the homage of the populace. "Send the girls to school," was one of the keynotes of his speech. Yet sensing the possibility of disapproval, he recalled that he had always faithfully followed the customs of Islam.

**THE FALL OF AMANULLAH** Amanullah wished to be the pendulum that made the clock of Eastern progress tick faster. But deeply-entrenched forces, foreign and Asiatic, saw safety in conservatism, or, faced with the threat of reform, in reaction. It became necessary to turn back the hands of time.

For nine years the British had suffered Amanullah. He gave them trouble in the North-West Frontier. He inspired movements in India. Now his trip had made him a symbol, and attempts in London to wean him from his former ways had proved unsuccessful.

Yet it is short-sighted to believe, as some Bolsheviks do, that British India and Colonel Lawrence of Arabia could have overthrown Amanullah. The revolt that swept Amanullah from the throne possessed deep roots in Afghan soil.

The Padishah had not governed very wisely. A devout Moslem, his educational reforms tended to alienate the Moslem hierarchy. He conscripted labor to build metal roads for autos. That labor became his enemy. The same roads cost him the support of the tribes through whose territory they passed; they were deprived of the former camel transport fees and the right to levy tolls on the ancient dirt paths. Amanullah's State, army, and school innovations entailed expenses. He had to collect more taxes. The people objected. In the army, the tribal chiefs saw a menace to their autonomous position. The King's efforts towards national unity impressed them similarly.

During the six months the ruler had absented himself from his domain, these hostile forces raised their head. Amanullah's intention on his return to press the reform program with Kemal-like vigor created an angry mood in wide circles.

Amanullah fell. Before he fell, Riza sent messengers offering military aid, on condition, however, that definite compensation be granted to Persia, perhaps in the province of Herat. Amanullah, though hunted, refused. Expelled from the capital and fled to Kandahar, the king's foreign minister flew over the Hindu Kush and thence to Moscow to sue for aid. Moscow was benevolently inclined, but not in a position to grant material assistance. A small Red Army push would have saved Amanullah. A battery of artillery slipped furtively into Afghanistan from Soviet territory might have driven Bache-Sakao, the "water boy," from Kabul. Instead, Amanullah soon saw himself in exile.

Nadir Khan, an uncle of Amanullah and a supporter of Amanullah's general political philosophy, took up the fight, and in November, 1929, he defeated Bache-Sakao. The "water boy" was executed, and in due course Nadir established himself on the throne. Amanullah apparently accepted the change with nonchalance. He lived in Italy, devoid of ambition, until his death.

**SOCIAL BARRIERS** Curzon wished to carve out geographical buffers between India and the Russian bear. Afghanistan and Persia served that purpose. But with the coming of the Bolshevik revolution, Russia ceased to represent a military threat. Yet England still needed buffers for India. Afghanistan and Persia expected to serve as non-conductors of the ideas being hatched in the Soviet East, and in Turkey. But the Afghanistan of Amanullah was not a non-conductor. It was a fine copper wire. The insurrection against Amanullah short-circuited the contact. It blew out the fuse: Amanullah. But historic processes bored from within India.

# 29

# THE MANCHURIAN CRISIS

THE CHINESE EASTERN RAILWAY has now and then been the subject of discussion in highest Moscow councils. It is realized that the road is a weak arm of the Soviet State in an exposed position difficult of defense. Ownership of the line, moreover, opens the Bolsheviks to accusations of Red Imperialism. But Soviet military authorities maintain that Vladivostok and the Maritime Provinces would become untenable if Moscow surrendered the thin connecting link between Siberia and the Pacific across Manchuria.

In 1924 Dr. Sun Yat-sen advised the Russians not to return the Chinese Eastern Railway (C.E.R.) to China lest the anti-Sun, anti-Kuomintang Mukden Government of Chang So-lin be so strengthened thereby as to be in a position to defeat the Southern Nationalists.

The Bolsheviks are too realistic to return the road irrespective of the effect of such a move on Chinese politics. They never determine policy in an idealistic vacuum.

It is clear from the historic record, and was admitted by no less an authority than the Sub-Committee on the Chinese Eastern Railway of the Washington Disarmament Conference whose report, read to the conference by Charles E. Hughes, stated that "The Railway is in effect the property of the Russian Government." The Chinese representatives made a number of reservations to this report, but did not object to its finding on the C.E.R.[1]

The C.E.R. is not indispensable to Soviet foreign trade. The Soviets could use the line if its ownership passed to China. This might be made the guaranteed condition of sale.

[1] *Conference on the Limitation of Armament*. Washington, November 12, 1921–February 6, 1922. (Washington, 1922). Official Protocol, p. 1376.

Chang So-lin seized the C.E.R. in January, 1926, and arrested M. Ivanov, the Russian director of the railway. Mukden was subsequently compelled to release Ivanov and the line. Chang So-lin's son, Chang Sueh-liang, seized the C.E.R. on July 10, 1929. The reason given was Bolshevik propaganda by the Soviet consulates in Manchuria. Several months after these accusations were broadcast the Chinese Government printed a pamphlet purporting to contain Bolshevik documents taken in the raid of the Soviet Consulate in Harbin and proving subversive Communist activity. Some of the papers were typed in the old, pre-revolutionary Russian orthography which was abolished by the Bolsheviks and is now never used in the Soviet Union. But the White Russian émigrés abroad still employ it as a mark of their protest against Bolshevik innovations. It is significant, moreover, that the Chinese, who had to put the alleged documents on record after having made them the much-advertised official excuse for the raid, took special pains to restrict the circulation of the pamphlet. As historical material, it is too vulnerable.

Dr. Theodor Sternberg, the *Berliner Tageblatt's* Tokyo correspondent, stated in its issue for August 15, 1929, that "in Japan they are convinced that China does not possess any evidence of revolutionary plans on the part of the Russian railway's or the Soviet consulate's officials." And even if such evidence were available, this bourgeois authority adds, China should have made diplomatic representations to Moscow before laying a violent hand on the C.E.R. "The real object in view," said the London *Bulletin of International Affairs* dated July 18, 1929, "is to be found in the long cherished desire of the Chinese Government to obtain complete control of the Chinese Eastern Railway to the exclusion of the Russian influence."

The explanation of the seizure of the C.E.R. must be sought in Chinese domestic politics. The Bolsheviks, to be sure, were prone, after their custom, to see in Mukden's violent act the hand of foreign imperialism. But there is no proof that London or Washington were implicated.

The internecine struggle in China was a continuous test of strength between various tuchuns or provincial leaders controlling different sections of the country and exercising independent sovereignty whether or not they formally acknowledged the authority of a central Chinese government. Feng, the "Christian" and "Bolshevik" general—both nicknames are equally misleading—even accepted office with the Nanking regime, but he never actually recognized his obligation to obey it, and when circumstances suited his purpose he fought it. Mukden might pay paper allegiance to Nanking, but in fact its co-operation with Chiang Kai-shek was restricted to the receipt of diplomatic support from him. Nanking won an international reputation as China's capital. The Chinese, however, knew that its voice was heard in only four neighboring provinces and that it could levy taxes successfully in only two.

Chiang Kai-shek, heir to the Kuomintang tradition and traitor to its principles, wished to win the support of Mukden, heir to Chang So-lin's tradition of implacable enmity to Southern Nationalism. Yen Shi-shan, the "peace lord" of Shansi province, dominated Peking in 1928 and 1929. He was an ally of Feng. Manchuria frequently sent forces below the Great Wall to Peking, or Peiping as it has been re-christened, and did not want to see Yen establish himself there. Feng, held fast in the famine provinces of Inner Mongolia, could at any time be forced to seek shelter and sustenance in Outer Mongolia which Mukden coveted. Feng was also a bane of Nanking's existence. He could dispute Nanking domination of the Yangtse, and he made uncertain Nanking's control of Hankow.

Nanking and Mukden thus had a common interest in destroying Yen and Feng. The seizure of the Chinese Eastern Railway, which, had it passed smoothly, was to have been followed by a Manchurian thrust toward Outer Mongolia, would have raised Mukden's prestige, increased its territory, and outflanked Yen and Feng. Nanking was prepared to play this dangerous game although it had no surety that Mukden would remain loyal.

The confiscation of the C.E.R. by the Manchurian Government became the preliminary of renewed civil war which broke out in the fall of 1929. But the seizure was a boomerang which returned to wound Nanking's position, for the strained relations between Russia and China in Manchuria paralyzed Mukden and prevented Chang Sueh-liang from giving Chiang Kai-shek the slightest assistance against Feng and Yen. On the contrary,

Mukden was inclined to ask Nanking for aid. Moscow, by virtue of the seizure of the C.E.R., was thus given the whip-hand over the Chinese internal struggle, and with the issue unsettled, Nanking lacked the ability permanently to eliminate its federalist enemies from the fray.

**JOINT MANAGEMENT OF THE C.E.R.** The Chinese had no complaint against the Russians on the score of the C.E.R.'s operation. Dr. R. Perech, a well-known Sinologue, showed in the Berlin *Vossiche Zeitung* of July 24, 1929, that since the Soviet Government took over the road in 1924, the C.E.R. earned an annual profit which was divided evenly between Moscow and Mukden. The number of passengers carried more than doubled between 1925 and 1928, and freight rose from 3,000,000 tons in 1924 to 5,459,000 tons in 1928. Millions of rubles were spent for the renewal of equipment, the construction of workers' homes, and new rolling stock. Wages, Dr. Perech writes, mounted 15 per cent during the Soviet period of management.

Most important were the changes in personnel. The Sino-Soviet treaties of 1924 provided for parity of nationalities in the working staff of the C.E.R. The Bolsheviks, accordingly, proceeded quickly to train and employ Chinese. The number of Chinese working on the line at the time Dr. Perech wrote was 17,841 or three times the number in 1924. As compared with 17,841 Chinese there were only 13,300 Russians. Chinese had received more and more positions of authority.

In all the press and platform controversy that followed the seizure of the C.E.R., the Chinese never expressed any dissatisfaction with the Sino-Soviet operation of the road.

**AMERICAN INTERCESSION** As soon as the Chinese took over the C.E.R., war-scare headlines blazed through the world's newspapers. No conflict in Manchuria could be localized. The situation was too important. America was as much concerned with the future ownership of the road as Japan. France had her interest, and Great Britain could not remain indifferent. People therefore began to prophesy an international war.

The writer was in Moscow at the time of the seizure, and he knew that, all threats, ultimatums, mass demonstrations, and diplomatic démarches notwithstanding, the

Soviet Union would not be provoked into war with China on the C.E.R. issue.

Eight days after the seizure, the United States, acting as guardian of the Paris Pact, urged peace on the Soviet and Chinese Governments. Both promised to remain mindful of their obligations. This, presumably, was sufficient assurance. But a few days later a mysterious memorandum came into being in Washington. Secretary Stimson, according to an official announcement, handed it to the diplomatic representatives of Britain, France, Japan, Germany, and Italy on July 25. It dealt with Manchuria, but the State Department withheld publication. Secrets, however, will out. The Moscow *Pravda* of August 6 printed a Vienna dispatch throwing light on the contents of the memorandum. It had suggested that (1) a neutral commission be appointed to study the Manchurian conflict; (2) the parties in dispute withdraw their troops from the danger zone and refrain from hostile action; and (3), and most important, a body of five Russians, five Chinese, and a neutral chairman operate the Chinese Eastern Railway pending a final settlement. The Bolsheviks suspected that the "neutral" chairman would be an American as in 1917 to 1922 when Colonel L. F. Stevens was director of the Chinese Eastern.

Previously, according to Mr. Kawakami in the Baltimore *Sun* of August 3, information of the same general character regarding the memorandum had filtered into the Japanese Press, notably the *Nichi Nichi* and *Asahi*. I have reason to believe that the sources drawn upon by the *Pravda* and *Asahi* were, indirectly, the German and Japanese Foreign Offices. Moscow, at any rate, felt that it had reason to be suspicious of Washington's lively interest in the Manchurian controversy. A declaration made at Williamstown on August 25 by Stanley K. Hornbeck, chief of the Far Eastern division of the State Department, confirmed Bolshevik suspicions. He did not deny the existence of the unpublished memorandum. "I am not in a position to make a statement on that point," he merely said. But he emphasized the fact that America's traditional policy in respect to the Chinese Eastern Railway was neutralization. He gave instances: the Knox proposals in 1907–10, and the period from 1917 to 1922 when an American managed the road.

Meanwhile, fighting proceeded on the Soviet-Chinese

frontier. On August 19 the Soviets handed the German Government a note (Germany was protecting Russian interests in China) which called attention to eight raids undertaken between July 18 and August 18 by Chinese and White Russian troops into Soviet territory. On September 9 the Soviets handed the German ambassador in Moscow, von Dirksen, a second note citing nineteen further attacks by Chinese and White Russian bands on Soviet steamers, border guards, and villages. A third protest to Dr. von Dirksen dated September 17 enumerated additional incursions into Siberia. In November the Soviet Government undertook armed reprisals. A Russian raid in force began on November 18. Air and artillery bombardments were reported, and newspaper dispatches announced the capture of Manchuli, the Chinese border town, Dalainor, and Hailar. Hailar had been gutted, telegrams said.

An Associated Press wire from Tokyo on November 21 informed the world that Mukden had decided to negotiate with Moscow for a settlement of the railway dispute. The Soviets had achieved their purpose. One big raid compelled Chang Sueh-liang, the Governor of Manchuria, to sue for peace. Hugh Byas, the Tokyo correspondent of the New York *Times,* wired his paper on November 28:

> The news from Manchuria confirms the Japanese anticipation that the Russians did not intend an invasion. The Russians apparently have not occupied any Chinese towns and are back on their own territory. They have given the Chinese a severe slap, humiliated them by disarming 10,000 troops, and scared Mukden into a settlement, all by a relatively small operation which led to no entanglements.

The moment the Red Army marched in, the Chinese and White Russians fled. Their commanders deserted, and the disorganized soldiers looted as they ran. The extent of the Chinese retreat was made out to be the extent of the Red advance. According to a United Press dispatch of November 26 from Harbin, the Soviet forces actually halted thirty-eight miles from the border and then returned to their base.

Chinese negotiators were now in touch with Melnikov, former Soviet consul at Harbin, and with Simanovsky at Khabarovsk. China had acquiesced, and the statesmen had initiated talks with a view to the restitution to Russia of the Chinese Eastern Railway. But Nanking demurred. To Chiang Kai-shek it was a question of prestige, of holding Mukden's paper allegiance, and perhaps of pleasing Washington. He wished to prolong the impasse in Manchuria. On November 29 the New York *Times* put the whole situation in a nutshell in its front-page headlines: "Nanking and Mukden at Odds on Policy as Hostilities Cease. Manchuria's Yielding Ignored by Chiang, Who Offers Reds New Counter-Proposals. Appeal Seen as Gesture. Tokyo Sees China Completely Beaten and Danger Over as Soviet Withdraws." Three things appear: the fighting had ceased; Manchuria had yielded; the danger of war was gone.

November 28 brought further light: Litvinov declared Nanking's counter-proposals superfluous as Mukden had already accepted Soviet terms. An A.P. message from Mukden stated that "despite denials and counter-denials peace is near." An A.P. telegram from Tokyo quoted the Japanese Foreign Minister, after a talk with the United States Chargé d'affaires, as stating that peace impended, and the prospect of an early direct settlement "makes intervention by the world Powers unnecessary and undesirable." Dispatches stated that Soviet airplanes had bombed the little Manchurian town of Buchatu with bombs, cabbages, and soot. This, probably, was a way of applying more pressure as negotiations proceeded. No further hostilities were reported along the Manchurian border.

Japan resolutely declined to join any move for foreign mediation, on the ground that an anti-war pact could not be invoked when there was no war and when peaceful negotiations promised immediate success. This represented the attitude of the German Government also. On December 2 Mr. Stimson announced his two communications on the subject: one to Moscow and Nanking recalling their Paris Pact obligations, the other to the signatories of the Pact urging their co-operation for peace. The German Government refused on December 2:

> At the present moment [the German rejoinder read] the German Government has before it reports to the effect that direct negotiations for the peaceful composition of the conflict have opened.

Mr. Stimson might have had from American officials

in the Far East the same information which prompted Germany to reject his proposal. He might have had it from the Germans. He certainly was told by Mr. Debuchi, the Japanese ambassador, that hostilities had ceased, and that an agreement between Moscow and Mukden was in prospect.

On November 28 the Associated Press wired from Paris that in view of reports regarding Mukden's acceptance of Moscow's conditions "the French Government, as one of the signatories of the Kellogg-Briand Pact, feels that the situation no longer requires the intervention of the signatories." France, Germany (which had undertaken to protect the nationals of China and Russia and was therefore very close to the problem), and Japan, the third party best informed on Manchurian affairs, all objected to the invocation of the Paris Pact. Then why did Secretary Stimson invoke it? Since he could not have been ignorant of the negotiations, the Bolsheviks concluded that his only purpose in intervening was to interfere with them. This may be an erroneous conclusion, but it will be readily understood how Litvinov might have reached it. Undoubtedly, Moscow also recalled the still secret Stimson memorandum of July 25, which continued to disturb Russia as well as Japan.

Replying to the Stimson note of December 2, Litvinov, on December 3, rebuked the Secretary of State for interfering in the negotiations then proceeding in the Far East. This, the commissar stated, "cannot . . . be taken as a friendly act." More important, possibly, was his assertion that "the Paris Pact does not give a single state or group of states the function of protector of this Pact." Finally, Litvinov expressed "amazement" that the United States, while refusing to recognize the existence of the Soviet Government, nevertheless gave it "advice and counsel."

The Litvinov note was no model of tact. The Bolsheviks had not yet learned to hold their tongue or to put it in their cheek. They reacted violently to outside interference and remembered the days of military intervention. Moreover, there must have been a tremendous temptation in Moscow to administer a whipping to Mr. Stimson for one of the worst faux pas in recent diplomatic history. For as a matter of fact, the Chinese Eastern Railway situation was settled a few days after Stimson invoked the Pact. The settlement accorded with Bolshevik demands. The road was returned to mixed Russian-Chinese management.

The vehemence of Litvinov's reply was a measure of the strong resentment felt in Moscow with Mr. Stimson's intercession, and, above all, by the fear that America's move would encourage Mukden's resistance to a settlement. That settlement, when it was finally achieved, left much to be desired. China was not reconciled to Soviet ownership of the Chinese Eastern Railway. And, under the circumstances, the feeling in Moscow grew more and more in favor of selling the railway.

# 30

# SOVIET-AMERICAN BUSINESS

PERHAPS the greatest improvement in Russia's foreign position during 1928 and 1929 was the favorable trend of relations with the United States. In the absence of diplomatic relations, a kind of extra-diplomatic relations came into existence which were occasionally as satisfactory as some of the Soviet Union's diplomatic contacts with European countries.

Although Secretary of State Kellogg wrote in a Republican campaign document in 1928[1] that "The American Government . . . does not object to banking arrangements necessary to finance contracts for the sale of American goods [to Russia] on long-term credits," and although on December 1, 1927, the State Department announced that "the Coolidge administration will not object to long-term credits [to Russia] if they are made after the sale of American goods has been arranged,"[2] nevertheless, the Department of Commerce, on occasions, told inquirers that long-term credits to Russia are inadvisable. In May, 1929, for instance, it was engaged in spreading statements alleging financial distress in Russia, difficulties in meeting payments on German credits, and an impending credit collapse. The State Department tried to discourage American firms from going into Russia, and attempts were made by its minor officials to dissuade the General Electric Company from signing the $26,000,000 long-term credit contract.

[1] Frank B. Kellogg: *Foreign Relations,* Republican National Committee, Bulletin No. 5, 1928, p. 49.

[2] New York *Times,* December 1, 1928.

In May, 1927, Dr. Alfred P. Dennis, the Vice-Chairman of the American Tariff Commission, applied for a Soviet visa and obtained it, but did not make the trip owing to the State Department's fear that the presence of an American official on Soviet territory might constitute recognition of the Soviet regime. But in April, 1929, two specialists of the United States Department of Agriculture obtained State Department permission to investigate the principal alfalfa growing sections of Turkestan and continued to conduct investigations in Central Asia without, needless to say, thereby compelling Washington to exchange ambassadors with Moscow.

The change in the State Department's position was further illustrated by the treatment of the Soviet fliers who piloted the "Land of the Soviets," an airplane of Russian manufacture, safely over a perilous, uncharted course from Moscow, via Siberia and Alaska to the United States in October, 1929. Earlier, the State Department frowned on an American-Russian Chamber of Commerce invitation to Commander Samoilovitch and Pilot Chukhnovsky of the Soviet ice-breaker *Krassin* which had participated in the rescue of Nobile's Arctic expedition, and the men, fêted and honored in many European capitals, failed to come to America. But the "Land of the Soviets" received the enthusiastic and very valuable co-operation of the State Department, the Navy Department, the War Department, the U.S. Treasury, the Department of Labor, and the Department of Agriculture. It is indicative also of a new popular attitude that the fliers were warmly welcomed by the mayor, officials, and citizens of every American city where they landed.

Hundreds of American tourists had travelled to Russia in the past years, and they invariably brought back reports of a stable government and peaceful conditions. The Bolsheviks invited a study of the Soviet Union. Clinton Gilbert wrote early in 1929 in the New York *Evening Post* of a conversation between a Soviet official and a United States official in Washington. The Russian likened the United States to an oriental physician who is prevented, by the practice of seclusion, from examining a woman patient. He must therefore base his diagnosis on second-hand reports. But the physician, said the Soviet official, at least learns about his woman patient from her friends. "You learn about the Soviet Union mostly from persons who are unfriendly to her. You really ought to have a look at the Soviet Union. You would find her quite a beautiful woman."

Moscow even gave every facility to a commission of twelve from the Veterans of Foreign Wars of the United States, which went to northern Russia in the summer of 1929 to exhume the bodies of American soldiers who had fallen in the frozen north fighting against the Bolsheviks in 1918–9. The Soviet Government volunteered to give the American corpses military honors as their ship left the Leningrad Harbor. This, however, was rejected.

**THE HOOVER ADMINISTRATION** Secretary of State Stimson wrote to Matthew Woll, Vice-President of the American Federation of Labor, on April 16, 1929, stating that "no change is under contemplation in the policy of this Government with regard to recognition of the present regime in Russia." The improvement of Russian-American relations since Herbert Hoover took office on March 4, 1929, was merely incidental to the increase of the business of the Amtorg (the Soviet Trading Company in America) and to the pressure of American firms for better facilities.

Recognition would give confidence to many American business enterprises that hesitated to deal with a country like Russia in the absence of diplomatic and consular protection. The Soviet Union bought much more than it sold in the United States. To make up for this unfavorable trade balance, the Soviet State Bank proposed, early in 1928, to consign $5,000,000 in gold to banks in the United States. The Assay Office, however, refused to accept the gold when it reached New York. The Treasury Department had objected, and Soviet-American trade was accordingly obstructed by being compelled to cancel its adverse trade balance through indirect and complicated banking operations in Europe. Recognition would obviate such difficulties.

The State Department's ban on Soviet railway bonds in February, 1928, was yet another illustration. The Chase National Bank, the Amalgamated Bank, and the Bank of Italy in San Francisco had undertaken to make payment on the coupons and principal of the bonds of the 9 per cent $30,000,000 Soviet Railway loan of 1927, payable in dollars. These banks would not float the issue in the United States. They merely agreed to pay interest and to redeem the bonds from the deposits which the Soviet State Bank had made with them. Nevertheless, the State Department, acting on its own initiative, but responding to a protest from the New York Life Insurance Company and, presumably, similar organizations, wrote to the Amalgamated Bank on February 3 and to the other financial institutions involved, firmly requesting them to discontinue a practice which was not in accord with State Department policy. The banks felt that to refuse to honor the maturing bond coupons presented for payment against the account of one of their clients—the State Bank—when that client had instructed them to make payment, contravened accepted and traditional business practice in the capitalist world. It was, they maintained, the recognized function which a bank should perform for its correspondents.

The State Department, however, rejected the bank's viewpoint, and made it clear to the Chase and Amalgamated that its ruling against the Soviet bond operation must be binding upon them. An official in Moscow quoted by the Associated Press declared that Secretary Kellogg's action "served no purpose save harassing the steadily growing trade relations between Russia and the United States." But the State Department's fiat remained. Washington's attitude, however, did not deter the business man seeking orders. The Amtorg's turnover continued to grow.

**THE FORD CONTRACT** The largest Soviet contract with an American firm was signed by Henry Ford and Saul G. Bron, for the Amtorg, on May 31, 1929. Ford would design a plant for the Soviet Government at Nizhni-Novgorod capable of producing 100,000 automobiles annually. Ford would give the Bolsheviks all his patents. He would send engineers to Russia to help build the factory. In the four years after the conclusion of the contract, the Soviet would buy from Ford cars, trucks, and parts equivalent to the cost of 72,000 Ford autos and trucks —approximately $30,000,000. The Amtorg would pay Ford his own cost of production plus a 15 per cent profit. The contract, which ran for nine years, provided for only very short-term credits. The agreement stipulated that Ford would train Russian automobile engineers and mechanics. Sixty Soviet citizens occupied a large room in the very midst of Ford's Detroit plant, studying and making designs.

The Ford agreement, like the agreement of October, 1928, with the International General Electric Company, would, in the coming years, swell the volume of American exports to Russia, even beyond its present unprecedented limits.

**SOVIET-AMERICAN TRADE** "Soviet-American trade" for the fiscal year ending September 30, 1929, Mr. Bron stated in *The Economic Review of the Soviet Union* (New York, October 1, 1929), "reached, according to preliminary data, the record total of $149,000,000 as against $113,000,000 in the previous year and $48,000,000 in 1913." Of the $149,000,000, $109,000,000 represented Soviet purchases in the United States.

But this was not the full extent of Russian-American trade. American firms bought oil and other Soviet products for distribution outside the confines of the United States, whereas many Russian goods brought to America could be purchased indirectly and are therefore missing from the record.

A new feature of American-Russian business was an arrangement whereby American companies gave of their experience, patents, and engineers to assist in the economic upbuilding of the Scviet state. On October 1, 1929, thirty agreements for such technical assistance had been signed. Among the companies were Du Pont de Nemours, Ford, General Electric, Radio Corporation of America, Hugh L. Cooper for constructing the Dnieperstroi Dam, Stuart, James and Cooke for sinking coal mines, Albert Kahn who designed the Stalingrad plant with an annual output of 40,000 tractors, and the Austin Construction Company of Cleveland.

# 31

# THE RESUMPTION OF ANGLO-SOVIET RELATIONS

AS LONG AS the Baldwin-Chamberlain Conservative Cabinet remained in power in England, no improvement in Anglo-Soviet relations was expected. After Litvinov's unsuccessful attempt in December, 1927, to bridge the gap by his interview with Sir Austen in Geneva, Moscow seemed discouraged and undertook no further measures. Downing Street permitted the situation to remain unchanged.

Meanwhile, the Soviet Government had received credits in Germany, and credits and a favorable reception from American business. In consequence of these circumstances, and partly reacting to the ill-will of the Baldwin Government, Moscow diverted much of its foreign trade from Great Britain.

**NEGOTIATIONS WITH URQUHART** In September, 1929, Mr. Leslie Urquhart, encouraged by a Soviet announcement on concessions, applied to Piatakov, then in Paris but subsequently appointed president of the Moscow State Bank, for a concession to some of his properties in Siberia. After preliminary conversations, Urquhart wrote a lengthy letter on October 15, outlining his terms and wishes to Piatakov. Less ambitious than the concession signed by Krassin and Urquhart on September 9, 1922, Urquhart nevertheless insisted on receiving £2,000,000 from the Soviet Government as compensation for damages suffered. He would invest that sum in his concession. He would also attract W. A. Harriman and the Guggenheim copper interests in America. Apropos of this offer, Litvinov recalled to the writer that the Soviet concession policy aimed to attract foreign capital into the country and not to finance foreign concessionaires with Russian Government funds. But the greatest difficulty, apart from the problem of currency exchange rates, was the disinclination of the Bolsheviks to pay compensation and thus establish a precedent.

The Soviets, however, did not reject Urquhart's offer, and in January, 1929, one of his representatives visited Moscow to negotiate with the Chief Concessions Committee. Details of operation, and questions of currency were discussed. But the Russians permitted matters to lag, and when Urquhart sent a telegram to Ksandrov of the Concessions Committee demanding a categorical statement of the Government's intention, Ksandrov did not even reply. Here the incident ended.

**THE BRITISH OIL DEAL** On the other hand, Soviet negotiations with Anglo-Saxon oil trusts reached a successful issue. The petroleum market of the United Kingdom is controlled by the Anglo-American Oil Company, an offshoot of the Standard Oil of New Jersey, the Royal Dutch-Shell, and the Anglo-Persian. But the Russian Oil Products, Ltd. (R.O.P.), caused these three giants considerable annoyance by underselling and by forcing them to pay retail distributors a "loyalty bonus" of one penny per gallon as an inducement not to sell Soviet oil. The Anglo-American is said to have lost $12,000,000 in 1928 on account of these conditions. The Anglo-Persian lost more, while Deterding of the Shell who distributed Anglo-Persian products on commission, had a large part of his deficit covered by the Anglo-Persian, in other words, by the British Government, and could therefore afford to continue longest the struggle against "stolen" Russian petrol.

Nevertheless, the Anglo-American and the Anglo-Persian wished to make peace with the Russians, and the combine of the three big trusts entered into discussions with the Soviet Naphtha Syndicate. The combine, however, made an agreement with Moscow conditional on the granting of a 5 per cent commercial discount which they could use as they saw fit. This was understood to be an attempt to win compensation in veiled form from the Bolsheviks.

Moscow rejected the demand. In December, 1928, accordingly, the negotiations broke down, but within a few weeks they were renewed by the Anglo-American, on behalf of the combine, after assurances had been given by the trusts that requests for compensation, direct or indirect, would not be presented. Discussions now proceeded smoothly, and in February, 1929, a contract was signed in London for the sale of several hundred thousand tons of Soviet oil to the combine. The agreement ran for three years and involved approximately $25,000,000. It also provided for supplementary sales.

The Naphtha Syndicate's agreement with the combine eliminated Deterding's claim to compensation, and strengthened Soviet trade with Great Britain.

**THE BRITISH DELEGATION TO RUSSIA** British business with Russia nevertheless lagged, and the trade balance continued highly unfavorable to England. With a view to correcting this situation, British interests organized a large delegation to visit Russia in the spring of 1929. They were welcomed warmly, and shown around wherever they wished to go. But they received very few orders. On April 5, G. L. Piatakov, the President of the State Bank, told the delegation why. Soviet purchases in Great Britain, he said, fell from 23,500,000 pounds sterling in 1924–5, to 5,800,000 pounds sterling in 1927–8. The Soviet Union, he added, bought 147,000,000 rubles' worth of machinery abroad in 1926–7 and 220,000,000 rubles the following year. But in the same period, imports of machinery from England, fell from 16,000,000 to 10,000,000 rubles. Piatakov indicated that this was the deliberate policy of the Soviet Government. If relations with Great Britain were not resumed, he stated frankly, Soviet imports from Great Britain "will be limited to just the bare essentials." But if an agreement was reached, "we shall without any difficulty be able to place orders in England amounting to 150,000,000 pounds sterling."

**THE RESUMPTION OF RELATIONS** When MacDonald's second Labor Cabinet came to power on June 7, 1929, the Bolsheviks thought they could expect immediate and unconditional resumption of diplomatic relations. They miscalculated.

Something important had altered in England since 1924.

Continued unemployment, unrelieved by the small immigration trickle to Canada and Australia, demoralized the labor market and undermined Labor's bargaining position. The membership of Trade Unions fell appreciably. During 1929 a widespread movement asserted itself among industrialists to cut wages. This, Labor economists argued, did not reflect the ill-will of the employer. It was more his reaction to the necessity of lowering the earning standards of the British working class in order to enable England to compete with Europe and Japan.

At the same time, the ideologists of British Labor moved to the Right, and men of the type of G. D. H. Cole modified their programme to conform to changed economic possibilities. Nationalization ceased to be a popular slogan.

Under these circumstances, the Left wing of the Labor movement who had championed the cause of friendship with Russia in 1924 no longer enjoyed the influence of a former day.

Nor was any sympathy or attraction for Russia felt in other than proletarian ranks. MacDonald did not have to reckon with any powerful popular demand for better relations with the Soviet Union. Under the heading of "Russia," the Labor Party program for the General Election of May 31, 1929,[1] declared that "A Labor Government . . . would at once take steps to establish diplomatic and commercial relations with it [the Russian Government], would settle by treaty or otherwise any outstanding differences, and would make every effort to encourage a revival of trade with Soviet Russia."

This was reiterated as an election pledge by Arthur Henderson in a broadcast speech on April 11. Moscow expected therefore that relations would be resumed a few days after MacDonald took office. Instead, he promised the Conservative Opposition that he would take no step without the previous approval of Parliament. Also, in reply to a Conservative question, he stated that he would stand by his policy as laid down in previous dispatches —which was taken to mean his note to Moscow in October, 1924, on the so-called "Zinoviev" letter. Both these promises were regarded as mistakes by many Laborites, and pressure was exerted during the summer of 1929

[1] *Labour and the Nation.* Revised Edition. Published by the Labor Party. London, 1929.

to invite the Russians before Parliament re-convened in November.

**MOSCOW CLAIMS A VICTORY** On July 17, accordingly, Henderson sent a note to Moscow through the Norwegian legation, asking that a Soviet representative meet him in London to discuss the procedure of a resumption of relations. Dovgalevsky, the Soviet ambassador in Paris, made his appearance in Downing Street on July 29. Their differences, it is said, were due to lack of a common language well-understood by both. But the Soviets' answer to Henderson's invitation had "emphasized," as Litvinov said in a published statement on October 4, "that preliminary negotiations must be restricted exclusively to questions of procedure, avoiding the substance of the controversial questions."[2] Henderson nevertheless raised controversial questions of debts and propaganda, the Bolsheviks charged. Henderson denied this.

The preliminary negotiations therefore proved abortive. Shortly afterward, Litvinov told the writer that they would maintain their stand even if it meant no relations with England during the entire term of office of the MacDonald Cabinet.

With the Russians adamant, the British gave way, and Henderson made a conciliatory offer to Moscow in a speech at Geneva which Litvinov acknowledged in an equally satisfactory statement. Notes were exchanged, Dovgalevsky returned to London, and on October 3 they signed a Protocol providing for the resumption of relations.[3] It included highly important provisions regarding future negotiations.

It accepted, as a basis for the forthcoming discussions, the treaties signed by MacDonald and Rakovsky in August, 1924, and subsequently rejected by the Baldwin-Chamberlain Cabinet—in other words, a vindication of Labor and Russia, and a blow to the Tories. After Parliament approved the resumption of relations, and after ambassadors had been exchanged—this too, the Bolsheviks regarded as a victory and an improvement on the 1924 exchange of chargé d'affaires—both states would define their attitude to the treaties of 1924. Once again it became necessary for the MacDonald Government to de-

[2] *Bulletin of International News*. London, October 11, 1929, p. 11.
[3] *Ibid.*, pp. 9–10.

clare its position on a State guarantee of a loan to the Soviets, or to arrange that a loan be somehow secured for Moscow, otherwise, and in view of Moscow's principle of "We pay if you lend," the problem debts remained insoluble. London would also have to define its attitude on Russian war debts and counter-claims, while the Soviet Government would have to say whether it would pay compensation to former foreign owners of nationalized property, or otherwise meet their claims.

**PROPAGANDA** The propaganda clause of the treaty of 1924 was immediately and finally accepted as going into effect on the exchange of ambassadors. Propaganda, therefore, should not obstruct the course of the future conference. The British Communist Party was laughably small, and had lost members despite widespread unemployment and labor discontent. The Labor Party and the trade unions no longer feared it.

The propaganda clause accepted by Henderson and Dovgalevsky was extremely far-reaching. According to one version, it was hastily adopted by A. A. Joffe and incorporated into Article 16 of the treaty before the Bolsheviks had offered many amendments. It read:

> The contracting parties solemnly affirm their desire and intention to live in peace and amity with each other, scrupulously to respect the undoubted right of a State to order its own life within its own jurisdiction in its own way, to refrain and to restrain all persons and organizations under their direct or indirect control, including organizations in receipt of any financial assistance from them, from any act overt or covert liable in any way whatsoever to endanger the tranquillity or prosperity of any part of the territory of the British Empire or the Union of Soviet Socialist Republics or intended to embitter the relations of the British Empire or the Union with their neighbors or any other countries.

This clause might mean much, and it might mean little.

The Anglo-Soviet Conference of 1930 faced greater difficulties than the negotiations of 1924. The subjects under examination would be the same. But the parties were five years older. The Bolsheviks set less store on an agreement than they did during MacDonald's first term of office. They felt stronger and more independent. They thought England had less to offer than the United States. "There is no disposition here," wired the *Manchester*

*Guardian's* Moscow correspondent on August 23, 1929, "to pay an exorbitant price for settlement" with Great Britain.

> One sometimes encounters a view, not yet predominant but stronger than it was five years ago, that economically the Soviet Union might find it more advantageous to continue industrial expansion with its own resources, receiving, as now, limited foreign credits but undertaking no obligations regarding the payment of pre-war debts and damage claims. This tendency is strengthened, the correspondent added, by the extremely rapid rate of Soviet industrial development. . . .

British coolness for a settlement was not to be outdone by Soviet indifference, yet these were not indispensable elements of agreement. As it was more difficult for Russia and England to agree in 1924 than before 1917, so it would be even more difficult in 1930 than in 1924.

## CONCLUSION

# PROBLEMS OF A REVOLUTIONARY FOREIGN POLICY

THE BOLSHEVIKS undertook changes in the economic structure of the Soviet Union. The agricultural system, basing itself on a poor, backward peasantry, held out a passive threat of crushing Communism by its inertia, its weight, and its opposition to reform. To destroy its negative political influence, the Soviet Government cast the torch of class war into the village, raising up the poor against the rich muzhiks. To undermine the power the village exercised as food purveyor of the city, the Bolsheviks brought the city into the country by mechanizing agriculture, organizing it co-operatively, and establishing State farms to yield the Government a bread surplus for feeding the town populations and for export. These processes affected intimately and daily the lives of 120,000,000 peasants and 25,000,000 peasant households. All Russia was rocking in the gigantic, dramatic struggle to stir, arouse, reform, improve, modernize, and weaken that most unprogressive of European economic units—the Russian village.

Simultaneously, and consequently, the Bolsheviks were faced with the task of rapid, large-scale industrialization. The Bolsheviks planned in a decade, to turn Russia upside down and inside out industrially. The Soviet Union had to catch up with Europe and then outdistance her. Moscow even aspired to run a race with America.

More goods could be had from foreign countries. No peasant philosopher, no anti-Bolshevik, however fanatic, would argue that Russia should become an agricultural colony of the industrialized West, and sell her grain for imported articles of consumption. Some industrialization stood on the programme of all factions. But the Bolsheviks represented the policy of greatest haste because they believed that in the present age of bitter competition by the Great Powers for new world markets, a foothold in the Soviet Union for one or several of them would prevent that measure of industrialization which conditions in Russia then demanded. The Soviet Government's tactics of using the monopoly of foreign trade strictly to limit imports of articles of consumption did work hardships on the population. But the opposite policy would have curtailed employment in the city without appreciably increasing employment in the villages. Industrialization made the cities a bigger, richer customer of the village. It was somewhat like the American idea of paying higher salaries so that the worker may be able to purchase more goods. The Russian village was, willy-nilly, paying the wage which would create a better Soviet market for its own output.

Mechanization of the village, plus industrialization of the cities, together with the accompanying social and cultural changes, absorbed the energies of the Bolsheviks and the Russian people. The observer noted a mounting disinterestedness in foreign affairs and foreign revolutionary possibilities.

In the Trotzky-Stalin party controversy, Trotzky contended that socialism could not be built in one country and that so backward a country as Russia. Stalin defended the contrary view. Stalin won. The old notion that the Soviet Government could neither persist nor succeed without revolutions in other lands is considered obsolete. Moscow then submitted the proposition that the capitalist and Communist worlds could live side by side in peaceful coexistence. Instead of concentrating energies on the overthrow of world capitalism, the Bolsheviks were bent on making good themselves.

The policy of industrialization created difficulties for Moscow in the realm of foreign affairs. Industrialization necessitated the importation of machines and mechanical equipment on long-term credit. A manufacturer can open short-term credits, but for long-term credits he must apply to the banks. In Germany, the banks disposed of very limited long-term credit. In England and America, the banks refused to grant long-term credits. Large American companies were either so rich or so intimately related to banks that they could without inconvenience, keep Soviet bills in their portfolios for years without discounting them. The same rarely applied to other countries, however.

Bolshevik insistence on industrialization together with the disappearance of grain exports, thus limited the growth of Russia's foreign trade and therefore the interest of the foreign business world.

Theoretically, a country in the process of industrialization should be as good a customer as an agricultural country. Whether the Bolsheviks bought from England textile-making machines or textiles, the turnover and the profit might be equally large. And yet, though this should apply generally, Britain's industry was best organized to export textiles, woolens, coal, ships, etc., and if Russia produced these herself, England lost. American industry, on the other hand, was developed later than England's and along different lines, and was better equipped to sell large quantities of machines than large quantities of articles for direct consumption. America's trade policy towards the Soviet Union was therefore unlike England's, and their political attitudes were unlike too.

For a number or years, and until 1925 approximately, German business circles also opposed Soviet industrialization and the monopoly of foreign trade which aided it. But the rationalization of German industry after the Dawes Plan and the reorganization of the German machine industry effected a change of attitude. Yet no one wished to see a strongly mechanized Russia which would compete for Germany's Asiatic and Baltic markets.

Industrialization also discouraged an active concession policy. Although the Soviet Government had from time to time announced more liberal intentions in the granting of concessions, the fact that domestic forces and funds were increasing industrial output tended to obviate the necessity of concessions. As long, for instance, as Baku and Grosni did not work well, Moscow weighed the advisability of inviting foreign oil companies to accept concessions. Now that is inconceivable.

Industrialization, accordingly, had the direct and indirect effect of limiting the number of foreign concessionaires and damping the interest of foreign traders. The Soviet political system likewise discouraged investors and lenders. The Azerbaijan Oil Trust or the Donetz Coal Trust or the Moscow Municipality was a tremendously rich, profit-earning, solvent business enterprise which, if it operated in any other country, could easily borrow in London, New York, Amsterdam, etc. But in case of default, bankruptcy or delinquency, no British or American or Dutch bank could attach the property of these undertakings in Gaku, Shakhti or Moscow. The property was Government property, and Communists would never permit its alienation by foreign capitalists.

The position of the Soviet Government as a whole presents a parallel difficulty. When Poland borrowed money from international banks, she guaranteed that loan by the income from customs, railways, and certain state monopolies. She employed Mr. Charles Dewey as the virtual economic dictator of the country. Similar guarantees were given and financial advisers accepted by Austria and Hungary. But Moscow would not pawn State-owned enterprises, nor could a foreign capitalist be invited to dictate the terms of Bolshevik economic construction and management.

Soviet failure to pay Czarist debts undoubtedly played an important role in the embargo placed on the Soviet Union by most foreign banks. Yet a probably greater factor was the impossibility of obtaining a real guarantee for loans to the Soviet Union. The immediate and more obvious causes were simpler. In the United States, banks seek State Department approval for foreign loans, and, in the absence of diplomatic recognition, the State Department withholds such approval. In England, political friction, and the disinclination to stimulate Soviet industrialization, served as obstructive influences. The banks of other countries frequently attune their activities too closely to those of the Anglo-Saxon financial world to step in where Wall Street and the City have imposed a boycott.

Accordingly, neither foreign investment, nor concession, nor trade possibilities affected Soviet foreign affairs decisively or favorably. Investments and concessions played no positive role at all in determining the policies of Government to the Soviet Union, while trade, however important, was too limited as yet to weigh very heavily in the balance of all nations.

The Soviet Government had also no wide political advantages to offer foreign countries. If Moscow was prepared to throw its weight to one and against another group of Powers, both would have courted Bolshevik goodwill. Russia had an army and an important geographical position, and her political voice would have been heard if she had cared to sell her support and friendship for the usual diplomatic quid pro quo. The Czarist Government approved of Italy's designs in Northern Africa, and in return Italy promised to smile on St. Petersburg's strivings toward Constantinople. More recent years witnessed similar gives and takes, but the Soviet Union refused to participate in them. And when a nation has no price, it ceases to be quoted on the world political bourse. Its name is not on the diplomatic Rialto. Bolshevism's principle of no entangling alliances weakened the Soviet foreign position.

The United States, for instance, was not so rich as to scorn intimate business dealings with the Soviet Union, but it was too rich to go far out of its political course to win that trade. If, however, Russia had signified a willingness to back American policy in China or in the Far East generally, diplomatic relations with Moscow might have become more attractive to Washington. Yet, although both America and Soviet Russia favored the unification of China, Russia's approach and principles, and her conception of the social basis of that unification, were so different from America's that the two could not walk together.

This Soviet aloofness largely explained Soviet isolation. Vis-à-vis Germany, however, as well as Lithuania, Turkey, Persia, and Afghanistan, Moscow pursued an active policy of co-operation. Moscow could have had alliances with one or more of these countries. It rejected them. Nevertheless, it was ready to buttress their international positions. "Our policy is to support the feeble," Chicherin said to the writer. If France became weaker than Germany there might be a readjustment of Soviet sympathies. This seemed a peculiarly inverted and impractical way of conducting foreign policy. Yet the chief bond between the Soviets and Germany was Germany's subjection to the Versailles system and to reparations. Between France and Germany, the Bolsheviks chose defeated Germany as political partner. Between Italy and Turkey, their choice was Turkey. Between Poland and Lithuania, it was little Lithuania. Such tactics were often a liability to Soviet foreign relations.

In relation to Turkey, Persia, Afghanistan, and, between

1924 and 1927, Kuomintang China, the Soviet Union was moved by its bias for revolutionary governments. Moscow wished to see these countries united, and strong enough to resist the efforts of other Powers to penetrate and dominate them and, perhaps, use them as spring-boards for attacks against Russia. In the case of Persia, the Bolsheviks might easily have reverted to the Czarist arrangement with England of spheres of influence. But such a policy was unthinkable.

The Soviet Union maintained truly warm relations with these Asiatic nationalist-revolutionary countries and with Germany and Lithuania. If any Power was to protect Soviet interests in some country where Russia was not represented or to act as mediator or messenger between any Power and the Bolsheviks, Moscow preferred Germany or Turkey, or a Scandinavian nation.

Vanquished and puny and anti-imperialist nations turned to Russia for comfort. This was a trump which the Bolsheviks could sell to the big Powers. Indirect bids had indeed been made, and direct bids too. Invariably Moscow said "No."

All these internal and external factors frequently made Soviet foreign policy immediately and, for practical purposes, fruitless. When Moscow negotiated its treaty of January, 1925, with Japan, it recognized the validity of the Portsmouth Treaty which ended the Russo-Japanese War; declaring, however, that this must not be taken to signify approval of Japanese action in Korea. Such championing of the Korean cause irritated Tokyo and could yield the Soviets no possible compensation.

Communist propaganda was another liability. Bolsheviks did not believe in assassination or similar terrorist pinpricks as methods of precipitating revolution. But they argued that capitalism, like feudalism, must outlive its usefulness, and that then it would be succeeded by Communism. Bolsheviks are not fatalists. Organization of proletarian forces and education of the masses were on their program. Such experience and training would, they contended, serve useful purposes when objective economic and political conditions in a given country made revolution imminent. The proletarian revolution was inevitable, the Russians argued; and they eagerly noted every landmark and milestone on the road to the goal. The road seemed to be lengthening, however. Bolsheviks were too realistic not to see that Western capitalism had stabilized itself.

Capitalistic stabilization alone would have compelled a change of tactics. But Soviet stabilization had accompanied capitalist stabilization. In the early years of the Bolshevik regime, all Bolsheviks accepted the thesis that the Russian revolution could not be successful unless a world revolution or at least a revolution in some important countries came to its support. Communism in Russia was in its infancy while the prospects of revolution in Europe were not altogether nil. By 1929, on the other hand, the Soviet Government was stronger, its economic position vastly improved, and the possibilities of greater success along the road to socialism decidedly encouraging to the Bolsheviks. If socialism could be built in one country by concentrating on its problems, the emphasis on world revolution naturally diminished especially as foreign conditions did not warrant sanguine hopes for the near future. It was significant, therefore, that Communists commenced to relate their prophecies of world revolution to the next world war. To be sure, they said the revolution might come first. Yet more and more spokesmen connected the international proletarian upheaval with an international military struggle. As Moscow, in its domestic policy, took a sharper course towards socialism, accordingly, the Powers noted a diminuendo of interest in foreign revolutionary issues. It would be instructive, if it were generally known how irritating Comintern activities and methods were to some of the persons responsible for Soviet diplomacy.

Europe generally admitted that a new world war would bring revolution to Eastern Europe and as far, at least, as Vienna. This fear of revolution undoubtedly tended to check militarist eagerness in some Western countries and could, in time of crisis, postpone the great struggle. The example and moral encouragement to revolution personified by the Soviet Union were thus at least a negative factor for world peace.

Somewhat of a paradox intervened, yet like many paradoxes, this one was quite natural. The workers of Europe were more friendly to the Workers' State in Russia when Bolshevism was weak than later when it was stronger. Be tween 1918 and 1920 foreign proletarian help, to which Lenin, Chicherin, and other Russians repeatedly appealed, contributed toward Soviet victory in the Civil War. But as

Bolshevism registered economic victories on the peacetime internal front, its foreign trade union friends cooled. Especially in England, they resented outside interference, refusing to believe that internationalism was becoming a dominating feature of modern capitalism, and that more outside interest in local British labor issues might, as the Bolsheviks contended, prevent German miners or American miners from ruining the chances of success of a British strike. The Bolsheviks asserted that more outside interference in national labor problems would strengthen national labor forces. They therefore subjected Social Democratic and Labor parties in bourgeois countries to bitter, unbridled criticism which—since these parties frequently participated in bourgeois Cabinets—created antagonism and complicated the task of Soviet diplomats.

The Bolsheviks tried to win Labor's friendship by inviting foreign workers to visit the Soviet Union and study its economic gains and social innovations. The results were varied. When even this weapon was blunted, it was realized to what extent Soviet diplomacy had no teeth. Moscow disposed of very few means of putting pressure on foreign countries in an international issue. The Russians were too intent on their internal problems and too dependent on peace to be able to threaten military aggression or actually to undertake it. Everybody knew that Moscow would avoid war at all costs, and that Moscow had few friends in Europe.

The Soviets could transfer their transit trade from Estonia to Latvia or vice versa in order to press their will on their small neighbors. In the Ruhr crisis, the passive threat of moving the Red Army paralyzed Polish action against Germany. In the East, Russia's policy toward nationalities and her social reforms produced a bond with the broad masses which reactionaries were unable to sever. Lithuania appreciated Soviet non-recognition of Polish rule in Vilna. Rumania sat uneasily in Bessarabia and the Balkans as long as Moscow refused to sanction the occupation of Bessarabia. Germany wanted Russian trade, and realized that friendship with Moscow strengthened her hand against the Western Powers. "The stronger our Russian partner," a German ambassador said to the writer, "the better we like it."

These factors, and the trade which stimulated a more

benevolent attitude in some American, British and other business spheres but could not seriously affect diplomatic policy, completed the list of chief influences which might fortify the Soviet Union's foreign political position.

A government so different, and so distasteful to capitalist Powers, as the Soviet Government, could not expect to achieve outstanding success in its foreign relations. Sometimes naïve Communists would marvel that Moscow had any foreign relations at all. If bourgeois nations were united among themselves, and if they attached less importance to material gain and more to principles, the Bolsheviks would probably be as isolated as they were in 1919 when all the world combined to overthrow them. The fundamental friction between non-Communist States prevented their combination against a Communist State, and Moscow sat back in safety and generally in inactivity with a diabolical smile on its face, thinking how sad it would be if the others could reach an agreement. Moscow did not divide its enemies. They were divided by natural causes. But Moscow encouraged and thrived on their conflicts.

Philip Kerr,[1] writing in the Conservative London *Observer* of September 22, 1929, lists three ruling influences in modern times: scientific invention, nationalism, and

> The third fact in the modern world is that the disciples of Karl Marx have succeeded in creating and maintaining for twelve years a state of 150,000,000 people on a Communist basis, and that there are no signs of an impending dissolution of the Soviet state . . . something has happened in Russia which is going to have just as much effect on the world in the long run as the French Revolution a century and a quarter ago. For Russia has dethroned usury from the altar on which it now stands in Western civilization, has rendered it almost impossible for anyone to live, or at least live comfortably, except by the fruit of his own work, and has made the huge engine of economic production and distribution function for the general good and not for private profit.

The Bolsheviks agreed that the revolution could not be ignored. But they submitted that the attention it provoked must be characterized by hostility rather than friendship. With the increasing suppression of private capitalism in the Soviet Union and the gradual enthronement of socialism, foreign antagonism to the Soviets could be expected

[1] Lord Lothian, later British Ambassador in Washington.

to grow. In fact, the Russians feared that the success of their Five-Year Plan of economic construction could so terrify the capitalist world as to make a foreign attack inevitable. There was perhaps more logic than realism in this approach. Yet, as the years went by, the Bolsheviks looked to the outside world less for aid and more for passive enmity or even violent obstruction.

# APPENDIX

(*Translated from the French original.*)

## CONVENTION BETWEEN FRANCE AND ENGLAND ON THE SUBJECT OF ACTIVITY IN SOUTHERN RUSSIA

"1. The activity directed by France is to be developed north of the Black Sea (against the enemy).

"The activity directed by England is to be developed southeast of the Black Sea (against the Turks).

"2. Whereas General Alexeev at Novo-Cherkask has proposed the execution of a programme envisaging the organization of an army intended to operate against the enemy, and whereas France has adopted that programme and allocated a credit of one hundred millions for this purpose and made provision for the organization of inter-Allied control, the execution of the programme shall be continued until new arrangements are made in concert with England.

"3. With this reservation, the zones of influences assigned to each government shall be as follows:

"The English zone: the Cossack territories, the territory of the Caucasus, Armenia, Georgia, Kurdistan.

"The French zone: Bessarabia, the Ukraine, the Crimea.

"4. The expenses shall be pooled and regulated by a centralizing inter-Allied organ."

This convention was negotiated by Lord Milner and Clemenceau, and signed in Paris on December 23, 1917.

# INDEX

LOUIS FISCHER was born in Philadelphia, Pennsylvania, February 29, 1896, where he graduated from the Philadelphia School of Pedagogy in 1916. For the year 1916–17 he taught in the public schools in Philadelphia. He began his career in journalism in 1921 as a contributor from Berlin to the New York *Evening Post*. His first trip to the Soviet Union was made in 1922. Since then he has specialized in Russian affairs, Far East and eastern-European politics, traveled extensively, and written a variety of studies. Among these are *Gandhi and Stalin* (1947) and *Russia Revisited* (1957). His newspaper columns have appeared in publications throughout the United States, Europe, and Asia. For the year 1959–60, Mr. Fischer has been a member of the School of Historical Studies at the Institute for Advanced Study in Princeton, New Jersey. He is married and the father of two sons. *The Soviets in World Affairs* was originally published in 1930.

THE TEXT of this book is set on the Linotype in a face called TIMES ROMAN, designed by Stanley Morison for *The Times* (London), and first introduced by that newspaper in 1932. The book was composed, printed and bound by The Colonial Press Inc., Clinton, Massachusetts. Cover design by CARL SMITH.

# VINTAGE RUSSIAN LIBRARY

*V-702* SIMMONS, ERNEST J. *Leo Tolstoy,* Volume II
*V-744* SIMMONS, ERNEST J. *Alexander Pushkin*
*V-346* TERTZ, ABRAM *The Makepiece Experiment*
*V-750* TERTZ, ABRAM *The Trial Begins* and *On Social Realism*
*V-713* TOLSTOY, LEO *The Kreutzer Sonata,* a novel
*V-749* TROTSKY, LEON *Basic Writings of Trotsky*
*V-711* TURGENEV, IVAN *The Vintage Turgenev*
Volume I: *Smoke, Fathers and Sons, First Love*
*V-712* TURGENEV, IVAN Volume II: *On the Eve, Rudin, A Quiet Spot, Diary of a Superfluous Man*
*V-724* WALLACE, SIR D. M. *Russia:* On the Eve of War and Revolution
*V-729* WEIDLÉ, W. *Russia: Absent & Present*
*V-751* ZOSHCHENKO, MIKHAIL *Nervous People* and Other Stories

## VINTAGE HISTORY—WORLD

*V-286* ARIES, PHILIPPE *Centuries of Childhood*
*V-59* BEAUFRE, GEN. ANDRÉ *NATO and Europe*
*V-44* BRINTON, CRANE *The Anatomy of Revolution*
*V-250* BURCKHARDT, C. J. *Richelieu: His Rise to Power*
*V-393* BURCKHARDT, JACOB *The Age of Constantine the Great*
*V-391* CARR, E. H. *What Is History?*
*V-67* CURTIUS, ERNST R. *The Civilization of France*
*V-746* DEUTSCHER, ISAAC *The Prophet Armed*
*V-747* DEUTSCHER, ISAAC *The Prophet Unarmed*
*V-748* DEUTSCHER, ISAAC *The Prophet Outcast*
*V-707* FISCHER, LOUIS *Soviets in World Affairs*
*V-277* GAY, PETER *Voltaire's Politics*
*V-114* HAUSER, ARNOLD *The Social History of Art* through V-117 (Four Volumes)
*V-201* HUGHES, H. STUART *Consciousness and Society*
*V-50* KELLY, AMY *Eleanor of Aquitaine and the Four Kings*
*V-728* KLYUCHEVSKY, V. *Peter the Great*
*V-246* KNOWLES, DAVID *Evolution of Medieval Thought*
*V-83* KRONENBERGER, LOUIS *Kings and Desperate Men*
*V-287* LA SOUCHÈRE, ÉLÉNA DE *An Explanation of Spain*
*V-43* LEFEBVRE, GEORGES *The Coming of the French Revolution*
*V-364* LEFEBVRE, GEORGES *The Directory*
*V-343* LEFEBVRE, GEORGES *The Thermidorians*
*V-92* MATTINGLY, GARRETT *Catherine of Aragon*
*V-703* MOSELY, PHILIP E. *The Kremlin and World Politics:* Studies in Soviet Policy and Action
*V-733* PARES, SIR BERNARD *The Fall of the Russian Monarchy*
*V-285* PARKES, HENRY B. *Gods and Men*
*V-719* REED, JOHN *Ten Days That Shook the World*
*V-176* SCHAPIRO, LEONARD *Government and Politics of the Soviet Union* (Revised Edition)
*V-375* SCHURMANN & SCHELL (eds.) *The China Reader: Imperial China,* I
*V-376* SCHURMANN & SCHELL (eds.) *The China Reader: Republican China,* II
*V-377* SCHURMANN & SCHELL (eds.) *The China Reader: Communist China,* III
*V-312* TANNENBAUM, FRANK *Ten Keys to Latin America*
*V-322* THOMPSON, E. P. *The Making of the English Working Class*
*V-749* TROTSKY, LEON *Basic Writings of Trotsky*
*V-724* WALLACE, SIR D. M. *Russia:* On the Eve of War and Revolution
*V-206* WALLERSTEIN, IMMANUEL *Africa: The Politics of Independence*
*V-729* WEIDLÉ, W. *Russia:* Absent and Present
*V-122* WILENSKI, R. H. *Modern French Painters,* Volume I (1863-1903)
*V-123* WILENSKI, R. H. *Modern French Painters,* Volume II (1904-1938)
*V-106* WINSTON, RICHARD *Charlemagne:* From the Hammer to the Cross

# VINTAGE POLITICAL SCIENCE AND SOCIAL CRITICISM

V-382 FRANKLIN & STARR (eds.) *The Negro in 20th Century America*
V-224 FREYRE, GILBERTO *New World in the Tropics*
V-368 FRIEDENBERG, EDGAR Z. *Coming of Age in America*
V-378 FULBRIGHT, J. WILLIAM *The Arrogance of Power*
V-264 FULBRIGHT, J. WILLIAM *Old Myths and New Realities* and Other Commentaries
V-354 FULBRIGHT, J. WILLIAM (intro.) *The Vietnam Hearings*
V-328 GALENSON, WALTER *A Primer on Employment & Wages*
V-277 GAY, PETER *Voltaire's Politics*
V-406 GETTLEMAN & MERMELSTEIN *The Great Society Reader: The Failure of American Liberalism*
V-174 GOODMAN, P. & P. *Communitas*
V-325 GOODMAN, PAUL *Compulsory Mis-education* and *The Community of Scholars*
V-32 GOODMAN, PAUL *Growing Up Absurd*
V-247 GOODMAN, PAUL *Utopian Essays and Practical Proposals*
V-357 GOODWIN, RICHARD N. *Triumph or Tragedy:* Reflections on Vietnam
V-248 GRUNEBAUM, G. E., VON *Modern Islam:* The Search for Cultural Identity
V-389 HAMILTON, WALTON *The Politics of Industry*
V-69 HAND, LEARNED *The Spirit of Liberty*
V-319 HART, H. L. A. *Law, Liberty and Morality*
V-283 HENRY, JULES *Culture Against Man*
V-95 HOFSTADTER, RICHARD *The Age of Reform*
V-9 HOFSTADTER, RICHARD *The American Political Tradition*
V-317 HOFSTADTER, RICHARD *Anti-Intellectualism in American Life*
V-385 HOFSTADTER, RICHARD *Paranoid Style in American Politics*
V-749 HOWE, IRVING (ed.) *Basic Writings of Trotsky*
V-201 HUGHES, H. STUART *Consciousness and Society*
V-241 JACOBS, JANE *Death & Life of Great American Cities*
V-332 JACOBS & LANDAU (eds.) *The New Radicals*
V-369 KAUFMANN, WALTER (ed.) *The Birth of Tragedy and The Case of Wagner*
V-401 KAUFMANN, WALTER (ed.) *On the Genealogy of Morals and Ecce Homo*
V-337 KAUFMANN, WALTER (tr.) *Beyond Good and Evil*
V-361 KOMAROVSKY, MIRRA *Blue-Collar Marriage*
V-341 KIMBALL & MCCLELLAN *Education and the New America*
V-327 LACOUTURE, JEAN *Vietnam: Between Two Truces*
V-367 LASCH, CHRISTOPHER *The New Radicalism in America*
V-399 LASKI, HAROLD J. (ed.) *Harold J. Laski on The Communist Manifesto*
V-287 LA SOUCHÈRE, ÉLÉNA DE *An Explanation of Spain*
V-280 LEWIS, OSCAR *The Children of Sánchez*
V-370 LEWIS, OSCAR *Pedro Martínez*
V-284 LEWIS, OSCAR *Village Life in Northern India*
V-392 LICHTHEIM, GEORGE *The Concept of Ideology and Other Essays*
V-384 LINDESMITH, ALFRED *The Addict and The Law*
V-267 LIPPMANN, WALTER *The Essential Lippmann*
V-204 LOMAX, LOUIS *Thailand: The War that Is, The War that Will Be*
V-193 MALRAUX, ANDRÉ *Temptation of the West*
V-324 MARITAIN, JACQUES *Existence and the Existent*

V-709 FEDIN, KONSTANTIN *Early Joys*
V-130 FIELDING, HENRY *Tom Jones*
V-45 FORD, FORD MADOX *The Good Soldier*
V-187 FORSTER, E. M. *A Room with a View*
V-7 FORSTER, E. M. *Howards End*
V-40 FORSTER, E. M. *The Longest Journey*
V-61 FORSTER, E. M. *Where Angels Fear to Tread*
V-752 FRIEDBERG, MAURICE (ed.) *Russian Short Stories:* A Bilingual Collection, Volume I
V-219 FRISCH, MAX *I'm Not Stiller*
V-8 GIDE, ANDRÉ *The Immoralist*
V-96 GIDE, ANDRÉ *Lafcadio's Adventures*
V-27 GIDE, ANDRÉ *Strait Is the Gate*
V-66 GIDE, ANDRÉ *Two Legends*
V-304 GOLD, HERBERT *The Man Who Was Not With It*
V-402 GOODMAN, PAUL *Hawkweed*
V-300 GRASS, GÜNTER *The Tin Drum*
V-182 GRAVES, ROBERT *I, Claudius*
V-217 GRAVES, ROBERT *Sergeant Lamb's America*
V-717 GUERNEY, B. G. (ed.) *An Anthology of Russian Literature* in the Soviet Period
V-255 HAMMETT, DASHIELL *The Maltese Falcon* and *The Thin Man*
V-15 HAWTHORNE, NATHANIEL *Short Stories*
V-227 HOWES, BARBARA (ed.) *23 Modern Stories*
V-307 HUMES, H. L. *The Underground City*
V-305 HUMPHREY, WILLIAM *Home From the Hill*
V-727 ILF AND PETROV *The Twelve Chairs*
V-295 JEFFERS, ROBINSON *Selected Poems*
V-380 JOYCE, JAMES *Ulysses*
V-716 KAMEN, ISAI (ed.) *Great Russian Stories*
V-134 LAGERKVIST, PÄR *Barabbas*
V-240 LAGERKVIST, PÄR *The Sibyl*
V-23 LAWRENCE, D. H. *The Plumed Serpent*
V-71 LAWRENCE, D. H. *St. Mawr* and *The Man Who Died*
V-706 LEONOV, LEONID *The Thief*
V-170 MALAMUD, BERNARD *The Magic Barrel*
V-136 MALRAUX, ANDRÉ *The Royal Way*
V-180 MANN, THOMAS *Buddenbrooks*
V-3 MANN, THOMAS *Death in Venice*
V-86 MANN, THOMAS *The Transposed Heads*
V-36 MANSFIELD, KATHERINE *Stories*
V-137 MAUGHAM, SOMERSET *Of Human Bondage*
V-78 MAXWELL, WILLIAM *The Folded Leaf*
V-91 MAXWELL, WILLIAM *They Came Like Swallows*
V-221 MAXWELL, WILLIAM *Time Will Darken It*
V-306 MICHENER, JAMES A. *Hawaii*
V-144 MITFORD, NANCY *The Pursuit of Love*
V-197 MORGAN, F. (ed.) *Hudson Review Anthology*
V-718 NABOKOV, V. (tr.) *The Song of Igor's Campaign*
V-29 O'CONNOR, FRANK *Stories*
V-49 O'HARA, JOHN *Butterfield 8*
V-276 O'NEILL, EUGENE *Six Short Plays*
V-18 O'NEILL, EUGENE *The Iceman Cometh*
V-165 O'NEILL, EUGENE *Three Plays:* Desire Under the Elms, Strange Interlude, and Mourning Becomes Electra
V-125 O'NEILL & OATES (eds.) *Seven Famous Greek Plays*

*V-753* PAYNE, ROBERT (tr.) *The Image of Chekhov:* 40 Stories
*V-714* PUSHKIN, ALEXANDER *The Captain's Daughter*
*V-24* RANSOM, JOHN CROWE *Poems and Essays*
*V-731* REEVE, F. (ed.) *Russian Plays,* Volume I
*V-732* REEVE, F. (ed.) *Russian Plays,* Volume II
*V-297* RENAULT, MARY *The King Must Die*
*V-16* SARTRE, JEAN-PAUL *No Exit* and Three Other Plays
*V-65* SARTRE, JEAN-PAUL *The Devil & the Good Lord* and Two Other Plays
*V-238* SARTRE, JEAN-PAUL *The Condemned of Altona*
*V-330* SHOLOKHOV, MIKHAIL *And Quiet Flows the Don*
*V-331* SHOLOKHOV, MIKHAIL *The Don Flows Home to the Sea*
*V-85* STEVENS, WALLACE *Poems*
*V-141* STYRON, WILLIAM *The Long March*
*V-63* SVEVO, ITALO *Confessions of Zeno*
*V-178* SYNGE, J. M. *Complete Plays*
*V-346* TERTZ, ABRAM *The Makepiece Experiment*
*V-750* TERTZ, ABRAM *The Trial Begins* and *On Socialist Realism*
*V-131* THACKERAY, W. M. *Vanity Fair*
*V-713* TOLSTOY, LEO *The Kreutzer Sonata*
*V-154* TRACY, HONOR *Straight and Narrow Path*
*V-202* TURGENEV, IVAN *Torrents of Spring*
*V-711* TURGENEV, IVAN *The Vintage Turgenev* Volume I: *Smoke, Fathers and Sons, First Love*
*V-712* TURGENEV, IVAN Volume II: *On the Eve, Rudin, A Quiet Spot, Diary of a Superfluous Man*
*V-257* UPDIKE, JOHN *Olinger Stories:* A Selection
*V-308* UPDIKE, JOHN *Rabbit, Run*
*V-751* ZOSHCHENKO, MIKHAIL *Nervous People* and Other Stories